DEATH, WOMEN AND THE SUN

ἀνατέλλοντός τε ἡλίου καὶ σελήνης καὶ πρὸς δυσμὰς ἰόντων
προκυλίσεις ἅμα καὶ προσκυνήσεις ἀκούοντές τε καὶ ὁρῶντες
Ἑλλήνων τε καὶ βαρβάρων πάντων ἐν συμφοραῖς παντοίαις
ἐχομένων καὶ ἐν εὐπραγίαις, οὐχ ὡς οὐκ ὄντων, ἀλλ' ὡς ὅτι
μάλιστα ὄντων καὶ οὐδαμῇ ὑποψίαν ἐνδιδόντων ὡς οὐκ εἰσὶ
θεοί...

… and at the rising and setting of the sun and moon [the children] saw and heard
Greeks and foreigners — in good times and bad — all prostrate in their devotions
to sun and moon, not as if there were no gods, but as if there most certainly were
gods beyond a shadow of a doubt ….

Plato, Laws 887e

Ἤλε μ', π' ἔχπάστες καὶ θὰ πάς καὶ ποῦ θ' ἀφίντς τὴ χόρα σ'; / ...
Ἤλε μ', ἤλε μ', ἤλε μ', ἤλε μ', ἤλε μ', καὶ ξὰν ἤλε μ' ! / Ἤλε μ',
ἀτζάπα π' ἔχπάστες ἐσύ 'ς σὴν ξενιτείαν; / ντό ἔν' τὸ μαῦρον τὸ
καράβ' ντὸ ἔρθεν καὶ 'ς σὴν πόρταν; / μαῦρα πανία ἔχ' ἀτό, 'ς σὴν
ξενιτὰν 'κὶ πάει, / ... ἀτὸ 'ς σὸν Ἅδην πάει, ... / κ' ἐσυντροφάες, νὲ
ἤλε μ', τὸν ἄσπλαχνον τὸν Χάρον !

My sun, where have you set off to, where are you going, where will you leave
your widow? My sun, my sun, my sun, my sun, my sun, and again my sun! My
sun, do you suppose you have set off for foreign lands? What is that black boat
that has come and is at the door? It has black sails, it is not going to foreign lands,
it is going to Hades … and you have become company, yes my sun, with
merciless Charos.

Modern Greek ritual lament of Pontic widow, Archeion
Pontou, 1951, p.189, after Alexiou, 1985

DEATH, WOMEN AND THE SUN

SYMBOLISM OF
REGENERATION IN
EARLY AEGEAN RELIGION

LUCY GOODISON

BULLETIN SUPPLEMENT 53

1989

University of London
Institute of Classical Studies

Published by
Institute of Classical Studies
31–34 Gordon Square, London WC1H 0PY

SBN 900587 56 3
ISSN 0076–0749

For my parents,
who encouraged me

CONTENTS

ACKNOWLEDGEMENTS

I am grateful to my PhD supervisor, Alan Griffiths, for his consistently good-humoured encouragement, help and positive criticism throughout more than fifteen years of hard labour, interruptions and setbacks in the writing of my PhD thesis and this revised version of it. Before I submitted my thesis, Alan and Christine Peatfield read the whole manuscript and generously contributed detailed critical comments. Helen Waterhouse kindly gave me her very helpful thoughts on Chapter 2 and gave much-appreciated moral support. Years later, Bob Arnott and Don Evely took trouble to read through parts of this revised version for mistakes which had crept in. I am most grateful to all of them; any remaining errors are, of course, my own. I also want to thank my thesis examiners, Nicolas Coldstream, Ruth Padel and Colin Renfrew for their positive criticism of my thesis and for the very generous advice and encouragement they have given me since, while I have been preparing it for publication.

George Hart gave valuable assistance with the Egyptian material, and John Betts and Dominique Collon kindly gave significant advice on their areas of speciality. Peter Warren kindly gave permission for me to reproduce an important item prior to publication, and engaged in an encouraging and informative correspondence. I have also been helped by correspondence, thoughts or information from Helen Waterhouse, Vronwy Hankey, the late George Thomson, John Cherry, Marisa Marthari, Joyce Morrison, R. L. N. Barber, Alison Gladstone, Nikos Efstratiou and Louise Martin; my thanks are due to all of these. For their practical help, friendship and support I want to thank Don Evely, Bob Arnott and, most especially, Margaret Williamson. For advice and help with preparing the pictures I am grateful to Hilary Arnott, Carlos Guarita, Louise London, Louis Mackay, Liz Moore, Paul Morrison, Joyce and David Morrison, Eleni Palaiologou, and Paula McDiarmid (who pasted up most of the pictures).

Especial thanks to Keith Horn, who started pasting up the pictures but was unable to finish them due to a serious illness which led to his death.

For funding I wish to express my thanks to the Dr M. Aylwin Cotton Foundation and to the British Academy, whose grants made publication possible. I am grateful to Jenny March for her patient work preparing the manuscript for publication.

I have also some personal thanks. Georgina Pollard first set me on my path by teaching me Greek out of school hours as it was not on the curriculum. I am grateful to my parents, Betty and Robin Goodison, for their belief in my work and their generous help in looking after my daughter, Corey, to free me to write. I must also thank Corey for always avoiding precious papers with a wisdom beyond her years, and Carlos Guarita for his tolerance and sense of humour; their affection has sustained me through long hours of work. Jenner Roth inspired me to finish. Over the years, I could never have carried the work through to completion without the patience, love and support of many friends, especially Jane Foot, Patti Howe, Stef Pixner, Joanna Ryan and Paul Morrison.

For permission to reproduce quotations I am grateful to the following:

Barrie and Jenkins for permission to quote from Mary Douglas, *Natural Symbols*, 1970.

Victor Gollancz Ltd. for permission to quote from Margaret Mead, *Male and Female: A Study of the Sexes in a Changing World*, 1962.

Harvard University Press for permission to quote from Carl W. Blegen, *Zygouries: A Prehistoric Settlement in the Valley of Cleonae*, 1928.

William Heinemann Ltd. for permission to quote from Hugh G. Evelyn-White (transl.), *Hesiod, The Homeric Hymns and Homerica*, 1914.

Kungl. Humanistiska Vetenskapssamfundet, Lund, for permission to quote from Martin P. Nilsson, *The Minoan-Mycenaean Religion and its Survival in Greek Religion*, 1927.

Lawrence and Wishart for permission to quote from George Thomson, *Aeschylus and Athens*, 1941.

Methuen and Co. for permission to quote from Colin Renfrew, *The Emergence of Civilization*, 1972.

The University of Chicago Press for permission to quote from Richmond Lattimore's translation of *The Iliad of Homer*, 1951.

Verso for permission to quote from Raymond Williams, *Problems in Materialism and Culture: Selected Essays*, 1980.

Lady Helen Waterhouse for permission to quote from the summary of her paper 'Priest-Kings?' in *Bulletin of the Institute of Classical Studies*, 1974.

For permission to reproduce pictures of objects prior to publication I am most grateful to Dr Kostis Davaras for Figs. 300 a-f, 310i, also 212c, and to Professor Peter Warren for Fig. 131f (as well as Figs. 140, 247c and 266a). I am also especially grateful to Dr Ingo Pini who generously gave me permission to reproduce over 300 illustrations from the *Corpus der Minoischen und Mykenischen Siegel*.

For kind permission to reproduce illustrations, I also wish to thank the following individual authors, publishers and institutions:

Dr Gudrun Ahlberg-Cornell (Figs. 295b, c, d, 296, 297a, b, 333b)

Professor John Boardman (Figs 17d, 25a, 26a, 54a, 55c, 57b, 67a, 68b, 128b, 133a, 148a, 156e, 164b, 166b, c, 172e, 176g, 178d, 181b, d, 193b, 248a, 252a, 253a, 263a, 268a, b, 269c, d, 275d, 277g, 280d, 299a, 318a, b, c, 321a, b, c, 322a, 323a, b, 324, 325a, b, c, d, e, f, g, 328b, 329a, b, 332a, b, c,)

Professor Keith Branigan (Figs. 9a, b, c, 32a, b, 48a, b, c, d, 49a, 64b, 72b)

Professor Nicholas Coldstream (Figs. 288a, 290, 292a, 310b, d, 316f)

Dr Dominique Collon (Figs. 12a, b, c, g, h)

Mr Andrew Fleming (Fig. 51b)

Dr Lyvia Morgan (Fig. 241 l)

Professor Colin Renfrew (Figs. 4, 44a, b, 45, 51a, 135d, 218g, 336a, b, d)

American Journal of Archaeology (Figs. 38g, 39f, 40a, b, 56a, 291f, g, 336c)

Antiquity (Fig. 215b)

Armand Colin, Paris (Fig. 251a)

Artemis Verlag, Zürich (Figs. 42d, e, f, g, 181i, 242a (drawing))

ACKNOWLEDGEMENTS

Butterworth and Co. (Publishers), 88 Kingsway, London WC2B 6AB (Fig. 216a)
Cambridge University Press (Figs. 242b, 292b, c, d, e, f, 299b, 326b, 327, 277a)
Jonathan Cape Ltd. (Fig. 51a)
Edinburgh University Press (Figs. 39b, 281a, b)
Edizioni dell'Ateneo, Rome (Figs. 28b, 66d, 76c)
Grafton Books, a division of the Collins Publishing Group (Figs. 179a, 188a)
Harvard University Press (Fig. 218f)
Hirmer Verlag, Munich (Fig. 188d)
Librairie Orientaliste Paul Geuthner, Paris (Figs. 67c, 71c, 87f, 104b, 112a, 131d, e, 196f)
Macmillan Publishers Ltd. (Figs. 42i, 63, 94a, b, 213a, b, 258b)
Methuen and Co. (Figs. 4, 44a, b, 45, 237b, 253d, 336a, b, d)
Oxford University Press (Figs. 19c, 55b, 72a, 114b, 115a, b, c, 133a, 135a, 243d, 280d, 299a)
Paul Åströms Förlag (Figs. 227a-h, 230c, d, e, f, 238b, i, 255c, 279f, 328f, g)
Penguin Books Ltd. (Figs. 236b, 248g, 78d, 12k)
Praeger Publishers (Fig. 102)
Princeton University Press (Figs. 39g, h, i, 41c, 42b)
Routledge and Kegan Paul (Figs. 42a, h, 64b, 72b)
Thames and Hudson (Figs. 18a-g, 25b, 93)
University of Massachusetts Press (Figs. 218d, e, 286b, c, 308a, b, 309)
Verlag Butzon and Bercker, Kevelaer, Neukirchener Verlag, Neukirchen-Vluyn (Figs. 12i, n)

The American School of Classical Studies at Athens (Figs. 189a, 260d, 304, 11b, c)
The Ashmolean Museum, Oxford (Figs. 133a, 206c, 214a)
The Trustees of the British Museum (Figs. 7, 41b, 42c, 92, 111b, 239b)
The British School at Athens (Figs. 11a, d, e, 76a, 78b, c, 121b, 125, 135b, d, 138a, 140, 179c, 199a, 214c, 218g, 241k, l, 247c, 266a, 277h, 280c, e, 293g, 305a, 306a, 310e, 326a)
Deutches Archäologisches Institut (Figs. 6e, 280a, 294b)
The Syndics of the Fitzwilliam Museum, Cambridge (Fig. 242a, photograph)
The Institute of Classical Studies (Figs. 275b, 292a, 306e, f, g)
Louvre Museum, Paris (Fig. 39e)
The Ministry of Culture of Greece (Figs. 49g, 60c, 109e, 119a, 120b, c, 122b, 138c, 243c)
Österreichische Akademie der Wissenschaften (Figs. 39j, 135c)
Royal Commission on the Historical Monuments of England (Fig. 78e)

INTRODUCTION

The intention of this book is to investigate some aspects of religious symbolism in early Aegean culture. It will not, however, focus on such symbolism in isolation or within a single phase of culture. It will select some specific and limited religious symbols so as to observe the process of change and transition through which they pass over time. It will also attempt to relate these changes to developments in the economic and social structure of early Aegean culture.

The study is concerned with religious symbols during an early phase of Aegean civilization, from the Early Bronze Age to the Early Iron Age. It is not intended as a comprehensive survey of all the religious symbols current during that period: many of the most familiar symbols characterizing Aegean Bronze Age religion, such as the double axe, the 'horns of consecration' and the bull, will receive little mention here. Rather its focus is on one particular area: that of solar symbolism. This has implications for other areas of symbolism, and therefore, within this overall brief, some consideration will also be given to the context and associated symbolic elements which locate solar symbolism within a broader understanding of the religion of the period. I am not presenting a comprehensive symbolism, but putting forward the case for the recognition of a widely unacknowledged strand of ideas and beliefs which, the evidence suggests, were present to a greater or lesser degree throughout several millennia of Greek history.

The study thus challenges assumptions which I would suggest amount to prejudices relegating sun symbolism as a 'disreputable' topic. In this area of research we have a situation such as West describes in relation to nature symbolism, as each generation turns away from those avenues of study 'in which its predecessors most obviously made idiots of themselves', which leads to a 'dereliction of knowledge' (1975, 15). It is against such a background of dereliction that I present evidence that solar symbolism is more complex and significant in prehistoric Greek religion than is generally recognized. On the basis of the archaeological record, I propose a scheme of beliefs and rituals associated with the sun which would throw some new light on our prevailing interpretations of early Aegean religion.

Approaching religion through symbols

It is not common practice to approach Aegean religion through symbols. Classical Greek religion, with its personified deities grouped in a clearly-defined Olympian pantheon, has cast a mould of thought which is hard to break out of even when we are tackling the prehistoric period. Characteristic is Furley's dismissal of animistic theories of Aegean religion as 'so far from the anthropomorphism of Greek religion as to be scarcely tenable' (1981, 13). Evans, though recognizing the symbolic significance of elements such as tree, pillar, stone, butterfly, etc., in Minoan religion, is nonetheless exercised with the search for Cretan Zeus. Nilsson, though likewise not limited solely to such concerns, is interested in identifying the anthropomorphic deities associated with snake, household, peak sanctuary and so on. The attributes of divinities are significant clues in such a search. However, they may be misleading, as Lloyd-Jones points out: 'In the earliest Greek religion, goddesses were little differentiated from one another: structuralists, with their tendency to neglect the historical dimension, would do well to remember that the precise marking off of one deity from another in terms of attributes and function may not safely be attributed to the remote past' (*JHS* 103, 1983, 90). That those symbolic attributes of divinities may at some early stage have played a less marginal role has been suggested by Jane Harrison (1927, 63): 'a thing is regarded as sacred, and out of that sanctity, given certain conditions, emerges a *daimon* and ultimately a god. *Le sacré, c'est le père du dieu*'. Furley's remark, though largely accurate for the Iron Age period of which he is writing, is not necessarily applicable to the Early and Middle Bronze Age, in which representations of divinity are controversial and the iconography is dominated by other motifs, including many elements from the natural world.

To approach a study of religion through the symbols themselves, with an awareness of the possible need to recognise the intrinsic significance of those symbols independently of their association with any personified deity, necessitates the questioning of certain assumptions about the nature of religion. The problem is highlighted by Onians' definition of religion, cited by Renfrew (1985, 11), as 'Action or conduct indicating a belief in, or reverence for, and desire to please, a divine ruling power ...: Recognition on the part of man of some higher unseen power as having control of his destiny, and as being entitled to obedience, reverence and worship'. Such a description does not fit all religions. Tylor was the first to give currency to the term 'animism' to describe a primitive religion which believes spirits to inhabit natural phenomena such as sky, sun, fire or sea, merged in those elements and only later emerging as anthropomorphic gods controlling those phenomena. The term 'naturism' has also been used to describe a religion which addresses elements of the natural world, including rivers, stars, plants, animals and rocks (see discussion in Lowie, 1925, 99-163, and Durkheim, 1926, 48-86). In this context obvious difficulties arise with Onians' definition. What if the divine power is not simply represented by, or associated with, but is *immanent in* a tree? The divine power is in this case neither 'unseen' nor 'higher' (although it may be taller than humans, its rooting in the ground disqualifies it from celestial status); nor would a tree necessarily be thought of as 'ruling' in quite the same manner as a personified deity. Similarly a severe problem is created by Leach's statement (1976, 37) that all metaphysical entities start out as 'inchoate concepts in the mind' which are then externalised in myths and in special material objects (also quoted by Renfrew, 1985, 13): what if the divinity starts as a tree and is later abstracted? This would be a reverse process. Similar problems are created in the use, in defining divine forces, of words such as 'supernatural' (suggesting a divorce from natural elements), 'superhuman' (suggesting an anthropomorphic deity), 'divine being' (again suggesting a personified figure), and 'transcendant' (suggesting something apart from, and not subject to the limitations of, the material universe). If the sun is the object of religious observance and worship, should it be described as a 'transcendental' power or do we need to recognise that the physical being of the sun is what is being worshipped? The term 'numinous' is useful here, in describing certain awe-inspiring or attractive qualities which may be immanent in aspects of the material and physical world.

It is evident that many of our assumptions concerning religion are challenged by looking down the telescope in this particular direction and focussing on the symbols themselves rather than on the divinities with which they were later associated. The intrinsic significance ascribed to such elements or symbols by primitive peoples is usually described as 'magical' rather than 'religious', but the too-ready use of the term 'magic' to hive off those beliefs and practices which are alien to our own religious outlook is itself due for careful scrutiny.

It becomes clear that we are running into difficulties in finding appropriate words to use. 'Ritual' is a word which is hard to avoid in tackling this subject matter. Here, drawing on Renfrew (1983, discussion), I will use it to refer to 'actions directed towards a divine entity or entities to gain their attention and/or intervention'. I have also found relevant Rundle-Clark's comment that 'Religious ritual is not just a series of actions performed for their own sake. These acts are symbolic; that is, they refer to things other than themselves, and this reference is always to something in the world of the gods' (1959, 27). The definition of a symbol is tackled in Chapter 4 below, but it may be helpful at this point to quote the same author's remark that 'Symbols are ... things which act as focal points for emotions or imaginative speculations ... They are not distinct entities, for they readily merge into one another, making patterns of bewildering complexity. Nevertheless, the combinations of symbols are not haphazard; it is just that the rules governing their use are not understood' (1959, 218). Where those emotions or imaginative speculations relate to the divine, we may regard ourselves as dealing with religious symbols.

The dating framework

The study of symbols and their arrangement in relation to each other within a belief system has in recent years been largely a preserve of structuralist enquiry. Chapter 4 below refers to various theories of symbol formation, clarifying the method used in this study and the way in which it differs from that of the structuralists. I make it clear that my aim is to undermine assumptions that there exists a 'universal' symbolism, and to point out evidence for a dynamic and changing relationship between a society and the symbols it produces. Here it is relevant to point out one specific divergence from the structuralist approach. Many anthropologists as well as classicists have criticised that approach for its tendency to view phenomena a-historically, without looking into the evolution or development and change over time of a particular ritual or cultural pattern. In this book the dilemma of trying to do justice to both the synchronic and the diachronic aspects of symbol formation has led to the adoption of a tri-partite structure which focusses consecutively on three phases or periods within Early Aegean culture. The changes in symbolism which evolve over time are thus crystallized as the differences apparent between the symbols of one period and that of the succeeding period. Within each period, however, a synchronic approach is adopted which involves casting the net wide both geographically and temporally. Thus cultural variations at a number of far-flung contemporary regional sites will be grouped under the general heading of one period, and developments within the period (for example, the emergence of peak sanctuaries during the first period) will again be subsumed under the general heading of that period.

The absolute dating framework for the Bronze Age is problematic; while Hankey and Warren's reappraisal of Bronze Age dating is not yet at hand, I will here use the scheme printed at the end of this Introduction, based on Betancourt (1985) and MacGillivray and Barber (1985), for dating the Early, Middle and Late phases of the Minoan, Helladic and Cycladic Cultures.

The three phases or periods are discussed in three chapters as follows:

Chapter 1

The emphasis here will be on isolating a geographical area and a time span which offers evidence pre-dating those new cultural features which have often been attributed to the arrival of 'Indo-European invaders' or 'Proto-Greeks'.

The starting-point of this period lies at the date often assigned to the beginning of the Bronze Age, the opening of the third millennium B.C. The terminal definition of the period rests on the appearance of certain changes in Aegean culture by around the middle of the second millennium B.C., including the emergence of Mycenae and other centres on the Greek mainland, the presence of new features in Grave Circles B and A at Mycenae, and the arrival of the battle chariot and the long sword. Although the reason for the appearance of these new phenomena is very far from clear, and we cannot assume discontinuity or 'Indo-Europeans', a significant prior sign of large-scale destruction or possible intrusion by new elements on the mainland lies at the junction between EH II and EH III, and therefore Chapter 1 can include mainland material only up to the end of EH II. At the base line, the aim here is to stop *before* the development of 'Mycenean' culture. As for the Cycladic islands, a long period of uniformity and gradual development was brought to a sudden close at the end of EC II, suggesting that they were influenced early by some new elements; this part of the study can therefore include material only from the Early Cycladic period, excluding material from Middle Cycladic and, where possible, from EC III proper. On Crete, however, it is a different story. Here there is strong evidence of an indigenous culture largely untouched by the new elements not only during the third millennium B.C. but also during much of the second millennium B.C. The decisive signs of mainland penetration of Crete have been dated as late as the start of LM II or even LM IIIA1/2 with the appearance of new grave practices and ceramic styles and shapes, and the abandonment of some sites; however, we are concerned here to predate any substantial influence by the new elements, and therefore I will include Cretan material only of the EM period and some of the MM period. Amidst the difficulty of determining the dating of MM I, II, III, and of the various destruction horizons of the period (see, recently, MacGillivray, 1986, and Warren, 1989, who proposes a major destruction in the MM IIIB/LM IA transition period), it remains possible tentatively to identify a catastrophe, generally thought to be an earthquake, causing destruction in Crete close to, perhaps just before, the end of MM III. I shall take this as the closing point for the Cretan material considered in my Chapter 1, which will therefore include MM IIIA and part of MM IIIB, including the earliest phase of the 'New Palace' at Knossos and stopping short of the Temple Repository material there. The line is harder to draw in some other areas of the island, for example East Crete (see Betancourt, 1985, 104). By MM III Crete was exporting increasing amounts of pottery to the mainland and Cyclades, but imports from those areas were fewer (see discussion in Betancourt, 1985, 112), and we can imagine that incoming influences from those areas were correspondingly insignificant. It should be made clear that this dividing line is not concerned with distinctions between 'Old' and 'New' Cretan palaces, but with predating by a generous margin any significant influence on Crete from 'Mycenaean' culture. Hooker has set the start of the Mycenean age at c. 1650 B.C. and has detailed the various ways in which, even during the succeeding century, cultural influence moved from Crete to the mainland rather than *vice versa* (1976, 34ff). Although the suggested catastrophe in late MM III was followed by immediate reconstruction, it enables us to draw a relatively clear line which apparently predates the proliferation of contacts with the Greek mainland and provides a workable *terminus ante quem* for the Cretan material to be reviewed in the first part of this study. (See discussions in Crossland and Birchall (ed.), 1973; see also pp.66-7 below.)

As far as dating seals is concerned, the situation is not always clear. Boardman has commented that 'for seals, the end of the Early Palace period is as difficult to define as its beginning' (1970, 28) and that for some types of seal, including four-sided prisms with hieroglyphs, 'no hard and fast distinctions between MM II and MM III can be drawn' (1970, 37). For these reasons I follow Boardman in including in my early phase some seals which are consistent with the Cretan seal tradition (such as three-sided prism seals) although their date is uncertain and they may overlap far into MM III: an example is the Oxford seal CS 167 (my **Fig. 26a**) which Boardman also includes in his Early Palace Period (1970, Black and White Pl. 27). Some seals which can be dated no more closely than 'MM III' are also included. All the Phaistos sealings (see *CMS* II, 5) are included in this first chapter. I have also taken a decision to include all hieroglyphs in this first part of my study, on the grounds that they are a form which started in MM I, which passed out of use at Knossos prior to the catastrophe that forms my horizon (Evans, 1909, 144-5), which declines and atrophies soon afterwards in other areas, and which represents a clearly indigenous Cretan tradition. The technical revolution in gem engraving identified by Betts (1986) in MM III provides a useful watershed.

Apart from seals, wherever there is some doubt with dating material, I have tended to place it later and treat it in Chapter 2 in order to be on the safe side.

Chapter 1 will thus consider some Cretan material from the Middle Bronze Age, in conjunction with Early Bronze Age material from three areas: the mainland, the Cycladic islands and Crete. Material from other areas of the Aegean features far less prominently throughout the study. In accordance with the theory of a cultural continuum in the Aegean in the Early Bronze Age, Chapter 1 treats both Cretan and Cycladic as well as mainland material together. Local variations are of course many and significant, as are local variations within Crete itself, but these are treated as variations within a cultural continuum rather than as manifestations of completely distinct and separate cultures. Similarly, chronological distinctions between the succeeding phases of culture within the Early Bronze Age may be recognized where relevant to the argument, but are regarded as phases within one overall period rather than being singled out for separate study. The Appendix develops more fully the considerations which lie behind this decision to treat the whole Aegean area and this whole phase of culture within one section of the study.

Chapter 2

This section deals with the remainder of the Bronze Age and witnesses the interaction between the indigenous culture described in Chapter 1 and the new cultural elements; whether those elements were the result of the arrival of 'Indo-Europeans' or 'Proto-Greeks' is not our concern here. The Late Bronze Age is not monolithic and it may appear surprising to find it treated as a whole; it would, however, add enormously to the length of this study to discriminate and treat material from its later phases separately in each case. Again material is drawn from the whole Aegean basin, and the differences which I pick out are those apparent between the two different traditions at various stages of the interaction as it developed over time from a more equal interaction and exchange of culture to a situation in which the 'Mycenaean' culture not only held sway on the mainland and the Cyclades but shows a strong presence in Crete itself. Nilsson's conflation of Minoan and Mycenaean religion has long been under question, and what is under scrutiny is perhaps a distinction not simply between Cretan and mainland religion but between indigenous Aegean and 'new' elements (see Renfrew 1981 and Hägg 1981).

Chapter 3

Here the area of concern is the Early Iron Age in Greece, from the earliest phases of the Geometric era to the appearance of writing. I place a final curtain at around 700 B.C. but occasionally venture beyond it into the Archaic period. The nature of this study does not require a strict *terminus ante quem* for this last period as it did for the earlier two, aiming as it does to trace continuities and discontinuities between the prehistoric and historic Aegean. Out of the historic material, the preference for emphasizing the earlier, Geometric, material derives from a need to limit the body of material tackled; moreover, this period's relative closeness in time to the Bronze Age highlights the possibility of continuity and renders changes more marked. In this section, literary evidence for religious symbolism will be examined along with the archaeological evidence. No attempt will be made to comment on the prominent local differentiations in cultural traditions during this period (for example, the distinct variations in the iconography of vase decoration). My concern is rather to highlight elements of apparent continuity from Bronze Age traditions which crop up at various times and places, as well as documenting those features which show a marked reversal or change from Bronze Age traditions.

A note on method

The nature, and use made, of the evidence for religious symbolism in each period is discussed at the beginning of each chapter. As my concern is to point to elements of continuity and discontinuity between the three periods, it is not appropriate to mix the evidence from the three periods but rather to keep it quite distinct; argument from later periods can therefore not be used to illuminate scanty or obscure evidence for earlier times. As Renfrew has pointed out (1985, 442), careful observance of this rule is necessary for an effective use of a diachronic method. Argument by analogy from other cultures is used sparingly and mainly where there is contemporaneity or some evidence of contact with the Aegean.

In each chapter the economic and social structure of the culture in question will be considered in conjunction with the evidence of religious symbolism. In discussion of this economic and social basis, my intention will not be to present new evidence or argument, but rather to follow, albeit critically and on occasion with reservations, the general consensus concerning the form this basis took during each period in question. Where new ground will be broken is in the interpretation of the religious symbolism traceable in already known and published archaeological material, and in the relationship suggested between this religious material and the social structure.

Throughout, an attempt will be made to present material which suggests a coherent, though complex, relationship between society and symbols. At the end of the study, in Chapter 4, some elements of this relationship will be discussed in more general terms.

DATING FRAMEWORK

ca. 3200 - 2800 B.C.			
	EM I	EH I	EC I
	EM IIA	EH II	EC II
	EM IIB		
ca. 2100 - 1950 B.C.	EM III	EH III	EC IIIA
	MM IA		EC IIIB
first potter's wheel	MM IB	MH	
	MM IIA		
	MM IIB		MC
ca. 1650 - 1550 B.C.	MM III		
(N.B. A groundswell of opinion would place this transition at ca.1800-1700 B.C.)	LM IA	LH I	LC I
	LM IB	LH IIA	LC II
	LM II	LH IIB	
	LM IIIA	LH IIIA	LC III
	LM IIIB	LH IIIB	
ca. 1150 - 1050 B.C.	LM IIIC	LH IIIC	

CHAPTER 1: BEFORE THE MYCENAEANS

1.1 TACKLING THE EVIDENCE

The nature of the evidence available for the study of prehistoric religion has been discussed most recently by Renfrew (1985, 11-26). Pointing out the absence of verbal testimony or direct observation of cult, he groups the evidence under the headings of non-verbal records (mainly depictions of religious practices or entities) and material remains of cult practices (including structures and symbolic objects). He suggests that this limitation may inhibit our ability to elucidate belief systems, as opposed to the reconstruction of rituals: 'In the absence of written testimony we must work with materials where the meaning has, to some extent, been made explicit: with signs, symbols and iconography' (1985, 13).

In this study, attempts to investigate some elements of Bronze Age symbolism will lead me to touch on the areas both of belief and of ritual, insofar as both are implicated in elucidating the meaning of those symbols. I am specifically interested in evidence for beliefs and rituals which will throw light on the meaning of solar symbolism. In brief, my line of argument will proceed as follows: (1) that the sun was significant in Aegean Bronze Age religion, and (2) that it carried a symbolic meaning which is indicated by the contexts and associations of its appearances. In order to establish (1), I first need to prepare some ground by ascertaining as closely as possible what we can reasonably take to be intended as a representation of the sun; this thorny task is broached on pp.11-15. I will also need to present evidence that these representations carry a religious, rather than a purely secular, significance. This requires establishing that we are discussing a religious climate where religious beliefs about the sun would not be inconsistent (as they would be, for example in an exclusively anthropomorphic or monotheistic religion); this issue is tackled on pp.4-11. It also requires evidence that the sun is involved in religious scenes or contexts: the appearance of the sun on a seal showing cult activity, or the east-facing doors of the Messara tholoi, might be taken as examples of such contexts. Lastly, it will assist my case if I can show that the items on which sun representations are found (for example, seals or 'frying-pans') can be taken to have a ritual function or magical significance. All this is required for me to establish my first point, namely that the sun was significant in Bronze Age religion.

Establishing my second point, that it carried symbolic meaning as suggested by the associations and contexts in which it appears, requires an investigation of those contexts. Renfrew (1985, 13-14) suggests that when symbols are habitually used together within the same context, 'an association of symbols with meaning in one case may be assumed in another when it is less apparent'. His example is of emblems associated with kingship in certain contexts, of which one emblem may singly indicate kingship in another context. I will use a similar line of argument in relation to the sun, and since a key word here is 'habitually', it will require the presentation of numerous and occasionally repetitive illustrations to establish the frequency of certain contexts and associations. It has also been pointed out that such symbolic associations may, in primitive religion, carry a force which it is hard for us to imagine. Thus Lowie remarks of a Hidatsa woman's statement that Indian corn and wild geese were one and the same thing: 'It was not that she was of pre-logical mentality in Lévy-Bruhl's sense, that is, incapable in ordinary life of separating the idea of the plant from that of the birds, but that in the given context both were associated in the same sacred complex and stood for that complex: whether one or the other cue was used to evoke the essential emotional state, was a matter of complete indifference' (1925, 287). We cannot assume in the inhabitants of the Bronze Age Aegean a state of mind similar to that of this woman; but neither can we assume an attitude to symbols similar to our own, and we must be open to whatever possibilities the evidence suggests about the range and depth of such associations in Early Bronze Age religion.

The seal evidence

At this point it remains to discuss briefly whether two of the main sources of apparent sun representations in this early period, engraved seals and 'frying-pans', can be thought to have any magical or religious function or significance. In the case of seals, a practical use is clearly indicated, as in the use of seal impressions to secure boxes at Lerna. Worn holes on some seals, as at Myrtos (Warren, 1972, 226), suggest that they may have been carried about the person and may partly have served the function of decorative jewellery in addition to their practical use. Many scholars, however, have attributed a further significance to the seals. Thus Evans suggests that they were designed to carry 'information about their owners' (*JHS* 14, 1894, 301).

We can speculate that the information might have been concerning the owner's clan, occupation, possessions, status, role in religion, personality, or a combination of these. If indeed it was the bearer of such information, the seal can be thought of as bearing a special relationship to its owner. Thus Branigan suggests that the designs on a sealstone were the equivalent of a man's signature and that it was in some way representative of that person: 'This being so, the seal was probably identified with its owner and regarded as part of him. Its ritual significance could thus be quite considerable' (1970, 97). Kenna also suggests that the seal in the ancient world had more than a practical use and that 'in its most primitive character it was believed to possess religious or magical qualities' (1960, 3). Citing examples from other parts of the Eastern Mediterranean, he concludes that '... a quasi-religious or amuletic character seems to be an almost invariable element of the seal in remote antiquity' (1960, 11). Platon (1974) has elaborated on the nature of the protection which the seal may have been believed to offer its owner in life, and on the possible reasons behind its burial with the owner: 'Les sceaux n'ont pas offert seulement leurs services à leurs maîtres pendant la vie, en caractérisant et en protégeant la personnalité, mais ils les ont accompagnés dans leur dernier demeure pour leur protection ultérieure et pour qu'ils ne soient pas utilisés par d'autres.'

It should in this context be pointed out that the connection of the seal with the dead person does not appear to have endured indefinitely as is witnessed by the disturbance of seals along with other grave goods at secondary burial. This practice does not, as Blasingham would have us believe (1983, 13), invalidate an interpretation of the seals as personal talismans. Whether due to their practical, artistic or magical values, seals sometimes became heirlooms used repeatedly over several generations. Platon connects the seal tradition with a pre-history where (1974, 102) 'le tatouage et la protection magique jouaient un rôle prépondérant', and he suggests influence from the Orient and Egypt, localities which 'eurent de l'avance dans le développement des idées de l'inviolabilité de la propriété et de l'assurance de personnalité par des signes parlants ou par d'autres qui conservaient toujours leur pouvoir magique.'

Blasingham's recent argument (1983, 11-21) for the interpretation of the Messara seals as indicating only the social 'office' of their owners remains unconvincing, resting as it does solely on the fact of the proliferation of motifs in early MM and on analogy with, or generalized remarks about, other primitive societies, in the absence of any other early Cretan evidence for the existence of such 'offices'.

The substantial arguments for the seal's special relationship with its owner and for its possession of a magical or religious significance, extending beyond a purely decorative or functional use, rest in its intrinsic worth; in the care taken with its engraving and the craftmanship involved which seems to reflect a high level of motivation; in its presence in the burial assemblage; and in parallels with other societies such as Egypt which had some contact with the Aegean and which provide fuller evidence for a tradition of amuletic seals.

The 'frying-pans'

The so-called 'frying-pans', dated to EBA I-II, made in stone or pottery and found mostly in the Cyclades but also in smaller numbers in Crete and on the Greek mainland, have long provoked debate concerning their purpose and use. A number of ritual uses have been suggested for them: for example, that hides were stretched across the top as drums in the funeral procession; that they were libation vases or incense burners; that they were filled with water to symbolize a sea deity or to serve as mirrors keeping away evil spirits and protecting the dead. Recently Faucounau (1978) has presented the ingenious suggestion that they were primitive astrolabes. While they are clearly not literally frying-pans, there is even doubt as to which way up they were used: as Caskey points out, the ornament is on the flat side and was meant to be seen (1971, 798-9); while one example, which as Doumas notes (1968, 171) clearly belongs in the 'frying-pan' tradition (**Fig. 102**), bears on its hollowed side a row of doves mounted on a ridge, which equally would be intended to be seen and could appear to float if liquid was placed in the vessel at the right depth to cover the ridge. The appearance of a pubic triangle on many examples leads Barnett to comment 'These are all womb-symbols of the Mother Goddess, and no doubt in the "frying-pans" seeds or other sacred items were inserted' (1956, 222). Some of the discussion concerning their use has been summarized by Doumas (1968, 18-19). (See also the recent review by Coleman, 1985, 202-4, who for unstated reasons finds it hard to imagine that the 'frying-pans' may have had both a practical and a symbolic application.) We have no pictures of them in use, although we might be failing to recognize them: see, for example, **Fig. 73c**; the circular object's relation to the figure here would be compatible with the frequent findspot of 'frying-pans' in graves near the head of the dead, sometimes in front of the head and on occasion resting on the bones of the hand as if being held up (Coleman, 1985, 206).

In this instance their specific use concerns us less than the question of whether or not that use belongs in the general area of ritual or religious observance. The arguments in favour of such a view would seem to lie partly in the funerary contexts in which they are often, though not exclusively, found. Another argument, as with the seals, lies in their intrinsic value and the craftmanship involved in making them. (See Renfrew, 1985, 19, on the frequent correlation between investment of wealth and religious significance.) The weight of the body in relation to the length of the handle would make them difficult to hold, and this again may incline us to think that they were not designed primarily for a functional everyday use. The appearance of the female pubic triangle on many examples may also incline us to consider seriously the possibility that they bore some relationship to the famous Cycladic female 'idols'. Lastly, we may again be influenced by the appearance of parallels abroad, in this case Anatolia, whose Aegean contacts were apparently stimulated by the East Anatolian metal-producing centres during the rise of metal-working and trade in the third millennium B.C. From this area, and from the third millennium B.C., we find a series of bronze mirrors which provide a contemporary metal counterpart to the 'frying-pan' (Mellink, 1956, 52-54) (see **Fig. 1**). In the context of other Anatolian borrowings, we can see parallels with the 'frying-pans' in common features such as the circular shape, the plain inner surface, the raised rim, and their considerable weight combined in some cases with a handle inadequate for holding it up. The decoration of the objects is very different and we cannot assume that their use was identical; arguments that the sun and ship designs on the 'frying-pans' could imply their horizontal use, water-filled, to reflect the sun are hypothetical and the parallel does not even prove that the 'frying-pans' were mirrors of any kind, as Mellink proposes (1956, 53). However, the similarities argue for some affinity in usage, and the appearance of the Alaca examples in graves would seem to strengthen the argument for some religious significance in the case both of the Alaca mirrors and of the Aegean 'frying-pans'.

1.2 MONOTHEISM, POLYTHEISM, ANIMISM?

It is appropriate to make some brief remarks about the religion which forms the background against which these objects, and the symbolism they carry, are to be investigated.

A 'Mother-Goddess'?

Any discussion of the religious symbolism of the Early Bronze Age Aegean must refer to the debate concerning the significance of the many female figurines which have been found dating from this period. These figurines, dating from Neolithic times onwards and including Cretan figures in addition to the well-known Cycladic sculptures, have led in some quarters to the suggestion that one unified goddess of fertility formed the main focus of religion in this early period. Thus Dietrich remarks:

> 'The majority of idols from shrines and sanctuaries representing the figure of a Mother Goddess are quite explicit in their significance … From at least the later periods of the Stone Age, ideas of fertility of vegetation and men were current in the settlements about and near the Aegean. This religious concept may have been universally shared by primitive cultures but more precisely took its origin in the Near and Middle East' (1974, 8).

Such generalizations cannot be regarded as valid for the Early Bronze Age Aegean without local and specific evidence. Many figurines from the Aegean are hard to sex (see **Fig. 2**). The theory of the 'Mother-Goddess', linked with earth and fertility, has been questioned as a general explanation for prehistoric figurines by Ucko (1962, 38-54) who points to the minority of figurines representing males, unsexed humans and animals and asks why these are not also considered as divinities. He identifies the cultural prejudices and suspect arguments by analogy from other cultures which have led to an over-ready assumption of a 'Mother-Goddess' interpretation for the Neolithic Aegean figurines (1968, 409-19); he emphasizes that our interpretation must be based on the evidence from the figurines themselves. As a Europe-wide phenomenon, the Mother-Goddess hypothesis has been questioned by Fleming, who argues that firm evidence for a Mother-Goddess is confined, in Europe, to the area Malta-Sardinia-France:

'The mother-goddess has detained us for too long; let us disentangle ourselves from her embrace.' (1969, 255, 259).

Function of the figurines

If the Aegean figurines are not to be assumed to be representations of a Mother or Nature Goddess, then a full range of possible interpretations must be investigated from scratch and their relative merits discussed. Such an investigation provides little support for the theory of a monotheistic Mother-Goddess comparable to the God familiar to us from the Jewish and Christian traditions. In fact, it reveals many features compatible with an animistic tradition.

The range of proposed interpretations for the Cycladic 'idols' has been usefully surveyed by Doumas (1968, 88-94). It starts at one end of the scale with the suggestion that the objects were toys; another suggestion is that they were simply an important possession of the deceased which it was thought necessary to bury with them. There is also the idea that the figures may have been intended to accompany or serve the dead person in some way, as nurse or protectress or perhaps as concubine, in the manner of the Egyptian 'Ushabtis'. Alternatively, they have been interpreted as companions of the dead dedicated to some supernatural agency. Another idea is that they are portrayals of votaries of a deity. Their significance would be different again if they were understood as votive offerings *to* a deity, in which case they might be portrayals of the deceased or another human being, of a votary, or of the deity (whether anthropomorphic, or only occasionally anthropomorphic, in nature). Another possibility is that they are cult images used as objects of worship (Renfrew, 1983, 14, and 1985, 22-3).

This is not the place to attempt to enter fully into the complex and thorny debate as to which of these possible interpretations is more credible. What is relevant is to make a few points about the evidence concerning the figurines which have a bearing on the discussion of other aspects of religious symbolism of the period. The focus here is on the Cycladic figurines, but the assumption will be that these and the numerous, often very similar figurines found from the same period in Crete reflect a similar body of ideas (see Appendix).

The interpretation as toys has been convincingly discredited on the grounds of the scale of the larger pieces, the use of marble for their manufacture in most cases, the workmanship involved in carving them, their funerary use, and the lack of correlation with children's graves. In any case, as Ucko reminds us, the archaeologist's distinction between dolls and magical figures is often conjectural (1968, 422). If the objects were simply personal possessions, the question arises why they are found only in a minority of graves. The number of apparently wealthy graves which contain no figurines and the absence of 'cheaper versions' such as terracotta figures in poorer graves suggests that some selection process must have been involved which did not rest on wealth. It seems that there must have existed some other qualifying factor or special link between the figurine and the person with whom it was buried. Renfrew tentatively suggests that: '... when figurations shown to have been used in cult practice, or relating to cult, are buried in a proportion of graves, the personal association thereby indicated is a reflection of a personal association during life. Were the grave finds very rare, they might be taken as an indication of a very special relationship of the deceased to cult, perhaps suggesting a status as priest or shaman. In this case the relationship may be as close as these but less specialized — involvement in cult at the personal level, possibly within the household' (1983, 9). Thus to say that the figurines were important possessions of the deceased still leaves us discussing the questions of their actual significance and what it was in their relationship with the deceased which qualified the deceased to be so accompanied in burial.

The question of whether the figurines were used in settlements prior to burial is still a matter of keen debate. In the Cyclades the instances of their discovery in settlements at Phylakopi and Aghia Irini are controversial (see recent discussion by Davis, 1983). The discovery of large numbers of such figurines on Keros also provides ambiguous evidence but combines with examples — admittedly less numerous than in Crete — of the repair of broken figurines to tilt the scales in favour of believing that they did have some use prior to burial. This would discredit the 'concubine' theory, already undermined by the lack of evidence to associate the figurines to male burials.

Breakage

The suggested function of the figures as 'psychopompoi' or as divine nurses or protectresses is thrown into question by their absence from the majority of graves: why should only a minority of the population have needed such assistance? (Doumas 1968, 89). It is also thrown into question by their breakage. Accidental breakage could not account for the high percentage of fragmentary figurines (Renfrew, 1983, 12); nor would it satisfactorily explain the absence of small chips and pieces and the predominance of large fragments which could have been recovered and re-used if breakage was unintentional (Davis, 1983, 9-11). Thimme has suggested 'the possibility that religious or magical practices unknown to us are connected with the breaking as well as the burial of these pieces' (1977, 588). Similarly Branigan (1974, 201) comments that at the Archanes tholos in Crete nine out of ten Cycladic figurines were represented only by either head or feet; he suggests that this might reflect deliberate ritual breakage and the careful selection of fragments put in the tomb. A later parallel for breakage in funerary ritual is provided by Egyptian religion: thus a passage from an Osiris mystery incorporated into Chapter 125 of the Book of the Dead has a soul, questioned by a Guardian of the Hall of Judgement, stating that it had been given a burning brazier and an amulet of faience. It states that it placed them both in a coffer, then: 'I wept over them, then I took them out, I extinguished the fire, I broke the amulet and threw them both into the lake' (Rundle Clark, 1978, 163-4, where he suggests that the amulet signified the god Osiris.) Of the Aegean figures we may ask, if they were intended to serve and protect the dead, why were they broken in such a way that might seem to impair rather than enhance such a role?

Votaries or votive offerings?

The suggestion that the figures represent votaries in the service of a deity might seem appropriate for the musician figures and particularly for the seated figure holding a cup from the Goulandris collection (Renfrew, 1983, 15), but it does not necessarily help us in interpreting the majority of female figurines which are so different in posture and sex, and which may have held a different significance.

To accept that the figures may be votive offerings to a deity would again leave us still facing the most difficult problem, namely that of investigating to what deity they were dedicated and what these offerings might be intended to portray. While they could be votaries, as mentioned above, they could also be images of the individual concerned. Thus Thomson suggests (1949, 247): 'As a representation of the worshipper they were dedicated by her in order to place her under the goddess's protection. This was done both in times of actual danger, sickness or childbirth, and in times of imaginary danger, such as initiation, marriage or bereavement.' Such an interpretation raises the question why so few male figures have been found: it seems unconvincing to argue as Doumas does (1968, 92-3) that the Cycladic musician type of figure is the male equivalent of the female figures and that women through childbirth face greater dangers and would therefore more often have call to use such figures for protection. Initiation, bereavement, and sickness would in all likelihood occur equally for men, and this explanation does not account for the difference in type between the male and female figures, with males portrayed mostly in specialized roles. A more plausible explanation for the discrepancy between the number of male and female figures could be created by supposing that the qualifying factor for being buried with a figurine favoured women (for example, that it was predominantly women who were involved in the organization of a household cult); or alternatively by suggesting that the figures were a non-literal representation of an aspect of the person which was conceived as female (e.g. soul, spirit-figure, genius, guardian-angel) whatever the actual sex of the person. Here, however, we are in the realm of pure supposition and, without the evidence to correlate the figures to the sex of the deceased, such suggestions cannot advance beyond speculation.

As votive offerings, the figures may represent a deity, or if interpreted as cult images they would again be understood as portrayals of a divine figure. The few larger figurines which would not fit into graves would qualify for use as cult images (Renfrew, 1983, 16-18); there are however several factors involved here which give information about the probable nature of such a deity and the qualities it displays which diverge from those commonly associated with a divinity.

Lack of evidence of centralized cult

There is no firm evidence for freestanding shrines in the Early Cycladic period, nor in Crete prior to the Mallia shrine and the peak sanctuaries which develop towards the end of our period. Full consideration of the Keros material may change this picture, as might more extensive excavation, but up to the present time the only foci of ritual to be unquestionably identified are the cemeteries. Especially large or consolidated structures which might have marked the site of centralized religious activities have not been discovered; nor has any specific building which might have been intended for such a use. The few figurine remains which have been discovered in settlement sites in the Cyclades were found dispersed over the site, possibly indicating a household cult which involved domestic rituals. If Rooms 89 and 92 at the Myrtos settlement are to be understood as rooms used for ritual, they would certainly suggest the existence of such a household cult in Crete at this early period. If this lack of excavated shrines reflects accurately a lack of such shrines in the Early Bronze Age Aegean, it would be appropriate to consider what the existence of a dispersed rather than a centralized cult of divinity might indicate about the religion of the period, especially in terms of the organization of such a cult and the relationship of the individual to the divine.

Diversity

Unity of practice and a sense of centralized purpose is also lacking from the burial context of the Cycladic figurines. Thus the number of figures found in a grave vary from none to two for canonical folded-arm figurines, while four figurines of Plastiras type have been found together, five of Louros type, and up to fourteen schematic figurines (Renfrew, 1983, 8). There is thus a range of different practices varying between the different culture phases of the Early Cycladic period. As Renfrew points out, '… there is no evidence that a single figurine was a necessary symbolic accompaniment of the dead', nor does the presence of even large folded-arm figurines suitable to be cult images 'necessarily imply that we have here a *single* deity. It is possible that different female deities could have adopted this gesture of epiphany' (1983, 8, 18). The discovery of paired 'idols' in Crete would again seem to argue against a single divinity (see **Fig. 3a**); a monotheistic deity does not come in pairs. This pairing of female figures recurs, as with the bell-shaped figurines (if figurines they are) from Tylissos (see **Fig. 3b** and **c**), and with the 'double-idol' shown on **Fig. 3d**. Thimme suggests a paired mother and daughter (1965, 79).

Different patterns of breakage between different types might also possibly suggest a 'systematic difference in use' (Renfrew, 1983, 5). Fitton (1983) has expressed the opinion that rather than one uniform explanation, there may have been 'a variety of thought processes' lying behind the figurines. Doumas has also stressed the 'variety of representations' and the difficulty of incorporating them all into one interpretation (Discussion at British Museum Cycladic Colloquium, 1983). One recalls Ucko's emphasis on the variety and likely diversity of usage of the Neolithic Aegean figurines (1968, 426, 434-7, 442-4). The range of Early Bronze Age representations includes a number of different approaches to the portrayal of the human body, several of which were current contemporaneously, as well as variations between pregnant and not. **Fig. 4** illustrates some of this variety.

A horizontal deity?

If indeed the figurines are intended as representations of deity, information about such a deity or deities is again afforded by the fact that the majority of figurines are so small. Doumas argues that it is unlikely they are divinities in view of the manner in which they are placed in the grave: this shows no signs of reverence, as they are generally mixed with other material, sometimes lying crushed underneath such material (1968, 91).

Encrustation and pick marks can be used to identify the lower and upper sides respectively of the figure in the grave and suggest a horizontal position, lying on front or back. Although museum displays generally place such figures upright, corresponding to our contemporary notion of what is appropriate for a deity, there is some evidence to suggest that a horizontal position might be more compatible with their original usage. Many of them are made with pointed feet which render them unsuitable for standing upright. Thimme points out that they cannot stand, and finds it significant that they were deliberately designed to lie (1965, 78, 80). Pat Getz-Preziosi has argued unequivocally that they were used in a reclining posture, and points out that even if propped up for display they would have a tendency to slip and fall (Discussion at British Museum Cycladic Colloquium, 1983). The frontal aspect of many of the figurines, and the lack of working on the back, might seem to suggest that they were intended to lie on their back.

This question would be illuminated by further, and more systematically excavated, examples of figures accompanied by a tray or cradle (**Fig. 6a**), reminiscent of the 'sleeping lady' type of figure from contemporary Malta (**Fig. 5**). **Fig. 6b** shows Getz-Preziosi's suggestion as to how the perforations on the cradle might have been used to secure the figure on it. Other cradles simply have a hole at each corner and some lack holes altogether (**Fig. 6c**). These cradles are discussed by Pat Getz-Preziosi (1978). Her ideas about the idols' horizontal position would seem to be confirmed by the stone plaque from a Koufonesi cemetery which bears an idol carved in one piece in relief (**Fig. 6d**) (Zafeiropoulou, 1970, 429). It is unclear how or why a cradle was suspended (Fiedler suggested that it served as a 'heilige Schwinge'), but a rather unusual relationship might seem to be suggested between the worshipper and the diminutive deity, if such it was, which was slung in a hanging cradle in such a way.

Relationship to the individual

A further notable feature of these figurines is the close relationship they seem to have borne to the individual. We do not know whether they were worn about the person, as in the case of the chalcolithic figurine from Cyprus which carries a small figurine around the neck as a pendant (**Fig. 7**). A very small stone figure from Crete slightly predating the Early Bronze Age bears a hole at its centre (**Fig. 8**). Doumas suggests that as the figure was a source of power to the individual during lifetime, so at death it had to be buried with them and at the same time neutralized in some way in order to remove its power. He suggests that such an intention may have lain behind the custom of pinning the figure down or wedging it between the stones of the grave walls (1968, 92-3). A similar idea might lie behind a custom of figurine breakage at burial. This line of thought, if substantiated, shows up interesting aspects of the relationship between the individual and the figurine, indicating that the latter, even if representing a deity, was closely identified with the former. A similar inference could be drawn from the parallel between the traces of red paint still discernible on some figurines and the red paint possibly used to paint the body of the deceased, as suggested by the presence of pestles, pallettes and pigments in the grave with red a predominating colour (see, for example, Doumas, 1968, 52ff). As Renfrew points out, even if the larger figures qualified as cult images, the funerary associations of the figurines 'would make the personal element in their use an important one also' (1983, 11). It would seem that even if the figures represent deities, they stand closer to, and are more identified with, the individual than a normal concept of deity would imply. Perhaps they stood somewhere between deities and humans, in a middle ground which Schefold enters with his suggestion that they portray ecstatic heroes and nymphs (1965), and Ucko with his proposal that the figurines' functions may have included their use as initiation figures, and as vehicles for sympathetic magic (1968, 434-7, 442-4).

While no conclusion will be drawn here about the use and significance of the figures, we are left, as Barber (1983, 12) points out, with a sense of their possessing special value, whether in an economic or psychological sense. He comments further that 'The strong predominance of female figures and the deliberate choice to emphasise sexual characteristics suggest that the main type (perhaps the only type in early times) is in some way connected with fertility ... the most common votary was one which drew attention to the fundamental role of women as the source of life and renewal in the community' (1983, 12, 13). It is this aspect of the figurines which has led to theories of a Mother-Goddess. At the same time, their generally small size combines with their varied use, apparent horizontal position, and close personal association to suggest that these ideas of fertility may not have been formulated in a unified or monotheistic manner.

Non-personified forms

It is worth noting, moreover, that some of the representations of divinity are barely personified, having only the most rudimentary resemblance to the human form. Renfrew's type I.D. of the Grotta-Pelos culture, for example (see **Fig. 4**) is barely more than a long rounded stone. **Fig. 9c** which, through the intermediary stage of **Fig. 9b** can be seen to belong to the same type as **Fig. 9a**, is hardly more representational; see also **Fig. 34c**. The religious beliefs we are investigating here have elements which in another context might be described as the worship of stones. The mountain peak sanctuary at Traostolos has a baetylic stone which may belong to this period. An interesting question is further raised by the stone weights which have created problems of interpretation, for example at Myrtos, by appearing scattered throughout the settlement, by being of different sizes which would impair their smooth functioning as loom-weights, and by in some cases bearing a depression rather than a full perforation which would render them impossible to hang (as in **Fig. 10**). For Warren the evidence suggests that the stones were not (or at least not primarily) loom-weights (1972, 237). He refers elsewhere to a very large collection of weights from the Knossos palace which were associated with shrine models and other ritual objects (see *PM* I, 220-4, 248-253).

The female 'idols' are also associated with another non-human form, the triangle, which is emphasised on Cycladic figurines. The triangle appears in a pronounced hatched form on the 'Goddess of Myrtos' (**Fig. 11a**), the squares perhaps suggesting material covering the pubic area (thus Warren, 1972, 210). It may carry a similar association with the female pubes or with fertility when it appears in isolation. Elizabeth Banks (1977), commenting on some curved triangular Neolithic objects from Lerna, mostly red, which were specifically made in that shape with perforations for hanging (**Fig. 11 b** and **c**), interprets them as pubic shields which 'probably had some part in a practice which focussed on the fertility of Neolithic womanhood' (1977, 330). Although of different use, an interesting parallel is provided by the triangular objects found in large numbers in the Neolithic 'shrine' at Nea Nikomedeia (ILN, April 18, 1964, 604-5, Fig. 12). Platt (1976), discussing some triangular plaques from Bronze Age and Iron Age Palestine which she also proposes as pubic coverings, points to links between the triangular form and female divinity which can be traced back to the Early Bronze Age Jemdet Nasr period in Mesopotamia. Now the Lerna pubic shields which, as proposed, were specially made for the job, often bear a decoration of mottling or streaky lines which might be taken as a representation of pubic hair. Dots and stripes are also used in the depiction of female pubic triangles on the 'frying-pans' (see, most clearly, **Fig. 38g**, and also **Figs. 38d, 40 a, b, d** and **f**). In the light of this one might wish to reconsider a series of triangular clay 'counters' from Myrtos. These objects (**Fig. 11d** and **e**), many of them curved, are re-used pieces of clay vessels cut into shape which had been 'deliberately chosen to show hatched or other painted patterns or incised and pointillé decoration from fine grey ware' (Warren, 1972, 217). It is possible that an association with the female pubic triangle was intended again here. These objects were, as Warren points out, called counters 'purely for want of a better name. We have no evidence for their use. One may speculate that they were for some kind of game' (1972, 217). The fact that the majority of them were found singly in different locations might suggest their use separately rather than, say, like a draughts or chess set, and their distribution over the site might suggest that they were items of common usage. One was found in the 'shrine-store' which also contained a stone, red ochre and bones (Warren, 1972, 85). Once again we may speculate whether these pieces bear any relation to the female figurines whose pubic triangle they so closely resemble.

Such use of stones, and triangles, is consistent with an 'animistic' religion which, as discussed briefly above, can see spirits or supernatural forces immanent in plants, animals, stones, streams and other elements of the natural world, and may moreover develop these into a schema of ideas about cycles of change in human life and nature before anthropomorphic divine characters enter the scene. Such a pluralistic, rather than monotheistic, basis for Aegean religion is acknowledged in talk of a Cretan 'polysymbolism': '… on est frappé de la multiplicité des invitations symboliques adressées aux puissances d'en haut: elles sont partout rappelées à l'attention, sous des formes diverses, coexistantes et comme insistantes. Dès 1930, il avait été parlé à ce sujet d'un *polysymbolisme* crétois … dont le principe est aujourd'hui admis' (Picard, 1948, 198). From the evidence of Cretan caves, Faure also argues for 'un polythéisme à la fois fonctionnel et géographique' (1964, 194).

The possibility that 'animistic' features may have been present in prehistoric Aegean religion has in some quarters been accepted. Thus Doumas (1968, 91) suggests that the level of civilization of Early Cycladic culture 'does not speak in favour of the view that they entertained explicit conceptions of divinity — hardly to the extent, at least, that they would give expression to such concepts in concrete pictorial terms'. Coldstream, though his own interest is in anthropomorphic representations, allows that 'A Minoan goddess may dwell in a tree, in a

pillar, or in a shapeless lump of stone; she may fly down to her shrine in the form of a dove...'
(1977, 3). Evans comments about the stone: 'the baetylic stone was always at hand as a
material home for the spiritual being, brought down into it by due ritual' (1931, 13). The stone,
according to Evans, only became charged temporarily, whereas 'The sacred tree might itself be
regarded as permanently filled with divine life as manifested by its fruit and foliage' (1931,
13).

In this discussion, it should be borne in mind that the concepts of one divinity and many are
not necessarily incompatible in the religion of a simple society. Thus in his study of the
religion of the Dinka of the Central Nile Basin, Lienhardt (1961, 31-2, 56 and passim) explains
how their unified concept of one Divinity (*nhialic*) can embrace a multiplicity of elements
including clan-divinities (mostly animals and plants) and more or less personified deities
associated with features of the natural world, as well as powers linked with a particular disease
or place, especially streams and woods. Lienhardt stresses that the attempt to outline a Dinka
'creed' or pantheon hinders understanding of a religion which 'begins with *natural* and social
experience of particular kinds' (1961, 96). The Hindu notion of *mātā* can also embrace one and
many (Pocock, 1973, 41-3, 89).

Conclusion

Leaving aside the question of whether the term 'Mother-Goddess' has any usefulness in
describing Aegean religion in this early period, the evidence presented in this section suggests
that whatever notions of female divinity may have existed, they had little in common with our
concept of a monotheistic religion and a considerable amount in common with traditions of
animistic religion. Thus the organization of religion was not centralized but manifested in
household cults, while the figurines, if they are representations of divinity at all, are generally
small; appear singly or in numbers in a variety of burial practices; bore a special relationship to
the individual and were perhaps in some way identified with her or him; were not revered in
our sense of the word and may belong in a horizontal position; are not always personified and
can appear as a stone and perhaps as a triangle. The concept of divinity, even if at some level
connected to a 'Mother-Goddess', is apparently decentralized and diffused. The figurines
therefore offer no evidence incompatible with the concept of animism or 'animate divinity' as
Evans terms it (1931, 13), against a background of which it may be possible to propose the sun
as another element in a schema which can embrace stone and tree as manifestations of divinity.
We are therefore not lacking a theoretical framework for the evidence of sun representations to
be discussed in this first chapter.

1.3 THE IMPORTANCE OF THE SUN

There has been a tendency to overlook or deny evidence for the importance of the sun and
moon in the religion of Bronze Age Greece. Thus Nilsson (1950, 413), discussing depictions
of the heavenly bodies, writes: 'The sun and the moon had a place in the religious ideas of the
Minoans, but these representations are not sufficient to prove that they also had a cult.' His
conclusion on the matter states (1950, 420): 'In the Minoan world there are consequently no
certain traces of a cult of the heavenly bodies; the evidence goes to show that they are
represented in religious scenes much as the anthropomorphic Sun God and Moon Goddess in
Greek art, e.g. in the west pediment of the Parthenon, viz. as the cosmological frame-work of

the scene. This presupposes some cosmogonic myths or at least beliefs relating to the Heavenly Bodies.'

The reference to anthropomorphic gods and the comparison with fifth-century Greek culture may be anachronistic here and are certainly questionable grounds from which to argue for the religion of this prehistoric period. Nilsson's views have exerted great influence and his arguments will be discussed more fully in Chapter 2 when we meet most of the material he reviews. Other scholars have been more open to the possibility of a cult of the heavenly bodies in the Bronze Age Aegean: thus Picard discusses it (1948, 197); Matz sees a 'Star of Ishtar' on some Cretan seals (1928, 86-7, 129); Evans and Kenna identify sun-worship on a seal (see below p.16). However, never has all the evidence been brought together, the whole case reassessed, and the implications for our interpretation of Aegean Bronze Age religion recognized.

Identifying solar symbols

Before we start, however, and quite apart from the question of whether an Aegean cult of the sun is a tenable idea, we face a major problem, that of the sun's iconography. It is hard to determine exactly the number of representations of the sun because it is hard to be certain which motifs are intended to signify the sun. In his list of points which may be helpful in understanding symbols, Renfrew (1985, 14) mentions that a symbol may relate graphically to the concept represented in a 'natural index'; he cites the example of the frequent use of a crescent to depict the moon. Unfortunately the sun is not so easy and lends itself to a variety of circular or rayed graphic motifs. An examination of the seals belonging to the early period reveals a large number of designs which might be interpreted as representing the heavenly bodies, particularly the sun. They have rarely been so interpreted, and an assessment of whether they should be so interpreted must be based on some methodological guidelines. The equivalent graphic motifs current in our own culture are clearly not a trustworthy guide. Here I will use three separate reference points: sun motifs on near-Eastern seal-cylinders; sun symbols in Egyptian religion; and sun motifs on Minoan hieroglyphic seals as interpreted by Evans.

The interpretation of sun motifs on the near-Eastern seal-cylinders presents its own problems of identification. Several motifs, however, which in a later period are positively identified through text or context as the sun, appear in representations contemporary with this early period in the Aegean. **Fig. 12** shows some motifs we might consider. Of these, **Fig. 12 a, b** and **c** appear as an Ur III innovation in the late third millennium B.C. and have been identified as astral symbols, perhaps solar symbols; **Fig. 12d** is rarer but is contemporary with these and is probably a simplified version of **Fig. 12b**. **Fig. 12 e** and **f** can be traced back as far as the eighteenth century B.C.; both are thought likely to be solar symbols at this date. **Fig. 12 g** and **h**, from the early second millennium B.C., had been regarded as astral symbols of some form, but a recent discovery allows the confident interpretation of the circle containing the outline of a many-pointed star as a solar symbol. The Stela of Dadusha, dating from circa 1800 B.C. and now in the Iraq Museum in Baghdad, bears (uniquely at this early date) a text identifying such a symbol as the sun (Khalil Ismail, 1986, and Islamaa Gailani, personal communication, 1985). The winged disc, **Fig. 12i**, appears from the early eighteenth century B.C.; later texts and contexts provide a clear identification with the sun. Other symbols we might refer to include **Fig. 12j** which is not definitely identified with the sun, although in the variation shown on **Fig. 12k** the context of the crescent suggests there may be a case for such an identification. The swastika, **Fig. 12l**, bears no clear solar identification, while the cross, **Fig. 12m**, appears post-1700 B.C., later than our period, but sometimes taking the place of the sun-disc or winged disc. (Collon, 1975, 1982, and personal communication.) Other astral symbols from the near-Eastern repertoire are shown on **Fig. 12n**.

We know that EM Crete had contacts with Egypt and the near East (see recent summary in Warren, 1984b); it seems that contemporary near-Eastern seals in general and, in one case, such a sun design in particular, were not unknown in Crete in this early period. Four seals can be referred to here. A near-Eastern haematite cylinder seal (**Fig. 13a**), which bears a likely sun symbol, is tentatively dated by Kenna to the eighteenth century B.C. and he suggests a deposition date of the end of MM II (1968, 329), but as its provenance is uncertain it offers no firm evidence. The other three, however, belong to our period: a silver cylinder seal with unclear design from an EM II context in a Mochlos grave (**Fig. 13c**); a cylinder showing two figures from Tholos B at Platanos (**Fig. 13b**); and a lapis lazuli cylinder from 40 cm below a MM IIIA floor at Knossos which is also likely to belong to our period (**Fig. 13d**). The latter bears a circular symbol with a star on it, and crescent below, parallel to those shown in **Fig. 12**. It can confidently be interpreted as sun and moon. There are thus some grounds to argue that the near-Eastern repertoire of astral symbols was not unknown in Crete.

Fig. 18 shows the motifs used to denote the heavenly bodies in Egyptian religious symbolism. These motifs show some overlap with the near-Eastern material. The Egyptian motifs on **Fig. 18d** and **f** have no parallel in the Aegean material. The scarab representing the sun at dawn (**Fig. 18e**) calls to mind the Messara scarab seals; these seals, along with other Messara finds, indicate some contact with Egypt, but we can only speculate whether any religious ideas were transmitted along with the artistic ideas.

Another useful reference point here will be Evans' study of Minoan hieroglyphic signs. Although he did not explicitly recognize the implications for his theory of Minoan religion, Evans commented that 'Among more symbolic ideographs the solar or stellar disk with revolving rays, and a four-petalled flower, are of frequent appearance' (1909, 133). In his catalogue of signs (1909, 221-2), he identifies four motifs as representing a 'star or rayed solar symbol' (**Fig. 16a**); a further five as representing a 'Day-star or sun with revolving rays' (**Fig. 16b**); two as representing the 'Solar disk without rays', commenting that it is hard to distinguish them from certain forms of the eye sign and that the second sign is identical with the Egyptian hieroglyph for 'sun' and 'day' and is also the Chinese sun symbol (**Fig. 16c**); one further sign is described by him as representing the 'sun and four moons' (**Fig. 16d**). Basing our analysis provisionally on his system of identification, we would identify as possible sun representations the selection of radiant or circular motifs on the hieroglyphic seals shown on **Fig. 17**.

Evans' selection of motifs could be challenged. However, as a coherent classification made by an archaeologist with no particular axe to grind on the subject of solar symbolism, his selection provides a further useful reference point.

Bearing these three different reference points in mind, we can turn to a selection of Cretan seals belonging to this early period, **Figs. 14** and **15** (by no means an exhaustive collection of such designs). In this material we find a motif of radiating lines in **Fig. 14 a - e**; the technique of marking out the shape of a circle with a series of small circles is evident in **Fig. 14 f - i**; lunettes have also been identified on **Fig. 14i** (Kenna, *CMS* VII, 37). A cross in a circle is found in **Fig. 14 j - o**; a series of concentric circles or a circle containing a central dot, generally with the addition of rays, are found in **Fig. 14 p - v**. In **Fig. 14v** we may again see a cradling lunette; while **14w** shows a plain rayed circle without a central dot. The rays may be set obliquely (**Fig. 14u**), or may curve into a whirl of which there are several varieties

(**Fig. 15 a - d**). These lead us into spiral forms (**Fig. 15 e - g**). The rayed motifs are also sometimes developed into the swastika (**Fig. 15 h - o**).

It is perhaps surprising, in the light of the oriental and Egyptian parallels and Evans' system of identification, that scholars have been so reluctant to take the risk of identifying any graphic motif as representing the sun, and moreover that they have been so strikingly inconsistent in the interpretations they have offered of the kind of motif shown on **Figs. 14, 15** and **17**. Thus **Fig. 19a** is described by Xanthoudides as a 'rich cross design' (1924, Pl. XIV), and **Fig. 19b** is identified by him as a 'nine-rayed star' (1924, Pl.XIV). A star is also the interpretation given to the whirling motif on **Fig. 19c** by Boardman (1970, 97). The Van Effenterres identify the motif on **Fig. 20a** as 'Motif étoilé au centre d'un cercle de dentelures en "tourbillon" ' (*CMS* IX, 18), but seem to take a leap of imagination in identifying the design shown on **Fig. 20b** as 'Table d'offrande (?) au centre. Étoile d'un côté' (*CMS* IX, 28). Kenna is fond of the 'star' interpretation, and applies it to **Fig. 21a** ('A curved-rayed star', *CMS* XII, 60) and **Fig. 21b** ('two stars', *CMS* XII, 140). Although it lacks any circular line round its circumference which could make it a wheel, and in fact has a scalloped edge, he interprets a green steatite discoid as 'A star motif or a wheel' (*CMS* XII, 41) (**Fig. 21c**), and an incomplete circular line near the circumference of the design prompts him to interpret **Fig. 21d** unquestioningly as 'A wheel' (*CMS* VIII, 152). In the light of his lack of interest in connecting any of these motifs even tentatively with the sun, it is perhaps surprising to find him describing **Fig. 21e** as 'Sonnenscheibe' (*CMS* VIII, 25) although he describes **Fig. 21f** as 'a solar symbol or a star' (*CMS* XII, 87) (the double axe shown on the central disc may be a later addition). In his collaboration with Sakellarakis, Kenna is perhaps more cautious: they describe **Fig. 22a** as a 'whirling pattern around a central cup-sinking' (*CMS* IV, 65), and **Fig. 22b** as 'Three centred circles, the outer of which is toothed' (*CMS* IV, 67); if any more ambitious description is applied, it is, however, again that of a star and we find **Fig. 22c** described as a 'Rayed star or sinking, surrounded by a rayed circle' (*CMS* IV, 83). Similarly, we find Platon describing **Fig. 23a** as 'four stars' (*CMS* II, 1, 507) and **Fig. 23b** as an eight-pointed star (*CMS* II, 1, 126).

Nilsson (1950, 414-5) has interpreted similar representations as portrayals of a sea-urchin. After concluding that the cross is a 'merely decorative scheme' (1950, 424) he states that he will not attempt 'a general discussion of the value and significance of the cruciform symbols including the *swastika*, which certainly has such a value' (1950, 425). His remark that 'The *swastika* is so rare that it can hardly be believed to have any important significance in the Minoan world' is unexpected in the light of the frequent appearance of this symbol on early seals (**Fig. 15 i - o** shows a small sample).

One might speculate about how many of the 'decorative elements' which the Van Effenterres (1974) record on 30% of the faces of a selection of 350 prism seals of the EM III - MM II period might turn out to be representations of the sun. These 'decorative elements' are almost the single most popular type of design categorized by the Van Effenterres, second only to the animal and bird designs found on 35% of the seal faces, and far more common than human figures which they record on 14% of the faces. It is interesting, however, that their study records 'cosmic symbols and religious objects' on only 1% of the faces. As the Van Effenterres themselves remark on the difficulties of making a classification of ancient seal motifs from a modern perspective, 'on peut s'inquiéter de savoir si une quelconque typologie moderne, avec sa logique propre d'interprétation, risque d'avoir quoi que ce soit de commun avec un antique système — s'il y en eut un — de choix des motifs': in this very vein of thought one might wonder whether the religious significance of the seal designs was originally intended to be limited to 1% of the motifs, and how many of the 'decorative elements' might, under the 'antique système', have been intended to fall into the category of cosmic symbols. We have already noted (pp.2-3 above) that the use and significance of the seals probably went beyond that of the purely functional.

What, then, are the criteria which we can reasonably use to determine whether or not any given representation is intended to show the sun? Parallels with the contemporary near Eastern or Egyptian symbols will affect our opinion; Evans' choice may also influence us. Where a motif fills the face of a seal it is perhaps impossible to determine its intention. However, if a motif appears in a larger design in an area of the field which could be sky, it might be thought of as a sun or star; if it appears to be in a meaningful relationship to human figures we may think its presence is not purely decorative. At the same time, other archaeological evidence suggesting the significance of the sun, which will be presented below, such as the easterly orientation of significant buildings, may make us more open to the possibility of such interpretations.

The possibility of sun-worship has been seriously considered as a feature of the early society of Malta, contemporary with this first period of my study, and of the culture which built Stonehenge. It is known that the sun played an important role in the religious ideas of contemporary Egypt, with which finds such as those from the Messara tholos tombs show that Crete had some contact. In the Egyptian context 'sun' and 'star' are not mutually exclusive interpretations, but are highly compatible within the same framework of religious belief which focussed on all the heavenly bodies. It is known that a sun-deity featured large in the religion of contemporary near-Eastern society, with whom again there are signs of contact; moreover, we have seen that there are some parallels between known oriental sun-signs and motifs common on the Cretan seals of this early period. It is perhaps surprising, therefore, to find how little serious attention has been given to the possibility that similar religious ideas may have played some role in early Aegean religion.

Conclusion

The Cretan seals shown above are only a selection from a very large number of seals bearing similar designs. A separate project would be required to make a full survey of such designs. I have omitted discussion of similar motifs appearing on different types of object such as the jug and pyxis lids shown on **Fig. 24**. The intention here is simply to question existing assumptions and to open up the possibility of attributing a greater significance to solar symbolism than has been done to date. I am not suggesting that all the motifs mentioned above are intended as representations of the sun. Some of them may indeed be sea-urchins. Many of them may represent stars or other objects unknown to us. Many shade off into stylized and purely decorative graphic designs. However, the recurrence of certain motifs in two separate Mediterranean traditions and in a selection made by a scholar who had no particularly cherished theory invested, will carry some weight. There seems a good case for advancing the hypothesis that some of these motifs *are* suns, and if even only one-third of them are to be so interpreted, a serious re-assessment is required of our interpretation of religious ideas of the period. Renfrew points out (1985, 21) that sometimes the scale or quantity of finds rather than their intrinsic nature commands attention, as when a commonplace object occurs again and again in a votive deposit. Applying this quantitative approach to the case in hand, we see a series of motifs recurring in great proliferation in a medium (seals) which can independently be argued to carry a magico-religious significance. As such, they command our attention and may do so even more when we explore the other contexts in which they appear.

1.4 A FEMALE SUN?

The firm association of the sun in classical Greek culture with male deities such as Helios and Apollo has tended to lead to an assumption, which has not been sufficiently rigorously examined, that in the prehistoric period also the religious symbolism of the sun, such as it was, would have gravitated towards a male divinity or divinities.   We have seen that the preoccupations of Early Aegean religion centred around female fertility; it will therefore be of particular interest to follow the evidence given above of the significance of the sun in this early period with a second set of evidence which suggests not only the significance of the sun but its association with female elements.

The seal evidence

Thus **Fig. 25a** shows a design on a steatite prism from central Crete in which two women are placed on either side of a low, and therefore possibly setting or rising, heavenly body in a scene which Evans describes as 'long-robed women ... adoring a rayed solar symbol' (*PM* I, 125) and which Kenna (1960, 43) describes as 'Two women adoring the solar symbol .... This is perhaps a representation of the sacred dance', although Nilsson describes the heavenly body concerned as an 'orb with hook-shaped protuberances' (1950, 386), and Boardman describes the design as 'Two women and a star' (1970, 97). The two women in this design each have an arm raised towards the 'sun' with the forearm rising diagonally from the elbow and the hand held horizontally. It shows a marked similarity to the position shown in the Egyptian symbol denoting worship of the sun (**Fig. 25b**). The similarity of the position of the arms of a woman on another seal (**Fig. 26a**), and the similarity of the sun's position in relation to her body, suggests that here again we might have a representation of the sun, although the depiction is slightly more unusual in this case, and Boardman describes this object as a 'blob whirl' (1970, 98). If it is indeed a sun, we might imagine that it is emitting only two rays, one up and one down. This might be by reason of the narrow space into which it is fitted in the design; however, a similar design of two-rayed concentric circles is found elsewhere (see **Fig. 26b**), and it is quite similar to one of Evans' hieroglyphic sun motifs shown above and reproduced again here for comparison (**Fig. 26c**).

Not entirely dissimilar is the scene shown on a Cycladic diadem of the third millennium B.C. (**Fig. 27**), which Renfrew has described as depicting two 'sun discs' next to 'adorants with arms raised' (1972, 421). For Zervos too the scene shows 'l'adoration du disque solaire' (1957, 258). The 'adorants' in this case appear to be wearing long robes or dresses and so we may perhaps think them to be women. Tsountas (1899, 124) compares their shape to the psi-shaped Mycenaean figurines, and the discs to the designs on the 'frying-pans'. Hood sees a 'bird-headed deity' (1978, 192) while Caskey sees 'divinities in semi-human form standing with raised arms' (1964, 65). We thus have three designs showing what seem to be women with arms raised next to an object which with greater or lesser certainty can be interpreted as the sun. In one case (**Fig. 25a**) the women may also be dancing. Renfrew (1985, 19) has pointed out the frequent correlation between special movements or dance and religious activity.

The next design is rather more problematic. **Fig. 28a** shows what might be a running female figure, described by Van Effenterrre as 'la déesse aux bras levés' (1980, 430), beneath a disc in the field above. The female sex is suggested by the use of a triangle for the lower half of the body: we have mentioned the strong association of the inverted triangle with female representations, and **Fig. 28b** shows a triangle with protruding legs used in a very similar way to portray the lower half of a female figure (herself described by Van Effenterre as probably a goddess of fertility, 1980, 433). However, we cannot be sure about the sex of the figure on **Fig. 28a**, nor can we be sure about the disc in the sky which may well be a break in the seal (Betts, personal communication, 1984).

Another problematic seal is shown in **Fig. 29**, the so-called 'Jester Seal' from Knossos. Its design shows a seated figure holding a disc which may have an addition above. But is the figure female? At first sight it might appear not, but the skirt, long hair and the breasts visible on the original must incline us to leave the question open. If we are looking for objects in ritual activity which might symbolize the sun, then people doing things with discs will interest us. The Egyptian quality of the design is also relevant. There is no reason to think the figure a jester, although playful activities are not necessarily incompatible with ritual. This point is relevant to the next picture. **Fig. 30** shows two figures which may be female: they have breasts but these may derive from the solid drilling technique used for engraving the body (John Betts, personal communication, 1984). Their heads have spikes radiating from them and they appear to be playing a very athletic game with two balls. Xanthoudides (1907, 163) describes the figures as two acrobats and the circles as 'two ornamental circles'. Might it also be a ritual scene?

We think of such ritual as a serious matter, but Renfrew points out that it is not necessarily so, and that rituals may be close to games, both sharing features such as rules and an element of display (1985, 14-15). It is thought that in some early cultures ball games were a cult practice intended to stimulate the movement of the heavenly bodies: a purposeful, symbolic, and in some ways serious game. Thus Frazer (1941 78-80, 644) refers to rituals of circumambulation, cup-and-ball games, and the throwing of fiery discs to assist the sun in its course and revive its strength. A similar significance has been ascribed to the ball-games which took place on the ball-courts beside the temples in pre-Spanish Mesoamerica (see, for example, Stern, 1948, Burland et al., 1970). Discussing **Fig. 30**, Grumach comments on the rayed heads of the figures and the possible connection of their circular movements with astral concepts (1968, 296). However, we have insufficient evidence as to what kind of activity is depicted. The acrobat on a sword from Mallia does not help us. We can only note the discs combined with acrobatic movement, the rayed heads, and the appearance of all these elements on a three-sided prism seal.

In order to do justice to the range of representations we should note briefly three other seals of highly dubious interpretation and significance. The first (**Fig. 20b**) has been tentatively described as an offerings-table with a star (*CMS* IX, 28); if it were so, it would interest us, but the interpretation of the offerings-table as such appears highly dubious, as does the interpretation of the smaller object as a star or sun or anything else. The second, **Fig. 31a**, depicts what might be a figure of indeterminate sex in energetic movement accompanied by a motif of discs enclosing a central point on either side; again, a game might be indicated but it is impossible to tell and the design may well be abstract as generally interpreted (see *CMS* II, 1, 108). The third seal (**Fig. 31b**) shows a seated figure seated under what looks on first inspection like the branches of a tree; however, it could equally be a whirl. If this motif could be convincingly argued to be either a tree or a radiant (possibly sun) motif, it would be relevant to this study, but the condition of the engraving renders any attempt at interpretation futile. On **Fig. 68b** two seated figures of indeterminate sex, set antithetically, raise an arm to a (?)star-shaped motif; the gesture is discussed below (p.40).

To summarize the evidence presented so far for the asociation of the sun with women in possible cult practices: we have seen female figures raising their arms to what is arguably a sun; a seated figure of dubious sex holding a disc; and scenes of (?)women dancing, running, and involved in an acrobatic ballgame, which activities might in some cases bear a relation to the sun. Of these only the first three, **Figs. 25a**, **26a** and **27**, present substantial evidence. Given the paucity in this early period of representations showing active human figures, let alone scenes where those activities seem to be of a ritual nature, to have three similar representations of this nature is impressive and, it could be argued, of considerable significance. If a recognized symbol such as the 'horns of consecration' were shown rather than a possible solar symbol, much weight would be attached to these scenes. On the basis of the parallels discussed above, I would like to propose that **Figs. 25a**, **27** and probably **26a** show sun-symbols, and reflect a seriously under-acknowledged strand of religious belief and activity in the Bronze Age Aegean, of which we will see many more examples.

However, from the representations mentioned so far, the association could consist simply of the relationship between female votaries or priestesses and a male sun divinity. For more explicit evidence about the nature of the connection between the sun and women, which suggests a closer association including elements of identification, we have to turn to evidence from the Cyclades in the shape of the objects known as 'frying-pans'.

The 'frying-pans'

The funerary associations and proposed ritual uses of these vessels have been discussed above (pp.3-4). What is under investigation here is the nature of the designs which these objects bear. The largest part of their circular face is filled in many cases with designs which depict items such as spirals, water with a boat, or a sun. What is of particular interest is that just above the handle can often be seen a clear delineation of the female pubic triangle. This raises the question whether one interpretation of these objects might be as representations of the human body. The handle would in this case be understood as suggesting a pair of tiny legs, as Zschietzschmann has suggested (1935, 663), and the round bulk of the vessel as a belly. Coleman finds it likely that the resemblance to the human body was suggested by the shape of the handles (1985, 196). One can note the principle of small tapering legs which splay out at the bottom on various figurines, for example those of Cycladic type from the Messara shown on **Fig. 32**. Some of the figures from the earliest times in Crete appear to dispense with legs altogether; **Fig. 33** shows some Neolithic examples, **Fig. 9 b** and **c** some from the Messara tholoi. As a compression of the female figure into circular form, the distortion is no more extreme than in, for example, the spherical representations from Crete shown on **Fig. 34 a** and **b**, and the spirit of schematization and stylization is certainly not alien to Cycladic art in which legs can be absent and the head can be minimal or non-existent, and some of the female figurines are known simply as 'pebble-shaped' (see **Fig. 34 c** and **d**). Zschietzschmann has argued that whatever other uses the 'frying-pans' had, we must interpret them as idols (1935, 664). **Fig. 35** shows how the 'frying-pans' might fall within a continuum of representations reflecting varying degrees of schematization.

That a similarly distorted representation of the human body with decoration on the central disc was not unknown in the Mediterranean generally at this time is shown by a series of clay disc-shaped figurines from a Bronze Age stratum in the second temple of Tarxien on Malta dating from the third millennium B.C. (Zammit, 1930, 53-54. His identification of the objects as phallic is surprising). **Figs. 36a** and **36b** show examples of these objects. Unlike the 'frying-pans' they have no raised rim on the reverse side; some have a hole in the centre. They have a projection behind which allows them to prop up in a diagonal position. They are mentioned here for their similar shape and for the comparable type and degree of stylization which they reveal; no comparison in terms of significance or use is intended. From the near

East, triangular Hathor pendants (see **Fig. 36c**) reflect a similar degree of stylization, representing for Barb 'a gradual development from the symbol to the anthropomorphic idol' (1953, 200).

(The necessity of excluding from Chapter 1 material which may date to EH III prevents me from including in the discussion here the circular-bodied figurine from Area G at Lerna, shown in **Fig. 247e**.)

Whether or not the identification of the whole 'frying-pan' as a portrayal of the human body is correct, the main point of interest here is the very close association on some of the 'frying-pans' of the sun with the female pubic triangle. The identification of the triangle has been made by several scholars. Thus Doumas (1968, 19) remarks on the 'incised portrayal of the female pubic area such as one finds on the marble idols of the period'. Renfrew (1972, 421) further comments: 'This symbol occurs so often, and compares so closely with the pudenda of the Cycladic marble figurines, that no other identification seems possible.' It is worth commenting that in some cases in the same position one can see a circle which perhaps represents the hole of the vagina, as occasionally in contemporary figurines: **Fig. 37** shows two examples where the 'hole' of the vagina, as well as the pubic triangle, is emphasised on two female figures from Crete. On **Fig. 38b** Coleman identifies 'Female genitalia represented by circular pattern of *Kerbschnitt*' (1985, 206).

The identification of the sun on the 'frying-pans' is also hard to dispute. Of the association of the central design with the sun, Renfrew remarks (1972, 421): 'The central rayed-disc may reasonably be identified as the sun. On the Louros pan it could hardly be a star ... The significance of symbols in this context is not clear; nor do we know why sun, sea and the female sex should be linked in this way.' It is precisely the problem of untangling this 'implicit religious symbolism' to which this study will address itself in discussing the sun symbolism of this early period. A further remark of Renfrew's at this point, that the sun was not 'the object of a cult in Crete' proves, from his reference, to be another example of the influence of Nilsson's views concerning the sun. The sun symbolism of the Cyclades and of Crete will here be investigated conjunctly.

At this point it is relevant to present some examples of the 'frying-pans' in question. **Fig. 38** shows some examples which carry both what appears to be a sun design and what may be taken as a female pubic design. **Fig. 38g** shows Coleman's collection of such pubic designs; one might perhaps also add the oval shown on **Fig. 38h**. **Fig. 39** shows other examples which bear the sun design but no pubic triangle; these serve to corroborate the strong association of the sun with this type of vessel. It should be noted that none of these collections are exhaustive. **Fig. 40** shows examples which carry the pubic triangle without a sun design and in conjunction with a different design; these will be referred to later in this chapter. **Fig. 41** shows some items which are included for the sake of interest: 'frying-pans' bearing spiral, seven-pointed star and rayed designs which might or might not be intended to represent the sun. (The spiral within rays on **Fig. 39b** suggests that both symbols may carry the same meaning.)

Higgins has taken these designs as the basis for suggesting that the 'frying-pan' was a 'fertility charm in the form of a womb' (1967, 55). Thimme goes so far as to claim that it represents 'the holy womb of the Great Goddess' (1964, 84); and it has been suggested to me (in discussion after Goodison, 1987) that these are female figures about to give birth. However that may be, the depiction of the sun on these objects argues strongly for its religious significance, while the close association of sun symbol and pubic triangle suggests that the sun was not only linked with women as possible ministrants of its cult but was in some way connected or identified with the female body in its functions of fertility and sexuality. Given the simplicity of the iconography of this period, it is unlikely that a male sun symbol would be depicted in sharp antithesis closely adjacent to female genitals.

Conclusion

This evidence suggests that in Early Bronze Age religious symbolism the sun was closely associated with the female sex. That this is rather a controversial suggestion to make for early Aegean culture does not reflect a lack of parallels for such an association in other cultures. Thomson (1949, 211-212) cites several cases where the sexual identification we think of as normal for the sun and moon is reversed, referring to the Murray Isles belief that the moon ravishes women thus causing menstruation, and the Maori belief that it is the moon which causes impregnation. He points out that the moon still carries the masculine gender in Slavonic and German, and that the early Greek word for it was 'mēn', a masculine noun which survived as the word for month. From the American continents Lévi-Strauss has listed several peoples who see the moon as masculine and the sun as feminine, including the Dakotas, the Maidu, the central Algonquin, the Cherokees, the Seminole, the Chimila, the Mocovi and perhaps the Tobas (1970, 332, 334).

Amaterasu, the main goddess in the Japanese pantheon and ancestress of the Imperial dynasty, was a sun-goddess. There are also Mediterranean examples of associations of female deities with the sun. A Sun- or Fire-goddess seems to be pictured on the Sargonid seal shown on **Fig. 42i** (see Frankfort, 1939, 129). As early as the third millennium Egyptian religion knew the goddess Nut as the sky (see **Fig. 42a**) who swallowed and gave birth to the sun (**Fig. 42b**); see also **Fig. 42j**. Later Egyptian iconography also offers us analogous examples of two female figures, usually Isis and Nephthys, adoring the rising or setting sun (**Fig. 42 c, d** and **e**) as well as evidence of a tradition in which the sun disc is shown placed at the womb (**Fig. 42 f** and **g**) and contains a child (**Fig. 42 g** and **h**). Many of these concepts can be traced back to earlier centuries in the textual evidence. Isis is sometimes identified with the goddess Hathor, who is described as bearing the sun-disc in her womb. As mother, wife and daughter of Re, Hathor both renews, and springs from, the sun (Bleeker, 1973, 48, 65-6) (see **Fig. 42j**).

We have seen that females were significant in the Aegean religion, and have reviewed evidence that the sun was also significant. Now we are putting the two together. At this point my intention is merely to point out that if, as I suggest, there was a cult of the sun in the early Aegean, its officiants appear to have been women, and the appearance of sun representations on objects explicitly sexed as female suggests that the association may have gone as far as the identification of the sun as female. While there is evidence to suggest that the sun may have been the object of ritual and may have been seen as a divine body or entity, there is very little to suggest any antecedent in this period for the later Greek male solar deity.

1.5 EVIDENCE FROM THE TOMBS

At this point it is relevant to make some general remarks about the burial practices of the Aegean in this early period. A survey of these practices has been made by Branigan (1970, 152-178), Doumas (1977) and Renfrew (1972, passim). Here what I will investigate is the possibility of the existence of certain underlying ideas about death in the Aegean area during this period. At first sight such a project might appear incompatible with the variety of burial practices apparent. In Crete alone this variety embraces cave and rock-shelter burials which continued to co-exist with rectangular chamber tombs and tholos tombs which were preferred in some areas, while towards the end of the period pithos burials and larnakes came into popularity. This range of practice might appear to have little in common with customs in the Cyclades, where cist graves were most common with some local variations to include corbelled graves and rock-cut tombs; Doumas (1977, 70) also comments on some chronological variations within the Early Bronze Age period. On the mainland of Greece an equally wide range of practices can be traced, from the Neolithic custom of burial within the settlement, occasionally with the use of pithoi for child burials, to the use of cist graves and rock-cut tombs with some exceptional local variations, as in the case of Levkas. It is no wonder that Renfrew comments, 'No clear pattern emerges from this multiplicity of customs' (1972, 431).

Branigan points to the distinct difference between the funerary architecture of different parts of Crete, but comments, 'Certain small scraps of evidence from Mochlos, such as the white clay fill in some graves, the heaping up of the skulls in one corner, and the building of a paved forecourt to at least some of the tombs, suggests that the differences in ritual may not have been so marked. So too does the evidence of the burnt bones at Kanli Kastelli and elsewhere' (1970, 177). It is precisely such scraps of evidence that this study will examine in some detail. Within the variety of practices there are certain recurrent themes, like threads which are sometimes woven in, but sometimes apparent in a piece of cloth; ultimately their consistent reappearance commands our attention.

The funerary remains are the expression of certain ideas about death which can only be inferred from those remains. This section will present the case that behind the variety of practices there lay a collection of beliefs which may have been shared in the Aegean, or at least in which there was considerable overlap between the different areas of Greece. As Renfrew comments of ritual generally, the 'full complexity of the Cretan symbolism' is not found outside Crete (1972, 427) and in this investigation the focus will again be on evidence from Crete, but with reference to other parts of the Aegean and the extent to which they may have shared, to some degree, in the symbolic ideas which the Cretan burial practices reflect.

Grave shape

In Crete the Late and Sub-Neolithic custom of burial in caves or rock-shelters continued into the Early Bronze Age in parts of the island. The use of caves for burial and ritual over many centuries after communities had stopped living in them has been remarked by historians and taken to suggest that some form of sanctity was believed to reside in the cave as such. In what did this sanctity lie? It has been suggested of the earliest European cave-dwellers that '... the essential belief seems to have been in the earth as a mother ... upon whose continued presence human life depended. Therefore the deep caverns of the earth were holy places; upon their walls and ceilings the revered and desired beasts were painted or incised in the splendid movements of full life, and the earth was thus impregnated with them' (Scully 1979, 10). The argument for the existence of an 'Earth-Goddess' or 'Mother-Goddess' in the early Aegean has been discussed above and found unconvincing. Whether the people of the early Aegean ascribed a sex to the earth, whether that sex was female, and whether the cave was imagined to be its womb, are all questions that must be answered on the basis of specific evidence from the cultures in question.

The building of the Juktas peak sanctuary altar over one end of a chasm (Karetsou 1981, 1987) certainly suggests the significance of the earth itself as a focus of cult. One of the arguments that the sanctity of the cave lay in more than its history as an early dwelling-place derives from the persistence with which its shape was recreated for burial places for centuries after it had ceased to be used for habitation. Thus in parts of Crete we find the appearance in EM I of the circular tholos tombs which are, Matz has suggested, 'reproductions in architectural forms of caves used for burials' (1962, 46). Evans argues: 'That in their origin the beehive ossuaries themselves were taken from a class of circular dwellings in vogue amongst the living can not be doubted' (Preface to Xanthoudides, 1924, xii), but as there is no indigenous evidence of circular dwellings (apart from the circular lamp from Lebena), he has to look to North Africa for prototypes and is obliged to propose Libyan immigrants at the start of the EM period. Branigan discusses the possibility that they might reflect influence from the Middle East or North Africa (1970b, 123, 140ff) but argues that they imitate the cave shape. One could also point to the circular buildings in use in third millennium B.C. Cyprus. Figure-of-eight shaped and curvilinear prehistoric houses are not unknown on the mainland (see, for example, *AR* 1982-83, 37). What remains unanswered, however, is the question why such a form should be borrowed, or preserved, for the use of the dead when it was not generally so preserved for the living. What was there about its shape which singled it out in this way as particularly appropriate for the use of the dead? The explanation offers itself that the tholos's circular domed or roofed cavity, with an entrance so small in many cases that it would need to be crawled through (the majority are less than a metre high), could be seen as mirroring not only the cave but the internal female anatomy with round womb and narrow birth canal (see **Fig. 43**). More evidence will be needed to establish whether this connection is viable.

The tenacity of this shape is apparent, though more sporadically, in other parts of the Aegean. Thus Branigan points out (1970, 145) that a tradition of circular or sub-circular graves may be traced in the Cyclades back to Late Neolithic times. Although the most common grave type, the cist grave, is not circular, we find on Syros the practice of building graves which were constructed in a corbelled fashion so that only a small opening remained at the top. On Melos we find rock-cut tombs which, like the rock-cut tombs of the mainland in the third millennium B.C., reflect different variations on the theme of passage leading to circular cavity (see **Fig. 44a**). None of these reflect what might seem to be the most economical or functional method of making a hole in the ground to place bodies in, and it is possible that the desired shape had some symbolic significance for those who cut it into the rock. Again, graves similar in shape and construction to the tholos tombs, though smaller in size, have been found on the mainland, at Aghios Kosmas in Attica, and on Euboia; they are built below ground level, with walls sloping inwards, an entrance with small dromos and a covering slab on the top (Mylonas, 1959, passim; Matz, 1962, 45-6). More exceptionally, a large grave complex has been excavated at Steno in Levkas where the dead were burned, often incompletely, on a circular stone-built platform before being buried in pithoi or small cists in the centre of the platform which was then covered by a mound (Renfrew, 1972, 431) (see **Fig. 44b**). At Archanes Fourni an unusual mortuary building, No. 21, containing pottery from the whole Minoan period, again shows a tholos-like underground structure, reached by six steps giving access to a pit (*AR* 1983-4, 61). The tenacity of the circular and passage shape throughout the Aegean area is one of the factors which must be taken into consideration when investigating the beliefs about death current in this period.

Link with vegetation cycle?

Another question to be considered is the association which has been suggested between agricultural or vegetational cycles and the human cycle of life and death (see, for example, Branigan 1970b, 137). The process of crop-growing depends on a seed being deposited in the earth, germinating, and growing forth into a new life. Many writers have pointed to the emphasis on fertility and pregnancy in the figurines of the early Aegean and have suggested that the link between the woman who bears children and the earth which bears trees, crops and life-sustaining fruits is an easy one to have made. However, whether it *was* made, and whether it affected ideas about death, is a matter which we have to assess rather than assume.

Perhaps relevant in this context is the very large hypogeum at Knossos which Evans attributed to the EM III period (see **Fig. 45**). This is a circular, dome-shaped underground chamber, which in its construction echoes the caves and circular tholoi used for burial and was, Evans believes, approached through a dromos 'like the doorway of a tomb' (*PM* I, 104). Interestingly this dromos, like the doorway of many tholos tombs, also faces east. If it was indeed used as a granary, this parallel in construction might imply a conscious parallel drawn between the earth as fertile storehouse for new vegetative life and the earth as storehouse for human life in the burial of the dead. However, the cooler temperatures underground could provide a secular motive, and we have in any case no evidence about what was stored there. A stronger case for the argument that the earth was symbolically seen as a womb for the reproduction of human life, parallel to the role it served for the reproduction of plant life, lies in the posture in which the dead were buried.

Contracted corpses

In the tholos burials he excavated in the Messara, Xanthoudides (1924, 134) reports that the dead were generally deposited in the first instance in a contracted position direct on the ground or in cists of wood or clay. Although extended inhumations are also found, the practice of contraction is confirmed from other tholos burials. Although again not universal, the practice of contraction was the norm in the Cyclades, where bodies were placed, usually on their right side, in a severely contracted position with legs bent up, forearms against the chest, and hands often in front of the face (Doumas 1977); see **Fig. 46 a - c**.

The argument that this position was dictated by the grave size is unconvincing; as Doumas points out, larger pits could have been dug and there are examples of larger tombs containing contracted burials (1977, 54). Similarly, in the graves of Zygouries on the mainland, Blegen points out that the contraction of the dead body was clearly not due to lack of space (1928, 44). It has been suggested that the position may have been achieved by tying the dead body (Doumas, 1977, 54) and that such tying might have been intended to prevent the dead from waking (Renfrew, 1972, 432), but the use of ropes is unproven and such an explanation does not account for the choice of this particular position for the body, which could equally have been bound extended. In the absence of any other explanation the position itself must be considered as being chosen on its own merits and for its own significance, and in this context the similarity to the position of the unborn foetus is hard to avoid.

The notion that, as the vegetation retreats back into the earth in winter, to await spring, so the human body returns to the earth in death to await rebirth, is one for which historians have been quick to point out parallels. Red ochre on bodies at Çatal Hüyük has been interpreted as symbolizing the possibility of rebirth from death (see, for example, Mellaart, 1964, 103, and Dietrich 1974, 105, 110), apparently by analogy with the blood-covered state of the new-born child. Red-painted bones are known from the Aegean Neolithic (see, for example, *AR*, 1978-80, 30). This raises the question whether red colouring was used on the bodies of the dead in the Bronze Age Cyclades, as we know it was used sometimes on the bodies of figurines. We have no evidence from the Cyclades that it was used but, as Doumas comments, this practice cannot be discounted entirely 'since countless graves contain marble bowls and palettes in which vestiges of red pigment are preserved' (1977, 58). Lumps of red ochre may also be found in a cemetery context, unassociated with any grave. Xanthoudides, however, records no traces of pigment on the palettes he found in the Messara tombs and does not believe them to be colour palettes.

The evidence is fragmentary and inconclusive, but a series of factors (such as tomb shape, body position, pigment) which in isolation make no sense could, if taken together, sketch out a coherent scheme of belief concerning death and rebirth.

Tomb outlook

One of the explanations given for funerary architecture of the Early Bronze Age is that it simply reflects an imitation of domestic architecture. I have pointed out (above p.22) the lengths to which scholars have needed to go to adduce any such prototype for the tholos tombs; moreover, Branigan (1970, 154-158) has argued convincingly against understanding the rectangular chamber tombs of eastern and central Crete as houses for the dead. For the Cyclades, Doumas has argued from the presence of doorways too small for use in some corbelled tombs that 'The significance of the doorway in each tomb is therefore probably symbolic, the representation of the doorway in an ordinary domestic house' (1977, 49). The presence of non-functional door openings in graves at Aghios Kosmas was also attributed by Mylonas (1959, 66) to the desire to give the grave the appearance of a house. Such a motive can perhaps not be disproved, but it is possibly more interesting here to ask why, of all the features of a house, a door was the one which was thought significant to reproduce, even in a non-functional and symbolic form, for the use of the dead person. **Fig. 95a (below)** conveys the impressive nature of some of these doorways. Why was it so important for the deceased to have a doorway? This raises the interesting evidence about orientation in the burial customs of the Early Bronze Age Aegean.

Of the Cretan tholos tombs, Branigan has pointed out that their doorways are remarkably uniform in size, orientation and construction and that they all face eastwards 'which is surely indicative of some particular funerary belief' (1970, 167). There is also some evidence of deliberate choice concerning the orientation of the corpse: at Vorou, bodies were mainly aligned in an east-west orientation with the head on the east; if daggers can be thought to be worn facing point downwards, the fact that the majority of daggers at Aghia Triadha point westwards (Branigan, 1970b, 89, Fig. 19), might again suggest that heads pointed east. The evidence from the Cyclades can, again, be found to be not literally identical but highly consistent in spirit. Cycladic graves show no consistent compass orientation, but the usual practice was to place the body with its back along the long side of the grave and facing the entrance. Doumas points out that this often meant that in hill-slope cemeteries the dead would be facing towards the valley, or towards the sea on coastal sites, a fact which has prompted the suggestion that 'a deliberate attempt was made to arrange the bodies in a position overlooking the open horizon' (1977, 55). Doumas himself is evidently not sympathetic to such an idea, although the suggestion that the eyeline of the dead was important is corroborated by the practice of often placing one funeral offering immediately in front of the face. Why was it important what the dead body looked towards? Why might it have been important for it to be provided with a doorway or an open view? Doumas is clear about the answer to this question: 'Such suggestions imply that the early Cycladic people believed in an After Life, a proposition which cannot be proven by strictly archaeological data' (1977, 55). (See also Doumas in *Aegaeum* 1, 1987, 15-18.)

Secondary burial

At this point it is relevant to discuss one of the major contradictions in the burial practices of this period: the contradiction between the care apparently taken on the occasion of burial, and the subsequent extreme disregard shown for the bones of the deceased. The initial burial often involved, as discussed, a choice of a certain position for the corpse and a certain orientation, possibly some treatment of the body with paint, certainly some selection of objects particularly appropriate to accompany the dead. Branigan (1970b, 112) suggests that such belongings were placed in the grave not simply to placate the dead, but to give them no excuse or reason to return to the house; he believes that these were not just possessions but 'palpable expressions and extensions of the man's personality or identity'. He cites some of the votive or religious objects selected, as evidence for a belief in a spiritual after-life of the dead (1970b, 113ff). He uses the evidence for food and drink being left with the dead, along with personal belongings, as indicating that the dead must have been buried intact as whole bodies (1970b, 170).

It is hard to reconcile such practices with the state of the bones which had subsequently been cleared to the side of tholos tombs, or jammed into the small cells or trenches around the tholos. Objects were found only with the last burials, and so presumably the property accompanying the earlier burials was removed when the bones were transferred from their original burial place: as Xanthoudides concludes, 'plundering of earlier interments must have been almost a regular part of Early Minoan funeral rites' (1924, 110). Branigan comments that the complete confusion of human remains in every tholos so far excavated 'suggests a complete disregard for the dead' (1970, 170). The mass of bones in the chamber ossuaries of East Crete present the same picture. In the Cyclades similar ideas seem to be reflected in the treatment of the dead. Multiple burials were made in some graves, which over a period of use came to comprise several storeys, as new storeys were added for new burials and the lower compartments came to serve as ossuaries for the older burials. A common feature of these cases is careful treatment of the skull at successive burials but 'general disregard of the remaining parts of the body' (Doumas 1977, 56). In the cemetery he investigated in Antiparos, Bent found that in most of the tombs the bones of the skeletons had been 'heaped together in confusion' (1884, 48). On the mainland, cist-graves with multiple burials have been found which, by their type and distribution, suggest Cycladic influence. Some rock-cut tombs also contain a number of burials, as at Zygouries: at this site Blegen reports 12 or 14 skeletons with their bones mixed up in confusion in a pit in Tomb VII, while 15 skeletons in Tomb XX were found in a mass mostly on one side of the chamber in utter confusion 'as if unceremoniously emptied into a rubbish heap' (1928, 49). Blegen is unhesitating in associating his graves with Cretan parallels; citing cave and rock shelter burials as well as East Cretan ossuaries (1928, 214). In some cases bones were so tightly packed that they must have been stripped first (e.g. Bent, 1884, 49; *AR*, 1977-8, 73).

The primary, careful burial was evidently followed by a secondary burial of a rather different nature. Anthropological literature provides examples of secondary burial from other areas of the world. For the Mapuche Indians (Faron, 1967, 230-33) the interval could last from days to months, reflecting the view of death as a slow transition. Hertz's study of the Dayaks of Borneo (1960, 27-74) refers to several other examples of the practice. In some cases the corpse waits up to a year, and the disappearance of the flesh is seen as significant. The soul may be believed to linger until the final ceremony when dance and (sometimes frenzied) incantations help it on its journey of transition to eventual rebirth in plant, animal or human form. Practices such as the retention of the skull in the home for good luck, or the pulverization of bones at the final ceremony to rub on the body or drink for protective powers, recall some aspects of the

Cretan evidence (e.g. Myrtos and Kaminospelio, see below); but these ethnographic parallels can only make us aware of possibilities. Nor can we use modern Greek secondary burial (see Alexiou, 1985) as evidence.

What seems clear from the prehistoric Aegean material is that again, underlying the varied burial practices of the different areas, there seems to be some such consistent set of ideas about the deceased which explains the apparent reversal in the treatment of the dead. What happened to the deceased which permitted such a reversal? Was it, as Mylonas (1948, 70) and Branigan (1970b, 113) suggest, that the possessions of the dead were no longer needed once the body had decomposed and the spirit was no longer in its physical home? At what point was the body determined to have sufficiently decomposed? Flesh takes several years to rot, but perhaps the bones were deliberately stripped. Was it simply a matter of convenience to sweep aside the previous burial when a new burial was made? Or did some other timing determine its transition from one state to another? Branigan makes the suggestion that: 'the burial of the dead with their personal belongings, food, and drink, the subsequent disregard for their skeletons, and the continuing practice of offerings to or on behalf of the deceased, taken together can only imply that the Early Minoans possessed beliefs which were mature enough to envisage a spiritual after-life which was not necessarily dependent on the survival of the physical body' (1970, 175-176). How and at what point might the dead have been thought to leave the body to enter that after-life? And of what did the after-life consist?

Containing slabs

At this point I shall pass over another method of burial, in pithoi, which will be mentioned below (pp.42-3), and shall move on to discuss an aspect of funerary architecture which has provoked some speculation. Tholos II at Porti in the Messara was closed with two large slabs, one inside and one out. Branigan (1970b, 110-112) points to the custom of placing lids on burial containers and suggests that a fear of the body while it was still articulated may have dictated the need to keep the body securely contained. He argues that the heavy stone door would have been intended to keep the dead in rather than the living out. He comments elsewhere that no Messara tombs have their doors opening towards the settlement, although the graves are placed close to the settlement. A rectangular stone slab 1.40m long covered Tomb VII at Zygouries (Blegen, 1928, 43), and slabs sealed the chamber tombs of the large EH cemetery at Manika (*AR* 1983-4, 17). Renfrew suggests that very possibly the heavy slab covers on some Cycladic graves may have been intended to keep the dead from rising, just like the heavy stones at the doorway of some of the Messara tholos tombs (1972, 432). He does not take this to indicate a belief in an after-life, but Doumas also notes the contradiction of burying the dead 'with special precautions to isolate the dead from the communities of the living' while at the same time the proximity of the cemeteries to the settlements 'could be interpreted as an acknowledgement of the continued membership of the dead in a viable community, provided that their actual bodies were safely interred' (1977, 30-31). He remarks that it could, of course, be a matter of convenience not to carry bodies further than necessary; however, what we have seen so far of the burial customs of this period, such as the depth of digging sometimes required, the care with orientation and position, the use of heavy stones and the practice of ritual, does not suggest that convenience was a prime consideration. Branigan also notes a significant contradiction in this aspect of the burial customs in the Messara, finding it very strange that in spite of their fears they kept their dead close to the living, building their tombs next to their settlements: 'In some way which we have yet to examine, the cemeteries were important in the life of contemporary society …' (1970b, 120).

part of the area in front of the tomb, and in front of the complex of chambers stood a large platform built of slabs of stone (Branigan, 1974, 201). Alongside the settlement of Pyrgos II, a fine paved road was built leading to a small courtyard outside a built tomb (*AR* 1977-8, 71). But what were these areas used for? The pavements may have been the site of rituals which were separate from actual interments, but their choice of location would appear strange if those rituals did not have some association with the same complex of ideas.

Branigan suggests that the cemeteries were, before the emergence of communal shrines and palatial courts, the focus of rituals and ceremonies important for the community as a whole, probably centred on a vernal deity related to the cycle of life and death (1970b, 138). He suggests (1970b, 136) that the rituals on these platforms may have involved dancing, citing a MM II plate from Phaistos which shows three female figures dancing, and a similar fragment from a second plate (**Fig. 49a**). He also mentions the famous *Iliad* passage (XVIII, 570-8) about the dancing-floor dedicated to Ariadne at Knossos. However, we do not have to look so late for evidence of dancing in Crete: this early period offers several other representations depicting dance. Thus an offerings-table from Phaistos (**Fig. 49b**) shows a scene similar to the plate; its depiction on such an object in the sanctuary of the Palace suggests a ritual significance for this dance, while the vegetation suggests it was performed outdoors. Other scenes of dance are perhaps shown on a seal from Platanos (**Fig. 49c**), and another seal where an animal head seems to be included in the design (**Fig. 49d**), or where an animal costume may be involved (**Fig. 49e**). Dancing or processing appear to be depicted on another seal (**Fig. 49f**). From the Cyclades, the Korfi t'Aroniou building which may or may not be a shrine has yielded what Doumas describes as a 'representation of dance' (1965, 57) (**Fig. 49g**); although it could also be a game.

We are therefore in a situation where we are aware of certain paved areas at cemeteries which appear to have been used for rituals of a more generalized nature and possibly involving more people than the specific rituals associated with an individual burial; we might also suppose from their location that these rituals were not completely dissociated in theme or orientation from burial rituals or beliefs. The suggestion has been put forward by Branigan that these rituals may have involved dance, and in fact we have a series of representations, at least one of which derives from a religious provenance, which show activities of processing or dancing which would have required just such an exterior paved area for their performance. So on the one hand we have some paved areas and are looking for rituals to fill them, while on the other we have scenes of dance and are looking for a dance-floor to place them on; in this situation we could entertain the possibility that the two may in some cases have belonged together. This possibility is discussed further below.

Conclusion

This section has looked closely at varied and localized burial practices in the Aegean area to draw out threads of continuity and suggest that there may have been some fairly widespread, although not uniform, ideas underlying them. Branigan remarks of the Messara practices and beliefs: 'Either we must see them as being entirely localized ... without any semblance of uniformity within the region, or else we must admit that they are far more complex and sophisticated than we have previously imagined' (1970, 175). He favours the latter solution for the Messara, and the same alternative could be posed for burial customs within the Aegean area as a whole. This section has itemised a number of factors such as tomb shape; contracted body position of the dead; possible use of pigment; the significance attributed to doorways or the outlook of the dead; the change from care to disregard of body remains after a certain period;

the tendency to segregate or contain the dead yet keep them close to settlements; the possible recycling of human bones in ritual; and the existence at cemeteries of pavements which could have been the site of more generalized rituals. Hard to explain separately, these factors become coherent and comprehensible if seen as reflecting a belief in the rebirth of the dead. Not all factors are present at once, but cumulatively they build up a jig-saw picture which is compatible with a sophisticated series of beliefs concerning death and rebirth. The idea that the death of vegetation and of humans, and the rebirth of both, were associated in the minds of the early inhabitants of the Aegean has often been mooted as a possibility or sometimes has been inferred by analogy from other cultures. This section has examined piecemeal the fragments of evidence from different parts of the Aegean which could give substance to this theory. I have argued that many different aspects of the evidence point towards the notion of some kind of rebirth for the human dead.

1.6 THE SUN AND THE DEAD

Easterly orientation

The previous section referred to the practice of building tholos tomb doorways to face east (p.24). Early exceptions include Lebena Ib, Trypiti, and Marathokephalon which face south-east, while Korakies N, Kaloi Limenes II and Kephali face south. Only one, at Myrsini, faces north-east. (The northern opening on Lebena IIa does not appear significant as this tomb is, uniquely, attached to Tomb II and uses that tomb's antechamber which does face east.) We have also seen above (p.24) that at some sites bodies were also aligned with head to the east. Branigan (1970b, 185) debates whether this was required by tradition or religious necessity, but comments: 'This orientation of the entrance, together with that of the bodies, to the east is at once suggestive of a connection with the rising sun. In a funerary context it may clearly be related to a belief in the revival of the body after death.'

Ucko makes some remarks about the difficulties of evaluating evidence from burial orientation. Referring to the work of Perry, he comments: 'It used to be claimed by ethnographers that the corpse was always orientated in the direction in which the spirit was to travel, a direction which correlated both with the position of the land of the dead and the home of the people's forefathers ... There is no doubt that there are many examples, such as some groups of the Shona of Rhodesia ... where this *is* the aim of orientation, but this is by no means invariably true' (1969, 272). He proceeds to give a list of many variations where the feet or the face or other factors indicate the significant direction in which the dead will move. These examples, however, indicate that there are many variations of meaning which can be drawn from burial orientations, rather than that no meaning can be drawn from them. In this instance the easterly orientation suggests a correlation with the sun's movements, which must be assessed in the light of other evidence for and against such an association.

Xanthoudides attributes this practice of using east-facing tombs to 'some tenet of religion, or perhaps merely to age-long conservatism' (1924, 134). It would be possible to argue the latter by analogy with the widely-forgotten belief which still dictates the east-west alignment of Christian churches and burials. However, as Shaw asks of the tholos orientation: 'what was the basis for the tradition if it were not connected in some way with the morning sun?'; he expresses his own opinion that there was a connection, direct or indirect, with one of the heavenly bodies (1973, 57).

That this concern with orientation was not limited to the Messara area is suggested by the orientation of the Chrysolakkos ossuary at Mallia, which is 12° from east-west. That this was the result of deliberate thought, and that the funerary orientation was further believed to have some relevance for the buildings of the living, is suggested by an identical orientation in the construction of the early Mallia 'agora', House Beta, and the network of MM I roads, approximately 500m away. Shaw has further pointed out that the internal dimensions of the 'agora' are identical with the external dimensions of the Chrysolakkos ossuary. The usual north-south orientation of Cretan palace courts, evident already in the proto-palatial period, does not conflict with this: as Van Effenterre points out, the significant factor is the orientation of the buildings. In palace construction the significant consideration seems to have been that certain rooms should face east (see p.77 below). (Van Effenterre, 1980, 209, 246, 256-7; Shaw, 1973, 52 n.26.) Karetsou (1987, discussion) has noted the 'very impressive' easterly orientation of the Juktas peak sanctuary altar from MM II on. Other interesting east-facing structures include the arc-shaped building built over the ruins of the settlement at Fournou Korifi, the door of the 'shrine' at Korfi t'Aroniou and the circular buildings recently excavated at Aghia Fotia (Tsipopoulou, 1986); while the central court at the same site is also oriented east-west.

As it has been noted above that one motif used to represent the sun in the early Aegean may have been the cross within a circle, it is perhaps relevant to mention in passing a type of shallow bowl bearing a cross painted in red which has been found in large numbers outside the tomb at Aghia Kyriaki, apparently for specifically funerary use (Branigan, 1974, 201). Warren has identified discs with convex bases bearing a similar design, from Myrtos, as potter's wheels (1972, 245); he also reports several jug bases bearing a black painted cross, and bowls with a red painted cross on the base (1972, 105, 120). A similar design was found on a bowl from Zygouries (Blegen, 1928, 82, Fig. 69). We shall return to this design below.

Other archaeological evidence

Firmer independent evidence of the association of the sun with funerary beliefs is provided by the 'frying-pans', those objects so often found in graves and so often, as we have seen, bearing a sun motif on their decorated face. A further parallel can be pointed out: in the last section evidence was presented suggesting that the grave may have been imagined by the inhabitants of the Early Bronze Age Aegean symbolically to represent a womb for rebirth of the dead; while the sun on the 'frying-pans' is placed in the circular area above the female pubic triangle, that is, in the womb area. If both 'frying-pan' and tholos grave symbolically represent womb, we can comment that both are round, while the former often bears a sun on it and the latter has its doorway facing east to the rising sun. We can note an emphasis on circular forms: circular graves, circular funerary vessels, and apparently a concern with the circular movements of the sun. Moreover, it is interesting that at least ten of the Messara tholoi also bear radiating spikes or projecting slabs, see **Fig. 50**, **Fig. 48b** lower left and **Fig. 48c**; Branigan points out the shortcomings of the various structural explanations for those slabs, which were in some cases carefully shaped, and concludes that no 'convincing explanation' has been offered for them (1970b, 41-44). Perhaps the tholoi themselves were sometimes 'rayed'?

It is also relevant to return here to the paved areas outside tombs which were discussed in the previous section. We reviewed evidence that those paved areas were a location for ritual and discussed the possibility that those rituals may have involved dance. Now, in addition to those representations of dance shown in the last section, we also have the scene of apparent dancing before a sun shown on **Fig. 25a**, and the scenes of 'adoration' of the sun with arms raised shown on **Figs. 25a**, **27** and perhaps **Fig. 26a**. We also saw evidence of acrobatics which may or may not have ritual associations and may or may not bear any relation to the sun, but which would certainly have required a smooth-floored open area for their execution (**Fig. 30**). The rituals which some of these scenes seem to portray have not been widely recognized as such, nor do we have any idea where they may have taken place or how they may have been integrated into the life and beliefs of the community. However, given the other solar associations of funerary architecture and vessels, it is perhaps not unreasonable to suggest that the cemetery pavements may have been the location for those activities. If this were to be considered, we might have to think about rituals on those sites which could have included raising arms to the sun, dancing to it, perhaps holding circular objects (as in **Fig. 29**) or performing athletic activities such as running or ball games. While most of these are speculative, raising arms and dancing to the sun are convincingly documented (see above). We can only speculate what timing might have determined the occurrence of such rituals, whether they were annual, seasonal, followed the cycle of crops or of death and birth in the community, or other factors.

A further matter for speculation is whether the sun was seen by these early people as in any way connected with the use of fire during burial ritual. Such a connection is not necessarily self-evident. The use of fire in funerary rituals has long provided a puzzle for archaeology. It is exceptional in the Cyclades and on the mainland, occurring at Steno in Levkas where the deceased were partly burnt on a pyre on a circular platform before being buried at the centre of it. There are, however, many examples from Crete which also involve some kind of partial burning of which the purpose is unclear. Cave burials at Kanli Kastelli, Pyrgos, Zakro and Trapeza have all revealed traces of burning. The unburnt bones indicate that it is not a question of a practice of cremation (Branigan, 1970a, 154). Lighting or fumigation has been suggested as another possibility, but this would not account for the extent of the fires, the heat of which splintered the floors in several of the Messara tholoi. At Porti, almost an entire thick burial stratum was blackened by fire and smoke; Xanthoudides comments, however, that the bones were blackened not by burning but by later exposure to close fire. Another alternative explanation is that rituals took place inside the tomb which included a funeral feast or the offering of burnt sacrifices, but as Xanthoudides points out, these would equally not call for so large a fire. Moreover, animal bones are absent from most Messara tombs and so animal sacrifices are not indicated. Xanthoudides concludes that a satisfactory explanation for the fires is lacking (1924, 135).

Recent excavation at a Knossos cemetery has presented puzzling evidence of a layer of burnt bones between EM and MM sherds (*AR* 1976-7, 11). The absence of fire traces in many cases shows that the use of fire was not a universal practice, but it is by no means clear how that use fitted into the scheme of other funerary beliefs and customs. Tholos B at Koumasa, one of the earlier Messara tombs, was found to have signs of fire not just at a hearth in the centre but at a fire-place in the south-eastern part of the tholos, and outside. In Tholos A at Platanos the signs of fire are most marked at the centre. Alexiou has pointed out that the lintel of Lebena Tomb II was blackened on the underside, perhaps by the passage of torches, and Levi has suggested that some of the burnt timber he found in Kamilari I came from torches. At Tholos IIIA and B at Megaloi Skoinoi traces of fire were found inside the tomb, and, from Tholos IIIB, quantities of charred bone in very small pieces from the antechamber area (Blackman and Branigan, 1977). We have seen (p.6) that extinguishing a fire could be part of Egyptian funerary symbolism.

However, this use of fire in the tholoi remains a mystery which none of the current explanations of Early Bronze Age religious practices can account for.

The hypothesis being proposed here is that Minoan burial beliefs in this early period may have associated the journey of the deceased with the movements of the sun, in particular envisaging some form of rebirth assimilated to the re-emergence of the rising sun in the east; that more generalized rituals at the cemetery site may also have been connected with the sun, whether this involved celebration, imitation, or stimulation of the sun's movements; and that the use of fire in funerary ritual may also have had some association to the sun in the minds of those practising the rituals.

Similar ideas have been arrived at independently by Van Leuven (1975), but unfortunately he is preoccupied with a later phase of the Bronze Age and does not present any substantial evidence which can help us at this stage of our investigation.

Parallels from other cultures

However, such an association between burial customs and the sun is not without parallel in other cultures of the third millennium B.C. Thus the passage grave excavated by O'Kelly at Newgrange in Ireland is constructed in such a way that once a year, on the shortest day, the dawn sunlight beams down the 70ft. long passage and into the burial chamber. Its shape is very like that of the tholos tombs (see **Fig. 51a**). Fleming places considerable significance on this form of construction: arguing against the existence at that time of a Europe-wide Mother-Goddess, he suggests that 'if there is really a single primary idea behind the megaliths, or any kind of initial spiritual unity, it must be searched for first amongst the Passage Graves' (1969, 249). He further comments: 'One possibility is that sun worship was involved' (1969, 257). Of the designs found in the Irish graves, including eyes, he comments (1969, 249-251) that there is no evidence that these eyes were intended to represent female personages: 'Many of the designs look as if they have some magical meaning, but the only tentative identification is that of sun symbolism.' His collection of 'possible sun symbols from the Irish Passage Graves' (**Fig. 51b**) shows interesting parallels to some of the symbols of Aegean origin which have been discussed above as possibly being intended to carry a solar symbolism (compare **Fig. 51b** to **Fig. 14** above). Fleming connects his designs to a clear sun and moon representation from Antelas in Portugal and to possible sun symbols from sites like Granja de Toninuelo, Badajoz (1969, 257). What is interesting here is that he is suggesting that a principle of grave construction orientated to the sun's movements was a significant and possibly even widespread principle in Europe in this period, and that certain symbols found in the graves (which closely recall symbols common in the Aegean) may have been sun symbols.

Closer to the Aegean, and in a culture which we know had some contact with the Aegean, we can trace rather more extensive parallels in Egyptian religion. It is suggested that burial was seen symbolically as a return to the earth of the Primeval Mound (Rundle Clark, 1959, 57); this idea has been endorsed by Dr. Edwards' recent argument, based on the history of pyramid construction, that the stepped pyramid was originally simply a development of the Predynastic primal mound from which life was believed to come at the time of creation (1984). We have here a schema of rebirth from the earth similar to that which has been suggested above for the early Aegean. Written material renders the evidence for Egyptian religious beliefs far more informative than that of the contemporary Aegean culture. However, the various ideas it presents are not completely integrated into one coherent system. Thus there were two quite distinct beliefs about the fate of the dead: one fate was to join your ancestors in living happily in the cemetery, as long as the tomb was properly attended. The other fate, which gained in credence around the end of the third millennium B.C., was that the soul soared up to join the sun and moon and stars in their round (Rundle Clark, 1959, 31). This latter idea is, according to Edwards (1984), reflected in funerary architecture: he has pointed out that entrance corridors to the pyramids can be found to point north towards the circumpolar stars, so that the king could have an exit route to the stars, as well as the route up to the sun offered by the pyramid's steps. In the temples attached to the pyramids, where cult was celebrated daily, the mortuary chamber faced east towards the rising sun; he also suggests that the very shape of the pyramids was an element of 'representational magic' offering a staircase to the sky. Thus the architectural arrangements composed a kind of 'mythical landscape' (Rundle Clark, 1959, 29) in a way which may not have been completely alien to contemporary Aegean religion. The notions of rebirth and of assimilation to the sun combine in the idea that the pink of the dawn sky is the blood of the Mother-Goddess as she gives birth to the sun (Middle Kingdom text from Gebelein, in Rundle Clark, 1959, 89).

I shall discuss below the part which the solar barque played in this schema. Here it will be relevant, however, to say a few words about Osiris, whose cult changed over the course of Egyptian history, and interweaves in an often unclear way with beliefs about other deities. His cult offers several features which have resonances in the Aegean material. Thus in early times he was worshipped in 'tombs' which consisted of a tumulus containing chambers reached by a winding passage; fragments in the Pyramid Texts make it clear that he was bewailed by a group of ecstatic dancers (perhaps priestesses personifying his sisters Isis and Nephthys); and a passage stating that at one point in his story the 'gates of the sky' were opened has been taken to suggest that at this point in the ritual the sanctuary doors were opened (Rundle Clark, 1959, 113, 123). The chamber in a tomb, the entrance through a passage, the dancing, and the emphasis on doors: these are all elements which have featured in my discussion above concerning Aegean funerary practices. It is interesting to note that the 'rebirth' imagined in the cult of Osiris is not a literal rebirth of the god: he is reborn not in his old form but as the vegetation of the new year. The transmission of Osiris' power to his living son Horus distinguishes these beliefs from those concerning Tammuz who is literally brought back to life in person. If proper observances were followed, the dead king could become one with the soul of the original Osiris. In entertaining the possibility of Aegean beliefs in rebirth we should bear in mind that such beliefs would not necessarily have taken the more literal form of rebirth of the soul familiar from the Hindu religion; the Osirian ideas provide a model of rebirth which can remind us of the range which such notions may cover.

Further parallels which can be found in the scenes shown on Mesopotamian cylinder-seals of this period will be discussed below.

1.7 DEATH AND THE SEA

It is relevant here to refer again to the problem posed by Renfrew in connection with the 'frying-pans', which was quoted above: 'The significance of symbols in this context is not clear; nor do we know why sun, sea, and the female sex should be linked in this way' (1972, 421). The sea factor and its relationship to sun and the female sex is precisely the element which will be tackled in this section. The linking of sun and sea is not confined to the 'frying-pans'. There is a substantial body of evidence which suggests that the sea and things of the sea such as boats and fish had some symbolic significance in the religion of this early period and were associated, as through the 'frying-pan' context, with the sun and with funerary beliefs.

Boats

Thus model boats are found in a variety of contexts, some of them religious, such as a grave or a peak sanctuary; **Fig. 52** shows some examples. (We might also wonder whether items of Neolithic pottery such as that shown on **Fig. 53a**, Evans' 'trays', were intended to represent boats: some of them bear holes for suspension and many bear wavy lines on the side.) However, all these objects could be explained as everyday objects indicating no more than that their owner was a fisherman. It could be harder to apply the same explanation to **Fig. 53b**, a recently published pottery object in the Mitsotakis Collection, which seems to be a model of a boat with a honeycomb inside; evidently no literal fishing boat. If, as Davaras tentatively suggests (*AE* 1984, 55-95), it derives from a MM I tholos tomb, it provides interesting evidence for the religious and funerary significance of the boat in this period. It can in any case be taken as pointing clearly towards a special symbolic significance for boats.

The many representations of boats which appear on seals could again be interpreted as literal portrayals of the sailor's trade. However, Betts concludes a study of such seal illustrations from the Bronze Age, in which he attempts to extract as much information as possible about the construction and functioning of Minoan boats, with the comment that they tend mostly to be represented as cult objects or symbols of some sort in stylized forms rather than as realistic illustrations of the actual vessels in which the Minoans sailed (1971, 325). He concludes that the seals and gems on which ships were commonly portrayed (it is the MM three-sided prisms which concern us here) had little sphragistic use but rather an amuletic function, apparently based as much on their range of symbolic motifs as on their material and shape. Commenting that naturalistic representations of ships are rarely found, he concludes that the ships which appear in Minoan art 'almost all have some kind of symbolic, semi-religious or occult significance. The illustrations tend … to over-emphasize certain features of the ship, perhaps those which had some special magico-religious significance' (1971, 333). **Fig. 54** shows some examples: if **Fig. 54b** is a ship, it displays some unusual features, while if **Fig. 54a** were taken to represent fishermen, we might comment on their lack of fishing equipment and ask why they are embracing. On **Fig. 54e** we seem to see a seated male and a standing female figure, who are, again, embracing — hardly suggesting an everyday fishing trip. The appearance of fronds accompanying the boat on **Fig. 54d** and **Fig. 55a** again suggests associations beyond the purely literal.

More speculatively, to take up Evans' suggestion that the different sides of a seal had a connected and cumulative meaning (a possibility also discussed by the Van Effenterres, 1974), we could trace another interesting feature of boat representation on seals, which is that it is not uncommon for a 'sun' motif to appear on one of the other faces. On **Fig. 55a** a boat with a frond is juxtaposed with two fish on one side and two stars or suns joined by a line on the other. On **Fig. 55b** a ship is juxtaposed with two quadrupeds and two swastikas on the adjoining faces. **Fig. 55c** shows a three-sided seal bearing a boat on one face and, on another, two seated figures each with an arm reaching up towards a rayed object which may be a star or sun.

One of the features of such ship representations is the occasional presence of a frond accompanying them, a motif suggesting an association with vegetation and fertility and endorsing the suggestion that these are nonliteral representations. The same feature is also apparent when the boat appears on 'frying-pans', which it does in a very large number of cases: examples can be seen on **Fig. 40d**, **Fig. 40f** as well as **Fig. 56**. In these, and the numerous other, cases the running spiral design surrounding the boat could be taken for the sea, and may have the same significance when it appears on its own on a 'frying-pan' without the boat (for example, **Fig. 40 a**, **b** and **c**). In some cases it can be noted that the boat is tilted at an angle from the horizontal as if the boat were on rough sea or sinking (NAM Nos. 5135, 5114, 6177.1). In very many of these cases the sea design is accompanied by the familiar pubic triangle, a juxtaposition whose significance we have already investigated in the case of the sun, but which remains to be elucidated in this instance. The appearance of both sun and sea scene in exactly the same position and with exactly the same juxtaposition to the triangle might suggest some degree of interchangeability, or that both designs represented in some respect a shorthand for the same aspect of experience.

Fish and shells

The fish is not only often included on seal designs of boats, and on those on the 'frying-pans', but also appears without the boat and in several of these instances is clearly juxtaposed with what could be identified as a sun symbol; see **Fig. 57 a**, **b** and **c** (on which latter Platon identifies 'fishförmige Gebilde' around the central motif, *CMS* II,1, 357). These juxtapositions with rayed, whirl, and dot rosette motifs are striking. On other seals the fish appears with other motifs (e.g. a bird on **Fig. 58**). The terracotta fish from the Traostolos peak sanctuary is also interesting, and may belong to this early period, although the site's dating is problematic (Peatfield, personal communication, 1988).

Some similar associations apparently extended to seashells. These are found in tombs in the Cyclades (**Fig. 59**) and also in small numbers at Archanes (Sakellarakis, 1967, 276) and at several tholos sites, as well as on the mainland (Blegen, 1928, 47). Of the tholos shells Branigan has commented that they are never numerous enough to suggest that they were deposited in the tombs as even token food offerings (for example, the tholos at Aghia Kyriaki yielded only 13 shells), and he remarks that they presumably possessed some other ritual significance (1974, 201). While it could be argued that these are simply attractive or personal objects which were placed in the tomb with the deceased, evidence from elsewhere corroborates Branigan's view that they may have held some further significance. Thus a conch shell trumpet was among the equipment found at the sanctuary of the Phaistos palace. In Warren (1972, 321) we read of a situation at the Early Bronze Age settlement of Myrtos where at a coastal site there is a total absence of fishbones and a very low number of seashells, only about 300 in all. This can be compared with the Neolithic site of Saliagos where 20,000 shells were found and these still comprised only 1% of the diet of the inhabitants. Moreover, at Myrtos some selective patterns of shellfish use seem to be revealed: conch and cowrie shells are not found much with limpets. To go by the rooms the shells were found in, the occupants appear to have eaten limpets but no other shellfish, whereas several cowrie shells were found in a cupboard in a completely different part of the settlement, at a higher level which suggests they may have been placed on shelves rather than left on the floor like the limpets. Shackleton comments that these cowries must surely have been intentionally put in a particular place (in Warren, 1972, 325). The two conch shells, one with a hole which would have made it suitable for sounding, were found in a different part of the settlement again, close to one another. There is also a faint trace of what could be red pigment on one of these shells. It seems that shells carried significance which we can only guess at, and which did not rest in their simply being pretty objects or simply being a convenient source of food. Their discovery in grave contexts could be taken to suggest that this significance may have had some relation to funerary beliefs.

To sum up the evidence reviewed so far, it can be seen that we have boats, fish and shells not only appearing in grave and sanctuary contexts, but also appearing closely juxtaposed with, or in some cases apparently substituting for, a sun symbol. The 'frying-pans', as we have noted, have strong funerary associations and the appearance of fronds and pubes on the 'frying-pan' representations might also suggest an association with fertility. The problem is to understand the ideas or beliefs behind this association of things of the sea with sun, death, and fertility. Thimme interprets the 'frying-pan' boats as cult boats with a funerary significance, and postulates a Sea-Goddess/Mistress of the Dead whom the deceased entered (1965, 83-4); but he omits to integrate the sun into his scheme. For Zervos the 'frying-pan' boat is the sacred 'barque solaire' (1957, 258) which carries the 'Mother-Goddess'.

A watery journey?

Now the later Greeks imagined that the sun travelled in a horse-drawn chariot, but there is also a later tradition that it travelled in a dish (see Chapter 3 below). The island inhabitants of this early period did not know the horse, and would more often see the sun set not over land but into the sea. I would like to put forward the hypothesis that they imagined it travelling in the form of a fish or in a boat. This idea would not seem strange to a peasant in modern Greece, where traditional ritual funerary lament refers to the black sailboat which takes away the deceased, who is described as 'My Sun' (Alexiou, 1985; 1974, 191-2); but the context here calls for convincing evidence from this period. Such an idea, of the sun making a sea journey, would account for all the puzzling representations and associations discussed so far in this section and bring them into a coherent schema; it is also endorsed by some other representations shown on **Fig. 60**. The first two of these, **Fig. 60 a** and **b**, are representations of a boat with a large disc in the field above to one side of the mast. Thomas and Kenna recognize the possibility of identifying the disc on **Fig. 60a** as the sun (*CMS* XIII, 105). Evans argues that the disc on **Fig. 60b**, like the crescents in other ship representations, can hardly be an accidental coincidence. He suggests that they are signs of time, two crescent moons signifying two months and the disc 'perhaps a yearly voyage of still greater length' (1909, 203).

Fig. 60c adds an interesting variation on the theme of disc and boat: the design, one of several EC designs found etched onto marble in the small room of Korfi t'Aroniou, also includes two human figures. The excavator Doumas describes the room as a small shrine and comments that it is difficult to define the meaning of these representations but that they may have had a magico-religious function, dedicated to a divinity and showing everyday scenes as thanks or as a plea for success (1965, 41-64). While his identification of the room as a shrine is questionable, an interpretation of the representations as showing everyday activities is hard to sustain. Overall they show a series of strange and interesting situations including dancing, a goat on a boat, a figure touching the tail of a 'catlike' creature, and a figure facing a fantastic creature which is barely recognizable as an animal (Doumas, 1965, Figs. 3, 4, 6, 8, 11, 12, see my **Figs. 49g, 118a, 119a, 120 b** and **c, 122b**). Such representations might seem more likely to represent scenes of cult than of everyday life. Among them is our picture, **Fig. 60c**, of two figures on a boat; beneath the arm of one of them we seem to see a small disc. Doumas, committed to interpreting this as an everyday event, suggests that this portrays work or argument between the figures on the boat, and thus has to interpret them as male figures and adduce (1965, 53) as a parallel for their undivided legs the example of some far-flung, dissimilar and unsexed Ligurian figures published by Isetti (*RSL* XXIII, 61ff). The long skirts of these figures, however, distinguish them clearly from all the other figures in the series which have divided legs and can perhaps safely be described as male (see, for example, **Fig. 49g**).

The appearance of female figures in this context suggests either a serious reappraisal of what constituted an everyday fishing trip in the Early Bronze Age Cyclades, or a recognition that this may be a ritual scene. *If* it is not just a dot, we have also to explain the presence of the tiny disc. It may, of course, be a ball, but then we have to explain why these two people are in a boat with a ball; moreover, unlike the objects apparently held on **Fig. 49g**, this disc does not actually touch the figure's arm. In the light of the evidence presented above, it is possible to suggest that this scene might depict the departure of a (female associated) sun by boat.

This interpretation may be corroborated by a close look at the seal from Archanes (Anemospilia) shown on **Fig. 60d**. Found with the body of what has been interpreted as a priest at a shrine, this seal shows a figure in a boat who has been described as male but whose skirt and perhaps breast might suggest that we have here another female figure (*AR* 1979-80, 50). We may wonder about the nature of this boat journey too. (If the site is to be dated as late as 1600 B.C. (Warren, 1988, 4), then this seal might belong with the later sets shown as **Figs. 208** and **212**.) The embracing figures on **Figs. 54a** and, especially, **54e**, might seem to confirm the possibility of boat rituals.

If, as has been suggested, the journey of the sun below the horizon (prior to its reappearance in the east) was seen as analogous to the process followed by the dead soul (prior to some form of rebirth), then it is possible to postulate that the dead person was sometimes believed to need a boat for the after-life journey. The presence of boats in graves might be associated with this belief. The reference to the boat as well as to the sun (or instead of it) might have arisen from the same associations: both sun and boat stood as a shorthand for the journey ahead of the dead soul. The notion of rebirth, and the link with fertility of vegetation, would account for the association of the boat on the 'frying-pans' with both fronds and pubic triangle.

It is futile to speculate what form of rituals might have given expression to such an underlying belief in different areas of the Aegean. It is interesting that Cycladic burial places often extend down towards the sea or face towards it, and the same is sometimes true in Crete (as, for example, at Mochlos and Aghia Fotia), although a secular motive based on the convenience of digging into a sloping hillside may be the explanation. Again it is impossible to tell whether the scene shown on **Fig. 60c**, if it does indeed show two women on a boat, reflects some ritual practice involving boats and the sea; such practices are certainly not unknown in modern Cycladic religion (Good Friday celebrations in many islands involve a seafront procession bearing the 'Epitaphios', and the celebration of Epiphany can involve blessing the sea and diving for a cross thrown into it).

Leaving such speculations aside, what can more substantially be argued is a connection between the sun and the boat, perhaps as its form of transport, and between both and the beliefs concerning the dead.

Egyptian and Mesopotamian parallels

Marinatos (1933, 232-3) draws a parallel with Bronze-Age Scandinavian representations of boats carrying the solar disc (**Fig. 61**), but we do not need to look so far afield. Parallels with Egyptian religious beliefs have already been discussed, and here it is relevant to refer briefly to the maritime angle of those beliefs. As an alternative to the Primeval Mound, the Primeval Waters were another Egyptian symbol for the source of all life. Thus in a passage of the Coffin Text 714, the High God says: 'I was (the spirit in?) the Primeval Waters … The most ancient form in which I came into existence was as a drowned one' (from Rundle Clark, 1959, 74). Similarly, one version of the underworld is that it lies in the waters under the earth. Burial in the sarcophagus was symbolically seen as a return to the waters (Rundle Clark, 1959, 57), and in one version of the Osiris story, Seth actually kills him by putting him into a chest and throwing the chest into the Nile. Simultaneously there exists a symbolism which sees the sky as a sea across which the heavenly bodies float or sail. Thus in one of the Pyramid Texts Geb tells Nut, the sky: '... you took up into you every god with his heavenly barque' (Rundle Clark, 1959, 49) (see **Fig. 42a**). The High God floats across the sky-ocean looking down on his creation, and to be able to join that boat was one of the ambitions of the dead soul; thus the symbolisms of sun and sea overlap and merge. **Fig. 62a**, using motifs which date back to the Middle Kingdom, shows the passage of the sun through the underworld illuminating the deceased, juxtaposed with the rising sun in the solar boat, symbolizing the rebirth of the soul. For comparison, **Fig. 62b** shows an Egyptian model of a funerary boat, which might remind us of those rather more rudimentary boats in Aegean graves; moreover, the two female mourners on board representing the goddesses Isis and Nephthys have an echo in the two seafaring women on **Fig. 60c**. Sometimes Isis becomes Hathor in this funerary duo with Nephthys. Since the time of the Coffin Texts in the third millennium B.C., the boat is one of Hathor's sacral attributes, reflected in her epithet 'mistress of the ship'. Texts tell us that she travels in the sun-god's boat through the realm of the dead. Hathor's voyage by boat was reflected in festive rituals symbolizing victory over chaos and death (Bleeker, 1973, 60, 69-70, 73, 92-3).

Perhaps less familiar than the Egyptian parallels are those which could be drawn with Mesopotamian religious ideas of the third millennium B.C., which include a sun-god in a boat. Thus cylinder seals from Early Dynastic times onwards show a sun-god who steers with a paddle a boat whose prow ends in a human or animal creature, as in **Fig. 63**. The god often has rays emanating from his shoulders, and his boat is sometimes accompanied by a scorpion; in this depiction, there are two scorpions fore and aft of the boat with the moon and stars in the curve of their tails. The god is also accompanied by a plough. Frankfort (1939, 68), debating whether this scene carries a purely astral or a chthonic significance, suggests that the journey of the sun during the night is depicted, as the moon and stars are sometimes part of the scene even when there is little room for their inclusion. As the seals show an accumulation of associations with agriculture he attributes a chthonic interpretation to the plough, and comments that the three symbols always found with the Sun-god's boat are a quadruped, a plough and a pot.

A sun which travels in a boat may also be, as suggested above, a feature of the religious symbolism of the Aegean in this early period. However, Frankfort's comments raise an issue which has not yet been tackled: what, if any, was the connection between the sun/boat/death symbolism discussed above and early Aegean ideas about agriculture and fertility? Frankfort mentions a quadruped, a plough and a pot. In our Aegean context the pot or jar is a good place to start.

1.8 SYMBOLISM OF THE VESSEL

'Potter' scenes

In his *Scripta Minoa* I, 132, Evans comments that 'The frequent recurrence of pots in the hands of human figures on the seals ... suggests that in many cases we have to do with the potter's craft'. Thus of the seal shown on **Fig. 64a** he comments that 'a pot is apparently being taken out of an oven' (*PM* I, 124), and he suggests that such designs reflect the pursuits of the seal's owner (1909, 131). Such an interpretation of these seals is common. Thus Branigan suggests that the seals shown on **Fig. 64b** show various stages of pot manufacture (1970, 74-76); Van

Effenterre identifies **Fig. 66a** as showing a potter (1980, 558); *CMS* commentaries often offer similar interpretations. Depictions of pots are indeed numerous on these seals, and in many cases this literal interpretation of them is quite adequate.

It is of interest, however, to note that parallel representations of people at work in other activities, such as sowing, harvesting or grinding corn, and weaving, are notably lacking: so why do we have so many potters? It has been pointed out to me that there is no Minoan tradition of showing people at work (Betts, personal communication, 1984). Moreover, if we look closely at some of these designs, we can start to notice some unusual features or ones which might be hard to integrate into an interpretation of all these seals as showing the potter at work. Thus in **Fig. 65a** the figure appears to be standing and simply touching a finished pot with one hand; perhaps he has just completed it. In **Fig. 65b**, however, we find two figures seated on either side of an amphora and, as Platon points out (*CMS* II, 2, 339), they seem to be reaching their hands *over* the vessel. In **Fig. 65c** we may remark on the appearance of what seem to be two branch motifs, as well as on the animal or bird shape of the seated figure's head. As Kenna's reasons (*CMS* VIII, 23) for considering it a later engraving are questionable, the strangely-shaped 'potter' on **Fig. 65d** should perhaps be added to the collection. Close examination of the examples shown in **Fig. 66** reveals several features which might seem incompatible with a scene of a potter at work. Thus, while two hands would seem to be essentially required for throwing a pot, the figures seem to be using one hand only; their upper body and head is bent forward in what gives the impression of a reverential posture; and in some cases we see traces of a high collar suggesting formal dress. The vessel seems to be either a jug or a two-handled amphora in each case, and in each case the figure has a hand resting on the handle. It could be pointed out that with their head bent down in this way it would be impossible for these figures actually to see the vessel which they are supposedly working on. We might suppose this a matter of economy to fit the figure into the seal, were it not that we find this posture reproduced exactly on other seals where the object touched is not a pot but a severed goat's head (**Fig. 67 a** and **b**). In this latter case a ritual context is surely indicated, and would seem to suggest that what we are looking at is a formalized ritual gesture. It recurs in another case where the goat is whole but perhaps trussed (**Fig. 67c**). The posture certainly recurs a number of times in almost exactly the same form, and on occasion the figures are set antithetically as in **Fig. 68 a** and **b**; on **Fig. 68b**, as I have noted above, the figures appear to be reaching towards a star-shaped motif of uncertain identity.

This crouching position, with one hand raised, seems to have a clear place in Minoan iconography, for it is crystallised in a hieroglyphic (**Fig. 68 c** and **d**), suggesting that it was a known and meaningful, rather than haphazard, posture. Evans (1909, 155) compares it to the ideographs of persons on Egyptian scarabs and comments that the gesture indicates a nuance of meaning different from the hieroglyph of the straight standing figure (1909, 181). One finds a slightly different posture adopted by the Egyptian potter-god Ptah, shaper of the world egg and of new bodies for the dead (see Budge, 1904, 500ff).

The jug containing mixed seeds (Sakellarakis, 1982) found in the central chamber of the shrine at Archanes (Anemospilia) might provide us with an example of the kind of vessels which were the objects of such reverential touch.

Although a significant relationship between designs on different faces of the same seal has not been established or clarified, it is interesting to note that, among other examples of similar conjunctions, the 'seated potter' of **Fig. 64a**, who again has one hand resting on a handle, is on the same three-sided seal as Kenna's 'Two women adoring the solar symbol' which I discussed above (see **Fig. 69**). We might wonder whether the activities shown on the different faces may have had any connection with each other. Grumach (1968, 295-6) identifies an animal head on both 'potter' and dancing women, and suggests that the latter scene points towards astral connections; finding the 'oven' interpretation unlikely, he suggests the rayed motif in this 'potter' scene (**Fig. 64a**) represents 'nichts anderes als den Himmelskreis'. We return to the 'oven' question below.

Other interesting features of these 'potter' scenes include an inversion of the human figure in relation to the pot (**Fig. 70a**), and a disproportionate size attributed to the pot (**Fig. 70b**), both suggesting that we are not looking at literal representations of everyday life scenes. In some cases the vessel seems to float in the air separate from the figure (**Fig. 70c**). In one case the vessel floats thus while the figure holds his arm up and perhaps holds something to his mouth (**Fig. 70d**). In another, two figures, one with one arm prominently raised, walk towards a jug and an amphora (**Fig. 70e**). The extra jug appears again on **Fig. 70g**. Like **Fig. 70b**, **Figs. 70g** and **h** emphasize the size of the four-handled vessel; and the nakedness of the male figure in both cases (so identified in *CMS* XI, 140, 218) would again suggest a ritual activity. One seal impression shows a jug juxtaposed with a double axe (**Fig. 70f**). In some other cases (**Fig. 71**) we seem to see a disc shown above the mouth of the vessel. In one case (**Fig. 71b**) we can clearly distinguish that it is a female figure touching this disc; female potters are of course well established as a feature of early societies, but in this case we might wonder whether her flounced skirt and high collar represent everyday working clothes. (We might again identify a disc above a vessel on **Fig. 71c**, in a design reminiscent of the later Aghia Triadha gold amulet.)

The second face of **Fig. 71b** is described by Evans as showing 'Two pots in oven' (*PM* I, 124). A similar design can be seen on several seals, for example **Fig. 72a** which Branigan suggests may represent the type of circular kiln with ash-pit and perforated floor which are still used today for firing pots at Thrapsanos in central Crete (1970, 76); the radiant lines extending outwards from the circumference of the circle (visible in Kenna's photograph and in Branigan's drawing) are typical of such representations. The same lines are very prominent on another three-sided seal from Crete (**Fig. 72b**). While it might seem natural to assume that these designs show pots in an oven, we should first perhaps pause to consider some other representations. **Fig. 73 a** and **b** show a similar circular 'oven' motif with radiating lines, but this time it is enclosing a 'sun-whirl' of the type we have met already several times. An interesting combination of these themes is found on **Fig. 73c** where a seated figure extends an arms towards (touching or holding?) what Sakellariou describes as 'ein von einem Kreis umgegebenes Feuerrad mit sechs Speichen' (*CMS* I, 435). As with our 'potter' figures, the other arm hangs down on the other side of the torso, while the 'Feuerrad' looks rather similar to the sun-whirl on **Fig. 73a**; the figure's bird-head suggests this is not an everyday scene and we may wonder what is going on. The radiant lines or hatching thought to indicate an oven on **Figs. 64a**, **71b** and **72 a** and **b** can also be found surrounding a number of other motifs apart from pots, including various creatures such as bird, fish and snake (**Fig. 74 a - d**); while a double row of such lines can surround a bucranium (**Fig. 74e**). Moreover, a similar antithetic arrangement of pots is found without any attempt to show a container around them (**Fig. 75a**) and pots can also be found in a similar container of oval shape (**Fig. 75b**). All this might seem to suggest *either* that this type of circle does not signify an oven and may be simply decorative, *or* that it does signify an oven, but that it also represents a symbolic idea which can be extended and applied to other objects and elements of the natural world.

Thus to summarize this review of 'potter' scenes we could comment that we have a highly disproportionate number of scenes of 'potting' in relation to other work activities; that we have scenes with a figure extending one hand to touch a pot with head bowed in a posture which appears elsewhere as a ritual gesture; that such figures sometimes wear a high collar or animal head; that we have scenes where a disc appears to be shown above the mouth of the vessel, handled by a male figure or a woman in a flounced skirt; that we have scenes where the circular so-called 'oven' is shown enclosing other motifs, including animals and what may be a sun symbol. All these factors point towards the conclusion that in at least some of these scenes what we are seeing is not simply a potter about his everyday business. Some further significance is suggested. To elucidate it we need to turn to other contexts of generally-accepted religious significance in which the pot also appears. Primary among these are its appearance as 'vessel-goddess' and as burial vessel.

'Vessel-goddesses'

There are numerous examples from this early period in the Aegean of vessels identified as female. Warren (1973) has reviewed these vessels and **Fig. 76** shows a selection, from the Cyclades as well as Crete: these vessels variously have heads, faces, arms, sometimes breasts which they may hold, or a pubic triangle. Sometimes they bear a snake (**Fig. 110a**). The 'Goddess of Myrtos' is also holding a vessel (**Fig. 76a**). Male pots are found in contemporary Cyprus, their long spout with two clay spheres at its base creating a male image, but in the Aegean area they appear to be exclusively female. Robert Arnott has pointed out that vessels like **Fig. 76b** provide a strong link between stone vessels and the Plastiras type of folded-arm figurines (personal communication, 1989). While the title of 'goddess' which is often applied to these vessels (as by Warren, 1973) could be questioned, the locations of their discovery, and their specialized, often impractical structure would seem to indicate a religious significance. It is interesting that the Egyptians had a birth-goddess Taurt who took vessel form (**Fig. 76e**) and that one of the forms taken by the Egyptian goddess Hathor was an urn with arms supporting breasts (Bleeker, 1973, 28). In the context of our enquiry, what these 'vessel-goddesses' establish for us is that the inhabitants of the Aegean in this early period commonly visualized the vessel as a symbol of the female body and in this context attributed a religious significance to it. In view of the emphasis in some cases on the breasts, we may think it likely that this significance was associated with fertility.

Pithos burial

A burial practice not discussed above, but one which recurs over a wide span both geographically and chronologically in the Aegean area, is that of burying the dead in a pot. Apart from the unusual discovery of cremated bodies in urn burials at Souphli in Thessaly, ascribed to the Larissa culture, the burial of child bones in a pithos inside the settlement was known on the mainland in the Early Bronze Age, as in the Korakou culture. At the cemetery discovered at Steno in Levkas partially-burnt remains were sometimes transferred to a pithos before burial on a circular platform covered by a tumulus.

Although evidence for child burials in pithoi is largely lacking for the Early Bronze Age period in the Cyclades, such burials were found at Kephala on the island of Keos dating from the Final Neolithic period. A Late Neolithic child pithos burial in a cave at Stavromyti is the only early example of the practice in Crete, but it reappeared in EM III, along with the use of larnakes, and became known throughout the island. Pot-burials of children and babies have been found in an Archanes burial structure of c. 2000 B.C. (*AR* 1987-8, 65). Several inverted pithoi of MM date were found by the tholos tomb of Porti, containing bones and some objects. At Galania Kharakia over three hundred such inverted pithoi were found, the earliest of which date from the EM II - MM I period. Thus although this practice is not in evidence over long periods of time, it was clearly compatible with funerary beliefs current in the Aegean area. Although an alternative to other burial methods dicussed so far, and apparently a very different alternative, it appears to constitute a different expression of similar underlying ideas about death. Above I pointed to evidence that the grave was symbolically imagined as a womb and the body symbolically prepared for, or orientated towards, some kind of rebirth. In the case of the burial vessel, the feminization of the pot described above again provides a womb association for this type of burial method; sometimes inversion makes the burial pithos mirror the internal female anatomy even more closely, although we cannot assume that this was the idea underlying the practice of inversion. Again we find the theme of a container used for burial from which some kind of egress or re-emergence is appropriate. **Fig. 77** shows a large funerary jar of the early palace period from Aghios Elias; it is displayed in the Heraklion Museum as it was found, with a skeleton curled up inside in the foetal position. The foetal position used in these pithos burials, combined with the examples of 'vessel-goddesses', would seem to argue that an a element of womb symbolism was present in such burials.

A parallel is perhaps traceable in EBA Western Anatolia, where burial in red/orange pithoi was combined with care with alignment of the pithos openings, an east-west alignment of the cemetery, and, in some cases, the presence of reddish colouring (Kâmil, 1982). See also Barb's speculations and references on funerary 'Mother-Pot' symbolism (1953, 206).

It is hard for us to imagine the kind of resonance which such an association, between pot and womb, may have held for these early Aegean people. The vessel was central to the daily survival of their communities. Vessels were used to store foodstuffs: a jar containing grain was literally a bearer of seed, a storehouse from which new life would grow. Forbes (1984) has recently pointed out how significant such storage jars remain for year-to-year survival even in a twentieth century household economy in rural Greece.

[The pot was also involved in two specific processes of transformation, both of them involving fire and both of them significant: one was its use in cooking to turn raw food into cooked, while the other was the baking of the vessel itself to turn it from soft clay to usable pottery. Again, it is not easy for us to imagine the connection which can be experienced in primitive communities between this latter type of manufacturing process and the process of transformation which takes place in the female body in procreation. Thus in Zimbabwe furnaces used for smelting iron were traditionally made in the symbolic form of a pregnant women with breasts, sometimes a bulbous stomach, legs and an orifice between them through which she 'gives birth' to the iron; **Fig. 78a** shows a photograph of such a furnace still in use. We know little about how pottery kilns were built and used by the early inhabitants of the Aegean. However, if the circular shape and domed 'tholos' roof traditional for later Bronze Age kilns were used also in this early period, then with their thick walls and small entrance (both required to keep in the heat), they may have borne some similarity in their construction to the 'tholos' tombs (see Davaras, 1973). **Fig. 78b** shows the plan of a MH kiln, built on a slope which was soon after used as a cemetery: the kiln's circular shape with an entrance passage is reminiscent of the plan of a tholos tomb. Another recently excavated prehistoric kiln of similar shape, as yet undated, is shown on **Fig. 78c**. The kilns from Mesopotamia and from Roman Britain shown on **Fig. 78 d** and **e** give some idea of similarities to the tholos which could arise quite independently simply from the exigencies of pottery baking. The use of fire in both kiln and tholos would certainly have constituted a common feature in the Messara; both pottery and bones were roasted rather than directly burnt. It is possible that the association between the pot and the womb may have extended to a link between the process of creation of pottery and of the recreation or regeneration of human life believed to take place within the tholos tomb. Such a possibility could only be substantiated or refuted by further excavation.]

Leaving aside such speculations, we can return to the concrete evidence suggesting that the pot may have been ritually touched and, in its appearance as 'vessel-goddess' and as burial jar, was linked to the fertile and reproductive functions of the female body. Whether this connection extended to the fertility and reproduction of vegetation remains to be discussed, and I will now turn to investigating this relationship between vessel and vegetation, between pot and branch.

1.9 VESSEL, STONE AND BRANCH

Nilsson has commented that the 'close association of the boughs with the libation jug … is … a proof of the importance of boughs in the cult' (1950, 263). It is generally recognized that the tree figured prominently in Minoan religion, and even in this early period the frequency of the appearance of bough and vessel together suggests a strong link between them. **Fig. 79** shows examples of this association on seals. More specifically, **Fig. 80** shows a scene centred on a tree, involving what may be (highly schematic) human figures, with a bird on one side of the tree and a vessel with a long spout on the other. If this is a scene of tree cult, a jug is apparently involved. However, to trace more closely the nature of the relationship between them, we will be helped by turning to some representations of Minoan 'genii' carrying jugs. The presence of the 'genii' indicates the ritual nature of the scenes and they feature both jugs and stones, throwing light on the role both seem to have played in early Cretan religion.

First, a few words about the stones. I referred above to evidence that the stone was sometimes seen as an embodiment of divinity, an idea favoured by Evans. We saw that 'pebble-shapes' have a place in the range of female figurines. One section of the 'shrine' at Anemospilia contained a raised block of unhewn rock in its south-west corner (Sakellarakis, 1981, 1982). That the sanctity of the stone was associated with vegetation seems to be clearly suggested by **Fig. 81a** which shows a cairn with fertile vegetation growing out of it. A bough grows out of stones again on **Fig. 81b**; however, on this sealing, a frond can also be seen growing out of the jug which the 'genius' is holding. A ritual of pouring would seem to be suggested. Such a ritual might again be suggested by **Fig. 81c**, in which a 'genius' again holds a jug, and would certainly seem to be indicated by the similar scene on **Fig. 81d** in which the jug is held in close proximity to a plant. The jug containing liquid to pour over the plant contributes to its fertility and this perhaps gives rise to the compression of ideas apparent in **Fig. 81b**, where the jug is shown as having the plant literally growing out of it. The jug which contributes to the fertility of the plant is shown as literally producing or creating it from inside itself. We saw that both stone and vessel can represent the female form; moreover, both stone and jug are shown as producing the fertile bough interchangeably.

I have already suggested above that certain vessels in certain uses (such as the 'vessel-goddesses' and the burial vessels) were symbolic of human processes of fertility and reproduction. We have seen that the fertile growth of the bough was also linked with vessels, in particular the jug. It now remains to be investigated whether, and if so in what way, the jug and bough may have been associated with human fertility.

The centrality of the plant in early Aegean religion has led scholars, by inference from other cultures, to look into Aegean material for 'celebrations in honour of a male deity symbolic of the growth and decay of vegetation', while it is suggested that 'the tree was symbolic of, in some way represented, the divinity — a goddess as we gather from the gems' (Dietrich, 1974, 74, 91). A goddess of vegetation accompanied by, and joined in 'hieros gamos' with, a son/consort who dies with the vegetation would seem to show a convenient concordance with religious beliefs of the eastern Mediterranean. However, there is very little evidence for such a belief in the Aegean, particularly in this early period. As Papapostolou points out, the iconography of hieros gamos is almost non-existent in Crete (1977, 83). The whole theory has been convincingly dismantled by Burkert, who comments: 'Frazer's "god of vegetation" is post-classic allegory transformed into a genetic theory of religion; we may leave it to rhetoric and poetry from whence it sprang' (1979, 99ff, here 100). What we do find in the Bronze Age Aegean is evidence of interest in, and perhaps rituals involving, human sexual activity, and indications that this activity was associated with both the bough and the vessel. Thus **Fig. 82a** shows a man and a woman holding hands accompanied by a bough in the field. **Fig. 82b** shows a similar scene of a man and a woman, this time accompanied by a dog and four jugs in a row along the bottom of the engraving; some middle-Eastern influence is apparent, particularly in the dress of the woman. In **Fig. 82c** the union portrayed is more explicitly sexual: Platon refers to the couple as being 'in Umarmung oder Begattung' (*CMS* II, 1, 529) and mentions the vegetation ('blumenartiges Dreiblatt') in the field. Unless we are to include what would be an extremely schematic representation of two human figures engaged with each other (**Fig. 82d**), these are the only representations from our early period indicating any kind of 'gamos'; however, there is nothing to suggest that any of them are 'hieros'. We do have a depiction of a 'twig-man' (**Fig. 83**), who again confirms a connection between fertile vegetation and human life, but again there is nothing to suggest that he is a divinity. Phallus-shaped objects were discovered at some tholos sites, for example at Koumasa near the paved area there (**Fig. 84a**); phallus-shaped beads found in a Cycladic grave are shown on **Fig. 84b**. Similar objects, with a hole in the top, were found by Blegen at EH Zygouries (see **Fig. 84c**), although he identifies them as figurines (1928, 186-9). That religious thinking of the period was concerned with the issue of human sexual intercourse is clear; its juxtaposition with pots and boughs suggest that this was symbolically linked with ideas about the fertility of vegetation, and the funerary context of the phalloi might also indicate a link with ideas about death. However, there is no evidence that personified deities were part of the thinking. The fertility of humans and plants may have been associated, but the evidence suggests that a cult of vegetation centred on plant life itself rather than on personifications of it.

Illustrations, as of every area of religious life in this early period, are few; but they suggest that not only were plants watered (**Fig. 81b** and **d**), they were also perhaps danced round (**Fig. 80**), or were the location or an accompanying feature of dance (**Fig. 49 a** and **b**, **Fig. 85a**), or were simply approached as in **Fig. 85b**, and **Fig. 85c** where two women appear to hold hands in the vicinity of a plant; their bird heads suggest this is a ritual scene. Less likely to be depicting any ritual scene, and probably secular, are **Fig. 86 a**, **b** and **c** where a man holds a pole or branch. The raised arms of the figures on **Fig. 86d** are suggestive, however (see the similar *CMS* XI No. 298), and the figure on **Fig. 86e** may hold a cup. **Fig. 86f** shows a man seated under a tree who may be playing some kind of game; we could, however, refer back to **Fig. 31b** which may also show a figure seated under a tree.

Earlier in this study I presented evidence for a symbolic connection between the sun and human fertility. Here I have presented evidence for a symbolic connection between pot/branch and human fertility. Did the two schemas relate? Is there evidence that the pot and bough were also linked to the complex of ideas around the sun and its sea journey which I discussed above?

We can point here to a number of seal motifs which may combine a representation of the sun and of plant life. Thus **Fig. 87** shows several which bear a circle or concentric circles juxtaposed with boughs; in some cases the boughs seem to be actually growing out of the circle. If we are to rely on the swastika as a sun motif, we can also point to a series of swastikas which appear to end in branches (**Fig. 88** shows a small sample). We might be less confident about believing the 'croix pommé'', decorated with vegetation motifs, to bear any relation to the sun (**Fig. 89**). Most interesting, however, is an Egyptian scarab, associated in Egyptian culture with the rising sun, engraved by a Cretan hand to show a group of Minoan hieroglyphs 'consisting of the solar disk with curved rays between two vases with high spouts' (Evans, *PM* I, 199) (see **Fig. 90**). The ideas of sun and vessel are thus selected to be paired in juxtaposition on this unusual seal. I have commented already on the conjunction of possible sun motifs with 'potter' scenes on adjacent sides of the same seal. Moreover, if **Fig. 26a** does, as has been suggested above, depict a scene of ritual focussed on the sun, it is of interest that an ear of corn and an animal's head are shown behind the woman involved in the ritual, suggesting that the fertility of plant and animal life was at issue.

As for watery connections for the pot and bough, I have already referred to the frequent appearance of fronds with boat representations on both seals and 'frying-pans' (see **Fig. 54d**, **Fig. 55a**, **Fig. 56 a** and **b**). **Fig. 91** gives a further example, together with examples of boughs juxtaposed with seashells, and the juxtaposition of a row of 'pots' with a fish. It is also interesting that fish appear at the other end of the ivory cylinder seal which shows a couple apparently lovemaking (**Fig. 82c**).

In the light of the many interesting contexts in which we find the vessel appearing, and in the light of the evidence presented for its association with human and vegetable fertility and with death, we can turn back to the puzzling 'potter' scenes with a fresh eye and perhaps fresh insight. So what are those people doing? Some of them may well be potters at work. But what of the figures touching pots with one hand and with head bowed? What of the discs involved in some cases, the possible juxtapositions with the sun, and what of those enigmatic rayed circles? We cannot answer those questions. We can however propose that some of those scenes may have had a religious or ritual significance linked to ideas about fertility and regeneration. We might suggest that a gesture of mourning, blessing, or 'calling forth' might be portrayed, and hope that further work may be able to throw more light on this puzzling area.

Parallels outside the Aegean

It will be helpful at this point to enquire how the schema of religious ideas I have been discussing might compare with contemporary religious beliefs and practices in other parts of the Mediterranean. Certain limited parallels are apparent. Thus **Fig. 92** shows a terracotta shrine model from Cyprus which shows a tripartite shrine crowned by three bulls' heads in front of which a female figure stands with outstretched arms before an amphora. A ritual scene is clearly intended; it is interesting to speculate whether, if this woman and amphora alone were shown on an Aegean seal, the scene would be described as one of a 'potter'.

Egyptian parallels have already been discussed. **Fig. 93** shows a cow-headed goddess pouring water to symbolize the annual inundation. Rising from the corn is a soul-bird with a human head, symbolizing the liberation of the 'soul'-form of Osiris (Rundle Clark, 1959, 101). Here two points will mainly interest us. One is the similarity to our jugbearing 'genii' shown in **Fig. 81 b** and **d**, both in the form of the Egyptian-derived 'genius' and in its action of pouring. The other is the association of the rising vegetation to the rising 'soul' of the dead Osiris. While I have argued against a personified god of vegetation in the early Aegean, an identification between the regeneration of vegetation and the regeneration of the soul of the dead would be highly compatible with the Aegean evidence. Osiris is both a mummy and the life-spirit of the earth and vegetation; as the disc of the sun passes through the dark cavern where he lies helpless, his phallus becomes erect, a sign of his reviving potency (Rundle Clark, 1959, 106, 169). We have here a clear model of the way in which ideas about the fertility of vegetation could be linked with the dead, and with the role of the sun in the revivification and regeneration of what is inert and infertile. It may illuminate the concern with both the sun and the phallus apparent at the Messara tholoi.

It could be argued that I have put forward two incompatible schemes for the after-life of the dead: that it sank into the ocean and rose again with the sun, and that it returned to a circular-shaped tomb or vessel to be reborn as if from a womb. For Barb (1953, 200, 206) the dolphin is a womb-symbol, and the marine conception of rebirth a consecutive development from earlier, chthonian symbolism. However, that both earth and sea symbolism could co-exist, and present little problem to the mythopoietic mind, has been seen from the Egyptian parallels; Mesopotamian religion presents an even clearer example of the co-existence and amalgamation of a number of different trains of thought.

Mesopotamian cylinder seals often show a sun-god who, as mentioned above, often appears in a boat and is regularly accompanied by a quadruped (often a lion), a plough, and a pot, which are 'an indispensable feature of the scene' (Frankfort, 1939, 108). Frankfort, as we have seen, proposes a chthonic connection for this sun-god on his nightly journey under the earth, and of the pot he proposes that 'The vessels may well contain the seeds, if we really believe the Sun-god to be on a journey to some field where ploughing and sowing are to be undertaken' (1939, 108). He debates how it is possible to interpret these chthonic connections. He asks whether they merely hint at the influence which the heavenly body exerts on the growth of vegetation but points out that such an explanation would not account for the explicit and manifold symbols referring to the earth and its fertility. For the interpretation of the boating scene he debates whether it merely represents a mythological view of the sun's daily journey through heaven, or reflects some belief in a direct and intimate connection between the sun's action and the success of man's labour in the field. He concludes:

> 'Both points of view are combined in a third and, to my mind, most probable explanation of the boating scene, based on beliefs which occur in Egypt as well as among the Hittites, namely that the sun passes through the nether-world during the night. The contact apparently established between sun and earth each evening in the west, to be broken each morning in the east, would create at the same time a connection with sprouting plant life which the usual equation of night, earth and death would reinforce ...' (1939, 109-110).

Other representations, such as in **Fig. 94**, show the re-emergence of the Sun-god from his mountain grave, often making this significant appearance through gates or portals (**Fig. 94a**). The appearance of a tree in some of these representations (see **Fig. 94b**) according to Frankfort 'proves clearly that the life of nature is affected by the occurrence' (1939, 105). We cannot assume a simple equation whereby the coming of the sun implies the burgeoning of vegetation for, as Frankfort points out, the Mediterranean sun also has the aspect of 'a power inimical to all life, withering the vegetation' (1939, 118). There is, however, for Frankfort a close association between the cycles: he remarks that in some cases '... it is impossible to decide whether the god emerging from the mountain is the Sun-god of the seals here discussed, the liberated Sun-god ..., or the resuscitated god of fertility ... Nor is this uncertainty a serious matter, since all three conceptions reflect an identical religious experience and the Ancients would probably not have understood our wish to distinguish between them' (1939, 100). This complex of ideas has been described at some length to give an idea of the kind of symbolic cluster which we might at some future date be able to disentangle for the Aegean material of the same period. There is no reason to assume that similar symbolic ideas prevailed in the Aegean as in Mesopotamia; it is however interesting that while ideas of the 'hieros gamos' have been suggested for the Aegean, by analogy with the eastern Mediterranean and with very little evidence to warrant it, this particular set of religious ideas has not been applied to the Aegean in the same way — although there appears to be considerably more material to warrant the drawing of parallels in this area of religious thought.

Of what then would the parallels between Mesopotamian and Aegean ideas consist? The idea of the 'mountain-grave' is compatible with Cretan cave burials and with the hillside location of many Cycladic graves. The 'portal' notion is consistent with the Aegean emphasis on grave doorways and egress described above, and apparent in the external appearance of some Cycladic graves (**Fig. 95a**) and perhaps the tholos tombs in their original state (**Fig. 95b**). I have pointed to evidence suggesting a similar association of the sun to ideas and rituals concerning fertility of vegetation in the early Aegean. There are also, as we have seen, links connecting sun-boat and sea themes to ideas about vegetation. The pot, that important chthonic element in the Mesopotamian sun-god's barque, may also be associated with sun and boat in early Aegean symbolic thought, if we are to identify a pot at the end of the boat shown on **Fig. 96**. This boat is particularly interesting as the other end terminates in the head of an animal (apparently a horse), like the prow of the sun-god's boat on Mesopotamian seals.

Conclusion

Thus a series of links can be traced between the themes of sun, sea and death and the themes of fertility expressed in the images of branch and pot. It is perhaps time to return to Branigan's suggestion that the people of the Messara had a vernal deity related to the cycle of life and death, and that for this reason 'the cemeteries were, before the emergence of communal shrines and palatial courts, the situation of ritual and ceremonial performed in honour of this deity' (1970b, 139). While I believe that the language of personified deities may be anachronistic for this period, the substance of Branigan's suggestion is compatible with the scheme of religious symbolism proposed in this study. I have proposed that burial customs of this period could be taken to indicate underlying ideas about the rebirth of the dead person; that such a process of rebirth may have been symbolically associated with the setting and subsequent reappearance of the sun; that the journey of the sun, and thus also of the dead person, was on occasion envisaged as being a seafaring one; that this process of rebirth was in some way associated with the reappearance of vegetation from the earth. I am not suggesting a rigidly schematic or consistent symbolism: I have proposed that the pot could constitute an alternative symbol of the vessel providing the vehicle for regeneration, and have pointed out its association with ideas or cult concerning the fertility of vegetation. It has also been suggested that the pavement areas of cemeteries may in some cases have been the location where rituals expressing this complex of ideas were enacted. The form of such rituals might have been various: a range of different activities have been very tentatively identified from illustrations and considered. They may possibly have followed seasonal or agricultural cues or may have been associated with the occurrence of birth or even death in the community.

The schema of religious symbolism proposed here for this early period, centred around the sun, is a tentative one. It does provide a coherent framework for a body of diverse evidence whch otherwise lacks explanation. It picks out only a few themes or threads in what must have been a complex tapestry of symbolic associations forming the religious ideas and practices of this early period. Even so, to my knowledge it is the first time that an attempt has been made to draw out such an extensive symbolic schema from the fragments and scraps of evidence inherent in the archaeological material of the period, rather than by inference from later material or by analogy from other cultures. The limited nature of that archaeological material, and particularly the lack of written sources, make the task a delicate one; the schema suggested here, proposing that the setting and re-emergence of the sun was symbolically linked with the regeneration of human, plant and animal life, is put forward as a basis or springboard for further investigation into this difficult area of symbolic thought.

1.10 ANIMAL AND INSECT SYMBOLISM

At this point, some reference should be made to animal symbolism.

In a study of 300 early prism seals, the Van Effenterres (1974) found that 219 had one, two or three faces bearing animal representations, as opposed to only 96 showing human figures. Animal symbolism, and also insect symbolism, clearly played an important role in the religious ideas of the Aegean in this early period. Here it is appropriate to refer briefly to a few creatures whose treatment in art, and apparent associations, are relevant to my theme.

Bird

The religious significance of birds is suggested by the frequent representations of what appear to be ritual scenes in which humans are shown with bird heads, as on **Fig. 49b** which is the decoration painted on a table of offerings from Phaistos, and also **Figs. 27, 73c** and **85c**. This significance is confirmed by the birds on the Knossos shrine model (**Fig. 98j**).   An association with the sun may be indicated by **Fig. 97** which shows four birds flying round a disc. There are also a number of designs with bird heads radially disposed which might reflect an attempt to integrate bird and sun symbols (**Fig. 98**); thus Kenna describes **Fig. 98a** as 'Five birds' heads issue from one central boss to make a star pattern' (*CMS* VII, 253) while Platon describes **Fig. 98e** as a 'Vogelkopfwirbel' (*CMS* II,2, 443). Was the bird associated with the movement of the sun through the sky? There may also be an association with women, if the skirts and long robes of the bird-headed figures indicate the female sex (as in **Fig. 27**, **Fig. 98 f, g**) although a minority appear to be male (perhaps **Fig. 98h**). Sometimes such figures appear with a plant motif (**Fig. 98i**). While (perhaps dubiously termed) 'duck vases' are found on the Cyclades and the Mainland (**Fig. 99**), some unusual examples of Cretan bird-shaped vases are given in **Fig. 100**. These last examples come from the tomb sites of the Messara, and other vessels with birds attached to the rim or inset in the depression of a bowl (as in **Fig. 101**) might seem impractical for daily usage and could suggest a ritual use for these vessels.

The usual interpretation of the bird in Minoan art generally is as the embodiment of a spirit, either of a divinity or of the dead. Thus Evans writes:

> Among primitive races at the present day the spiritual being constantly descends on the tree or stone in the form of a bird, or passes from either of them to the votary himself in the same bird form, as the agent of his inspiration … It may be noted that where the sacred doves appear in their simplest European form they are generally associated with a sepulchral cult. It is in fact a favourite shape, in which the spirit of the departed haunts his last resting place (1901, 7).

Vermeule suggests that the 'Egyptian *ba*-soul was the model for the Greek soul-bird' (1979, 75), though this seems hard to prove from the iconography. Interesting in this context is the appearance of a row of birds, possibly doves, across the centre of a flat circular vessel in the Goulandris collection (see **Fig. 102**). Very similar to the 'frying-pans' in shape, this vessel may perhaps have served a similar funerary function. Doumas (1968, 174), commenting on the frequent appearance of the dove in Early Cycladic art and Aegean art generally, remarks that their exact significance is not understood but that at an early stage of human society generally people began to 'attach special significance to the birds, believing them to be imbued with supernatural qualities'. He rules out a practical use for the vessel, rendered impractical by the presence of the birds: 'We are, therefore, justified in believing that the dove vessel had a special magico-religious function, related probably to funeral rites for the dead.'

Noting the significance of the bird in religious symbolism, and its possible associations with sun, women, and death, we can pass on to the discussion of other animals and insects.

Lion and Lioness

The lion is another creature which occurs with some frequency on representations of this period. Here, however, one is reminded of the necessity of questioning assumptions concerning symbolism which may exist in the modern mind. Whereas modern phraseology refers to the lion as 'King of the Jungle', in looking at representations of this early period we need to be wary because a male sex is not clearly indicated. Thus in **Fig. 103** a female figure with a long dress bears a cat- or lioness-head, while the representation of lions in groups suggests the habit of lionesses hunting in company rather than the solitary male. (**Fig. 103** recalls the Egyptian story about the savage lioness Tefnet who metamorphoses into a benevolent goddess, see Bleeker, 1973, 49.)

The lion also appears with other associations. **Fig. 104** shows seals which bear lions on one end and a swastika on the other end. Such conjunctions which are not actually on the same seal-face may carry little significance, but when we find lions and scorpions on either end of the same seal Xanthoudides remarks: 'The representation of lions and scorpions on the same seal, which we shall meet with again, is probably not fortuitous; the reason for it lay perhaps in the religious beliefs and superstitions of the time' (1924, 112). **Fig. 105a** shows four lions on one end of a seal with two scorpions on the other end; **Fig. 105b** shows lions and spiders on one end of a seal and three scorpions on the other; while the seal on **Fig. 105c** shows three lions and what Xanthoudides describes as a debased design for scorpion (1924, 113). **Fig. 105d** is very similar to this last. The juxtapositions do seem to be recurrent. Although it appears in other contexts (**Fig. 105 e** and **f**), Branigan does not attribute any symbolic meaning to the use of the scorpion in such cases, commenting that it may have been a favourite 'simply because it could be so easily adapted for use as a pattern' (1970, 141). However, in the same passage he admits that 'The same cannot be said however of the lion, for this animal does not have the same potential for use as a pattern and indeed the seal engravers make no attempt to use it in this way'. He ascribes the popularity of the lion as a motif to the increased contact with the eastern Mediterranean during EM III and MM IA; however motifs are generally not borrowed unless the borrowing culture has a use for them. He points out that while the agrimi appears in pairs or alone, and scorpions in two's and three's, the lions are most often shown in groups of four or more. Hood takes the abundance of lion representations to suggest the possibility that lions existed in Crete in early times (1973, 104); the recent bones from LH Tiryns suggest that this is not out of the question for the early Aegean.

Insects

Two other creatures which make frequent appearances are the bee and the butterfly. Bees are perhaps intended on the seal shown on **Fig. 106a**, and on one seal the insect has arms and there appears to be an allusion to the skirt and hair of a woman, as if a bee-woman is intended (**Fig. 106b**). The MM IA brooch from the Chrysolakkos ossuary at Mallia recreates two bees in gold (**Fig. 106c**). The bee also appears on hieroglyphic seals (**Fig. 106d**). Some kind of symbolic significance would have attached to the representation of a honeycomb in a model boat (**Fig. 53b**). **Fig. 107** shows a jug with a 'butterfly' pattern of a type which is already found in Crete on Sub-Neolithic pottery from burial caves. Dietrich (1974, 119-122) points out that in Çatal Hüyük bee and butterfly are connected in a cult concerned with the dead, and suggests by analogy that these creatures may have had a similar significance in the Aegean; he points out that their life cycles qualify them to symbolize 'the continuous appearance of life from death'. Evans, writing about Minoan religion generally, puts forward similar views: discussing a later seal, he comments (1931, 28) that 'The butterflies and chrysalises above the Goddess are naturally emblematic of resurgence, and certain other relics … go far to show that this symbolic idea played a large part in the Minoan conception of the chief divinity'. He points out that the popular belief that departed spirits could take the form of butterflies can be found world-wide and has survived to this century in the folklore of Crete and modern Greece where butterflies are 'little Souls'.

Such interpretations concur very satisfactorily with the symbolic scheme proposed in this study. However, if all that were required were argument by analogy, from modern parallels, or from what is 'naturally emblematic', the discussion of religious symbolism would be a very much easier matter. More specific evidence is needed concerning the symbolic significance of these creatures in the Early Bronze Age, and the most that such analogies can offer is a possible interpretation to be borne in mind.

Similar interpretations have been offered for the beetle. The beetle appears depicted on seals; we also find seals in the shape of the scarab beetle, as in **Figs. 90** and **108**. It has puzzled archaeologists to find model beetles appearing as offerings at mountain peak sanctuaries: surely a beetle would not be a suitable offering to a deity? It has, however, been pointed out, (for example by Dietrich 1974, 292), that they could be compared with the Egyptian scarabs which were associated with regeneration and renewal of life. Rutkowski (1972, 175-9) suggests that as the beetle lived off sheep droppings, it was associated with the prolific reproduction of the herd, and was regarded as a representative of the Goddess. We have seen that in Egyptian symbolism the beetle also represented the 'sun at dawn' (see **Fig. 18e**), and a scarab is found with a Minoan 'sun' engraved on it (**Fig. 90**), but again more evidence is needed.

Snake and others

Another element which clearly carried some significance, though it is not clear exactly of what nature, is the snake. Though hard to distinguish with certainty from other curving lines, snakes appear to be shown occasionally on seals, as on **Fig. 109 a - c** and **Fig. 74c**. **Fig. 109d** shows a seal apparently made in the shape of two snake heads. A snake may be intended on one of the Korfi t'Aroniou pictures (**Fig. 109e**). **Fig. 110a** shows a vessel shaped like a woman with a snake entwined round her shoulders, while **Fig. 110b** appears to show a female with a snake coiled around her head; there are other similar examples. There has been much discussion about the symbolic significance of the snake in the later Aegean, ranging from interpretations of it as a symbol of the household, of death and rebirth, or of the phallus as an adjunct of a female deity. It could be argued that its habit of sloughing its skin qualifies it to be an appropriate emblem of regeneration. For this early period, however, there is little evidence. As .with the scorpion, lion, bee and other creatures mentioned here, it is hard to tell what its associations were; one can only comment that it clearly was important in the network of beliefs about the natural world current in this period, and pass on.

This network of beliefs seems to show clear divergences from the (often implicit) beliefs about the relative worth or status of various animals which may be present in the modern mind. Dietrich (1974, 292) comments on the difficulty of explaining why 'pests' or 'lowly creatures such as pigs and stoats or weasels' should be dedicated as part of religious ritual, as at the peak sanctuaries. We could accept Peatfield's (1988) argument that even the weasel could perform tasks useful to man. We are, however, investigating a culture where a toad can be made in gold (**Fig. 111a**). Also in gold is a tiny teardrop-shaped charm from the peak sanctuary on Mt. Juktas, now in the Heraklion Museum, which bears a snake, a scorpion and an insect in relief. From the Cyclades the Goulandris collection includes a container in the shape of a pig which is one of the few zoomorphic vessels made in marble (**Fig. 111b**). An ivory seal from the tombs of Platanos is also made in the shape of a pig (**Fig. 111c**). Spiders (?) appear, in one case with a 'whirl' (**Fig. 111 d** and **e**). Symbolic, and possibly religious, significance apparently attached to animals which might appear unlikely to modern eyes.

Dog

Another creature which to modern eyes might appear unsuitable for depiction in a reverential way or in a ritual context is the dog. However, it appears frequently on Minoan seals, and in several cases it appears to be involved in scenes with people. **Fig. 112a**, showing what is perhaps a dog with a man, may be a secular scene, but in **Fig. 109c** the dog (again questionably identified) seems to appear with a man and a snake, while on **Fig. 82b** a dog is clearly shown juxtaposed with a human couple holding hands in a scene whose associations with fertility and whose religious implications have been discussed above. From the Cyclades, we can again with some confidence identify the dog on the diadem showing 'sun discs' and 'adorants with arms raised' (**Fig. 27**). Other arrangements in which we find the dog shown include the 'foreparts of four dogs in a swastika arrangement' (Kenna, *CMS* VII, 315) (**Fig. 112b**); a dog in the type of hatching pattern discussed above (**Fig. 112c**); a dog with an animal head between its legs (**Fig. 112d**); and what is perhaps a dog with a disc between its legs (**Fig. 112e**), or what seems to be a disc or ball in front of it (**Fig. 112f**), or above it (**Fig. 112g**). *CMS* XI No. 331 seems to show a dog with a 'star'. **Fig. 112h** shows an elegant dog on a lid from the cemeteries of Mochlos. While some of these designs may be secular or decorative, the appearance of the dog with the human couple and with the bird-headed adorants, as well as with a severed animal head and on grave equipment, suggests that it had some place in religious symbolism and was linked to the preoccupations of Aegean religion.

Goat

The wild goat or agrimi was one of the native animals of Crete which were probably hunted from early times. Its importance in the economy, however, is perhaps not a sufficient explanation for the frequency of its appearance in Cretan art of this early period. Branigan points out that agrimi models from Petsofas may have been votive offerings to secure help in hunting, but that bronze models of agrimi horns from Palaikastro and Platanos were found in tomb deposits, as were several seals depicting the agrimi: 'Votive offerings seem unlikely in these contexts and again the appearance of agrimi on prism seals suggests that they had a more important role to play in ritual than that of a hunted animal whose capture was sought' (1970, 112).

Evidence from Myrtos (Warren, 1972, 319) suggests that at some settlements the sheep played a more significant role than the goat in daily life and in economic survival, and yet the sheep is rarely represented. This would seem to confirm that the goat had a particular symbolic meaning for the inhabitants of Crete in this early period; Branigan suggests that this meaning lay in an association with strength and virility and that the models and depictions of the animal may have been 'intended to secure for those who deposited or wore them the same vital characteristics' (1970, 112).

Some association with sex or fertility might seem to be confirmed by seals showing two goats possibly mating (see **Fig. 113a**), as well as another seal (**Fig. 113b**) and a protopalatial model (**Fig. 113c**) which very clearly show such a mating. It has been pointed out above that certain motifs, such as the sun and the bird, appear most frequently adjacent to, or combined with, female figures. In contrast, the goat appears most frequently with male figures on the same face of a seal (**Fig. 114**) or, with less clear significance, on adjacent faces (**Fig. 115**). It also appears frequently with branches (**Fig. 115 a** and **b**, **Fig. 116 a** and **b** and **Fig. 117 a** and **b**), and possibly with a snake as in **Fig. 116c**, though such snake representations are hard to identify with any confidence. Another interesting feature of goat representations is that the goat often appears with a circle or disc, which may be above the animal in the field, or below the body between the goat's legs (see **Figs. 117a** and **b**) or both (**Fig. 117 d** and **e**); in **Fig. 117 c** and **d** the goat almost appears to be leaping over the disc-shaped motif. The recurrence of the disc shape, and the variety of ways it is shown, suggests more than a random decorative addition. On occasion the disc becomes a star-shape (**Fig. 117f**).

That the goat may have had a similar symbolic significance in the Cyclades is suggested by the representations carved on the walls of the small semi-circular 'shrine' at Korphi t'Aroniou. Though the excavator's identification of this site as a shrine is questionable, the scenes shown on the walls are perhaps not simply 'everyday scenes' as he suggests (see above p.37). While he proposes that the scenes have a magico-religious function, consisting of everyday scenes dedicated to a divinity as thanks or a plea for success, I have suggested that the scenes themselves may portray ritual situations. Thus in one scene, as Doumas notes, one figure holds out a hand to touch the head of another figure, while a third figure with a strange head stretches out his right hand as if to touch the head of an animal, apparently a goat; his left hand holds an object which could be a short club (1965, 54). Between the horns of the goat is a small disc (**Fig. 118a**). This scene could be compared to a Cretan seal showing a standing man touching the head of a recumbent goat (**Fig. 118b**) and another showing a seated man touching the head of sideways-set quadruped (**Fig. 118c**), as well as to the scenes we have discussed above showing a seated (male?) figure with head bowed touching a goat's head (**Fig. 67 a**, **b** and **c**). Touching goats' heads was evidently a frequent and meaningful activity, and the examples where the head is severed may incline us to believe that even where the goat is living it is an activity with ritual significance. The strange head, strange positions of the figures, and disc on the Korfi t'Aroniou picture would seem to confirm such a view. Other scenes from Korfi t'Aroniou show humans accompanying, or touching, animals which are hard to identify for certain, but one scene shows an animal, which may be a goat, embarked on a boat followed by a figure armed with some implement, possibly a bow (**Fig. 119a**). Like the scene I discussed earlier in this study (p.37), this scene of the seafaring goat hardly seems to resemble an incident from everyday life or an ordinary departure by boat: where is the goat being taken to? Goat and boat may be found on adjacent sides of the same seal (**Figs. 54c, 55b**). The goat also appears with the pot (**Fig. 119b**). Another interesting context in which we find the goat is posed antithetically on a cairn (**Fig. 120a**). Boardman's description of this representation as 'two goats on rocks' (1970, 98) omits the fact that these rocks are built into a triangular cairn such as we see at the centre of ritual in other scenes, while a fertile bough is featured prominently at the side. The suggestion that the stone itself was regarded as sacred by the Minoans has been referred to above.

Thus, while it is impossible to make any firm statement about the symbolic role played by the goat in religious beliefs of this period, we have a series of tentative associations: its depiction with the bough and in the process of mating suggests an association with fertility. Juxtapositions also suggest an association with males; perhaps with the snake; and also with the discs, boats, pots and stones which have come up for discussion earlier in this study. A number of ritual events or actions present themselves as possibilities, including some kind of games, ritual touching of the animal alive or dead, and the placing of the animal on a barque. Any of these could represent a belief rather than an actual event.

It is perhaps relevant to mention briefly in passing two illustrations which may or may not be intended to represent the goat (**Fig. 120 b** and **c**). The tail is unlike a goat's. While Doumas (1965) identifies weapons sticking into the back of the animal on **Fig. 120b**, and interprets **Fig. 120c** as a hunting scene, the arrow interpretation is not convincing for the regular vertical spikes on the animal's back, and the generally strange shape of the animal, and the animal-head apparently worn by one of the human figures, must incline us to look for other explanations of these scenes.

Bull or cow

The bull, as one of the best-known elements in the later religion of Crete during the palace period, appears perhaps surprisingly infrequently and is pictured far less frequently than the goat. It is possible that it played a similar symbolic role to the goat and gradually replaced the goat over time. Evans suggests that the votive remains of the Diktaean cave as well as the traditions of Amaltheia tend to show that it (the goat) 'was sacred to the indigenous "Zeus" at an earlier period than the bull' (1901, 84); while questioning the terminology of an 'indigenous Zeus' one could accept his underlying point about the continuity of the symbolic associations carried by these two animals. Perhaps the conservatism of the seal-engraving traditions explains the relatively rare appearance of the bull on seals in this early period. (An apparent exception is shown on **Fig. 121a** where a bull is shown with discs.) We do, however, find bull figurines in settlements and cemeteries in this early period. Some bull's head figurines were found, for example, at EM II Myrtos, and **Fig. 121b** shows some bull statuettes, probably of MM IA date, from the burial complex at Fourni in central Crete. Some vessels in the form of bulls from the tholoi of the Messara show small human figures attached to the horns (see, for example, **Fig. 121c**); much discussion has not resolved whether or not such representations reflect an early form of the 'bull-leaping' which may have taken place in the later palace period. Significant for us in this context are the funerary context of such finds and the nature of the contact practised, or imagined, with the bull. It is also important to bear in mind that some of these representations are unsexed and may show the female of the species; what we assume is a bull may in fact be a cow.

Suffice it here to mention that other creatures such as deer and apes or monkeys also played a less prominent role in the pictorial and symbolic vocabulary of this early culture (see **Figs. 122** and **123**); **Fig. 122b** is particularly interesting for its portrayal of a deer with emphasis on the phallus and with the appearance of the now-familiar disc in a prominent position in relation to that phallus.

It is also noteworthy that certain animals appear recurrently juxtaposed with each other, such as the goat and the bird (**Fig. 124**).

Summary

In this brief review my intention has partly been to draw attention to certain creatures which might have been associated with the symbolic scheme of regeneration linked to the sun which was outlined earlier in this study. My intention was also to fill in very briefly some of the main features of the symbolic topography which surrounded the cluster of symbols linked to the sun which has been proposed above. If solar symbolism had the significance proposed above, then synchronously these other elements of the natural world also had some significance, were landmarks, so to speak, in the surrounding symbolic horizon. Branigan comments (1970, 112) that the 'complexity in the religion of the palatial era is of the greatest interest and one is anxious to know whether the intricate relationships between these various elements were established during the Early Bronze Age'. Although some associations and relationships have been tentatively suggested here, the main intention has been simply to point out which other elements of the natural world figured largely on the same symbolic map. In making some suggestions concerning sun symbolism, this study has picked out only a few threads in a complex tapestry of religious belief, and it is useful to be reminded of the texture of the surrounding fabric.

Attitude to animals

Relevant too, perhaps, to this study is not simply the relationship between the different elements, but the relationship between all these significant elements of the natural world and the human beings who focussed their religious beliefs or activity on them. The way humans saw, approached and handled animals in the religious area may give us clues as to how they saw and approached other elements of the natural world such as tree, stone, and the sun. One model that has been proposed for this relationship between primitive people and the natural world is based on the very early function of animals, as well as plants, as the totem or emblem of a clan. This pattern, thought to have been common among early peoples, is described by Willetts (1962, 6):

> Membership of the clan was determined by descent from an assumed common ancestor, a totem. Totems are either edible species of animals and plants or natural objects. Organic totems must be presumed to have come first because of their connection with the food supply; while inorganic totems, such as stones, man-made implements, rain, wind, are later types developed by analogy.

Rituals around a plant totem may originally have involved eating the plant and symbolically 'becoming' the plant; rituals celebrating an animal clan totem may similarly have involved humans identifying with the animal, for example by dressing up in an animal head and skin.

There are other models for identifying with animals, such as the adoption of 'ox-names' and the mimicking of cattle movements in dance which Lienhardt (1961, 16-27 and passim) describes as part of the religion of the Dinka people of the Central Nile Basin. Lienhardt notes that the Dinka do not sentimentalize the animals or anthropomorphize them, but 'The moral closeness and interdependence of cattle and men is rather brought about by the human imitation of the characteristics of cattle' (1961, 21).

We have no evidence for totemism in early Aegean religion, and cannot use the Dinka for argument by analogy. However, a parallel process of becoming close to, or identifying with, animals can be recognized in some of the representations which have survived. Of animals being ritually sacrificed and eaten we have little evidence for this early period. The goat was, however, apparently ritually touched, alive or dead; the snake was handled and possibly the bull too. In some scenes animals appear to leap, rear or dance with humans (**Figs. 109c** and **112a**). People apparently dressed themselves up as birds, identifying with them to perform sacred gestures or dances (as in **Fig. 27**). People wearing bird or animal heads have been identified on a wide range of representations. Connections with fertility, with death and with the sun are suggested in some cases, and the keynotes of the relationship of the human to the animal world in the ritual sphere seem to be physical involvement, identification and participation.

The number, and range, of scenes depicting such activities apparently focussed on plant and animal life might seem to confirm an interpretation of early Aegean religion as exhibiting largely an 'animistic' character in which elements of the natural world were revered and celebrated in their own right and had not yet become attributes of personified deities as in the later period. For example, whereas later the olive tree is sacred as an attribute of the goddess Athena, at this point it seems in many cases to be plants themselves which are the focus of religious activity and belief. This interpretation of early Aegean religion has been discussed above and if it is to be credited it must influence our understanding of the relationship that may have existed between the people of this early culture and the sun. It would corroborate evidence presented above from representations, which may involve the sun itself, showing individuals raising their arms, dancing, perhaps running and jumping, and also showing sun representations placed on the female belly. The combination of evidence might seem to suggest that the relationship of human beings with the sun, as with other natural elements, was one of physical participation and even some degree of identification.

1.11 THE ECONOMIC AND SOCIAL BACKGROUND

Preceding sections have investigated some aspects of religious symbolism which may have been associated with the sun in this early period, and have outlined some other aspects of the symbolic framework which may have existed contemporaraneously and may have formed the context of that solar symbolism. This study is also concerned with considering the relationship between such religious symbols and the social structure of the culture which produced them. The question to be investigated is to what extent artistic and religious creations are the products of a particular time and situation. Specifically, we are enquiring whether it is possible to establish any connection between the scheme of solar symbolism proposed above and the society which, it is suggested, produced that symbolism. This connection is discussed in Chapter 4. Here it is relevant to offer a brief review of the evidence and opinion concerning the social context of this early period.

Consistent with the approach used throughout this part of the study, the main focus of attention will be Cretan culture. Evidence concerning the Cycladic islands and the mainland is drawn in occasionally. A discussion of the advantages and difficulties inherent in regarding these areas as part of a cultural continuum with Crete is presented in the Appendix.

Bintliff (1984) has recently highlighted the legacy we bear from Evans' original vision of Minoan Crete as an idealized peaceful, humane and aristocratic society. This vision has vied with later Greek traditions of a Minoan thalassocracy and a King Minos. Bintliff describes a recent reaction to the idealized view, in which scholars have emphasised early social stratification, competition and exploitation, and have identified evidence of human sacrifice and cannibalism in Minoan Crete. Thus Starr (1984, 9) has recently warned us that the Minoans loved flowers, but so did Himmler. In this minefield it is necessary to step extremely warily, and even the consensus which I am attempting to describe is hard to present, particularly for this early phase of Minoan society.

For the EM I period we have very few extensively excavated settlements, as Renfrew points out (1972, 88): 'The scanty and virtually unpublished remains at Mochlos and Ellenais Amariou establish merely that rectangular houses were still in use. It seems likely that the neolithic agglomerate plan seen already at Knossos, which is repeated at Early Minoan II Vasiliki, was prevalent also during the Early Minoan I period.' The excavation of Debla has provided only a little further information, with its triangular building and evidence of separate single-room structures (Warren and Tzedhakis, 1974). For the EM II period, however, the situation changes. The site of Myrtos or Fournou Korifi in southern Crete stands out as one concerning which we are relatively well provided with information, thanks to the detailed excavation of Professor Warren (1972). The dates Warren suggests for the occupation of the site are approximately 2,600 B.C. to 2150 B.C. Even here, the evidence leaves many important questions unanswered, but Myrtos seems a useful starting-point for an investigation of how the inhabitants of Early Bronze Age Crete may have lived.

Myrtos

On a high slope a few kilometres from the village of Myrtos, the surviving remains of stone walls mark out over ninety small rooms or areas (see **Fig. 125**). There appear to have been corridors and staircases, and traces of red plaster were found on some of the inner walls. Before full details of the excavation were published, Branigan suggested that 'The building would seem to represent yet another wealthy man's mansion' (1970, 48), and since their publication he has continued to present that view (1975, 117). However, Warren concluded from his excavation that the site consisted of a settlement complex which had housed about 100-120 people. Remarking no trace of individual self-contained houses and no larger room such as might be suitable for a lord or chief, he suggested that it might be some form of communal living unit: 'A settlement, then, in the form of a single large complex without separately defined houses suggests a social organization based on a single large unit, a clan or tribe living communally and perhaps not differentiated into individual families, and quite without any apparent chief or ruler' (1972, 267).

From the evidence of the site, Warren estimated that its inhabitants had up to a thousand olive trees, cultivated over 12-15 acres, and grew barley, wheat and grapevines. Cereal was probably a large part of their diet and they seem to have made wine. They also kept sheep, goats and a few cattle. They ate some shell-food. They stored oil, olives and cereals. Eight 'potter's turntables' suggest that they made pottery, mostly turning it by hand. Spindle and loom equipment bears witness to spinning and weaving activities. The inhabitants may also have done some dyeing, in red and possibly purple. Metal and obsidian were, it is suggested, traded in from elsewhere.

As for the domestic and religious life of the inhabitants, there appear to have been several eating rooms scattered throughout the settlement, identified as such by the high concentration of animal bones and limpet shells found in them. It is suggested that some rooms may have been used for ritual: Room 89 was found to contain an unusual hearth, a green steatite human figurine, and fragments of the skull of a young man; Room 28 contained some bulls' head figurines; Room 92, which Warren identifies as a shrine, contained a small clay figure of a woman holding a jug in her left arm (**Fig. 11a**). Warren suggests she may be a 'household goddess' (1972, 87). Next door to this room is one which he describes as the shrine store, which contained an enormous quantity of broken vases, of which only five were large in size, as well as a group of bones, a small stone disc, a stone weight, a triangular clay counter and a scrap of red ochre. Interesting in terms of the symbolic scheme discussed above is that the rooms believed to be associated with ritual or religious use are on the west side of the settlement. The site also yielded some seals and sealings. No graves have yet been found.

Many questions remain unanswered about the community who inhabited this site. Did they live on a cliff-top for reasons of defence? Why, living so near the sea, do they appear to have eaten no fish? How did they provide themselves with water at such a dry site high above the sea? Was the female figurine holding the jug a goddess protecting the water supply as Warren suggested? What was the cause of the fire which eventually destroyed the settlement?

Even what little seemed sure about the site has recently been open to question. A recent study by Whitelaw (1983) has led him to suggest that the settlement was divided into units for nuclear families of four to six people, and that it housed only 25-30 people altogether. His argument is based on the existence of several separate cooking areas with rooms for food preparation and storage nearby, although he suggests that weaving may have been a shared activity. He also points out that types of pottery fall into clusters, for example a group with white chevrons, again suggesting independent households. He suggests that the settlement expanded gradually from one original family unit to eventually include five or six units. He is, however, in agreement with the general hypothesis that the site represents a 'small, egalitarian, rural community', and his detailed analysis of room usage convincingly counters Branigan's view. Whitelaw proposes that, in its basic social organization around the unit of the nuclear family, it is fairly typical of rural settlements in the island at that time: settlements which, he believes, may have coexisted with larger and more differentiated settlements at sites such as Mochlos, Mallia and Knossos. These last two, he suggests, may have held a population of 690-1,030 people and 1,290-1,940 people respectively in the EM period.

It remains possible to draw out a few general points from the evidence at Fournou Korifi. The surviving number of weapons and implements do not suggest a warlike way of life. There is no evidence of marked signs of inequality among the inhabitants of the settlement, and there appears to have been some degree of collectivity. The most striking figurine found on the site, that bearing the jug, is female; a factor which might suggest that some significance or special role attached to the female sex in religious matters, although we cannot therefore assume that the organization of religion was a prerogative of women.

The number of grinding querns found at Fournou Korifi suggests that cereal was a large part of the diet; animals were kept, but the food supply was apparently not supplemented by hunting. According to some theories about the development of early human society, the importance of agriculture as opposed to hunting or stock-raising may have implications for the sexual division of labour within the community. Thus Thomson writes (1966, 13):

> Each of these modes of production is marked by a distinctive division of labour between the sexes. In the pre-hunting stage there was no production, only simple appropriation of seeds, fruit and small animals, and therefore there can have been no division of labour at all. With the invention of the spear, however, hunting became the men's task, while the women continued the work of food-gathering. This division is universal among hunting tribes, and it was doubtless dictated in the first instance by the relative immobility of mothers. Hunting led to the domestication of animals, and accordingly cattle-raising is men's work. On the other hand, the work of food-gathering, maintained, as we have seen, by the women, led to the cultivation of seeds in the vicinity of the tribal settlement; and accordingly garden tillage is almost universally women's work. Finally, when garden tillage had given place to field tillage and the hoe to the cattle-drawn plough, the work of agriculture was transferred to the

men.   These ever-shifting tensions between the sexes correspond to the gradual transition from matrilineal to patrilineal descent.

Depending on our understanding of how agriculture was carried out at Fournou Korifi, this theory might lead to the suggestion that women played a large role in the organization of the settlement there.   It would, however, be argument by analogy.   Branigan, basing himself partly on the number of female figurines from early Crete but partly also on analogy, suggests that women played an important role in Early Minoan communal life, albeit a role in decline: 'Traditional female tasks moved into the hands of specialists and one suspects that agriculture too became almost completely the preserve of the male' (1970, 124).   The fact is that we have no evidence about who carried out the pot-making, weaving or agriculture at the settlement of Fournou Korifi, and the only substantial clue as to the role or importance of its women lies in the jar-carrying figurine and some other fragments.

Other settlements

It is uncertain to what extent the settlement at Fournou Korifi may be taken as typical of Cretan settlements in the EM II - EM III period to which it belongs.   In the case of another excavated settlement of the period, at Vasiliki, the 'mansion' interpretation may give way to a view which sees the settlement as another village on the agglomerate plan, as pointed out by Renfrew (1972, 90); a full reinterpretation will depend on the results of the current re-excavation.   There has been some hesitation about applying the term 'mansion' or 'proto-palace' to the newly-excavated 35-roomed building at Aghia Fotía (Tsipopoulou, 1986, and discussion).   Moreover, although Whitelaw estimates the size of population at EM Knossos as at least 1,290 and comments that this would require relatively complex forms of social organization, he also points out that the case has not been proven that structures found at Knossos, Phaistos, and Palaikastro represent parts of mansions or protopalaces.   He places the figure of 1,290-1,940 for Knossos at the upper limit documented for egalitarian societies (1983, 339, 344, 345).   Cherry further points out that a large building does not necessarily imply an élite or forms of organization similar to the palaces (1983, 39).   The assumption of substantial differences in wealth or status between different members of the population, which is carried in the term 'mansion', is thus questioned and the possibility is raised that the organization of social living at other contemporary sites may have been consistent with that which has been suggested for Fournou Korifi.

Such a possibility would be endorsed by an acceptance of Van Effenterre's identification of a public square and 'council chamber' in the Agora and Hypostyle Crypt at Mallia, where political organization could have taken place independently of the palace (1980).   Indelicato (1982) identifies similar areas at Knossos and Phaistos and presents stratigraphic evidence (such as changes to roads) which suggest the gradual encroachment and final dominance of the palace over those civic areas.

Tomb evidence

Another important source of information concerning the social organization of the inhabitants of Early Minoan Crete lies in tomb sites.   The tholos tombs of the Messara plain have been referred to above.   Apart from the body remains these tholos sites have yielded pottery, tools, daggers, clay phalloi, seals and amulets, models of animals and a number of figurines, most of them female.   Some of the artwork suggests Egyptian influence; a cylinder seal was apparently imported from the East; ivory, obsidian, tin and liparite would also apparently have been imported.   There is debate concerning the date and intensity of Crete's contacts with Egypt and the Near East (see, for example, a recent re-evaluation by Cherry,

1983, 41). However, what maritime trade there may have been apparently co-existed with the prosperous pursuit of agriculture and stock-raising, according to Xanthoudides, who comments on the density of the tombs in the area: 'This density of population implies that the Minoans lived a comfortable life in peaceful conditions. We have found nothing that suggests war, nothing to imply civil strife or even defence against foreign raids' (1924, 133). Commenting on the discovery of daggers in the tombs as the only indication of a warlike disposition, he suggests that this might reflect a tradition surviving from a previous more warlike era, or might simply reflect a Minoan fashion; he cites here the MM I figures from Petsofas showing peaceful people in worship with a dagger at the waist. There are no traces of fortification in this area, and as no knives have been found we might also suppose that the daggers served the function of knives, as domestic implements or as agricultural tools. Xanthoudides further concludes from his excavation of the tholos sites: 'The peaceful untroubled existence of the Minoans is shown by the objects buried with their dead, and particularly by the stone vases, which make it clear that they had leisure to expend a vast amount of time and trouble on vessels of which the only use was sepulchral' (1924, 133). He suggests that the gold, ivory, and precious stones used for ornaments or seals, and the toilet implements, all speak of wealth, ease, and care for appearance.

There has been some discussion concerning the distribution within the society of this wealth and the social power it may have carried with it. Xanthoudides (1924, 135) remarks finding close to the large tholoi some small rectangular tombs 'used either to supplement them when full, or possibly for a lower class of person'. Given the custom of secondary burial and looting at that time, it is difficult to assume an alternative system of burial based on the presence of some ossuaries which have poor burial objects. For example, a similar disparity of wealth can be found between the upper and lower (older) layers of bodies within the same tholos, and at Koumasa Xanthoudides reports that nothing at all was found with bones which had been moved. Branigan comments (1970b, 107) that objects of gold and bronze would have been most attractive plunder for people cleaning out the earlier tomb deposits, and their complete absence from these magazine-like rooms suggests that the contents of these rooms were skeletal remains deliberately cleared from inside the adjacent tomb. This understanding, as well as the occasional valuable find from the cells (such as the ivory figure No. 229 from southern cell 4 at Platanos) discounts Xanthoudides' theory that these areas were for the burial of 'poor people' or 'slaves' (1924, 9).

The assumption of wealth and status differences appears, however, to be a difficult one to shake off. Thus Blasingham (1983) has suggested that the seals denote the different ranks of their owners within the society. She dismisses the notion that the seals might have belonged to heads of households, on the basis that the occupant of Archanes tomb A (who had a seal and three gold rings) was a woman (reflecting another assumption); instead she suggests that the proliferation of seal designs over this early period reflect the development from communities headed by one chieftain to the more complex organization of the early palaces. Arguing from the way motifs cross between different tombs that they cannot have indicated clan or group membership, she proposes that the society was developing from simple clans to stratified clans and that the seals depicted a whole range of offices and ranks in society. She proposes that the continuity and embellishment over time of certain motifs could reflect the growing complexity of social distinctions, while the presence of the plough indicates that there must have been some form of hierarchical organization (1983 and personal communication in Cambridge, 1981). These arguments, based as they are largely on analogy, on the absence of evidence, or on deduction from other equally questionable suppositions, are hardly convincing. The process of deducing social structure from the internal artistic evidence of motif variation on seals remains unsatisfactory in the absence of external archaeological evidence to corroborate it. The number of motifs appearing render her hypothesis unlikely in view of the small scale of Messara communities suggested by Branigan (below). The conditions in which bodies are mostly discovered makes it hard to draw any conclusions as to the ownership of the seals; the hypothesis that seals denoted chieftains is itself too tenuous to serve as the basis of a further argument that the proliferation of seal motifs indicated a growing complexity in the social structure.

One significant fact which can be deduced from the condition in which the bodies are found is that these were collective graves. Our own century is so accustomed to the principle of one body, one grave, that joint burials of bodies are known only in the exceptional and unwelcome conditions of famine, epidemic, war, or social persecution. In this context, however, we are dealing with a social situation in which these early occupants of Crete arranged as a preferential method of burial to be interred with hundreds of bodies in what Xanthoudides refers to as 'communal vaults' (1924, 134). The method of organization of burial is in itself significant. Preconceptions that investigation might lead to the discovery of separate individual graves of a 'chieftain' or 'leader' have proved ill-founded. The discovery of two or even three neighbouring tholoi apparently in use concurrently next to some settlements has led to the suggestion that each was used by a clan which formed the most significant unit within society. Branigan presents this case in some detail (1970b, 128-30) and comments 'In death, at least, the Early Bronze Age societies of the Messara were egalitarian' (1970b, 130). Even in his recent re-appraisal, Branigan focuses on the possibility of wealth discrepancy between, rather than within, settlements (1984). Such differences of wealth, or size, between settlements remain inconclusive evidence for hierarchical relations between settlements (see, recently, discussion after Branigan, 1988).

Investigations in the Agiofarango valley enabled Branigan to make further suggestions about the relationship between tombs and settlements in the Messara region (1974, 202-3). The numbers of burials indicate, he suggests, that a kin-group of about 15 people may have been the norm in the Asterousia mountains and he finds that 'each tomb can be associated with a spring, a sanctuary, a sufficient area of arable to maintain a population of about 15 persons, and settlements capable of housing a kin-group of this size. One larger site (at Megaloi Skoinoi) may have housed 45-50 people using three tombs, while some tombs appear each to be associated with two or three smaller settlement sites consisting probably only of a farmstead. While recognizing that there were already large centres in existence, as at Knossos and Phaistos, he suggests that sites such as Megaloi Skoinoi, as well as Fournou Korifi and Vasiliki, may have been exceptional and proposes that an average figure in the Agiofarango would have been about 10 persons per settlement site. After a further study of the area Branigan adhered to his view of settlement based on a number of clan or extended family holdings (Blackman and Branigan, 1977, 71).

Social structure

It is difficult to ascertain what forms of social organization and social distinction may have existed within the settlements of this period, and what type of relations may have existed between them. After commenting on the significance of the clan as a unit, Branigan remarks 'Over and above the structure within the clan, and the responsibilities to the clan, however, there must have been differences of status and wealth within the larger, village community, and there must have been responsibilities to the community' (1970b, 130). Admitting that the tombs yield no evidence of the latter, he suggests that they perhaps provide a little evidence of the former in the shape of the seals and gold diadems, which may, he believes, have indicated status of some sort. At the same time he concedes that 'There is no clear evidence at all for the burials of persons with little or no material wealth, or for those with no political or social status (1970b, 130). Branigan's views about the pattern of settlement are accepted by Whitelaw, who would substitute 'nuclear family' for 'clan' as the basic unit for social organization but also believes that 'the limited evidence for wealth in the Messara tombs need not carry with it an implication of developed social ranking' (1983, 337). Cherry (1983, 40) concurs with a picture of 'a wholly undifferentiated social landscape, comprising very small-scale autonomous local units … The Messara data, at any rate, give few indications of *any* dimensions of social differentiation'. Even where not all tombs are equally wealthy, he finds little sign of social differentiation (1986).

There is also little evidence that craft specializations such as pottery were the prerogative of a distinct group dedicated solely to such work. The suggestion has been made that such activities may have been carried out largely on a part-time basis by inhabitants who were also involved in farming as an important source of their livelihood (Branigan, 1983). The lack of clear evidence of separate religious buildings throughout most of the EM period, and the indications, as at Fournou Korifi, of religious activities at a domestic shrine integrated in the living quarters, also tends to argue against a separate caste or class in charge of religious affairs. Whitelaw has underlined the similarity between the south-west cluster, where the unique figurine was found, and the domestic assemblages of the other habitation clusters (1983, n. 10). Evidence for the existence of hierarchies of wealth, power and status within these early communities are thus remarkably inconclusive.

In summary, then, of the evidence discussed so far, one can point to several features which might be seen to contrast with subsequent cultures in Greek history. One is a lack of warlike preoccupations; another is an apparent collectivity in the organization of both living and burial habits; a third is the lack of convincing evidence of wealth differences within the community; while a fourth is the predominance of female forms in religious representations.

It is questionable whether this evidence from a small area of Crete can be generalized over the island as a whole, or over the whole of the period considered in this section, which extends into the Early Palace period. From other parts of the island, for example from Mochlos, we find more striking examples of the amassing of wealth. Renfrew remarks on the riches of Tomb II at Mochlos, where eighty-five gold ornaments were found accompanying only three seals and three dagger blades: 'The presence of secondary burials and the possibility of disturbance complicate the situation, and yet we can say that one or more of the individuals buried in Tomb II at Mochlos were very much richer in grave goods than the average occupant of the Messara tholoi could possibly have been' (1972, 378). Richer in grave goods, yes, although it is not clear how useful such evidence is in informing us about wealth in the society of the living, as Ucko has pointed out: 'the richness or poverty of offering may in no sense reflect either the actual material conditions of a society or the actual wealth of any individual, for these may both be subordinated to social and ritual sanctions' (1969, 266). One recent ethnographic study has suggested that fewer than 5% of cultures of any type of social organization use grave goods to signify social status; Blasingham, citing it (1983, 13), seems to undermine her own argument about office and authority in the Messara. Moreover, as Renfrew himself points out in the same passage, cited above, the general practice of collective burial, found at Mochlos as elsewhere in Crete, makes it hard to ascertain individual burial associations. Perhaps distinctions in funerary architecture are more telling. Branigan points out that while evidence for such distinctions is lacking in the Messara: 'The evidence from the north and east of the island is not so clear, but the contrast at Mochlos between the well built chamber tombs and the simple cist graves might perhaps suggest that here social distinctions were observed' (1970 , 177-8). Soles (1986) has recently used architectural evidence to argue for social ranking at the prepalatial cemeteries of Mochlos, Gournia and Mallia, but Branigan (1988) has pointed out that the richest finds are not always from the best-built tombs. Whitelaw also suggests that 'very great differences in the wealth of offerings and in the structural elaboration of the tombs, argue for differential status within the community' (1983,337) although Cherry concludes that '*Unambiguous* evidence for either horizontal or vertical distinctions within society is still difficult to detect before the first palaces themselves' (1983, 40).

Peaceful or warlike?

The debate concerning the peacefulness or otherwise of Minoan society is another vexed question. The evidence will rest on three points: evidence of fortification and defence considerations in choice and construction of settlement sites; evidence of weapons; and representations of scenes of war or fighting. Arguments by analogy are not helpful (as in Alexiou, 1979, 41-2).

As regards the evidence of hill sites and fortifications in early Crete, Alexiou (1979) provides an impressive list. However, many of the sites he mentions are not fully excavated and the evidence from excavated sites by no means unambiguous (see, for example, Warren's comments on the 'fortification wall' and the limits of the settlement at Fournou Korifi, 1972, 86, 268). Alexiou's case is a strong one, but not sufficient to prove internal hostilities rather than external danger: he omits to point out that sites showing an EM II destruction such as Fournou Korifi, Vasiliki, and Pyrgos are all near the sea, and fails to establish how such Cretan fortified sites, several of them short-lived, differed from contemporary Cycladic examples. The fortification wall directed towards the sea suggests fear of piracy at the newly-excavated Aghia Fotia site in East Crete. Until further excavation provides more evidence, it seems wise to leave an open verdict here.

As regards weapons, much depends on one's interpretation of the daggers in Messara tholoi. For Alexiou (1979, 50) they are evidence of day-to-day arm-bearing, while Branigan comments that in EBA Crete 'weapons which one can confidently ascribe to military use are very few indeed. Dagger blades are common, but there is reason to think that they were not used as weapons of war but rather as an all-purpose knife. Some of the longest daggers produced in EM III and MM IA might perhaps be regarded as short rapiers. Apart from these there are perhaps half a dozen spearheads — which could have been used for fishing — and just two arrowheads, one of copper from Mochlos and one of stone from Sphoungaras. Clearly hostilities were rare ...' (1970, 124). Similarly at Mallia the weaponry from Room VI indicates for Renfrew 'the princely status of the ruler of Mallia' (1972, 386), while Van Effenterre (1980, 247), describing the funerary deposits, comments on the striking 'totale absence d'armes, défensives aussi bien qu'offensives'; for him the weapons from Room VI are of a ritual nature (1980, 216). Again the question is vexed, but here the general paucity of other arms such as shields or spears will influence our interpretation of the Messara daggers, and severely weakens the case for weaponry.

As to the third issue, that of representations of weapons or fighting, the evidence for such representations is generally lacking. While figured scenes are relatively rare and there is, as has been pointed out, no tradition of showing people at work, we might expect to find at least one or two scenes of fighting if this was an aspect of life into which as much interest was directed as into ritual activities (witness the later Mycenaean examples). No such interest is, however, apparent.

This vexed question was thoroughly aired at the recent symposium on Minoan Thalassocracy (see Hägg and Marinatos, 1984, passim). Despite the enthusiastic presentation of evidence for Minoan militarism, the evidence for this early period pales in comparison with what came later. Scenes of fighting increase from the end of MM onwards; helmets are represented in Crete from MM III (Hiller, 1984, 28-9); the figure-of-eight shield hardly occurs in Crete before 1600 B.C. (Hood, 1978, 160). Weapons found in Minoan graves in this period are strikingly few compared with Mycenaean graves and with later Minoan graves of the Warrior Grave period. As Warren commented, 'It is in comparison with the Mycenaeans that the Minoans appear to have been, *relatively* speaking, peaceful people' (in Hägg and Marinatos, 1984, 12). One could submit that the evidence suggests a society, not necessarily without conflict, but one which had little investment in the celebration or preservation of the actions or equipment of war: a society generally without warlike interests and certainly not based on a military way of life. Branigan, commenting on the strangeness of this evidence in a situation where so many Bronze Age societies have left evidence suggesting that the military ability of their leaders was highly important, concludes that 'Minoan civilization reveals little interest in military affairs, although from MM III onwards offensive weapons and armour become more common' (1970, 124).

The early palaces

This raises the question of how far the particular features of early Cretan society discussed above may have continued into the early palace period. Branigan's view is that 'With the development of palatial civilization and the growth of towns and overseas commerce, it seems certain that social distinctions must have multiplied and increased. The number of specialized trades and crafts grew rapidly, in the palaces the rise of a bureaucracy inevitably gave birth to new social distinctions, and so too, one imagines, did the proliferation of organized ritual in the peak sanctuaries' (1970, 130-1). He suggests that the effects of these changes on the village communities of the Messara would have been to render the populations more mobile and less egalitarian, as well as breaking down the clan unit, as reflected by the increased popularity of individual methods of burial. The emergence of the peak sanctuaries can be seen as a reflection of greater centralization of social organization; Rutkowski suggests that they played a special role in giving divine authorization to the palace rulers: 'The kings and the whole of the ruling group had a vested interest in the welfare of the peak sanctuaries' (1972, 175). There is debate, however, about how closely the peak sanctuaries and cave cults should be linked to the emergence of the powerful palace centres (see Cherry, 1986 and discussion). Peatfield (1988) posits an originally popular cult co-opted by the palaces not for the *establishment* but for the *maintenance* of their power. Nor is it clear whether power was centralized in the hands of any one group: Cherry has pointed out that the remarkable cultural koine evident from the early days of the Cretan palaces does not necessarily imply an over-riding ruling system and might be the product of a number of politically autonomous centres of power.

There is some controversy, too, concerning the reasons for the emergence of the palaces and the process whereby these developments took place. Thus Cherry, (1981), in a summary of his argument, suggests that they did not necessarily emerge through a gradual, evolutionary process. He finds little evidence from third millennium B.C. Crete for the presence (even incipiently) of central authority, social differentiation, industrial production, or economic organization much beyond the household level — factors which he sees as among the key elements in palatial civilisation. He points out that 'The recent re-excavation of Vasiliki and the re-analysis of Fournou Korifi ... have largely undermined their claimed status as the architectural and organizational precursors of the old palaces. Detailed studies of the communal tombs and the social landscapes in which they were set likewise militate against any view which sees Early Minoan settlements as anything but essentially autonomous and serving the same limited range of basic functions.' Arguing that the evolutionary model is itself a reflection of Darwinism and other late Victorian modes of thought, he suggests that the changes involved in the emergence of palatial culture in Crete took place relatively abruptly and extremely rapidly, and that the period EM III-MM I sees a cluster of radically new features (1983). The fragmentary remains of the EM III Knossos 'proto-palace' built on the same alignment as the later palaces (Hood and Smyth, 1981, 6) offer little evidence to illuminate the controversy either way.

Thus the changes seen in the early palaces may have come late. Moreover, while the growth of population and of trade which they testify indicates a need for centralized organization, and growing specialization indicates the emergence of classes of specialists, we have little evidence as to the forms of social organization employed. In the lack of written testimony or of representations of figures of authority, inferences about the nature of the hierarchy involved rest largely on analogy.

However one understands the process of transition, it is clear that the features I have isolated in Early Minoan culture had a limited lifespan and possibly a limited regional extension within Crete. Whether or not any of these features may be apparent to a lesser degree in the contemporary culture of the Cyclades and the mainland is discussed in the Appendix. Nor is it clear what one can deduce from these elements in the way of information about the social organization of these early communities. The fact that women appear more frequently than men in religious representations does not, for example, imply that women held a greater measure of social control, although it may reflect some degree of social status unusual in terms of later Greek society. The fact remains that we know very little about the economic and social organization of these early communities. From the little evidence we have it does, however, appear that Cretan culture in this early period included some unusual elements, such as a degree of collectivity in the organization of both life and death; an absence of clear indications of hierarchies of wealth outside the early palaces; a way of life not geared to warlike activities; and signs of value or significance attached to women in the religious sphere. The question of how these elements may have related to the symbolic scheme which has been proposed is discussed in Chapter 4.

CHAPTER 2: THE HEYDAY OF THE CRETAN PALACES AND THE MYCENAEAN AGE

For the time span and geographical area considered in this chapter, see the Introduction.

This chapter starts by reviewing elements of *continuity* between the period considered in the last chapter and the remainder of the Bronze Age in the Aegean area. I shall suggest that certain aspects of solar and related symbolism continued to be current in an only slightly modified form in this later period.

The second half of this chapter then proceeds to isolate *changes*, to point out the new symbolic elements that enter the schema of religious ideas, and the aspects of symbolism of the preceding era which are changed and modified in this new period.

Again, there will be an attempt to relate the religious symbolism apparently current in this period to its economic and social structure. More specifically, it will be relevant here to note changes which distinguish the social organization of this period from that of the preceding period. Some suggestions as to how these might correlate with the changes observed in religious symbolism are presented in Chapter 4.

This chapter therefore opens with a brief review of current thinking about the social structure of this later period, placing especial emphasis on noting new elements which do not seem to have been present in the earlier period.

2.1 WHAT KIND OF SOCIETY?

The conventional historical outline of this period in the Aegean used to focus on the arrival of an Indo-European people who invaded Greece from the North at the end of the Early Helladic period, bringing with them a characteristic grey ware known as Minyan, the horse, and other new cultural features. Thomson (1966, 28) has suggested that while the earlier inhabitants of Greece were primarily agricultural in the basis of their subsistence, these new arrivals were a pastoral people, their life based on a form of subsistence which tends to give economic and therefore political power to men rather than to women. The conventional profile of this period portrayed a phase of interaction between this newly-arrived people and the sophisticated palace culture of Crete, in which the former was influenced by the latter; then the mainland society is described as becoming dominant in the interaction and finally holding sway even in Crete itself.

More recently this scenario has come under question, and a rather more complex picture has emerged. It has been pointed out that on the Greek mainland there are signs of peaceful penetration as well as violence; some sites bear witness to a change in cultural equipment without destruction, others may have been by-passed. Signs of disruption at the end of the

EH II period may have been an earlier phase of the same process. The grey Minyan ware may not have been associated with these supposed invaders, as a parallel ware is found in Early Helladic contexts. Three different phases of transition, between EH II/EH III, between EH III/MH and between MH/LH I, are under scrutiny for evidence of discontinuity. Although some form of discontinuity in material culture is generally recognized, we no longer have a simple picture of Greek speakers arriving at the end of EH III. (See discussion in Hooker (1976), Best and Yadin (1973), Dickinson (1977), Van Royen and Isaac (1979).)

The thorny problem of who these invaders were, if indeed they existed, and the problem of establishing the date and the nature of their suggested incursion into Greek lands fortunately does not concern us here. We are not concerned with the nature, but with the *result* of the introduction into the Aegean area of new cultural elements. Without entering the debate as to how such developments came about, we are concerned simply to establish that by the Late Bronze Age certain very marked changes had taken place in the social organization of the Aegean area as compared with the social organization of the earlier period discussed in Chapter 1. I shall now review these changes before moving on to describe the changes in religious symbolism which appear to have accompanied them.

Largely due to the relative wealth of evidence that survives from this later period, the nature of its social organization is the subject of a greater consensus among scholars than exists for the earlier period. For this reason some of the main points can perhaps be summarized fairly briefly. After a 'poor, backward, and unorganized' MH period (Dickinson, 1977, 107), the start of the late Bronze Age sees an increase in population and prosperity. Although the culture of mainland Greece in this Late Bronze Age period is generally termed Mycenaean, archaeology records the existence of important centres at a number of other sites. Thus Linear B tablets from Pylos reveal a picture of a complex and bureaucratic palace life: the palace staff is listed as 669 women, 392 girls and 281 boys, who may mostly have been slaves from the Eastern Aegean; excavations unearthed nearly 3,000 cups in the palace pantries; the tablets refer to many specialized groups of craftspeople, such as woodcutters, bronze-smiths, ship-builders, and unguent-boilers. Bath-pouring, carding, spinning and weaving appear to be clearly allocated as occupations of women (see Kirk, 1965, 45-54, Chadwick, 1976, 80, 151-2).

The palace appears to have controlled much of the surrounding area. On the Pylos tablets 160 place-names are mentioned, each place probably representing a small village which appears to have made contributions to the palace of goods such as bronze or linen, and to have received various items in exchange. Systems of land-ownership current during this later period are difficult to unravel with any certainty, but it was apparently hierarchical, with those in authority each owning a 'temenos' of graduated sizes. Each village appears to have had a mayor or headman, and some tablets suggest privileged classes of military personnel. At Pylos one tablet appears to mention 443 rowers, and we also find a list of military groups, some of whom appear to be guarding the coast; among equipment, armour is listed. Grave customs seem to confirm the impression of an unequal society, revealing different grave types of widely varying size and quality, apparently used by different groups depending on wealth and status; although a social distinction between cist graves and chamber tombs has recently been questioned by Dickinson (1982). The ruler or head of state is referred to by the term 'wanaka': we now have evidence for a male ruler or rulers. As Finley has summarized the situation: 'The picture that emerges from ... an analysis of the tablets and the archaeology combined is one of a division of Mycenaean Greece into a number of petty bureaucratic states, with a warrior aristocracy, a high level of craftmanship, extensive foreign trade in necessities (metals) and luxuries, and a permanent condition of armed neutrality at best in their relations with each other, and perhaps at times with their subjects' (1981, 53). It has been suggested that at least part of the income of these people came from piracy, raiding, and booty from wars.

Among the differences between the social organization of this and the earlier civilization of Crete reviewed in the last section, the most significant in this context are perhaps the militarism, the clear evidence of hierarchy and of pronounced differences in wealth. In farming, stockbreeding is thought by some to have been more important than the production of grain and oil (see, for example, Howe, 1958). We also now have marked evidence of a division of labour between the sexes with women confined to certain forms of work; one can only speculate about the effect militarism may have had on the position of woman, representing as it did an activity and a source of wealth apparently controlled mainly by men.

It is unclear to what extent, through prolonged contact and influence, similar social structures developed in Crete even before the putative phase of Mycenaean domination of Knossos which, it has been suggested, may have begun around the time of the LM IB destructions in Crete. Social hierarchies will have developed some time earlier in the Cretan palaces. Linear B tablets found at Knossos record a system of requisition and exchange as complex as that at Pylos, although debate continues as to the nature of the relationships behind these exchanges (see, recently, Hooker in Hägg and Marinatos, 1987, 313-6). It has been suggested that the Minoan palaces may have combined the functions of Buckingham Palace, Whitehall, Westminster Abbey and perhaps even Wembley Stadium (see Halstead, 1981, 201). The labyrinthine Knossos palace can be seen primarily as an élite residence, or as a temple to which religious offerings were brought and at which rituals were performed, or as a storehouse and central clearing house which served to recycle and redistribute goods among the population, or as basically comprising a town or living complex with a religious area at its centre. Social structures, for example the relationships of craftspeople to the palace, remain hard to gauge (see, recently, Evely, 1986). The palace does not appear to have been fortified and resembles a miniature city rather than the small fortresses which were centres of power in the mainland. The early building of a road system linking the palaces, and their apparently even development in the early period, suggests peaceful internal relations, as Waterhouse has pointed out (1974). Debate continues about the date and indeed existence of the 'Minoan thalassocracy' of Greek tradition, which some would rather see as a later, Mycenaean, thalassocracy (for example Van Effenterre, 1984, arguing from linguistic evidence) (see also Hägg and Marinatos, 1984, passim). Evidence such as the figure of 400 chariots mentioned in the tablets of Knossos does however suggest that by c.1400 B.C. Knossos, even if not a thalassocracy, was militarized to some considerable degree. The tablets afford a picture of a highly stratified society and much power may have lain in the hands of specialized groups. During the fifteenth century Knossos seems to have established a hegemony over the other Cretan palaces, and during the same period the amicable contact between Crete and the mainland seems to have changed character. Cretan influence on the mainland dwindles, and Knossos becomes more warlike. Debate continues about the cause of the destructions which brought down most major Cretan sites during this century, prior to the fall of Knossos itself.

Evans' theory of a 'priest-king' ruling at Knossos has been seriously questioned by Waterhouse, who presents an unorthodox but convincing argument pointing to the paucity of unambiguous representations showing men in positions that suggest authority or status, and the relative wealth of representations showing women in such positions. (**Fig. 256** shows one such example; the Chieftain Vase, **Fig. 251a**, may simply show a military scene; the torso of the 'Priest King Fresco' now seems to be crownless (see Niemeier, 1986); and the recently-excavated 'Master Impression', **Fig. 255c**, if it depicts a human, remains unique in showing a male figure alone in a position of superior power, see Hallager, 1985, 32.) Waterhouse argues 'that the existence before LM II of a king, let alone a priest-king, is not supported by the bulk of the surviving monuments: that Greek traditions about Minos and the Thalassocracy refer to the period immediately before the destruction of the palace at Knossos in the 14th century: that other *Greek* traditions about the Cretan past were either derived from ritual or other religious practices or, if secular in content, were distorted in transmission by Greek political and social ways of thought: and that Minoan culture was in essence unlike its contemporaries, especially that of Mainland Greece, and so it is reasonable to suppose that its social structure was equally *sui generis*' (1974). Her conclusion, that it was over a long period a priestess or priestesses who held sway at the palace of Knossos, is convincing. She does, however, concede that 'To suggest that at the highest level Minoan centres were directed by high priestesses is not to deny the co-existence of important male hierarchies, in charge, perhaps, of shipping or overseas trade; the envoys painted in Egyptian tombs are all men, as is the procession on the Harvester rhyton ... Were naval matters decided in the Knossos theatral area, whose separateness from the palace Evans emphasised? ... By LM Ia, when priestly figures in long Syrian-type robes appear on seals, and are seen as evidence for oriental cults beside the native Minoan ones, priests must have come to share the service of the palace goddesses and some of the power of the priestesses ... There is evidence that in general the predominance of the priestesses was in decline throughout LM I. A social structure so abnormal *could* only have survived in comparative isolation and prosperity' (1974). She also points out that the increasing attention paid to the building of rich private houses from MM IIIB onwards could reflect a shift of emphasis from communal to individual well-being.

What this signifies for our argument is that even if priestesses held sway in Knossos, many of the features which characterized earlier Cretan society (the apparent egalitarianism, and absence of hierarchy and militarism) were by now in steep decline (viz. the inequality apparent in **Fig. 256**), and the social power of women was also on the ebb. Thus even while accepting Waterhouse's argument, we still have to recognize that we are now dealing with social structures in Crete which have substantially different forms from those of the earlier period discussed in Chapter 1.

This study is concerned with investigating the relationship between social organization and religious symbolism in the Bronze Age Aegean. This second chapter, dealing with the last part of the Bronze Age, is, as described above, broaching a new situation in terms of the social organization of this period. This new situation does not, however, present such a unified face as that reviewed in Chapter 1. Though social organization has certainly changed, we are dealing with a situation of continuous interaction between two apparently differing tendencies or forces. Traditionally this used to be expressed as a tension between the indigenous culture of Crete and the culture of the newly-arrived invading 'Indo-European' people based on the mainland of Greece. Given the problems of that theoretical framework, one can still however describe the situation as one of interaction or tension between certain cultural traits characteristic of Crete or originating in Crete during this period, and other traits characteristic of the mainland culture or apparently emanating from there. The degree of communication and the intensity of exchange between the two areas appears to have varied considerably over the centuries in question; the significant point, however, is to establish that what we are examining is a process of exchange between two different cultures; an exchange which affected religious ideas as it affected social organization. This point has often been overlooked in conventional treatments of the period: thus Nilsson writes of the difference between the religion of Minoan Crete and Mycenaean Greece, 'Scholars state almost unanimously that no difference exists, the monuments with religious representations from the mainland being absolutely indistinguishable from those found in Crete.' Although he proceeds to list some of the many obvious differences between the two cultures, he himself in his study of religion proceeds to treat them as one assimilated whole: 'Practically, in the details of research, we must treat both as one; for no separation can be made between the small monuments, gems, etc. whether found on the mainland or in Crete' (1950, 6).

This tendency to assimilate the Cretan and the Mycenaean will not be followed here. While the movement of personnel (including craftspeople) and objects between the two areas may make some small monuments impossible to separate, it does perhaps remain possible even in the area of religious symbolism to distinguish between the two different tendencies or forces evident in varying degrees in different aspects of the archaeological and artistic record. Thus this second chapter will fall into two halves: the first half reviewing what, in the cultural mix, remains consistent with what we have remarked as characteristic of the earlier period particularly in Crete (see Chapter 1); the second half investigating what appears to reflect the introduction of new elements not markedly present in the earlier period, especially in Crete.

The evidence to be used in this chapter will now be briefly reviewed.

2.2 TACKLING THE EVIDENCE

In this period seals and gems continue to supplement the archaeological record in providing a substantial body of evidence about religious symbolism. While the earlier seals discussed in Chapter 1 revealed symbols in a sparing, often inexplicit way, the later seals and gems of this period often offer full and elaborately engraved scenes; in some cases these may make it possible to unravel what was condensed, and in some cases they serve to confirm or clarify symbolic connections which were suspected or speculated for the earlier period. In some cases where symbols appear to reflect a continuation of religious ideas from the earlier period, it is possible to draw from them an elucidation of the meaning which was suggested by the earlier materials in fragmentary or enigmatic form.

For the earlier period it was argued (pp.2-3) that many of the seals served an amuletic function and that the motifs they carried often held a magical or religious symbolism. Though seal usage and function does not continue unchanged in this later period, this second part of the study will continue to look to seal designs for evidence of religious symbolism. Such a procedure appears justified by the many unambiguous cases of ritual scenes and cult objects appearing on the seals. The greater complexity and clarity of the apparently secular scenes on seals does not necessarily imply that the intention is invariably to show a situation or narrative based on everyday life. **Fig. 126a** offers one example: described by Kenna as 'Young bull attacked in the front by a birdlike creature and above by a flying bird; an octopus beneath' (*CMS* VII, 216), its depiction of the octopus in this context makes it clear that what could otherwise be interpreted as a 'scene from life' of animal interaction, albeit an unlikely one, might perhaps more accurately be interpreted as a collection of meaningful symbols in a particular relation to each other. That the seal-engraver was not inhibited by too great a concern with literality is shown by the frequent depiction of similarly unlikely juxtapositions (such as the lion and bird on **Fig. 126b**) and the appearance of outright mythological creatures like the griffin (as in **Fig. 126c**) alongside what are probably literal and secular scenes.

A feature of this later period is the appearance of the 'talismanic' gem on which objects taken from everyday life become stylized motifs repeated as symbolic forms. Kenna (1960, 44) points out the similarity between this treatment and the early stylization of forms on the EM three-sided prism beads (which have featured prominently among the seals discussed in Chapter 1 above). The fact that the talismanic seals are often not cut in such a way that they can give a fair impression prompts Kenna to suggest that 'The inception of this class of stone seems designed for those who required the seal to possess an amuletic quality; and indicates that other seals were being made whose amuletic content was not the first consideration' (1960, 45). He suggests a growing specialization in the making of seals, a specialization which is also indicated by advancing technology and the move in some cases towards harder stones. This raises the question to what extent certain seals were luxury items oriented towards the tastes and beliefs of a minority group or élite.

The material to be approached thus offers us a complex face. Hägg (1981) has recently pointed out that we can isolate two strata in Mycenaean religion, the official and the popular level. He suggests that the official religion is more likely to reflect Minoan beliefs adopted by the upper classes in Greece. Renfrew (1981) has further suggested that there may have been a reflux of Minoan elements borrowed by the mainland returning to Crete in a more or less changed form. Hägg also remarks that mainland popular cults, especially those linked with natural phenomena such as caves and water sources, may have been inherited from the 'pre-Greek' population: 'In the end some typically Minoan traits allegedly borrowed by the Mycenaean Mainland may turn out to be aboriginally Aegean, surviving through the millennia' (1981, 39). The criterion with which I will approach this confused situation will be that of ascertaining which elements show *continuity* from Chapter 1, and which show *change*. Having devoted some attention to establishing, in Chapter 1, some features of 'pre-Mycenaean' religion, we should be in a position to isolate elements which show continuity with or discontinuity from it, whether these elements appear in Crete, the Cyclades or the mainland. Approaching the material with this criterion may in turn throw up evidence which illuminates the questions raised above, but our concern will remain that of distinguishing between the 'pre-Mycenaean' elements and the new elements. Material post-dating the destruction of the palaces is thus of equal relevance, suggesting again what in the area of religious belief survived, and what did not survive, the new social phenomena of the later centuries of the second millennium B.C.

Scenes on pottery are another source of interesting iconographic material for this period. Pottery, however, lacks the seals' long tradition of amuletic usage and of use as an appropriate medium for religious scenes; for this reason scenes and motifs on pottery cannot be used as evidence for religious symbolism in the same way.

While for the earlier period we are working with a 'picture book without a text' (in Nilsson's phrase), the decipherment of Linear B provides us with some written material for this later period.

The tenuousness of the connection of Homer's poems to life in Bronze Age Greece renders them unsuitable for use in any way as evidence in this context. This is not to deny that there are Mycenaean elements in Homer. Moreover, Nilsson has argued (1932, 24) that details of mythology are likely to be preserved longer in such a medium than details of social life. However, the accuracy of the preservation in Homer of concrete details of Bronze Age social life is so controversial that we must regard the poems as equally unreliable and inappropriate to use as evidence for Bronze Age myth and religion.

2.3 CONTINUITY: THE SUN AND ITS SYMBOLS

Religion and symbols appear to adapt slowly and are not transformed overnight by social changes. They tend to survive, sometimes in vigorous shape, sometimes in formalized or lifeless elements which suggest the survival of traditions whose original meaning is forgotten. In this period, in which forms of social organization were evidently in process of change, the beliefs and symbols of the earlier period appear to have survived to some considerable degree. This appears to be true not only in Crete but also on the Cycladic islands and on the mainland, whether due in the latter instance to what might be construed as the surviving traditions and conservatism of a 'pre-Mycenaean' population, or to the influence which Crete exerted on the mainland during most of this period. There are important changes, but before investigating them I will first describe these survivals.

Evidence for ritual scenes with female figures

One aspect of religious symbolism which continues to be documented is the importance of the sun and its association with female figures. Moreover, the more explicit and elaborate representations of this later period confirm the more tenuous evidence of earlier seals. Thus **Fig. 127 a** and **b** show the sun and moon associated with what is indubitably a scene of ritual in which a female figure is central. The presence of the moon makes the identification of the motif as the sun hard to contest in either case: Nilsson identifies the motif on **Fig. 127a** as the sun (1950, 347); and of **Fig. 127b** he writes, 'In the centre there is a six-spoked wheel, with the spokes projecting a little beyond the ring, viz. the sun' (1950, 413).

The sun is represented in one case (**Fig. 127a**) by a disc with tapering rays engraved on it, in the other case (**Fig. 127b**) by a six-spoked wheel. Possible sun symbols are also scattered on the 'Homage' krater, a Mycenaean vessel exported to Cyprus apparently showing a similar approach to a 'seated goddess', in this case by warriors (see Vermeule and Karageorghis, 1982, 197). On this krater (shown on **Fig. 127c**) the symbols at first glance appear decorative, but it is noteworthy that they appear in conjunction with bird and horns, while all three are markedly absent from the adjacent parallel scene of approach to seated goddess (on the right). The same symbols appear again with what Pottier (1907, 233) regards as 'sacred plants' on the other side of the krater: perhaps their appearance is not purely random. There has been little doubt about the identification of the sun and moon on a ritual scene on a Cypro-Mycenaean cylinder from Salamis in Cyprus (**Fig. 128a**): of this representation Evans remarked that 'the orb and crescent signs and the bovine head in the field above point to a combination of solar and lunar divinities' (1901, 71). In this case a plain disc, with crescent beneath, is used. Nor is the significance of the winged disc (see **Fig. 128b**) disputed. The function and associations of the sun in such contexts has, however, been more open to debate. Thus Nilsson will see the function of these representations as merely setting the cosmological scene (1950, 420). And where a pair of solar and lunar deities are proposed, it has often been assumed that the sun is associated with a male, and the moon with a female, divinity. Thus Persson (1942, 99) writes of **Fig. 127a**, 'The sun and the moon in the sky have undoubtedly something to do with the divinities: the moon with the Great Goddess ..., judging by the myths which will be treated later, the sun, as already emphasized, with the male god.'

On **Fig. 129**, however, we see what Nilsson describes as 'a rayed orb, the sun' (1950, 179) (a dot rosette motif is used) prominently associated with a scene in which a 'worshipping man is standing' before 'a very fine representation of the epiphany of a goddess before her shrine': the divinity with solar associations in this case thus appears to be female. Other representations confirm that an association of the sun with female divinity was still a living current in the religious thought of this later period. In two religious scenes centering on a female priest-figure or divine epiphany, it is possible but doubtful that the sun is intended by two concentric arcs in the sky, (**Fig. 130 a** and **b**); they recall, as Nilsson remarks of the latter (1950, 280) similar lines on the great gold ring from Mycenae (**Fig. 127a**), and they also recall the line circumscribing the sun on **Fig. 129**.

More consistent with the evidence examined in the last section, particularly the representation on **Fig. 25a** of two women dancing, is the Cretan seal shown on **Fig. 131a**, where a woman is dancing with a 'large many-rayed star' on either side of her in what is described by Xanthoudides as 'most probably a religious representation' (1907, 174). In the light of the evidence presented in Chapter 1, I would suggest that again the sun is intended here. A religious interpretation of the scene might be corroborated by the fact that the woman's head is 'bird-like' and is surrounded by a circle of dots. A similar scene is shown on **Fig. 131b** where a woman again dances by a rayed symbol; one of her arms is raised. A similar position is adopted by a woman dancing by a similar motif on **Fig. 131c**. A similar scene is shown on two other seals attributed with a Knossos provenance (**Fig. 131 d** and **e**). We thus have quite a series of similar representations: too many to dismiss or ignore. It is hard to avoid the conclusion that some cult of the heavenly bodies is depicted. Recent excavation has yielded a further interesting example, also from Knossos, of which Professor Warren has kindly allowed me to reproduce a preliminary drawing (**Fig. 131f**): here again an arm is raised to the sun and the similarity to the arm position of the women on **Figs. 25a** and **26a**, as well as the similarity of all three to the Egyptian symbol for 'sun-worship' (**Fig. 25b**), is noteworthy. A raised arm is again seen on **Fig. 131g**, a recent chance discovery from the Unexplored Mansion at Knossos and an impressive addition to the set. Also worthy of comment is the low position of the star or sun symbol which shows a noticeable consistency between the representations shown on **Fig. 131 a - g** and those of **Figs. 25a** and **26a**; the rising or setting sun might be intended. Again, it is perhaps noteworthy that Egyptian spells are very often addressed to the rising or setting sun — cf. Spell 15 in the Book of the Dead (Allen, 1974, 12-26). Of his seal Professor Warren comments that he had been inclined to take the symbol as a sun symbol, as it is not unlike the clear sun on the Tiryns ring and is large in size; given the gesture he suggests that the lady may be thought to be adoring the symbol (personal communication 1984). In his recent study of seal iconography, Younger identifies sun symbols on the seals which I have shown as **Fig. 131 a**, **b**, **c** and **e** (1988, 133 and 290).

In a different medium, pottery fragments from Phylakopi show a similar scene (**Fig. 131h**) which Zervos (1957, 36) describes as an adorant with the object of adoration, a solar disc, although Warren points out that a flower head perhaps cannot be ruled out (personal communication, 1988). The gesture of the figure here parallels that on the seals (especially **Fig. 131 b**, **c**, **e**, **g**), and again we have a bird head. (Zervos also identifies **Fig. 131j** as a scene of adoration, 1957, 39.)

Fig. 131i is interesting for its similarity to **Fig. 131a** and **Fig. 159**, but because of its unclarity I hesitate to include it in the set. I omit completely two other possible candidates, HM No. 919 (*CMS* 11, 3 No. 124) and a recently-excavated seal from Archanes (*Ergon*, 1985, Pl. 97) because in both cases seal damage makes any conclusion impossible.

The representations on **Fig. 131 a** to **h**, assembled here for the first time, add up to a substantial body of evidence. If they do not show scenes of sun-worship, they require some other explanation equally compatible with the other evidence. I find the 'sun' interpretation most convincing.

That we are not dealing with a situation where female priestesses may be attending to a male solar divinity is confirmed by an interesting mould from Palaikastro (**Fig. 132**). Whereas in the earliest period we found 'frying-pans' with sun motifs apparently depicted on schematically-indicated female bellies, here we find a small female figure 'dont le corps est garni d'une roue solaire décorée d'une croix' (Picard, 1948, 197). Next to her stands a larger bell-shaped female cult idol, and next to her again 'une grand roue, dentelée au pourtour' which Evans identified as a representation of the cruciform figure of the day-star coalescing with the rayed disk of the sun (*PM* I, 514). For Zervos too it is a 'roue solaire' (1957, 258). The importance of these circular symbols and their association with the female figures is indubitable; their juxtaposition, and the presence of a small crescent symbol within the orb of the smaller disc, make their interpretation as sun symbols highly convincing. The location of the solar disc actually *on* the female body is reminiscent of the earlier 'frying-pan' material and will be remarked again later in this section. The depiction of the bell-shaped idol indicates that the context is religious.

We again find the sun appearing prominently in a religious context on a bronze tablet from Psychro (**Fig. 133**). Here the presence of three sets of horns of consecration makes a religious significance likely for the scene, and the presence of a crescent suggesting the moon makes the interpretation of the rayed disc as the sun hard to dispute; one wonders how often a similar rayed motif, in the absence of the moon and therefore conventionally interpreted as a 'star', might also have been intended to represent the sun (as, for example, in **Fig. 131**). What is of particular interest here is that, while a male figure stands on one side of the plaque beneath the crescent moon, at the other end the sun is closely grouped together with a bird and a fish, two of the most important elements which, it was suggested in Chapter 1, were associated with the sun's journey in the earlier period. Faure, interpreting the plaque as dedicated to a cosmic female divinity of sky, earth and water, relates it to other sun and moon symbols found in the Psychro cave (1964, 156-7).

This clear grouping of sun, bird and fish might suggest that some rayed motifs associated with a bird and a fish on a vessel from the 'Tombe dei nobili' at Phaistos are intended to represent suns (**Fig. 134a**), although the context and rendering here seem rather to be decorative. A very similar symbol, however, recurs with birds on a Cretan larnax of unknown provenance (**Fig. 134b**).

Evans makes much of the cruciform stellar sign as a 'symbol of the Great Minoan Goddess under her chthonic aspect' (*PM* I, 516-7). Without agreeing with all his interpretations along these lines, we can recall that the cross in a circle was among the near-Eastern repertoire of solar symbols discussed in Chapter 1. Interesting therefore for its motifs of a cross within a circle (similar to the motif on the Palaikastro mould), and for its representation of a bird and perhaps a fish (compare **Fig. 74b**) with a figure apparently involved in some ritual activity, is a LH III vessel from Tomb 521 at Kalkani, the so-called 'Circus Pot', whose unusual decoration has been much discussed (**Fig. 136 a - e**). A ritual scene is suggested by the figure's bird-head, distinctive skirt and raised arms (**Fig. 136a**); the costume, body position and gesture are not unlike that of the 'sun adorants' on the Syros diadem (**Fig. 27**) and the more contemporary Phylakopi pottery fragments (**Fig. 131h**). The other side of the vessel shows two figures who may be jumping and dancing respectively (**Fig. 136 b** and **c**). Bird, goat, and two other motifs which are perhaps a fish (**d**) and a branch, are disposed around the lower half of the pot.

Wace describes the central figure on this vessel as 'dancing or jumping' (1932, 30) but fails to note its bird-head; his identification of this figure as male therefore seems unlikely in view of the overwhelming predominance of female figures appearing in long skirt combined with bird costume, many of them dancing (see **Figs. 156-159**). Wace's identification of the other two figures as both female could also be questioned, but this need not detain us here. He makes heavy weather of the motif by the goat's head, which looks very much like its familiar accompaniment, the branch (see, for example, **Figs. 115a**, **117a**, **120a**) and is so interpreted by Stubbings (1975, 17). What interests us most, however, are the wheel-shaped motifs. Wace, deferring to Nilsson, states his hesitation in pronouncing them solar symbols and it is only the strong suggestion from the picture itself that it shows a 'ritual dance', combined with independent indications for a ritual function of the vase, that sway him to suggest a 'ritual significance' for the scene (1932, 177-8). His discomfort about the presence of the animals is surprising in the light of the parallel afforded by the Psychro tablet (**Fig. 133**). Furumark (1941, 459-461) follows Wace in identifying the central figure as male, although he notes the bird-heads and suggests that the central figure holds the wheels. Making his peace with Nilsson by suggesting that this is a 'special case' in which the wheels are not ornamental but form part of the pictorial representation, he notes 'striking parallels' in Scandinavian bronze age rock-carvings which indubitably show sun rites. Referring to the Palaikastro mould he concludes 'there is thus some evidence in favour of the view that sun rites were among the religious customs of the Minoans and that the wheel was a solar symbol in Crete'. More recently, Stubbings (1975, 17-18) has argued that we should be 'less shy' of the solar interpretation here; his near-Eastern parallels (see **Fig. 136f**) do not undermine, but rather corroborate, our closer Aegean parallels.

The crossed circle

Similar motifs of crossed circles are identified by Forsdyke (1925, 194) as 'sun-symbols' when they appear on a false-necked jar in the British Museum (**Fig. 137**): goats and birds are again present, among the creatures arrayed between the tentacles of an octopus, in a decoration of which Forsdyke comments that 'these designs doubtless had a religious significance'. Furumark, however, does not agree (1941, 458).

The 'wheel' shape appears in Linear B as the syllabogram 'ka', and as an ideogram of unknown meaning (Hooker, 1980, 37). In Linear A it also appears, sometimes in the hands of a skirted figure, known as the 'armed warrior' ideogram. Thus **Fig. 138a** is described as showing a πολεμιστὴν κρατοῦντα ἀσπίδα καὶ ξίφος (Papapostolou in *AAA* IV, 1973, 434), although no sword seems visible.

The same symbol crops up in another interesting context: on an open krater from Karpathos (**Fig. 138 b** and **c**), as part of another 'unique' decoration, which includes alongside the 'wheel' a pilgrim flask, a 'wand-shaped' object and two kylikes (Charitonides, *A Delt* 17, 1961-2, 62-3). The wand-shaped object is similar to those held in the hands of figures on the Episkopi larnax (**Fig. 217a**), suggesting that they have a ritual significance. Charitonides refers to the 'cosmic' associations of the wheel and compares the design to that on the Palaikastro mould (our **Fig. 132**). He suggests that the vessels shown in this manner on the krater bore a religious use, and we might take the depiction of the 'wheel' in their company as independent evidence for its religious connotations.

We find the same 'wheel' symbol, enclosed within another concentric circle, painted on the base of the female figurine described as the 'adorant of Myrsine' by J. and E. Sakellarakis (1973) (see **Fig. 138d**). Lastly, we find the same wheel-shape above 'snake frames' on a sealing in the Heraklion Museum (**Fig. 138e**); its position recalls the appearance of 'star' symbols above bucrania (**Figs. 178 b**, **f** and **g**) and suggests yet again the religious significance of this symbol.

Several other interesting appearances of the crossed circle could be mentioned. One is its appearance juxtaposed with a frond on a seal in the Ashmolean (**Fig. 135a**). Others are on two bridge-spouted jars from the Pyrgos IV Tomb deposit (Vronwy Hankey, personal communication, 1988). Another is shown on **Fig. 135b** and **c**, a series of plaques found with LH III larnakes from Tanagra, and bearing a tang for insertion into the larnax lids (*AR* 1969-70, 16-17). The disc is mounted on a pair of 'horns of consecration' and bears a bird, and thus provides further confirmation of the association of the motif with both bird and death. Funerary associations are again suggested by the prominent appearance of the crossed circle on a larnax from Messi in Crete (**Fig. 135 e - g**). Lastly, we have the interesting recent find at Phylakopi (**Fig. 135d**) of fragments of a neck-handled jug decorated with a crossed circle juxtaposed with parts of (?)dogs. Mountjoy interprets the disc as a chariot wheel rolling downhill (in Renfrew, 1985, 204) and suggests a hunting scene (in Macgillivray and Barker, 1984, 328). However, the earlier-documented association of the dog with a funerary context (**Fig. 112h** — echoed in the similar find from the Gorge of the Dead at Zakro) and with discs (**Fig. 112 d - g**), in one case almost certainly the sun (**Fig. 27**, Cycladic diadem with dogs, 'adorants' and sun-discs), must make us wonder whether Mountjoy's line of interpretation is appropriate.

This ubiquitous 'wheel' deserves a separate study in its own right. It will be recalled that a similar cross within a circular bowl formed the decoration of ritual vessels in the Messara (p.31 above). The design clearly has a secular and decorative application. At the same time, indications of its religious significance are too many to ignore. In the early period these suggested an association with death; in this later period we also find an association with female religious figures (**Fig. 132, 138d**), while in the light of this evidence the similarity of the symbol to that on the Tiryns ring and the similarity of the position of the figure on the 'Circus Pot' to that shown on **Fig. 27** suggests that it may also in some cases represent the sun as an object of cult.

In passing we can refer to a seal showing a similar radial motif surmounting a double axe, again suggesting a religious connotation (**Fig. 147**).

Evidence for dance

The jumping and dancing apparently shown on the 'Circus Pot' (**Fig. 136 b, c, e**) is reminiscent of evidence for dancing discussed in Chapter 1 for the earlier period. Other examples from this later period suggest that jumping, dancing and processing still played a significant role in ritual. Thus **Fig. 139a** shows a (male?) figure performing a leap; behind him a second male figure raises his arm to touch the leaper's head, while behind him again a third figure makes the same gesture to touch this second man's head. Kenna's description of this is: 'Three men enact a cult scene' (*CMS* VII, 170). (One is reminded of the male figure touching the head of another on the earlier Korfi t'Aroniou picture, on **Fig. 118a**, and the similar gesture on **Fig. 86d** and *CMS* XI No. 298.) A vigorous procession appears on a sealing from Pylos (**Fig. 139b**), described by Sakellariou as 'Drei Adoranten (?)' (*CMS* 1, 382). A round dance is perhaps intended by the figures on the rim of a conical bowl from a tomb in Ialysos in Rhodes, of a type generally taken as mourners because some raise hands to head in the gesture of mourning (**Fig. 139c**), and by the figures in a late Minoan terracotta model from Palaikastro (**Fig. 139d**). **Fig. 139e** also seems to show dance. Basing himself on its architectural unsuitability for other purposes, and mentioning the presence of a patch of beaten earth floor slightly below it, as well as the discovery in the vicinity of several seals depicting dancing or cult gestures, Warren suggests that the LM II - IIIA Great Circle at Knossos (7.64m upper diameter) may have been a dancing platform (*AR* 1982-3, 69; *BSA* 79, 1984, 307-23) (**Fig. 140**). In Chapter 1, I discussed representations suggesting that scenes of dancing may have been oriented towards the sun; for this later period we have again reviewed several scenes suggesting that dancing may have been oriented towards the sun (as in **Fig. 131** and perhaps **Fig. 136**). Thus we might reasonably speculate whether the sun might have been involved in any ceremonies taking place on the Great Circle. The Circle was not used after LM IIIA2.

Designs associating circular forms with the female sex are of interest to us in this context, and I await with interest the publication of a conical clay mould from Archanes (Tourkogeitonia) with the representation of 'two women within a circle' (*AR* 1981-2, 54 and *Ergon* 1980, 49).

Other archaeological evidence

There are other unexpected contexts in which we may note the appearance of circular forms possibly representing, or associated with, the sun. Thus **Fig. 141a** shows a disc appearing immediately above a vessel. As Nilsson remarks, the disc is in an inappropriate place above the cup (1950, 414). However it could also be pointed out that the scene clearly has ritual significance, and a literal representation may not be intended; a parallel could be provided in the disc above a vessel on **Fig. 71b** and perhaps **Fig. 71a**. The presence of the bird is interesting. A disc may again be shown on **Fig. 141b**, in this case beneath the feet of a figure whom Nilsson describes as 'a woman, presumably a goddess' (1950, 156).

Independent evidence for the significance of the sun is provided by the compass orientation of Minoan palaces. That rituals performed in the large courts of the palaces may have borne some relation to the sun is suggested by their north-south-east-west axis and their apparently deliberate alignment for maximum sunlight, especially during the winter, which Shaw has noted 'whether for purely practical reasons relating to climate, or religious reasons, or a combination of the two' (1973, 54, 58) (see, for example, **Fig. 142**). Associating this fact with the east-west orientation of the tholos tombs, he comments that many religious structures at Knossos are set on an east-west axis and open towards the east (1973, 56-7). He further comments that: 'it becomes clear that the relationship between the rooms intended for ritual along the Western side of the court and the court itself must have been an important one. If not, and the eastern orientation was the chief factor, then the ritual rooms could simply have been placed on the eastern side of the east wing'. Hood (1971, 65) also allows that ritual reasons may have been important in the alignment of the courtyards. Independently, Hägg has proposed three rooms at Knossos as suitable for the enactment of epiphany; all three have an approximately east-west orientation in which the focus of attention is at the western end (1983b, 185). Other interesting east-facing structures include the latest shrines at Tiryns; the rectangular chamber housing the Aghia Triada sarcophagus; and the West Shrine at Phylakopi, opening east on to a courtyard, and lit principally by its eastern doorway (Renfrew, 1985, 369). A stone found on top of the east-facing Juktas peak sanctuary altar bears a carved 'star' design composed of intersecting lines to which Karetsou (1987) has attributed a religious significance.

Recent excavation has uncovered a paved court east of the MM III / LM I cult building at Kato Syme Viannou (see *AR* 1984-5, 60-1). There are several other buildings whose function is debated (see, recently, Fotou, 1987) which seem to reveal a substantial room with columns opening on to an east-facing courtyard, e.g. Nirou Khani and the Royal Villa at Knossos. Van Leuven refers to a number of south-east-facing shrines, which he attributes to orientation towards the sun's movements (1978, 141).

We also find what may be sun designs shown on articles of apparently religious function. Thus **Fig. 143a** shows such a design on a circular object of roughly 'frying-pan' dimensions, hollow underneath, but without a handle and bearing a series of perforations in rings. The careful execution and distinctive shape of this object suggest that it may not have been intended for daily domestic use; its perforations and hollow underside render it comparable to a 'lamp-cover' found near a cave containing larnax burials at Palaikastro which Bosanquet interprets as a ceremonial vessel on the basis of its size and decoration (1923, 91) (**Fig. 143b**). Two sun symbols might also perhaps be identified on a gold amulet from Aghia Triadha (**Fig. 144**), where these symbols appear juxtaposed with a beetle, a snake, a scorpion and a hand. An object in the form of a crescent supporting a disc, discovered at Tylissos, and a similar one from Phaistos, (**Fig. 145a**) have been identified as sun-and-moon symbols by Hatzidakis (1934, 104 and Pl. XXX). The moon has also been identified on a serpentine lentoid from Ligortyno, where a crescent shape appears beneath or within a shrine approached by a 'priestess' (Van Effenterres, *CMS* IX, 188) (**Fig. 145b**); I find this latter case unconvincing.

Less clearly representing a sun symbol, but nonetheless interesting, are the red dot rosettes decorating the face of a painted stucco head from Mycenae (**Fig. 146**), perhaps referring to a practice of decorating the skin.

It is not suggested that all of these designs were intended to represent the sun; it is being suggested that a proportion of them were. If even a proportion of them were, then taken together they would still require that some reinterpretation of Bronze Age religious symbolism be made which recognizes and assimilates them.

Nilsson's arguments

At this point the question arises as to why these symbols have not been more fully recognized by scholars in the past. As we have seen with various individual cases above, Evans often recognizes solar symbols but offers only a limited integration of this recognition into his overall theory of Minoan and Mycenaean religion. Nilsson takes a rather different approach. His overall theory (1950, 412ff) is that there was no cult of the heavenly bodies in Minoan-Mycenaean religion. In practice he recognizes certain highly explicit cases of solar symbols (such as **Figs. 127 a** and **b** and **Fig. 129**); in a number of other cases, however, he tends to prefer almost any other interpretation to that of 'solar symbol'.

In a few instances he is no doubt right. Thus he seems correct in identifying the rayed object on **Fig. 148a** as a sea-urchin; the irregular length of the rays distinguishes it from our other motifs. However, Lyvia Morgan has recently commented on the frequent erroneous interpretation of motifs such as **Fig. 148b** as a 'starfish', which in fact has only five limbs. Identifying this motif as a 'star' design, she points out its consistent attachment to every prow on the Thera ship painting (see **Fig. 148c**) and suggests that it 'takes its inspiration not from a living creature but from an idea: an association between the star as a nautical emblem and its context the sea' (1984, 172). A similar interpretation could be perhaps applied to the similar radiant symbols appearing in a marine context with a fish on one side of the famous Palaikastro larnax (**Fig. 195a**). The main thrust of Nilsson's argument against solar symbolism does not stand up to scrutiny. Thus he proposes that the motifs accompanying a fish on one side of the Palaikastro larnax (**Fig. 195a**) are sea-urchins, and then deduces that a similar motif accompanying a griffin on the other side (**Fig. 149**) must have the same interpretation, degenerated into a purely decorative motif (1950, 415). He might equally well have argued from the griffin side that the motif on the fish side was a sun motif. The depiction of double axe and horns of consecration do in any case argue strongly for the non-realistic nature of the decoration. He uses 'this circumstance' (the unproven argument that the Palaikastro symbols are sea-urchins or a decorative motif whose meaning had been forgotten) as the basis for questioning a rayed orb which appears above a flower or octopus on a Cretan seal (**Fig. 150**). He perhaps starts to strain credulity when he uses the same basis for questioning that the motif on **Fig. 151** (described by Evans as a rayed sun) is anything more than a star or rayed orb, or when he uses the same basis for questioning the motifs seen on **Fig. 131a**. He thus builds a flimsy edifice on the questionable Palaikastro interpretation. Proposing a geometric origin and an ornamental purpose for various sun-like designs, he questions that any of the rayed hieroglyphs are intended to represent heavenly bodies. He may be on stronger ground with pottery: thus he dismisses a collection of symbols on sherds from Mycenae (**Fig. 152a**) as 'merely decorative' (1950, 419). Although Forsdyke comments of a similar collection of designs (**Fig. 152b**) that 'the cruciform types resemble a solar symbol of universal currency' (1925, 206), unlike with the larnax or seals we have no reason to attribute any religious significance to this pottery context which by LH III often shows a degeneration of decorative motifs. It is a different matter, however, when symbols occur in figured scenes with religious connotations. Having adopted his line of argument, Nilsson is obliged to dismiss the large disc on the Palaikastro mould (**Fig. 132**) as a four-spoked wheel, in spite of the difficulty of explaining the presence of the 'wheel' juxtaposed with objects of religious significance, and of reconciling it with the presence of a parallel smaller disc actually mounted on the body of one of the female figurines shown on the mould. This smaller disc he does recognize as the orb of the sun, with moon inset, but he associates it with 'cosmic beliefs or myths' rather than a 'cult of the sun'.

Nilsson thus puts forward a battery of different arguments against attributing significance to solar symbolism, and if one cannot be applied he uses another. One begins to wonder if he protests too much. Various motifs are dismissed as sea-urchins or as purely decorative motifs. Those that cannot be so disposed of are allowed as sun-symbols, but in an insignificant scene-setting role despite their prominence in a clearly religious context (**Figs. 127 a** and **b, 129, 132, 133**). Others again of our examples are not referred to in his discussion at all (such as **Figs. 131 b - h, 144, 145, 25a, 27**); some have been excavated since he wrote and further undermine his case. He cannot be blamed for his ignorance of this material, which might have inclined him to change his mind. While one would not necessarily suggest that all the symbols dismissed in this way by Nilsson are sun symbols, it is reasonable to argue from their specific shape and contexts that a considerable number of them are: cumulatively there is a case which he does not answer.

Iconographic guidelines

Nilsson is committed to a line of argument which will minimize the number of representations thought to indicate the sun. Among other scholars one finds a high degree of inconsistency as to what is and what is not thought to be a solar symbol in this later material, as in the earlier material. Kenna sometimes opts for a 'sun' interpretation: thus he describes **Fig. 153a** as 'The solar symbol within a circular frame from which spring curved rays' (*CMS* XII, 196), and **Fig. 153b** as 'A star or sun symbol enframed with lunettes' (*CMS* XII, 242). If identical motifs appearing in ritual scenes are also to be understood as solar symbols, the implications for our interpretation of Bronze Age religion are worth considering. The extent of variation of opinion between scholars as to what can confidently be identified even as a heavenly body is highlighted by **Fig. 154**. Here we find **Fig. 154a** described by Betts as 'Star surrounded by nine circles with central dot' (*CMS* X, 101), while the Van Effenterres describe an almost identical central motif (**Fig. 154b**) more non-committally as 'un motif central rayonnant' (surrounded in this case by 'Semis irrégulier de cercles à point central') (*CMS* IX, 210). Platon and Pini (*CMS* II, 3, 171) stick to the 'star' interpretation even for a fine long-rayed specimen (**Fig. 154c**). The achievement of greater consistency in the interpretation of such symbols would seem to require an overall reassessment based on a more general recognition of the place of solar symbolism in the religious ideas of the Bronze Age.

Fortunately, in reviewing this material of the later period we have more guidelines to assist us in identifying solar symbols than in the earlier period discussed in Chapter 1. Thus symbols appearing in an elevated position in conjunction with a crescent moon may confidently be so identified: these include a disc with tapering rays engraved on it (as on **Fig. 127a**); a wheel shape (**Fig. 127b**); and a disc with protruding rays (**Fig. 133**). Such motifs appearing in a different context may well be thought to represent the sun. We might add to the list the motif on **Fig. 129** which has not been disputed as a sun symbol (the rays are almost separate from the disc as in a dot rosette). We may also note rare examples of the winged disc (**Fig. 128b**). **Fig. 128a** shows that a plain disc could also on occasion signify the sun.

Many more possible cases of solar symbolism will be presented and discussed later in this part of the study. At this point, however, it is relevant to review briefly which elements of the animal symbolism current in the early period can be seen to survive in this later period alongside the apparent continued significance of the sun.

Associated symbols: bird, lion, griffin and others

One of the creatures which clearly retains some significance in the system of religious symbolism is the bird. **Fig. 155** shows birds associated with a triple altar and horns of consecration. In several of the possible sun representations discussed above, a bird also appears. As examples of this we could point to **Fig. 127b** and **c** (in both cases a bird appears behind the seated priestess or goddess) and **Fig. 133** (where it appears perched on a bough proceeding from a pair of horns of consecration, adjacent to the sun symbol); with less certainty, depending on our interpretations of the scenes, we could also consider **Figs. 134, 136e, 137** and **141a** as further examples of this association of the bird to the solar disc. In many of those same possible sun representations, we saw that women figured prominently as part of apparently religious or ritual scenes. In addition to the sun-bird association and the sun-women association, we also seem to find a strong association between bird and women. **Fig. 156** shows some of the many representations of women dressed as birds, or 'bird-women'. These are variously described. We find **Fig. 156a** described by A. Sakellariou as 'Geflügelte Frauengestalt' (*CMS* I, 504), but Kenna describes **Fig. 156b** as 'Weibliche Gottheit in Vogelgestalt' (*CMS* VIII, 104), and **Fig. 156 c** and **d** as 'Goddess as bird' (*CMS* VII, 238 and *CMS* XII, 368). Boardman concurs with the divine interpretation and describes **Fig. 156e** as 'A bird goddess' (1970, 106). We are not concerned here with the question of whether these pictures are intended to represent the epiphany of a divinity; we are interested in several other points. One is the continuing apparently firm association between bird and woman. Bird-men are not unknown (see **Fig. 157a**), but bird-women predominate by far, and their female sexual characteristics can be emphasised (**Fig. 157b**). Another point is that the raised head and spread wings of many of these bird-women suggest that they are dancing (see **Fig. 158 a, b** and **c**); Kenna writes of **Fig. 158d**,'Emphasis upon the bird attributes but the body curvature derives from the sacred dance' (*CMS* VII, 182). This suggests a continuity from the ritual dances of the earlier period which were indicated by representations such as **Fig. 27** showing raised-arm figures in bird dress. The parallel between **Fig. 27** and **Fig. 136** has already been noted, both showing figures in bird-head and long robe with raised arms adjacent to large discs, which in one case at least have been identified as sun-discs. These bird-women scenes also have resonances in representations of dance from this later period: thus the position of the woman with 'bird-like' head on **Fig. 131a** closely parallels that adopted by the bird-woman on **Fig. 159**, and might incline one to suggest that the two circular 'cult-objects' (Kenna, *CMS* VII, 181) on either side of this latter bird-woman may also be intended as suns. Such an identification would support the hypothesis, consistent with many of the representations discussed here, that bird costume and dancing were part of rituals directed towards the sun.

Further evidence of a female figure associated with both birds and discs is offered by **Fig. 160a**, late bell-shaped Cretan idols who wear a crown of discs and birds, while the earlier **Fig. 160d** wears a radiant crown with birds. **Fig. 160b**, female figures in gold foil from Grave Circle A at Mycenae, are surmounted by birds; while **Fig. 160c** shows a female figure handling a bird. Higgins has recently suggested that some of the pieces in the Aigina treasure may include depictions of the sun, for example the 'Master of Animals' pendant (my **Fig. 271a**) and earrings Nos BMC Jewelry 763-6 (which also feature birds) (Lecture at Manchester University, November 1986).

Another area where we might be tracing continuity is in the association of the lion with the female sex. Thus the depiction of a female figure ('Potnia Theron') between lions is common, as in **Fig 161a**. In **Fig. 161b** the female figure assumes an elevated and commanding position; in other examples she sits or kneels to touch them on the nose, in pairs (**Fig. 161c**) or singly (**Fig. 161d**). In another case it is the lion who rears between two figures whose breasts suggest they are female (**Fig. 161e**). On **Fig. 161 f** and **g** a female figure is perhaps riding a lion. A bronze lion was yielded by the Aghia Irini shrine site, noted for its many female cult images. That the lion itself was not symbolized primarily as a virile kingly beast is suggested by **Fig. 162a**, which shows a lioness giving suck; again, it is the lioness and not the lion who is represented in the alabaster libation vase in the shape of a lioness's head from Knossos (**Fig. 162b**), although the Mycenae gold rhyton is a lion. *CMS* XI No. 330 shows a 'lion-woman'. We saw from **Fig. 151** that lions can be shown, in this case heraldically posed with their forefeet on an altar, with what Evans described as a rayed sun. **Fig. 163a** shows what Kenna describes as a lion and crab with 'sun' (*CMS* VII, 80); although this creature could also be a cat. Consistent with these other examples, it might be reasonable to suggest that the motif on **Fig. 163b**, which Kenna describes as a 'star in the field between the legs' (*CMS* XII, 339), might also have been intended to show the sun. **Fig. 151** parallels the appearance of lions on either side of the sun disc in Egyptian art (**Fig. 164a**); a further similar example could be cited in **Fig. 164b**, where again the animals have their forefeet on an altar; however, Boardman (1970, 96) suggests that these are dogs, and their precise identity is hard to establish. In **Fig. 164c** we can more confidently identify a lion, with what Younger (1988, 44) identifies as a sun; see also *CMS* II, 4 No. 76.

It has been pointed out that both bird and lion are found juxtaposed with, or linked to, female figures and what are very probably solar symbols. It is interesting therefore to notice what happens with representations of that lion-bird hybrid, the griffin. We find the griffin clearly shown as female on **Fig. 165**. We also find the griffin accompanying a female figure on **Fig. 166 a**, **b** and **c** although the figure on **Fig. 166 d** and **e** is of uncertain sex. On **Fig. 149** we saw the griffin on the Palaikastro larnax accompanied by what may be a sun motif, and on **Fig. 167a** we find it tethered to a column with what Kenna describes as 'A star or solar symbol' (*CMS* XII, 383) in the field between its legs. In this context it is perhaps worth drawing attention also to a tiny disc which accompanies a griffin on **Fig. 167b**. **Fig. 167c** shows both a lion and a griffin accompanied by what the Van Effenterres describe as 'étoile dont la gravure est peut-être plus tardive, sur un motif effacé dont on devine la trace' (*CMS* IX, 172); although the similarity of the execution of this motif to that on **Fig. 167a** is worthy of comment. A sphinx appears with a similar motif on **Fig. 167d**. These symbols accompanying animals in the field will be the subject of a fuller discussion below; see also Younger, 1988, 290-1.

Snakes also appear to continue to hold a significant place in cult, and are closely associated with female figures, as with the famous 'Snake Goddesses' from Knossos (**Fig. 168**). The butterfly continues to be a popular motif, perhaps with funerary associations, cf. the Mycenae butterfly scales (**Fig. 169a**), while the butterfly-woman of the Zakro master suggests the existence of a conceptual link between the butterfly and the woman (**Fig. 169b**). Elements such as the scorpion continue to appear, as in **Fig. 170a** where it is juxtaposed with the symbol of a fertile bough; the crab is also popular (**Fig. 170b**). The scorpion further appears with birds, jugs and what may be sun-whirls on an interesting prism seal in Germany (**Fig. 170c**). On these elements, see also Younger, 1988, 203ff.

It is now time to return to the circular symbols which often appear in the field accompanying quadrupeds, especially the goat, to investigate what connection, if any, they bear to solar symbolism.

2.4 CIRCULAR SYMBOLS WITH QUADRUPEDS

In Chapter 1, some comments were made about the apparent symbolic significance of the goat (pp.52-4). I also commented on the appearance of certain disc-shaped objects in the field accompanying goat representations (**Figs. 117, 118a**). Some continuity is indicated by the appearance of similar iconography in this later period.

Thus we again find evidence that the goat was significantly associated with cult. **Fig. 171a** shows a man approaching a shrine, followed by a goat, while **Fig. 171b** shows both a goat and a saluting man at a shrine where a male deity is making an epiphany (so interpreted by Sakellariou, *CMS* I, 329). **Fig. 171c** from Mega Monasteri appears to show a procession leading or following a goat; **Fig. 171d** from Knossos shows a very similar scene. It will be noted that in each of these instances, as in the earlier material, the goat is accompanied by a *male* figure or figures. Frequent appearances with a bough or 'sacred tree' (Evans, 1901, 56) suggest that the animal may have been linked in ritual with a cult of fertility (see **Fig. 172 a, b, c**). The appearance of horns of consecration in some cases may be noted (**Fig. 172d**). It is interesting that on **Fig. 172e** what might be the ithyphallus of each goat could also be taken as the trunk or stem of the plant; that the sexual attributes and activity of the goat were seen as significant is again confirmed by explicit representations of goats mating (**Fig. 172 f** and **g**). Close examination of **Fig. 171b** (original) shows that the man accompanying the goat is also ithyphallic.

Apart from these associations, however, we also find the association with discs recurring. We saw above that lions and griffins may appear with what have been identified by scholars as a 'star', 'sun motif' or 'solar symbol' in the field above or below the animal's back (see **Figs. 149, 163, 167 a** and **c,**). We also find a cylinder seal in the British Museum which shows an agrimi and a winged griffin 'interset with solar symbols' (Kenna, *CMS* VII, 213) (see **Fig. 173**). The symbols here, perhaps because of their association with the griffin as well as the goat, are identified as solar symbols, but they are very similar to motifs which are described as a 'star' (Kenna, *CMS* VII, 75) and a 'toothed centred circle' (Sakellarakis and Kenna, *CMS* IV, 185) respectively when they appear with a goat alone on **Fig. 174 a** and **b**; perhaps these latter may also be intended as solar symbols. Boardman describes the motif on **Fig. 174b** as a 'star' (1970, 93). The motifs which Kenna describes as 'stars' (*CMS* XII, 375) appearing in the field with a goat-headed animal on **Fig. 175a** are also closely similar to motifs which he identifies as solar symbols (*CMS* XII, 280, 252) when they appear with fish on **Fig. 175 b** and **c**. It is possible that we have here a consistent and recurring association of the goat with solar symbols of which the extent and significance has never really been charted or considered.

It is perhaps appropriate to review some of the other possible examples of this juxtaposition. **Fig. 176a** shows a goat-man with figure-of-eight shield and an 'oursin ou symbole solaire' (Van Effenterre, *CMS* IX, 152); **Fig. 176b** shows a horned goat-like animal with a 'five-point "star" ' above its rump (Betts, *CMS* X, 174); **Fig. 176c** shows a 'Cretan goat' with 'two tubular drill sinkings' in the field (Kenna, *CMS* VII, 79); **Fig. 176 d** and **e** show quadrupeds with 'boules' between their legs (Van Effenterre, *CMS* IX, 223 and 224); **Fig. 176f** shows two animals with 'two dots' in the field (Betts, *CMS* X, 169). On a Cypriot seal (**Fig. 176g**) the goat and disc are accompanied by a scorpion.

Not all these animals are goats. Those on **Fig. 176f** are suggested by Betts to be bulls or deer. It is perhaps worth reviewing some of the other examples of these dots, discs or stars appearing with different types of quadruped. Thus **Fig. 177a** is described as a deer with a 'cup sinking' above the back (Kenna, *CMS* VII, 235); on **Fig. 177b**, a star appears to be attached to what Nilsson describes as a man-stag (1950, 375); on **Fig. 177c** a 'Stier' has 'zwei Punkte' beneath its belly (Kenna and Thomas, *CMS* XIII, 137); **Fig. 177d** shows a 'deer' with 'tubular drill sinking' in the field (Kenna, *CMS* VII, 79).

One might refer here to some even more various, but perhaps not entirely unconnected, representations. Thus on **Fig. 178a** it is a moon-shaped 'Kreissegment' which appears beneath the belly of a stag (Kenna, *CMS* VIII, 116); on **Fig. 178b** we see a bucranium with a 'star' above it (Betts, *CMS* X, 106) (see also **Fig. 178 f, g** and **i**). These last recall a very ancient Egyptian tradition of depicting cattle with a sun-disc between their horns. These represent Hathor, who is also associated with the stars (see **Fig. 178h**). One Egyptian conception of the sky was as an immense cow (as in **Fig. 178j**). The cowhead could also represent the female soul (Bleeker, 1973, 58, 61). **Fig. 178c** offers the unusual spectacle of a man 'playing with two balls … between two bulls' (Kenna, *CMS* VIII, 203), while **Fig. 178d** shows a man apparently leaping over a goat in a manner reminiscent of 'bull-leaping' scenes. As noted above, some of these 'bulls' are unsexed and may be cows; in some cases — e.g. *CMS* II, 3 No. 88, which shows a calf — a cow is clearly suggested. **Fig. 178e**, strictly a hieroglyph, offers an interesting after-note to **Fig. 120 b** and **c**. In that context Doumas suggested that the spikes rising from the animal's back represented weapons lodged in its back; however this representation (**Fig. 178e**) plainly suggests that we are dealing with a stylized manner of depicting the animal, rather than the literal hunting scene which Doumas would see.

In some quarters extraneous disc-shaped motifs on seals have been attributed to a penchant of craftsmen for becoming 'trigger-happy' with a tubular drill. Thus Nilsson writes of the tube-borer: 'the Minoan gem-engravers were so fond of this tool that they sometimes used deeply bored circles as mere ornaments, even when not altogether suitable' (1950, 414). However, the consistent and recurrent association of quadrupeds (especially goats) with not only circular but also radiant and star-like motifs which elsewhere have been clearly identified as solar symbols; the preference for placing these in certain unusual positions, particularly beneath the belly; the parallels to similar representations of such motifs associated with exotic or mythical creatures such as the lion and the griffin; the juxtaposition on occasion of religious motifs such as the bough and the figure-of-eight shield, together with a recognition of the traditional amuletic function of the seals, all serve to indicate that what we have here is neither the random application of space-filling graphic motifs nor a factual depiction of everyday scenes of animal life. It will be recalled that the goat appears with circular symbols in other representations of this later period, such as **Fig. 137** and the apparent depiction of a cult scene on the 'Circus Pot' **Fig. 136**. These factors, together with the evidence of continuity from the earlier period (see **Figs. 117** and **118a**), might rather seem to suggest that in origin a magical or religious association lies behind these juxtapositions.

In this context I would wish to advance the hypothesis that some at least of these symbols are sun motifs; that they reflect the continued significance of the sun in the religious symbolism of the Bronze Age Aegean; and that some of the pictures may represent imagined or mythic events or relationships, or alternatively may show actual rituals enacted variously with animals or with humans in animal costume, perhaps involving balls representing the sun. (These last two alternatives are not incompatible or mutually exclusive, and some of the pictures might represent a combination of both.)

Having presented material suggesting the continued importance of the sun in religious symbolism of this later period, and having presented the case for its continued association with various creatures which we noted as significant in the religion of the Early Bronze Age period, I shall now move on to investigate whether we also find a continued association of the sun with funerary symbolism, the sea, and vegetation rituals. The first topic to be tackled is that of funerary symbolism.

2.5 CONTINUITY: THE SUN AND DEATH

Here we are investigating whether any of the symbolic associations between the sun and funerary beliefs and practices which were proposed in Chapter 1 continue to be current in this later period.

The tombs

Among the many changes noticeable in social organization and customs in this later period, there yet remains some continuity in burial practices. In Chapter 1 it was suggested that certain burial practices of the early period were highly consistent with a doctrine of rebirth associated with the sun's movements. Some of these, such as contraction of the corpse, the disregard shown for it after a certain period of time, secondary burial, the separation of the skull, the tinkering with bones, the use of pithoi for burials and the use of fire, continue to be sporadically in evidence during this later period.

Moreover, although they were not the universal form of burial, the chamber and tholos tombs of this period show that principles of grave construction prominent in the earlier period continued to be known. The mainland tholoi, often covered with a tumulus, and sometimes with a stone peribolos to revet the edge of the earth mound, have a different pattern of usage from the collective tholos tombs of Crete and have been regarded as royal or dynastic tombs. However, the structural similarity is striking and Branigan (1970b, 156-160) has argued convincingly for a direct line of continuity from Cretan to mainland tholoi; Hooker (1976, 36) also argues for some continuity. In both tholos and chamber tombs of this period, the circular shape and the entrance passage continue to offer a parallel to the female anatomy of the womb which, it was suggested, may have carried meaning for the people of the earlier period (**Fig. 179 a** and **b**). The continuing importance of the circular principle is particularly apparent in the tholoi (see **Fig. 179c**). It was also evidently thought significant in the grouping and enclosure of the shaft graves at Mycenae, witness the Grave Circles.

A principle of orientation towards the sun's movements continues to be evident in a few cases (see, for example, **Fig. 179b**). In a study of chamber tombs at the mainland site of Prosymna, Van Leuven reports detecting a concern with orientation towards movements of the sun: 'Within each group, particular tomb locations were determined primarily by choosing the terrain that would permit a desired orientation, towards the sun at certain times of the year and day, in accordance with solar characteristics of the funeral cult. The favourite times were just after sunrise or before sunset on the date of the winter solstice or, less popularly, the summer one' (1975). He also comments on the circular plan of the cemetery as a whole, and on its westerly position in relation to the settlement. Having reached my own interpretations independently, and on the basis of different evidence, I am interested to note that he suggests the tomb alignment to sun movements was based on the optimum time for the 'rebirth' of the sun to promote an after-life for the dead. Dickinson (1977, 46, 51) comments on the east-west orientation of most bodies in Mycenae Grave Circle A, and suggests that grave circles may have been more common than is realized. It is noteworthy that on the east side of Mycenae Grave Circle A (see **Fig. 179d**) there is a space inside the later wall which might have been used for rituals (but see Laffineur in *Aegaeum* 1, 1987, 117-25). Shaw (1973, 57) finds it 'most suggestive' that the axis of the Temple Tomb at Knossos, a religious structure which also served as a tomb, is aligned east-west with its entrance on the east.

Perhaps of relevance in the context of this question of architectural alignment, and the possible orientation of courtyards and religious rooms (see p.77 above) and tomb doorways to the rising or setting of the sun, are the sample of seal engravings shown on **Figs. 180, 181** and **182**. Here we find in **Fig. 180a** a very worn seal from the Messara which shows quite simply the design of a doorway; its similarity to the tomb doorways shown on **Fig. 95** may or may not be deliberate. The Messara doorways were, it will be recalled, aligned to the east and have been compared above to the portals through which the sun rises on Mesopotamian cylinder seals (see **Fig. 94a**). **Fig. 180b** shows a similar doorway with a 'star' motif and crescents visible through the doorway, while another crescent is visible above the doorway, with crosshatching around. The 'star' motif visible at, or perhaps through, the base of the doorway will interest us here: are we looking at a tomb doorway juxtaposed with heavenly bodies? Some other motifs of an architectural nature appear with a disc adjacent to them (**Fig. 181**). These have been interpreted as rustic shrines, but also as vessels. On a representation like **Fig. 181d**, the latter interpretation seems most plausible. Vessels do appear with a similarly hatched top (**Fig. 181e**), although the disc on **Fig. 181a** would hardly be practical as a vessel handle and the appearance of similar motifs altogether without handles (**Fig. 181f**) must incline us to leave the question open. Certainly **Fig. 181g** looks quite unlike a vessel, as do **Fig. 180 a** and **b**. Perhaps the Bronze Age artist was content with an ambiguity which we find puzzling; it is a similar ambiguity to that apparent in the Lebena house-lamp and the 'fire-cover' shown on **Fig. 143b**. One reason for interest in this case is the existence of a possible Egyptian model: compare **Fig. 180b** with **Fig. 181i** (from an eighteenth to nineteenth Dynasty tomb), which the Book of the Dead identifies as showing the flying soul and shade next to the tomb, while the roof of the tomb represents the horizon with the sun rising between the two mountains (see Allen and Hauser, 1974, 76 n.151).

Another apparently architectural motif which appears with a star or sun motif is shown on the hieroglyphic seals on **Fig. 182 a** and **b**. As hieroglyphs these should properly have been considered in Chapter 1, but they are included here for purposes of comparison with **Fig. 180**. Evans identifies this motif as a decorator's 'template' for stencilling and suggests that as an official title it denotes a 'Wall-painter/Beautifier' (1909, 268). Its possible hieroglyphic significance does not concern us here so much as its origin as a motif. It appears not only with a 'star design' beneath it but also with a tree design beneath it (as on **Fig. 182c**); the positioning of the 'star' in relation to the facade is certainly similar to that on **Fig. 180b**.

Funerary iconography

Whatever might be the correct interpretation of such designs, it is worth noting that several of the possible sun representations referred to in the discussion of sun motifs above (pp.72ff) derive from a funerary context: the vase shown on **Fig. 134a**, for example, is from the 'Tombe dei nobili' at Phaistos, while, perhaps more significantly, **Fig. 149** is one of several examples where a 'sun' appears as part of the decoration of a larnax; the sun motif is repeated twice on the lid of the same larnax (**Fig. 183a**). Other possible suns on larnakes include **Fig. 134b** and **Fig. 198a**. Evans identifies a 'decorative motive in the form of a six-rayed star' on a burial jar from Knossos (**Fig. 183b**), which he relates to a 'clearly religious symbol' (*PM* I, 584).

It was suggested in Chapter 1 that dances oriented towards the sun may have taken place on the paving close to graves. It is therefore of interest that some possible representations of circular dance (such as **Fig. 139c**) derive from a funerary context. A further example, the model of four dancers from the tholos site of Kamilari, is shown on **Fig. 184**. The dating of this item is uncertain; for iconographic reasons I have placed it late. Here the horns of consecration indicate that this dance has a religious significance. Other models from Kamilari (e.g. HM No. 15074) have been identified as showing a cult of the dead. The sex of the Kamilari dancers is unclear, while only one of the dancers on **Fig. 139c** can be identified as female by her breasts. It is reasonable to suggest that these scenes of circular dance may represent part of funerary ritual. As to other evidence concerning funerary ritual, larnax decorations suggest that women played an important part in funerary rituals and mourning (see **Fig. 185**); on one larnax from Tanagra (Tomb 22) women are shown actually placing the corpse in the larnax (Long, 1974, Pl. 10, Fig. 24). In some cases (e.g. **Fig. 245a**) a female deity is perhaps represented (see p.104 below). The figures on coffin ends have an Egyptian parallel in the custom of painting Isis and Nephthys on the ends of coffins to watch over the head and feet of the deceased (compare **Fig. 185a** with **Fig. 185e**, see Hayes, 1935, 74-5, 122-3). Long compares these goddesses with the Aghia Triadha sarcophagus 'griffin goddesses', and we might also compare the winged figure on **Fig. 245a**. The function of the Egyptian goddesses includes protecting and reviving the deceased. While there has been much discussion about the possible interpretations of the famous 'toasting' model from Kamilari, another model from the same site will interest us more for its representation of a female figure in a circular setting (**Fig. 186**). Apparently kneeling or squatting with a slab or table before her, we might think she was kneading dough (as Hood, 1978, 105) were it not for the bird and horns of consecration around the edge of the circle which again suggest a ritual scene; interesting too is the emphasis on the doorway with a lintel and the appearance of a (male?) figure framed in it. Its significance is unclear, but its find context suggests that the ritual may be funerary. Alexiou believes it represents a 'Totenmahl' rather than the preparation of food (*Gnomon* XLIII, 1971, 279). We might wonder if this figure is involved in one of those acts of 'preparing and mixing concoctions, fermentations, dishes' which Mauss defines as the essence of one type of magical ceremony (1972, 53). The factor which most interests us is the recurrence of circular themes in funerary iconography.

Mirrors and fire

Reference was made earlier in this study to the 'frying-pans', one interpretation of whose use is that they served as mirrors. It was noted that some were found in graves in front of the head, on one occasion resting on the bones of the hand. It is therefore of some interest to explore the significance of the mirrors which are often found in graves of this later period. Mirrors are also shown in the hands of women in several scenes on seals and mirror-handles of this later period. Webster (1958, 34) comments of these scenes that we can suppose that the Mycenaean goddess needed a mirror simply for purposes of her own adornment. Such an interpretation is however highly inconsistent both with the details of those scenes themselves and with the grave contexts in which mirrors have been found.

Thus Taylour (1964, 76) cites a burial in a tholos tomb near Pylos in which the body had a dagger by its left side and an arrow shaft between the legs as well as a bronze mirror on the lower abdomen; it would seem that either we have here a woman concerned with warlike pursuits, or we must recognize that mirrors were popular with men. An LM IIIB chamber tomb burial at Aghios Ioannis (near Chania) contained sword, knife and mirror (*AR* 1984-5, 67). Similarly in grave No. 7 at Zafer Papoura Evans found a corpse buried with a bronze mirror at its left shoulder and a bronze knife near its right arm (see **Fig. 187a**). A bronze mirror was also part of the funeral offerings of the 'Chieftain's Grave' (No. 36) at the same site (see **Fig. 187b**). Evans comments that at Zafer Papoura, as at Mycenae, bronze mirrors 'were as much part of the furniture of the men's graves as of the women's' (1906, 115). Nor are the mirrors created by the rivets on the ivory mirror-handle from the tholos 'Tomb of Clytemnestra' at Mycenae shown in use for self-adornment; rather they are being placed against the belly by the two women holding them (**Fig. 188a**). If we are to identify plants on the outer shoulders of the two figures, this would also affect our interpretation of the scene and incline us to interpret it as a ritual scene. Persson has commented of the 'Goddess with mirror' scene shown on a gold signet ring from Mycenae (**Fig. 188b**) that the mirror may sometimes represent a solar symbol, used in magic rites to make the sun shine (1942, 89); he bases this idea on Syro-Hittite reliefs. One recalls **Fig. 73c**. Other Aegean representations seem to confirm that the mirror appears as an object with a specific religious function rather than as a vanity item for self-adornment. Thus **Fig. 188c**, the decoration on an ivory mirror-handle from a chamber tomb at Mycenae, shows two seated women facing each other, holding up a circular object which Poursat (1977, 80) identifies as a mirror, as well as a bough and some other, indistinguishable, objects. The bough and other objects suggest this is not a simple scene of toilet. On the plaque from the mirror-handle shown in **Fig. 188d**, circular objects created by the rivet ends are again pointedly placed at the belly, rather than being used for self-adornment, and the presence of birds in the women's hands would again seem to suggest that we are looking at a cult or ritual representation rather than a scene from daily life or involving toilet preparation. One might conclude that one use at least of mirrors or shiny circular objects pertained to ritual or religious beliefs. An association with the sun is possible.

The placing of the (usually shiny) disc at the belly in the Pylos burial and in **Fig. 188 a** and **d** provides an extremely interesting parallel to the sun motifs placed on the belly of the 'frying-pans' of the earlier period. An emphasis on the significance of the belly seems again to be indicated by the placing of one or both of the dead person's hands in their lap for burial in Mycenaean tombs (Wace, 1932, 139). The mirror motif will also recall suggestions that the 'frying-pans' were used, water-filled, as mirrors; even, according to Faucounau, for the purposes of measuring the movements of the heavenly bodies. Thimme (1965, 85-6) has argued for a long-standing association between the mirror and death in Greek religion.

In the light of earlier comparisons drawn with Egyptian religion, it is worth noting that during the 3rd and 2nd millennium B.C. it included a vigorous cult of the goddess Hathor, daughter of the sun-god, a sky goddess who sometimes travels in the solar boat, and as early as the First Dynasty is described as being present in the sun temple. Traditionally called 'Golden', she is also 'queen of the stars', and is associated with the Sirius star heralding the inundation of the Nile. She is usually shown with cow horns and sun disc between them. The cow represents fertility and plays a role in funerary cult, associated with renewal of life for the dead. Hathor was also associated with the plucking of the papyrus, another ritual performed in her honour symbolizing renewal. Linked with a nature-substratum, the creative forces of life and the colour red, she is a grim goddess who, when placated, embodies enthusiasm, exuberance and plenty. Other attributes include the uraeus or snake. Her cult involves epiphany and ecstatic dance, and as the bestower of children she has phalli in her sanctuary. She was also a tree goddess, particularly associated with the sycamore under which she sits, and under which the deceased aspire to sit with her. Sometimes it is shown as a bare tree, an emblem of death. The later Greeks apparently identified her with Aphrodite Ourania. (Bleeker, 1973, 1-105; Allam, 1963; Derchain, 1972; Hornung, 1971, passim.) Hathor's cult, which has many reverberations in Aegean religion, also involved mirrors which may have represented the sun (Bleeker, 1973, 53). Mirrors were dedicated to Hathor, and were a common feature of funerary representations which showed the mirror held by the deceased or placed under their chair in a case. The British Museum contains a large collection of such ritual mirrors, dating from c. 1900 B.C. onwards. The inscriptions on several make it clear they were the property of men (e.g. Nos. 2736, 22830); in one example from the late 2nd millennium the mirror handle incorporates the head of the goddess Hathor and the bronze mirror is shown as the sun-disc between her horns (No. 29428). Such material relating to Hathor is highly compatible with our LBA Aegean material. In this context one thinks particularly of the possible mirror and 'bare tree' of **Fig. 188b**.

Another element of funerary practice in the early period was the occasional use of fire, which, it was argued above, may not have served a purely practical function. It is interesting to comment in this context on the discovery of bronze lamps in some tombs of this later period: **Fig. 189a**, for example, shows a bronze lamp from a Mycenaean chamber tomb at Athens which, it has been suggested, 'may have been left symbolically alight by the doorway' (Immerwahr, 1973). **Fig. 189b** shows a bronze lamp from chamber tomb No. 14 at Zafer Papoura which bears a similarly long handle with a tapering end 'convenient for insertion into the chinks of walls' (Evans, 1906, 40). It is interesting to remark on the similarity in the shape and size of this object to the bronze 'frying-pan' found by Evans at shaft grave No. 36 (the 'Chieftain's Grave') at the same site. This vessel, shown on **Fig. 190**, is compared by Evans to a small bronze pan found in Grave No. 14 (visible on **Fig. 191a**), another found in the necropolis of Phaestos, and another in a tomb of the lower town of Mycenae; he regards all these as small 'frying-pans' (1906, 39). If he is correct, one must remark on an apparent continuity in usage, and perhaps religious symbolism, from the 'frying-pans' of the Early Bronze Age period.

Persson asserts the importance of lamps in ritual and suggests that like the big fires lighted at the start of spring they operated through sympathetic magic to give control of the greatest source of light and warmth, the sun (1942, 62, 89). Excavation certainly continues to provide fresh, if fragmentary, evidence of the role of fire in Aegean burial customs in this later period.

In some cases traces of burning are found on the bodies themselves (see, for example, the description in *AR* 1981-2, 58, of a recently-excavated LM III tholos tomb in West Crete); in another case traces of fire may be present on the tholos floor without any human remains (see *AR* 1982-3, 26, report on recently-excavated tholos at Kokla in the Argolid); fires in the dromos are also suggested at the recently-excavated LH 'Tomb of Thrasymedes' at Voïdikilia (Pylos) (see *AR* 1980-1, 20). Chamber tomb No. 14 at Zafer Papoura, which contained the 'frying-pans', also yielded a substantial tripod plaster hearth (**Fig. 191a**). Braziers, firejars and fire-bowls are a common feature of funerary equipment (see **Fig. 191 b**, **c** and **d**). Moreover, a carbon analysis by Georgiou of the contents of several Cretan 'incense-burners' indicates that they were not incense-burners but 'rather braziers filled with the coals of long-burning hard woods better suited for fuel than aromatising' (1977, 136-7). In his study of chamber tombs at Prosymna, Van Leuven found that tombs containing evidence of fire, amber or mirrors showed a high correlation with each other, with location in the south-east area of the cemetery, and with orientation towards the solstice directions.

The evidence here is extremely fragmentary, but it suggests that a continuing association of funerary beliefs and practices with the sun is by no means to be excluded. It also remains a possibility that beliefs associating death with solar symbolism were reflected in the ritual use of fire and mirrors.

2.6 THE JOURNEY BY SEA OR CHARIOT

Recently recognition has been paid to the increasing evidence for the connection of Minoan religion with the sea (for example, in Hägg and Marinatos (edd.), 1981, 172, 214). Evidence for the symbolic significance of elements associated with the sea, such as shells, fish and boats, continues to appear throughout the Aegean and amplifies our understanding of those associations tentatively suggested on the basis of the more inexplicit representations of the earlier period.

Shells and fish

Shells are found in sanctuaries, for example at Juktas among offerings (Karetsou, 1987) and at Knossos paving a shrine floor (**Fig. 192a**). They continue to be found in graves (as in **Fig. 192b**). Sometimes their shape is reproduced in other materials, as with the red faience conch shell from the 'shrine' of Pyrgos IV (*AR* 1977-8, 77), while a blue one is known from the shaft graves at Mycenae. From Mallia we find a triton shell of chlorite, with a decoration in relief which includes a libation scene involving daimons (*AR* 1981-2, 55). Ritual vessels are often made in the shape of shells, as with the famous examples from Knossos and Zakro (**Fig. 192 c** and **d**). Such skeuomorphs can be taken as evidence of the shell's importance as a cult object (see, for example, Montagu, 1981). A well-known crystal lentoid from the Idaean cave in Crete shows a female figure standing near an altar with a conch shell in her mouth, perhaps sounding it (**Fig. 193**). Recently a shell perforated for use was found with other evidence of cult activity at Petras near Siteia (*Archaeologia* 16, 1985, 90) and two conch shells were found at the shrine site at Phylakopi (Renfrew, 1985, 328). That shells were deemed appropriate for religious or ritual uses is clear, but the exact nature of the symbolism they carried is harder to determine. **Fig. 193** offers some clues. Here the shell appears in conjunction with the horns of consecration and bough, suggesting links with a cult of fertility; it appears in the hands of a female figure, and moreover beneath the altar we see what might represent a schematic female figurine of the 'violin' type and a familiar item which Boardman describes as a 'star' (1970, 105), and which Younger describes as a 'sun/star' (1988, 129). A close look at the photograph, rather than the drawing, of this motif reveals that the rays are superimposed on a disc, as in the sun design on **Fig. 127a**. The links associating the shell with females, with vessels and with fertility which can be traced in this material may cast some light on our interpretation of the seal shown on **Fig. 194**. Boardman describes it: 'A bull. The device below resembles a shell' (1970, 95). Closer examination, however, reveals that the bull appears to be ithyphallic with the phallus inserted into the shell-shaped motif. The idea of the shell as a (female?) receptacle, and as associated with fertility, would thus seem to be reiterated in this design.

I suggested above that in the early period the fish was one of the forms in which the sun was thought to have travelled as it sank into the sea, and was thus perhaps associated with an analogous journey of the dead person. A continuing association between the fish and death might seem to be indicated by the sarcophagoi of this period which, in both chest and bath-tub varieties, often carry a prominent fish decoration: see **Fig. 195** and there are many more examples.

I suggested above that during the daytime part of its journey, the movement of the sun may have been seen as analogous to that of a bird, and evidence for a close association between the sun and birds has been presented. A link between the bird and fish might be traced in the many representations of flying fish, some examples of which are shown on **Fig. 196**. Birds also appear juxtaposed with fish on the same seal face (**Fig. 196f**). That their association was not random or purely aesthetic in inspiration is suggested by **Fig. 197** where, as Forsdyke remarks, the horns mark the 'sacred character' of the scene (1925, 150). An association between all three elements bird, fish and sun might seem to be represented on the sarcophagus design on **Fig. 198a** and, in a more decorative vein, on **Fig. 134a** and on **Fig. 198 b** and **c**; all three would seem to have a strong funerary symbolism. On **Fig. 198d** disc-shaped motifs and lunettes may be intended in the field. The presence of the bird in these cases undermines Nilsson's interpretation of the radiant motif on the Palaikastro larnax (**Fig. 195a**) as a sea-urchin (1950, 415). Clearly the fish is not always shown in a literal setting. This association would seem to be confirmed by the design on the bronze tablet from Psychro where the three elements of bird, fish and sun are closely linked, ranged together on one side on the tablet, in a manner which leaves little doubt as to the identity of the three motifs (**Fig. 133**). The appearance again in this context of horns and boughs suggests a link with ideas concerning fertility as well as with the sun.

This Psychro tablet may affect our interpretation of other designs where fish appear with rayed motifs. While some of these rayed motifs may represent sea-urchins it is unlikely that they all do. Thus although Kenna describes the rayed object on **Fig. 199a** as a 'putative sea-urchin' (in Coldstream, 1973, 125) and the circular elements between two dolphins on **Fig. 199b** as 'zwei Seeigel' (*CMS* VIII, 189), he describes that between two dolphins on **Fig. 199c** as a 'Sea urchin or sun' (*CMS* VII, 110). The Van Effenterres describe the rayed object between two fish on **Fig. 199d** unequivocally as 'un oursin' (*CMS* IX, 88), and on **Fig. 199e** we find only a central perforation 'die von strahlenförmigen Strichen umgeben ist' (Sakellariou, *CMS* I, 490). The four rayed motifs shown accompanying fish and dolphins on **Fig. 199 f - k** are, however, unanimously described by the *CMS* editors and Xénaki-Sakellariou respectively as stars. **Fig. 199 e**, **j** and **k** recall the earlier fish circling rayed motifs on **Fig. 57**. **Fig. 199j** and **k** are identified by Younger as sun symbols (1988, 206, 208). We have already seen that the very similar rayed motifs appearing with fish on **Fig. 175 b** and **c** were described by Kenna as solar symbols (*CMS* XIII, 280, 252). There is clearly some inconsistency of interpretation here. Perhaps the examples which definitely show the sun (such as **Fig. 133**) could guide us, encouraging us to interpret similar motifs with disc and protruding rays (as in **Fig. 199 d - g** and **k**) as solar symbols, while variations with more irregularly disposed or unsymmetrically bending rays, or a more floral appearance, may be degenerations of such motifs or may indeed have other interpretations such as sea-urchin or flower (e.g. **Fig. 199 a, b, h, i**).

We saw that such an association of fish with the sun was evidenced in the earlier period (**Fig. 57**). The vegetable sprays and talismanic boughs present in several of these representations make it clear that we are not looking at literal scenes of underwater life. The recurrence of the juxtaposition further suggests that we are not looking at a random conjunction of two sea creatures. If this study has been correct in suggesting that the whirl may be used to represent the sun, a further connection between fish and sun might be recognized in the motif shown in **Fig. 200** where fish make up the radii of a whirl. One could compare this to other designs where birds are similarly used to make up a circular motif or whirl (see **Fig. 98 a - e**).

It will be noticed that on several of the designs discussed above, boughs appeared associated with the fish (see, for example, **Fig. 199 d** and **g**). This association recurs in several cases, as shown in **Fig. 201**. The appearance of a talismanic jug in several cases (**Fig. 202**) would seem to confirm that what we see here is a connection between the fish and a cult of fertility of vegetative life, rather than literal underwater scenes. That the fertility of animal life was also to some extent implicated might be drawn from the appearance of the fish juxtaposed with goats and deer in a manner that is not lifelike; although it might be possible to find some other explanation for these scenes (**Fig. 203**).

From the evidence presented here one might suggest that the fish was symbolically linked with the sun and with the fertility of plant life, as well as with death, as on **Fig. 198**; Vermeule (1965, 136) notes that marine motifs are 'suggestively common' in Minoan funerary imagery. That it was also associated with a female element, perhaps a goddess, is indicated by the designs shown on **Fig. 204**. **Fig. 204a** shows a 'Frau zwischen Delphinen', as Sakellariou describes the scene (*CMS* 1, 369); the position of the hands and of the fish make it clear that this is not a portrayal of a fisher bringing in a catch but rather of a symbolic association. Similarly **Fig. 204b** shows a female figure whose familiar arm position indicates she may be dancing, with two fish-shaped entities on either side of her skirt; Kenna describes the scene as 'Göttin mit Fisch' (*CMS* VIII, 174). The female figure flanked by fish on **Fig. 204c** has her arms raised in a gesture which is also familiar and might confirm a religious significance in these representations. We might also wonder whether the discovery of a terracotta dolphin (**Fig. 204d**) in the Aghia Irini shrine on Kea, which contains so many female statues, reflects similar religious ideas. (Fresh examples of fish in shrines continue to emerge; cf. the recently-excavated fish from an LM I B shrine at Archanes, **Fig. 204e**.)

The boat journey

The Kea site has also yielded part of a bronze boat model from corridor VII of the temple. I referred above to Betts' suggestion that most of the ships depicted on Minoan seals are not realistic illustrations of the vessels which were used for sailing but rather are cult objects or symbols of some sort with a magico-religious significance (see p.35). Gray (1974, 46) also notes that Late Minoan Crete yields very few realistic representations of useable ships. In at least one case a boat is carved on cult apparatus (see Warren, 1966) at an inland sacred cave. We find ships represented in a 'talismanic' style (as in **Fig. 205a**); plant motifs may be incorporated (**Fig. 205b**) or added to the design in a non-naturalistic way (**Fig. 205c**). **Fig. 205d** shows a pot design along similarly stylized, unnaturalistic lines, with a bird perching or fish ensign on the end of the boat. If one again asks, in the context of this later period, wherein the symbolic significance of such boats might have laid, an association with death is one of the elements which appears to be indicated. Thus we find a boat with birds decorating a sarcophagus on **Fig. 206a**, and another boat decorating a sarcophagus on **Fig. 206e**. **Fig. 206b** shows a clay model of a boat which was among the offerings to the dead in a Mycenaean chamber tomb (NAM No. 3099). We also find a boat among the offerings made to the dead on the Aghia Triada sarcophagus (see **Fig. 206 c** and **d**). Six boats are carved on the door jamb of a tholos tomb at Dhramesi in Attica (Blegen, 1949). Apparently a boat was useful to the dead in some way. For Grumach (1968b, 24-6), shellfish offerings in graves and the marine scenes on larnakes suggest a close association between the sea and death. Alexiou (1972, 95-8) does not believe that the ship on **Fig. 206a** indicates a sailor's grave. Pointing out the absence of other occupation-related funerary representations, and of everyday life themes generally from larnax decorations, he comments on their preoccupation with religious themes and suggests that the boat symbolizes transport of the dead to the other world. He cites the Egyptian and near-Eastern parallels. In this he follows Nilsson (1950, 623-9), who suggests that a sea journey to Elysium was a Minoan idea originating from Egyptian beliefs. Persson (1942, 85) presents a similar idea, suggesting that like the boat of Osiris, the dying vegetation god of Egypt, boats in representations of this period may stand for the boat of the setting sun; he proposes a connection between a god of fertility and a sun god. We do, as in the earlier period, see discs juxtaposed with the boat, in the field above it, on seal designs (**Fig. 207**), although the significance of this motif is unclear. More interestingly, while Persson writes of a male deity, the occupants of an interesting series of Aegean boats are largely female.

Thus **Fig. 208a** shows a boat bearing what Chapouthier describes as 'une sorte de cabine' and containing two figures wearing costume typical of 'scènes religieuses'. He thinks they are probably priestesses (or transvestite priests) rather than deities, and suggests it shows an actual boat journey with ritual significance (in Amandry, 1953, 26-7). **Fig. 208b** shows a similar scene: a boat containing two figures in female robes and what may be a structure at the rear of the boat. Two human figures are again shown in a model larnax in the Heraklion Museum (**Fig. 209**), reinforcing a larnax/boat association; in this case their sex is hard to determine. I shall not discuss here a seal impression from Knossos showing a male figure in a boat with a dog below (see Nilsson, 1950, Fig. 5). A ritual scene is suggested by another boat seal in which the occupants of the boat appear to be male (**Fig. 210**); they are accompanied by a bird which is perhaps being released by the larger, kneeling male figure; one recalls the seal impression from Knossos (**Fig. 141a**) which also suggests the release of a bird as part of a ritual scene. Also comparable may be **Fig. 211a** which Kenna interprets as a divine female standing on the waves with two birds in attendance (*CMS* VII, 175); again the birds could be in a process of being released, but it is hard to have confidence in his interpretation of the 'waves' beneath the female figure's feet. A different representation of sea is identified by Evans, who sees a marine goddess reposing on the waves in **Fig. 211b** (*PM* IV, 955-6); John Betts, however, points out that the design could equally stand upright and that the wavy lines could have a variety of other interpretations (personal communication, 1988). Returning to boats, we find a remarkable series involving female figures in boats (**Fig. 212**) which show certain recurring themes and which may affect our interpretation of the seals shown in **Fig. 208**.

Thus in **Fig. 212a** we see an animal-headed boat containing a single figure whose long hair might suggest she is female. **Fig. 212b**, the famous gold ring from Mochlos, shows a seated female, in an animal-headed boat which has its prow pointing away from the shore. We also see a tree and a ladder-like construction which, as Sourvinou-Inwood (1973) and Chapouthier (in Amandry, 1953, 26) have argued, are in the boat and not behind it as Nilsson suggested (1950, 269). This interpretation is validated by the similar construction and tree, alongside a female figure, which appear on a more recently discovered ring from Makrygialos in East Crete (**Fig. 212c**). Davaras identifies here a sacred enclosure or shrine, a sacred tree, and a worshipper or priestess (*A Delt* 28, 1973, 590). Her hand is raised to her head. Davaras suggests that the ring provides evidence for the existence of sacred boats in Minoan religion. The gold ring from Tiryns, **Fig. 212d**, bears a more complex scene showing what is generally accepted as a scene of arrival or departure by ship (in this instance I am not concerned with the possible identification of characters from myth, but rather with the ideas underlying this scene). Its similarities to the others in this series suggests it may belong with them rather than to a class of literal narrative scenes as Nilsson suggests (1950, 39). In **Fig. 212e** the theme of departure again seems to occur; in this case a female figure, 'the goddess' according to Persson (1942, 82), is shown with arm outstretched above a crewed boat and in the field near to her, also above the boat, we see a small irregular disc and what Evans describes as a tree (*PM* II, 250).

The authenticity of **Fig. 212f**, the 'Ring of Minos', was questioned by Persson on the grounds of its similarity to other seals and as a result of certain preconceptions held about Minoan religion (for example, that it was a misunderstanding to place the structure *in* the boat). If it is to be reconsidered as possibly genuine, it will interest us for its representation of a female figure in a boat with an animal head, consistent with our series. (Persson's dismissal of this as a copy of the Mochlos ring fails to recognize sufficiently the difference both in the structure and in the woman's position which is closer to **Fig. 212c**, while her use of the oar or pole parallels **Fig. 212a**.) The spectacular ceremonial attire and the decoration of divine symbols of the ships in the Ship Fresco of the West House at Akrotiri have been taken to indicate that these too are ritual ships. If the fresco does indeed show 'the festive arrival of ... the divine bridegroom in the sacred wedding ritual' (Säflund, 1981, 207) then we might include it in our series.

These scenes may reflect some kinship with the Egyptian journey of the sun and the parallel journey of the dead through the underworld, in which boats are also vegetational and winged creatures appear. **Fig. 62b** shows a long-standing Egyptian tradition of two female figures accompanying the dead on this imagined boat journey, parallel to the pairs of female figures in our series (**Fig. 208**). We have seen (above, p.39) that the funerary goddess Hathor, who was also associated with fertility, was imagined to travel by boat.

The most striking parallels, however, to this series of boats are found in representations of ritual boats on Mesopotamian seals. Thus the Mesopotamian boat on **Fig. 213a** bears a ladder-like structure similar to that on the Mochlos and Makrygialos rings (**Fig. 212 b** and **c**) and not entirely unlike that on the Stathatos seal (**Fig. 208a**). A second Mesopotamian seal (**Fig. 213b**) shows a shrine in a similar relation to the boat as the building on the Mochlos ring (**Fig. 212b**), while the figure above the boat recalls our **Fig. 212e**. The trees on our seals are echoed in plant motifs on both these Mesopotamian boats, and we have already seen (p.39) that the animal head was a feature of the Mesopotamian sun-god's boat.

What distinguishes the Aegean material is the presence on board ship of predominantly female figures. The paired figures shown on **Fig. 208** have a parallel in the earlier Aegean material, particularly the Korfi t'Aroniou picture, **Fig. 60c** (and perhaps also **Fig. 54a**); **Fig. 60d** may also show a departing female. It will be recalled that the earlier material also showed vegetation and discs associated with boat scenes. We also saw boats replacing sun symbols adjacent to the female pubic triangle on the 'frying-pans'. What is suggested is a continuing

Aegean tradition of beliefs or rituals based around the concept of sea departure by a female element associated with vegetation and perhaps with the sun.

We can perhaps return now to the evidence presented above of the boat's association with the sun and with the dead. It was suggested in Chapter 1 that in the early period the sun was associated with the female sex, and with a regenerative process believed to be undergone by the dead parallel to the regeneration of vegetation. It was suggested that the boat might have been imagined as a vehicle of the sun on the nightly part of its journey. It is interesting then, in the material reviewed above from this later period, to find boats represented in contexts which suggest an association with a journey of the dead, and of a female priestess or divinity, and perhaps of the sun. This association may also provide a context for the associations of other marine items (such as the shell) to cult, and in particular to their apparent association with women and with fertility.

Chariot and horse

For an island people who did not know the horse, a boat may have seemed the most suitable vehicle to imagine for the sun and for the dead. For a mainland people who prized the horse highly, the chariot, or horse and chariot, may have appeared a more appropriate form of transport. Nilsson suggests that the chariot represents 'another conception of the supreme voyage' which was 'a later accretion' (1927, 629). This consideration may explain why the boat was gradually replaced by chariots drawn by the horse, and other creatures (some fabulous), in funerary contexts during this later period.

Thus the Aghia Triadha sarcophagus, which shows a boat apparently carried as an offering to the dead on one of its long sides (**Fig. 206 c** and **d**), features a chariot on each of its short sides (**Fig. 214a**). At one end the chariot is drawn by goats; at the other it is drawn by a griffin surmounted by a bird. The appearance of the griffin makes it clear that we are dealing here not with a literal but with a symbolic form of transport, perhaps transport for the dead or for divinities relevant to the dead person's welfare. Frankfort (*BSA* 1936-7, 121) would like to regard the griffin as an 'Angel of Death'. Long (1974, 32) suggests that these 'griffin goddesses' are a 'divine escort for the soul'. It is particularly interesting to note that the occupants of the chariots in each case, like the occupants of the boats shown in **Fig. 208**, are two female figures. We may also note two fragments of larnakes showing a horse and chariot, one perhaps not used funerarily, from the mainland (**Fig. 214 b** and **c**). There is also a chariot on a larnax from Zafer Papoura (Evans, 1906, 29, Fig. 26a). A more recently-excavated larnax from Kavrochori near Heraklion (**Fig. 215a**) shows, juxtaposed with fish and bird, an empty chariot and horses depicted schematically from above with the horses apparently lying on their sides. For Rethemiotakis (1979, 256-7) it recalls the horses sacrificed at Marathon (see. **Fig. 219b**). He suggests that the larnax representation is inspired by some popular religious myth and that the chariot was needed for the journey of the dead to the other world.

In addition to these examples of boats on larnakes and chariots on larnakes, there is one very interesting larnax which brings both forms of transport together, and suggests a strong association between both and the sun. This is the larnax from Kalochorafiti in the Messara, to be published by Alexandra Karetsou. One side of this larnax shows a boat with fish below, above which a horse-drawn chariot with one or two occupants descends, again suggesting, as Rethemiotakis comments (1979, 258), transport for the dead to the other world. In addition the scene is scattered with a number of 'wheels', concentric circle and rayed motifs which Lembesi (in *A Delt* 29, 1973, 886) tentatively, and Schachermeyr (1979, 83) definitely, identify as sun symbols. The iconography established here (above) would indicate that at least some of them are indeed suns. We seem to be seeing here two alternative forms of transport for the occupant of the sarcophagus, offered simultaneously on a 'belt and braces' princple and associated with the sun.

Interestingly, we again find a North European parallel in the conjunction of chariot, boat and circular symbols on funerary rock carvings (see **Fig. 215b**).

The juxtaposition of the two ideas of boat and horse may be traceable in the putative 'horse-head' of some of the cult boats discussed above (as in **Fig. 212 a** and **b**). One thinks too of the controversial 'Horse on shipboard' sealing (**Fig. 216a**) although in this case it is probably safest to agree with Betts (1971, 330) who concedes that 'some kind of mythological or cult scene may be depicted' but prefers to understand horse and ship as two separate engravings made at separate times. We find the horse linked with marine themes in other contexts, such as the 'sea-horse' and the juxtaposition of horse and fish on pottery, although too much weight cannot be attached to such juxtapositions in pottery decoration (**Fig. 216 b** and **c**). The juxtaposition of fish and horse on different sides of the same seal is also interesting but inconclusive (**Fig. 216d**).

Larnax decorations do on occasion appear to show funerary scenes or rituals, as in the case of the Aghia Triadha sarcophagus and the Tanagra mourners (**Fig. 185**), and so we may wonder whether the chariot shown on the Episkopi larnax (**Fig. 217a**) is taking part in any such rituals. Such a suggestion would be corroborated by the appearance next to the chariot of a procession, and perhaps by the appearance of a lollipop-shaped object in the hands of one of the chariot occupants, as well as in the hands of a female figure in the next panel; again the protagonists of this scene might seem from their skirts(?) to be female. A similar interpretation of funerary rituals might also be advanced for the chariots shown on a Tanagra larnax (**Fig. 217b**), which appear below a row of mourning women.

That the chariot, or horse and chariot, in these instances may represent not only the vehicle of the dead but simultaneously the vehicle of the sun is a satisfying notion; it is however one which neither foreign parallels such as the Bronze Age horse-drawn sun from Trundholm in Denmark (referred to by Nilsson, 1950, 421) nor the later Greek chariot-driving Helios can prove as a current idea in this period. Visual parallels are apparent in the closeness of the chariot wheel shape (as on the Aghia Triadha sarcophagus, **Fig. 214a**) to possible sun-symbols on the Palaikastro mould (**Fig. 132**) and, less certainly, the 'Circus Vase', but we cannot draw much from this. The Kalochorafiti larnax is certainly the strongest indication that boat and horse-drawn chariot were in some way interchangeable, and that both were associated with the sun.

That there was some notion of the funerary chariot travelling over the sea might be suggested by the Episkopi sarcophagus (**Fig. 217a**) which shows the chariot riding over an octopus described by Vermeule as representing sea waves (1979, 67). Perhaps a similar idea is intended by the wavy lines beneath the chariot on a krater from Ialysos (**Fig. 218f**); again the driver here could be female, and there are (careless and degenerated) 'sun' motifs around the scene. As the funerary significance of the chariot kraters is debatable, I have omitted them almost entirely from my discussion. However, Vermeule (1964, 205), finding a prototype in the Aghia Triadha sarcophagus, inclines to the view that chariot compositions on kraters 'satisfied a demand for funerary symbolism rather than appealing to retired soldiers as a memento of past exploits'; she suggests that in some areas kraters substituted for the more expensive sarcophagi (see also 1965, 131, 141).

While many representations of chariots in this period are clearly male-driven, secular, and apparently military in nature, there are some others which may not be. Thus **Fig. 218a** shows a fresco from Tiryns which, if it is correctly reconstructed, is interesting for again showing two (?)women in a chariot, perhaps part of a procession. This may depict a social scene, but the seal motif shown on **Fig. 218b**, where a chariot is drawn by lions, is clearly not a literal representation: the chariot evidently had some role in the imaginative and symbolic ideas of this period. Horse- and griffin-drawn chariots appear in a religious scene featuring a 'goddess' on a LM II cylinder seal from Astrakous (see Long, 1974, 30 and Fig. 6). Moreover, the 'horns of consecration' on **218 c** and **h** suggest a priestess or deity on horseback. Chariot groups are found in Mycenaean graves (listed by Long, 1974, 34 n.37), and in shrines, as at Aghia Irini and at Phylakopi (see **Fig. 218g**; the chariot holds three figures and the remains of a (?)'parasol'. Other fragmentary charioteers from Phylakopi (Nos. 839, 862) wear a polos and so may be female, as French has pointed out (in Renfrew, 1985, 223).). A three-handled jar from a Late Minoan necropolis at Chania (**Fig. 218d**) offers what Benson describes as an extraordinary confirmation of the 'special funerary appropriateness' of the combination of chariot and bird (1970, 29). We may note the circular symbols around the horse. **Fig. 218e** shows a bird resting directly on a horse's back. The chariot and horse have evidently taken a place among the cluster of recurrent symbols which were apparently linked with each other and with notions of death in the earlier period. That the horse had a role in burial rites in this later period is confirmed by the appearance of horse skeletons in graves. Thus, for example, remains of a horse were recently found in one of the tholos tombs in the LM cemetery of Apodoulou Rethymnis (*AR* 1981-2, 58); the skeleton of a horse cut into pieces was found in Tholos Tomb A at Archanes, on one side of the door to the inner chamber (**Fig. 219a**); while at Marathon a MH tumulus contained most of a horse, and the skeletons of two horses were found laid out in the dromos of a later tholos tomb (**Fig. 219b**).

The evidence suggests that both boat and horse and chariot were in some way envisaged as transport for the dead, linked with vegetation and with female deities or attendants. In some cases an identification with the journey of the sun is also suggested.

2.7 SYMBOLISM OF VESSEL AND BRANCH

Plant symbolism

The centrality of the plant in religious beliefs and activities continues to be evident in this later period. Thus the plant appears between the horns of consecration and in association with female figures (**Fig. 220**); plants are held by adorants on the gold ring shown on **Fig. 127a**; poppyheads seem to be held by a seated priestess or goddess on the same ring, and are perhaps intended in the crown worn by a late female idol from Gazi (**Fig. 221**). Plants appear in the context of processions of women and men (**Fig. 222 a - c** and on the gold ring **Fig. 127a**). Actions of touching or picking branches or fruit (as on **Fig. 127a**) seem sometimes to have involved energetic movement (**Fig. 223**); perhaps acrobatics were also part of a plant cult, as in **Fig. 224**, though these scenes may well be secular. The fertility of plant life is associated with dance and worship on the ring from Isopata (**Fig. 225a**); branches are associated with women dancing on **Fig. 225b**; and a tree-bearing shrine is the location for dance on **Fig. 225c**. A tree itself appears to be the focus for dance and worship on **Fig. 225 d** and **f**. A plant is the centre of a scene involving a familiar combination of birds, fish, and humans in bird costume in **Fig. 225e**. It is noteworthy that the last five examples involve female participants. In this later period we continue to find daimons 'watering' plants (**Fig. 226a**) or a cairn of stones (**Fig. 226b**), also carrying jugs alone (**Fig. 226c**) or in procession juxtaposed to plants as on the famous ring from Tiryns (**Fig. 127b**). Of **Fig. 222a** Mylonas comments: 'There can be no doubt that, like the trees of the enclosures pictured on the rings, the boughs here are cult objects' (1966, 149). (See also Warren's recent discussion of flower rituals, 1988, 24ff.)

That the plant can take on the quality of sanctity is clear. The sacred plant is on many seals closely associated with a pot: often a jug, a spouted jug or a two-handled vessel. A selection of 'talismanic' seals bearing this juxtaposition of symbols are shown on **Fig. 227**. Evans has commented on the apparent 'religious value' of the spouted vessel (1909, 197). That these vessels had a religious use is shown by their appearance next to the horns of consecration (as on **Fig. 228**). That they carried some sanctity in themselves is suggested by their appearance actually between the horns of consecration (**Fig. 229**). That they symbolically represented a source or *producer* of fertility is suggested by engravings which show the plant growing out of the vessel itself (**Fig. 230 a-e** and perhaps **f**). The sanctity of some vessels, and their symbolic role as objects out of which things grow, is a feature showing continuity from the earlier period discussed in Chapter 1. From the evidence of that earlier period it was suggested that the identification of the pot as female led to an association between the bulbous part of the vessel and the female womb; evidence for a similar identification and association in this later period will be presented below.

We also saw in the earlier period that sun motifs were often clearly associated with the motif of the bough or vegetable spray. In this later period too we find that the sun appears in scenes of religious or ritual significance in which plant life is involved: for example on **Fig. 127 a** and **b**, **Fig. 132**, **Fig. 133**. On occasion we find what may be solar symbols entwined with boughs and mingled with vegetative motifs (**Fig. 231**; some of these examples include a double axe). We also find the pot and branch combination juxtaposed with a sun or star on **Fig. 232 a** and **b**; Evans describes **Fig. 232a** as showing 'two-handled chalice, plant and sun' (1925, 20). **Fig. 232c** shows what Sakellarakis and Kenna describe as a 'Talismanic combination of a *kantharos* and two stars' (*CMS* IV, 218). A design showing jug-bearing daimons and a plant is crowned by what is probably a sun in **Fig. 233a** (the motif of rays carved onto a disc is familiar from uncontested cases like **Fig. 127a**); cf. the parallel arrangement with winged disc on a cylinder-seal from Cyprus (**Fig. 233b**). Less clearly significant but nonetheless interesting is the combination of discs and perhaps plants appearing with daimons in **Fig. 233c**, rather in the way that discs appear with quadrupeds (see **Figs. 173-77**). Vegetation or cereal grains can perhaps be identified onsome of the 'sun-dancing' pictures discussed above (**Fig. 131 c, f, h**).

Pot symbolism

An association of the sun with the fertility cult represented by pot and branch is indicated by this evidence. Kenna suggests of the talismanic seals showing this association that 'when a symbol or representation of the sun appears, there is little doubt about the conclusion of events which are hoped for — after the drought, rain and vegetation' (1960, 45). Evans also recognizes 'the rayed disk representing the sun' and describes some of these amuletic seals as 'rain charms' (1925, 20, 21). The evidence for the association of the sun with the rebirth of the dead which is presented in this study would suggest that the sun may have played rather a different role from that of the drought-bringing element which accentuated the need for rain; it may also have played a part in ideas of fertility as a bringer of fruitfulness and a symbol of regeneration.

Perhaps I should refer briefly to an unusual seal design (**Fig. 234**). If, as Kenna states, this design does indeed show a 'Kantharos mit Feuer' (*CMS* VIII, 147), we have a further hint about the use of the vessel in cult and its possible association with sun ritual. However, in view of the ambiguity of the design and the absence of any parallels, it is hard to have confidence in Kenna's interpretation.

The pot, then, as in the earlier period, continues to be associated with the bough and the sun, and to symbolize a source of fertility. Another continuing feature is the association of the pot with the female sex, whether it is carried by a woman (**Fig. 235**) or, as in the earlier periods, itself becomes a women with breasts (**Fig. 236**). In this schematic identification of vessel with woman, the belly of the female figure is located at the belly of the vessel.

We do still find an occasional representation of human sexual activity (as perhaps in **Fig. 237a** and **b**), but the association of some vessels with the union of male and female which we noted in the earlier period (**Fig. 82b**) is not apparent in this later period.

[It is, however, interesting to note an unusual feature present on some of the false-necked jars characteristic of this later period. On these jars, dark lines are sometimes drawn between the two necks which, on the analogy between the vessel and the human body suggested by **Fig. 236**, would represent the neck and head of the human. In some cases these lines faintly suggest embracing arms. In many cases they are non-committal, as in **Fig. 238 a** and **b**; in some cases the contour of the lines tapers in such a way as to suggest human limbs (**Fig. 238 c, d**); on occasion we even seem to see a tailpiece of hair on the back of one of the 'heads' (**Fig. 238 e, f, g** and **h**). There are further numerous examples of such lines between the two necks of the vases. It is perhaps coincidental that several of these jars (**Fig. 238 b, h, i**) bear rayed or dotted concentric circles or other designs which we have discussed above as possible sun symbols. Although not false-necked jars, the slightly later sub-Minoan vase on **Fig. 239a**, as well as the jugs on **Fig. 236 a** and **b**, show that the spout of a vessel could represent a head. That two people could be merged in the same vase in Cyprus is shown by **Fig. 239b**, though I know no closer parallels.]

Evidence for rituals

Leaving aside such speculations, we can note that certain vessels continued to carry similar associations to those carried by vessels in the earlier period. But what of the evidence from the earlier period that some kind of ritual may have been practised which involved touching vessels? Here we can avail ourselves of the range of far more elaborate and informative seal engravings which this later period has left to us, and which present a much fuller picture of the vegetation rituals practised. Thus a MM III prism bead, **Fig. 240**, shows a figure touching or bending over vessels in a manner which has often been interpreted as a literal scene of a potter at work (this one is described by Kenna as 'A potter with two pithoi' in *CMS* XII, 158), while we can now compare such designs to fuller scenes in which a very similar posture and situation are shown in what is clearly a ritual context, such as that shown on **Fig. 241a**. On **Fig. 241b** the ritual of touching or shaking the tree with energetic movement is accompanied by dance, while what Boardman describes as a storage jar (1970, 104) appears to stand at the foot of the tree; in other cases the tree touching can also be accompanied by bending over a vessel (**Fig. 241c**). The central figure is usually female in these scenes, but the bending or shaking is performed by a male or female, and **Fig. 241g** and **j** show a male and female figure confronted (compare *CMS* I No. 101 and *CMS* IX No. 115) (the problem of determining whether these central figures are human or divine is discussed later, pp.103ff). In some cases the object looks rather like an ovular stone (**Fig. 241 d, j** and **k**, perhaps **a** and **e**). (On **Fig. 241 d** and **k** we can recognize the familiar bird in flight.) Further examples have recently been found, including a seal from Knossos with a naked woman clasping a baetyl (Warren, 1988, Pl. 9, 16ff, where he also discusses an impression from Zakro). Sometimes the object, vessel or stone, does not appear with a figure bent over it but appears at the side of the picture (**Fig. 241 f**, **g** and **i**). Sometimes it appears to be sprouting (**Fig. 241 a**, **f** and **g**), rather like the sprouting rocks and vessels we have met already (**Figs. 81 a** and **b**, **230**). Sometimes a figure bends, not over a vessel, but over a table or altar-like structure (as on **Fig. 130a**, where the structure has been identified by Persson and Evans as a tomb). It is hard to tell whether or not a similar ritual might be intended on **Fig. 241h** in which a woman stretches her hands out over a circular outline enclosing what Pini describes as spindle- or egg-shaped objects topped with horizontal blocks, perhaps 'Pithoi mit Deckeln' (*CMS* V, 322). The circular outline is of interest here: if these are indeed burial pithoi, we might imagine it to be a circular tomb. (The presence of plants in this representation would again indicate an association with vegetation cult.) It is also of interest that a large pithos-shaped vessel appears at one side of the boat departure scene shown on **Fig. 212e**; while the two orbs with something sprouting from them shown in the field on the boat-ring from Mochlos (**Fig. 212b**) might, through their similarity to the sprouting pithoi or stones shown on **Fig. 241 a**, **f** and **g**, be understood as the same motif carrying a similar association with the vegetation cult (thus Sourvinou-Inwood, 1973, 157), suggesting that boat and bending belong to the same scheme of ideas. (Warren's (1984) ingenious but unconvincing 'squills' argument (also favoured by Persson, 1942, 83) fails to account for the fact that some of these objects are sproutless and others patently need to be large enough to be leant over, while they all clearly have a place within the same set of religious ideas and practices. While stones and pithoi are clearly indicated in a number of cases, as Warren himself admits, we have no reason to be attracted to a special case that a few out of this coherent set should be squills. See also Younger, 1988, 349.)

The courtyard at Phylakopi, with its baetyl, pots and adjacent shrine (Renfrew, 1985, 102, 374), and the central court of the Mallia palace with its rounded stone, might be considered as possible locations for the kind of rites shown on **Fig. 241**.

The debate as to whether the objects in these scenes are stones or pithoi need not detain us here. We have seen in Chapter 1 that both could in certain circumstances acquire sanctity through identification with female divinity. Similar associations have been suggested for some vessels in this later period and the stone continues to play a role in cult, as with the fetish stones in the shrines of the Little Palace at Knossos, and at Kommos, while excavation has recently yielded the fresh likely example of a baetyl from Phylakopi (see **Fig. 247 a** and **b**). Female (?)divinities stand or sit on rocks (**Fig. 161b** and **d**). In the context of these bending and touching scenes, as Sourvinou-Inwood has pointed out, the oval stone and pithos are closely associated and in fact interchangeable (1973, 156-7). We may wonder again for this later period whether the practice of contracted burial and other ideas about death made the burial pithos into a symbolic womb; also whether the stone symbolized, as in the earlier period, specifically the fertility aspect of female divinity. The apparent nakedness of some of the figures clasping the baetyls certainly indicates sexual connotations, and suggests that the beliefs underlying the ritual incorporated ideas about human reproduction.

The question arises: what is the desired result of the touching or bending? The emergence of foliage from the objects in some cases suggests that the fertility or the return of vegetation might have been the aim. The ecstatic quality of the movements of those involved in these vegetation rituals, to which wine might have contributed, has often been remarked. Persson (1942, 34) and Hood (1971, 138) have suggested that some of the pithoi may be burial pithoi, pointing to a scene of mourning. The association with vegetation has been taken to suggest that these scenes show a ritual vegetation cycle linked with the death and resurrection of nature (thus Sourvinou-Inwood, 1973, 156). A scene from a LM III larnax from Knossos (**Fig. 241l**) might seem to confirm that vegetation rituals were linked with rituals for the dead. The, to us, perhaps strange conjunction of mourning and fertility was evidently not alien to Bronze Age thinking and is evident in other forms; see, for example the nude figure of a pregnant woman with hand raised in an attitude of mourning from LM III Gournia (**Fig. 236c**). Persson (1942, 88) has suggested that the bending over is an act of ecstatic mourning as part of a vegetation cult, and he traces several stages of the ritual suggesting an order or seasonal cycle in the cult scenes. In Chapter 1 a certain cycle of ideas associating the disappearance of vegetation with death and with the disappearance or withdrawal of the sun was proposed for the earlier period. The fuller material available for this later period would, with Persson's interpretations, present a fuller and clearer picture of the way in which such ideas might have continued to be expressed. Thus, in a purely speculative vein, it could be suggested that the first stage involves death and departure: the disappearance of the sun associated with boats and the sea, witnessed by the boat scenes shown in **Fig. 212 b**, **c** and perhaps **e**, in which fertile vegetation seems also to leave on board ship; it will be recalled that the dead also were thought to need a boat for their journey of departure after burial. The second stage would then involve mourning and bending over jars, stones, or graves which literally or symbolically contain what is dead, whether the inert seed, the buried body, or a symbol of either. Persson suggests that there was a simultaneous ritual of calling on divine power to aid regeneration, attracting the attention of the divinities 'by shaking the tree … or by conjuring up the heavenly power through an ecstatic dance … or by gifts' (1942, 89). Hood asks whether a search is being made for a magic fruit or bough to restore life to 'the dead god'. This is perhaps followed by a stage which involves the use of fire, lamps and mirrors to respark and revitalize what is apparently dead. Scenes of festive dance may mark the return of life as in the spring, while processions with offerings may indicate some kind of 'harvest festival'. The evidence for a symbolic correlation between funerary beliefs and the movements of the sun, and for the association of the sun to the vegetation cult, suggests that a similar cyclical process might have been seen as applying to the sun (which undergoes both a daily and a yearly 'death'); to the dead person; and to vegetation. The common feature in all three cycles might have been conceived as disappearance followed by regeneration.

One point of interest is to refer to the earlier so-called 'potter' scenes, discussed in Chapter 1, which show figures touching vessels with head bent forward (as in **Fig. 66**). The possibility that those earlier designs represent a simpler, cruder version, more restrained and thus harder to identify, of these same rituals of touching or mourning over the vessel would strongly suggest that we have here some continuity of belief and practice from the earlier period.

Egyptian parallels

Parallels with Egyptian beliefs have already been mentioned, and it is worth noting that sorrow followed by elation was part of the cult of Osiris. **Fig. 242a**, the decoration on a coffin interior, shows an interesting sequence. Rundle-Clark (1959, 255-6) suggests that, reading from the bottom, we see first the soul lying in the tomb with its mummy, immobile and helpless. In the next picture the night sun enfolded by arms, probably the arms of the goddess of the underworld sky, penetrates to the underworld and its rays fall upon the soul in its new form as the body of Osiris. Out of his inert body sprout five plants. In the next scene the rising soul has become the sun as it climbs above the eastern horizon, adored by apes (morning stars?); while the next picture shows Nut as the sky 'who gives birth to the gods (i.e. the stars)' with the sun boat carrying Re the sun god sailing on her back. Rundle-Clark interprets this sequence as a process of transformation and salvation of the soul. What is of particular interest in the context of this study is the identification of the soul not only with the sun but also with the death and revival of vegetation. (Cf. also the vegetation associated with the rebirth of the sun on **Fig. 42j**.)

Certain parallels could be drawn between this sequence and the ideas that seem to underlie our Aegean representations. The prominence of the female element and the prominence of the pot which, as we have seen, was closely integrated into Mesopotamian ideas about the sun-god's journey, are paralleled in the Egyptian scheme by the goddess Hathor, who can take vessel form (see **Fig. 242b**) and is the goddess of the nocturnal and underworld sky instrumental in Osiris' revival. Her funerary cult with its erotic dance seems to bear affinities to scenes of Bronze Age Aegean ritual. From the prehistoric era Hathor was associated with the vegetation god Min; she also had a special link with Osiris. Music, song and dance were sacred to her, and her funerary rituals involved inebriation, ecstatic dance and acrobatics as well as feasting at the grave and offerings to 'the godly souls'. It is thought that such rituals were linked with harvest rites (Bleeker 1973, 47, 51, 53-8, 66-7, 85, 94-5).

Some questions of interpretation

Let us return to the Aegean material to mention some outstanding questions. Even if one accepts that the links and overlaps in the rituals and symbolism suggest that the processes followed by the dead, the sun and vegetation were linked in the minds of the celebrants, and even though the pictures give some clues as to what the rituals consisted of, it is hard to estimate their time scale. It is possible to speculate that the whole cycle of ritual (mourning, revitalizing, celebration) was performed together on one occasion in the funeral rites of the dead person; or that the regeneration of the dead was believed to coincide with the yearly cycle of cult concerned with the regeneration of vegetation; or that some seals show, telescoped together, a series of rituals which were enacted over considerable intervals spread out during the year. At this stage the evidence does not allow us to argue convincingly for one of these hypotheses rather than the other. We need to bear in mind that in Greece cereals are harvested earlier in the summer than in Northern climes and the midsummer sun can wither. We must also be open to the possibility that, in spite of the prow in some cases pointing away from the shore, the boat scenes in question might depict the *return* rather than the departure of vegetation: thus Palmer interprets the Linear B 'po-ro-wi-to', apparently a significant date for rituals, as 'Plowistos', the 'sailing month' or month when sailing becomes possible again in the spring. Persson's scheme for the ritual cycle receives some confirmation from Palmer's interpretations of the Linear B texts, which include the identification of a 'festival of the New Wine', a 'festival of Lamentation' and a 'festival of the Thirsty (Dead)' (1963, 240-256). However, Palmer's interpretations rest in part on arguing back from the later Attic festival of the Anthesteria, a procedure which is not appropriate within the framework of this study.

Another point which is uncertain is the relationship of these rituals to individual divinities. The Linear B tablets, as deciphered by Ventris, make it clear that we are now dealing with personified deities, and we must accept that by this period the sun or vegetation was probably to some extent symbolized by an anthropomorphic deity. There has been a tendency to assume, from an analogy with oriental religion, that the figure at the centre of the cult was a male vegetation god such as Tammuz (see, for example, Palmer, 1963, 252 and Chapter 1.9 above). However, as we have females at the centre of mourning and celebration, and females arriving or departing by sea, there is a stronger case for arguing from the representations discussed so far in this study that the divine figure involved was female. It is with some surprise and reluctance that Nilsson, arguing (independently of these representations) from the later evidence of myth, recognizes that Ariadne may originally have been such a deity (1950, 527):

> It appears … from … legends that her death is the salient feature in the myths of Ariadne … No other heroine suffered death in so many ways as Ariadne, and these different versions can only be explained as originating in a cult in which her death was celebrated.
>
> The Naxian rite gives us the clue. It closely resembles a type of vegetation-festival, well-known from the Oriental religions but foreign to the true Greek religion. The death of the god of vegetation is celebrated with sorrow and lamentations: his resurrection with joy and exultation. In these cults it is a god who is worshipped: here it is a goddess, and this seems to make the originality of the cult certain. As far as I know, the death of such a goddess is unique.

Here then we find a complex of ideas around the issue of death and regeneration which may have informed rituals directed towards several different divinities. What is striking is how many of the cult practices and symbolic associations recognized in the earlier period continue to be current. We have seen that women continued to be associated with funerary rites (see **Fig. 185**). Interestingly, we again find some indications of the significance of the colour red: for example, red material wrapping a skeleton in Tomb E6 at Pylos, red paint in the pillar crypt and shrine of the Temple Tomb at Knossos and in the background of the 'griffin goddesses' on the Aghia Triadha sarcophagus, which leads Long to suggest that it 'might have been considered an appropriate colour for deities associated with death' (Long, 1974, 29, see also 50 n.2); but unfortunately the evidence remains inconclusive. More substantial evidence of continuity is offered by the iconography of goats. I have commented above on the continuing association of the goat with male figures and with plants (see p.82). A more specific instance of continuity in cult seems to emerge from some rare cases in which a woman is shown with a goat. On the seal shown on **Fig. 243a** a woman in a flounced skirt with apparently bare breasts stands facing a goat and touching its nose. **Fig. 243b** shows a detail of the Episkopi sarcophagus in which a woman again stands facing a horned animal, probably a bull which perhaps replaces the goat, touching its nose. **Fig. 243d** again shows a woman touching the nose of a quadruped, in this case probably a goat or stag. In Chapter 1 we mentioned scenes of touching the heads of goats, whether dead (**Fig. 67 a** and **b**) or alive (**Fig. 118**). The most striking similarity perhaps lies between the two later scenes (**Fig. 243 a** and **b**) and that shown on one of the Korfi t'Aroniou pictures (**Fig. 118a**); the latter is reproduced here as **Fig. 243c** to assist the comparison. In each case, in **Fig. 243 a, b** and **c**, the figure facing the animal has the rear arm bent so that the hand rests on the waist or slightly higher, while the other arm reaches out to touch specifically the *nose* of the animal. The ritual dress shown on the seal, and the funerary context of the decoration of the sarcophagus (which we know from other cases were used on occasion to show specifically funerary ritual) must incline us to take more seriously the suggestion made above that the earlier Korfi t'Aroniou pictures show scenes of ritual and perhaps funerary significance. It is worth noting that goat heads were sometimes found buried with human skeletons, for example in Tanagra chamber tombs; while at Zygouries goat skeletons were found in a grave dating back to MH (Blegen, 1928, 41). One might also comment tentatively on the parallel between the disc shown between the horns of the goat on **Fig. 243c** and the circular motifs between the horns of the animal on the sarcophagus (**Fig. 243b**). The appearance of discs and other possible sun symbols with quadrupeds has been discussed above (see p.53 and pp.82ff). Kanta (1980, 323) suggests that LM III sarcophagi, such as this, bear a flowering of longstanding popular traditions which was allowed by the passing of palatial art. (See also Renfrew, 1985, 436ff on the survival of 'folk' elements in Late Bronze Age religion.)

We have no parallel in this period for the earlier 'goat-in-a-boat' (**Fig. 119a**), although the goat on **Fig. 244d** steps or rather leaps onto an unusual platform (see also the similar *CMS* XI No. 159).

In more general terms, representations such as those shown on **Fig. 244 a - c** indicate that animals continued to participate, or to be imagined to participate, in cult scenes. Some survival of a relationship of identity with animal life can perhaps be traced in the continuing custom of dressing up in animal and bird costume (including unusual examples like **Fig. 244e**). Masks may have been used (see Younger, 1988, 352). The dance and frenzied movement portrayed on the seals (cf. **Fig. 241** and also bizarre scenes like **Fig. 244f**) has been understood as a way of entering 'mystic union' with the deity (Taylour, 1964, 61). One can only speculate on the nature of this identification or union of the worshipper with the divinity, whether that divinity was envisaged in animal, plant or anthropomorphic form. One can also only speculate whether those divinities may have been believed to respond with gifts of healing, illumination or prophecy to their entranced followers.

2.8 DEPICTING DIVINITY

Identifying Divinity

In this later period, the Linear B tablets as deciphered by Ventris and Chadwick describe offerings to named personages, who are known to us as members of the later Olympian pantheon, and thus indicate that we are dealing with a religion involving personified deities. However, whether any of the pictorial and glyptic representations which have survived are intended to represent these personified deities is a difficult matter to determine. Are those figures honoured by processions (as in **Fig 127**), or seated at shrines (as in **Fig. 129**), or standing as the central focus of dance and other ritual activity (as in **Fig. 130**) priestesses or the epiphany of a goddess? Various criteria might be taken as indications of divinity, such as upraised arms (as in **Fig. 160a**), non-human characteristics such as a bird's head or wings (as in **Figs. 136a** and **156**) or the ability to associate with mythical or semi-mythical beasts (as in **Figs. 161** and **166**). However, a position at the centre of rites, or a posture of raised hands, could be adopted by a priestess, and equally a costume such as a bird costume could be donned, as seems to have been a practice since the earlier period (see **Figs. 27, 73c**). It is hard to be certain which creatures were viewed as mythical and which as creatures which inhabited other lands; nor can we be certain that an imaginary scene implies that those involved in it are necessarily deities (what of participants in scenes of lion fighting? Or bull-leaping if, as suggested, that had imaginary elements?). There is a dearth of surviving figurations of divinity in the Middle Helladic period, and in Cretan shrine contexts where one might expect to find them. In some religious systems there are divinities which are not amenable, or suitable, to be figured. Nor does a name which is recognizable from later Greek religion imply that at this point the deity took a similar form to that familiar to us from later evidence (as pointed out by Renfrew, 1983b). The passage of various characteristics and attributes from the divinities of this period to those of archaic and classical Greece was by no means a straightforward one.

A few examples may highlight the problems in determining divinity. The winged figure which appears on the end of a sarcophagus from Tanagra, depicted either within or before a rectangular building crowned with horns of consecration (**Fig. 245a**), is described by Orlandos as 'sufficiently clearly' representing the epiphany of the goddess (*Ergon*, 1977, 19). The two winged figures on the long side of the sarcophagus (**Fig. 245b**) are not, however, placed in the same category, and for Vermeule a similar figure on the end of a larnax in Kassel 'may show the soul or psyche of a dead woman' (1965, 129). The winged female figure on the seal shown in **Fig. 245c** might fit more easily into the category of a woman in costume, especially as she is holding out her girdle, indicating that her clothing is shown literally and has explicit mechanics: no suggestion here of a divine epiphany or of a blurred or mystical fusion of human and bird form. Is size a factor to consider, as with the impressive clay statues from Aghia Irini on Keos? The raised arms of the female figure on **Fig. 246a** might not in itself be sufficient to indicate divinity, but would her find-spot on an altar, and the presence of horns of consecration on the Karphi figure of **Fig. 246b**, strongly argue divinity for these particular figures, and by extension for all others adopting the same stance? What of the appearance of a female figure in similar posture visible through the doorway inside a round hut-shaped urn from Knossos (see **Fig. 246c**)? Would her presence at the centre of the little building imply divinity for her, and by analogy for others of her stance?

This question need not be pursued here. The concern of this study does not centre on the choice between understanding such representations as priestess or as goddess; whether priestesses or goddesses, we are more concerned with the sex of these figures who were so significant in religious ideas, and with the symbols associated with them. Nor need the evidence of the tablets plunge us into a full discussion about which of the deities there mentioned correlate with which of the later Olympian deities: we are concerned with the contour of cult and with the clustering of symbols, not with the labels attached to the divine which may, as argued above, tell us little.

Evidence for continuity

What, then, does concern us from the religious evidence offered by the decipherment of the Linear B tablets? And what can the pictorial and glyptic representations of religious personnages, whether human or divine, tell us about continuity in religious symbolism? One of the most significant single factors is perhaps the predominance of females in religious representations and cult scenes; again, the question whether they are appearing as epiphanies or representatives or officiants of divinity does not detract from the clear indication that the female continued to play a central role in religious ideas. The list of recipients of offerings referred to in the tablets, though not so overwhelmingly female as the representations, also bears witness to the continued strength of female connections with divinity. A highly interesting factor which emerges from the tablets is the multiplicity of deities referred-to; even if one allows that some may be different local names for the same deity, we appear to have a far greater numerical strength of deities than in the historical period. This vindicates Nilsson's (1950) option for many deities rather than a single deity in Minoan-Mycenaean religion. In terms of glyptic, it has been pointed out that one iconography may have been used to represent a multiplicity of divinities. Renfrew (1985, 432-3) has argued that the terracotta female figures of the LBA Aegean could represent a variety of divine personages. This plurality of deities would be consistent with the arguments against an early monotheistic 'Mother-Goddess' put forward in the first section of this study.

A further aspect of the tablets' evidence which is of interest to us in the light of this study is the implication from the names of some of the divinities that their origin and derivation may have lain in elements of the natural world. Thus the tentative identification which scholars have made of references to a 'Dove Goddess' and a 'Priestess of the Winds' (see, for example, Palmer, 1963, 237, 262) corroborates the argument proposed earlier in this study that in the Early Bronze Age divinities were not necessarily envisaged in human form. The 'Priestess of the Winds' is a particularly convincing translation from the texts and is of especial interest to us as indicating that elements of the weather were regarded as sacred. The fact that the winds could be regarded as sacred and cultivated as divinities in this later period provides a strong strand of continuity from the earlier period when, it was suggested, the sun was so regarded.

Comment has already been made above on another manifestation of non-anthropomorphic or semi-anthropomorphic divinity in the form of what seems to be a 'pot-goddess', for example **Fig. 236d**. This item, found in an apparently religious context, identified as female by a small pair of breasts, and reminiscent of Early Cycladic figurines in the position of her arms, might provide a strand of continuity from earlier figures such as the 'Goddess of Myrtos'.

Another strand of continuity can perhaps be traced in the persistence of circular and tri-partite forms in association with the architecture and sculpture of divinity. Thus, for example, the unit of three is strongly apparent in the tri-partite shrines (discussed by Shaw, 1978). Baetyls and 'fetish stones', which have already been mentioned, offer well-rounded embodiments of divinity (**Fig. 247 a** and **b**), and it is interesting that in this later period round 'loomweights' continue to turn up in contexts more strongly linked to cult than to looms, leading Warren to comment of the 79 such objects which he found in the Cult Room Basement at Knossos, some of them extremely heavy and of differing weights (see **Fig. 247c**) that 'It could perhaps be that their final usage was not for weaving, but in some way connected with the cult vessels with whch they were associated' (*AR*, 1980-1, 85). (See also Warren, 1988, 20.) Moreover, although the Phi shape of Mycenaean figurine (**Fig. 247d**) is usually understood as a stylization of a folded arm position (see French, 1971, 112-23), it is interesting for its use of a circular shape to represent the torso of the female body, as has been suggested for the EBA 'frying-pans'. Caskey (1955, 43) also traces a parallel between the Phi-figurines and the fragmentary circular-bodied EH figurine from Lerna (**Fig. 247e**).

The idea that the terracotta figurines represent elements of continuity has been put forward independently from different sources. Thus Barber in a discussion of EC figurines asks whether 'the reappearance of schematic figurines in the LBA represents the emergence of a native element in the population which had been subdued since EC IIIA' (1983). Parallels between the patterns of usage of EC and LBA figurines have also been suggested; particularly interesting are the piercing of the LBA figurines for hanging (Hägg, 1981, 38) and the close personal association suggested by the placing of a figurine on the body of the dead (Taylour, 1964, 76). It is therefore very interesting to find Blegen writing fifty years ago of a figurine found in EH Zygouries; 'Is it utterly impossible that … late Mycenaean figurines represent the reemergence of a persistent underlying native type and that their real ancestors are to be sought in the Early Helladic period in figures such as the one under discussion?' (1929, 185-6). We may note the continuation of the appearance of such female figurines in pairs (see Chapter 2.11 below). Their sex (female), their size (generally small) and their usage (for example, their appearance in graves) are among the factors shared by both Early and Late Bronze Age figurines, although the lack of material from the intervening period makes it hard to prove a continuous tradition.

The question of size raises a more general point of continuity, in which continuity between the early and late periods becomes more apparent by a comparison with, for example, religious practices in the East at this period. The relatively unassuming nature of most of the images and premises used for cult in the Aegean are consistent with a religious tradition which had never provided awe-inspiring housing for its deities or included massive public display as part of its religious practice.

Up to this point we have discussed many different aspects of religious symbolism which reveal continuity from earlier times in the Aegean. Now it is time to turn to an examination of aspects of religious symbolism which have clearly changed.

2.9 DISCONTINUITY: NEW THEMES AND MOTIFS

Parallel to, and contemporary with, the many elements discussed above which show continuity from the earlier period, the evidence from this later period also reveals significant changes. One aspect of change is manifested in the appearance and popularity of themes and motifs which were almost completely absent from earlier representations.

Thus, if one is simply to refer to the type of scene depicted on the seals, we find a new element in the appearance of scenes not simply showing hunting but showing hand-to-hand attacks on animals with spear or fist, and celebrating the moment of kill, as in **Fig. 248** (see also examples listed in Younger, 1988, 159ff). Also introducing a new motif are the scenes which show one animal — often a lion — attacking another, as in **Fig. 249** (for further examples, see Younger, 1988, 100-118). Another new element appears in scenes where humans are in combat with each other, as in **Fig. 250**; also in the portrayal of military situations and personnel, as in **Fig. 251**. New too is the celebration of items of military equipment as symbols in isolation, in the way in which the motif of the helmet is used on **Fig. 252**. It is unclear whether or not the so-called 'figure-of-eight shield' is indeed primarily a shield, but in either case this is also largely a new motif and one which is popular in a variety of contexts, including some of those discussed here as new. Thus it appears with animals fighting in **Fig 249d**, and with an animal and a severed limb on **Fig. 253a**, as well as on scenes of procession such as **Fig. 253c** and the great gold ring from Mycenae **Fig. 127a**. We also find it with ears of corn which appear to associate it with the vegetation cult, as in **Fig. 253 b** and perhaps **d**. (On its links with vegetation cult, and hunting, see, recently, Marinatos, 1986, 52-8.) **Fig. 253f** shows it in a clearly military context. On occasion it appears to be personified, as on the great gold ring from Mycenae **Fig. 127a** and on **Figs. 252c** and **253e**. It is worth noting that the white arms protruding from the shield in the latter example indicate that it may be personified as female; however, the most significant point about the 'shield' for us in this context is the fact that it seems to have been largely unknown in the earlier period and is found predominantly on the mainland. Mylonas postulates the 'War Goddess' as the Mycenaeans' only creation. He suggests that, with their aniconic tendencies and lacking a suitable prototype in Crete, they 'built her up from the armour they employed' at an early date when the figure-eight shield was still in use, perhaps in LH I (1966, 160-1).

Another new feature of the representations of this later period is the popularity of female figures, in contexts which may be religious, carrying an implement such as a stick or sword, as in **Fig 254**. Also new is the popularity of the 'position of command', with one arm outstretched holding a spear or pole, which **Fig. 251a** shows had a place in the contemporary repertoire of military postures. This position can be seen assumed by the so-called 'Mother of Mountains' on **Fig. 161b**, by a female figure of the 'Mistress of Animals' type accompanied by a lion on **Fig. 255a** (although Hallager, 1985, 23, doubts this is a female), and also on **Fig. 255b** by a male figure in what may be a cult scene, if one is to judge by the rhyton, jug, vegetation and possible altar which accompany him. Most dramatically, it is assumed by the male figure in the recently published 'Master Impression' (**Fig. 255c**).

While from the earlier period we have several examples of female figures portrayed in a religious context in a way which suggests that they played a significant role, what is new in this later period is the popularity of scenes in which women are the focus of a procession which may be both numerous and formal, as in **Fig. 256** as well as the great gold ring from Mycenae **Fig. 127a** and the well-known Tiryns ring **Fig. 127b**. In the earlier period activities such as dancing and touching were prominent, not so much that of processing towards a figure who by virtue of size or other factors is clearly discriminated from those processing in her honour. We also find that now some figures are distinguished by their elevation (**Figs. 161b, 255c**). The impression is of the increased significance of status and authority.

Similarly new is the elaborate religious architecture which is a focus for worship in **Fig. 257a**, and which surrounds the female figure with upraised arms in the seal shown in **Fig. 257b**. The 'column surmounted by a bird on each side' which Betts points out (*CMS* X, 241) confirms the impression that this is a shrine. Nothing quite so grandiose is evidenced for the early period. Perhaps a further expression of the same trend towards a more exaggerated obeisance to, and elevation of, divinity or its representatives, can be identified in the new custom of representing figures of apparently religious significance as small figures elevated in the air. We can see such a figure on the great gold ring from Mycenae, **Fig. 127a**, on the gold ring from Isopata, **Fig. 225a**, on **Fig. 258d**, and on a gold ring in the Ashmolean, **Fig. 241a**; perhaps also on **Fig. 171b** and **Fig. 258c**. Another example is shown in **Fig. 258a** where a small female figure is raised in the air with attendant griffins on each side. A similarly diminutive figure appearing behind the throne of a vegetation goddess of the Mesopotamian religion is taken by Frankfort to represent a statue of that goddess (see **Fig. 258b**), and Kenna and Thomas refer to the central motif of **Fig. 258a** as a cult pillar (*CMS* XIII, 42). Our small figures do, however, often appear without a base suspended in mid-air and it is not clear that we should necessarily think of them as cult images. Whether we think of them as raised cult images or as imagined visions of an air-borne divinity, they tell the same story of exaggerated respect for an elevated and increasingly abstracted deity who is no longer firmly embedded in living physical manifestations of divinity, whether human, animal or vegetable, as in the earlier period.

The implication of these new tendencies in representation would appear to be that a more exaggerated status was accorded to religious personnel and that religious ideas included the notion of a divinity more clearly separated from the world of her or his followers than in the earlier period. This impression is corroborated by archaeological evidence revealing the burial of individuals of a high degree of status and wealth with apparently religious concerns, as in the 'royal' burial of a woman in Tholos A at Archanes (J. A. Sakellarakis, 1967, 281). Independently, the Linear B tablets, with their proliferation of terms for apparently religious personnel, have been taken to indicate the existence of a hierarchy in the organization of religious affairs (see, for example, a recent discussion by Hooker, 1983).

In general terms one can therefore comment that this later period saw the emergence of several new themes and preoccupations in glyptic and pictorial representations, including some reflecting aggression, combat, militarism, and a new interest in items of military equipment.

Priestesses or goddesses are portrayed in different terms in positions of command, exaggerated status, elevation, and apparently a greater degree of abstraction. It is now time to investigate more subtle changes in the specific symbolic associations established for the earlier period; the first area to be examined is the symbolism associated with the sun.

2.10 DISCONTINUITY: A MALE SUN?

The apparently growing significance of male figures in religious contexts during this later period is a topic which provokes serious debate as to the origin of such figures and the route by which the notion of a male deity arrived in the Aegean. At this point we are concerned only with the question of how such a phenomenon relates to the schema of sun symbolism which was proposed in Chapter 1. It will be recalled that evidence from the earlier period suggested that the sun played a significant role in religion and that it was associated with, if not identified with, the female sex. The discussion which follows here will centre on a series of pictures which are shown in **Fig. 259**. Some of these have been reviewed earlier in this study, but are reproduced at this point to give the sense of a process of development from a symbolic schema in which the sun is associated with the female sex, to one in which it is associated with the male sex and appears to be identified with a male divinity. There has been no attempt to range the illustrations in chronological order but rather to show the various stages they represent of a process which would have taken place very differently in different parts of the Aegean, but which we know ultimately resulted in the Geometric period in a male sun god.

Fig. 259a shows a priestess or goddess seated in front of a shrine, while in front of her a male figure stands with his arm raised in a gesture of respect; he is clearly a worshipper or attendant. At the centre of the scene, above the two figures, a large sun is shining. Many similar examples of a female religious figure associated with the sun have been shown above (see **Fig. 127 a** and **b**, probably **Figs. 131** and **132**), but here we can see particularly clearly a prominent sun centrally shown in a religious scene in which a female figure is the representative or manifestation of divinity. Webster's argument (1958, 44) that because a wavy line segregates the sun it is not to be identified with the 'goddess' below is unconvincing. If the sun carries overtones of divinity in this representation, it is certainly a female divinity.

Fig. 259b, a gold ring in Berlin, shows a rather different scene. Again we have a prominent sun, a shrine, a male figure and a female figure. The implication is again that we are looking at a religious scene in which the sun plays some central role. Nilsson (1950, 266) describes this scene as 'a man adoring a goddess', but if we look carefully we notice that in this case it is not the woman but the man who is standing in front of the shrine facing the woman, and his arm is outstretched in the familiar gesture of command which we have seen above in military scenes (see **Fig. 251a**) as well as in religious scenes, assumed by representations or representatives of divinity (see **Fig. 161b**). (See also **Fig. 255**.)

Very similar in structure is the scene shown on the gold ring from Knossos reproduced on **Fig. 259c**. Again we have a shrine with a tree appearing at the top of it; again we have a male figure in front of it with his arm outstretched horizontally in the gesture of command; again a woman stands facing him. The differences in this case, however, are that the woman clearly has her arm raised in a gesture of worship; that the outstretched arm of the male figure holds a pole or spear; and that behind him, in front of the shrine, there stands a large column while another small column is visible inside the shrine. Even more strikingly, we notice that in this case the male figure is small in size and is elevated in the air, with short lines radiating from above his shoulders. Evans (1931, 15) identifies the female as 'the Goddess' in the act of bringing down a small 'Warrior God'. Nilsson (1950, 256) suggests that what we see is a 'woman worshipping a god who hovers in the air'. The latter might seem more plausible, but whichever is the case the figure on whom attention is focussed, and the figure whose right to residence or occupation of the shrine is most strongly suggested, is the small male figure. The short lines emanating from the head and shoulders of this figure are described by Kenna (1960, 125) as a 'nimbus'. Evans suggests that they represent flying locks (1931, 15); such a method of portraying hair is, however, inconsistent with a wide range of representations on seals of figures in vigorous activity whose locks might be shown to be flying (see, for example, **Figs. 139a, 223, 225, 241 a - d**). Alternatively one can look to the Mesopotamian sun deity who is regularly shown on seals with rays emanating from head and shoulders (see, for example, **Figs. 94 a** and **b**). If this parallel is the significant one, we could view **Fig. 259c** as another version of the same scene that is shown on **Fig. 259b**. The two main differences would lie firstly in the fact that in **Fig. 259b** the sun actually appears, whereas in **Fig. 259c** the elevated male figure perhaps embodies the sun; and secondly in the appearance of a prominent column in association with this second male figure.

Armour and rays can perhaps again be identified on the flying male figure shown on one end of a Cretan larnax from Milatus (**Fig. 259d**). Evans pointed out the parallel between these rays and those of the Babylonian sun-god Shamash (1901, 74), but, later, flying locks shown on Knossian wall-paintings inclined him to the view that we have to do with hair rather than a rayed emanation (1906, 99-100). Comparisons with other larnax paintings left him convinced, however, that this figure represented a divinity. The parallel to the Mesopotamian representations of the sun divinity is marked and is hard to explain away as a coincidence. One could, moreover, comment that in neither of these two cases do the lines around the shoulder and head convincingly suggest hair: in the one case (**Fig. 259c**) they are too short and discontinuous, while in the case of the larnax (**Fig. 259d**) they emerge from the shoulders themselves rather than from the head. Vermeule (1965, 136) compares these latter lines to the wings of a supernatural figure in the same position at the end of a larnax in the Kassel Museum. (Compare **Fig. 245a**.) It is interesting to note that the figure on the Milatus larnax is associated with a fish, a creature whose symbolic association with the sun seems to have a long history which has been pointed out in this study.

I am uncertain whether to add one last representation to this group. The sarcophagus decoration on the Kalochorafiti larnax (discussed on pp.94-5, above) shows an elevated and apparently descending chariot which may contain one or two people. It is clearly associated with a fish, a boat, and a variety of circular-based symbols some of which we may take to be intended to represent the sun. The presence of these symbols, as well as the fish, suggests that a sun deity may again be intended in this figure; however the sex of the chariot occupants is not clear and if they are two their closest parallel may lie in the Aghia Triadha sarcophagus female chariot drivers.

Webster (1958, 45) further identifies a male sun god on a gold ring in the Ashmolean Museum (**Fig. 241a**); he suggests that the eye and ear show that the small male god with bow is the sun god who sees and hears everything. However, this is based on Homeric ideas of the sun (*Iliad* III, 277). He also suggests that an archer sun god (who shoots rays) and the archer master of animals (who shoots animals) and the archer healing god (who fires diseases) were later combined into the classical god Apollo.

This study has proposed that in the Early Bronze Age period the sun was associated with the female sex and was on occasions imaginatively located on the belly of the female. We know that in the Geometric period the sun was visualized as a male charioteer. What has been put forward in the paragraphs above is a series of transitions in the visual representation of religious scenes which may reflect different phases of the process whereby a sun symbolized as female and as a womb symbol becomes a sun symbolized as an elevated male deity associated with arms, a column, and perhaps a chariot, within the time span of the Late Bronze Age.

2.11 A MALE GOD OF VEGETATION AND CHANGING SYMBOLISM OF VESSEL AND COLUMN

A vegetation god?

The precise date, origin, and method of arrival, of a male god or gods in the Aegean during the second millennium B.C. has been the subject of much debate. In this context we are concerned with this phenomenon only insofar as it relates to the network of symbolic ideas about vegetation whose currency in the earlier Aegean was proposed in Chapter 1.

Representations of male figures have, of course, always been a part of the Aegean repertoire since the third millennium B.C. There has, however, been discussion about various changes in the nature of such representations in the Late Bronze Age (for example, the appearance of a majestic or 'striking' male figure as opposed to a praying or attendant one) and the relationship of such changes to the emergence of the male sky god Zeus. Recent excavation at the Phylakopi shrine, with its north-east (male-associated) platform replacing the south-west (female-associated) platform in use, has helped to fill out our picture of a male god increasing in importance during the Late Bronze Age (Renfrew 1985, 362, 371, 420). Males are well represented in the Linear B tablets, less well represented in art, which perhaps takes some time to catch up; the 'Master Impression' (**Fig. 255c**), if it shows a god, goes some way to fill the gap, but remains unique (see Hallager, 1985, 32). The preceeding section discussed evidence for the identification of the sun with a male deity. Here we will examine certain other specific changes in the contexts in which male figures appear.

One such change lies in the almost unprecedented appearance of female figures carrying or holding a small child, some examples of which are shown on **Fig. 260**. (There are a very few earlier cases, for example from Cyprus and Neolithic Sesklo.) We may note with interest that contrary to our Christian iconography of madonna and child, a *pair* of female figures sometimes appear in this context too (**Fig. 260 c, d**), thus perpetuating a tradition of pairing female figures which we have seen in the early period (**Figs. 3**, **60c**) as well as in this late period (for example, **Fig. 208**). The child in such representations is often thought, without conclusive evidence, to be male; Fig. 260a, for example, is described by Alexiou as 'la déesse tenant l'enfant-dieu dans ses bras' (1973, 69). Some have suggested that we are dealing with a son/consort of 'the goddess', who joined with her in 'hieros gamos' and became the centre of fertility cult, dying and being reborn with the vegetation. Some writers, citing analogies with other cultures, have linked this young god with traditions of a 'year-god' sacrificed at the end of his reign. It should be made clear that there is no evidence indicating such a cult in the Aegean at this time; in the absence of such evidence, argument by analogy is unsatisfactory.

There is, however, some evidence suggesting the appearance of a god or gods of vegetation. Thus in a central position between the horns of consecration with a 'genius' on either side, where generally we see a plant (as on the gem from Vafio, reproduced here again as **Fig. 261a** for purposes of comparison), we occasionally see a male figure appearing; it is as if he is growing out of the horns of consecration as the plant does on **Fig. 261a** (as well as in other instances such as **Fig. 228** and **Fig. 133**). **Fig. 261b** shows a male figure in this central position between the horns, with a jug-bearing genius on one side and a winged goat on the other. (Reasons given for doubting the authenticity of this seal, as expressed by Gill, 1964, are unconvincing. Betts has withdrawn his doubts: see Hallager, 1985, 30 n.175.) This emerging male figure exhibits signs of authority: in **Fig. 261c** a male figure appears, again between two genii who are still holding vessels as if for pouring water or libations on the plant, but in this case the horns of consecration which cradle the plant are absent and the male figure stretches out his arms to grasp them by the head or forelock in a gesture of command. In **Fig. 261d** the vessels are absent and, all links with plant tending and horns of consecration apparently forgotten, the male figure grasps the two genii by their tongues in an unmistakable display of domination.   The suggestion is not being made that these seals follow a chronological sequence, but rather that they appear to reflect different stages in a complex process of development whereby a plant is replaced by a personified deity of vegetation, who becomes increasingly divorced from his plant roots and increasingly the master of a distinct measure of control over the genii who were the traditional attendants of the vegetation rites. One can only speculate about the nature of the interplay between Cretan and mainland influences in this process. It might be tempting to suggest that a ritual of plant fertility was not so relevant for some sections of a society in which, while agriculture remained important, stock breeding perhaps grew in significance and a new and important source of livelihood and wealth lay in trading and in the assertion of martial power through the wars and raids led by male chieftains such as are often ascribed to Mycenaean society; this shift of emphasis in social organization could be seen as analogous to the process whereby the plant fades and a strong male figure grows in significance.

The growing importance of the column

This development in religious iconography appears in parallel with another new phenomenon apparently associated with the vegetation cult. Whereas in some representations the jug-bearing genii appear to be concerned with pouring liquid over a cairn of stones (**Fig. 262a**), in others we see them with their jugs poised over what is a newly prominent motif in Aegean symbolism, the column or pillar (**Fig. 262b**). **Fig. 262c** shows how the significance of the act of pouring could be forgotten: the artist has put one column in the wrong place out of reach of the genii's jugs. That the columns became more important than the pouring suggests that the artist did not know or had lost touch with what the ritual was originally about. We might imagine a mainland craftsperson reproducing Cretan motifs. It is hard to avoid the suggestion that the growing emphasis on the pillar or column was part of a dislocation from direct links with a cult of vegetation as it had been practised. This would seem to be confirmed by other representations in which the column appears totally dissociated from jugs, genii, or any such elements.

We might also comment on the increased size of some of these pillars in relation to human and animal figures. Pillars are, of course, found in the early period, for example the bird-pillars from the 'model shrine' at Knossos (**Fig. 98j**), but they do not appear dwarfing figures in a religious context as they do in this period. Thus on **Fig. 263a** we find two genii, jugless, flanking a column which is markedly taller than they are: in a tradition noted for its small figures human and divine, and its absence of monumental structures, for the first time the focus of attention or worship in such scenes is a man-made object which dwarfs its attendants. In

Fig. 263b we find a woman, who is perhaps dancing, between two shoulder-high columns; but in **Fig. 263c** the columns dwarf the human figure. **Fig. 263d** shows an analogous representation, Mycenaean from Cyprus. Though this is usually called the 'Window' krater, the familiar gesture of the female figures (see **Fig. 263c**), and their focus on the central upright, suggest that Evans' interpretation of 'pillar shrines and votaries' (1901, 14) is more appropriate. In none of these last three representations is there any sign of an association with vegetation. Links with vegetation are also not prominent in **Fig. 259c** where a very tall column appears as an object of veneration between a tree-bearing altar and a descending armed male deity. Again we see a shift of emphasis away from a cult of vegetation towards a cult associated with height, authority and martial power, whether armed or unarmed. This study has discussed the continuing tradition, originating in the Early Bronze Age, of cult centred on stones, jars and other round objects, and has proposed that in many instances these round objects were symbolically associated with the womb. The shift of emphasis from circular to vertical motifs could be seen as a reflection of social changes involving the increasing importance of hierarchy and authority.

It is perhaps relevant to add a few further comments about the contexts in which the pillar or column appears, in particular about the motifs for which it can apparently be substituted. Thus on the gold ring from Tiryns (**Fig. 127b**) it appears as the last of a row of upright fronds, which it apparently can replace. Evans has commented on this interchangeability of tree and column: 'The two forms, moreover, shade off into one another; the living tree, as will be seen, can be converted into a column or a tree-pillar, retaining the sanctity of the original' (1901, 8). The pillar and the tree alternate in the same position between heraldic animals. On **Fig. 264a** two griffins are tethered to a central column. Some form of taming or subordination is implied, as with the lions tethered on **Fig. 273**. On **Fig. 264d** we see how the column appears on the Lion Gate of Mycenae between heraldically positioned lions, in exactly the position where the sun appears on a seal representation (**Fig. 264b**, reproduced here again for comparison). In this position, replacing the sun, altar or cairn (**Fig. 264c**), the column apparently constitutes a suitable signal emblem for the substantial military fortification of Mycenae. This substitution, if it is not fortuitous, would offer us another example of the replacement of circular and triangular motifs by a vertical linear one. On **Fig. 265** a column appears behind a quadruped, its lower part appearing below the animal's body where we are accustomed on occasion to find a phallus, as, for example, on **Fig. 172e** and **Fig. 194**.

The vessel

We have seen above that some elements of cult centred on stones and vessels continued in this period in forms which show recognizable continuity from the earlier period. However, there are also changes. Analogous with the apparent shift from stone and vessel to pillar, we find that the vessel itself begins to be portrayed in new ways. Thus recent excavations at Knossos have produced a tall cup decorated with what Warren describes as a 'unique, grotesque face' (see **Fig. 266a**) which he suggests may be 'an apotropaic shield device' (*AR* 1979-80, 49) perhaps associated with a 'Great Minoan Goddess of Nature' (1986). The grotesque face is not entirely alone, however, as equally grotesque faces appear as what Evans (*PM* I, 704) describes as 'goblin types' on Melian vases of the MBA II period (**Fig. 266b**). (It will be recalled that MBA Cycladic material was excluded from Chapter 1, and is considered together with the later material here in Chapter 2, for reasons explained in the Introduction.) **Fig. 266c** shows one of these 'goblin' designs in its context on a nippled jug: the jug is clearly identified as female, in accordance with a symbolic connection which we have seen to be widely current, but it now appears as the bearer of designs which lend it a more grotesque quality than it has previously displayed in its appearances in vegetation cult. Such gorgon faces have appeared earlier on Cretan *seals* (see Weingarten, 1983, 90), but not on *vessels* falling within my Chapter 1 period. In his presentation of the Knossos material in London (1982), Warren associated the grotesque face on the cup with the fragments of children's bones belonging to an adjacent room on a lower floor, which bones, he suggested, might have been the remains of a human sacrifice to a Cretan Mother-Goddess. The recent discovery of a cup containing the skeleton of an infant at Palaikastro (MacGillivray, 1988) may prove to give rise to similar interpretations. The issue of whether and how such sacrifice may have taken place is not relevant here (see Warren's recent discussion, 1988, 28). It is however relevant to point out that the Knossos phenomena show elements which are discontinuous with any Cretan cult of our earlier period, leaving aside the speculative status of the 'Mother-Goddess'. Thus the LM IB Knossos cup-rhyton bears, alongside the grotesque face, a frieze of helmets(?) and figure-of-eight shields which we have seen were also new elements becoming popular only in the Late Bronze Age in Crete, practically unknown in Early Bronze Age and Middle Bronze Age Crete and hardly occurring there before 1600 B.C. (see Hood, 1978, 160). Although the onion-shaped objects are hard to identify with confidence as helmets, Warren's 'squills' interpretation is less attractive, failing, as he recognizes, to tally with the objects' most noticeable feature, the rows of short, thick lines (1984, 21) (compare the helmets on **Fig. 253f**). The fact that the Cult Room Basement was built and used only in LM IB (Warren, *AR*, 1981-2, 52) also fails to suggest any continuity of site or religious practice. It is of some interest that the matt-painted technique of the Melian vases has been attributed by some to mainland influence (Sakellariou and Papathanasopoulos, 1970, 81).

This chapter has thus traced several marked changes in religious symbolism in the Late Bronze Age: the replacement of the plant by a personified male deity with qualities of authority; the shift of emphasis from low or round religious objects to a high vertical column; and the attribution of grotesque aspects to the vessel, which elsewhere had been associated with fertility of plants and human erotic activity. One could see each of these changes as the reflection of an underlying shift of emphasis in religious matters from the celebration of an organic process of reproduction to the veneration of authority and of monumental man-made constructs.

2.12 CHANGED RELATIONSHIP TO THE ANIMAL KINGDOM

In the last section we noticed some changes in the cult of vegetation which became apparent in the Late Bronze Age. We can also comment on changes in the ways in which animals appear in cult representations, and particularly changes in the relationship between those animals and the human figures shown, whether those human figures represent cult officials or personified anthropomorphic divinities.

The most marked change is perhaps not one to which we can attribute much weight: this is the appearance of animals which are in process of being sacrificed. **Fig. 267** shows some examples. The appearance of such representations does not necessarily mean very much as we have more numerous illustrations of every aspect of cult activity in this later period. It is, however, perhaps significant that although we see severed heads of goats and bulls there is not one seal celebrating the actual act of animal sacrifice from the earlier period.

I have commented above on the appearance of an increased number of representations of hunting in this later period, often showing humans attacking animals with spears or bows and arrows (**Fig. 248**). Here we can add that this later period also offers many more representations of dead or captured animals being carried (as in **Fig. 268a**) or apparently being prepared for carrying (**Fig. 268b**). Kenna (*CMS* XII, 364) describes one of these as 'Mother goddess carrying a captured quarry over her shoulder' and another (*CMS* VIII, 197) as 'Göttin mit gefangenem Tier' (see **Fig. 269a** and **Fig. 269b** respectively). While we might hesitate before applying the terminology of 'Mother-Goddess', and may indeed question that terminology itself, a cult context rather than a scene of return from hunting does seem to be suggested in all the examples shown on **Fig. 269** by the ritual dress of the female figures shown. In other cases a religious context can perhaps also be inferred from the fact that the dead creature is carried by a 'genius' (as in **Fig. 270**); in other cases we might perhaps, less certainly, draw the same inference from the fact that the animal shown is the semi-mythical lion, as on **Fig. 268**.

Another feature which becomes more prominent is the appearance of what are generally referred to as the 'Master of Animals' and 'Mistress of Animals' in representations which explicitly celebrate the expression of domination over living animals. Thus the 'Master of Animals' grasps two birds by the throat on a gold pendant from Aigina probably dating from MM III (**Fig. 271a**) and 'holds two captive lions subdued' (Kenna, *CMS* VIII, 212) by their hind feet on a cylinder from Cyprus (**Fig. 271b**). In **Fig. 272 a** and **b** he assumes the familiar posture of command with arms horizontally outstretched on either side apparently grasping the lion's forelock, and on **Fig. 272c** the helplessness and indignity of the beast in relation to the central male figure is again emphasised by one of the lions being held upside down. (Further examples of the 'Master of Animals' are listed in Younger, 1988, 156ff.) The motif is known in our earlier period (see HM No. 1578), but this kind of scene never achieved the same popularity. A similar position of command can be adopted by a central male figure towards two flanking 'genii', as we saw above (**Fig. 261c**). Regardless of the conclusion we might reach concerning the nature of the male figure between the lions, a changed attitude to animals is evident. In some representations, the central male figure is absent but the lions are tethered to a central column, as in **Fig. 273**; their subordination is again suggested.

In scenes where animal quarry is being carried, female figures seem to predominate, but the appearance of female figures with living animals differ slightly in character from those of the male figure discussed above. While she may command them (**Fig. 161b**) or apparently receive respect from them (**Fig. 161a**, **Fig. 244a**, **Fig. 255a**), some representations indicate the continuation of a more symbiotic relationship (**Fig. 161d**, **Fig. 166c**, **Fig. 243 a** and **b**) in which communication and participation are suggested. In none bar one of these scenes is the female figure placed physically higher than the creatures involved, nor is she touching or holding them in a manner which suggests the subordination, discomfort or passivity of the animal. Participation and identification are particularly suggested in cases where dressing up as the creature is shown (as in **Figs. 156, 157, 158, 159**). In the case of the well-known female figures with snakes (**Fig. 168**), the grasping of the snakes suggests a measure of control which is absent from those representations where the snakes simply entwine themselves around the figure.

In the representations reviewed in Chapter 1, we saw a seated human figure bend to touch an animal head (**Fig. 67**); we saw animals accompanying a human (as in **Fig. 109c** and **Fig. 112a**); we saw snakes wrapped around a human (**Fig. 110**) and humans apparently dressed as birds (**Fig. 27**). We saw that the most prominent themes are of association, accompaniment, respect for, and identification with, the creatures shown. In one instance a male figure stands with arms outstretched between two goats (**Fig. 114a**), and we also find bull horns being grasped (**Fig. 121c**); nowhere, however, is the expression of domination so pronounced, or the depiction of tamed, dead and carried animals so frequent, as in the later period.

CHAPTER 3: INTO THE IRON AGE

Chapter 3 brings the investigations of Chapters 1 and 2 to a conclusion in the Early Iron Age. Its purpose being largely comparative and retrospective, it will deal somewhat more economically with the material under review than the preceding two chapters. It will highlight elements of continuity and change in some aspects of the religious symbolism of the Early Iron Age. As in Chapter 2, elements of continuity will be discussed first, followed by a review of some of the evidence for change.

For the time span considered in this part of the study, see the Introduction. We are not concerned here to enter into the discussion about the causes of the collapse of the 'Mycenaean' civilization which had flowered in the Aegean area during the latter half of the second millennium B.C. It is, however, relevant to review briefly some of the features of social life during the 'dark age' and of the civilization which emerged from that 'dark age' during the first centuries of the first millennium B.C. A mention of these features is necessary to provide a background to the observable changes in religious symbolism and to provide an insight as to how these changes may have related to the new social structures and economic realities of the Early Iron Age.

It will also be necessary in this context to outline possible channels through which we might believe the apparent elements of continuity in symbolism to have survived from the Bronze Age to the Geometric period over the intervening 'dark age'.

3.1 ECONOMY AND SOCIETY

Continuity through the 'dark age'?

Due to the paucity of surviving material goods or enduring buildings, the 'dark age' appears to us as a period of slumber in Aegean culture. The evidence of depopulation, the decline in standards of building, the loss in many areas of technical skills and the apparent loss of the art of writing and of geographical knowledge all suggest a deep hiatus after the 'Mycenaean' civilization. The sense of discontinuity can, however, be tempered. Snodgrass (1971, 383-5) points out parallels between the 'dark age' and MH periods and suggests that certain elements of Mycenaean society (for example Cyclopean walls, palace bureaucracies and large-scale painting) were intrusive features to Greece which came and went: 'Beneath all this there lay a substratum which we may now recognize as essentially Greek'. There are also other factors which suggest channels through which cultural traditions of the Bronze Age could have been preserved during this period.

The appearance of the Dorian dialect is problematic for historians of this period, although Chadwick's (1976b) controversial suggestion that the Dorians might have been an indigenous and previously subdued population whose 'substandard' Greek had previously coexisted with the 'standard' Greek of upper-class Mycenaeans would, if it were accepted, affirm one channel through which traditions from the Aegean culture of the second millennium B.C. could have survived into the first millennium B.C. Snodgrass also prefers to see the 'Dorians' as intruders belonging to the same cultural milieu, perhaps from the outer fringes of the Mycenaean world (1971, 385-6). The refertilization of, for example, Athenian pottery by a Cypriot influence reflecting elements carried there by 'Mycenaean' refugees has also been proposed. We may also imagine that clan structures survived and preserved traditions.

The problem of establishing the possibility of continuity in religious practice is a vexed one. The building of later shrines over secular Bronze Age buildings may reflect little more than the visibility of Bronze Age ruins. However, there are several sites where Mycenaean religious activity was followed by intermittent offerings throughout the 'dark age' (see Coldstream, 1979, 329-331); and the existence of other sites where continuity must be assumed from the survival of a pre-hellenic deity, indicates that even the absence of 'dark age' evidence does not necessarily mean a discontinuity of religious tradition (such as at the sanctuaries of Aphaia on Aegina, of Zeus in the Dictaean cave and of Demeter at Eleusis). The survival of the names of many Olympian deities from the Bronze Age also speaks of continuity of religious tradition, and at an exceptional site like Kato Symi in Crete we can find archaeological continuity from the MM period into the historical period with virtually no interruption. All in all, the picture suggests that channels existed through which some memories of the Bronze Age were able to survive. Snodgrass points to the significance of surviving traditions of festivals which were an important and ancient part of Greek religion, originally not linked with official worship; he suggests that the religious revival in the eighth century B.C. drew not only on Homer but on 'faint recollections' of Bronze Age religion 'kept alive but not on the whole practised' during the intervening period (1971, 399).

Surviving artefacts also evidently played a role. Benson (1970, 114-118) lists Mycenaean objects found in Geometric sanctuaries and graves with which the Early Iron Age population were evidently familiar. The appearance of contemporary seals in graves and sanctuaries or in use as amulets in this later period reflects a perpetuation of Bronze Age usage, and a long-standing tradition of wooden seals throughout the Geometric era is perhaps a possibility (Boardman, 1970, 108). A continuity of format (for example, the three-sided prism seal) and of graphic motifs (for example, severed limbs and the principle of torsion) can be found to link Early Iron Age seals with those of the Bronze Age. The survival of some Bronze Age motifs (such as the double axe and the antithetical panel) on pottery decoration of the Geometric period is also significant.

The identification of Linear B as an early form of Greek indicates a continuity of language and suggests that other cultural features could also have survived. We can fairly safely assume the existence throughout the 'dark age' of a textile tradition which may have preserved and perpetuated some motifs and symbols from the earlier periods. Innovations, such as the partial introduction of cremation, were few, and this, as well as the shift from multiple burials and chamber tombs to individual burial in cist tombs or earth-cut graves, was partly anticipated in Mycenaean times. The use of jars to contain the remains of the dead was, of course, not new. All in all, the evidence suggests that there were plenty of channels open through which certain elements of religious symbolism could have been preserved during the 'dark age'. As Renfrew has pointed out, we need no longer see only 'a few fragile strands of continuity across a great divide ... The process now seems one of transformation rather than of substitution' (1985, 441).

Finley points out that we can assume the destruction of the Mycenaean palaces and fortresses meant the disappearance of the particular pyramidal social structure which had created them (1981, 61). What was left? Of the structure of 'dark age' society itself we can gain only the sketchiest of pictures. Desborough points out that potters were professional craftsmen in this period and suggests that in the absence of money they were paid by barter. Referring also to the existence of metalsmiths, he proposes that there must have been a few communities which we might describe as 'urban' containing artisans.

After the 'dark age'

It is hard to draw any clear conclusions about the prevailing forms of social organization in the 'dark age'. Of the society which emerged after the 'dark age' we are slightly better informed. Again here there will be no attempt to present new evidence or new interpretation of evidence but simply to summarize the picture generally painted by historians of the period. From a monarchical society we now have a predominantly aristocratic one. The generally accepted picture is of small independent communities with a small urban centre containing a town square and, eventually, a temple. The archaeological evidence of the eighth century settlement at Emporio on Chios reveals two types of house 'belonging to two different social classes' (Coldstream, 1979, 308). The larger *megara* are thought to have housed the aristocracy, while the largest is understood to belong to the local chieftain, 'a concrete illustration of the kind of social system which we would infer from literary and historical evidence' (Snodgrass, 1971, 424). The chieftain's house shared the acropolis at Emporio with an altar and sanctuary of Athena, suggesting that the performance of centralized priestly functions was the prerogative of those in political power, as was the administration of justice. In the absence of written law-codes, this situation left much in the hands of individual discretion, and we have Hesiod's much-quoted attack on the 'gift-devouring' judges of his time. Hesiod gives a vivid account of the farmer's year in his part of Greece, telling us about the warm smithy where people crowd in winter and the swollen feet of the improvident man, about the 40-year-old ploughhand who concentrates better than a young man, and the problematic sailing trips to sell corn which might be part of the year's work. He provides less information about the organization of land ownership in Boeotia, although it was evidently privately owned and a man who got into debt could apparently eventually lose his land and become reduced to a dependent status on the new owner. Hesiod refers to the 'θής' who was of poor social standing but free, unlike the 'δμῶες' who are variously interpreted as house-serfs or slaves. Snodgrass also sees evidence of social differentiation in the graves of the period (1971, 192). Hägg has developed this point in his study of burial customs as evidence for social differentiation in eighth-century Argos (1983, 27-31). 'Stasis' arising from the wide gap between rich and poor, as well as from squabbling within the aristocracy, has been cited as one cause of the colonization process from the late eighth century onwards. Although spinning and weaving were apparently the tasks of household women rather than specialist craftsmen, Hesiod refers to potters and minstrels as well as to the smith, and potters perhaps had their own quarters in some cities by the late eighth century. The emergence of a 'middle class' of relatively prosperous small farmers, traders, and craftsmen during the Geometric period has been proposed by historians of the period. Society was still based on farming, and Snodgrass suggests that stock-breeding rather than arable farming was the norm (1971, 379-80).

The sharp divide between peasants and nobles and the apparent lack of mobility led Burn (1936, 1) to make a comparison between this society and the medieval European feudal system.

(Burn, 1936; Coldstream, 1979; Desborough, 1972; Dietrich, 1970; Finley, 1981; Snodgrass, 1971; West, 1978).

The period of history reviewed in this chapter contains many internal changes and transitions, not only from the 'dark age' to the Geometric age but also with the eighth century's signs of increased trade and population growth, the emergence of sanctuaries such as that at Olympia, colonization and the rediscovery of writing. There are many differences in regional traditions and development. However, for our purposes it will be considered as one period, seen rather like a bunch of variegated and disparate threads which each nevertheless bridge the same span between the Bronze Age and historical times. In this context, what is of most interest in historians' accounts of the period is their emphasis on the sharp divide between the aristocracy and the people, and the clear evidence that one section of the population stood in a dependent or servile relationship to another. It will be recalled that clear evidence for pronounced differences of status or wealth between different individuals or classes in society was a feature that was noticeably lacking in areas of Crete examined in Chapter 1 of this study, and was suggested by evidence from the Late Bronze Age period reviewed in Chapter 2, although the problems of interpreting the surviving written texts from that period left much unclear. It will be useful to bear in mind this information about the social structure of the Early Iron Age in relation to the changes in religious symbolism which will be reviewed below.

3.2 TACKLING THE EVIDENCE

The evidence for the religious symbolism of this period is far more copious and complex than for the two preceding periods. In some instances this evidence will be similar to that used for the two earlier periods: pottery shapes and decorations, seal engravings, and other archaeological evidence.

But this period also witnesses the appearance of a new form of evidence: the literary, which, with its use of symbols for writing, in turn affects other symbolic usages. The focus in this study will be largely on Homer and Hesiod and on some of the Homeric Hymns rather than on the lyric poets.

The Homeric and Hesiodic poems

The Homeric epics, while unsuitable to qualify as reliable evidence for the Mycenaean age or for social organization during the 'dark age' and Geometric era, can be regarded as a rich source of evidence for the *religious and symbolic ideas* current in the centuries between the end of the Bronze Age and the date of their composition in the form we have.

The relationship between Homer and the Geometric world is complex and has not been fully elucidated. Coldstream (1979, 346ff) has pointed out that certain phenomena, such as the popularity of hero cults, appear soon after the knowledge of the *Iliad* spread across to the Greek mainland; what appear to us as signs of 'continuity' from the Bronze Age may thus be simply a contemporary response to Homer's version of the heroic past. However, Coldstream simultaneously discusses examples where worship of heroes 'may well embody a continuous memory about them through the Dark Ages', and practices such as the brief return to inhumation in Attica which were likely to have derived from an awareness of ancestral custom but could not have derived from the influence of epic (1979, 351). Snodgrass doubts that unbroken poetic traditions similar to that of Homer could have survived in areas with discontinuity of occupation, but points out that a revival of interest in the Bronze Age, as at Mycenae, seems to begin before the diffusion of epic; he suggests that a similar sequence can be detected in the changes in pottery decoration (1971, 430-1). Hiller has also recently argued that 'the folk-memory of the heroic past had an unbroken continuity' (1983, 11). Vase painters show an interest in the whole Trojan cycle as part of an even wider set of stories long before they focus on specifically Homeric themes. The recent excavation of a 'heroic' burial at Lefkandi dating from the last half of the tenth century (Popham, 1984) is also noteworthy; even allowing for the exceptional development of Euboea, this find must again enhance our sense of Iron Age familiarity with the 'heroic' world well before the diffusion of the Homeric poems.

Moreover, where the Homeric influence does represent a reflux of Bronze Age ideas and practices carried back from Ionia, we do not have to regard this as an extraneous interpolation alien to the mainstream of Greek culture, but rather as a form of continuity, albeit an indirect one. By virtue of their presence within the poems, such elements can be regarded as having some currency in Geometric culture, even if as archaisms. Through repetition they were evidently familiar and influential. On the other hand, where the Homeric influence reflects ideas and practices which have accrued to the poems during the 'dark age' and Geometric period, this material is again relevant and interesting for us. We are concerned here not with the social realities but with the ideas current in our period. As Murray recently remarked (Discussion at Aegean Archaeological Seminar, Oxford, 1984), Homer is either a reflection of reality or is an invention which satisfies his audience. In either case he provides valuable material for a study of current symbolic ideas.

A more serious problem in the appraisal of the evidence for the symbolic ideas current in Early Iron Age society arises from the increasing complexity of that society. Once one finds marked social stratification one faces the question: whom does the evidence represent? Where we may suppose the existence of clearly distinguished social groups or classes, we need to ask which group our evidence provides information about. This problem is particularly acute when we come to literary evidence. Herodotus claims (II, 52) that Homer and Hesiod defined the pantheon of the Greek gods; insofar as there is truth in this, we have to be aware of any bias in that process of definition, any tendency in Homer and Hesiod to propagate some elements in preference to others. In this context it has been suggested that the Homeric poems, as epic poetry orientated towards an aristocratic audience, reflect a 'class bias' and emphasize the Olympic pantheon at the expense of more popular elements which slip in more parenthetically, as if by oversight. (It is noteworthy that much of our proposed evidence for continuity from the Bronze Age is derived from precisely such parenthetical or even metaphorical passages.) Poetry designed for an aristocratic audience will not tend to reflect or promote the world view of the peasant. The Hesiodic poems spring from a slightly different context, that of a working owner-farmer: although not the poorest peasant, Hesiod does not belong to the landed gentry. The wealth of magical and superstitious ideas in Hesiod provokes comment on how rarely such elements appear in Homer (see, for example, Burn, 1936, 44-5). It has been suggested that the difference in emphasis in Homer could be accounted for by a difference of class or tribal origin, or of economics (an uprooted warrior people not so closely linked with the soil and with agricultural rituals?).

Be that as it may, the difference between Homer's and Hesiod's accounts of religion is quite pronounced if we review Hesiod's treatment of the Olympian gods, who feature so prominently in the Homeric poems. While Zeus and the Olympians get very full coverage in Hesiod's mythological sections, the *Works and Days* tell us extremely little about how these deities were worshipped and offer a plethora of detailed instructions about observances of a very difference kind oriented around the sun, streams, the natural world, the dates of the month and daily life. The *Works and Days* perhaps reflect more closely than the Homeric poems the preoccupations of men working the soil on a day-to-day basis. Attempts to condemn passages concerned with such observances as interpolations are dismissed by West (1978, 333), who remarks that superstitions are instilled by upbringing and if these superstitions were current in Hesiod's time he would have respected them. He also quotes Thorndike's comment that 'one remarkable corollary of the so-called Italian Renaissance ... has been the strange notion that the ancient Hellenes were unusually free from magic compared with other periods and places ... so far has this hypothesis been carried that textual critics have repeatedly rejected passages as later interpolations or even called entire treatises spurious for no other reason than that they seemed to them too superstitious for a reputable classical author' (1923, 20ff). For the purposes of this study the authenticity of the authorship is irrelevant as long as the lines are not too late to be considered within our period. Thorndike's comments about the common attitude towards superstition in Greek writings are, however, extremely relevant and care must be taken to avoid such prejudices in evaluating the relative accuracy of Homer and Hesiod in the picture they offer of the religious practices of their period.

While Hesiod may speak more particularly for those of the population involved in daily working of the soil, as an intellectual, and an idiosyncratic one, he is by no means a typical farmer. It should also be noted that the *Works and Days* reflect very clearly the world view of men rather than women involved in this work. Hesiod makes no bones about his derogatory attitude towards women (see Chapter 3.14 below) and we shall not expect to find in his *Theogony* or *Works and Days* an emphasis on material reflecting the work and interests of women, or any myths, cults or religious activities which might have been of specific concern to them. With the constraints and limitations placed upon them by their situation, audiences, specific geographical origins and the rules of their genre, Homer and Hesiod hardly present evidence which is 'typical' for the period; however, we have to be grateful for the evidence they do provide.

Similar questions may be asked about the vase decorations of this period. Schweitzer has pointed out that in Late Geometric art pictures of the gods, especially Zeus and Poseidon, have been suggested but never really proven (1971, 53). Although we often find scenes of cult (mostly funerals) and human figures on jars, we very rarely find anything resembling an Olympian deity, and there are few links between vase iconography and epic generally (see Coldstream, 1979, 352-6). This suggests that the vase decorations reflect an originally radically different tradition from the Homeric poems and one into which Homeric themes were not fully integrated. Since some of the ornamental motifs suggest the influence of textiles, we might imagine that this ceramic tradition ran parallel to a lost textile art and that both had a more popular basis than the Homeric poems.

Another problem that arises with literary evidence is the question: how much weight should be lent to symbolic associations which occur in the course of the poetic use of the metaphor? It is widely recognized that Homeric metaphors often reflect a different strand of culture from the rest of the text, representing moments when the poet can drop the self-conscious archaizing evident in the mainstream of his narrative and allow contemporary allusions to slip in. While these metaphors often serve a purely descriptive function, as when, for example, a wounded warrior may be described as crashing down like a falling tower (*Iliad* IV, 462), it occasionally seems that the choice of metaphor reflects traditional symbolic associations which may have their origins in religious beliefs or rituals; a metaphor comparing horses to a gravestone might be considered in this light (*Iliad* XVII, 434).

One further source of literary evidence is the 'Homeric' Hymns. There has been much debate concerning the function, and the date of composition, of the Hymns. In this context I will use the Hymns to *Demeter*, *Apollo*, *Aphrodite*, and occasionally *Hermes*. Although these four longer Hymns are variously dated between the eighth and sixth centuries B.C., their style and language belong to the same tradition as Homer and Hesiod and their circumstances of composition may also be thought to be traditional (despite the increase of false archaisms and innovations in the later works; see, recently, Janko, 1982). The 'Hesiodic' *Catalogue of Women* is used for similar reasons. Translations of the Hesiodic poems and Homeric Hymns will be from the Loeb edition translated by Evelyn-White (1914) (with some emendations), while translations from the *Iliad* will be from Lattimore (1951) and *Odyssey* translations from Rieu (1946). Hesiodic fragments are numbered as in Merkelbach and West (1967).

With the advent of literacy, we are confronted by theories suggesting that oral and literate societies will of necessity have a completely different mentality (see Thomas's recent application of this thesis to early Greek society, 1986). However, we shall be venturing very little beyond the earliest days and the first creations of the written word, when its effects cannot have reverberated throughout society; so the complex debate as to the exact nature and extent of those effects need not detain us here.

Vase decoration

In using vase decorations as a basis for the discussion of symbolism, a question can be raised concerning the extent to which the grouping together of certain motifs may be thought to reflect a symbolic association between those motifs. The question also arises whether such associations reflect current beliefs or ossified artistic conventions, like the dead metaphor in literature. Where double axes are scattered all around a figured scene, one may conclude that we are dealing with an empty pictorial tradition, a mere casual space-filling device. However, where certain elements consistently and frequently appear in association with one another, we may have grounds for believing that some meaningful and current symbolic association underlies the choice of motif, especially where the same juxtapositions are echoed in bronze work and in poetry. A tendency among historians to scan the decorations of Geometric vases keenly for the first examples of narrative art has tended to detract from an awareness of the non-literal qualities of many of these representations. Factors which might tend to disqualify the representations from literal interpretation include distortions of size (such as a bird almost as large as a ship), an emphasis on unlikely features, and a juxtaposition of incongruous elements which make nonsense in any literal terms. Such features may reflect the use of distortion to create emphasis, or a monstrous effect, but in many cases they may be best explained in terms of a significant and often consistent symbolic link.

In view of the tendency to favour literal or purely ornamentative interpretations of vase decorations, it is salutary to bear in mind that many of the vases in question are funerary, in a culture where even domestic vessels appear to have carried a strong numinous significance, and dire ill-luck could arise from an untimely placing of a jug on a mixing-bowl, or the failure to charm a pot (*Works and Days* 744-5, 748-9). It is reasonable to suppose that a similarly powerful significance attached to their decoration.

A note on method

The meshing together of the archaeological and literary evidence is no easy task. Here the following procedure will be followed: in the longer sections, the archaeological material will be reviewed first and the evidence it provides will then be set against the literary evidence for comparison. Where the one type of evidence corroborates the other, we evidently have a stronger case.

In some instances 'Indo-European' sources could be proposed for the evidence of solar symbolism in this period. Such sources may well be reflected in the evidence, particularly where discontinuity and changes in solar symbolism are apparent. However, Renfrew has recently stressed the dangers of arguing back from the Greek religion to supposed Indo-European belief systems (1985, 434). In this chapter, in cases where we find early Iron Age material which shows continuity from ceramic, glyptic and other archaeological material not only of the Late Bronze Age but also of the Middle and Early Bronze Age in the Aegean area, these Aegean sources will be preferred. The view will be taken that we can regard such material as more substantial evidence for continuity within the Aegean area than the often tenuous linguistic evidence dependent on theories of Indo-European invasion.

Another factor which should be mentioned briefly is oriental influence. Near-Eastern culture is often used as a source for argument by analogy to fill gaps in our knowledge about Aegean culture at various points, and is also an alternative source for various cultural traits which can be thought to invalidate continuity from Mycenaean cults as an explanation for the appearance of certain motifs in Geometric art. While the evidence for Eastern influence on Aegean art in this period is not questioned here, it will not automatically be preferred to Aegean Bronze Age material as a source for certain artistic or religious influences. The view will also be taken that motifs and symbols are borrowed only when appropriate to the borrower. The point is made clearly by Thomson (1966, 4), 'it must be remembered that, since the function of all social institutions, alien or indigenous, is to satisfy some need, the origin of this or that custom is not explained by saying that it was borrowed from abroad' and by Finley, 'originality never means creation out of nothing, and it is no less valuable and consequential when it starts from an idea borrowed from elsewhere' (1981, 19)

3.3 CONTINUITY: ANIMISTIC IDEAS

In Chapter 1 of this study the importance of the sun in the religious ideas of the Early Bronze Age was argued in the context of a religion in which other natural elements such as stones, plants and animals were the recipients of cult practices and reverence as the embodiment or home of some sort of immanent divinity. Often termed 'animism', this form of religion is evidenced in the material reviewed in Chapter 1 by scenes of people actually tending or touching such natural elements as animals, stones and plants, and apparently dancing before or saluting the sun, as well as dressing up as animals and birds and undertaking other activities which suggest a desire in the worshipper to achieve some kind of participation or union with the creature concerned. As we saw, certain features of this 'animism' continued in the Late Bronze Age although other trends, particularly that towards an elevated anthropomorphic male deity, pulled away from it.

In the Early Iron Age we continue to find traces of an 'animistic' type of religious thinking and we need to review the evidence for it in order to provide a background against which we can seriously consider the possibility that the sun continued to be important in religious ideas. As Webster comments: 'Homeric man ... was surrounded by things physical, animate, and invisible which were insufficiently understood. They all seemed to have some kind of life ...' (1954, 16).

Thus Homer provides us with many examples of the divinity of rivers. We have reference to the River-God Scamander, who has his own priest, Dolopion, in *Iliad* V, 76-78. In *Iliad* XXIII, 147-8, we have a reference to an offering of fifty rams to be made to the River Spercheus next to its waters, where it has a precinct and an altar. That the divinity was still to some extent regarded as immanent in the waters of the river itself is, moreover, indicated by *Iliad* XXI, 131-2, where Achilles refers to the sacrifice to Scamander of bulls and of horses which were thrown into the water. It is true that the rivers are to some extent personified: this is implied by the claim of some heroes to be descended from River-gods (for example, Asteropaeus in *Iliad* XXI, 141-3, and Diocles in *Iliad* V, 544-5) and is confirmed by Scamander's excursion into human form at *Iliad* XXI, 212-3. However, when Scamander takes Achilles on, it is in his watery form as the actual flood of the river itself; and he calls to his brother Simois to fill his channels with water from the springs and lend his flood to join in the battle against Achilles. On a less heroized and more personal note, Odysseus prays to a river before swimming into its mouth (*Odyssey* V, 445ff); and again, in a tradition of country life rather than of epic, Hesiod at *Works and Days* 737ff suggests a sanctity intrinsic to the water of the rivers themselves by the instruction not to cross them without washing the hands and uttering a prayer while looking into the waters.

Homer has, of course, a sea-god, and several references to wind-gods who can receive prayers and offerings (e.g. *Iliad* XXIII, 194-6). We also have references in Homer to sacred woods (such as that of Poseidon at Holy Onchestus at *Iliad* II, 506) and sacred trees (such as the oak whose sacredness to Zeus is mentioned at *Iliad* V, 693, and *Iliad* VII, 60). We also have the olive trees at *H Demeter* 23 who might have been expected to hear Persephone's cry for help. Natural sites and trees were also associated with nymphs. In *Odyssey* XIII, 103-4, for example, we read of a cave sacred to the Naiads, and at *Odyssey* XII, 317-8, we hear of a cave used by the nymphs as a place to meet and dance. In the *H Aphrodite* 264ff we are told that pines or oaks spring up when nymphs are born, grow with them, and die with them. Hesiod describes a bronze race of mortal men sprung, perhaps, from ash trees (ἐκ μελιᾶν) (*Works and Days* 145);and in *Theogony* (187) he refers to nymphs termed Meliae or ash-nymphs, which were born from Earth along with the Erinyes and the Giants from the blood that Kronos shed at the beginning of the world when he castrated his father Heaven. Epithets such as 'owl-faced' and 'ox-eyed' applied to the deities in Homer show that their anthropomorphic suit is a relatively new one which does not always sit comfortably; Kirk derives such phrases from 'primitive theriomorphic cults' (1965, 320). Thetis rises from the water 'like a mist' (*Iliad* I, 359) while Apollo descends like night (I, 47).

The issue of birds and animals will be discussed further later, but it is clear that other natural elements were also important in religious practices and ideas. It is not simply that a natural setting was thought to be appropriate for many rituals, such as the sacrifice to the gods at Aulis which takes place on their holy altars by a spring underneath a plane tree (*Iliad* II, 305-7). It is also that the elements of the natural setting were protagonists in religious rituals and themselves carried a sanctity. The stuff of the physical world and of daily life appears to have been imbued with a religious significance in a manner which still shows signs of resemblance to animism. This attitude can extend to human architecture, artefacts, and activities. Thus in *Iliad* V, 499, we find a reference to the chaff being blown across the 'sacred' threshing floor (ἱερὰς κατ' ἀλωάς) when Demeter, helped by the wind, separates it from the grain, and again in *Works and Days* 597 we find the grain itself referred to as holy (ἱερὸν ἀκτήν): the act of separating the grain from the chaff is evidently not a mechanical one but one in which animistic or divine forces are involved. Similarly we find in *Works and Days* 465ff an instruction to pray before ploughing and at 748-9 a reference to the need to 'charm' pots. Such ideas, commonly described as superstitious or 'magical', abound in Hesiod. Another way of describing the situation would be to say that everyday phenomena and activities were still to some extent the stuff of religion. Listing the activities through which the gods were honoured (including singing, dancing, processions, possession, taking part in games), Finley concludes that 'Religion, in sum, was not set aside in a separate compartment but was meshed into every aspect of personal and social behaviour' (1981, 129). Evidence for the organization, location and activities of religious ritual in our early period, discussed in Chapter 1, suggested that this was even more true of that early period, and we may reasonably suppose that animistic elements in Early Iron Age religion represent a survival, perhaps considerably attenuated, of religious ideas current since that earlier time. While some beliefs, such as the sanctity of rivers, may reflect 'Indo-European' ideas, and Zeus himself is noted for his thunderbolt, those that show a marked continuity from material dating back to the Early Bronze Age, particularly that concerning plant and animal life, may well be thought to reflect indigenous Aegean traditions.

Among the natural elements which we are discussing we must consider the heavenly bodies. Mentioned frequently in Hesiod, they slip much more occasionally into Homer, as when at *Iliad* XVIII, 483-489, Hephaistos decorates Achilles' shield:

> He made the earth upon it, and the sky, and the sea's water,
> and the tireless sun, and the moon waxing into her fullness,
> and on it all the constellations that festoon the heavens,
> the Pleiades and the Hyades and the strength of Orion
> and the Bear, whom men give also the name of the Wagon,
> who turns about in a fixed place and looks at Orion
> and she alone is never plunged in the wash of the Ocean.

This passage is interesting for the astronomical knowledge it reveals, a knowledge otherwise not strongly manifested in Homer, although the *Works and Days* make it clear that such a knowledge played an important part in the working life of the farmer. The continuing significance of Earth and Sky as elements carrying not only a practical but also a numinous significance in themselves is again revealed when at *Iliad* XIX, 258-60, Agammemnon needs to make a very solemn oath that he has not touched Briseis, and we find that Earth and Sun are part of that oath when he declaims:

> Let Zeus first be my witness, highest of the gods and greatest,
> and Earth, and Helios the Sun, and Furies, who underground
> avenge dead men, when any man has sworn to a falsehood.

When Hera herself needs to make an oath she calls to witness Earth and 'the wide heaven above us' and 'the dripping water of the Styx' which she describes as 'the biggest and most formidable oath among the blessed immortals' (*Iliad* XV, 36-8).

It is against this background of the survival of some forms of 'animism' that evidence will now be examined for the continuing significance in religious ideas of the most prominent of the heavenly bodies: the sun.

3.4 CONTINUITY IN SOLAR SYMBOLISM

Here, in the face of the weight of currently-accepted opinion (see pp.140ff), we shall review several aspects of apparent continuity in solar symbolism: one aspect involves investigating the evidence for the continuing significance of the sun and its place in cult (often overlooked or denied by scholars); another concerns an investigation of continuing evidence for an association between the sun and female figures, and between the sun and funerary beliefs, both of which were suggested above for the Bronze Age Aegean. This section will also refer briefly to the survival of forms of architecture and ritual which might derive from the same cluster of ideas.

As will be the procedure throughout Chapter 3, we shall first review the archaeological evidence, and then turn to the literary evidence to see if there is material which confirms or corroborates the impression given by the archaeology.

(a) The Archaeological Evidence

In the Geometric material we may note the recurrent appearance on vessels, many of which are funerary, of designs which were among the repertoire of possible sun symbols discussed in Chapters 1 and 2. These designs include concentric circles, the cross within a circle, and the rayed circle (**Fig. 274** shows some examples). We also find swastikas. As Courbin points out, all these designs have been liable to interpretation as solar symbols; however, as he points out of the solar interpretation of the swastika 'Il faudrait le démontrer plutôt que l'affirmer' (1966, 476). Without the context of figured scenes or of other juxtapositions, such a case is hard to prove. I certainly would not wish to suggest that all, or even most, of such circular symbols were intended as sun symbols. In isolation there is little to suggest that these are any other than decorative motifs, as Courbin believes. It is to figured scenes, then, that we turn to investigate whether any significance, solar or otherwise, should be attached to such motifs. Proving a symbolic significance for some does not preclude the use of similar motifs in other contexts as purely decorative designs.

Of interest here are some unusual fragments from Thera (**Fig. 274e**) on which Coldstream (1965, 37, n.25) finds it 'tempting' to see a solar myth: 'a reclining figure (Phaëthon? Icarus?) looks up in amazement at a vast disc, above which a quadruped prances through the sky'. While expressing reservations about wider theories of solar symbolism as proposed by Roes (1933), Coldstream comments that 'the more elaborate of the Theran discs are remarkably sunlike' and refers to epigraphic evidence suggesting a sun cult on Thera. Such an interpretation, if it is correct, will influence our interpretation of other similar discs which may or may not be incorporated in figured scenes.

The 'crown of light'

We can turn now to circular object in the hand of a female figure on a famous krater in the British Museum (**Fig. 275a**). Often described as a wreath, the object appears here in the familiar context of a boat embarkation. Coldstream (1979, 355) favours the suggestion that the design shows Ariadne displaying the crown of light with which, according to Pausanias, she had illumined the Labyrinth. A crown of light to illumine the labyrinth is not necessarily incompatible with solar symbolism. It may recall for us the notion of the sun lighting the underworld which has been mentioned above in relation to the Bronze Age and will come up again below in relation to Geometric symbolism. Moreover, the idea of a crown is compatible with Bronze Age scenes of possible sun-cult reviewed above, in which we saw female figures whose heads were rayed or surrounded by a circle of dots (**Figs. 30**, **131a**, perhaps **129**). Further light, however, is cast by another figured scene, on an oinochoe of Euboean style from Italy (**Fig. 275b**). Here again Coldstream, pointing to the Minoanizing dress of the female figures and the presence of what seem to be two oars, argues persuasively that the scene may show Ariadne with the crown of light in her hand (1968, 91-3). He remarks that dancing women carrying similar objects in other Geometric figured scenes (see, for example, **Fig. 275c** extreme right) may depict a later episode in the same legend: the Delos dance of the crane (the same bird is intended, he suggests, on the left of the Italian oinochoe). In this context we are not so much concerned with whether the scene depicts Ariadne or the Crane Dance or indeed a contemporary ritual connected with the legend; we are interested in the substratum of religious ideas which might be underlying both ritual and legend. In particular we will recall from the Bronze Age scenes of apparently seafaring female figures accompanied by a disc (**Fig. 60c**), and of female figures holding up circular objects in a religious context as on the Palaikastro mould (**Fig. 132**) and perhaps the 'Circus Pot' (**Fig. 136 a, e**), reproduced again here (**Fig. 275e**) to highlight the close visual parallel with the Italian oinochoe.

We might add to the Iron Age scenes a seal from Megara (**Fig. 275d**) showing a male and female figure holding between them what Boardman (1970, 134) describes as a 'wreath'. I am not aware that anyone has interpreted this couple as Theseus and Ariadne; however, what is interesting to note is that the 'wreath', like all the circular objects under discussion, shows no sign of foliage. Moreover, also like all the others, it belongs in the repertoire of possible Bronze Age sun symbols reviewed in Chapters 1 and 2.

The 'Crane Dance' theory might affect our interpretation of a dance scene on a vessel from the Argive Heraion (**Fig. 276a**); in this case we have no 'wreath' or 'crown', but we do have a bird. Moreover, on the bird, and loose in the field, we have another familiar symbol, the swastika. That the sun could be associated with scenes of dance, in a symbolic rather than a scene-setting way, is shown by **Fig. 276d** where a ring of (bird-headed?) dancers is set upside down to a ring of vessels interrupted by a 'sundisc with twelve rays' (*Antike Gemmen*, I - 1, 31). Another dance scene (**Fig. 276b**) shows a vigorous dance, similar to that on **Fig. 276a**, and a disc surrounded by dots in the field above. In such a context the explanation of filling ornament can readily be proposed, but in the context of **Fig. 276d** we may wonder whether the sun is intended. The interpretation of filling ornament does not even arise with another circular object, in this case the familiar cross within a circle, surrounded by dots, which appears in the hand of a female figure approaching a seated priestess or goddess on a bowl from the Kerameikos (**Fig. 276c**). As with the scene on **Fig. 276a**, the female figure is part of a line of frond-bearing women holding hands; the context seems to be not so much mythical as religious. (Although Oriental models can also be cited, **Fig. 276c**'s depiction of a procession approaching a female figure of religious significance with vegetative associations closely parallels Bronze Age scenes shown in **Fig. 127** in which a sun or dot rosette patterns also appear.)

Thus we have a series of representations showing dancing women associated with, and often holding, objects which recall our 'sun' motifs from Chapters 1 and 2. As to the 'crown of light' theory, the underlying ideas of a female figure involved in a theme of rescue/reappearance from the dark/labyrinth/underworld are highly compatible with what we have seen of earlier sun symbolism. However, if the object in question is a crown, we may wonder what is the function of the crossed bars which appear across its centre in some cases and which might make it difficult to place round the head; we might also wonder why, in all the representations discussed, we never seem to see the object actually worn on the head. It is, moreover, inconsistent with my method in this context to use later parallels or explanations retroactively.

Other circular and radiant forms

For illumination we may turn to an interesting bronze pendant of Luristan type from Tomb P at Fortetsa near Knossos (**Fig. 277a**). This takes the form of 'a nude female set inside a ring which she grasps with outstretched hands ... Flanking lions on the outside of the ring at the top ... vertical groove for pudenda' (Brock, 1957, 136). It is the familiar crossed circle or 'wheel' symbol, with a female figure not simply holding it but enclosed in it. Her divinity is suggested by her nakedness and by the presence of the lions, which also remind us of their Aegean Bronze Age symbolic associations. Although almost certainly of Anatolian origin (see Brock, 1957, 199), the presence of this pendant in a Cretan grave suggests that its symbols were familiar in Crete and bore some meaning and currency there. This object suggests that the crossed circle or wheel shape may have continued to hold religious associations compatible with those apparent in the Bronze Age, and perhaps more connected to them than to later myth. Other articles from Crete tell a similar story. Thus a Dedalic plaque of about 600 B.C., 'perhaps representing Cybele' (Higgins, 1967, 28), will interest us for its representation of a female figure holding a disc over her abdomen, again reminiscent of Bronze Age iconography (e.g. **Fig. 132** and the 'frying-pans') and again showing a circular motif in an evidently meaningful, rather than abstract, decorative, or space-filling role, in a religious representation (**Fig. 277b**).

While a similarly-held smaller disc is often interpreted as a tympanon (**Fig. 277f** shows examples from Lindos), a scarab from Cyprus with a six-winged figure carrying a rayed disc (**Fig. 277g**) shows that reminders of the religious significance of such discs were not far away; perhaps that significance had never been forgotten in the Aegean area.

A further example will perhaps incline us to draw the swastika too into the same category of religious symbol. Again from Fortetsa, the frieze on an amphora from Tomb OD includes a scene showing what Brock (1957, 36) describes as two 'mourners' on either side of a swastika (**Fig. 277c**). Coldstream doubts that these are mourners, who should have at least one hand to the head (personal communication, 1985). However, what is significant for us here is that the parallel between the position of women and symbol on both this and Bronze Age representations is too marked to be dismissed (see **Fig. 277d** for comparison). Although the vessel has possible Attic connections (Snodgrass, 1971, 82), the (perhaps acrobatic) scenes on other panels of the frieze (**Fig. 277e**) also have Minoan antecedents apparent in the clothes and gestures of the figures as well as in the style of drawing, as Schweitzer notes (1971, 72). Some survival of the practices and beliefs proposed in Chapters 1 and 2 seems to be clearly indicated. Such indigenous examples may influence our attitude to Archaic seals showing scenes of apparent sun-worship in an oriental vein, such as **Fig. 277h** and **i**. These seals, from Chios and Lindos respectively, show two figures on either side of a tree or pillar, with one arm reaching towards it and the other raised to a winged disc (indisputably the sun in this period). Such scenes not only embody current Eastern influence, but also resonate with earlier scenes of tree-touching or saluting the (?)sun within the Aegean area itself (see, for example, **Figs. 25a**, **26a**, **27**, **129**, **131 b - h**, **225d**, **223** above).

Crete is, of course, a special case as far as survivals are concerned, so it is of particular interest to find terracotta rings, radiating disc and star shapes in association with an assemblage of largely female figurines from a cult context at Tiryns (**Fig. 278**). In this, as in several of the examples discussed here, a female divinity associated with the sun may be indicated.

Circular and radiant forms in funerary contexts

These items may affect our interpretation of circular and radiant motifs in Geometric funeral scenes. Such motifs often appear scattered over the scene in an apparently random way which suggests a decorative intention. However, they also occasionally appear in prominent, recurring and apparently significant positions. As Boardman has commented, 'where special patterns recur in special places we must think again' (1983, 16). Their use as decorative 'fill' in some contexts does not preclude the use of circular symbols in other contexts as significant symbols, any more than the decorative use of vegetation precludes the occasional purposive representation of fronds; while the scattering of 'butterfly' shapes coexists with the use of the 'true' double axe (with handle) as a meaningful symbol (as Courbin observes, 1966, 476).

Ahlberg believes that the placing and context of the circular emblems on funerary vessels indicate a 'special significance'. She proposes that the zones bearing the emblem denote a locality outside the house, perhaps a court, for example on **Fig. 279f**. Having come thus far, it is hard to understand why she concludes that the emblems may represent curtains, drapery or architectural decoration (1971b, 144-6). This interpretation fails to account for the lack of any supporting structures which those features would require; nor does it explain why those features should assume such prominence. On the other hand, a solar symbol would fit the exterior context well; its funerary associations would also be compatible with the appearance of rayed symbols in interior prothesis scenes and other significant contexts. Thus the radiant motifs on a krater from the Kerameikos (**Fig. 279a**) are prominent and recurrent: appearing, again at waist height, between female figures seated with their arms raised in a gesture of mourning, these radiant motifs might be thought to be related to ideas underlying the funerary ritual. On the neck of an amphora in the Benaki Museum, **Fig. 279b**, we see circular radiant motifs apparently strategically placed in a prominent position by the head and feet of the corpse. A similar motif again appears by the corpse on **Fig. 279c** (by the head) and **303d**. On **Fig. 279d** concentric circle and swastika motifs again figure prominently, although the concentric circles may simply be a conservative formal survival from Protogeometric. The deliberate and significant association of the swastika symbol with mourning is suggested by an item in a different medium: the terracotta figurine of a mourning woman (**Fig. 279e**) who bears on her breast large swastikas juxtaposed with a picture of another mourning woman. In this design, the placing of the swastikas in relation to the mourning woman is reminiscent of the Fortetsa amphora (**Fig. 277c, e**), while the association of radiant motifs with a seated mourner recalls **Fig. 279a**. A consistent and pointed pattern of association seems to emerge.

A more decorative use of circular motifs seems to be indicated on **Fig. 280a**, bell-shaped clay dolls and a pyxis from Protogeometric Athens; although it is interesting that these objects are found only in tombs and only with the burials of women and children. Decorative also, probably, are the circular and radiant motifs found on fragments of coffins from Assarlik (**Fig. 280b**); it is, however, noteworthy that again the context is funerary. On the other hand, for a pendant from Tekke Tomb 2, almost certainly representing sun and moon (**Fig. 280e**), no specifically religious or funerary significance can be inferred.

A word should perhaps be said about the readiness of scholars to identify certain crossed circle or radiant motifs as chariot wheels. Thus the crossed circle and fish which flank a 'winged gorgon' with rayed head on an unusual archaic seal, probably from Melos (**Fig. 280c**), suggest to Boardman an indication of 'ability to travel over land and sea?' (1963, 50). The juxtaposition of circular motif and fish is, however, familiar to us from the Bronze Age, and with a figure looking so like a personification of the winged-disc, we may again wonder whether solar symbolism is intended. The 'chariot wheel' interpretation is also often applied to the votive 'wheels' found in many parts of the Greek world (e.g. **Fig. 280d**). Blinkenberg, however (1931, 127), points out that their structure is in several respects incompatible with that of a chariot wheel or miniature chariot wheel and concludes that 'On ne peut donc assigner aux petites ruelles en question une destination nettement définie'.

We thus have a pattern of usage of a range of circular and radiant motifs which is highly consistent and which is not adequately explained by interpreting one variety as a chariot wheel or as a 'crown', however accurate such an interpretation might be in specific cases. What are the ideas behind this use of motif and, indeed, behind the Ariadne myth itself? The motifs appear to be to a certain extent interchangeable, and appear consistently either in a funerary context or in association with a female figure (whether in the hand of a female figure; adjacent to a female figure with raised arm; decorating a female figure; or enclosing a female figure). In many of the cases cited both funerary and female associations are present. A close association between women and death may further be traceable in the prominent role played by women in scenes of mourning and in the occasional appearance in graves of female figurines who 'look like successors to the Mycenaean mourner figures' (Boardman, 1971, 64). These associations closely parallel associations apparent in Bronze Age religious symbolism. Moreover, they appear in a variety of different iconographic forms (swastika, crossed circle, rayed disc, dot rosette, concentric circles); in a variety of different media (terracotta, bronzework, vase decoration); and in several distinct areas of Greece with different processes of development (Crete, Attica, the Argolid). It is thus apparently not a case of the unthinking imitation of iconographic motifs. On the basis of this evidence I would propose that some tenuous and sporadic survival of the Bronze Age religious ideas discussed in Chapters 1 and 2 can be traced in the Early Iron Age.

Let us investigate whether a rather different form of archaeological evidence, architecture, can offer any material to support or refute this proposition. It was argued in Chapters 1 and 2 that the circular shape of some tombs may have constituted a reflection of the circular shape and cyclical motion of the sun, and of notions concerning a cycle of death and rebirth linked to the orbit of the sun, with its daily disappearance and reappearance. The burial customs of the Early Iron Age differ in many respects from those of the Bronze Age, but in some areas we see not only the continued use of, but also in some cases the continued construction of, both chamber and tholos tombs (for examples, mainly from Crete but also from Thessaly and Messenia, see Desborough, 1972, 272-3, 368-70, 372-3, 376-7) (see **Fig. 281a**). The continued use for burials of the cave, the cairn of stones and the circular tumulus (see **Fig. 281b**) also reflect forms and possibly ideas current in the Bronze Age. Excavation of a Geometric burial site in Naxos town has recently uncovered several circular features consisting of a stone setting 1.5 - 2m. in diameter, for which an association with grave cult has been proposed (*AR*, 1985-6, 76). Similar settings had been noted by Hägg at Asine, Mycenae and other sites (1983, 189-94). Three round funerary periboloi were recently excavated at Palaio Gynaikokastro in Macedonia (*AR*, 1986-7, 37).

Apart from tombs, the circular shape was also sometimes used for buildings of a more general religious use. At the sanctuary of Apollo at Eretria a circular mass of masonry was found surrounded by a succession of deposits; these are dated from the eighth century onwards and include miniature hydriae with designs of a procession of women wearing diadems. Southeast of the Apollo temple, a single course square structure was also found to encapsulate a circular construction of between three and five courses, associated with Geometric pottery, some of it burnt; its use in the eighth century B.C., possibly as an altar, is suggested (*AR*, 1982-3, 18).

While tomb orientation is not consistent, we may note the custom of aligning temples to face east, suggesting either a vital or a purely formal tradition of concern with the sun's movements. On the other hand, Hägg notes that in eighth-century Argos pithos burials almost always have a west or south-west orientation, a practice which is less strictly observed by those using cist tombs. He suggests that this custom 'was based on beliefs that were stronger on the popular level than among the nobility' (1983, 28, 31). Mylonas comments on the use of an east-facing court, and (?)east entrance, in the cult of Eleusinian Demeter (1961, 68). The role of fire in Bronze Age burial customs was referred to above; the use of cremation in the Early Iron Age places fire in a prominent role, although the ideas underlying this practice remain inaccessible to us. Perhaps on this, as on other aspects of symbolism discussed in this section, we will be helped by the literary evidence to which we now turn.

(b) The Literary Evidence

The questions which literature might usefully illuminate for us include the problem of discovering whether the sun played a significant role in religious ideas and beliefs; whether it was associated with death; and whether it was associated with the female sex. Given the particular bias of the Homeric and Hesiodic evidence (as discussed above in Chapter 3.2), a positive answer to any of these questions will constitute an independent confirmation of the trends traced in the archaeological evidence discussed above.

Tackling first the general issue of the significance of the sun in cult, we have already noted that the Sun, like the Earth and the Heavens in general, can be called on in the Homeric world when a very serious oath is required. To the examples already quoted in the previous section (3.3) we can add that of Agammemnon at *Iliad* III, 276ff, where he calls on the sun immediately after Zeus:

> Father Zeus, watching over us from Ida, most high, most honoured,
> and Helios, you who see all things, who listen to all things,
> earth, and rivers, and you who under the earth take vengeance
> on dead men, whoever among them has sworn to falsehood,
> you shall be witnesses ...

We might imagine that the formulae of oaths were traditional and harked back to earlier times. However, we also have an example in Homer where the Sun is the recipient of offerings on the same basis as Zeus, even mentioned before him. Thus in *Iliad* III, 103-4, Menelaus accompanies an oath with the offering of:

> ... two lambs: let one be white and the other black for
> Earth and the Sun God, and for Zeus we will bring yet another.

Odyssey XII, 346-7, makes it clear that the Sun is a fitting candidate to have a rich temple (νηòν) with many fine ἀγάλματα. In the *H Demeter*, too, the Sun is described as sitting in his temple receiving offering from mortals (28-9). At *H Hermes* 381, Hermes, trying to prove he is an honest citizen, claims greatly to reverence (αἰδέομαι) Helios and the other gods (δαίμονας); note the order. In *Works and Days* 338-9 we have the instruction to perform propitiatory rituals to the gods on going to bed and when the φάος ἱερόν comes. *Works and Days* 414-7 suggests some discomfort from the μένος of the sun, but generally it is seen as a benign force: τερψίμβροτος, in the words of *Odyssey* XII 269. The *Works and Days* (727) also refers to the necessity to avoid urinating towards the sun. In his commentary on Hesiod's instruction about morning observances, West notes Plato's references to the later Greeks performing prostrations at the rising and setting of both sun and moon, and to Socrates praying to the sun at sunrise

(*Laws* 887e and *Symposium* 220d). If this entry in the commentary is relevant — that is, if the remarks of Hesiod and Plato reflect one and the same tradition — it would speak of the tenacity of that tradition. However, in this context our method requires that we focus on the Early Iron Age evidence and this has provided us with a few references 'en passant' which reveal the existence of a tradition of reverence for the sun involving practical observances; the strength and significance of that tradition are hard to assess. The source of such ideas about the sun is also debatable. While 'Indo-European' influence is often proposed, and may indeed be present, some elements of the symbolism seem to be anchored by close parallels to the Aegean Bronze Age past which we reviewed in Chapters 1 and 2.

Symbolism of gates and doors

One such possible thread of continuity in which ideas about the sun can be traced involves symbolism of gates or doors. Earlier in this study it was argued that in the Bronze Age some significance was attached to the doorways of tholos tombs and other types of tomb (see Chapter 1.5). It was noted that in some cases 'false' doors were constructed. In the case of the tholos tombs of the Messara a fairly consistent easterly orientation of the doorways has been remarked; I followed other scholars in believing that this was associated with the rising sun and that some notion of the egress or rebirth of the dead was involved. The appearance of the sun through portals or gates was suggested as a motif current in religious ideas and in iconography, and Mesopotamian parallels were drawn. It is interesting, therefore, to review the contexts in which the symbol of the doorway appears in the Early Iron Age. Thus we find that the underworld was frequently imagined as having doors: for example, at *Iliad* XIII, 415, Hades is described as strong 'Hades of the Gates'; and at *Iliad* XXIII, 71 and 74, we hear about the 'gates of Hades' and 'Hades' house of the wide gates' (εὐρυπυλὲς Ἀϊδος δῶ) which the shadow of Patroclus cannot pass. (Christiane Sourvinou-Inwood, 1983b, 36, lists several other similar Homeric references.) In Hesiod too we hear about entering the gates (πυλέων) of Tartarus and about its doors (θύρας), in passages of dubious authorship (*Theogony* 741 and 732); at *Theogony* 811 we read about its shining gates and bronze threshold (μαρμάρεαι πύλαι, χάλκεος οὐδός). West (1966, 364-5) discusses this idea and comments that 'Gates are constantly associated with the house of Hades and the abode of the dead'; we might, however, question whether his remark that 'They symbolize the (irreversible) transition to another realm' was necessarily true before Hesiod's time in the period when this symbol took shape; aside from the experience of prison, gates and doors imply thoroughfare.

In view of this symbolism in relation to Hades, it is of interest to find that in the Early Iron Age the sun is also visualized as having gates. Thus in *Odyssey* XXIV, 11ff, we read that the souls of the suitors are led by Hermes past Ocean Stream, past the White Rock (Λευκάδα πέτρην), and past the gates (πύλας) of the Sun, which are evidently visualized as lying on the route of the dead. This expression does not occur elsewhere in Homer, but it has echoes in several passages of Hesiod. Thus, in *Theogony* 749-50 we read that Night and Day also have a bronze threshold (οὐδὸν χάλκεον) to cross, of which West comments 'A threshold has the same symbolic power as a gate' (1966, 367). We may notice that in this passage it is Ἡμέρη, a female Day, who holds the all-seeing light (φάος πολυδερκές) for those on earth, and the idea of birth is not completely absent as we read at *Theogony* 124 that day was 'born' from Night.

The underworld, then, has gates; and Day or the Sun emerge from gates. That these might be the same gates is suggested by the *Odyssey* passage (XXIV, 11ff). Moreover, the association of parts of the sun's cycle with death, suggested earlier in this section on the basis of the archaeological evidence, is echoed in literature by the firm location of the dead and the underworld in the west, which would be reached by making a journey parallel to that of the setting sun. (Cf. the westerly orientation of the pithos burials studied by Hägg, 1983.) Thus, the idea expressed by Achilles at *Iliad* XXI, 55-6, that the dead might rise up against him from the western gloom (ὑπὸ ζόφου ἠερόεντος) suggests they have made a journey similar to that of the sun. We know that the sun is thought to go ὑπὸ γαῖαν, as in *Odyssey* X, 191, while the soul of the dead also goes beneath the earth (as at *Iliad* XXIII, 100). Nor is the idea of the sun shining in the underworld unknown: it is what the Sun threatens Zeus he will do if the slaughter of his cattle is not avenged (*Odyssey*, XII, 383). It is perhaps also present in an interesting passage in a dubious part of the *Theogony* (986 ff) where we read that Eos' son, Phaethon, was snatched by Aphrodite and made a guard at her temple νύχιον, by night, a night-guard. West, 1966, 428, amends to μύχιον without strong grounds, especially in view of the riddle he cites from *A.P.* 14.53.4 about νυκτιπόλος Φαέθων, the 'midnight sun'. However, even his emendation implies a stay in the underworld, as Nagy (1973, 171) points out, referring to the usage of μυχός in phrases like μυχῷ χθονὸς εὐρυοδείης (*Theogony* 119)).

Fire, funerary contexts and female figures

Does literature provide any other evidence for a continuing tradition connecting the sun with death or rebirth? The association of sunrise with birth is preserved in the epic epithet for dawn, ἠριγένεια, or 'early-born'. Also some connection between the sun and death can perhaps be traced in references to the 'magical' or ritual use of fire. In Chapters 1 and 2 of this study the possibility was raised that the use of fire may have been a component in Early Aegean funerary rituals which, it was suggested, were oriented towards the idea of rebirth. For the Early Iron Age, archaeology speaks of the use of cremation; does literature inform us about any thinking underlying this practice? What we do have are several interesting references to torches in epic poetry and myths of the Iron Age period, which repeatedly associate torches with death, the underworld, and the preservation of human life. Thus, when Persephone is snatched to the underworld Demeter searches for her for nine days with flaming torches (αἰθομένας δαΐδας) in her hands (*H Demeter* 48, 61). This is the kind of episode that has the ring of a retrospective explanation for a ritual practice, and has been tentatively associated with the practice of the later Thesmophoria or the Mysteries (Allen, Halliday and Sikes, 1936, 136-7). Demeter also meets a torch-bearing Hecate (52). Later in the story, at 239, we hear that unknown to them Demeter hides the son of Celeus and Metaneira in the heart of the fire to make him like an immortal (κρύπτεσκε ... ἠύτε δαλόν). Halliday has suggested that ideas of an initiatory 'death to new life' might have been involved (*CR* 25, 1911, 8ff), while Richardson suggests that the Demophon episode may relate to the Mysteries themselves. The significance of the act of 'hiding the torch within' is again suggested by the preservation of the short quote referring to those οἳ πρόσθε φανὴν ἔντοσθεν ἔκευθον (*Catalogue of Women* 121). We find another trace of the identification of the brand with human life in a metaphor in the *Odyssey*, V, 488-491, where we read that Odysseus covers his body as a lonely crofter in the corner of an estate buries a brand in ashes to keep the fire alive. The Greek refers to the 'seed' of fire. There is emphasis on the act of 'hiding' in all these contexts. That the flaming torch might also have been associated with the heavenly bodies is not necessarily self-evident, but it is interesting that in the Demeter references the divine bearers or manipulators of fire are female, a phenomenon which we might expect if these references are throwbacks to rituals or beliefs of the religion of the Bronze Age. The above examples seem to suggest a tenuous link between fire, death and survival.

Also predominantly female in literature are mourners, a factor which again echoes Bronze Age associations and the archaeological evidence reviewed earlier in this section. Thus, in the opening sequence of *Iliad* XVIII, (28ff), when Achilles starts to mourn, the maidservants join in, screaming and beating their breasts, and the cry is taken up beneath the sea by his mother, Thetis, and the troop of Nereids. At *Iliad* XVIII, 339-340, Achilles promises that until Hector's death Patroclus will be wept for day and night by female captives from Troy, in what sounds close to 'professional' mourning. At *Iliad* XXII, 429-431, the citizens of Troy also mourn Hector's death while Hecabe leads the Trojan women in lament, whereas at *Iliad* XXIV, 720ff, the only leaders of lament are again women: Andromache, Hecabe, and Helen (see also *Iliad* XI, 394-5, and *Odyssey* III, 260-1).

Earlier in this section we reviewed a number of representations in which not only were women the ones associated with, or performing some ritual possibly involving, the sun or a sun symbol (Figs. **277c**, **279a**, **279e**, and perhaps **Fig. 275 a** or **b**), but also in some cases we found the implication that a female divinity linked with the sun may have been involved (**Figs. 276c**, **277a**, **278a**). We reviewed in Chapters 1 and 2 the evidence associating a female divinity with the sun in the Bronze Age; if there is some indication of the continuation of such an association in the Early Iron Age, we must ask which of the female divine names which we know from literature might have been attributed to the deities involved.

Here we need to be aware of countering a long-standing assumption that if a female goddess was associated with any heavenly body, it must have been the moon. Thus Persson concludes from the nomenclature 'Pasiphae' and other terms of later times that 'the original Great Goddess was also the goddess of the moon' (1942, 136) as well as the goddess of fertility. Clearly it is not enough for us to find terms associating a female figure with brightness or luminosity: a specific reference to the sun will be required for us to establish a connection in the face of this weight of opinion. *Prima facie* a likely candidate because of her name and Minoan connections, Pasiphae is later described as daughter of the sun, but is associated with no such specific reference in our literature and indeed receives little emphasis in it. Persephone again might be a likely candidate: her disappearance for one third of the year before reappearing in the spring (*H Demeter* 401ff) might be symbolic of the sun's yearly cycle of withdrawal in winter, and she is sought with torches. Her later association with the ball has been attributed with 'a double connotation, one chthonic and funerary, the other nuptial and pre-nuptial' (Sourvinou-Inwood, 1978, 108). But again, there is no specific association with sun, sky, or heavenly bodies. We would expect literature to be reticent about any vestiges of such connections, but in the case of some other female divinities they do appear. In this context an interesting character is the witch Circe, who is linked with the sun in various ways in writings of this period.

Circe

Circe is referred to as the daughter of Helios in *Theogony* 956-7 and 1011, and Hesiodic fr. 390 refers to her travelling on the chariot of the Sun. The doubtful authorship of these passages throws their date into question, but in *Odyssey* X, 133ff, she is also referred to as the daughter of the Sun. She is referred to explicitly as a goddess (θεός), albeit a δεινή one with a human voice, and she has powers such as assuming invisibility and sending winds as well as her more witchy ones of casting spells with the use of φάρμακα. Circe's name itself derives from κίρκος which, as well as meaning a hawk or a falcon, also means a circle. Liddell and Scott suggest that 'circle' or 'ring' was the original notion and that the hawk was so called for its wheeling flight. Circe's menageries of men turned animals could also be seen as carrying some reminiscence of the theriomorphic cults which have been suggested for the Bronze Age.

Her attendants, the daughters of springs and groves and sacred rivers, also suggest a heritage from an earlier, animistic religion.

Circe also has an interesting geographical relationship with the sun. On arrival at her island with his crew, Odysseus remarks that they no longer know where east and west are, nor where the sun is rising or setting (*Odyssey* X, 190-2). Rhys Carpenter takes this to suggest a northern forest (1946, 18), but it might also suggest that the vicinity of Circe is a kind of limbo world, beyond or beneath the circling motion of the sun. It is perhaps significant that it is Circe who gives the instructions to Odysseus about how to make the journey to converse with the dead. On his return to her island Odysseus describes it as (*Odyssey* XII, 3-4):

νῆσόν τ᾽ Αἰαίην, ὅθι τ᾽ Ἠοῦς ἠριγενείης
οἰκία καὶ χοροί εἰσι καὶ ἀντολαὶ Ἠελίοιο.

This is Circe's island, on which she lives and has her home: it is some surprise, then, to hear it described not only as the place where the sun has its risings, but also the place where the home of Dawn is located and where she has her χοροί. The reference to dance strikes a familiar chord and as no other οἰκία is mentioned on the island, the possibility is raised that the home of Dawn and the home of Circe might be one and the same place. Moreover, Nagy (1973, 151) points out that when Odysseus first arrives at Circe's island the overall plot suggests that he is wandering in the realms of the extreme west and it is from here that he travels to the underworld; however, on his return to her island it is described (in the passage above) as the abode of dawn and sunrise, i.e. in the east. An intimate relationship between Circe and the sun is suggested throughout these passages and we may wonder whether at some point she had herself been a sun deity, now reduced to a witch in a folk tale. (See also Cook, *Zeus* Vol. I, 1914, 238ff.)

Dawn and Aphrodite

The association of Circe with dawn might prompt us to follow up some other references to Dawn in writings of this period. Thus we read at *Theogony* 371-4 that Dawn is sister of the sun and moon in a passage where, as West points out, 'the natural dyad Sun-Moon is extended to a typical triad ... by the addition of Eos, Dawn or Daylight' (1966, 270). She is also associated with the sun and moon at *Theogony* 19. In a later passage of the *Theogony*, whose authorship is dubious, 984ff, we read about Dawn's liaison with Tithonus and with Cephalus. West describes her as 'one of the most predatory of goddesses'. What interests us particularly here, however, is the reference to her giving birth to a son, Phaethon. Now Phaethon is often described as the son of Helios, and in Homer the word appears five times as an epithet of the sun itself. Phaethon thus appears to be very closely associated with the sun, and in some cases identified with it (a similar confusion occurs with Hyperion who is sometimes the sun and sometimes his father). In this context such an identification of Phaethon with the sun would make Dawn not the sister, but the mother, of the sun. Elsewhere the name Phaethon is used for one of the horses drawing Dawn's chariot (*Odyssey*, XXIII, 246); whereas in Homer the sun does not have a chariot, it appears that Dawn, like Helios in Hesiod, rides in a chariot across the sky.

This leads us to the interesting sequence of events described in *Theogony*, 990-1, whereby Phaethon is snatched by Aphrodite to be posted in her temple, whether 'in a corner' (West's emendation, 1966, 428) or 'by night' (as MSS). A sun-figure such as Phaethon might seem a strange occupant for Aphrodite's temple until we recall Aphrodite's epithet Οὐρανίη. This term appears elsewhere used for various minor female divinities. Thus at *Theogony* 78 it appears as the name of one of the Muses, of which West comments that 'the idea of a Μοῦσα

Οὐρανίη may have been suggested to Hesiod by the tradition that the Muses were daughters not of Zeus but of Uranos' (1966, 181). At *Theogony* 350 we also find an Oceanid with the same name, described as θεοειδής. As an epithet for Aphrodite, however, the term is harder to account for. There is the story at *Theogony* 188ff about Uranos' genitals, but of this West comments: 'It is less obvious why the foam forms round the genitals of Uranos ... The probable answer is that Aphrodite's cult title Οὐρανία suggested that she was Uranos' daughter ... Given this, it only remains to link the castrated Uranos somehow with floating foam ... This is an excellent example of how a complex aetiological myth is created' (1966, 212-3). If the Uranos story came after the 'celestial' epithet, we are left without an explanation for Aphrodite bearing that epithet. We are also left with nothing to account for the interesting fact that she is born from the sea. West offers no alternative explanation, but we could trace some suggestion of a celestial goddess, rising from the sea, in whose temple a sun-figure such as Phaethon would not be an inappropriate attendant.

Nagy (1973) points out various parallels between Dawn and Aphrodite: Aphrodite's abduction of Phaethon is compared to Dawn's abduction of Tithonos, Kleitos and Orion, and in all but one case the verb used to describe the act derives from ἁρπάζω, 'to snatch' (*Theogony* 990, *H Aphrodite* 218, *Odyssey* XV, 250 and V, 121). The same verb is used of the actions of the death-bringing θύελλαι, but, as Nagy points out, the snatching in these cases leads not to death but to preservation. Of Phaethon's liaison with Aphrodite, Nagy comments (1973, 162), 'I imagine a setting sun mating the goddess of regeneration so that the rising sun may be reborn'. He cites Rig-Vedic sources for a goddess of solar regeneration, the dawn Uṣas, who is both mate and mother of the sun-god Sūrya (names which, he states, are formally cognate with Ἥλιος and Ἠώς). He has some difficulty, however, in explaining why Ἠώς does not appear in Homer with the formal cognates of the appropriate Rig-Vedic epithets (1973, 162-3), and observes (174) that Aphrodite has 'usurped' the epithet of 'the Indo-European dawn-goddess of the Greeks', Eos, as well as the roles that go with the epithet. Perhaps the traditions associated with Aphrodite were stronger; it could certainly be suggested that the 'pre-Indo-European' archaeological evidence from the early Aegean (cf. the seals and 'frying-pans' discussed in Chapter 1) offer more concrete and telling evidence of ideas of female fertility and regeneration associated with the sun than do tenuous linguistic arguments.

Before leaving Aphrodite, we can note Faure's suggestion that the Psychro tablet reflects a cult of a cosmic deity of earth, sea and sky: 'On pense alors à celle qui sera, plusieurs siècles plus tard, Aphrodite Ourania' (1964, 157). In support of such a notion, he points out that the character of the Psychro cave offerings fit with characteristics of the later Aphrodite Ourania, and that several important later traces of her cult are found in the Lasithi area; he suggests (1966, 158) that Aphrodite was prefigured by three Minoan figures: Pasiphae, Ariadne and Phaidra, aspects of the same goddess. The limits of the scope of this study do not allow further discussion of several relevant aspects of Aphrodite's personality which emerge clearly from the later evidence, including the epithets 'black', 'of the grave' and 'horseback'.

Hecate

The remaining character to be considered for possible solar associations is Hecate. Here we will be concerned with two main loci referring to her: *Theogony* 411ff and the *H Demeter*. The authorship of the *Theogony* passage has been questioned, although West argues that it is authentic Hesiod (1966, 277-280); this issue does not concern us, for the reasons pointed out above (p.121). What does interest us is to read (412-415) that she received a share of the earth and the sea, and also received honour in heaven: in a three-part universe, she has a share of honour in each part including a celestial aspect. This tri-partite division is reminiscent of that referred to in *Iliad* XV, 187-192, where Poseidon claims that he was allotted the sea when Zeus was allotted the sky and Hades the nether world. These claims might seem to encroach upon Hecate's, but it becomes clear that her claim is of an older generation: whereas at *Theogony* 412 Zeus is awarding Hecate honours, at 421ff we read that as a child of Earth and Sky she had a portion from the earliest times from which Zeus *took nothing away*, leaving her privilege in earth, sea and sky. This passage clearly states her membership of an older generation of gods, the former gods, μετὰ προτέροισι θεοῖσιν. We are impressed to read that Zeus himself honours her: Ζεὺς τίεται αὐτήν. West suggests that several of the functions attributed to Hecate were prompted by a desire to appeal to the audience at the Games of Amphidamas (1966, 45). However, what interests us is to find that these functions include increasing fertility, childbirth and child-care, and an interest in games, horses and the sea, all of which themes appear to have been associated with sun rituals in the Bronze Age according to our evidence. It is interesting, too, to find horses and the sea mentioned in one breath, a juxtaposition familiar from the Bronze Age and one which we will find again (see Chapter 3.12 below). West refers to Hecate's other oceanic connections, including a dedication to Hecate on the archaic altar in the shrine of Apollo Delphinius at Miletus which is the earliest known archaeological evidence for Hecate-worship (1966, 278).

This passage is quite exceptional in the context of evidence for Greek religion in the Early Iron Age, and can be attributed to Asiatic influences brought to Boeotia by Hesiod's family. West explains the absence of this Hecate from the Homeric pantheon by the fact that 'She was always a goddess of private rather than public cult' (1966, 277), though we are left to wonder why some deities were never thought appropriate to be honoured in public cult. His discussion of her 'origin' does not concern us, as we are interested in the source not so much of the name as of the cluster of symbols, whatever name is applied to those symbols in different cases. We might comment, however, on his description of her as a 'healthy, independent and open-minded goddess' who lacks the 'lunar, magical, chthonic, and bloody' associations of later centuries; we could point out that her concern with fertility was precisely one which could be seen as chthonic and magical in later times, but had apparently not yet in this context accrued such associations in a negative sense. As for her 'lunar' associations, the other passage we shall review suggests that not only did she have a celestial aspect, but also offers some tenuous possibility that she was indeed at this early period associated with at least one of the heavenly bodies, an association perhaps eclipsed in the world view of the Hesiodic and Homeric poems.

We now turn to the *H Demeter*. When Persephone is seized by Hades, she calls out loud, but (22ff) no one among gods or humans or in the plant world hears apart from two figures: Hecate and Helios. Both are sitting in an enclosed space at the time, Hecate in a cave, Helios in his temple. One wonders what lies behind the choice of these two characters. Later Demeter also hears her daughter, and wanders distracted for nine days. But when the tenth dawn has come, a figure bearing a torch meets Demeter. A figure appearing at dawn with a torch might be expected to be the sun, but no, it is Hecate. What is more, Hecate can tell her nothing. They go together to approach Helios the Sun-god, and get an eye-witness account from him. The structure of this story is extremely awkward. Only one character is needed to witness the seizure and to help Demeter by giving her the information she needs; the duplication is obvious. Helios' role is highly inconsistent as he gives an account of seeing an event which we have been told he only heard from the inside of his temple. Hecate is, as Richardson points out, very much a 'Nebenfigur' (1974, 155); he suggests that her appearance is due to her position in the cult of Eleusis, but in this case she would not need to have heard Persephone's cry, but could have simply joined Demeter to help her. The strange coupling of Hecate and Helios as the two witnesses is explicable in the case of Helios who often plays the role of witness. It is, however, hard to see why Hecate should be paired with him: unless, of course, there was an earlier version in which she was the Sun who witnessed the event and gave Demeter the information she needed. The pairing of her with Helios could perhaps be explained if we were to understand her as the Moon; however, although this would have been an easy identification for the poet to make explicitly, no such reference is present — moreover, as Richardson points out, the Greek moon-goddess does not have torches (1974, 156). It would in any case appear a strange time of day at which to meet the moon. Before leaving this topic, we could refer to the later vase-paintings which show Hecate assisting in bringing Persephone up from the underworld, and to the Ugaritic *Poem of Baal* in which, as Richardson points out, the Sun-goddess assists Anat in the recovery of Baal's body (Gaster, 1950, 194-7, 202). Such themes are highly consistent with the role of the sun in funerary beliefs which was suggested for the Bronze Age.

Conclusion

In this discussion of Circe, Aphrodite, and Hecate, we may wonder if we have put our finger on any of the female deities associated with solar symbols in Geometric representations such as **Figs. 276c** and **278a**, or on memories of earlier such deities. West (1975) has made out a similar case for Helen, arguing that she went to the south (Egypt) like the sun in winter, and that her return was celebrated at the Heleneia. Skutsch has taken up the theme, pointing to her identity as a tree goddess (Δενδρῖτις) who returns in the spring, and agreeing that 'there are indeed indications connecting her with the sun' (1987, 189), although the derivations he is interested in investigating are Indo-European. Other named Olympian divinities could also be investigated for such associations. The ambiguity and overlap between different divinities need not discourage us, familiar as it is from the overall pattern of attribution of qualities to Olympian deities, which includes many inconsistencies and regional variations (as recently stressed by Sourvinou-Inwood, 1978).

We have, then, some evidence for continuity in solar symbolism from the Bronze Age to the Early Iron Age: traces of evidence in a variety of media associating the sun with death, with gates, with female figures, and some indications of survivals or memories of a female sun deity. The main version by now is, however, that the sun is a male god; to this, and to the other conspicuous changes in solar symbolism, we shall come soon. But first we shall survey other areas of symbolism to see if we can find any further traces of continuity.

3.5 CIRCULAR DANCE

We noted in Chapter 1 that in that earlier period circular forms were favoured in religious usage and perhaps ideas. We noted examples of circular dance, and perhaps a circular dance floor in LBA Knossos. We will therefore be very interested in any religious practices involving the circular form in this later period, which might represent a strand of continuity from the Bronze Age. We will be particularly interested in representations which may show a circular dance such as was suggested by some of the Bronze Age material, and in evidence of a religious significance for dance.

Such evidence is available from funerary vessels: Ahlberg comments on the 'magical significance' of the *circumambulatio* round the bier, and cites examples of 'funerary dancing' actions at the prothesis scene itself (1971b, 300, 302-3). She suggests there may have been a 'kind of female lamentation performed in a dancing way' and concludes that 'representations of dancing in Geometric art have a strong funerary character' (1971b, 306-7).

Some of the Geometric designs show a line of figures holding hands who are certainly processing but leave us in doubt as to whether a circular dance is intended: see **Fig. 276 a, b** and **c, Fig. 282 a, b** and **c**. This last Schweitzer sees as a round-dance, 'Has the vivacity of a dance ever been more vividly expressed than in the round-dance of long-legged women on a large cauldron in Athens?' (1971, 51); however, their hands are not linked and Cook (1947, 149) interprets it as a foot-race of young men. Some of these representations show a mixed group (**Fig. 282d**), others may show a men-only group (**Fig. 282e**).

Now we can move on to those representations which do seem to show a full circle, such as **Fig. 276d** and **Fig. 283a**, this latter being one of a series of bronzes from Olympia showing groups of four, five and seven naked women respectively dancing in a circle (Schweitzer, 1971, 155); a similar group in Athens includes a flute-player (**Fig. 283b**). **Fig. 283c** shows rows of women and men meeting, and a mixed group is again suggested by **Fig. 283d**, a frieze from the neck of an amphoriskos from Crete, interpreted by Schweitzer as a 'round-dance of men and women' (1971, 72). A similar round-dance is performed by what may be 'upright stag creatures' (Schweitzer, 1971, 155) in a bronze group from Arcadia (**Fig. 283e**). (Does this show animal costume?) For further examples of round-dances, see Tölle.

Now **Fig. 276d** is interesting for its association of the dance with vessels and rayed sun-disc. However we might regard the other examples of circular forms and round dances purely as (in some cases perhaps secular) evidence for the Early Iron Age, with no implication of continuity from the Bronze Age, were it not for the famous passage in *Iliad* XVIII, 591-605. Here, as part of the decoration of the shield of Achilles, we read that Hephaistos depicted:

> a dancing floor, like that which once in the wide spaces of Knosos
> Daidalos built for Ariadne of the lovely tresses.
> And there were young men on it and young girls, sought for their beauty
> with gifts of oxen, dancing, and holding hands at the wrist. These
> wore, the maidens long light robes, but the men wore tunics
> of finespun work and shining softly, touched with olive oil.
> And the girls wore fair garlands on their heads, while the young men
> carried golden knives that hung from sword-belts of silver.
> At whiles on their understanding feet they would run very lightly,
> as when a potter crouching makes trial of his wheel, holding
> it close in his hands, to see if it will run smooth. At another
> time they would form rows, and run, rows crossing each other.
> And around the lovely chorus of dancers stood a great multitude
> happily watching, while among the dancers two acrobats
> led the measures of song and dance revolving among them.

I have quoted this passage in full because it includes many interesting features. Round forms are a common form of primitive dance in many cultures. However, we are interested in investigating the meaning and history specific to such dances in Early Iron Age Greece, and here this passage throws valuable light. The dance it describes is very consistent with our illustrations, both of circular dances (**Fig. 283a**) and of round dances where rows meet each other (**Figs. 282d, 283c**). We also have an emphasis on the circular form of the dance, with the interesting metaphor from pottery, and a reference to acrobatic games for which we have noted evidence in Chapter 1 and Chapter 2 as well as perhaps in Early Iron Age Crete (**Fig. 277e**). We also find the event placed in the context of a female divinity (Ariadne), and an explicit reference to the fact that Crete was the kind of place in which such dancing floors could be expected to be found in the 'heroic' past. This last point must be taken as an indication of a memory that Crete was an important origin of such dances and a suggestion that the Geometric dances shown above may reflect a survival of Minoan dancing rites.

When discussing Bronze Age representations of dance, I suggested that some of those dances may have been associated with observances towards the sun. It is interesting that Lawler suggests that the aim of the funerary dances described in Homer was to put life back into the deceased; she also posits that circular dances were mimetic of the heavenly bodies and notes that at *Odyssey* VIII, 370ff, a dance blends into a ball game (1964, 42, 46, 49). Courbin believes that some of the Early Iron Age Argive dance scenes involving vegetation show 'un culte d'adoration ou de vénération' (1966, 491). However, we have also seen that some Early Iron Age dance scenes feature a circular or radiant motif. In some cases it may play a decorative or scene-setting role (**Fig. 276b**); however, in some cases it is clearly not in that role (cf. the sun on **Fig. 276d**), and in **Figs. 275b** and **Fig. 276c** a circular symbol is prominently held. On **Fig. 275b** it has, as we have seen, been associated with Ariadne through an independent line of argument. An interesting appendix to the discussion of the meaning of that motif is provided by a Boeotian terracotta figurine of the late Geometric period (**Fig. 284**). This female figure bears on her dress a decoration showing a 'frieze of dancing women' (Coldstream, 1979, 202) above whose heads, and interspersed between whom, we see dot rosettes, while her neck bears the swastika motif.

As the dances themselves recall a Cretan tradition, we may wonder whether any of these motifs preserve traces of a memory of an association of those dances with the sun.

3.6 SYMBOLISM OF THE BIRD

We noted earlier in this study that in the Bronze Age Aegean, from the time of the Early Bronze Age onwards, the bird played an important role in religious symbolism and that one aspect of this role seemed to be an association with the sun.

(a) The Archaeological Evidence

Vase decoration

Greek Geometric pottery offers us a wide range of decorations closely juxtaposing the bird with every variety of motif which have been argued as representing solar symbols in the Bronze Age. Thus we find birds with concentric circles (**Fig. 285**) and with dot rosettes (**Fig. 286**). We also find birds with the crossed circle and swastika (**Fig. 287**). In approaching the problem of the interpretation of such motifs we again have to face what West (1975, 15) has described as a 'dereliction of knowledge': in the area of solar symbolism, as in the nature myths West discusses, the result of past overstatement of the case is that 'it became bad form to inquire in those directions at all'. Conscious of this prejudice, we need to tackle the evidence of solar symbolism on its merits, not hesitating to scrutinise the arguments of its critics.

A good example is the unpopularity of the 'solar bird' interpretation applied to circular motifs in Geometric art by Roes (1933) and others. Boardman expresses a typical scepticism with his recent comment that he sees 'little likelihood of any serious revival of support for sun symbols' (1983, 16). Critics have focused, rightly, on the circular motifs themselves: as

Courbin points out, if the motif does not represent the sun, then the bird with it is not a solar bird. He further finds a contradiction between the solar and funerary interpretations that have been made of such designs. Benson (1970, 67) writes that 'A particularly interesting problem is afforded by the motif of the four-spoked wheel with a dot rosette or similar motif in each interstice' as in **Fig. 287c**. His objection to suggestions that such symbols represent a sun-disc rests on the argument that the near-Eastern influence adduced to account for such an identification is not sufficiently proven (1970, 67, 142 n.71). He takes 'a wheel to be first and foremost a wheel' around which a funerary iconography accreted; at some point perhaps this was overlaid with an oriental significance, the date and method of whose appearance must be seriously considered, 'if this significance cannot be shown to be part of a native Bronze Age heritage'. There are of course examples from the Aegean suggesting a familiarity with oriental iconography which explicitly links the bird with sun symbols, see **Fig. 287 e** and **f**; in the latter the presence of the 'ankh' sign with winged disc and birds confirms a religious association. However, the solar significance of the 'wheel' as part of a native Bronze Age heritage has indeed been thoroughly argued earlier in this study. We have reviewed evidence for the association of the bird with this and a variety of other similar symbols since the time of the Early Bronze Age, and we therefore have no need to adduce the near-Eastern influence of which Benson is so sceptical. His case is further weakened by the appearance of the bird with a number of other circular motifs apart from the wheel: by focusing attention on the wheel, he fails to account for the appearance of the bird with a variety of similar motifs some of which are perhaps more obviously 'sun-like'. Thus we find the circle intersected by more numerous radii, as in **Fig. 288**, and the rayed circle, as in **Fig. 289** (Benson was obliged to explain the radiating lines on **Fig. 287c** as a 'purely decorative needlework embellishment'). In some cases the rays form a whirl shape (**Fig. 290**) and in some cases they take the familiar form of the swastika, as on **Fig. 287d**. While I would certainly not suggest that all these motifs were intended as sun symbols, the association of the bird with such a variety of circular forms suggests an underlying idea which could explain the presence of all these motifs including the 'wheel'.

Rather than affirming a plethora of solar symbolism borrowed wholesale from the East without apparent cause or motivation, as Roes has been criticised for doing ('so ist alles solar' exclaims Schweitzer, 1934, 351), I am here proposing a set of specific associations to the sun deriving from a coherent system of beliefs about death dating back to the Aegean Bronze Age and witnessed by the material remains of that period.

Courbin's objections can also be answered. Firstly, the combination of solar and funerary interpretations, so far from being incompatible, is exactly what we would expect to find in terms of the Bronze Age material reviewed earlier in this study. Moreover, the solar interpretation of such circular motifs does not rest simply on argument from Bronze Age traditions: I feel that Roes underestimates the significance of the Geometric bronzes to which she refers. Boardman has pointed out that we may regard associations as more than fortuitous 'when they are repeated often and especially if they are repeated on different wares' (1983, 16). While the circular motifs on vase decorations do not always derive from religious contexts and often appear static, stylized and formal, as one might expect of a purely decorative tradition, the same cannot be said of the bronzes.

Bronzes

These small votive bronzes, often found near shrines, associate the bird with the 'wheel' and other circular motifs in an entirely different medium. In some cases the 'wheel' motif appears in a context suitable for a wheel (as in **Fig. 291a** where two such motifs seem to make up a miniature chariot in which the bird rides). In other cases, however, the 'wheel' is horizontal (**Fig. 291 b** and **c**) and is evidently not conceived as a form of transport. In other cases, again, a globular shape is associated with the bird (**Fig. 291c**), and sometimes the bird simply surmounts a flat disc (**Fig. 291d**) in a manner which suggests that the salient connection is between the bird and the circular or disc shape. Another variation is that birds appear around the circumference of the disc (**Fig. 291e**). Bouzek (1967), in a study of such bronzes from a range of mainland sites including some with a Mycenaean past, identifies the circular forms as sun symbols without stating his reasons for this. Moreover, his conclusion that they derive from the sun-symbolism of prehistoric European art is undermined by his failure to note pre-LH IIIC examples in traditions of the Bronze Age Aegean itself which clearly link the bird with the sun and with discs, often in very analogous forms (see, for example, **Figs. 97, 98 a - e, 133, 159**). Nor can one agree with his opinion that such symbols retained only a declining significance. Such a variety of forms speak not of meaningless formal repetition, but rather of living ideas which can be expressed in a variety of ways. A Geometric iynx-wheel in Boston (**Fig. 291 f** and **g**) shows their currency in a tradition of 'magical practices' to whose continuing vigour many later references testify (see Nelson, 1940). (The later amalgamation of wryneck, wheel, love charm and solar emblem (see Tufnell, 1983) is less 'enigmatic' in the light of our Bronze Age traditions.) The bird is thus consistently and recurrently associated with circular shapes which may take the form of a chariot wheel, a horizontal wheel, a globe or a flat disc; from the find contexts, these shapes would in many cases seem to have a religious connotation. If they do not symbolically represent the sun we might have a serious problem to discover what alternative explanation could be proposed for them.

Some funerary evidence

Birds are of course frequently depicted on funerary vessels (e.g. **Fig. 279d** and **293b**), in some cases evidently used as properties in the funeral ritual, and their 'funeral character' has been readily recognized (Ahlberg, 1971b, 156-7).

Interesting archaeological confirmation of the significance of the bird in religious ideas is provided by a recently-discovered straight-sided cremation pithos from the North Cemetery at Knossos (see **Fig. 292a**). The pithos shows two contrasting scenes, probably summer and winter, where birds appear accompanying a winged female divinity: small birds appear in her hands, while other, larger birds appear surmounting (in three out of four cases) the trees that flank her; these larger birds are, Coldstream suggests, supernatural. He comments that 'this contrast of seasons must in some way be related to the alternation between birth, death, and rebirth — an entirely appropriate theme for the decoration of a receptacle for human ashes' (1984, 99).

In this context several points will interest us especially. These particular birds are clearly not decorative: the pithos provides independent evidence of the religious significance of birds in association with ideas about seasonal change. Moreover, it belongs in the Minoan tradition, and while Coldstream suggests that the pithos painter may have been influenced by Minoan larnakes in the same graves, we do not necessarily need to see the pithos as the result of imitation or revival rather than of continuous transmission of ideas. The ideas expressed are coherent and vivid and evidently had meaning for the artist rather than being cribbed; the discovery in Fortetsa Tomb X of a model tree and birds probably intended to perch on it (**Fig. 292b**) suggests that such a motif was in other cases also thought appropriate for the grave. The survival of Minoan traditions seems the most likely explanation.

Apart from the continuity in ideas from the Bronze Age, there are also several direct iconographic parallels which could be traced. The contrast in scenes (bleak/fertile) could perhaps bear affinities with the contrasting paired scenes of approach to a goddess (also with bird) on the Homage krater (**Fig. 127c**), where one scene is markedly bleaker. The theme of bird perched on bough has a precursor in the Psychro tablet (**Fig. 133**); while the bird flying from the goddess's hand has antecedents in several birds released or in flight in Bronze Age representations, some of them certainly religious (see **Figs. 141a, 155b, 210, 211a, 241d, k** and **l** and perhaps **160b, 188d**).

Coldstream's 'nature goddess' pithos shows no sun. However, an oinochoe from Fortetsa Tomb 1 shows what Brock (1957, 98-9) describes as a 'sacred tree' accompanied by two birds, a 'tripod cauldron (?)' and, on either side of the tree, 'two suns' (**Fig. 292c**). To this we can add a quite striking collection of lids whose shape, dimensions and funerary context strongly recall the EBA 'frying-pans' as well as similar LBA objects shown on **Fig. 143**. Like those earlier examples, these lids bear concentric and radiant motifs (**Fig. 292d**). Like one of those earlier examples (see **Fig. 102**), two of these lids bear a bird ornamentation, in this case painted in white-on-black decoration (**Fig. 292 e** and **f**). The lids constitute at most a remarkable sign of continuity, at least further confirmation of the bird's funerary significance and its firm association with circular shapes and radiant motifs. Crete is, of course, a special case, but these significant Cretan birds will affect our attitude towards the birds decorating the (often funerary) vessels of the Greek mainland. The association of bird and female figure on the Knossos pithos (see also the figurine **Fig. 292g** where a radiant motif is added) will remind us of earlier Aegean material linking female figures with the motifs of bird and sun.

(b) The Literary Evidence

Literature, as we might expect, emphasizes slightly different areas of symbolism, but also speaks volubly of the significance of the bird in religious ideas. The significance of bird calls and movements as omens in the process of soothsaying and prophecy emerges clearly from the pages of Homer and the Hymns (e.g. *Iliad* VIII, 247; XII, 201, *H Hermes* 544). We have no way of telling whether prophecy was part of the function of the bird in BA religion. We may wonder whether later accounts of the doves associated with the oak tree at Dodona reflect a very ancient oracular tradition and might be related to the importance of trees and birds in Bronze Age religion, including apparent traditions of religious officiants dressing in bird clothing; but the lack of direct evidence from the Early Iron Age makes it impossible for us to trace a direct link.

In literature of the Early Iron Age there are two other kinds of reference to birds which might seem to represent continuity from the Bronze Age. One is the association of birds with the dead and the other is their association with deities. Birds were evidently thought a suitable motif for funerary objects, and in literature we find the soul compared to winged or bird-like creatures. Thus at *Iliad* XXII, 362, we read that Hector's soul flutters free (πταμένη), and at *Odyssey* XI, 605, the shades of the dead clamour like the call of wildfowl scattering in panic; there are other similar references. These are of course only metaphors, but some metaphors seem to emerge as a reflection of underlying symbolic connections. Thus the interpretation of the bird as a symbol of the soul, often proposed for the Bronze Age though never proven, could arguably be seen as continuing into the Early Iron Age.

We also find in Homer recurrent metaphors in which the gods are compared to birds. Thus Hera and Athena strut in eagerness like pigeons (*Iliad* V, 778); Poseidon has the speed of a hawk swooping from rocky heights (*Iliad* XIII, 62-4); Thetis is like a hawk swooping (*Iliad*

XVIII, 616); Athena swoops like a shrieking long-winged bird of prey (*Iliad* XIX, 350); while in the *H Demeter* 43, Demeter searches for Persephone speeding like a bird (οἰωνός) over land and sea and in the *H Apollo* 114, Iris and Eileithyia go to Leto's aid like shy pigeons. There are several other examples in Homer. While some of these are simply metaphors in the same vein as other metaphors comparing, say, Penelope, her maidservants, or Achilles to birds of different types, some of them verge very closely on the actual identification of the deity with the bird. Thus when Athena and Apollo sit on the oaktree sacred to Zeus 'like birds of prey', at *Iliad* VII, 59 (ἑζέσθην ὄρνισιν ἐοικότες αἰγυπιοῖσιν), we may presume that they actually took the form of birds as it would seem inappropriate for them to perch on branches in anthropomorphic form. Other examples of the embodiment of a deity as bird can be found, for example at *Iliad* XIV, 290, *Odyssey* III, 372 and V, 337 and 353.

The animistic ideas argued for the Early Bronze Age, in conjunction with the evidence indicating the significance of the bird in religion at that time, would be highly consistent with a picture of a religion which attached to birds in the early period a sanctity that later became differentiated between a number of named deities. The representations showing birds accompanying cult officiants or anthropomorphic divinities in the Late Bronze Age (as on **Figs. 160, 211a**) also have their counterpart in the appearance of birds as messengers of the gods in literature of the Early Iron Age.

3.7 THE WATERY GRAVE?

Earlier in this study I suggested that during the Bronze Age the sun was associated with the boat, perhaps seen as an appropriate vehicle for the sun as it set into the sea, and, by extension, as a vehicle for the dead. The association at that time appeared to have extended to other phenomena of the sea such as fish and shells, which were also represented linked with the sun. It was further suggested that over time, and with the advent of the horse, the horse and chariot replaced the boat in popularity as the mode of transport which the sun, and the dead, were imagined to use.

(a) The Archaeological Evidence

When is a literal interpretation appropriate?

Our review of the possible survivals of this association between the sun and things of the sea draws in a question of interpretation. The figured scenes on Geometric vases often include representations featuring boats. While the chariot scenes found on funerary vessels are widely interpreted as associated, perhaps in a symbolic way, with the funerary ritual (see below, Chapter 3.8.), there is a tendency to interpret other types of scene in a purely literal or narrative way. Thus Schweitzer writes of 'fighting on land and sea' or (1971, 43) 'a warship under sail, warriors on the shore, the return of a victorious ship after a hard-fought battle with warriors waiting for it on the beach (?)'. In his consideration of the significance of such scenes he discusses, without conclusion, the possibilities that they may depict deeds in the life of the dead man or may be harking back like epic poetry to heroic themes of the Mycenaean era (1971, 43-4, 35-6); although he points out that there were certainly plenty of real battles such as these in the Geometric period. Ahlberg, (1971, 58-9, 66-70, 108-110) proposes that they represent scenes from the 'floruit' of the dead man, arguing from the use of the huge grave kraters as (individualized, she believes) grave markers and from a historical context in which such battles, whether against pirates or neighbours, may have taken place and may have provided a political reason for the sudden halt in the production of vessels with such decoration in Athens in the eighth century B.C. She places little emphasis on the absence of naval battles in the epic poetry that has survived to us, and does not make explicit the argument that could be based on such scenes of fighting being found only on the funerary vessels of men.

For those boat scenes which show no action or glorious exploits at all, she is obliged to take a different tack. In the case of **Fig. 293e** she deduces, from the presence of the same Dipylon warrior type in both, a relationship between the prothesis zone and the ship zone, a funerary association (1971b, 209). She finds such an association accentuated in the ship scenes on the New York krater 34.11.2 and on **Fig. 293b** by the presence of birds whose 'sepulchral significance' she recognizes (1971b, 157). She concludes that on **Fig. 293e** the presenting of the oars shows a ceremonial act in honour of the deceased alluding to a real ceremony at the funeral. She suggests the same interpretation may be valid for the ship on **Fig. 293b**, commenting that there is no way to prove or disprove this (1971b, 306, 309). She does not address the question of *why* such ceremonial acts were thought appropriate for a funeral. If they reflect the nautical occupation of the deceased, why were other occupations not similarly represented? Moreover, her approach provides no explanation for the funerary boats which are totally unoccupied, such as **Fig. 293f**, the decoration on a mid-ninth century pyxis from a (?)woman's grave at Lefkandi (*AR* 1986-7, 13-14). While such a representation could be argued as symbolizing a naval exploit on the *pars pro toto* principle, the dominant and unnaturalistic association of birds and fish, as well as the suggested sex of the deceased, suggest that a less literal approach would be more appropriate. Commenting on the number of boat scenes without fighting, Kirk suggests that 'in the development of Geometric ship-painting at first the ship itself was the main interest' (*BSA* 44, 1949, 144).

Ahlberg's adherence to a purely literal approach raises other problems. Her view that the funeral scenes shown are real is undermined by her argument that the presence of numerous funeral participants and heavily armed warriors on vases does not reflect the reality of prosperity or martial strength in contemporary society nor the reality of funerals: 'It is not, as it generally seems to be thought, necessary that multiplicity of human figures, of chariots, warriors and archers means the presence of these figures and chariot teams in the activities represented.' However, it is on her view that the funeral scenes shown are real that she bases her argument that the fighting scenes are also real. It is not enough to say that motifs are reduplicated as 'filling', reflecting the 'interest' of the community in such themes; in this case, whole scenes could also be added as 'filling', reflecting the 'interest' of the community in other themes. Perhaps the key to the problem is that the wrong questions are being asked. The choice is not between literal representations of the 'floruit' or funeral of the dead man on the one hand, or narrative representations showing events from myth or epic on the other (an alternative which Ahlberg rejects). The debate can be short-circuited by recognizing a traditional association of the boat with the journey of the dead. This opens the possibility that such scenes show personages and actions associated with funerary ritual and ideas about death, even if they were not actually performed at the specific funeral of this person; equally, other scenes could be added which were not drawn from the life or from the narrative of extant epic, but from themes and actions which find their source in traditional funerary beliefs. From the underlying association of the boat with death, funerary rituals derive, and from that association and its iconography, the narration of mythic themes and the depiction of real life exploits are developed.

Ahlberg unwittingly supports this view when she points out (1971, 17): 'The fact that chariot races and processions of warriors are with certainty connected with the funeral scenes, usually represented in the zones above, may be regarded as a support of the assumption that scenes in different zones on a vase may be connected.' If all the chariot scenes are, then why might all the boat scenes not be, specifically *funerary* in origin? Boardman (1983, 19) has also recently argued that motifs set in separate panels may be read together. If different scenes on the same vase may be connected, what is the theme that unites **Fig. 293a** and **Fig. 293b**, which appear so closely juxtaposed on the same vessel? We may note that Bronze Age larnakes were used to depict rituals and ideas about death, as in the famous Aghia Triadha and Tanagra examples, and many of the decorative themes of Geometric funerary vessels are inherited from that time. From the iconography of such Bronze Age larnakes, the depiction of mourning women (**Fig. 185**) survived, with the same two-handed gesture of mourning familiar from Mycenean iconography (as Ahlberg notes, 1971b, 303); the prothesis scene survived (as on the Tanagra larnax from Tomb 22); and so did the depiction of the horse and chariot (**Figs. 214, 217**). It seems extremely likely that the depiction of boats (**Fig. 206** and the Kalochorafiti larnax) could also have survived and could be reflected in these boat scenes on funerary vessels of the Early Iron Age. On **Fig. 293 a** and **b** the boat appears near to the horse and chariot as on the LM Kalochorafiti larnax. Vermeule has suggested that already in the Bronze Age such funerary iconography was being transferred from sarcophagi to kraters (1964, 205). Ahlberg herself comments on the 'hereditary' agreement between Mycenean and Geometric funerary customs and iconography (1971b, 303-4).

I am not disputing here the narrative nature of some of the fighting scenes on Geometric vases, such as those showing the twin-bodied figure widely identified as Aktorione-Molione, though even that identification has been doubted (as by Carter, 1972, 52-3; Boardman, 1983). Nor am I disputing that many of the boat scenes may draw from the reality of experience in the Early Iron Age; nor that their intention in some cases may be to glorify events in the life of the dead man. However, Carter (1972, 38-9) has pointed out that the frequency of ship-fights in art does not mean that this was the commonest form of encounter in this period; he comments on the typical rather than the specific nature of such scenes, and on their disappearance from the repertoire of Greek painting before the end of the eighth century. Whatever the narrative causes of death shown in the picture, whether fighting or man-eating fish, the number of representations of boats linked with, or carrying, corpses (as in **Fig. 294**) hints strongly at a deep-seated association between boats and the dead. What I would suggest is that the relationship of boat scenes to contemporary Early Iron Age ideas about death is perhaps not seriously enough considered, and that, underlying some elements in the representations, there lies an iconography which can be traced back to funerary ideas of the Bronze Age.

Continuity from the Bronze Age?

In some cases the survival of such a tradition from the Bronze Age is indicated by the presence of various graphic motifs. Thus we see on **Fig. 293b** a boat accompanied by birds whose disproportionate size and unnaturalistic positioning make their interpretation as gulls who are accidentally perched on the boat or fluttering over it rather implausible. The ship on **Fig. 298a** also has a bird placed next to it. That such unnaturalistic birds had been part of funerary iconography since the Bronze Age is shown by the birds associated with a boat on a larnax from Crete (reproduced again here as **Fig. 293c** for purposes of comparison). Another similarity will be noted between the boats on **Fig. 293 b** and **c**: they each bear a circular symbol closely juxtaposed with or integrated into one end of the boat. A boat is paired with a large swastika on the bow fibula shown on **Fig. 293d**. We also find circular symbols, usually rayed symbols, appearing frequently in the field accompanying such boats on Geometric vases (as on **Fig. 293b**). A rayed symbol appears prominently above a solitary, empty, static boat on **Fig. 293g**, an Attic cup. We are reminded of possible sun symbols closely associated with boats not only on LBA examples such as **Fig. 206a**, the Kalochorafiti larnax and the Thera ship painting (**Fig. 148c**) (see Morgan, 1984, 171-2), but also as far back as the EBA 'frying-pans'. The interpretation that in these Geometric decorations we are seeing a sun literally portrayed shining down on the scene is belied by the appearance of several such motifs together, and also fails to explain the recurrent appearance of this motif integrated into the construction of the boat itself (**Fig. 295** shows some examples: compare the LBA **Fig. 148c** from Thera). It could be argued that these are simply filling motifs, like the equally ancient but apparently insignificant double axes scattered over many of the Geometric vase decorations. However, the prominence and recurrently specific location of these rayed symbols call for our serious consideration.

The suggestion that these circular symbols may be sun symbols and may be symbolically associated with the boat might encourage us to look more closely at some particular scenes. Thus **Fig. 296** shows a boat with three horizontal figures in the field above, which Ahlberg (1971, 37) describes as 'certainly corpses'. There is, however, no fighting apparent to explain the provenance of these corpses. At one end of the boat stands a figure holding what is probably the steering oar, while with another hand he is handling the sail (*ibid.*). At the other end of the boat a figure is turned towards it and touching the horn; by analogy with the famous ship scene on the British Museum krater (**Fig. 298a**) Ahlberg concludes that this figure also 'may be regarded as entering the ship. That he is not shown in a hostile attitude is clear from the lack of weapons. The ship is evidently not beached, but about to leave'. A boat carrying dead; a figure in a non-hostile attitude climbing aboard; and above the boat we note two dot rosettes. With these features in a krater decoration, is it fanciful to think that we may be seeing a representation of the journey of the dead? Such an interpretation would be highly consistent with the scenes of departure with boat and perhaps sun which were associated with ritual and funerary contexts in the Bronze Age.

In the same vein of thought, we might question Ahlberg's interpretation of the female figure seated in a boat on **Fig. 297** as a 'captive woman' tied to the sail (1971, 28-9). The figure is reminiscent of the female figures we saw seated in boats in Bronze Age representations (particularly **Fig. 212 a** and **b**) and could be argued to owe something to the iconography if not the religious beliefs of that time. The cabin is similar to that shown on the Bronze Age representations on **Fig. 208a** and **Fig. 212d**. Here we might be encouraged in our questioning by the British Museum krater shown in **Fig. 298a**. This last shows the embarkation of a male figure clasping the wrist of a female figure who holds in her other hand a disc-shaped object which we have already discussed above in Chapter 3.4. The scene is very similar to that shown on a Late Bronze Age signet-ring from Tiryns (**Fig. 212d**), and to that on another ring from Crete, reproduced again here for comparison as **Fig. 298b**. On the Bronze Age **Fig. 298b**, the presence, floating in the air above the ship, of a small female figure, a tree and a disc, as well as its similarity to more explicitly religious representations, indicate that the scene carried some religious significance and is not simply narrative. In our Late Geometric parallel, **Fig. 298a**, we see summarily executed fronds of vegetation on either side of the female figure, and in her hand she carries a disc-shaped object; it is likely that this representation, whose narrative content is more apparent, is drawing on the same pool of religious ideas which form the basis of the Bronze Age scene. The characters on the British Museum krater, as we have seen above, are often identified as Theseus and Ariadne (thus, for example, Schweitzer, 1971, 57 and Schachermeyr, 1964, 314); however, we could equally argue that what we see is Helen being abducted by Paris, and perhaps the truth is that it is not a major dilemna as to which name we choose. Nilsson (1932, 170-2) suggests that 'Helen is a pre-Greek goddess of vegetation whose peculiarity it is to be carried off, just as Kore was carried off by Pluto. Thus we have a pre-Greek hieratic myth, the rape of the goddess of vegetation by a god, which was made a heroic myth in various ways'. He also identifies Ariadne as a pre-Greek vegetation goddess (see pp.101-2 above where this suggestion is linked with Bronze Age representations of female figures embarked on boats). Fittschen's (1969, 53ff) preoccupation with choosing between the (to him contradictory) interpretations of the 'wreath' on the British Museum krater as 'Liebessymbol' or as an attribute of cult, and between interpretations of the whole scene as a divine epiphany, an event from epic or from daily life, is put into perspective by recognizing that all those strands may be traced to a common origin in one specific Bronze Age tradition, the possibility of survivals from which he dismisses rather summarily (1969, 57). In **Fig. 298a** the fronds of vegetation, and the disc (whether 'crown of light', or sun-disc, or both) in the female figure's hand, suggest that religious ideas underly the scene. In the Bronze Age we saw representations of two female figures in a boat, of single women in a boat or of a man and woman departing together (**Figs. 54e, 60c, d, 208, 212**). In the Late Geometric period we find this last motif clearly represented; perhaps what is important is not whether the scene shows Ariadne or Helen but that in either case it derives from Bronze Age religious ideas centred on a departing goddess.

Two other objects might be mentioned in passing. One is a fragment of an open-work bronze stand from Crete showing an apparently similar scene with a male and female figure standing together on board ship (**Fig. 299a**); this object might seem to reflect, yet again, the same set of ideas, and has been so identified by Benton (*BSA* 35, 1934-5, 98 n.7) who proposes that the figures show Ariadne and Theseus. Helen is another candidate who has been proposed (see Demargne, 1947, 243 n.1). Also from Crete, and perhaps confirming a continuing association between the boat and ideas about death, is a model boat found in Tomb X at Fortetsa (**Fig. 299b**). Its diminutive occupant reminds us of the LBA figures in the model larnax in the Heraklion Museum (**Fig. 209**).

A Geometric oinochoe in Hobart shows another scene of departure by boat (**Fig. 299c**). What will interest us here particularly are the gestures of mourning by the female, and perhaps the male, figures on shore (see Hood, 1967); the dot rosettes (suns?) appearing prominently between the heads of these figures; and the representation of two figures who are not rowers sitting touching at the centre of the boat. Hood (1967, 87) cites comments from Vermeule and Coldstream which present the possibility that this may be a funeral scene involving a 'ship burial': an idea not identical with, but highly compatible with, my hypothesis that such scenes derive from Bronze Age ideas about the boat as transporter of the dead. Another noteworthy item is an early sixth century ivory relief from the sanctuary of Artemis-Orthia at Sparta which shows a similar boat scene (**Fig. 299d**).

Moreover, apparently bridging the gap across the 'dark age' lying between the Bronze and the Geometric age, we have some very interesting small votive figurines from a cave at Inatos (Tsoutsouros) in South Crete which has been ascribed to the Goddess Eileithyia (Alexiou, 1963, 310). While some of these represent a pregnant woman (**Fig. 300a**) or couples embracing (**Fig. 300b**), one shows a couple embracing in a tub or primitive boat (**Fig. 300c**), and another shows the remains of what appear to have been two figures, at least one of them female if we are to judge by the dress, standing in a wide shallow boat (**Fig. 300d**). This object reminds us of parallels as early as the EBA (**Fig. 60c**) and spanning the LBA (**Fig. 208**). The significance of the boat in cult at this cave is further impressed on us by another, empty, model boat (**Fig. 300e**). The offerings, apparently made to a female divinity, cover all stages of reproduction including a baby nursing at the breast and in a cradle (**Fig. 300f**). Faure points out that this is a divinity concerned not only with labour but also with love and fertility, and that the term 'Eileithyia' is a later appelation for a divinity 'qui fut peut-être anonyme et multiforme, et qui, ailleurs, fut nommée Artémis, Athèna, Hèra ou Dèmètèr avec des fonctions courotrophes analogues' (1964, 94). We cannot, however, join Faure in seeing the boats simply as the dedications of sailors or as being concerned with the protection of travellers. The presence of a boat containing an embracing couple indicates other concerns. The presence of the boat among these symbols associated with fertility, and, as in other examples, directly linked with male-female union, and again shown carrying a woman or women is entirely consistent with Bronze Age traditions reviewed in Chapters 1 and 2. The survival of such traditions in this cave is, moreover, suggested by apparently continuous offerings — including characteristic items such as the double axe — from LM III through the Sub-Minoan to the Geometric period. Alexiou (1973,97) comments that 'Les modèles de bateaux sont à rapprocher éventuellement de la nature lunaire de la déesse', but we have no evidence for an Aegean moon goddess associated with a boat at this or any earlier period, whereas we do have some evidence for a female deity and a boat associated with the sun. The finds from this cave remain largely unpublished, but if the claim for dark age votives can be substantiated it would provide an impressive example of continuity.

From Geometric vase decoration we also have evidence of the continued presence of a marine goddess; the deity with fish on her skirt on the 'Artemis' amphora shown on **Fig. 301** is highly reminiscent of those Bronze Age female figures with fishes sometimes described as 'goddess with fish' (see **Fig. 204**). Vermeule (1979, 71-2) draws a parallel between the later Charon, ferryman of the dead, and Egyptian mythology; but, as we have seen, the boat theme and its Egyptian connection can be traced much further back, into the Bronze Age.

Before leaving this topic, we could comment on the survival of an iconography in which the fish and the bird were linked, which we saw was well documented in the Late Bronze Age (as in **Figs. 133, 134a, 197, 198**). **Fig. 302** shows some examples of the continuation of this association. It is also noteworthy that fish appear under the handles of the new pithos from Knossos featuring the 'nature goddess' with birds (**Fig. 292a**). Fish are engraved in antithetical pairs on either side of a central swastika on four ninth century bow fibulae from Kerameikos Grave 41, of which Carter comments that 'the composition seems rather to reflect an older tradition than to adumbrate the future' (1972, 34). Swastikas are also prominent with the fish on our **Fig. 302c**. We saw that in the Bronze Age fish and bird were often grouped together with the sun (as in the examples just cited), and we may speculate whether any traces of the religious thinking which shaped that grouping was surviving in the Early Iron Age.

In conclusion, we may perhaps say that the archaeological evidence shows us some scenes where a boat is involved in a mythological scene recalling themes of departure familiar from the Bronze Age. A circular object appears prominently held in one such scene (**Fig. 275a**), and in another showing perhaps a ritual dance in which oars feature (**Fig. 275b**). Other vase representations of ships show recurrent circular or radiant motifs and other unnaturalistic features which suggest that Bronze Age funerary iconography, if not beliefs, influence the artist. It could be argued that the Bronze Age tradition underpins the suitability of the boat for funerary vase decorations, may be expressed in several scenes which are often interpreted as literal and narrative, and underlies the development of such narrative scenes when they do clearly emerge.

(b) The Literary Evidence

The suggestion that some of the circular symbols under discussion are sun symbols, and that boats on Geometric vases owe something to the tradition of a sun-boat traceable to the Bronze Age, would gain credence if we could show that the notion of the heavenly bodies travelling by sea was also reflected in literature. It is relevant therefore to find that in *Works and Days* 566 the star Arcturus is described as rising from the holy stream of Ocean; at *Iliad* V, 6, we read of the star of summer rising from its bath in Ocean; at *Odyssey* V, 275, we read of the Bear being the only constellation that does not bathe in Ocean; at *Iliad* XVIII, 489, the same comment is made of the Bear. The sun is, of course, no exception: at *Iliad* VIII, 485, we hear about the shining light of the sun dropping into the Ocean, and at *Iliad* XVIII, 240, we hear again about the sun sinking into Ocean. If the sun needed a chariot to cross the sky, a boat might have been convenient for this part of the daily journey. In later Greece we still hear about the sun's 'cup' which Herakles borrows for his journey. A view of Ocean as a circular entity embracing the entire earth is apparent in the description of the shield of Achilles (*Iliad* XVIII, 606-7), and West points out that at this time Ocean is not entirely supplanted by Olympus as the dwelling-place of the gods or as a focus for religious ideas: 'If the Olympians do not live by Oceanus, they go there often enough' (1978, 193). Citing the many examples of feasts with the Aithiopians and the Hyperboreans, the visit of Hera to Oceanus, as well as the 'garden of the gods' where Hera and Zeus celebrate their marriage and where Hera plants the golden apples, he comments that 'we have here a conception which can be traced back to Minoan Crete and ultimately to Egypt' (*ibid.*).

Moreover, literature also provides us with passages where the sea is linked with ideas about the journey of the dead. The presence of the Oceanids in *H Demeter* 5 suggests that the rape of Persephone may have taken place near the sea (Richardson, 1974, 149). We cannot make too much of the oar on Elpenor's burial mound (*Odyssey* XI, 77-8 and XII, 15) or of the enigmatic oar which Odysseus must carry inland at the end of his travels before death comes to him out of the sea (XI 121-137); although these oars are evidently significant and remind us of the 'oars' on the Italian oinochoe discussed above (**Fig. 275b**). However, what emerges clearly from the pages of Homer is that Ocean not only carries the heavenly bodies sailing in it but is also closely associated with the transition to the underworld. As Nagy (1973, 150-1) points out, it is from Ocean that the sun rises (*Iliad* VII, 421-423) and into which it falls at sunset (*Iliad* VIII, 485); however, those who die also fall into Ocean, as when Penelope says (*Odyssey* XX, 61-5):

> Ἄρτεμι, πότνα θεά, θύγατερ Διός, αἴθε μοι ἤδη
> ἰὸν ἐνὶ στήθεσσι βαλοῦσ' ἐκ θυμὸν ἔλοιο
> αὐτίκα νῦν, ἢ ἔπειτα μ' ἀναρπάξασα θύελλα
> οἴχοιτο προφέρουσα κατ' ἠερόεντα κέλευθα
> ἐν προχοῇς δὲ βάλοι ἀψορρόου Ὠκεανοῖο.

We have seen that Odysseus also reached the underworld by sailing beyond the sea until he reaches Ocean (XI, 13ff). By dying Penelope will have fallen into Ocean, but she will also have gone underneath the earth (XX, 80-1):

> ἠέ μ' ἐϋπλόκαμος βάλοι Ἄρτεμις, ὄφρ' Ὀδυσῆα
> ὀσσομένη καὶ γαῖαν ὑπὸ στυγερὴν ἀφικοίμην

which, as we have seen, is also what happens to the sun after it has fallen into Ocean (*Odyssey* X, 190-2, *H Hermes* 68). Arguing from a completely different standpoint from mine, drawing on the language of Homer independently without reference to any of our Bronze Age material, Nagy concludes that 'when you traverse the Okeanos, you reach the underworld, which is underneath the Earth. From the solar standpoint, the significance of Okeanos is that when the sun reaches the extreme West at sunset, it likewise drops into the Okeanos; before the sun rises in the extreme East, it stays hidden underneath the Earth. When the sun does rise, it emerges from the Okeanos in the extreme East ... Thus the movement of the sun into and from the Okeanos serve as a cosmic model for death and rebirth. From the human standpoint, the sun dies in the West in order to be reborn in the East' (1973, 161).

A further point is worth mentioning in passing. Although one might question Frame's (1978) interpretation of almost all Odysseus' fabulous adventures as cycles of solar return associated with the triumph of νοῦς over death, his return journey from Phaeacia does certainly show some convincing traces of solar associations. Thus Odysseus, impatient to be off, keeps turning his head towards the Sun, urging it to set (XIII, 29-30); as soon as it is down he leaves; on the journey he sleeps 'like death' (XIII, 80); he arrives at Ithaca at dawn and wakes up near a cave (XIII, 93ff). While Frame is interested in deriving such patterns from 'Indo-European' ideas, we will surely prefer to trace sea-faring themes to traditions of an indigenous sea-dwelling Aegean people rather than to those of invaders often alleged to have come from an inland northern continent; especially when those indigenous traditions include evidence suggesting a solar boat.

We now turn to the form of transport which, it was suggested, began as early as the Late Bronze Age to supplant the boat as the main form of transport imagined to be suitable for the sun: the horse and chariot.

3.8 SYMBOLS OF HORSE AND CHARIOT

Earlier in this study I suggested that during the Late Bronze Age the horse and chariot partially replaced the boat or fish as the vehicle or form in which the sun was thought to travel. I also noted that the horse and chariot appeared to be associated with funerary practices and ideas (see Chapter 2.6). Comment was made on the appearance of horse burials associated with human ones, and on the appearance in some cases of female figures driving a chariot (as on the Aghia Triadha sarcophagus) which were interpreted as a possible continuation of the role of women in boats associated with the journey of the dead. From the Early Iron Age we find a substantial body of evidence suggesting a continuing association between the horse (and horse-and-chariot) and both the sun and death.

(a) The Archaeological Evidence

The horse and death

Linking the horse and chariot with funerary themes, we find a very large number of funerary vessels which show, near to the representations of the funeral or of mourning, a procession of horses and chariots. **Fig. 303** shows several examples. The exact nature of the association can be debated. On occasion the horse is clearly shown as the drawer of the hearse, and the procession of chariots which often appears below could be understood as a representation of the funerary procession. Ahlberg argues that the representations of chariot scenes, races and processions refer to the ceremonies and games held at the actual funeral, perhaps a bit exaggerated (1971b, 307-8). Benson (1970, 24) points out that the Geometric friezes showing a military parade of chariots have their exact analogy both in the funeral procession of Patroclus and in the latest Mycenaean kraters of the mainland. We may also note their LBA precursors on larnakes, as on the H. Triadha sarcophagus or **Fig. 217**. **Fig. 279b** shows an infantry procession which also tallies closely with the details of the funeral honours paid to Patroclus. It is not our concern here to establish whether the Geometric vases are copying Homer; what is significant is the horse and chariot's part in the imaginative framework which the Early Iron Age Greeks brought to the idea of death, and the exact nature of the role it played in that framework.

Benson (1970, 22) points out that the association between the horse and death could be on a mundane level: that since the horse and chariot was a sign of status, they represented honour for the deceased. While many of those buried with vessels bearing such processions may not have had the resources to finance such lavish display at their funeral, we could understand such illustrations as having the intention of ennobling the deceased. Such considerations may well have played a part in the choice of motif. However, as Benson recognizes (1970, 24), there is also the possibility that the horse had a role as transporter of the dead to the after-life. He points out that the type of chariot used in the Late Bronze Age reappears on Dipylon vases, and suggests that the knowledge of the funerary associations of the horse in the Bronze Age had not vanished from the Greek world (1970, 24-5). Ahlberg identifies the *circumambulatio* of chariots round the corpse as an 'old magic rite' (1971b, 306).

The possibility Benson mentions (1970, 23), that the chariot rather than any particular animal is the main factor in the concept (the horse just happening to be the animal most commonly used for drawing it in the Aegean world), would seem to be is belied by the frequent independent appearance of the horse in funerary contexts. Thus the horse appears depicted without chariot on some Geometric funerary vessels; **Fig. 304** shows an example of a pyxis with horses on its lid, from the grave of a woman. The suggestion that the horse was thought appropriate for transport in the after-life also receives some validation from the practice of burying horses with the dead, which we saw was also known in the Late Bronze Age. We may note the practice of burying horses (and chariot) in Cyprus during the eighth and seventh centuries B.C., and the four horses that are thrown on the pyre of Patroclus in *Iliad* XXIII now have their counterpart in the four horses buried next to the 'heroic' burials of a man and a woman in the Toumba area of Lefkandi (see **Fig. 305**). Tomb 68 has yielded two further horse skeletons (see *AR* 1986-7, 12-13). These burials predate the spread of Homer's popularity on the mainland, but again, we are not concerned whether this is a case of 'life copying art' but with establishing the presence of such ideas in the contemporary symbolic framework of the Early Iron Age.

The idea that the presence of the horse on an item of pottery indicated military occupations or activities on the part of its owner is undermined by pieces such as that shown on **Fig. 306a**, where a horse and infantry figures appear on a large Late Geometric krater found in the grave of a woman. The central figure is described as 'a groom with a horse' (*AR* 1973-4, 19). That the ownership of horses indicated wealth and prestige cannot be discounted as a significant factor in the use of horse motifs. This is not, however, incompatible with the horse also possessing a symbolic significance, such as is proposed by Schweitzer, who argues from the wings they occasionally bear and the symbols displayed around them that they are supernatural (although winged horses hardly occur before the seventh century). He suggests (1971, 54) that the horse played a leading role in Attic religion and cult of the dead, linked with the Ionian cult of Poseidon and with the god of death (though Coldstream sees 'too many possible Poseidons' in the figures with horse and fish on Argive vessels, 1977, 12). Schweitzer suggests that the male figure who often appears standing between two horses (as on **Fig. 306 b, c**, and **d**) is the 'God of the Dead'. He also identifies as Kore an eighth century seated terracotta goddess from an Attic grave (Grave 1 at Kallithea) on the back of whose throne a horse is shown (1971, 160).

The horse and the sun?

Since we are concerned with establishing the presence or absence of an association between the horse and the sun in the Early Iron Age, we shall be interested to note the presence of swastikas and dot rosettes with several of these man-horse groupings. Coldstream (1965) has argued from their protome form that a man holding the reins of a horse (**Fig. 306 e, f, g**) on an early seventh century Theran vase represents a mythical scene, and suggests it is the Rising of Helios. Interestingly, the vessel's burnt interior might indicate a funerary use. If such an interpretation is correct for the Theran vessels, one wonders how applicable it may be to scenes which show not protomes but full horses, accompanied by familiar 'sun' symbols (e.g. **Fig. 306 a, c, d**). The bird perched on the head of the central figure in **Fig. 306d** suggests a non-literal intention, and echoes the bird juxtaposed to the figure on the Theran vase (**Fig. 306e**). In an even closer parallel, what appears to be a large rayed sun is shown juxtaposed to a horse-rider on an amphora from the Kerameikos (**Fig. 307**). Motifs which appear in other contexts to represent sun symbols crop up in many instances closely juxtaposed to chariots (see, for example, **Fig. 308 a** and **b** as well **Fig. 303b**). Overlooking the Bronze Age evidence associating the horse and chariot with the sun in the context of funerary beliefs, Benson is at a loss for an explanation for the appearance of such symbols on Geometric funerary vessels, and can suggest only that, like chevrons, they were used to recall the glamour associated with olden times and add a Mycenaean or heroic 'flavour' to the composition (1970, 50-1). He therefore can offer 'no better explanation' for the 'unusual circles' scattered over the chariot scene shown on **Fig. 309** than that they were the work of another trigger-happy designer inspired by drilling of similar shapes from the hands of earlier Aegean gem-engravers (1970, 58). He cites a gem in Oxford (our **Fig. 26a**) as an early example of such decorative drilling, ironically choosing a seal for which I have argued a very specific intention.

While it seems that circular motifs on Geometric vases, like other motifs such as chevrons, have in some cases, such as **Fig. 309**, proliferated to the point of ornamental filling, it remains important to investigate the original motivation behind the use of the symbol, especially when we are dealing with artefacts and themes which have funerary associations. In the case of these representations, an original motivation, and in fact a long history, for the association of the horse and chariot to the sun, and to death, can be found. Decorative flourishes can, as we have seen, coexist with examples where the same symbol is given meaning and prominence. In some instances in Geometric art, the association of the horse with possible sun symbols is pointed in a way that strongly suggests a current and meaningful relationship between the two motifs rather than the unpurposeful repetition of juxtapositions seen on the works of a previous era: **Fig. 310 a, b** and **c** show the swastika, the cross, and a type of dot rosette combined with the horse, while **Fig. 310d** shows the horse with the standard which Roes (1933 passim) proposes is also a solar symbol. **Fig. 310e** shows crossed circles and fish on the side of a horse askos with a diminutive slumped rider (the deceased?) from Tomb Q at Tekke. Here again, funeral as well as solar associations may be suggested.

Figurines, fibulae, fish

Archaeology also offers some evidence for the continued association of the horse with a female rider, mentioned above in Chapter 2.6. Thus a number of statuettes have been found depicting a naked female on horseback; in some instances she carries a child. (See, for example, **Figs. 310 f, g, h.**) Examples from Cyprus and Arcadia lead Schweitzer (1971, 156-9) to suggest a Bronze Age survival, and their provenances associate them with Artemis, Hera and Demeter. Such items, and similar evidence among the votive offerings at the Cretan cave of Tsoutsouros (**Fig. 310i**), further strengthen our sense of the independent religious significance of the horse.

It was suggested in Chapter 2.6 that horse and boat have a special relationship as two forms of transport visualized for the sun, and we noted that they are juxtaposed, together with probable sun symbols, on a Late Minoan larnax from Kalochorafiti. I suggested in the previous section (3.7) that a similar affinity between the two elements is reflected in their juxtaposition on adjacent zones of Geometric funerary vessels. Further evidence of their connection is perhaps afforded by an examination of some Geometric fibulae.

The general nature of these fibulae is indicated by **Fig. 311 a** and **b** where we see that on the decorated plate the representation of a horse, accompanied by a cluster of birds and a rosette, backs onto a representation of that semi-mythical creature the lion, similarly accompanied by birds and rosettes. The motif of the lion backing onto the horse suggests that the medium is not necessarily being used for literal portrayals, and the appearance of a tripod in front of the horse on **Fig. 311b** will further incline us to believe that these scenes may carry some kind of mythical or cult significance.

Bearing this in mind, we can turn to a series of representations on fibulae which recurrently juxtapose the horse and the boat. Thus on two plate fibulae from Thebes (**Fig. 312 a** and **b**) the horse (with bird) backs onto the boat (with birds). The birds are not naturalistically positioned in any of the representations, the boats are in each case accompanied by disproportionate fish, and one of the boats is unmanned; hardly what one would expect if a naturalistic representation were intended. In **Fig. 313**, a horse and chariot is similarly backed onto the representation of a boat. Here the boat is accompanied not only by fish but by a swastika (= sun?), and in the panel above the boat we see a lion attacking a doe. Schweitzer's suggestion (1971, 55) that the lion and sphinx are symbols of death, would endorse an interpretation of these scenes as showing an assemblage of symbols associated with death. (Compare the fish on **Fig. 215a**.)

This is where the interpretation of various other scenes as narrative must come under question. Thus Schweitzer's interpretation of one of the representations on **Fig. 314** as a 'warship … used as a horse transporter' (1971, 213) appears stretched when we look closely at the unmanned boat, bearing a single horse, with a fish beneath the boat, a bird perched on it and a large radiant sun-like motif (which Schweitzer describes as a 'star') prominently placed beside it, in the area where we often find such motifs on representations of boats on Geometric vases. The other three scenes on the fibula each include snakes and birds, and one is dominated by a swastika. It will be recalled that the interpretation of 'horse transporter' has also been offered for the appearance of a horse on a boat of the Late Bronze Age (**Fig. 216a**); the implication is of an unusual predilection for the transporting of single horses by boat.

Credulity is again stretched by Schweitzer's narrative interpretation of scenes on a plate fibula in the Thebes Museum (**Fig. 315**). On one side he would have us see a 'beach or quay' on which two excited horses are prancing about while a ship of ambiguous character ('probably commercial but also equipped as a warship') can be seen on the beach. A fight is in progress on board while two birds are 'fluttering around the ship' (1971, 205). On a closer look we find nothing on the meander pattern at the base, framed by semi-circles above and below, to indicate that it is intended to represent a beach or quay; moreover the birds are not fluttering but are in static positions. It seems more plausible to see here simply a collection of associated motifs:

bird, horse, boat, and a scene of armed combat. Even harder to interpret as a literal scene is the other side of the plate, which Schweitzer would have us see as 'Two horses seem to be running off ... Stable boys are trying to catch them. On the top left there is a lion. In the background an erotic scene appears to be taking place' (1971, 205). Little as we know about day to day reality in Geometric Greece, it is hard to believe that such a conjunction of events shows a situation from everyday life. It is hard to imagine whether the stable boys would be more frightened of the lion or shocked by the couple in the background: perhaps that is why the horses have run away? Surely, rather, we may again interpret it as an assemblage of motifs, each of which are familiar to us from Bronze Age iconography. (We may also add to the assemblage what are perhaps two birds, unremarked by Schweitzer, at the left of the scene.) While many of the Bronze Age motifs we are discussing may have degenerated over time into purely decorative themes, the artists of the Geometric era still apparently knew that they belonged together and were interested in experimenting with new combinations.

The independent association of the horse with the fish can be seen on the Cretan askos (**Fig. 310e**). It is also attested on many Argive vessels, often with the familiar circular or rayed symbols (**Fig. 316**). Perhaps it is time here to return again to Courbin's objections to a symbolic explanation for such juxtapositions. Again he puts forward, for the fish, the — for him — ' contradiction qu'il y a entre l'interprétation solaire et l'interprétation chthonienne' (1966, 481). From the fact that the placing of the fish under the horse represents neither a rigidly followed nor an exclusive association, and from the fact that it degenerates, Courbin argues that it is a purely formal juxtaposition: I find this a weak explanation for such an inherently improbable and persistent association. Out of the horse/fish compositions we see narrative and event emerging (as in **Fig. 316f** where the horses fight); this does not solve the problem of identifying the thinking behind the original and tenacious juxtaposition. While the interpretation proposed here cannot be justified purely in terms of the internal evidence of Argive pottery, Courbin's own explanation based purely on that internal evidence is also highly unsatisfactory. The scenes do, however, make sense if seen in the wider context of the contemporary representations of the Early Iron Age, as discussed here; the solar interpretations put forward are further strengthened by the evidence from literature to which we now turn.

(b) The Literary Evidence

The association between horse and sun for example, which is suggested by the ceramic evidence, is reaffirmed by literature. In the Homeric Hymns Helios is described as having a chariot and horses, as in *H Hermes* 69 and *H Demeter* 63 and 88, where we read of Helios:

᾿Ὡς εἰπὼν ἵπποισιν ἐκέκλετο· τοὶ δ᾿ ὑπ᾿ ὁμοκλῆς
ῥίμφα φέρον θοὸν ἅρμα τανύπτεροι ὥστ᾿ οἰωνοί.

The notion of sun as charioteer was clearly well established in this context. However, as Richardson points out, the Sun's chariot does not appear in Homer (1974, 171). We have already seen (in Chapter 3.4 above) that in Homer Dawn has a chariot. There are other shreds of evidence associating the horse, or horse and chariot, with a female divinity. We have already noted the archaeological evidence of an enthroned goddess with a horse and of statuettes showing naked, and sometimes child-bearing, female riders. We read at *Theogony* 439, that Hecate stands by horsemen, and in *Iliad* VI, 205, we find reference to Artemis 'of the golden reins'. Tradition, then, associates the horse with the sun, and with a male charioteer sun-god, but also includes a strand of ideas linking it with female divinities.

Whereas in the early period discussed in Chapter 1 we found evidence suggesting that death may have been linked with ideas or ritual of boat departure, and we also found evidence of ball games which, it was suggested, may have been thought to simulate and stimulate the movement of the sun and the return of life, we might now expect to find funerary games centred around the form of transport currently most favoured for the sun: the horse and chariot. It is noteworthy then, that we find a chariot race as the first event of the games at Patroclus' funeral, which also included a foot race and other athletic contests. We may also note that before the chariot race, and before the funeral ceremonies, Achilles and the Myrmidons drive their horse-drawn chariots three times round the body of Patroclus in mourning (*Iliad* XXIII, 13-14). One could speculate that the returning or circular motion of the racing or processing chariots echoed the chariot journey of the sun and reflected an earlier belief that this activity would encourage the return of the soul from its journey on the sun's chariot.

The possibility that the tradition of games in Greece, formally established in the Early Iron Age, derived its origin from rituals of movement which were part of Early Bronze Age funerary rituals is one which would require a separate study fully to evaluate. However, returning to the specific issue of the chariot race in *Iliad* XXIII, we may note with interest the inclusion of a garbled and incoherent reference to some surviving ancient historical object or landmark which suggests in the poet an awareness of some ancient associations of the race. Nestor gives Antilochus the following detailed description of the turning-post (XXIII, 327-333):

> There is a dry stump standing up from the ground about six feet,
> oak, it may be, or pine, and not rotted away by rain-water,
> and two white stones are leaned against it, one on either side,
> at the joining place of the ways, and there is smooth driving around it.
> Either it is the grave-mark of someone who died long ago,
> or was set as a racing goal by men who lived before our time.
> Now swift-footed brilliant Achilleus has made it the turning-post.

We shall discuss other stones attributed with high antiquity below (Chapter 3.12). This passage has baffled Homeric commentators. However, the reference to a tree, stones, to their status as survivals of an earlier age, as well as the specific suggestion of a connection with an ancient burial, make perfect sense within our schema and must all prompt us to consider seriously the possibility that the chariot race owes something to Bronze Age funerary traditions. If this is the case, we have another layer of ideas underlying the deployment of circling chariots on funerary vessels.

Literary evidence would further seem to confirm a deeper association between death and the horse and chariot than that based simply on funerary practice or prestige: thus in the *H Demeter*, 16ff, we read that the earth opened and Hades sprang out with his immortal horses, seized Persephone and carried her away on his gold chariot (ἐπὶ χρυσέοισιν ὄχοισιν); in this context death is clearly horse-transported. We hear of Hades' chariot again at 375-6, where the same chariot is used to return Persephone to the daylight.

In several passages of the *Iliad* we have reference to 'Hades of the famed horses' (κλυτοπώλῳ) (as at V, 654 and XI, 445). When, at XVII, 434, we read that Achilles' horses stand as firm as a grave monument over the barrow of a corpse, we may wonder whether this is a fortuitous comparison or one of those metaphors reflecting a symbolic connection.

The argument proposed here, that many of the horses in Geometric art have a symbolic significance, and that the horse and chariot is a substitute for earlier ideas of the boat as a means of transportation for the sun, will be further supported if we can find independent evidence associating the horse with boats and things of the sea. *Theogony* 439ff announces in one breath that Hecate is good for horsemen *and* for those who work the sea. A similarly two-pronged interest is more familiarly ascribed to Poseidon. At *Iliad* XVI, 150-1, we read that

Achilles' magic horses were born beside Ocean. In the 'days' section of the *Works and Days* we find activities associated with horses and with the sea coupled several times in a manner that defies a pattern of logical thought; (this will be discussed more fully below, p.167). Thus we can see that the literary and archaeological records combine to provide numerous examples of the association of the horse with the boat and with fish, and of both horse and boat independently with death. The curious and repeated juxtaposition of the horse and the boat is hard to explain without the ready explanation provided by the common denominator they share as traditional transporters of the sun associated with the journey of the dead.

3.9 SOME OTHER SURVIVALS OF BRONZE AGE SYMBOLISM

So far I have discussed various elements which, I have argued, were significant in Bronze Age religious symbolism: the sun, the bird, the boat and the horse. Various associations have been traced between the sun and each of these other elements. This is not the place to locate these symbols within the wider context of the overall picture of religious symbolism in the Geometric era, but it is relevant to remark in passing on the web of juxtapositions and associations which also unites each of the elements with the other. It is moreover relevant to point out that two other symbols discussed above in the sections on Bronze Age religious symbolism, the snake and the goat, also appear closely associated with these same symbols.

I have commented on the frequent juxtaposition of horse and fish. We also find the horse associated with the bird. Thus we see a horse with a bird between its legs (**Fig. 317**) and a winged horse on seals (**Fig. 318**). Of winged horses Boardman comments that we are not obliged to recognize them all as Pegasus as teams of them are often shown on island vases pulling divine chariots (1970, 120). Literature confirms the association, as in *H Demeter* 89, where Helios' horses speed off with his chariot 'like long-winged birds'. These are only a few examples of an association which prompted Benson to comment (1970, 30) 'The bird had not only reappeared in Attica by the Middle Geometric …, but from this time it was deliberately linked, maybe equated, with the horse'. So there is a strong link between bird and horse, for which **Fig. 218 d** and **e** provide some Bronze Age antecedents. I have commented above (see Chapter 3.7) on the Geometric association of the bird and the fish (as on **Fig. 302**), and on the Bronze Age precedents for that association.

The snake appears on Geometric funerary vessels (as on **Fig. 319a** from Rhodes, **Fig. 279b**, **Fig. 303 d - f**, and other examples from Attica); from Fortetsa we even find what is perhaps 'a chthonic goddess with snakes attached to her dress' (Coldstream, 1984, 97) (**Fig. 319b**). The goat appears with birds and familiar cross symbols (as on **Fig. 320**). In various other combinations on seals we find winged goats, sometimes coupled with horses and fish (**Fig. 321**); I have commented above on the horse-fish combination on vases. We also find the horse with bird, swastika and snake (**Fig. 322**); and bird with snake and fish (**Fig. 323a**). Of some of these combinations Boardman comments (1970, 121) 'Odder still is the way both the winged horses and winged goats are grafted on to fish bodies'; however we have seen that the bird connection and the marine connection of the horse and goat can be traced back to the Bronze Age. To underline the Bronze Age antecedents of these combinations, we also find recurring double axe motifs, and heraldic compositions (such as on **Fig. 317a** and **Fig. 324**) which are highly reminiscent of the earlier period.

Another sight familiar from Bronze Age seals are representations of the lion with a disc or star, and the goat or other quadrupeds with discs (**Fig. 325**). While Boardman describes the discs as 'gouged holes which produce blobs on the impression' appearing 'where empty space is to be filled' (1970, 120), the similarity to Bronze Age examples (such as **Figs. 117, 163, 167, 173, 174, 176**) must make us wonder whether the choice of motif is completely decorative or fortuitous.

While some of these parallels may reflect an iconographic, rather than a living symbolic, inheritance from the Bronze Age, some of the scenes and juxtapositions which we find in Early Geometric art seem to reflect traditions which, in view of their idiosyncrasy and their expression in different media, are unlikely to have been preserved only on the superficial level of iconographic imitation. Thus, for example, we saw that in the Bronze Age the goat played a significant role in cult (**Figs. 67, 171**), including perhaps funerary cult and ideas (as on the Episkopi larnax, **Fig. 217a**, and the Aghia Triadha sarcophagus, **Fig. 214a**). We also noted an unlikely EBA scene of a goat apparently on a boat followed by a figure carrying a (?)weapon (**Fig. 119a**). In the LBA goats often appeared on seals with possible shafts or arrows adjacent to them (e.g. **Fig. 174a, 244d**). Mycenaean grave stelae favoured hunting scenes, and LM III larnakes can also show goats and scenes of chase (e.g. Nos. 1707 and 1709 in Chania Museum). Such hunting scenes may, as Coldstream has pointed out (1984, 93), partially if not exclusively represent symbols of death. It is noteworthy therefore in this later period to find not only the reappearance of hunting on the funerary vessel (**Fig. 326a**), but also the appearance of the goat prominently placed in prothesis scenes (as on **Fig. 303c**), and, from Fortetsa, the unlikely juxtaposition on a bell krater of goat and boat (see **Fig. 326b** and compare with the Korfi t'Aroniou picture **Fig. 119a**). On **Fig. 244d** the goat seems to stand on a platform and, again, to be victim of a shaft. The closeness of these Bronze Age parallels must again make us consider the possibility of continuity in religious symbolism.

3.10 CONTINUITY IN SYMBOLISM OF EARTH

In Chapters 1 and 2, I highlighted evidence suggesting ideas of 'immanent' rather than 'transcendent' divinity. In this, the earth itself was significant: its topography (mountains, rocks, stones) and its products (such as plant life) featured prominently in cult. Caves were used for cult and burial, and it was suggested that some forms of built or dug graves imitated the cave shape with a notion of reproducing the shape of the female womb. In Early Iron Age religious symbolism we can trace what may be survivals of such beliefs.

Although the continuing evidence of religious cult at caves is significant, archaeology otherwise tells us little here. Perhaps most significant is the design on a lid from Tomb P at Fortetsa (**Fig. 327**), which shows a human protome beneath a tripod; this figure is interpreted by Brock (1957, 123) as 'the authochthonous Cretan goddess (Gaia?)'. We cannot with confidence put a name to this figure, but she is apparently female and evidently bears a close relationship to the earth from which she appears to be rising. If she represents Earth, it is in a personified form, while the cave evidence speaks of a sanctity still to some extent associated with physical location.

Literature tells a similar story, of an Earth whose physical topography and whose emergence as a personified divinity both play a significant role in religious ideas. We have seen that she is frequently called upon in Homer for solemn oaths (as at *Iliad* XIX, 259, XV, 36). Earth's barrenness at the time of Demeter's grief suggests an affinity with that goddess (*H Demeter*, 305ff). Earth plays a major role in several early myths, as we shall see further below. Moreover, there are intimations that she had previously held greater power: thus at *Theogony* 505 we read that thunder, the thunderbolt and lightning had been hidden by Earth before they were given to Zeus by his brothers, perhaps suggesting a memory of a time when Zeus had not yet acquired all the attributes and powers he held in Hesiod's time.

While in literature Earth is to some extent personified, and she plays an active personal role in the Kronos story, the physical topography of the earth remains significant. Thus at *H Apollo* 333 Hera prays by striking the ground with her hand, and in response the earth moves. Underground places are more than once described as 'holy' (e.g. ζαθέης ὑπὸ κεύθεσι γαίης *Theogony* 483). We have seen that literature also frequently regards caves as sacred (as at *Odyssey* XII, 317-8, and XIII, 103-4). We have seen (above, p.150) that both the setting sun and the souls of the dead were thought to travel 'under the earth'. She is also, however, the 'mother of all' who bears the fruit of the earth (γῆ πάντων μήτηρ καρπὸν σύμμικτον ἐνείκη, *Works and Days* 563); and from the number of mythological births which take place in caves, we may conclude that a symbolic link between cave and womb retains vitality. She is thus symbolically linked with processes of both disappearance and appearance (of vegetation), of both birth and death.

One other aspect of Earth is noteworthy in this context. This is the survival of various references which associate her with prophecy. Thus at *Theogony* 624ff Earth advises Zeus and other gods to bring Obriareus and Cottus and Gyes up to the light, telling them everything that would happen Γαίης φραδμοσύνῃσιν ... αὐτὴ γάρ σφιν ἅπαντα διηνεκέως κατέλεξε. In this context West (1966, 339) notes her prophetic role and her benevolence to Zeus, except in producing Typhoeus. At *Theogony* 463 it is both Earth and Heaven who inform Kronos that he will be overcome by Zeus. West (1966, 295) notes that Heaven does not appear elsewhere in an oracular capacity, and suggests that he appears here merely as a complement of Gaia, citing many later references to Earth's oracular connexions. It is noteworthy that at Dodona, the prophets are described as sleeping on the ground with feet unwashed (*Iliad* XVI, 235), suggesting a close relationship with earth. These early traditions of prophecy will be further discussed as we turn to investigating evidence of continuity in the religious symbolism of earth's landscape and products: plant and stone.

3.11 THE FERTILE BOUGH

Earlier in this study it was pointed out that items which in classical times were an attribute of divinity were in the Early Bronze Age themselves seen as manifestations of divinity. Thus we saw a cult centred on the tending of, and display of reverence towards, plant life. I also suggested that this cult appeared to be associated with the sun and that cults aimed at procuring the fertility of vegetation may have been related to funerary cults. At this point it is relevant to review what survived of such ideas in the Geometric era.

(a) The Archaeological Evidence

Of the continuing significance of the plant in religion, vase decorations inform us extensively with their numerous representations of cult scenes in which plants feature. I have already commented above on the large number of depictions of circular and dancing rituals; of these, very many show the participants holding branches (see, for example, **Figs. 276c, 276a, 282b**). The ritual action of holding a branch near the head or feet of the corpse at prothesis scenes (noted by Ahlberg, 1971b, 302) (see **Figs. 303c, 328f, 328g**) suggests that plant life still had a place in ideas about death. In some cases we see a priestess or goddess holding an item of plant life, as on **Fig. 282a** from Cyprus. **Fig. 328a** shows two women placed on either side of a frond, holding it between them in a posture reminiscent of that on the Bronze Age Phaistos sealing (**Fig. 85c**). For many further similar examples of vase decorations showing groups of women holding boughs between them, see Tölle. Similar activities associated with branches also seem to appear on seals, as on **Fig. 328b** on which Boardman sees two women with branches, bird and snake (1970, 134); other examples include **Fig. 328d**, described as a naked dancing man with raised arms and two branches, and **Fig. 328e**, described as a figure seated on a throne, holding a sceptre in front of him (both in *Antike Gemmen* Vol. I-1, 32).

At some of these scenes of vegetation ritual, individuals appear to be performing pronounced leaps which stand out from the general round of dancing (see, for example, **Fig. 276 a** and **b**). A fine example of a leap also appears strikingly on the base of a pot from Siteia (**Fig. 328c**). These leaps recall Bronze Age parallels (e.g. **Fig. 139a**) and also Lawler's comment that leaping dances are common among primitive peoples, to quicken the growing force in nature and induce fertility (1964, 30). The question arises as to whether these athletic activities, as well as the round dances themselves, may be derived from similar activities in the Bronze Age. It will be recalled that activities such as vigorous ball games, leaping and running, were suggested by seal engravings dating back to the early period discussed in Chapter 1. It is of interest, then, to find Geometric representations which show similar activities. Apart from the jumping referred to above, there is a seventh century seal (**Fig. 329a**) which shows a woman running, juxtaposed with another face which shows a close-up view of a woman carrying a branch. Although Boardman hesitates to do so, the prominent breast in each case would incline us to identify both figures as female. The familiarity of the running motif from the Bronze Age (as on **Fig. 28a**) is endorsed by its three-sided prism shape, of which Boardman comments: 'Two seal shapes hint at an unexpected source of inspiration. One is a three-sided prism ..., exactly the form of the Minoan Archaic Prisms and the other a bell-shaped stamp with spiral markings, which resembles Minoan seals of the same period' (1970, 118). There is also a seventh century seal (**Fig. 329b**) which shows a figure running juxtaposed with two branches (the long hair and buxom contour throw into question Boardman's identification of this figure as male). On the reverse side of this last seal we find what Boardman (1970, 135) describes as 'Two naked human figures, one apparently carrying the other'; a close look at this scene shows a marked resemblance to other scenes identified as love-making (see the Bronze Age seal **Fig. 82c**, described by Platon (*CMS* II,1, 529) as 'Umarmung oder Begattung', and also **Fig. 332b** below).

Thus we have three separate activities which may, from the presence of vegetation, be associated with ideas concerning the fertility of plant life: one is dancing, the second is running, and the third is love-making. We will take each of these activities in turn and see what light literary references can throw. But first we can enquire what literature tells us about current ideas concerning the frond and about vegetation cult in general.

(b) The Literary Evidence

Literature makes it clear that in this period plants were significant attributes of divinities, like the palm tree near the altar of Apollo at Delos which Homer tells us was looked at with awe (comparable to the awe with which the shipwrecked Odysseus looks at Nausicaa) (*Odyssey* VI, 162ff). The concern here, however, is to investigate the evidence of plants retaining some intrinsic numinous power independently of an associated Olympian deity. There is evidence that ideas concerning the sacredness of plant life survived in some contexts. Thus the importance of the staff is stressed in Homer on several occasions: in *Iliad* I, 233ff, Achilles swears on the staff; in *Iliad* II, 46, Agammemnon goes to the Assembly with the immortal sceptre of his fathers (σκῆπτρον πατρώϊον, ἄφθιτον αἰεί). We find references to a king bearing a staff and judges or elders administering justice with staff in hand (*Iliad* I, 238, and *Iliad* XVIII, 505 and 557). Such references suggest that the staff served as a symbol of family inheritance and also as a guarantor of true or just speech. (An archaeological parallel can be seen in the formal position of the figure seated on a (?)throne holding a branch on **Fig. 328e**.)

Hesiod's *Works and Days* make it clear that religion and agriculture were still very closely interwoven; I have commented above on expressions such as the 'sacred grain' and the instruction to pray before ploughing. Moreover, occasional references slip into Homer which bely the Olympian world view generally propagated by those poems, and reveal knowledge of a tradition in which plants are used as a power in themselves to achieve healing or magical purposes. Thus, for example, we hear at *Iliad* XI, 740-1, of Agamede who knew all the φάρμακα that grow in the wide world; in *Odyssey* X, Circe uses powerful φάρμακα mixed in their food to transform Odysseus' companions to animals, and Hermes gives Odysseus another φάρμακον which he needs only to hold in order to counteract hers. Both Circe and Hermes use wands to transmit their magical powers. At *H Demeter* 228, ὑποτάμνον has been taken to refer to the cutting of herbs for magical purposes (cf. Richardson, 1974, 230).

Evidence for rituals

Homer also provides several references to festivals orientated around vegetative life. Thus at *Iliad* IX, 534-5, we hear of an overdue harvest offering which King Oeneus should have made to Artemis along with the other gods. At *Iliad* XVIII, 569ff, he gives a description of a vineyard scene where boys and girls dance to a boy singing the song of Linus to a lyre; the same Linus, according to a Hesiodic fragment which describes mourning songs to him (305), was the son of Ouranie. While the information which Homer gives of such activities is extremely sparse, and Hesiod is hardly more forthcoming, it is worth investigating what further information literature can offer about the ideas and purpose underlying the three activities which we have seen witnessed prominently by archaeology in association with vegetation: dancing, running, and perhaps also love-making.

Dancing, as we have seen above, is frequently shown on Geometric vases, is often circular, in Homer connected with Cretan traditions, and in some representations is accompanied by what may be a sun motif. That dance was associated with sexuality is implied by the residence of Himeros next to the Muses in *Theogony* 64, of which West comments 'That the Charites and Himeros live next to the Muses means, of course, that they have related interests and that they have much to do with each other' (1966, 177); it is also suggested by the adjective ἱμερόεντας being applied to χορούς at *Theogony* 8, and on two separate occasions in Homer (*Iliad* XVIII, 603, and *Odyssey* XVIII, 194). However, we have no further information about how dance may have been related to fertility of human or plant life in ritual.

Running as part of a cult centred on plant fertility is suggested not only by the seals cited above, but also by the story of Atalanta which is referred to in Hesiodic fragments (see, *inter alia*, fr. 76). The story of the woman who sought to avoid marriage by running, but eventually lost a race because of the three apples given to Hippomenes by Aphrodite, combines themes of human and plant reproduction with an athletic contest.

As for the evidence of an association between plant fertility and human reproductive activity, we have, apart from these seals, some references in literature. Thus, at *Theogony* 194-5, Hesiod tells us that grass grew up around the feet of the new-born Aphrodite, while at *Iliad* XIV, 347, grass and flowers grow during the love-making of Hera and Zeus. An actual ritual involving sexual activity, such as the seals cited above may show, is more closely suggested by *Theogony* 969-971, where a thrice-ploughed fallow field is given as the location for the love-making of Demeter and Iasion, which resulted in the procreation of Ploutos. The same union, with the same location of the thrice-ploughed field, is mentioned in *Odyssey* V, 125-7. West (1966, 423) comments that 'The practice of reinforcing the efficacy of the ploughing by simultaneous sexual activity, often in the fields themselves, is well attested from various parts of the world'; he regards this union as the mythical correlate of 'the ancient agrarian ritual'. However, the ubiquitousness of such a practice does not mean that it necessarily took place in Greece; it is important to bear in mind that the relevant evidence for Greece consists only of such scraps of pictorial and literary evidence as have been presented here, combined with similar but equally enigmatic scraps of evidence from the Bronze Age. We might, however, imagine that a seal like **Fig. 329b (below)** bears some relation to the Demeter story, perhaps showing a ritual underlying the story. The correlation of human fertility with not only plant but animal fertility is implied at *Works and Days*, 232-5, where Hesiod tells us that the just city prospers with plentiful produce from the earth, woolly sheep, and children who look like their parents; West points out how closely the fertility of flocks is followed by that of humans in the list (1978, 215).

Association with death and birth

We also have evidence from the Early Iron Age that vegetation rituals may have been closely associated with funerary beliefs and rituals. Specific plants or fruits were associated with death, like the pomegranate which figures so prominently in the Persephone story as the fruit whose seed ensures her return to the underworld (*H Demeter*, 371ff), and which recalls Bronze Age parallels. In *Iliad* VI, 420, Homer recounts that the mountain nymphs planted elms round the grave of Eëtion; evidently a grave was an appropriate location for a tree. However, what emerges most strongly in this context is again some form of identification between human and plant life.

In many cases the medium through which the idea is transmitted is a simile. Thus at *Iliad* VI, 146ff, Glaukos says that the generations of men are like the leaves of trees which the wind blows to the ground, after which the trees bud and fresh leaves grow in spring. A similar simile recurs at XXI, 464ff. Sourvinou-Inwood has associated such imagery with a traditional 'accepting' attitude towards death as a familiar and necessary event, within the context of a community whose continuity offsets the discontinuity of the individual (1983b, 34 and passim). We are told at *Iliad* XVIII, 56-7, that Achilles was nursed by Thetis like a little plant in a garden bed and shot up like a sapling. The metaphor of the 'flower of youth' occurs as early as Homer (e.g. *Iliad* XIII, 484). We have already referred to Hesiod's description (*Works and Days* 145) of the third race of men who were made, perhaps, from ash-trees (ἐκ μελιᾶν), and will discuss further below Homer's knowledge of an ancient tradition of a man made from oak or stone; other references also associate antiquity and the early generation of humans with trees and tree nymphs (cf. *Theogony* 35, 187 and 563). In the *Iliad* there are many descriptions of men in battle being felled like trees, whether it is a poplar (Simoeisios in IV, 482) or an oak, poplar or pine (Asios at XIII, 389); the recurrence of the image may suggest that the association lies deeper than the convenience of tree-felling to convey the impact of a man being killed.

It will be noted that although the tree is associated recurrently with death, it is also associated both with the first genesis of humans and with birth in general. Thus Leto bears Apollo in Delos by a hill near a palm tree (*H Apollo*, 18). She holds the tree during birth (*ibid.*, 117). The tree is apparently an important accompaniment or agent of the birth; one is reminded of the substitution of a male deity for a plant at the centre of the horns of consecration during the Late Bronze Age and one wonders whether originally in the story the tree *was* Apollo. Of the Minoan deity partially assimilated to Zeus in myth, West comments: 'It is universally acknowledged that he was a vegetation- or year-god like the Semitic Adonis and the Egyptian Osiris, and not unlikely that he was the son of the earth or of the great goddess of Minoan art' (1966, 291). Again, one should question the assumptions implicit in this passage, both concerning the existence of a 'great goddess' in Crete, and concerning the Minoan antiquity of a 'year-god'. The specific evidence for such ideas in the Aegean again consists only of scraps such as those I have dealt with in this study; for the Early Iron Age this evidence, ranging from the literary evidence cited above to the sometimes sketchy representations of plants in Geometric funerary scenes, speaks most volubly and suggestively not of a 'year-god' but of a funerary cult which combined ideas about the fertility and rebirth of vegetation with those concerning the fertility and rebirth of human beings. In this the material is very consistent with evidence from the Bronze Age.

Plants and prophecy

Before moving on from this discussion of the symbolism surrounding vegetation, it is relevant to mention briefly the recurrent tradition associating trees with prophecy. Thus it is clear that the oak at Dodona played a significant part in the prophetic practices (*Catalogue of Women* 240), and we are also told that Apollo has a laurel tree 'from' which he prophesies (*H Apollo*, 396). The same word ἐκ is used of Zeus' prophecy from the Dodona oak at *Odyssey* XIV, 328 and XIX, 297. At *Odyssey* XI, 91 the soul of the prophet Teiresias holds a gold 'sceptre'. At *Theogony* 30 the Muses give Hesiod a σκῆπτρον of laurel on the same occasion as they breathe into him a divine voice to tell the past and future: a function of the sceptre highly consistent with its use in Homer to help men speak in public and give judgement. Commenting on these references to oak and laurel, as well as on the association of bees with divination at *H Hermes* 552ff, and on later references to doves at Dodona, Sourvinou-Inwood notes the significance of plants and animals in prophecy and suggests it may derive from 'a common "mentality" operating at a particular stage in the history of Greek religion — a stage in which physical objects and animals were of paramount importance, and which in historical terms I would identify with the Dark Ages' (1979, 242). In the context of this study, however, we have evidence suggesting that such a stage can be traced back much further, to the Bronze Age. In the Bronze Age material, we saw many representations of people dressed as animals and touching trees in different ways the significance of which, in the lack of any relevant written texts, could not be guessed. Though any method of verification is lacking, it is a possibility that the later association of trees with prophecy reflects a survival of a Bronze Age tradition in which humans were believed to receive communication from the divine through contact with vegetation.

Demeter and Persephone

Lastly, we should perhaps also refer to some specific features of the Demeter and Persephone story, as told in *H Demeter*, which have resonances in the Bronze Age material. The dearth of small finds from the earliest buildings on the sanctuary site at Eleusis leave the cult's origin in doubt; a Cretan or local origin cannot be excluded (*pace* Mylonas, 1961). I shall not enter here into the thorny debate as to whether 'Demeter' can be identified in any Bronze Age representations; rather I am interested in pointing to some underlying strands in the story's structure which seem to show continuity from Bronze Age Aegean religion. One significant feature is perhaps that its protagonists are two female figures: a pairing of two female figures has, as we have seen, been a recurring element in the religious iconography of the Aegean since the Early Bronze Age (see **Fig. 3**). In some of the Bronze Age examples they are explicitly shown in the kourotrophic role which is prominent in the Eleusis story (see **Fig. 260 c, d**). Bronze Age depictions of a pair in a boat (**Figs. 60c, 208 a** and **b**) or a chariot (**Fig. 214a**) perhaps have parallels in Archaic representations such as **Fig. 329c** showing two female figures, probably Demeter and Persephone, in a cart. It is also noteworthy that flowers, important in many Bronze Age representations of cult (e.g. **Figs. 127a, 132a, 225a**) play a significant role in the rape of Persephone (*H Demeter* 5ff); Richardson (1974, 143) has pointed out that they are also prominent in Underworld topography in Homer (as at *Odyssey* XI, 539, 573, XXIV, 13). The parallel between Persephone as a disappearing vegetation goddess and the female figure we saw apparently departing (by boat) taking vegetation with her on Bronze Age seals (e.g. **Figs. 212 b, c** and perhaps **e**) is apparent. Richardson (1974, 14-16) has questioned theories dividing the development of the Eleusinian Mysteries into two separate stages, the primitive agricultural and the personal or eschatological, and suggests that an original 'non-Greek' cult may from early times have held a dual significance including both elements. Such a dual significance combining vegetational and funerary cults was clearly suggested by the evidence for Bronze Age religion discussed in Chapters 1 and 2 above. Moreover, two elements important in the Demeter story and in Eleusinian ideas, the action of sitting down to grieve and the more light-hearted element of jesting, also have resonances in the Bronze Age material. Thus Demeter's actions of looking down (194) and sitting down, to grieve (emphasized at *H Demeter* 98, 191-201) recall those Bronze Age scenes of figures sitting or kneeling with eyes down to mourn over a vessel or stone (which has a further parallel in later traditions of Demeter sitting to mourn on the Agelastos Petra). We think here of the 'potter' scenes discussed in Chapter 1 (e.g. **Fig. 66**) and of the more explicit LBA scenes shown on **Fig. 241 a, c, d, e, k, j**. We are also reminded of **Fig. 279e** and the Geometric funerary vase decoration (**Fig. 279a**) showing a row of female figures seated on stools with arms raised in mourning to a (?)sun symbol. Richardson (1974, 181-2) refers to Isis sitting at a parallel point in her mourning of Osiris, and to many instances showing the importance of sitting or lying down to grieve in Homer (1974, 218-9). Iambe's cheering of Demeter with jests, which Richardson (1974, 216-7) relates to parallels in funerary and solar rituals of many other cultures, could also perhaps be compared to the more light-hearted elements of (partially naked) dancing which appear to accompany mourning on some Bronze Age seals (as on **Fig. 241 a, c, d**). (A further Cretan parallel, Demeter's association with the snake of Cychreus, is noted in Chapter 3.17 below.)

It is interesting that while near-Eastern parallels to the Demeter story are often adduced (see, for example, Richardson's comparison with the myth of Tammuz, 1974, 258), there is a tendency to overlook parallels with Bronze Age Aegean religious ideas which are close not only in specific details but also in their underlying emphasis on a female rather than a male deity of vegetation.

3.12 SYMBOLISM OF VESSEL AND STONE

Earlier in this study it was argued that, in Bronze Age religious symbolism, (1) the pot was imaginatively viewed as female and (2) it was in some way envisaged as a womb which (3) symbolized not only birth but also rebirth of the dead. This idea was reflected in, for example, the sporadic but recurrent Bronze Age practice of burying the dead curled up in the foetal position, and in pithos burial. It was argued that the stone played a similar symbolic role, and that in each case the regeneration of human life from the vessel or stone was associated with the regeneration of plant life.

(a) The Archaeological Evidence

In the Early Iron Age the use of vessels for burials continued to provide a practical framework within which such ideas could exist. With the intermittent change of practice to cremation for adults, children continued sometimes to be inhumed in a large pot or pithos, as in the infant burial shown in **Fig. 330**. Cemeteries with pithos burials for adults also continue to be found in the Geometric period. Moreover, with the practice of cremation, funerary customs included the use of vessels to hold the ashes and, sometimes monumentally, mark the grave. That these vessels were not seen purely functionally but had some significance in themselves is suggested by the careful choice of funerary and other specific scenes to decorate them; that it was thought necessary for the vessel to bear some relation to the dead person is indicated by the Attic Protogeometric practice of using neck-handled amphorae for the ashes of men and belly-handled or shoulder-handled amphorae for women.

Is there any evidence to suggest that in the Early Iron Age, as in the Bronze Age, the jar (though used for burial of both sexes) was itself symbolically seen as female and perhaps as a womb? We lack the numerous clearly anthropomorphic vessels of the Bronze Age, whose breasts informed us as to their female sex; however examples from Crete, such as the vessel in the shape of a female figure on **Fig. 331a**, show that the concept was not entirely lost there, and the nipples on **Fig. 331d** clearly indicate continuity. There is also what might be described as a 'woman-in-a-jar' from Crete in the shape of the late ninth century model sanctuary shown on **Fig. 331b**. The small circular model, fitted with lugs like a suspension pot, contains a female divinity; her debt to a Bronze Age tradition is evidenced not only by a similar item from the post-palatial period (**Fig. 246c**), but also by her arms which are raised in the familiar Minoan gesture. Hiller has recently highlighted the revival of this traditional gesture in the Geometric period (in Hägg, 1983, 92-3, 99). It is also interesting to note a marked resemblance between the positioning of the dog(?) on the roof of this sanctuary, and that of the dog on an Early Minoan lid from the cemetery of Mochlos (**Fig. 112h**). Coldstream comments: 'One would expect the model to have some bearing on the mysteries of death and the afterlife, since it was found in a tomb; I see the building as Hades, the House of the Dead, where a corn goddess such as Persephone is compelled to spend six months of each year' (1977, 10). Such an interpretation, if correct, would provide a further hint about the Bronze Age derivation of the Persephone figure. A ritual connotation, and an association with women and with funerary ideas, is again suggested by an unusual kernos, also from Crete (**Fig. 331c**). This shows two apparently female figures, one of whom from her gesture of raised arms would seem to be mourning, forming a circle with six pithoi. An interesting placing of the jug is at the tail of a horse-shaped askos (**Fig. 310e**) from a tomb at Tekke. Two pots appear on the back of a horse from the fill of Tomb 51 at Lefkandi (**Fig. 310j**). Moreover a speculative suggestion made above (p.43) is recalled by the recent discovery at Protogeometric Torone of a potter's kiln in the cemetery area (*AR* 1982-3, 43).

The identification of the jar with fertility in Bronze Age symbolism was partly reflected in the appearance of vessels in conjunction with a scene suggesting male/female union (see **Fig. 82b**); it was also noted that of animals the goat and the goat alone is the one which is shown engaged in the act of coupling in the Bronze Age (see **Figs. 113** and **172 f** and **g**). These associations continue in Iron Age iconography. An archaic gem from Athens in the shape of a cube shows love-making on one face, and two women standing by a jar (one playing pipes) on another face; the other two faces show two goat at a tree, and joined goats with bird and lizard, respectively (**Fig. 332a**). A Cretan seal shows goats mating and, on the reverse face, a scene of love-making juxtaposed with a jar (**Fig. 332b**). Matz took this for a Bronze Age seal (1928, Tafel IX, 24). We do not need to follow Boardman's interpretation of this last scene as 'A seated man and a standing woman' (1970, 137). His recognition that 'the artist meant to convey some sort of bodily contact with the man' leads him to consider Davies' suggestion that the scene shows Clytemnestra killing Agamemnon, but we do not have to look so far. A close inspection of the bodily contact reveals that it is of a very intimate nature and the similarity to the positions shown on **Fig. 82c** and **Fig. 329b**, as well as the juxtaposition with the goats whose activity is quite explicit, suggest that sexual activity is the most plausible explanation. Nor is the theme an uncommon one for the period: one can point not only to **Fig. 332a** but also to **Fig. 332c**, a sixth century Melian gem on which an unambiguous scene shows 'Love making, with a swan in attendance and a swastika' (Boardman, 1970, 137) and again linked with the goat motif, backing onto a chimaera with a star and disc in the field. It would seem, then, from **Fig. 332 a** and **b** that in the Early Iron Age the vessel continued to be associated not only with the woman, but also with ideas about fertility.

Earlier in this study I discussed the role played in Bronze Age religious ideas by the stone, a role which has often been emphasized, as for example by Evans: 'the baetylic stone was always at hand as a material home for the spiritual being, brought down into it by due ritual' (1931, 13). In this study the apparent interchangeability of the stone and the jar in certain Bronze Age rituals in which they were leant over, or plant life emerged from them (see **Fig. 241**) was used as the basis for the argument that the two elements played a similar role in Bronze Age religious symbolism. A continuing link between the stone and fertile vegetation is suggested by a Melian seal (**Fig. 323b**) which shows 'A centaur holding a branch and a stone' (Boardman, 1970, 136). (It is interesting that such centaurs became a symbol of primitive and anarchic opposition to Greek warriors.) Moreover, the stone continued to play a significant role in funerary practices, used both as a grave marker set vertically over the grave and, as in earlier centuries, to seal the burial container (see, for example, **Fig. 330**).

(b) The Literary Evidence

What evidence does literature provide of a continued numinous significance attached to jar and stone? Or of specific associations to death, rebirth or the female sex? A loaded and sentimental, rather than a purely functional, attitude to the funerary urn is expressed most poignantly in *Iliad* XXIII, 91-2, where the ghost of Patroclus pleads with Achilles to 'let one single vessel, the golden two-handled urn the lady your mother gave you, hold both our ashes'. A deep-seated symbolic identification of the jar as the home of the dead might be construed from an interesting couplet in *Theogony* 726-7, where Hesiod says of Tartarus that ἀμφὶ δέ μιν νὺξ τριστοιχεὶ κέχυται περὶ δειρήν; we have here a Tartarus which has a neck, and West points out that the implication is of a narrow entrance like a jar (1966, 360). A sense of the possible cosmic significance and numinous content of jars is also given by the *Iliad* passage (XXIV, 527ff) describing how Zeus has two urns from which he metes out the fate of humans.

The female jar

Achilles' jar came from his mother, and at *Iliad* XVIII, 348, we have reference to the 'belly' (γάστρην) of a cauldron; this raises the question whether Early Iron Age literature preserved the Bronze Age symbolism of visualizing the jar as the female body.

Hesiod's association of the jar with the female sex in the Pandora story is discussed below, but at this point it is relevant to discuss briefly his reference to the jar in the last section of *Works and Days*. This centres on the information he gives about fourth days. At the start of the section he informs us that the fourth is a holy day. At 797-99 he warns to avoid trouble on the fourth of the beginning and the ending of the month as it is a day fraught with fate. At 800-801 he instructs that the fourth of the month is the day to bring home your bride (with due regard to the omens). On the fourth day of mid-month, which is favourable for a girl to be born (794-5), it is a good day to tame sheep, oxen, dogs and mules to the touch (795-7), and to start building ships (809). Then he states (814-818) that the twenty-seventh of the month (which West, 1978, 358 believes should most likely be equated with the fourth of the waning month) is best for starting a jar, putting yokes on the necks of oxen, mules and horses, and for launching a ship. Then he states (819-820) that the fourth day is the day to open a jar, followed by the comment that the fourth of mid-month is holy above all. In this complex web of instructions a certain consistent pattern of symbolic associations can be traced. Of the instruction about yoking horses at 816 West comments that 'those who lived in places suitable for this form of travel could not seriously be expected to concentrate on a single day of the month' (1978, 361); perhaps Hesiod means yoking for the first time (Alan Griffiths, personal communication, 1989). Even so, it is clear that instructions such as this are of a symbolic nature, giving information about associated images as much as about what you might expect to do or not do on certain days of the month. While a sequence following the monthly lunar cycle could be imputed to the instructions, it does not hold throughout the passage. At 785 West points out that 'chronological sequence now yields to associative sequence ... The corresponding days in different decades sometimes have similar properties ... This shows that superstitious feelings attached to the numbers themselves: it was not all based on the aspect of the moon' (1978, 356). Thus 'the idea may be that any kind of 4th is holy *qua* 4th' (1978, 362). We can also pick our way through this passage to find more specific links between the fourth days of the month. Thus different fourths are good for a girl to be born, to bring home a wife, to open a pithos, and to start a pithos. A woman-jar symbolic identification appears to be suggested. Moreover, West points out that there is a certain logic in the middle fourth being put forward as the day to open a jar, to break in animals and to start ship-building, while the last fourth is the day to start a jar, to yoke animals and to launch a ship. Given the unwieldiness of this sequence as a practical work plan, we are again entitled to look for symbolic links, and in view of my argument about the identification of ship and horse as sun transporters and the association of both with a cycle of regeneration centred on jar symbolism, it is extremely interesting to find the horse and ship yet again paired together here and tied to instructions about when to open a pithos.

'Oak and stone'

Turning to the symbolism of stone in literature, we again find significant material. There is an interesting passage in *Iliad* XXI, 403-5 where in part of the landscape Athena picks up a large boulder 'which men of a former time had set there as boundary mark of the cornfield';

here again we find stones associated with the usages of people of the past.   An interesting phrase in the *Theogony* (35) is a proverbial expression traditionally thought to mean 'Why enlarge on worn-out or irrelevant topics?' Literally translated as 'Why all this about or around oak and stone?', its exact meaning is in fact highly debatable (see West, 1966, 167-9). That it was connected with the past is however suggested by the appearance of the same phrase in *Odyssey* XIX, 163, where Penelope asks the beggar Odysseus about his descent 'for you certainly did not spring from the traditional tree or rock', οὐ γὰρ ἀπὸ δρυός ἐσσι παλαιφάτου οὐδ' ἀπὸ πέτρης. The 'White Rock' (Λευκάδα πέτρην) past which Hermes led the souls of the suitors at *Odyssey* XXIV, 11, has also provoked much thought. Thus Nagy (1973, 141-7) draws from a variety of references in Archaic and Classical authors his conclusion that 'the White Rock is the boundary delimiting the conscious and the unconscious — be it a trance, stupor, sleep, or even death'. Interestingly Furley argues independently, from a different basis, that the use of stones or cairns as terrestrial boundaries led to their significance as boundaries between life and death (1981, 59). However that may be, in the *Odyssey* passage the White Rock is clearly a significant landmark in the journey of the dead.

But as well as signifying death, the stone also appears as a source of life. The theme of the stone as a womb or receptacle for regeneration is reflected in Penelope's reference to the tradition of birth from of tree or stone (cited above). West (1966, 167) refers us to a parallel Hebrew tradition of birth from rocks, at *Jeremiah* ii 27. In the Deucalion story, stones are again involved in the creation of people (*Catalogue of Women*, 234). The theme recurs in the story of the birth of Zeus in which at *Theogony* 477 Rhea is sent (tellingly) to Crete to bear Zeus, and then gives to Kronos a stone wrapped in swaddling clothes as a substitute for the baby; he puts the stone into his belly (*Theogony* 485-7). The account that the stone, when vomited back, was placed at Delphi as a marvel for men (*Theogony* 497-500) also reflects a continuation of the tradition of sacred stones. The later name of 'omphalos' given to the stone again affirms a belly/womb connection, and West cites an interesting Orphic account of a stone given by Apollo to Helenos who dressed it and treated it like a baby, and rocked it until it cried at which point it could be consulted for prophetic truths; 'One wonders whether the Delphic stone too was supposed to have mantic properties', West concludes (1966, 303). That it had is suggested by the scholiasts on the 'oak and stone' dilemma: Δωδώνη γὰρ δρῦς, πέτρα δὲ Πυθώ. If so, we have a solution to the dilemma in which 'tree and stone' are explicitly associated with birth, but also, as West points out, with speech (1966, 168): we could postulate Bronze Age religious beliefs associating tree and stone with fertility and with the regeneration or birth of human life, beliefs which also attached mantic powers to those elements, which could be reached in ecstatic states. The 'babbling' or 'chattering' qualities associated with oak and stone in Hesiodic and Homeric references could thus be seen as the disparaging attitude of a later age to such practices which were displaced by the more formalized organization of prophecy.

However that may be, our main concern here is to affirm the survival of a tradition which associated both the jar and the stone with death and with human regeneration. The continuing significance of stone symbolism in later Greece is affirmed by Page Dubois (1988, 86ff).

3.13 THE NUMBER THREE

It was argued earlier in this study that Bronze Age symbolism attached significance to the number three, and that triple and circular forms predominated in religion and in symbols of the natural world.

In the Iron Age we find that the number three retains some of its numinous significance, and is often used, especially in the context of events and activities relating to magic, fertility, birth, death and the underworld.

A selection of instances can be listed at random. Hesiod tells us that the snake in a secret place in the mountains gets three young every three years (*Catalogue of Women*, 204, 130); Demeter searches for Persephone for three times three (nine) days (*H Demeter*, 47); Persephone spends two parts of the year with the gods and one third of it in the secret places of the earth (*ibid.*, 398-400); in the *H Apollo*, 91-2, we read that Leto was nine days and nine nights in labour with Apollo; Hermes has three branches on his magic staff (*H Hermes*, 529-30); three holy prophetic sisters are entrusted to Hermes (*H Hermes*, 552ff); Hesiod tells us that at the ends of the earth, for heroes, the earth bears honey sweet fruit three times a year (*Works and Days*, 173): also that Tartarus is as far below earth as it would take an anvil to fall for nine days and nights and land on the tenth (*Theogony*, 725); moreover, night is spread around its neck in a triple line 'like a neck-circlet' (726-7). In *Iliad* XVIII, 344ff, the washing of Patroclus' body involves the use of a three-legged brass kettle (cauldron) and an unguent nine years old. West comments of Hesiod: '... he does very often arrange families in threes or multiples of three. There are three Cyclopes, Hundred-Handers, Gorgons; Kronos has three sons and three daughters; Hyperion has three children ...; so do Kreios, Ares, and Zeus with Hera; there are three winds, Horai, Moirai and Charites; thrice three Muses' (1966, 36 note 2).

The list could be extended, but there is also evidence of a more fundamental tri-partite symbolism, in a three-way vision of the universe. Thus in Poseidon's outburst in *Iliad* XV, 185ff, where, as brother of Zeus, he claims equal privilege to Zeus along with Hades, he states:

> All was divided among us three ways, each given his domain.
> I when the lots were shaken drew the grey sea to live in
> forever; Hades drew the lot of the mists and the darkness,
> and Zeus was allotted the wide sky, in the cloud and the bright air.
> But earth and high Olympos are common to all three.

Other views of the universe are of course also put forward, but the tripartite universe is a recurrent idea. Thus in the *H Demeter*, 13ff, we read about a flower so sweet-smelling that 'all the wide heaven (οὐρανός) above and the whole earth (γαῖα τε) and the sea's salt swell (ἀλμυρὸν οἶδμα θαλάσσης) laughed for joy'. Later in the same hymn (33ff) we read that Persephone remained hopeful as long as she still saw earth (γαῖαν) and starry heaven (οὐρανόν) and the strong flowing sea (πόντον) and the rays of the sun. Later still (85ff) we find another reference to the idea that Hades had received a share when a three-way division was made in the beginning. I have already referred above to the passage in the *Theogony* where Hesiod states that Zeus gave Hecate a share in the earth and the sea (γαίης τε καὶ ... θαλάσσης) and she received honour also in heaven (ἀπ' οὐρανοῦ) (412-4). The same idea is repeated a few lines later (423ff) with a slight difference: this time Hesiod states that Zeus took nothing away of her portion among the former Titan gods, her share as it was in the beginning, of honour in earth, sky and sea. As it predates Zeus, a great antiquity is implied here for this three-way division of the universe.

It is interesting to note that evidence also remains of the circular world view which is suggested by some of the Bronze Age material discussed earlier in this study, as when the Homeric poems refer to the circular stream of Ocean (see, for example, *Iliad* XVIII, 399 and 606-7).

Having picked out, in the last eleven sections, some apparent threads of continuity from the religious symbolism of the Bronze Age, I shall now turn to evidence of discontinuity, reviewing changes that were simultaneously developing in attitudes towards women and in the symbolism of sky and earth, sun, earth and vegetation, the jar and the human body.

3.14 DISCONTINUITY: WOMEN'S ROLE AND STATUS

Evidence for the social organization of the Early and Middle Bronze Age Aegean is disappointingly slender, as we have noted. However, it was pointed out above that what evidence exists does not indicate any marked discrimination between the sexes in areas like manner of burial, and moreover that much of the visual evidence, especially from Crete, shows women in central roles or roles commanding respect, particularly in the religious sphere.

Evidence for the social organization of the Early Iron Age is again disappointingly insubstantial, but literature now informs us clearly about a sharp division of labour as well as of well-developed attitudes requiring the two sexes to adopt distinctly different occupations and behaviour.

Thus in *Iliad* VI, 490-3, Hector sends Andromache home to the loom and the spindle, explicitly stating that the business of war with which the poem is concerned is 'men's work' (πόλεμος δ' ἄνδρεσσι μελήσει πᾶσιν). Penelope is similarly sent out of the public eye by Telemachus at *Odyssey* XXI, 350-3, as well as at *Odyssey* I, 356-9, where it is 'talking' that he claims to be 'men's work'. In *Iliad* XVI, 7, Achilles compares Patroclus' tears to those of a little girl with her mother, suggesting that such displays of feelings are more common in the world of females. Which roles and which behaviour are regarded as the better in the context of the poem is not left open to question. We repeatedly find that a comparison to a woman is used as an insult to a man. Thus in *Iliad* II, 289-290 Odysseus tries to stop the wailing of the homesick Achaean troops by comparing them to little boys or widowed wives. At *Iliad* VII, 96, when Menelaus wants to reproach the Achaeans for failing to respond to Hector's challenge he calls them 'women not men' (Ἀχαιΐδες, οὐκέτ' Ἀχαιοί). When Hector wants to taunt Diomedes in *Iliad* VIII, 163-4, he compares him to a woman and a wretched doll or puppet (γλήνη) and says the Danaans will dishonour him. Homer's romanticization of the male-female relationship, to which Arthur refers (1984, 14-15), does little to counteract the values expressed in such passages.

Nor are such attitudes confined to the heroic world of epic war. Starr (1962, 315) refers to a 'hardening of masculine claims to superiority' reflected in Hesiod and later aristocratic writers alike. Hesiod's description of farming life reflects a pronounced division of labour. It is clear that a slave-woman may follow the plough, but a wife may not (*Works and Days* 406), and that the place for a young girl is inside the house with her mother (*Works and Days* 519-20). The decisions involved in running the farm are evidently made solely by the man, to whom the poem is addressed. Hesiod also displays little respect for, or confidence in, women and is sceptical about women's motives. 'Do not let a flaunting woman coax and cozen and deceive you: she is after your barn. The man who trusts womankind trusts deceivers' he tells us (*Works and Days*, 373-5), referring, West believes, not to a coquette who wants to marry you for your property but to a wife, neighbour's wife, or slave who is caught poking into the granary and tries to get away with it by charming you. The misogynism of the passage is not lost on West, who comments that 'Women stole food because they were kept half-starved by their husbands, who resented their habit of eating' (1978, 250-1). Again, at *Works and Days* 701-5, Hesiod urges his readers not to make a marriage that will be a joke to the neighbours and warns against a bad wife who is parasitic and 'roasts' her husband without fire, ageing him before his time.

Hesiod is also explicit about attitudes to women in the area of sexuality. Phrases such as that in which he tells us that Theia was 'subject in love' to Hyperion before giving birth (ὑποδμηθεῖσ' ... ἐν φιλότητι) (*Theogony* 374) and that Rhea was δμηθεῖσα by Kronos before bearing his children (*Theogony* 453) imply a certain attitude to sexual activity: the same verb can be used for taming an animal or for killing someone. Whereas in the earlier Bronze Age material we find representations of women displaying sexual parts of their bodies independently of a male presence and with apparent pride, sexual activity is now associated with the subjection of the woman. We have here the early signs of that imagery whose later forms Gould charts (1980, 53), a way of thinking which 'associates women and their role in sex and marriage with animals, especially the taming, yoking and breaking in of animals'.

We have then in this period evidence suggesting a situation in which a sharp division of labour confines women to certain activities and roles, in which a certain degree of authority over the woman appears to rest in the man, and in which women are the object of disparaging attitudes in general and of ideas of mastery or domination in sexual activity. Arthur (1984, 23-6) has suggested that control over the woman, and especially her sexuality, was felt to be both essential and problematic as the result of specific social conditions, such as crucial dependency on the existence of an heir for the continuance of family rights over land (whose availability was increasingly restricted), and also woman's very exclusion from political responsibility, and liability to be transferred from one family to another, which made her allegiance to any particular social order, or even any particular family, dubious. Saliou points to the appropriation of daughters' allegiance by their fathers in early Greek mythology, and the emphasis on that relationship over the mother-daughter relationship; she suggests that in early Greece 'It is women's inferior status, their incapacity to exercise power directly, combined with their role of carriers of that power, which makes them valuable and dangerous for the paternal lineage' (1986, 190). Sussman (1984) has suggested that the need to control population growth led to changes in attitudes towards female sexuality, while urbanization and specialization of what had been women's household industries led to a devaluing of women's work.

Other aspects of social life in the Early Iron Age were discussed above, including features such as the social power of an aristocracy and a pronounced discrepancy between the wealth of different sections of society which was by no means so apparent in the material discussed above in Chapter 1. It now remains to be explored how these changes in the division of power, wealth and work roles, and in social attitudes, particularly towards women, may have been reflected in changes in those aspects of religious symbolism relating to women which were discussed earlier in this study.

3.15 THE DIVIDING OF SKY AND EARTH

In the Bronze Age we saw that much of the religious activity for which we have evidence related to the celebration of the earth and its produce, whether vegetative or animal life. We have seen that some of those ideas survived in the Early Iron Age. However, in this period we also see a shift of focus from the earth to the sky. Zeus, as we are repeatedly told, lives in the sky (ὑπέρτατα δώματα ναίει) (*Works and Days*, 8). While Poseidon at *Iliad* XV, 185ff, claims that he and Hades, as masters of sea and underworld respectively, have equal status with Zeus and an equal share of earth and Olympus, his very capitulation to Zeus later in the same passage reflects a shift of power away from the tri-partite balance he asserts. Zeus himself comments that if it had come to blows it would have been quite a fight (224-5), but he seems in little doubt as to who would have prevailed. Zeus' supremacy over the gods of Olympus is often stated, and is apparently maintained by brute force. Thus, for example, at *Iliad* XV, 128ff, Athena urges restraint on Ares: 'Madmen, mazed of your wits, this is ruin! ... he (Zeus) will at once leave the Achaians and high-hearted Trojans, and come back to batter us on Olympos'. As for the world of earth, we are explicitly informed of Zeus' power over the fate of humans; we are also told, as at *Iliad* XXI, 194-199, that Zeus is more powerful than rivers and Ocean:

> Not powerful Acheloios matches his strength against Zeus,
> not the enormous strength of Ocean with his deep-running waters,
> Ocean, from whom all rivers are and the entire sea
> and all springs and all deep wells have their waters of him, yet
> even Ocean is afraid of the lightning of great Zeus
> and the dangerous thunderbolt when it breaks from the sky crashing.

The power of Zeus, embodied in the thunderbolt, carries fear and punishment. It is significant that this punishment is clearly seen as being brought by Zeus from the sky, οὐρανόθεν (*Works and Days*, 242). The relationship of earth to this power is clearly subservient: in *Iliad* II, 781-2, for example, we are told that earth groans beneath the troops as she does beneath Zeus the thunderer in his anger when he lashes the earth about Typhoeus. The sky has become occupied by a masculine god and in this context the earth that suffers passively under the lash of Zeus has come a long way from the earth celebrated in Bronze Age religion. Whereas in the Early Bronze Age we found a heavenly body, the sun, placed as a decoration on a human belly, the separation between the heavens and the earth with all its inhabitants is now much sharper. West (1966, 198) argues that in Hesiod the sky is not thought of as a dome: 'Rather is the sky as flat as the earth and parallel to it.' In the context of the separation of heaven and earth it is relevant to review Hesiod's account of the creation of the world.

The story starts at *Theogony* 116ff: 'Verily at the first Chaos came to be, but next wide-bosomed Earth, the ever-sure foundation of all.' So Earth came first, but a few lines later she gives birth to 'starry Heaven, equal to herself, to cover her on every side ...'. Heaven takes exception to the children he fathers from Earth and forces them to hide in a secret place within her away from the light of day, until she, groaning, makes a sickle which her son Kronos undertakes to use. There follows the climax of the story (176ff): 'And Heaven came, bringing on night and longing for love, and he lay about Earth spreading himself full upon her. Then the son from his ambush ... took the great long sickle ..., and swiftly lopped off his own father's genitals.' The problems around childbirth attached to the stories of both Kronos and Zeus will be discussed more fully below. At this point it is relevant only to point out how clearly several themes familiar from later thought and literature appear in this story. Alongside the conflict between father and son familiar from the Oedipus story, and the alliance of mother and son against the father, we find a clear representation of the deceitful and potentially castrating nature of the female. Although Hesiod points out Heaven's wrong-doing in confining his children, the end of the story leaves us with a superior and desexualized Heaven and with an irreparable breach between sky and earth. The separation of a male Heaven from a female earth speaks of changes in the symbolism attached not only to sky and earth but also to up and down, male and female, light and dark. It remains to be seen what changes have occurred in this period in the symbolism associated with that dominant occupant of the sky who, I have suggested, may at one point have been seen as female: the sun.

3.16 CHANGES IN SOLAR SYMBOLISM

The many traces of continuity into the Iron Age of the solar symbolism which characterized the Bronze Age have been discussed above in Chapter 3.4-3.8. Evidence was presented suggesting that the sun continued to be associated with death, with rites conducted by women and in some cases with female deities, with the boat and the horse/horse-and-chariot, and with creatures such as the bird and the fish. However, in this later period we see a continuing process of assimilation of all these elements to a male deity or deities. Of the slender list of sites where continuity of religious observance can be traced through to the Geometric period from the Bronze Age, Coldstream (1979, 329-331) cites no fewer than four major sites (including Delos, Delphi and Olympia) where a change from a female to a male divinity seems to have occurred during the 'dark age'. Divine attributes will have been changing hands during this period and it will not surprise us if those symbolic elements with which we have been concerned, including perhaps the sun, are among them.

That the deities now associated with the sun are several, often confused in identity, and that various qualities and attributes symbolically associated with the sun are carved up unevenly between them might serve to confirm the thesis that it was not originally a male deity at all. Thus at *Theogony* 374 and 1011 (as well as once in the *Odyssey* and twice in the *H Demeter*) Hyperion is the sun's father, whereas in half a dozen passages in Homer and in the *H Apollo* Hyperion is the name given to the sun itself (as pointed out by West, 1966, 202). The name often applied to the sun is Helios, a male chariot driver according to the *H Demeter* though not in Homer. Whereas in the Bronze Age we saw the sun often linked with vegetative motifs, the Sun now has not agricultural but pastoral concerns: he owns flocks (*H Apollo* 411-13) and herds (*Odyssey* XI, 108), which Odysseus' men wrongfully kill with such disastrous results in *Odyssey* XII.

What distinguishes this solar symbolism from material such as the Early Bronze Age frying-pans is not only the male sex of the sun but the recurrent emphasis on the sun's power of sight. His eyesight which makes him a watchman of both men and gods is emphasized in *H Demeter* 62, whereas *Odyssey* XI, 109, and XII, 323, inform us that his eye and ear miss nothing in the world, and in *Iliad* III, 277, Agamemnon prays to him with a similar description. *Iliad* XIV, 345, refers to the sun whose light beyond all others has 'the sharpest vision'. The Sun plays the role of spy informing Hephaistus about Ares and Aphrodite's love affair in *Odyssey* VIII, 270-1 and 302. The sun is also described as 'looking' with his beams in *Theogony* 760 (ἐπιδέρκεται ἀκτίνεσσιν). It will be recalled that on the Early Bronze Age 'frying-pans' the sun was placed above a female pubic triangle in the position of the belly. The part of the body now associated with the sun in the Iron Age is evidently the eye. From female belly to male eye is quite a shift. What in the earlier period appears to have been seen as a symbol or source of regeneration is now imagined in a supervisory role. Paul Friedrich, commenting on the Orion story which we shall discuss further below, proposes an identification between sight and male sexuality: '... here and elsewhere sight and male sexuality are closely linked symbols' (1978, 41). We are told (as at *H Demeter* 70) that the sun sees 'with his beams', and Richardson points out that this is imagined not as a receptive but as an active function: 'The Greeks thought of the eyes as seeing by the light emanating from them, rather than that received by them' (1974, 173). One thinks also of Apollo's arrows, discussed below.

It is also interesting that the absence of light is associated with what is unpleasant: 'black Ker' at *Odyssey* XVII, 500, black anger at IV, 661. The sinister Erinys is described as mist-walking (*Iliad* XIX, 87). A value judgement is implied in which the invisible and darkness are seen as negative. This phenomenon will be discussed more fully below.

It is interesting, however, to note that Helios is not the only deity associated with this overseeing role. The *Works and Days* refers not only to Zeus' myriad immortal watchers but also to his eye which sees everything and understands everything (πάντα ἰδὼν Διὸς ὀφθαλμὸς καὶ πάντα νοήσας) (*Works and Days* 267) in order to keep watch for wrong deeds and, Hesiod hopes, to mete out justice accordingly. West suggests that we are dealing here with a piece of Indo-European heritage and proposes that 'Hesiod's Zeus with his spies and his all-seeing Eye, and Homer's Sun ... are evidently fragmented survivals of this Indo-European system' (1978, 219, 223). He finds in these passages traces of Zeus' original celestial nature in that system: 'The constant use of the singular, 'eye' not 'eyes', seems a legacy of the time when the sun was involved', although by this period Zeus was largely detached from the physical world (1978, 224). Again, we have a confused picture, with the emphasis on eyesight characteristic of Helios also partially ascribed to Zeus, not only in Hesiod but also in Homer (cf. *Iliad* XXIV, 296, 331), suggesting not the direct transmission and continuity of one tradition, but the collision of different religious traditions which results in the scattering of various symbolic elements to different divinities and different pockets of religious thought.

Listing those divinities who in Early Iron Age sources get a report of mortal misdeeds, West refers not only to Helios (who gets a report from his daughter in *Odyssey* XII, 374), and Zeus (*Works and Days* 252ff), but also to Apollo, who in a Hesiodic fragment and once in Pindar receives information from a crow (West, 1978, 221). More significant than Helios in the Olympian pantheon, Apollo seems also to have inherited certain attributes which belonged to the sun in Bronze Age religious thinking. There are some interesting elements in the *H Apollo*'s account of how the god staffed his shrine at Delphi:

> Then Phoebus Apollo pondered in his heart what men he should bring in to be his ministers in sacrifice and to serve him in rocky Pytho. And while he considered this, he became aware of a swift ship upon the wine-like sea in which were many men and goodly, Cretans from Cnossos, ... These men were sailing in their black ship for traffic and for profit to sandy Pylos ... But Phoebus Apollo met them: in the open sea he sprang upon their swift ship, like a dolphin in shape, and lay there, a great and awesome monster ... he kept shaking the black ship every way and making the timbers quiver. So they sat silent in their craft for fear ... (388ff).

A deity who can take the form of a dolphin and who travels in a boat: all this is highly reminiscent of the sun symbolism of the Bronze Age, and the fact that the sailors are Cretans would seem to confirm the source of this symbolism. Again at *H Apollo* 29 he rises from the waves. Christiane Sourvinou-Inwood has recently stressed the Cretan basis of Apollo's personality, and has suggested that many elements of his personality frequently ascribed to oriental influence can in fact be traced in Cretan sources (1983). Some association with the sun could also perhaps be detected in the behaviour of Apollo on arrival, when he leaps from the ship 'like a star at noonday' (ἀστέρι εἰδόμενος μέσῳ ἤματι) (441) and many flashes of fire flew from him and their brightness reached heaven (τοῦ δ᾽ ἀπὸ πολλαὶ σπινθαρίδες πωτῶντο, σέλας δ᾽ εἰς οὐρανὸν ἷκεν) (441-2), although similar language is sometimes applied to other deities. The dolphin connection is confirmed in the establishment of his cult of Apollo Delphinius, but now a new element appears in his instruction to his new officiants to 'keep righteousness in your heart' and to avoid disobedience and 'any idle word or deed and outrage as is common among mortal men' otherwise 'other men shall be your masters and with a strong hand shall make you subject for ever' (539ff; part of the text is dubious but its gist is clear). The dearth of written texts from the Bronze Age does not permit us to assume from the absence of textual evidence that such ideas about correct and obedient conduct were absent from religious ideas at that time; however, we have seen in Chapter 1 that in the early period there are few signs of the obeisance to an elevated divinity which is the prerequisite of such ideas. The moral superiority of divinity and the concept of punishment are explicitly associated here with this divinity who is in other ways reminiscent of the earlier Cretan sun-deity. Interestingly enough, the weapon Apollo makes use of for punishment is the arrow, as in *Iliad* I, 43ff:

> So he spoke in prayer, and Phoibos Apollo heard him,
> and strode down along the pinnacles of Olympos, angered
> in his heart, carrying across his shoulders the bow and the hooded
> quiver; and the shafts clashed on the shoulders of the god walking
> angrily. He came as night comes down and knelt then
> apart and opposite the ships and let go an arrow.
> Terrible was the clash that rose from the bow of silver.
> First he went after the mules and the circling hounds, then let go
> a tearing arrow against the men themselves and struck them.
> The corpse fires burned everywhere and did not stop burning.

In the material of the Late Bronze Age, evidence was found for the assimilation of the sun to a 'descending' male deity who is perhaps depicted with a long pole, a shield, or a fish (see **Fig. 259**). A small figure with a bow and arrow is also seen elevated in the field juxtaposed with an eye and an ear in one religious scene of the Late Bronze Age (**Fig. 241a**). The horse and chariot is ascribed to Helios in Iron Age symbolism; while there is no explicit early Iron Age identification of Apollo with the sun, he has inherited the fish and is perhaps also the heir of the elevated armed male figures of the Bronze Age. It is interesting that in the passage quoted above he is described as coming down 'like night'. His association with the boat might prompt us to identify him in some of the archer figures appearing on boats on Geometric vases (as on **Fig. 333a**) if I have been correct in suggesting that some of those scenes are not literal representations of warfare; but here we can only speculate. Sun symbols are certainly often present in boat and fighting scenes, as I have pointed out, and are sometimes closely linked with the protagonists (**Fig. 333b**). Apollo is himself, incidentally, also no enemy to the horse as *Iliad* II, 763ff, testifies.

A close relationship to the sun is again suggested by the partnership of Apollo with Helios to defeat the serpent (δράκαιναν) which the *H Apollo* tells us was at Delphi before Apollo. After shooting her with an arrow, Apollo claims ' "... here shall the Earth and shining Hyperion make you rot". Thus said Phoebus, exulting over her ... And the holy strength of Helios made her rot away there; wherefore the place is now called Pytho ... because on that spot the power of piercing Helios made the monster rot away' (368ff). It is not relevant here to enter the debate as to whether this passage can be used as evidence for the existence of an oracle of a female divinity at Delphi before Apollo was established there. What is, however, relevant is not only the teamwork of Apollo and Helios but also this antagonism to a serpent or snake which stands in contrast to the Bronze Age evidence in which the same religious ideas which appeared to honour the sun also honoured the snake. This passage recalls *Catalogue of Women*, 204, 138, in which the arrows of Zeus lay low the snake; perhaps the bow is a natural weapon for a sky god, and the snake now a natural enemy. In Homer the snake now appears in a prophetic context as a portent of horror, as at *Iliad* II, 308ff. In the Delphian context, we are witnessing marked changes, if not in the ritual practice of prophecy, certainly in religious ideas and symbolism.

In this context it is interesting to note that while the snake becomes a discredited and monstrous opponent in the above story about the prophetic establishment at Delphi, another creature celebrated in Minoan art, the bee, is placed in an ambiguous light in another passage about prophecy in the *H Hermes* 552ff which describes

> ... certain holy ones, sisters born — three virgins gifted with wings: their heads are besprinkled with white meal, and they dwell under a ridge of Parnassus. These are teachers of divination apart from (Apollo) ... From their home they fly now here, now there, feeding on honey-comb and bringing all things to pass. And when they are inspired through eating yellow honey, they are willing to speak truth; but if they be deprived of the gods' sweet food, then they speak falsely, as they swarm in and out together.

These bee-women (three of them, significantly) recall the half-bee half-human figures on Bronze Age Cretan seals, and may reflect a tradition surviving from that time (cf. the bees appearing on Cretan seventh century pottery). More will be said below about the fate of various Minoan cult animals.

To sum up the changes in sun symbolism to which I have referred: we see the symbolism associated with the sun in the Bronze Age falling unevenly to a group of male divinities. The chariot-driving role falls to one, and we see an emphasis on the sun's power of eyesight. If our interpretation of Apollo Delphinius is correct, the fish and boat attributes fall to an archer god who carries power of healing but also of punishment and who uses the bow and arrow to effect that punishment: a shift of emphasis away from the circular disc of the sun to its external and potentially destructive rays? While some of the Sun's attributes are assimilated to male divinities, meanwhile many of the creatures prominent alongside the sun symbolism of the Bronze Age become discredited and monstrous, as we shall see further below.

3.17 CHANGES IN SYMBOLISM OF EARTH AND VEGETATION

I pointed out above that the association of the earth, and particularly the cave, with the womb in Bronze Age religious symbolism appears to have continued into the Iron Age. However, these elements are evidently viewed in a very different light from the way they were seen in the Bronze Age. Whereas in the Early Bronze Age sun and womb were linked on the 'frying-pans', now what is stressed is the elevation of the sun in an overseeing role and the separation and superiority of the sky and its occupants as opposed to the earth and its inhabitants. Whereas in the Bronze Age we found the pregnant womb frequently celebrated, now we find stories of divine succession in which the workings of female pregnancy and childbirth are interfered with or taken over by male divinities. Whereas in the Bronze Age the vegetative and animal creations of earth were celebrated, now what is emphasized is not the earth's creativity but rather its secretness, its hiddenness, the awfulness of some of its creations and of the activities which take place inside it. Whereas in the belief system investigated in Chapter 1 the earth was apparently a womb for regeneration, and the grave a stage in a cycle of rebirth, it is now seen as a dead end, a cold dark place where people go when they die, never to return. Let us look more closely at some of these changes.

Firstly, those mythological stories in which the procreative functions of the womb are interfered with: we have already referred to the story of Heaven and Earth in which Heaven, disliking his children, hid them away in a secret place (ἐν κευθμῶνι) of Earth as soon as each was born; an action which caused Earth great discomfort and led to the castration of Heaven by his son Kronos (*Theogony* 154ff). What is interesting is to find a variation on this story recurring when Kronos himself swallows his own children, born by Rhea, so that no son of his could usurp his ruling position (*Theogony* 459ff). It is interesting that Crete is the place where Rhea is sent to give birth, and where Earth receives her son Zeus to bring up. West (1966, 298) suggests that in an earlier version Earth may herself have been the mother of Zeus, or Rhea more clearly a personification of Mother Earth, 'This would explain the part played here by Ge'. However that may be, what we see here is the same story reduplicating: both are about the father not allowing childbirth to happen normally. In one case he forces the babies to go back inside, in the other he swallows them himself as soon as they are outside. The child, creation of the woman's womb, is met in two ways: either by suppression or by assimilation. We have, if not 'womb envy', certainly disregard for, interference with, and disempowerment of, the workings of the womb. The succession problems of the divine royal family are not solved until the next generation, when Zeus settles the matter once and for all by swallowing his wife Metis in entirety, which West recognizes as a 'reduplication of the Kronos-motif' (1966, 401). As Arthur (1984, 24) comments, 'Hesiod makes a polar tension between male and female a primary fact of his cosmogony ... It is only Zeus who finally succeeds in escaping from the cycle, and he does so by learning to assimilate, rather than simply repress, the forces which threaten him'. He then gives birth himself to Athena, a female lacking in female sexual attributes. The myth could be interpreted as showing the attempts of male divinities over three generations to assimilate and appropriate the procreative power of the womb in the vocabulary of myth.

Earth's monsters

Meanwhile, many of the creatures born, and living, in the earth become objects of horror. The snake was an object of reverence in Minoan religion and its appearance on some Geometric funerary vases shows that it still had a place in cult; but it is also now given a very different kind of image and, if it is to be identified in the following passage, is stated to be the enemy of Zeus: '... in the mountains the Hairless one in a secret place of the earth bears three young every three years ... But when she becomes violent and fierce, the arrows of Zeus lay her low ... Only her soul is left, and that, weakened, about a small unformed den ... lies ...' (*Catalogue of Women* 204, 129-143). Instead of being celebrated as the source of life, earth becomes the home or birthplace of monsters. Thus Hesiod tells us about Callirrhoe who gives birth in a hollow cave (σπῆι ἔνι γλαφυρῷ) to the fierce Echidna, a monster who is 'half a nymph with glancing eyes and fair cheeks, and half again a huge snake, great and awful, with speckled skin, eating raw flesh beneath the secret parts of the holy earth (ζαθέης ὑπὸ κεύθεσι γαίης) (*Theogony* 295ff). Dreadful acts, like the eating of raw flesh, are consigned to 'hidden parts' of the earth, and the symbiosis of woman and snake, celebrated in the well-known figurines from Crete, is transformed into a grotesque hybrid monster. Echidna, the inhabitant of a cave under a hollow rock (κοίλη ὑπὸ πέτρῃ), gives birth to a family the members of which are all familiar to us from the same source:

> ... first she bare Orthus the hound of Geryones, and then again ... Cerberus who eats raw flesh, the brazen-voiced hound of Hades, fifty-headed, relentless and strong. And again she bore a third, the evil-minded Hydra of Lerna ... She was the mother of Chimaera who breathed raging fire, a creature fearful, great, swift-footed and strong, who had three heads, one of a grim-eyed lion, another of a goat, and another of a snake, a fierce dragon; in her forepart she was a lion; in her hinderpart, a dragon; and in her middle, a goat, breathing forth a fearful blast of blazing fire ... Echidna ... brought forth the deadly Sphinx ..., and the Nemean lion, ... a plague to men' (*Theogony* 309ff).

The dog, the lion, the snake and the goat: the very creatures who appear as motifs revered in Bronze Age religion are now selected for inclusion in a list of anti-social monsters. These animals receive an equally bad press in other aspects of Early Iron Age literature. The dog of Hades is mentioned also in Homer (e.g. *Iliad* VIII, 368), and there are several uncomplimentary references to dogs in the *Iliad*, as at XIII, 623, where Menelaus refers to the Trojans as dogs. The Chimaera also appears in *Iliad* VI, 179, and a three-headed serpent is among the terrifying symbols on Agamemnon's shield (*Iliad* XI, 39). In the *Catalogue of Women* 226 the snake of Cychreus was driven out by Eurylochus as defiling the island, but interestingly was received by Demeter at Eleusis and became her attendant. The lion, celebrated in Minoan art, is described as the eternal enemy of man at *Iliad* XXII, 262.

Are we to think it a coincidence that these monsters are derived from Minoan religious symbolism? And what are we to make of the fact that the same creatures appear as the enemies of Heracles in story (*Theogony* 313ff) and picture? Thus the bow fibula on **Fig. 334a** shows on one side the slaying of the Stymphalian birds, and on the other the scene of Heracles killing the Nemean lion, behind whom on the picture Schweitzer identifies a scorpion (1971, 214). The bow fibula on **Fig. 334b** shows Heracles struggling with the Hydra while 'His feet are being menaced by Hera's crab' (Schweitzer, 1971, 214). Sourvinou-Inwood sees such phenomena as the result, not of coincidence, but of attitudes to women and to death, suggesting that 'this image of dangerous female monsters bringing about death is ... the mythological expression of two fundamental fears, the fear of death and the fear of the alien female nature, as seen through the eyes of the "establishment world" of men, two fears which have been fused into one, into a model of death caused by a polarized version of the female' (1979, 245).

Earth and a new view of death

The changed conception of earth does go together with what seem to be different ideas about death. In the belief system discussed in Chapter 1, it was suggested that the earth was associated with birth and also with rebirth: graves often faced east and had doors. Now, however, those who go into the ground stay there; their disembodied ghosts cross the Ocean to the gloomy realm of Hades from which they never return. When Odysseus visits the dead he finds ineffectual disembodied ghosts who flutter to and fro with 'a moaning that was horrible to hear'. In his famous speech, Achilles tells Odysseus that he would rather be a serf in the house of a landless man than king of all these dead men. The shades of the Trojan War heroes are there, battle wounds gaping, still nursing anxieties and resentments from their lives with all the cares of the living and none of the joys. The celebrated individualism of the heroic ethos is perhaps inconsistent with the older belief system in which certain of such mortal associations seemed to be shed (as the body became disregarded after a time in Bronze Age funerary customs) prior to some form of rebirth in a cycle of regeneration. Sourvinou-Inwood has blamed the widening horizons of the Greek world and the break-up of the small tight-knit community for a change in attitude towards death which started in the eighth century: 'the feeling of one's personal identity which death terminates becomes stronger than that of death as a collective phenomenon, part of the world's life-cycle' (1983b, 45). She cites factors such as the shifting of the funeral feast away from the grave, the trend away from intramural burials, the hardening of death-related pollution beliefs and the use of more individualized grave monuments as evidence of feelings of anxiety about survival, and fear and revulsion towards death which continued to increase from the Archaic age onwards. (See also Parker, 1983, 34ff.)

In this new and grimmer picture of death, the earth is seen as a female being who receives the dead in her 'bosom' or 'lap' (κόλπος) and who holds them down fast (*Iliad*, III, 243; XXI, 62-3, etc.). Death is variously described as dark, dank and chill, and earth contains 'the houses of the dead ... ghastly and mouldering, so the very gods shudder before them' (*Iliad* XX, 63-5); we can detect a decisive shift from the time when the bones of the dead were ground for ritual, and a skull could live in a domestic shrine, as in Early Bronze Age Crete. While I have argued that in the Bronze Age a belief in some form of regeneration left people free to sweep aside or use bones, it now seems that bones can be the objects of exaggerated respect; an example is the anxiety of some Geometric gravediggers at Eleusis to placate some bones they had accidentally disturbed, as described by Mylonas (1961, 62). Parker points to evidence for death pollution in Homer (1983, 66ff). *Odyssey* XI makes it clear that the idea of punishment after death is now present. Death now appears to be a completely negative experience and the Earth a powerful and devouring female personification who has many strong men in her lap and 'holds them down'. The female personification of earth was strengthened, according to Saliou, when women were removed from work on, and ownership of, the land; she suggests that it represents the opposite of the valuation of women (1986, 204).

The general picture is of a discrediting or demotion of the role of Earth simultaneous with the affirmation of the superiority of sky deities. Another item which in the Bronze Age appeared to be a womb symbol, the jar, also now starts to be seen in an ambivalent or negative light. The changes in symbolism of both earth and jar are crystallised in the story of Pandora, to which we now turn.

3.18 PANDORA'S JAR

Many of the changes in the symbolism of the jar which seem to appear in the Early Iron Age are embodied in the story of Pandora. The most important expressions of this story in this period are in Hesiod *Works and Days* 42-105 and *Theogony* 561-612. A short excerpt from each version will call to mind the salient points of the story. We start when Zeus is telling Prometheus that as a punishment for his stealing fire:

> "I will give men as the price for fire an evil thing in which they may all be glad of heart while they embrace their own destruction" ... And he bade ... Hephaestus make haste and mix earth with water and to put in it the voice and strength of human kind, and fashion a sweet, lovely maiden-shape ...; and Athene to teach her needlework and the weaving of the varied web; and golden

Aphrodite to shed grace upon her head and cruel longing and cares that weary the limbs. And he charged Hermes ... to put in her a shameless mind and a deceitful nature ... And he called this woman Pandora ...

For ere this the tribes of men lived on earth remote and free from ills and hard toil and heavy sicknesses ... But the woman took off the great lid of the jar with her hands and scattered all these and her thought caused sorrow and mischief to men. Only Hope remained there in an unbreakable home within under the rim of the great jar, and did not fly out at the door ... But the rest, countless plagues, wander amongst men; for earth is full of evils and the sea is full (*Works and Days*, 57-101).

... from her (Pandora) is ... the deadly race and tribe of women who live amongst mortal men to their great trouble ... And as in thatched hives bees feed the drones whose nature is to do mischief ... even so Zeus who thunders on high made women to be an evil to mortal men, with a nature to do evil. And he gave them a second evil to be the price for the good they had: whoever avoids marriage and the sorrows that women cause, and will not wed, reaches deadly old age without anyone to tend his years ... And as for the man who chooses the lot of marriage and takes a good wife suited to his mind, evil continually contends with good (*Theogony*, 590-610).

West has pointed out the difference between the two versions: in the *Theogony* version woman is the evil in herself, whereas in the *Works and Days*, with the addition of the jar motif, she is the instrument of a comprehensive calamity explaining the hardship of life in general and not just the hardship caused by women (1966, 307). He cites sources for similar traditional stories from other parts of the world and comments that 'It is different with Eve, but noteworthy that her eating of the forbidden fruit brings about a κρύψις βίου as well as loss of immortality and suffering for women' (1978, 155).

West also reviews later evidence identifying Pandora as the name of a chthonic goddess, sometimes identified with Ge. Among the evidence he cites are vases showing a female ascending from the earth, including a fifth century Oxford krater on which this figure is named as 'Pandora'. He adopts a contradictory position in which he denies that Pandora has a chthonic nature while concurring that Pandora represents the earth and suggesting that the myth states that man was born from the land. There seems little doubt about the identification of Pandora with earth. She is made of earth mixed with water (*Works and Days* 61), and apart from the vase illustrations we have examples of the use of the epithet πανδώρα with Ge, as well as the association of Pandora with Ἀνησιδώρα, a similar title of Ge or Demeter (West, 1978, 164); West also notes the recurrence in Early Iron Age poetry of the epithet ζείδωρος with earth, as in ζείδωρος ἄρουρα at *Works and Days* 173 and elsewhere in Hesiod and Homer (*Works and Days* 117, 237, *Odyssey* IV, 229, IX, 357): evidently epithets concerned with 'giving' have a strong and deeply rooted connection with Earth. The problem remains to explain how the title 'all-giving' is attached to a woman who brings disaster to the human race (the associations with Earth render Hesiod's explanation for Pandora's name at *Works and Days* 80-82, that all the Olympians contributed to her making, clearly spurious). The contradiction can best be explained by recognizing that the story must have changed from an original version in which the name Pandora was more aptly applied. West admits this possibility: he sees the jar as 'probably a pre-Hesiodic motif' (1966, 307) and suggests that 'the old story that man is descended from Prometheus and Pandora was modified in order to make the first woman a plague sent by the gods' (1978, 166). Such a modification, drastic as it must have been, can be seen as a highly consistent part of the process described above, whereby the celebration of the creativity of earth is replaced by mistrust and fear of its workings and of those of the woman and the womb with which it was associated. A similar shift of definition can be seen in the role played in this story by the jar.

This is not the place for a full analysis of the Pandora story, for which see, recently, Vernant (1980). Here we are concerned with reviewing this one particular aspect of the story: the role of the jar and the extent to which it reflects changes in attitude and religious ideas since the time of the Bronze Age.

We saw that in Bronze Age religious ideas the jar held an important and apparently positive place: it was touched reverentially, plant life grew from it (**Figs. 66, 230, 241**). In this story it plays a confused role, provoking debate as to whether good things were allowed to escape from it, or whether bad things were spread abroad from it. If the latter, why was Hope inside? The difficulty and inconsistency can best be explained by again recognizing that we have a story in transformation. West seems to settle for Friedländer's view that the Prometheus story and pithos motive were originally unconnected and 'that Hesiod has adapted an older version in which the jar contained only good things' (1978, 170). (See Friedländer, 1907, 44-5.) The confusion in the story seems to arise from the fact that the jar originally contained good things, but now contains bad things. A similarly ambiguous role is played by the jar in *Iliad* XXIV, 527ff, where Achilles states that Zeus has two jars in his palace from which to mete out to humans: one containing his blessings and the other containing his evils. We will think also of another container whose opening causes disaster, the leather bag containing the winds given by Aeolus to Odysseus (*Odyssey* X, 19-55); while the bronze jar in which Ares is imprisoned (*Iliad* V, 385ff) is a cause of suffering, almost death. Since jars were used for the storage of provisions, the only 'bad' things they might have contained were 'evil spirits', as West points out (1966, 307n). The notion of 'evil spirits' implies religious ideas of a kind for which we have little evidence in the Bronze Age. The shift in values as regards the jar reflects perhaps a changed attitude to death (the burial jar) as well as a changed attitude to the woman who was shaped as a pot from the Early Bronze Age and who again in this account is herself fashioned rather like a pot (duBois, 1988, 46) and is the one who is in contact with the fateful jar of the story and is the agent of unleashing its destructive powers. So perhaps the significant question is to account for the extremely negative attitude towards women in this story.

Furley (1981) asks the same question. Pointing out that both Hesiod's versions of the story take the viewpoint of the husband whose wealth is eroded by drone-like women, whose welfare is destroyed by the lifting of the pithos lid and who consequently is obliged to work in the fields, he comments, 'I cannot say *why* Hesiod's myth is so mysogynist in tone: the fact is, the advent of a wife seems to have been equated in the male view with the origin of evil and difficulty' (1981, 191). He draws an ingenious parallel between the Prometheus/Pandora story and later Greek marriage rituals in which fire (signifying warmth and contact with the gods) is brought to the groom's house at the same time as the ambivalent benefit of the new wife who will deplete his stores (just as Pandora opened the jar). He argues that this social reality underlying the myth accounts for Hesiod's detailed retelling of it, and states his interest in showing 'how myth draws on, and is nourished by, the everyday soil in which it is rooted' (1981, 199).

This analysis is helpful as far as it goes, but he does not take the matter one stage further to account for the male-centered view of the world in which the woman (who evidently worked as hard as the man) is the source of all evil and the depleter of stores while the man (who presumably ate as much as the woman) is not. If we dig deeper into that 'everyday soil' at the roots of the myth to which Furley refers, we find forms of social organization and beliefs which inform both the myth and the marriage rituals. These, as mentioned above, appear to have included the accordance of second-class citizenship to women and a generally derogatory attitude towards their social role and worth. As women are also the sexual partners of man in the reproductive act, we might expect these beliefs inevitably to draw in their train a derogatory or at least ambivalent attitude towards sexuality. Hesiod shows amply that this is indeed the case. When Aphrodite sheds desire onto Pandora, it is cruel desire (πόθον ἀργαλέον). The woman who looks so sweet has a bitch's mind and a deceitful nature (*Works and Days*, 67): among Aphrodite's portions at the first are not only delight and love, but also deceit. Women, as social inferiors, taint what they carry and sexuality becomes something potentially harmful or degrading. Furley comments of the Pandora story that 'the various attributes of human versus divine existence are made to focus on the unfortunate dependence on women' (1981, 199). Vernant (1980, 177) makes the same point, commenting that in the story one of the main things differentiating men from gods is the woman, seen both as wife and as bestial stomach. The belly's creative reproductive role no longer valued, it becomes seen as destructive, baneful, importunate, bitchy (see *Odyssey* XV, 344, XVII, 473, XVIII, 54, VII, 216). To feed it man, unlike the gods, has to work in the fields, and this lot is inextricably linked with the existence of woman: 'The figure of Pandora represents this "bitchiness" of the belly which characterizes the human condition once it has been separated from the gods ... But the appetite of the female belly craves not only food but also sex' (Vernant, 1980, 179).

In this attitude to the belly we have perhaps the first signs of a symbolism which Padel has traced in later Greek material (1983). While pointing out that the 'splanchna' remain important in divination, and the belly is the medium into which the divine is thought to penetrate, she comments that it becomes a dark inner space, linked with the underworld, a creative place but its products frightening. Women are identified with this dark enclosed space; Padel refers to the notion of women's sexuality as polluting men, while woman becomes, as often in tragedy, 'a sexual and social emblem of inner suffering'. From a creative and radiant vessel to an inwardly pained one is a long transition, and in the ambivalent jar of Pandora it has perhaps just started.

DuBois traces a parallel in the later changing mataphors of the female body from a self-sufficient and parthenogenetic earth to a field and then a furrow dependent on male sowing: from the 'fruitful inside' to 'mere receptacle' (1988, 106-7, 39ff).

By the time of Hesiod, woman has become a symbol of mortality. Since the woman is inferior, the sexual feelings of desire which attract a man to her are suspect; this leads to the paradox where he delights in embracing something evil to him (τέρπωνται κατὰ θυμὸν ἑὸν κακὸν ἀμφαγαπῶντες) (*Works and Days*, 58). West cites various examples of this paradox of taking pleasure in an affliction (1978, 157). By creating an enemy in his home, man has also created an internal enemy in his breast: his sexual desires and pleasures. Man is condemned to an eternal tension, for even if he gets a good wife, evil continually contends with the good (ἀπ' αἰῶνος κακὸν ἐσθλῷ ἀντιφερίζει ἐμμενές) (*Theogony*, 609-610). Internally, he is also condemned to a continual tension and struggle with an apparently new-found enemy, the sexuality carried in his body. Henceforth, as Vernant has it, 'L'existence humaine ... est placée sous le signe du mélange entre biens et maux, de l'ambigu, de la duplicité' (1974). Thus Gould can trace in later Greek myth and tragedy themes of male ambivalence, anxiety, fear and antagonism towards women and their sexuality, which is imagined as bringing destruction and death (1980, 54-7). Whereas in the Bronze Age we saw representations of apparently religious connotation celebrating the pregnant female body, in the context of the Pandora story the womb and the woman are seen primarily as a vehicle for the man to have heirs. Whereas in the Bronze Age the body appeared to be celebrated in its own right, it is now highly ambivalent, and through his sexual connection with the woman it is that which marks man down as less than divine.

3.19 AMBIVALENCE AND THE DIVIDED BODY

The changed symbolism of the body in this period is reflected in several ways: in the application of dualities of good and bad to different sides of the body in a growing emphasis on binary symbolism (as opposed to the trinary symbolism noted in the Bronze Age); in ideas about flesh and mortality apparently reflected in sacrificial rituals; and in beliefs about bodily control which classify certain of the body's more physical functions as inferior to others. I shall refer to each of these aspects and then investigate how this body symbolism combines with the changed symbolism of earth and sky, male and female in some mythological stories of the period.

One way in which a new binary symbolism of the body is reflected is in the discrimination between the right side as positive and the left side as negative in the telling of portents, as for example when lightning on the right is described as a good sign at *Iliad* II, 353, and there are many other instances in Homer. Another example of binary symbolism is in the appearance of a distinction between the mind or soul and the body. This is perhaps reflected in the Pandora story discussed above, and in other literary accounts referring to sacrificial rituals, which will now be discussed.

The distinction between spirit and matter

Of the *Theogony* version of Prometheus' trickery towards Zeus about the ox sacrifice, West comments that 'The Homeric practice of laying pieces of raw meat upon the bones (ὠμοθετεῖν) probably originated as sympathetic magic, assisting the flesh to grow again. It was only later, when the god was held to come and feast with the men ... or when the smoke and vapour was held to carry the god's share of the meal up to him in heaven, that a sense of the unfairness of the apportionment developed and gave rise to the Prometheus myth' (1966, 306). He is here following Meuli's and Burkert's interpretation of the act of ὠμοθετεῖν as being a symbolic reconstitution of the whole animal's flesh. Vernant suggests that sacrifice recalls a golden age when men dined with the gods free from afflictions such as work, old age and women, but by the division of the animal serves as a reminder that that age is definitely over (1979, 43-4). Furley follows Vernant's analysis of the sacrificial division as offering smoke and savour to the gods because that is incorruptible, while men get the meat 'as befitting their corporeal and perishable condition. Thus the physical division of the animal matches the existential distinction between men and gods' (Furley, 1981, 5). He points out the concurrence of this with Leach's view that as sacrifice is a gift to a being in the Other World, the 'soul' or metaphysical essence of the gift must be sent along the same route as the dead man travels to reach the other world, and must therefore first be separated from its material body by killing (Leach, 1976, 82-3). Furley points out at length the parallels between funerary and sacrificial rituals in order to strengthen the case for accepting this conceptual analysis of Homeric sacrifice. If he is right, his argument raises two relevant issues for us. One is the clear distinction between spirit and matter evident in such beliefs. Another is the question of the source of these forms of sacrifice with their attendant beliefs. Furley cites Burkert's location of the classical and Homeric burnt offering on a raised open-air altar within the Semitic tradition rather than that of the pre-dark age Aegean, and comments 'It seems to me then that there is no intrinsic implausibility in the theory that Homeric cremation and sacrifice grew up together in the Dark Age and formed an integral whole within the religious system' (1981, 36). His argument, based on the type of altar used as well as on the rarity of cremation in the Mycenaean world, would confirm my thesis that the appearance of a spirit/matter split in this period represented a discontinuity from the symbolism current in the Bronze Age Aegean. Furley traces other manifestations of this split, for example in the story of Thetis trying to eliminate the mortal element of Achilles (the body) by burning in order to make him immortal, parallel to the method used in sacrificial ritual to burn the god's portion of the animal into an essential form in which it can be transferred to the world of the gods (1981, 76).

It is relevant here to refer briefly to Greek vocabulary for the 'body' and 'spirit'. It has been pointed out that the common later term for body, σῶμα, is used in Homer only of the dead body, while a variety of words, μέλεα, γυῖα, δέμας, χρώς, etc., are used in Homer to refer to the living body. West is sceptical about Snell's inference from this that Homer had no conception of the body as a physical unity, but admits that while Homer had other words for the body as a visual object (δέμας, εἶδος) and as a repository of energy and strength (μέλεα, γυῖα), the term σῶμα encroached upon their territory in later Greek, as ψυχή encroached upon that of the Homeric θυμός (1978, 295). The encroachment of these comprehensive and paired terms for 'spirit' and 'body' on an earlier usage which featured a whole range of words might surely incline us to think that each of these paired concepts were becoming conceptualized in a more taut and focussed way in contrast to earlier ideas. In spite of various formulations (e.g. Adkins 1970, Claus 1981 and, most recently, Gill 1988), the central problem remains the same: that of charting the beginning of the emergence of the term ψυχή as a centre of self 'which is not body and which is related to body as master is to slave' (Claus, 1981, 1).

The pure and the impure: controlling the body

Mary Douglas suggests that concern with the definition of bodily boundaries can be correlated with a concern to preserve social boundaries. It will be relevant here to quote a passage of hers which will lead on to our discussion about beliefs concerning bodily control in the Early Iron Age. Douglas suggests that the more value a society sets on social constraints, the more value it will set on bodily control:

> The human body is the most readily available image of a system … the body tends to serve as a symbol of evil, as a structured system contrasted with pure spirit which by its nature is free and undifferentiated …

> … along the dimension from weak to strong pressure the social system seeks progressively to disembody or etherealize the forms of expression; this can be called the purity rule …

> … the human body is always treated as an image of society … If there is no concern to preserve social boundaries, I would not expect to find concern with bodily boundaries. The relation of head to feet, of brain and sexual organs, of mouth and anus are commonly treated so that they express the relevant patterns of hierarchy. Consequently I … advance the hypothesis that bodily control is an expression of social control …

... the more the social situation exerts pressure on persons involved in it, the more the social demand for conformity tends to be expressed by a demand for physical control ... (1973, 17, 100, 98-9, 12).

We have noted above prevailing views of Geometric Greece as a static and hierarchical society with a sharp division between the powerful oligarchs and other sections of the population, and we have also commented on the social control of women. It is therefore extremely interesting, in the light of Mary Douglas's remarks, to approach the specific series of controls to be exerted on both the sexual and excretory functions which are listed in the *Works and Days*. Here are some of the more interesting of the strictures which Hesiod lists about the boundaries to be placed on bodily activities:

> The best treasure a man can have is a sparing tongue, and the greatest pleasure, one that moves orderly...

> Never pour a libation of sparkling wine to Zeus after dawn with unwashed hands, nor to others of the deathless gods; else they do not hear your prayers but spit them back.

> Do not stand upright facing the sun when you make water, but remember to do this when he has set and towards his rising. And do not make water as you go, whether on the road or off the road, and do not uncover yourself: the nights belong to the blessed gods. A scrupulous man who has a wise heart sits down or goes to the wall of an enclosed court.

> Do not expose yourself spattered with sperm by the fireside in your house, but avoid this. Do not beget children when you are come back from ill-omened burial, but after a festival of the gods.

> Never cross the sweet-flowing water of ever-rolling rivers afoot until you have prayed, gazing into the soft flood, and washed your hands in the clear, lovely water. Whoever crosses a river with hands unwashed of wickedness, the gods are angry with him and bring trouble upon him afterwards.

> At a cheerful festival of the gods do not cut the withered from the quick upon that which has five branches with bright steel. (i.e. do not cut your finger-nails) ...

> Take nothing to eat or to wash with from uncharmed pots, for in them there is mischief.

> Do not let a boy of twelve years sit on things which may not be moved (i.e. tombstones), for that is bad, and makes a man unmanly; nor yet a child of twelve months, for that has the same effect. A man should not clean his body with water in which a woman has washed, for there is bitter mischief in that also for a time. When you come upon a burning sacrifice, do not make a mock of mysteries, for God is angry at this also. Never make water in the outpourings of rivers which flow to the sea, nor yet in springs; but be careful to avoid this. And do not ease yourself in them: it is not well to do this (719-59).

Although several of these precepts are practical (for example, not excreting in the water supply), the overall impression is of a natural world which is dangerous unless it is approached with a series of restraints and precautions. The emphasis on right living and religious observance through bodily control (over talking, excretion, timing and cleanliness) contrasts dramatically with the glimpses of energetic and ecstatic religion in the representations of the Bronze Age Aegean. We gain a clear sense of a body hierarchy in precisely the sense Mary

Douglas describes: thus the genitals are not pure enough to be displayed facing the sun, or even to be uncovered at night; urine and faeces are unacceptable and incompatible with the sun and rivers; sperm is incompatible with the hearth. West (1978, 336) comments that sexual intercourse is widely held to impair ritual purity. What will interest us here particularly is the role played by the sun. West cites later Greek sources which also suggest that 'Pollution in general is supposed to be hidden from the sun, as if its purity were defiled by the sight' (1978, 337). He quotes other sources suggesting an antipathy between a person in an unclean state and the sun or fire, particularly the hearth, which could be polluted by such a person (1978, 337).

Other body products, such as nail clippings, are also ill-omened and are to be excluded from religious occasions. While the Earth appears to have been one of the elements celebrated in earlier Aegean religion, now hands must be washed before the gods are approached. Women and what they touch (e.g. their washing water) is impure and dangerous to men; West comments that 'the danger is again, no doubt, loss of masculinity' from 'the contagion of the weaker sex' (1978, 343). One wonders also whether the potential danger in pots, if uncharmed, derives from their traditional connection with the female principle. Death again apparently is a feminine influence, for sitting on tombstones can make a man unmanly. West cites later Greek sources showing that 'the taint of death, avoided especially by those who especially sought purity ... was obviously inauspicious for conception' (1978, 337). This contrasts with the Bronze Age evidence for the association of human fertility with funerary practices (as, for example, in the discovery of phalli at tholos sites). The discrimination of women from men, and of the earth from the sky, appears to bring fear of what is now suppressed. Whereas in Bronze Age religion death was significant in ritual activity, apparently linked with rebirth and integrated to the extent that the remains of the dead were used in cult, we now find that funerals and even tombstones are anathema and dangerous to the whole process of religion and childbearing as well as endangering manhood. It is interesting that while sperm is unclean, the actual process of procreation (presumably in order to get the required heirs) is sanctified and has to be protected: another of the contradictions which the discrediting of women and of sexuality creates in this world view.

Overall, we can see that a circular model incorporating day and night, life and death, has been replaced by a linear model with purity at one end and impurity at the other; male at one end, female at the other; sun, gods and the male principle at one end, genitals and body products at the other. It is possible to draw from this passage of Hesiod two lists of incompatible warring elements of which, in each case, the impure threatens to endanger and pollute the pure and the incompatibility of each pair is clearly stated:

Impure	Pure
Unwashed hands	Zeus and the gods
Making water	Sun
Uncovering genitals	Blessed gods
Genitals spattered with sperm	Hearth
Burial	Begetting children
	Festival of gods
Unwashed hands	Rivers
Cutting fingernails	Festival of the gods
Uncharmed pots	Washing and eating

Tombstone	Manhood
Women's washing water	Man's washing
Mocking mysteries (literally: finding fault with unseen things)	The divine (literally: 'God')
Urination and excretion	Outpourings of rivers, springs

Here we are not dealing simply with an antithesis between male and female or between sky and earth: it is possible to see how those antitheses have become part of a complex web of symbolic antitheses including oppositions between the divine and the mortal, between religion and physical activities, between purity and impurity. It is striking to notice how women and burial rites, both apparently central to religious activity in the early part of the Bronze Age, are now regarded as dangerous or contaminating; similarly the genitals and the jar, both motifs which were apparently a focus for reverence in Bronze Age Aegean religion, are now opposed to the pure and to the divine. Parker comments: 'Sex is dirty ... By banning birth, death, and also sexuality from sacred places, the Greeks emphasize the gulf that separates the nature of god and man' (1983, 76, 66).

The attitude to physical activities expressed in this passage, together with the apparent crystallization of vocabulary for mind and body discussed above, and Hesiod's emphasis on Pandora's deceptive beauty and the ambivalence of the pleasure she brings, seem to offer us the first signs of what Vernant (1965) has described as a 'prise de distance à l'égard du corps', traced by Snell (1953) in the later lyric poets' development of the concept of the soul as a non-spatial element, separate from the body, reflected in their exploration of the contradiction between desire and action, past and present, involving themes of nostalgia, separation, longing, bitter-sweet love, emotional ambivalence and the pain involved in pleasure.

Polarity in the stories of Teiresias and Orion

It will be of interest to turn now to two more examples of mythological tales deriving from this period to investigate further how the female/male antithesis appears to be reflected in a conflict between sexuality or matter and spirit or spiritual vision. The Hesiodic *Melampodia*, 275, offers us the following story:

> They say that Teiresias saw two snakes mating on Cithaeron and that, when he killed the female, he was changed into a woman, and again, when he killed the male, took again his own nature. This same Teiresias was chosen by Zeus and Hera to decide the question whether the male or the female has most pleasure in intercourse. And he said: 'Of ten parts a man enjoys one only; but a woman's sense enjoys all ten in full.' For this Hera was angry and blinded him, but Zeus gave him the seer's power.

This passage raises the broader and complex question of the relationship of prophets to snakes in early Greek mythology. This relationship is clearly an ambivalent one: while snakes appear in a negative role in relation to prophecy (as portents in the *Iliad* and in the *H Apollo*'s story of the Python at Delphi), we also find attributed to snakes the power to impart the prophetic gift (as in the case of Melampous, *Great Eoiai*, 261). This will not surprise us, as we have seen that other symbols of Bronze Age antiquity, such as the jar, retain old associations lingering on, even while new and more negative associations are accruing to them. This Teiresias story shares with the Delphi story the pattern of aggression by a male figure towards snake(s), which culminates in the establishment of the male aggressor as a prophet; this may again reflect the discrediting of old symbols (the snake) and the appropriation of their imagined powers and qualities by the developing male figures of Early Iron Age religion. Structural analysis is not always the best tool for delicate areas of mythological ambivalence such as this, but here again we may use it tentatively as a sample of an approach which can be used as Greek religious ideas seem to reflect an increasing move towards duality and polarity. I have made this analysis independently, and rather differently, from that of Brisson (1976). While Teiresias' sex-change implies some form of association or identification with the snakes, his action of killing them is in the forefront here, and it is this new aspect of antagonism to the snake that we will focus on in this review of changes in symbolism. That they were mating at the moment he found them further illuminates a possible cause for his antagonism. It is clear that they were associated with sexuality, and his killing of them in the act suggests his hostility to this. We have already met the snake as the enemy of Zeus above (Chapter 3.17). In the second half of the story we have two opposing sides drawn up: one the one side Hera, the female who has a closer affinity with the pleasures of sexuality and whose power is used to inflict blindness; on the other side is Zeus who (apparently in spite of his many sexual exploits which perhaps have more to do with power than sex?) is pronounced by Teiresias to get less out of sexuality and thus to be superior in some way (witness Hera's wrath), and who is also able to confer the power of prophecy, the power to 'see'. In this story the female, sexuality and blindness are in counterpoint to the male and to spiritual vision. The tools which structural analysis has made available could be applied to this story and would provide us with a chart of polarities looking rather like this:

snakes	Teiresias
female	male
full enjoyment of sexuality	less enjoyment of sexuality
Hera	Zeus
blindness	prophecy or 'seeing'

A brief critical discussion of structural analysis follows in Chapter 4; this example, however, provides a context in which a structural analysis into binary opposites can be seen not simply in isolation or as a reflection of a universal symbolic law, but rather in a dynamic relation to a historical process and to a specific social structure.

Similar themes of sex, blindness and death interweave in the Orion story to which we now turn. I need to state here the difference of my approach from that of the structuralists, as followed by Fontenrose, which involves taking all versions of the myth as if they were synchronic and of equal value: 'So a feature found in a late literary version, though absent from earlier literary versions, must be taken into consideration, especially if we find a corresponding feature in a cognate myth. We must not too readily attribute it to late invention' (1981, 3-4). Nor, however, can one assume without evidence that a late feature is also early. Here I will adopt a contrary approach more suitable to my thematically limited and historically specific review of the myth: that each individual version tells its own story. Thus, although a different version appears in *Odyssey* V, 121-4, here we will focus on the story as recounted in the Hesiodic *Catalogue of Women* 148(a):

> When he was come to Chios, he outraged (literally: forced) Merope, the daughter of Oenopion, being drunken; but Oenopion when he learned of it was greatly vexed at the outrage and blinded him and cast him out of the country. Then he came to Lemnos as a beggar and there met Hephaistos who took pity on him and gave him Cedalion his own servant to guide him. So Orion took Cedalion upon his shoulders and used to carry him about while he pointed out the roads. Then he came to the east and appears to have met Helius (the Sun)

and to have been healed, and so returned back again to Oenopion to punish him; but Oenopion was hidden away by his people underground.   Being disappointed, then, in his search for the king, Orion went away to Crete and spent his time hunting in company with Artemis and Leto. It seems that he threatened to kill every beast there was on earth; whereupon, in her anger, Earth sent up against him a scorpion of very great size by which he was stung and so perished. After this Zeus, at the prayer of Artemis and Leto, put him among the stars, because of his manliness, and the scorpion also as a memorial of him and of what had occurred.

Here again my intention is a modest one of sampling the usefulness of structural analysis in charting particular tensions in the story. In this version the punishment of a sexual offence is blindness, which Orion is helped to remedy by the counter-acting power of Hephaistos the fire god and Helios the sun-god. As Fontenrose comments (1981, 11): 'If his eyes were gone, ... he had to get light from Helios or fire from Hephaistos to replace them. If his eyes were blinded but still present, he needed light or fire to rekindle them. In fact, we find Hephaistos identified with Helios: fire and light have an obvious relation.' What is new in contrast to earlier tradition is their association with the eyes of a male rather than, as in the EBA, the belly of a female (see Chapter 3.16 above). Moreover, here both Helios and Hephaistos appear clearly as representatives or champions of the male element, rescuing a man who has transgressed against a woman. We have already met Helios in this role above in conjunction with Apollo (Chapter 3.16).   The agent who inflicted the blindness, the woman's father in this case but acting on her behalf, goes *underground*. When hunting in Crete Orion threatens to kill every beast on earth, which apparently constitutes a statement of hostility to Earth and thus provokes her to send the scorpion to kill him (we are reminded of the scorpions apparently linked with the Early Bronze Age religious beliefs on the Messara seal-stones). The suspicion that this story is concerned with a challenge to those beliefs might seem to be confirmed by its reference to Crete. It is in Crete that the Earth is militant enough to react in this way to Orion's aggression towards her animal creatures, and why if not because of her strong tradition in this region? Here the opposing pairs into which the story can be seen as falling are:

Female sexuality	Orion
blindness	Hephaistos (Fire-god)
	Helios (the Sun)
	Eyesight
underground	
animals	hunting
	Artemis
Earth	
scorpion	
death	
	Zeus
	stars
	manliness

The clear lines of binary opposition are confused here by the role of Artemis and Leto intervening on behalf of Orion, slightly reminiscent of Athena's intervention against the traditional deities of her own sex on behalf of Orestes in the *Oresteia*; we know that in other contexts Artemis can respond very differently to the slaughter of animals (see, for example, recent discussion by Lloyd-Jones, 1983), and in the *Odyssey* version of the myth she responds very differently to Orion, being the agent of his death.   Here the punishment connected with a sexual offence, and the weapon of retribution by the female or someone acting on her behalf, is again blindness.   From other contexts we are familiar with the notion that blinding can represent a symbolic castration (as in the Oedipus story, the Grimm story of Rapunzel, the Victorian threat that 'masturbation blinds'); given its use as a punishment for a sexual crime, we may speculate whether it carried any such connotation here.   What is apparent, however, is that Orion twice offends against a female: once by raping a mortal woman, once by violating the female divinity Earth through senseless overkill of her animal stock.   Orion's penchant for hunting, making sexual advances and boasting emerge as common themes in the many versions of the myth discussed by Fontenrose, who comments that 'In these myths the sexual transgression may be replaced by a hunting transgression, as when Orion boasts that he will kill all wild animals on earth … Hence hunting appears to have a sexual meaning, among others' (1981, 255).   In our version Orion's punishment is blindness for the first crime and death for the second, but in each instance a male divinity effects his rescue, and the conclusion of the story sees him vindicated and elevated to a position of astral immortality in the sky.

In the Orion story, as in the Teiresias story, we can see a very marked change from the symbolic ideas reviewed in Chapter 1, not only in the apparent shift from a circular to an antithetical symbolic structure, but also in the proliferation of oppositions between male and female, purity and sexuality, sight and blindness, sky and earth.

CHAPTER 4: HOW ARE SYMBOLS FORMED?

The Greek root of the word 'symbol' points us towards something which is 'put together': an agreement, connection, comparison or link. Language itself is nothing but a set of symbols, and as Mary Douglas remarks: 'All communication depends on the use of symbols, and they can be classified in numerous ways, from the most precise to the most vague, from single reference signs to multi-reference symbols' (1973, 29). Thus at one end of the scale is a sign like the '+' or '-' sign in arithmetic, at the other end a symbol like a national flag with the plethora of emotional, social, political and historical associations which it carries. Cassirer has classified symbols by categories, dividing them according to subject matter into symbols of science, language, art and religion. He defines man as the 'symbolizing animal', suggesting that the symbol underlies all human expression and culture. He points out that whereas mathematical symbols are lucid and precise, the other categories are increasingly vague and equivocal, referring to something which may not be present or obvious. Symbols appear to be particularly potent and essential in the field of the metaphysical and it is with this area that this study in religious symbolism is concerned. Furley's (1981, 98) summary of Leach's definition of symbols as 'signs drawn from one cultural context (where they acquire meaning in relation and contradistinction to other signs) applied metaphorically in another' (1976, 9-16) will serve us adequately enough here. The pattern established by the relationship of a number of such signs to one another, sometimes termed a classificatory grid, is referred to in this study as a symbolic system. Our main concern here is with the process of symbol formation, seeking to address questions about what determines the use and form of symbols in a society, and how symbols change.

Symbolism is a wide-ranging area of study in very many different disciplines, including anthropology, theology, sociology, psychology, and literary criticism. All that is possible here is the briefest mention of some of the most significant theories of symbol formation to help locate the approach used in this study.

Theories about symbol use which have been current in this century have tended to be dogged by the notion of the 'universality' of certain symbolic associations, from Freud's postulation of a primordial symbolic language, and Jung's 'archetypes', to Lacan's ostensibly contrasting but arguably equally universal and static 'Symbolic Order'. This is not the place for a critique of such universalist theories of symbols, a critique already convincingly made by many anthropologists and sociologists (see, for example, Lane 1970, Jameson 1972, Sperber 1975, McDonnell and Robins 1980). These critics have pointed out a number of questionable assumptions underlying such thinking, including the assumption that humans have an innate mechanism to structure their experience in a certain way, and that symbols are a code, like language, rather than a cognitive process. Critics also point out that such theories have tended to omit any historical perspective and discuss symbols in the abstract, disconnected from any social context.

In contrast, this study discusses symbols against the background of their social setting and presents the case that this setting may play a part in their formation. Such a project questions the universality of symbols and requires an awareness of the relativity of the symbolic representations of our own society. This awareness is essential to an empirical investigation of symbolic schemes which may differ from our own. In particular, in the context of this study, we may need an awareness of our assumptions concerning male-female symbolism, an area which has often been prey to assertions of universal symbolism, although in fact it takes many diverse forms from one society to another. As Margaret Mead has remarked (1962, 30-1):

> The differences between the two sexes is one of the important conditions upon which we have built the many varieties of human culture ... In every known society, mankind has elaborated the biological division of labour into forms often very remotely related to the original biological differences that provided the original clues. Upon the contrast in bodily form and function men have built analogies between sun and moon, night and day, goodness and evil, strength and tenderness, steadfastness and fickleness, endurance and vulnerability. Sometimes one quality has been assigned to one sex, sometimes to the other. Now it is boys who are thought of as infinitely vulnerable and in need of special cherishing care, now it is girls ... The periodicities of female reproductive functions have appealed to some peoples as making women the natural sources of magical or religious power, to others as directly antithetical to those powers; some religions, including our European traditional religions, have assigned women an inferior role in the religious hierarchy, others have built their whole symbolic relationship with the supernatural world upon male imitations of the natural functions of women.

Thus in our own contemporary culture the 'Busie old foole, unruly Sunne' is generally envisaged as male, while, in spite of the 'man-in-the-moon', the moon is most generally imagined as female, as 'Diana's orb'. The Christian God is male, and what is morally good in him is associated with what is higher rather than low: thus the Book of Common Prayer refers frequently to the 'Lord most high', and the instruction is to 'Lift up your hearts'. Co-existent with the analogy of high and low is that of light and dark, life and death: thus, the 'God of God, Light of Light' is contrasted with 'us, miserable sinners, who lay in the darkness and the shadow of death'. We also find an analogy between soul and body: thus 'our sinful bodies' need to be chastised and 'washed'. The spirit is willing but the flesh is weak, and the embodiment of flesh in the Adam and Eve story, as in other Christian literature, is the woman. Thus upon the contrast in bodily function which Mead refers to, we have constructed a series of analogies between high and low, light and dark, good and bad, life and death, mind and body, spirituality and sexuality. As Leach describes this split as it expresses itself in myth: 'God against the world and the world against itself for ever dividing into opposites on either side: male and female, living and dead, good and bad, first and last ...' (1969, 8).

A further example which could be given is the split between the right and left hand. In his well-known study Hertz pointed out that qualities of strength, good and life are often attributed to the right hand, while weakness, evil and death are associated with the left, a distinction which, Hertz emphasizes, arises from social factors. He claims that a positive emphasis on the right hand appears in some societies as a result of educational bias, for there is no strong preponderance towards the right hand in the majority of people and 'the testimony of nature is no more clear or decisive, when it is a question of ascribing attributes to the two hands, than in the conflict of races or the sexes' (1960, 89).

The pervasiveness of such symbolic sets is highlighted in a recent study of 'Gender Advertisements' by Goffman, who comments (1976, 111-2): 'Floors are associated with the less clean, less pure, less exalted parts of a room — for example, the place to keep dogs, baskets of soiled clothes, street footwear and the like. And a recumbent position is one from which physical defense of oneself can least well be initiated ... The point here is that it appears that children and women are pictured on floors and beds more often than men.' Suggesting that in our culture 'high physical place' symbolizes 'high social place', Goffman goes on to point out that in commercial advertising photographs men are recurrently placed higher in frame than women, even when 'a certain amount of contortion is required'. Such analogies, then, between high and low, are apparently evidenced in a wide range of visual and symbolic representations within our culture.

This very brief mention of some of the most pervasive symbolic representations in our twentieth-century western culture has been included in order to highlight the assumptions which we may unconsciously be carrying into a study of Early Aegean culture, whose symbolism may emerge as being as unlike ours as its forms of social organization were different from our own. As Page duBois points out, 'We cannot equate our experience with "being human" everywhere, always, and forever ... the metaphors used by our culture are just that, metaphors' (1988, 186, 14). Some writers who accept that much symbolism is socially determined will still claim that there is something natural or universal about a dualistic view of the world, and much work has been done with the intention of proving that this tendency of Western culture to classify by binary opposition carries a universal validity. Thus Lévi-Strauss has found in the myths of primitive cultures many series of pairing contrasts between life and death, summer and winter, north and south, cooked and raw, family and non-family, and so on. This approach has proved attractive to many anthropologists and has led Leach to state that 'Binary oppositions are intrinsic to the process of human thought ... An object is alive or not alive and one could not formulate the concept alive except as the converse of its partner 'dead'. So also human beings are male or not male, and persons of the opposite sex are either available as sexual partners or not available. Universally these are the most fundamentally important oppositions in all human experience' (1969, 9-10).

Here again we find a 'universal' pattern of symbol being postulated. It is a significant leap from the recognition that some cultures employ binary opposition in their symbolic system to the claim that all do or that such a pattern is fundamental to human experience. A dispassionate perusal of anthropological literature suggests that this last is far from being the case. For a society which believes in reincarnation, life and death may be seen in terms of cycles or a wheel. In our society life/death may appear a clear division, but in cultures where people believe they communicate with spirits or leave their inert bodies to travel astrally during dreams or trance, the line is by no means so clear-cut or two-sided. Anthropological literature reveals that world views can come triangular, four-fold, or in a variety of shapes and sizes (see, for example, Needham 1979).

The symmetrical quality of certain aspects of the structure of the human body (eyes, ears, hands, feet, brain), sometimes adduced as an argument for the inevitability of polarized thought, represents only one pattern selected from several potentially recognizable within the body: thus there is the model of the digestive system (taking in and putting out); the blood (circulation); the principle of balance. In certain symbolic systems the circumference of the human being is defined as an egg-shape, wheel or circle, surrounding the extremities. The duality model is present, but its predominance in certain cultures is the result of a process of selection. Similarly, physical differences between male and female exist but, as Mead points out (above), those differences may be polarized in various societies into extreme and culturally specific symbolic dualities. The failure to question the universality of such dualities leads into far-reaching assumptions about the nature not only of human symbolic systems but also of human social organization. Thus Leach, writing on Lévi-Strauss, comments that 'The *basis* of human exchange and hence the basis of symbolic thought and the beginning of culture, lies in the uniquely human phenomenon that a man is àble to establish a relationship with another man by means of an exchange of women' (1970, 44). Such a far-ranging and loaded statement requires careful and historically specific validation from open-ended empirical work before we accept the view of the origin of human society to which it commits us; we must be open to the possibility that such theories may be inapplicable or inappropriate to the early Aegean culture examined in this study.

The entire process of tracing binary oppositions in other societies has recently been questioned. Structuralists have been criticized for turning a method into a theory. Mary Douglas has suggested that anyone going into a cultural field looking for pairs of contrasted elements will inevitably find them, and has questioned the usefulness of simply juggling symbols and their relationship with each other without regard to their role in relation to society; she comments that Lévi-Strauss '… cannot come up with anything interesting about cultural variations (which are local and limited) since his sights are set on what is universal and unlimited to any one place or time … To be useful, structural analysis of symbols has somehow to be related to a hypothesis about role structure' (1973, 95). We must therefore be on guard against a tendency to assume a universality of symbolic language or to draw out from Early Aegean material binary oppositions such as our own symbolic set will predispose us to find; we need to be open to the possibility of finding different forms of symbolic organization and of discovering meaningful relationships between those symbols and the society which uses them.

Non-structuralist anthropologists have postulated different causative factors in the formation of symbols, including the role played by the social structure of the specific society in question. Relevant here is Durkheim's view that all symbolic divisions and classifications are based on divisions within society. His argument is that the first categories which humans made were social categories, and the first groupings or classes of things were classes of people. These categories were then transferred to nature, and nature was seen through the same model, falling into the same groupings. The social order is thus strengthened and validated by its reflection in the natural world. Social divisions and classes are endorsed by appearing to be part of a vast metaphysical scheme of things. Symbols are thus a collective creation, a collective representation which reflects and endorses the unity of the group. Particularly concerned with religion and religious symbolism, he proposed that collective forces become represented and externalized as gods which then serve as a rallying point to ensure social cohesion. The reality behind religion is a social reality. The connections made between things, and the sacredness of certain objects were, he suggested, not intrinsic but attached to them due to social factors.

Durkheim presented a strong case for seeing the match between a society and its symbols, but in seeing symbols as a means of endorsing certain social groupings, he omitted to tackle the question of the origin of such groupings and thus ignored some significant factors including material and economic factors, and questions of conflict between different groupings. As a result, social groups are seen as rather floating and static, eternally married to their matching symbols, and there is no clear model for non-conformity or change in a society or its symbols.

The model for change and development absent from Durkheim's theory is present in the work of Marx who postulates that the means of production, the material subsistence of a society, is the base on which all other social institutions, groupings and ideology are founded and from which they are derived. The precise relationship which Marx postulated between economy, social institutions and symbols has been open to various interpretations. Here I will follow Raymond Williams in questioning the interpretation of 'superstructure' as simple reflection of the economic base, and seeing it instead as determined by 'the base' in a subtle rather than a crude or predictable way: Williams suggests that we understand the process of 'determination' as 'the setting of limits and the exertion of pressure' rather than 'a predicted, prefigured and controlled content' (1980, 34). He proposes that an accurate interpretation of Marx might result in seeing society as a totality in which the different elements to some extent also affect each other in a 'field of mutually if also unevenly determining forces' (1980, 20). According to this theory, the symbols of early Aegean society are not crudely 'caused' by, but can be seen in some meaningful relationship to, its means of economic survival and institutions of ownership and power. As Renfrew has pointed out, surprisingly little work has been done on the societies of Crete and Mycenae to examine 'the degree to which the prevailing religion was … used to legitimize the existing social system' (1985, 443).

Marx's theories were evolved primarily from his analysis of Western capitalism and it has been suggested that they are not applicable to primitive or ancient societies. For a people living so far from contemporary Western culture as the Early Minoans, and who did not necessarily make the distinction between 'economic', 'social' and 'religious' which we assume, it is hard to isolate their 'economic organization'. For example, if members of a society who depended on crops for their subsistence prayed while they watered them, is this to be considered of 'economic' or 'religious' significance? Should we consider the water 'economic' and the prayer 'religious', discriminating between them even if both had equal significance in the mind of the waterer, and the need to do both had equal influence in shaping other customs of that society? In relation to the problem of defining ritual, Renfrew highlights a similar difficulty: discussing Leach's distinction between 'technical' and 'expressive' actions, he asks: 'How are the two to be distinguished? The former are functional in a materialist sense. The latter are purposive also, and certainly functional if the intention is to alter the world … any given action may at once be both. This point, indeed, raises the whole question of the embeddedness of religious actions within the everyday practices of life' (1985, 15). Mauss too has pointed to the close historical association between magic and techniques, from hunting and farming to pharmacy, and has commented on the role of the 'magician-craftsman' (1972, 19, 142, but also 20). It has been pointed out that our distinction between 'sacred' and 'secular' may have no relevance to a Bronze Age society; a concrete example lies in the close association of workshop and storage areas to shrines and sacred areas in the Bronze Age Aegean palaces (see Hägg and Marinatos, 1981, 215, 217). The same dilemma occurs with the interpretation of many sealstones: **Fig. 335**, to take just one of dozens of possible examples, shows an everyday scene of potting or, more probably, wine-pressing juxtaposed with hieroglyphic signs and symbols on a Middle Bronze Age seal which probably combined a functional with an amuletic significance.

On the basis of similar arguments some writers on the ancient world have dismissed Marx as irrelevant for this period. Finley (1973) has argued that the ancient world was never a 'class society' in Marx's sense, and that status was a more powerful determining factor than economic considerations such as profit. Similar views have been expressed by Sally Humphreys (1970). This is not the place for a detailed discussion of their arguments. There are, however, specific writings of Marx in which he reveals an awareness that categories applicable to capitalist societies are not appropriate to pre-capitalist societies. He appears to have recognized that in a community organized by kinship and based on farming, economic considerations would be likely to assume a far broader form. He suggests that 'The establishment of the individual as a *worker*, stripped of all qualities except this one, is itself a product of *history*' (1964, 68); in primitive societies 'work' would not be separable from the individual's entire relationship to the community and to the land. Thus the object of labour is not 'the acquiring of wealth' but 'self-sustenance', a person's 'own reproduction as a member of the community' (1964, 74). Instead of alienation we find posited 'the natural unity of labour with its material prerequisites' (1964, 67). Human beings' relationship with the material source of sustenance, the earth, is compared to their relationship with their own body: 'The *attitude* to the land ... means that a man ... has an *objective mode of existence* in his ownership of the earth, which is *antecedent* to his activity and does not appear as its mere consequence, and is as much a precondition of his activity as his skin, his senses, for while skin and sense organs are also developed, reproduced, etc., in the process of life, they are also presupposed by it' (1964, 81). Living as he did before the development of anthropology as we know it, and before excavations in the Aegean area yielded significant information about the prehistory of that area, Marx is no authority for the specific problems it offers. What is relevant here, however, is that whereas in any society Marx suggests that social, religious and philosophic considerations are significant, and not simply reflections of an economic base, he here recognizes specifically that the actual economic relationship between primitive peoples and the earth has far broader ramifications than for those farming in a predominantly urban Western society. He thus posits the possibility of a culture in which humans do not exist in a landscape inhabited by reified objects upon which they act in a subject/object relationship (compare discussions of 'animism' earlier in this study). If individuals 'live in' the natural world as they 'live in' their bodies, their work on it and investigations of it will not be merely mechanical or manipulative but characterized by a sense of participation: the separation between production and religion becomes less meaningful. He makes it clear that he regards the essential elements of his theory as being applicable even to such apparently different societies. It is thus possible for us, while accepting that a contemporary category of 'economic' as a defined sphere might not have existed in the early Aegean in any such restricted sense, and that we may need to extend the category of 'economic' to be broader and embrace more factors than in contemporary society, to continue to regard it as a significant factor in the process of symbol formation. We may thus be able to look at a society as a whole, paying particular attention to those questions which are often omitted from a study of symbols: questions such as 'Where did the food come from?', 'Who held power and made decisions?', 'Who did what work?' and 'Who owned what?'.

We stand here, as it were, between two extreme paths. The one tendency which I have mentioned above is to write about symbols ahistorically, as if they were separate independent entities which descend arbitrarily out of the ether at certain points in time to be adopted by a particular society. The crude Marxist alternative might appear to be to tackle them, again as separate entities, but in this instance ones which follow directly from economic factors of production, ownership and wealth. A middle path, incorporating the theories of Durkheim as well as those which Marx clearly regarded as appropriate to primitive societies, would be to look at symbols as an integrated part of a society, involved in a complex and dynamic relationship with other aspects of that society's life, never totally separable from material factors but positively interacting with them and merging with them. Prayer, dance, religious images, status, respect, spiritual achievement, may all carry a significance and influence of their own in a society; but somewhere beyond them will lie a connection with physical factors such as the need for food, shelter and sex, and the way in which the satisfaction of those needs is organized within the society. The nature of the connection remains to be explored. This approach gives us a social context for symbols and also provides us with a model for change in symbols, concomitant with changes which may be traceable in the economic organization and social groupings within society.

Following this approach, it will be recalled that in Chapter 1 I reviewed some interesting characteristics of the Early (to Middle in Crete) Bronze Age Aegean society with which that part of the study deals. Among these characteristics were a strong agricultural base, a way of life not significantly oriented towards martial activity; a degree of collectivity in the organization both of the living community and of the burial of the dead; an absence of clear evidence of hierarchies of wealth or power; and signs of value or significance attached to women in the religious sphere. The question of how these elements may have related to the symbolic system current in that society remains to be tackled. The scope of this study does not include a discussion of the nature of this relationship for any of the three periods under discussion. The intention is merely to point out possible parallels or correlations which can be traced in this material without detailing how such similarities might have come into existence. The establishment of the existence of such parallels would help to lay the groundwork for a future more wide-ranging discussion which might have significant implications for our understanding of ancient Aegean religion.

Coming as we do from a culture in which, as noted above, binary opposition is a prevailing symbolic pattern, one of the features of the symbolism reviewed in Chapter 1 which may strike us most forcefully is the ubiquitousness of circular and triangular forms, whether apparent in grave construction and equipment, the designs which have been suggested as sun representations, the emphasis on the pubic triangle or the grouping of items in units of three. Pairs and two-fold representations are of course also found, but the circular and triangular appear to be integrated into patterns of graphic representation and symbolic thought to a degree which is perhaps unusual to us. The scheme of regeneration outlined in the discussion of this material in Chapter 1 would in itself indicate a focus on circularity, on the *return* of the sun, of vegetation, on the renewal of human life. This symbolic scheme, if it is accepted, shows sharp differences from a system of binary opposition which counterposes 'life' to 'death': the funerary customs outlined, with the use of the foetal position, the orientation to the reappearance of the rising sun, and so on, suggest that the relationship between life and death was visualized in a rather different way. In a culture which focussed on the cycles of the sun, light and dark might equally appear not as incompatible opposites but as different phases of one cycle. Several writers have pointed out the inapplicability of our notions of linear and progressing time to the view of the Greeks, who even in the historical period preserved a tradition of time as circular (West, 1978, 376; Cornford, 1950, 44-5). As to the discrimination between 'high' and 'low' which is part of the symbolic framework of Western Christian culture, it is perhaps significant that in our early period the sun does not appear to be symbolized as 'up' as opposed to what is 'down': rather we find an emphasis on its process of setting or rising, and at the same time find an image of the sun located at the centre of the female body, on the belly of the 'frying-pans'. The 'heavenly body' of the sun is not contrasted with the physical body, but resonates with it and in some way is identified with it. In the light of Mead's remarks quoted above, it is also interesting to note that in this culture it appears generally to have been the woman rather than the man who was most closely associated with the sun. We may speculate how this apparent identification of the female sex with the more powerful and generative (as opposed to reflective) of the heavenly bodies might have correlated with the relatively strong social position of women in comparison with later Aegean and contemporary Western societies. We might also comment on the apparent association with women of that powerful animal, the lion, to us a male symbol (the 'King of the Jungle').

Notions of death based on the sun's disappearance and return and the symbolism of the fertile female pot or vessel appear to have been based on the recognition and celebration of the female reproductive cycle and its association with the cycle of fertile vegetation. Such a symbolism could be correlated with, in fact it might be difficult to imagine in the absence of, a significant agricultural basis and a degree of social status attributed to women. Though the paucity of the evidence makes it hard to draw any firm conclusions, there are few traces of any formalized system of enmities between the animal and insect world and that of humans, or indeed between animals and insects themselves; the appearance of 'lowly creatures' and pests in religious contexts has provoked debate. If this last point is valid, it only serves to add to the picture of a symbolic system based on circularity and inclusion rather than opposition and antithesis. Attitudes to death seem to show a similar tendency, as suggested, for example, by the handling of the bones of the dead at Aghia Kyriaki and Kaminospelio and the paved areas close to cemeteries, which imply that the bodies of the dead lacked the alien or untouchable quality they possess for us.

Whereas various symbolic oppositions within twentieth-century Western culture (light/dark, life/death, high/low) could be correlated with an exaggeration of sexual differences between men and women, or to differences in social status, wealth or power, as Mead and Goffman suggest above, this early culture with its traces of collectivity and egalitarianism and apparent lack of marked discrimination between the sexes would seem to reveal a corresponding lack of marked oppositions or contrasts in its symbolic schema, preferring the circular and the triangular.

A further point of correlation is perhaps between the evidence presented in Chapter 1 for a pluralistic and animistic rather than a monotheistic religion in the early Aegean and the evidence for a social organization without apparent hierarchy within some settlements, and without obvious relations of domination between settlements. The evidence, as described above (Chapter 1.11), is rather for co-existent but decentralized and autonomous communities in the different localities of Crete, each flowering in distinctive forms of culture. The notion of an all-embracing Mother Goddess, Earth Goddess or Nature Goddess depends on the concept of 'Nature' being one centralized entity: an idea which, as Williams points out (1980, 68-9), is itself the product of a particular culture and moment in history rather than being a self-apparent or prior truth:

> The central point of the analysis can be expressed at once in the singular formation of the term [Nature]. As I understand it, we have here a case of a definition of quality which becomes, through real usage, based on certain assumptions, a description of the world ... The association and then the fusion of a name for the quality with a name for the things observed has a precise history. It is a central formation of idealistic thought ... Now I would not want to deny, I would prefer to emphasize, that this singular abstraction was a major advance in consciousness. But I think we have got so used to it, in a nominal continuity over more than two millennia, that we may not always realize quite all that it commits us to. A singular name for the real multiplicity of things and living processes may be held, with an effort, to be neutral, but I am sure it is very often the case that it offers, from the beginning, a dominant kind of interpretation: idealist, metaphysical, or religious.

One function of seeing nature as a unified entity has been the search for an 'essential principle' behind and distinct from her physical manifestations; another result has been a growing sense of separation and alienation between 'Nature' and 'Man', which Williams traces not only from the domination and exploitation of nature through recent industry and urbanism, but also from the growing complexity of our interactions with the natural world. In the early Aegean, in contrast, we saw that participation and identification were keynotes in the interaction of humans with elements of the natural world. The lack of evidence from the early Aegean for a centralized or abstracted deity of the natural world could thus perhaps be correlated with the method of organization of agriculture as well as with the absence of clear evidence for centralized or hierarchical forms of social control.

It should be stressed that in the discussion both of social organization and of symbolism in the period reviewed in Chapter 1, there is no claim that this study gives a comprehensive description of all the factors present. The intention of this study is merely to establish the existence of certain characteristics of symbolism and social organization, present variously in patches or as strands or tendencies within the overall picture. The exact extent of their currency is hard to determine, but their presence to some degree, as witnessed by a substantial body of evidence, is what is significantly at issue here.

The main feature of Chapters 2 and 3 is the steady movement they show away from the characteristics of both the society and the symbolism reviewed in Chapter 1. While there are many indications of continuity, in particular of symbolic ideas surviving as a steady if diminishing strand among the symbolic ideas of the Late Bronze Age and Early Iron Age, we also have pronounced signs of directly contrary developments. In the sphere of economic and social organization in the period covered by Chapter 2 these perhaps include a shift of emphasis towards pastoral farming; they certainly include evidence of war as part of a way of life and perhaps of subsistence; male rulers; a bureaucratic and hierarchical organization of land ownership and a clear hierarchy of wealth and power; a marked division of labour between women and men; signs of increased activity by men in the performing of religious functions. There are new phenomena in the sphere of art and religious symbolism which could be correlated with these changes.

Among graphic motifs prominent for the first time in Chapter 2, I have pointed to representations of attacks on animals, scenes celebrating hunting, and scenes of animals attacking each other, as well as the appearance of straightforward military scenes and representations of items of military equipment which are isolated and celebrated in what might be termed a fetishistic way (e.g. helmet, figure-of-eight shield). We could comment on this that aggression and its implements are apparently celebrated in new ways.

Moving away from a view of sanctity as widespread through many elements of the natural world, we see a concentration of the sacred onto named and, in varying degrees, personified divinities which are abstracted from the natural elements in which they had apparently been embodied in the earlier period. In the representations of such divinities or their priest/priestesses we have found certain new features: they often carry a weapon and may adopt an aggressive stance with it; they may assume a 'position of command'; they are placed in an elaborate architectural setting, are distinguished from their followers, or appear to carry increased status as suggested by their greater size and/or vertical elevation. The extent of these characteristics present singly or together adds up to an indication of a distinct shift in ideas about the nature of the divine. Signs of qualities of dominance attached to religious figures coincide with a decline in the significance of their association with vegetation: in the earlier period we saw that the focus of attention could be on a plant or tree, whereas now a procession honours an anthropomorphic figure seated beneath a tree (**Fig. 127a**) or we may find that such a figure replaces the plant altogether (**Fig. 261**). This could be interpreted as a shift away from a society based overwhelmingly on agricultural fertility associated with female reproductive cycles, towards a perhaps more pastoral society also concerned with martial activities, the preservation of hierarchy and the celebration of centralized authority. This might also be reflected in the decreasing occurrence of circular forms and the growth of the column which increasingly dwarfs human individuals. The shift of emphasis from low, round circular motifs to high, vertical linear motifs could be correlated with the social changes described. The celebration of the organic processes of reproduction (human, animal and plant) are now perhaps relatively less crucial for the survival of the social fabric than the veneration of authority and of monumental man-made constructs.

Certain specific changes are apparent in the relationship between humans and animals. Whereas in the period reviewed in Chapter 1 we saw gestures of touch, dressing-up and other activites which suggested close association with, identification with, and respect for, animals, we now find numerous representations of dead and captured animals. In the representations of religious personnel (divine or officiant), we find that humans are as often accompanied by animals as dressed up like animals in a manner suggesting identification; moreover, representations now often seem to celebrate domination over those accompanying animals (**Figs. 271, 272**).

Certain changes in symbolism, for example the apparent substitution of the horse and chariot for the boat, could be seen simply as reflecting innovations in society such as the introduction of the horse. However, the apparent sexual division of labour and the more significant role played by men in the organization of government, religion and war may contribute to other changes in symbolism such as the gravitation of the sun towards a male divinity, perhaps armed (**Fig. 259**). While the sun appears to 'change sex', other symbols such as the vessel remain female but start to acquire different values and associations. Whereas in Chapter 1 we saw that the vessel was apparently touched with reverence and associated, perhaps as a womb symbol, with the fertility of plants and with human erotic activity, in this period it remains prominent in cult (**Figs. 226-230, 236, 241**) but starts to acquire negative associations, as for example when it appears bearing sinister faces (**Fig. 266**).

Chapter 3 sees many of the tendencies witnessed in Chapter 2 exaggerated. The social structure reveals a rather different kind of hierarchy, the general widespread rule of townships and communities by aristocratic minorities who also appear to have had some hand in the organization of religion. Historians write of a wide gap between rich and poor, and a distinction between free and non-free citizens also appears to have been present in some form. Hesiod and Homer now offer ample evidence of a sharp division of labour in which women are assigned to certain work (such as weaving) and to certain places (the house), and are associated with certain forms of behaviour. The term 'woman' is applied to men as an insult, and Hesiod makes it clear that women have to be kept in place by men in the running of the household. It appears that women have little social control, and in relation to men are disparaged, discredited and disempowered. Moreover, whereas representations of women of the Bronze Age often showed them displaying sexual parts of their body in a proud and active way, often independently of the presence of men (e.g. dancing with other women), we now find evidence that women were expected to play a more passive role sexually and to be 'mastered' in love.

Alongside these social developments there are a number of pronounced developments in religious symbolism. Whereas in Chapter 2 we found a tendency for deities to be shown elevated, we now have a firm notion that gods lived in the sky; whereas in Chapter 2 we found that divinities started to appear as aggressive or dominating, we now find one chief divinity, Zeus, dominating not only humans but the other gods, with brute force as the last resort in the assertion of his power. Sky is now opposed to earth, which is subservient to the sky god. Whereas in Chapter 1 we picked out what seemed to be a circular view of the sun's cycle, setting and rising, now the earth and sky appear to be perceived as two distinct and vertically separated planes. The antithesis between them is expressed in a crystallized form in the breach between Heaven and Earth in Hesiod's creation myth. The most powerful occupant of the sky, the sun, undergoes analogous symbolic changes. Whereas in the earlier period it was associated with agricultural fertility, the sun now has pastoral associations and is the leader of herds; whereas previously we saw that it could be associated with the female belly, it is now linked with the eyesight and 'watchman' role of a male god.

In Chapter 1 we saw that the pregnant female belly was celebrated, as in the Cycladic and other figurines representing a pregnant woman. In this period we find that the stories of divine succession around Cronos, Zeus and Metis give a series of examples of the reproductive processes of the womb being interfered with according to the priority of ensuring the succession or security of male rulers. Whereas in Chapter 1 we saw that the earth's products of vegetative and animal life were a significant focus of attention in religious activity, we now find that what is emphasized is also the hidden nature of the earth and the awfulness of some of her creations. Creatures like the snake, thought to be significant in chthonic cult in the earlier period, now appear in a negative light as monsters or enemies of man. Ideas about burial in the earth have also changed: whereas in Chapter 1 we noted a series of phenomena, such as graves facing east, or having doors, which suggested some notions about rebirth, the grave now has nothing but negative connotations and death is a dead end. The negative view of women current in this society co-exists with a negative view of the vessel or jar, witnessed in the Pandora story and in other passages of Hesiod, as when he warns against uncharmed pots in the *Works and Days*. At the same time we find the clear expression of negative attitudes towards sexuality. Certain examples of binary symbolism make their appearance, such as an antithesis between left and right in the body (right being positive, left negative) and a distinction between the soul or essence and the mortal, physical body. Hesiod's passage of injunctions in the *Works and Days*, and other texts, betray a sharp series of antitheses between purity and impurity, between sun and genitals, between the spiritual and sexuality, and so on. In this symbolic system pots and death both carry ambivalent or completely negative connotations. The sharp divide between sky and earth, male and female, purity and impure body functions, life and death, are as different from the circular symbolic system described in Chapter 1 as the sharp divide between social groups in this period is different from the apparently more egalitarian social organization of that earlier period.

APPENDIX: THE CASE FOR A CULTURAL CONTINUUM IN THE AEGEAN DURING PARTS OF THE EARLY BRONZE AGE

The main focus of Chapter 1 of this study is Crete and the evidence for religious symbolism which derives from there. At points, however, the net is spread wider and evidence is drawn in from other parts of the Aegean world, notably the Cyclades. The use of such evidence relies on an understanding that, during parts at least of the period in question, these different areas of the Aegean world had sufficiently strong cultural links for them to be effectively regarded as a cultural continuum. The existence of such a cultural continuum during the second phase of the Early Bronze Age has already been recognized. Thus Renfrew remarks (1972, 183):

> The number of cultural links seen at this time in the Aegean is quite remarkable. The one-handled cup, for example ... suddenly becomes a widespread form, where previously links of this kind between any two local regions in the Aegean were unusual, and between all of them totally unknown. Nor does any one region dominate the others to a preponderant extent. Certainly a high proportion of the forms, such as the *depas* ..., are of Anatolian origin, but the 'sauceboat', usually considered a Helladic type, has an equally wide distribution. And the Cycladic folded-arm figurine is widely found in the mainland as well as in Crete which otherwise seems to hold rather aloof from the Aegean world during the early bronze age.
>
> It is this international flavour, a widespread distribution of forms with different origins, which leads one to think of a continuum rather than of cultural influence emanating from a single source.

Tracing the cause of this situation to an outburst of metal trading, he comments that 'This is a new phenomenon, for the preceding phase shows very little of this international spirit' (1972, 170) (see **Fig. 336a**).

The patterns of cultural connection between the different areas of the Aegean which lead Renfrew to this statement are described in his book *The Emergence of Civilization* (1972). Since he wrote, certain items, such as the one-handled cup, have been redated, but further evidence of Aegean interrelations continues to be brought forward: see, for example, recently, Warren (1984b), who concludes, 'At the very least we can postulate a previously unsuspected, strong degree of linkage, economic and perhaps populational, between the Cyclades and northern Crete in late EB1 or transitional EB1/2. In full EB2 these links are much expanded' (1984b, 60). The onus here is thus, perhaps, not to establish this 'international spirit' as a general phenomenon, but rather to discuss to what extent it expressed itself specifically in the area of religious symbolism with which this study is concerned, and to what extent it also might relate to similarities between different Aegean areas in the forms of social organization which this study also reviews. It is, then, in these two specific areas of religion and social organization that we need to examine the extent and pervasiveness of this cultural continuum, largely within the second phase of the EBA, as from the end of EB II onwards Crete is treated in isolation.

First, attention will be focused on the area of religious symbolism and on the glyptic, graphic and ceramic representations which are our source of information for such symbolism. To what extent are there similarities in such representations as are found in the three geographical areas of Crete, the Cyclades, and the mainland? We must tread warily here, as Renfrew remarks: 'It is frequently felt to be sufficient for the suggestion of cultural connections that two objects found at distant places should show some similarity of form, without a detailed consideration of their respective contexts, or even of the chronology' (1972, 135).

To start with the female figurines discussed above in Chapter 1.2, it is perhaps not redundant to point out that Crete shares with the Cyclades not only a predominance of female figurines over male figurines or other types, but also the use of such figurines as grave offerings. The fact that Cycladic originals as well as local copies of them have been found in Crete corroborates the impression of a continuum of religious ideas. **Fig. 336b** shows the findspots of folded-arm figurines in Crete, and Doumas comments of such finds: 'The fact that idols (both imported from the islands and made locally) have been found outside the Cyclades indicates that in certain areas at least a similarity in beliefs and customs must have existed among the Early Bronze Age cultures of the Aegean basin. Moreover, the presence of these idols outside the Cyclades proves that the islanders were in contact with their neighbours' (1968, 81). It is noteworthy that such finds in Crete are not confined to the EBA II period.

The discovery of such locally made figurines, specifically in Cretan tombs, leads Barber to point out that 'They were therefore presumably, in Cretan eyes, a Cycladic variant of something *which was also important in Crete*, where the Cycladic style of representation was regarded as an adequate substitute for local objects' (1983, 6, my emphasis). Excavation continues to fill out the picture, as with the discovery of Cycladic figurines at Archanes (Fourni), whose special connection with the Cyclades is also suggested by quantities of fragmentary obsidian blades (*AR* 1975-6, 29; *AR* 1976-7, 63; *AR* 1979-80, 50). Cycladic figurines are also found on the mainland. The relative lack of evidence of imports of Cycladic figurines before the appearance of the folded-arm type has been ascribed by Tamvaki (1983, 6) to the increase of trade and communication at the time of their appearance, if not to their artistic merit. This lack of export in the first phase of the Early Bronze Age should, however, perhaps be set against a Neolithic background in which it has been argued that female figurines from many parts of the Aegean area show marked similarities: thus Weinberg, for example, remarks of one group of figures: 'It is clear from the comparison of these details that our group of seated figurines belongs to the general family of Aegean Neolithic human representations, or sculpture, having striking resemblances to those from the mainland of Greece at least as far north as Thessaly, from the Cyclades and from Crete' (1951, 128).

The similarities and differences in the funerary customs of the three main areas under discussion (Crete, the Cyclades and the mainland) have been reviewed at some length in Chapter 1.5, with emphasis on certain consistent and recurring factors which suggest underlying shared beliefs.

The next source of evidence for religious symbolism which should be discussed is perhaps the 'frying-pan'. Findspots of 'frying-pans' in the Cyclades and southern part of the mainland are indicated on **Fig. 336c**, showing that this form, which one might think of as essentially Cycladic, was fairly widely known on the mainland; moreover it is again interesting to note that the mainland produced its own version of the 'frying-pan' (Renfrew, 1972, 536-7), indicating that we have here more than an instance of the straightforward importing of items without a sense of their purpose or an assimilation of their meaning. Coleman (1985, 200) comments on the 'local character' of some mainland 'frying-pans', and argues for local manufacture in Attica. Renfrew points out that some finds of 'frying-pan' type in the mainland predate the Korakou culture and can be traced back to the Eutresis culture. Coleman suggests that the shape may even have originated on the mainland (1985, 203). 'Frying-pans' are not widely found but are not unknown in Crete: Aghia Fotia in east Crete, thought to be a cemetery of Cycladic immigrants, has yielded two vessels of 'frying-pan' type (see **Fig. 39f**), and a wide shallow dish from the cave of Platyvola in western Crete has been identified as a 'frying-pan' (in Chania Museum, No. 2001). There is also a 'frying-pan' in the Giamalakis collection, identified by Marinatos and Hirmer (1960, Pl.5) as a Cycladic import, EM II-III. Some MM dark-faced incised lids from Knossos (see **Fig. 24b** and **d**), which are comparable to the 'frying-pans' in shape and (?)sun design, have been interpreted as belonging to a parallel Cretan tradition, rather than being Cycladic imports (see MacGillivray et al., 1986b; *PM* IV, 87ff).

The situation with seals and sealings is different again. Here the Cyclades are largely excluded from a cultural pattern which Crete and the mainland appear to share. A sealstone from Aghios Kosmas may be a Minoan import, but this apparently may not be true of two from Asine and Rafina (Renfrew, 1972, 112). Seals and sealings from the mainland apparently show a fairly homogeneous style and repertoire of motifs, and it is of some interest that the motifs used are consistent with, or similar to, motifs used on Cretan seals. For example, impressions from Lerna dating from the EH II or 'Korakou' phase include depictions of a bee, jugs, cruciforms, a few plants and, rarely, swastikas (Caskey, 1955, 41, Pl.22). None of these motifs are unknown in Cretan seals of this period and some, like the cruciform arrangements, are common. Blegen points out the similarity between an engraved seal from Zygouries (1928, Pl.XXI No.4) and a terracotta seal from Aghios Onouphrios and others from the Messara tombs. Some of the unpainted ware from the same site also seems to bear seal impressions, one showing a 'circular labyrinthine pattern' (Blegen, 1928, 107) whose 'Early Minoan affinities' have been remarked; others show familiar concentric circles and spiral designs. Fresh examples of spiral decoration continue to appear, for example on a lead object from the EH settlement at Voidikilia (*AR* 1982-3, 29).

Maintaining a focus on the site of Zygouries which belongs to the Korakou phase of culture and which Renfrew suggests gives 'a very clear impression of a fairly typical settlement of the time' (1972, 110), we find that other objects which may have had religious or symbolic significance show affinities with Minoan and Cycladic culture. Thus we find a palette (Blegen, 1928, 194) which shows a similarity to Cycladic palettes and to those which Xanthoudides excavated in the Messara; miniature dishes (Blegen, 1928, 107) like those found in Crete and the Cyclades (although the context here is not specifically funerary); a seashell in a grave (Blegen, 1928, 47), as in Crete and the Cyclades; and a small foot with a suspension hole which Blegen suggests may be an amulet and for which he lists the Cretan parallels (1928, 197, 218). The similarity of other, apparently secular, objects from Zygouries, such as daggers and tweezers, to Cycladic and Early Minoan equivalents (Blegen, 1928, 182-3) fill out our picture of the busy channels of communication through which religious objects may have changed hands, and through which a loose consensus of religious ideas may have been imparted or sustained. Of the contact between Zygouries and the Cyclades Blegen concluded (1929, 212): 'We are justified in concluding that related customs and practices prevailed in both areas, and that there was also regular intercommunication between the two.'

Renfrew gives the following estimate of the degree of continuity of religious symbolism which can be recognized in Crete, the Cyclades and the mainland during the third millennium B.C. Referring to some similarities in ritual vessels in use in the Cyclades and Crete, in particular the 'kernos' and the pitted offering table, he comments: 'These scattered indications effectively demonstrate that at least in the Cyclades, and in Crete, a formal religious symbolism developed during the early bronze age. Moreover the different regions had their own beliefs; the Cretan double axe and horns of consecration are not seen in the Cyclades, nor the sun, sea and sex symbolism in Early Minoan Crete. The megaron hearth is a specifically mainland feature. And yet at the same time the symbolic significance of birds, and the widespread presence of the Cycladic folded-arm figurine indicate a community of outlook, anticipated by the finds of seated, cross-legged figurines in the neolithic of Crete, the Cyclades and the mainland' (1972, 426-7).

Perhaps our sense of this 'community of outlook' can be enhanced. One point here is that the horns of consecration are found relatively rarely in Crete in this early period and even the double axe is by no means a dominant symbol (Branigan, 1970, 110-113). Moreover, the evidence proposed in this study for the importance of solar symbolism in Crete, and for its association there with the female sex, would further diminish our sense of the differences between Cretan and Cycladic symbolism of 'sun, sea and sex' in this early period. The similarities suggested between sealstones of Crete and of the mainland would, if we accept the amuletic or talismanic role of seals, again imply some continuity of religious symbolism between these two areas. The picture which emerges by no means indicates a uniformity of culture, and one would not wish to deny the clear signs of local variations; however, it would appear that different areas held different elements in common in varying combinations. Although each area had its own specialities in the way of ritual or religious objects (double-axes, 'frying-pans', folded-arm figurines and so on), the ease with which one area could adopt another's particular products or coincide in the use of them again implies an underlying 'community of outlook' between the three areas.

Having reviewed briefly the extent to which an international spirit can be traced in the area of religious symbolism, it is perhaps time to move on to the question of whether the unusual features of Cretan social organization, which I have correlated with Cretan symbolism, were also present in the Cyclades and the mainland during this period.

The subsistence of the small communities on the Cycladic islands during the Early Bronze Age is thought to have been based on the cultivation of wheat, grapes and olives, alongside the keeping of goats, sheep, pigs and some cattle. The diet is thought also to have included fish and shellfish, and it is suggested that the general level of subsistence afforded the existence of some specialized craftspeople. As Doumas has briefly summarized the situation: 'Hunting, fishing, animal husbandry and agriculture were the everyday activities of the Cycladic islanders in the Early Bronze Age; this is indicated by food residues and implements found in settlements and cemeteries. It seems, too, that some kind of "industry" had developed. Metallurgy, marble-sculpting, pottery, quarrying, and working of obsidian presuppose cooperatives — albeit primitive — of artisans specialized in their crafts. There is strong evidence that some marble figurines can be attributed to certain individual sculptors, or to schools of sculptors' (1983, 31). In the absence of extensive evidence from settlement sites, much of the evidence for social organization comes from the cemeteries used by this early population. The clustering of graves, and the later use of multiple burial, has been taken to suggest the existence of some kind of social groups within the community (Doumas, 1983, 29): possibly this was some form of kin-group. We have a slightly different situation, however, from that pertaining in Crete. Doumas also points out that graves are of different sizes, and suggests that this, combined with the variety in the quality of construction and the difference in the wealth of the objects found in them, 'may be taken as indicative of the existence of differences in social status among the inhabitants of a Cycladic community' (1968, 14). Renfrew draws the same conclusion from the evidence: after a detailed analysis of the contents of a selection of graves, he remarks: 'These

finds give a clear picture of the emergence of a social stratification during the early bronze age
— at the beginning marked by a slight variation in the quality and quantity of grave goods; by
the end indicated not only by greater quantities of finds, some concentrated in the wealthy
graves, but also by the avoidance of "common" types and the rare inclusion of princely (or at
least "chiefly") objects' (1972, 377). Even bearing in mind Ucko's comments about the
difficulties of drawing meaning from differences in the wealth of grave goods (referred to in
Chapter 1.11), it is hard to avoid reaching a similar conclusion. The varieties in the quality of
grave construction are persuasive. In this respect, then, we appear to have a very different
situation from that which has been suggested above as existing in parts of Crete.

Two other interesting points, however, arise from Renfrew's investigation. Thus he
comments of the graves studied (1972, 375): 'I have been able to detect no systematic
association among the finds which could indicate a sexual distinction: we cannot assume that
men did not use needles or take special care over their appearance. No weapons are found in
the graves, nor indeed copper axes or chisels, although the settlement finds show that the
inhabitants possessed them.' In relation to the position of women, then, this evidence is
compatible with that from Crete and fails to suggest a marked difference in social status
between men and women; while the Cycladic figurines suggest that in the area of religion at
least women were afforded some significance or status.

The question of weapons and fortifications is rather more complex in the Cyclades than in
Crete. The appearance of the dagger does not in itself tell us a great deal: 'Although in many
cases primarily a weapon, the dagger was a dual-purpose object, serving also as a knife. Not
until the late bronze age were these two functions clearly differentiated' (Renfrew, 1972, 393).
Renfrew, however, describes the evolution of the dagger to the long sword and remarks that
'The correlation between personal status and the possession of richly-adorned weapons cannot
be over-emphasized' (1972, 394). As far as fortifications are concerned, they are not found in
the Cyclades during the Early Bronze Age I period, nor was any great advance in fortification
seen in the Early Bronze Age II period. However, in the first part of the Early Bronze Age III
period (EC IIIA), fortifications became more common both on the Cyclades and on the
mainland of Greece (see **Fig. 336d**). (Some prefer to date these from EC IIB, cf. Rutter, *AJA*,
87, 1983, 69-76.) Whilst it has been thought that these fortifications may be related to the
activities of pirates or sea-raiders (Renfrew, 1972, 398-9), Doumas has now suggested that
these fortifications may have been the settlements of intruders and that the threat to these
intruders may not have been external (in French and Wardle, 1988, 28). Opinion thus remains
divided as to whether the militarism evident in the Cyclades at this time reflected concern with
defence against external attack from other parts of the Aegean or warlike relations within or
between the populations of the islands. It is of some interest that scenes of fighting are not
among the subjects celebrated on surviving representations of the period, for example on
'frying-pans' or on the walls at Korfi t'Aroniou.

To what extent any of the features of social organization remarked in Cretan culture of the
Early Bronze Age were also present on the mainland of Greece in the same period is perhaps
even more debatable than in the case of the Cyclades. Blegen's summary concerning life at the
settlement site of Zygouries is perhaps of interest here (1928, 220):

> The village was evidently a prosperous agricultural community. It seems to have
> imported goods on a fairly considerable scale from comparatively distant quarters, and
> perhaps it had commodities of its own to give in exchange. Among these latter may
> have been agricultural produce, livestock ... perhaps also potter's clay. Imports
> included above all obsidian from Melos, lava or volcanic stone for millstones and
> grinders, marble vessels and figurines from the Cyclades, gold, silver, and bronze; and

trade connections with Crete are apparent. Such open commercial intercourse between a small town in an upland valley on the mainland and regions across the sea implies an age of tranquillity and security from hostile incursions; it also implies power and organization to patrol the highways of traffic, but whence came the power and who controlled it are questions which cannot yet be answered.

We have, then, at the Zygouries settlement a similar method of subsistence as at the Cretan and Cycladic settlements; also similar is the background of apparent tranquillity, and the custom of mass or collective burial which has been described above in Chapter 1 is another common feature which this site shares with Crete.

The question of the social organization of this settlement might be illuminated by a thorough reappraisal of the evidence in the light of Warren's discoveries at Myrtos (Fournou Korifi), which have opened new possibilities in the interpretation of settlements of this period. Although Blegen leaves this question open, it is clear which way his thought is leading when he remarks that the presence of gold in these tombs of people of 'humble standing' at Zygouries 'gives some intimation of what we may expect when the grave of a chieftain is found' (1928, 55). The fact that such a grave has not been found and may never have existed except as an assumption of the excavator may make us wonder about how similar assumptions may have influenced his interpretation of other materials at the site. For example, the ground plan of the main part of the settlement (**Fig. 336e**) is not dissimilar in its agglomerate nature to the ground plan of the Myrtos settlement (**Fig. 125**). In the absence of doorways between many of the rooms, the division of the site into houses must remain tentative. Thus Blegen identifies one house as having 'especially large dimensions; perhaps this was the house of the chieftain or headman of the village' (1929, 220). Reference to the material excavated and to the ground plan, however, reveals no very strong argument for grouping these three rooms (3, 4 and 5) together as one 'house'. One could contrast Blegen's interpretation with the interpretation which Warren makes of a somewhat parallel group of rooms at Myrtos (Rooms 80, 88, 89, 91, 92). Interestingly, both groups are at the western end of the settlement and border on an open area. Each group includes an exceptionally large room (Room 4 at Zygouries is 5.60m x 5.55m while Room 80 at Myrtos is 4.85m x 5.00m) containing a large number of storage jars and a central structure which at Zygouries is a circular fire-baked hearth. The Myrtos group also contains a hearth, in Room 89, conspicuous in this case for the benches on either side which Warren found too elaborate for a room that was simply a kitchen (1972, 81). The floor of Room 4 at Zygouries was made of trodden clay laid on a prepared bed composed of whitish clay; interestingly, Room 89 at Myrtos, the room of the hearth and the skull, also had white clay packing on the floor. This method of floor covering was by no means universal in either settlement and is noteworthy for its similarity to the layer of white substance (earth or sand) used at some tholoi to seal over the floor after a clean-out of previous burials prior to re-use. Of this practice Branigan has remarked: 'Whether or not the white earth has some significance we do not know, but apart from Lebena and Platanos A, it was also found covering swept-aside burials in tholos E at Koumasa; and in the small graves on Mochlos in the east we find a filling of white clay which is said to have been taken to the small island from the mainland' (1970, 172).

While Room 4 at Zygouries yielded a coarse cooking pot containing beef bones and many shallow bowls, Room 91 at Myrtos contained a large number of shallow bowls and a 'group of bones' (Warren, 1972, 85). Querns were found in both sets of rooms. While the Myrtos rooms are distinguished by the finds of a figurine, fragments of a human skull, and the vase-carrying female figure shown on **Fig. 11a**, the Zygouries rooms' most remarkable product is perhaps a 'sauceboat' with a ramshead spout, although the adjacent Rooms 6 and 7 contained a bird vase and a figurine.

Though there are many differences, there are substantial parallels between these two groups of rooms in their westerly position, their closeness to an open area, their use of white clay flooring, the exceptional size of one room in each case, the evidence of food storage and preparation, and the presence of a conspicuous or unusual hearth. These similarities would not appear to justify such divergent interpretations as have been placed on them by Warren and Blegen respectively. Further investigation might reveal that Warren's interpretation of his group as food and ritual rooms for a collective settlement could with equal validity be applied to the Zygouries rooms; evidence such as the absence of hearths in several of Blegen's 'houses' might be drawn in to corroborate such a hypothesis. Whitelaw's interpretation of a rather differently organized, but still egalitarian, Myrtos might also be tested out against the Zygouries evidence.

Of course the settlement at EH Lerna presents a rather different picture. The intention here is not to present such a hypothesis at length but rather to indicate one of many ways in which mainland material of the Early Bronze Age might be open to fresh interpretation in the light of recent excavations.

It will be seen from this brief survey that, in the context of the 'international spirit' prevalent in the middle phase of the Early Bronze Age, there is also evidence of cultural similarities between Crete and the Cycladic and mainland areas in the specific aspects of culture with which this study is concerned. Thus, although there are many local variations (as, indeed, there are within Crete itself) and although, as Cherry points out, 'the frequency and significance of inter-regional interaction at this time are still far from clear' (1983, 40), there are sufficient common threads both in the religious symbolism used in each area and in the organization of their communities to warrant their consideration within the scope of the same study.

BIBLIOGRAPHY

Arthur W.H. ADKINS, *Merit and Responsibility: A Study in Greek Values*, Clarendon Press, Oxford, 1960.

A.W.H. ADKINS, *From the Many to the One: A Study of Personality and Views of Human Nature in the Context of Ancient Greek Society, Values and Beliefs*, Constable, London, 1970.

Gudrun AHLBERG, *Fighting on land and sea in Greek Geometric Art*, Skrifter Utgivna Av Svenska Institutet i, Athen 4, XVI, Stockholm, 1971.

Gudrun AHLBERG, *Prothesis and Ekphora in Greek Geometric Art*, S.I.M.A. 32, Paul Åströms Förlag, Göteborg, 1971 (1971b).

Margaret ALEXIOU, *The Ritual Lament in Greek Tradition*, Cambridge University Press, 1974.

Dr. M. ALEXIOU, 'Death, Marriage and Re-birth in Greek Tradition', paper presented to the Society for the Promotion of Hellenic Studies, London, 6.6.1985.

Stylianos ALEXIOU, 'Kriti' in *A Delt*, 18 B 2, 1963, pp.310-11.

S. ALEXIOU, 'Larnakes kai aggeia ek tafou para to Gazi Herakleiou' in *AE* 1972, pp.86-98.

Stylianos ALEXIOU, *Guide Sommaire du Musée Archéologique d'Héraclion*, Direction Générale des Antiquités et de la Restauration, Athens, 1973.

Stylianos ALEXIOU, 'Walls and Akropolises in Minoan Crete (The Myth of Minoan Peace)', in *Kretologia*, 8, 1979, pp.41-56.

Schafik ALLAM, *Beitrage zum Hathorkult (bis zum Ende des Mittleren Reiches)*, Verlag Bruno Hessling, Berlin, 1963.

Thomas George ALLEN (transl.) and Elizabeth Blaisdell HAUSER (prepared), *The Book of The Dead or Going Forth by Day*, University of Chicago Press, Chicago, 1974.

T.W. ALLEN, W.R. HALLIDAY, and E.E. Sykes (ed.), *The Homeric Hymns*, Clarendon Press, Oxford, 1936.

Pierre AMANDRY, *Collection Hélène Stathatos: Les Bijoux Antiques*, Institut d'Archéologie de l'Université, Strasbourg, 1953.

Shirley ARDENER (ed.), *Perceiving Women*, Malaby Press, London, and Halsted Press, New York, 1975.

Marylin ARTHUR, 'Politics and Pomegranates: An Interpretation of the Homeric Hymn to Demeter', *Arethusa*, 10, No. 1, 1977, pp.7-47.

Marylin B. ARTHUR, 'Early Greece: The Origins of the Western Attitude Toward Women' in John Peradotto and J.P. Sullivan (ed.) *Women in the Ancient World: The Arethusa Papers*, State University of New York Press, Albany, 1984, pp.7-58.

T.D. ATKINSON et al., *Excavations at Phylakopi in Melos*, B.S.A. Supplement No. 4, Macmillan, London, 1904.

Elizabeth C. BANKS, 'Neolithic *Tangas* from Lerna', in *Hesperia*, 46, 1977, pp.324-39.

A.A. BARB, 'Diva Matrix' in *Journal of the Warburg Institute*, 16, 1953, pp.193-238.

R.L.N. BARBER, 'Early Cycladic Marble Figures: some thoughts on function', paper presented to British Museum Cycladic Colloquium, 1983. See FITTON, 1984, pp. 10-14.

R.L.N. BARBER, *The Cyclades in the Bronze Age*, Gerald Duckworth and Co., London, 1987.

Richard D. BARNETT, 'Ancient Oriental Influences on Archaic Greece', in Saul S. Weinberg (ed.), *The Aegean and the Near East: Studies Presented to Hetty Goldman*, J.J. Augustin, Locust Valley, New York, 1956.

J.L. BENSON, *Horse, Bird and Man: The Origins of Greek Painting*, University of Massachusetts Press, Amherst, 1970.

J.T. BENT, 'Researches Among the Cyclades', in *JHS*, 5, 1884, pp.42-59.

Jan G.P. BEST and Yigaël YADIN, *The Arrival of the Greeks*, Adolf M. Hackert, Amsterdam, 1973.

Philip P. BETANCOURT, *Minoan Pottery*, Princeton University Press, Princeton, New Jersey, 1985.

J.H. BETTS, 'Ships on Minoan Seals', Vol. XXIII of the Colston Papers (Proceedings of the Twenty-third Symposium of the Colston Research Society, held in the University of Bristol, April 1971), Butterworths Scientific Publications, Butterworth and Co. (Publishers) Ltd., London.

John H. BETTS, 'Engraved Gems in the Collection of the British School' in *BSA*, 66, 1971, pp.49-55 (1971b).

John H. BETTS, 'A Technical Revolution: Gem Engraving in MM III', paper presented at University of London, Mycenaean Seminar, 15.10.86. See *BICS*, 35, 1988, p.163.

J.H. BETTS and J.G. YOUNGER, 'Aegean seals of the Late Bronze Age: Masters and workshops. Introduction', in *Kadmos*, 21, 1982, pp. 104-21.

John L. BINTLIFF, 'Structuralism and Myth in Minoan Studies', in *Antiquity*, 58, 1984, pp.33-38.

D. BLACKMAN and K. BRANIGAN, 'An Archaeological Survey of the Lower Catchment of the Ayiofarango Valley', in *BSA*, 72, 1977, pp.13-84.

Ann C. BLASINGHAM, 'The seals from the tombs of the Messara: Inferences as to kinship and social organisation', in O. Krzyszkowska and L. Nixon (ed.), *Minoan Society: Proceedings of the Cambridge Colloquium 1981*, Bristol Classical Press, 1983.

C.J. BLEEKER, *Hathor and Thoth: Two key figures of the ancient Egyptian religion*, E.J. Brill, Leiden, 1973.

Carl W. BLEGEN, *Zygouries: A Prehistoric Settlement in the Valley of Cleonae*, Harvard University Press, Cambridge, Massachusetts, 1928.

C.W. BLEGEN, 'Hyria' in *Hesperia Supplement 8*, 1949, pp.39-42 and Pl.7, No. 6.

Chr. BLINKENBERG, *Lindos: Fouilles de l'Acropole 1902-1914 Vol. I*, Walter de Gruyter and Cie Libraires-Editeurs, Berlin, 1931.

John BOARDMAN, *The Cretan Collection in Oxford*, Clarendon Press, Oxford, 1961.

J. BOARDMAN, *Greek Island Gems*, Supplementary Paper No. 10, Society for the Promotion of Hellenic Studies, London, 1963.

John BOARDMAN, *Excavations in Chios 1952-55: Greek Emporio*, British School of Archaeology at Athens and Thames and Hudson, 1967.

J. BOARDMAN, 'The Khaniale Tekke Tombs, II' in *BSA*, 62, 1967, pp.57-75 (1967b).

John BOARDMAN, *Archaic Greek Gems: Schools and Artists in the Sixth and Early Fifth Centuries B.C.*, Thames and Hudson, London, 1968.

John BOARDMAN, *Greek Gems and Finger Rings*, Photography by Robert L. Wilkins, Thames and Hudson, London, 1970.

John BOARDMAN, 'Symbol and Story in Geometric Art', in Warren G. Moon (ed.), *Ancient Greek Art and Iconography*, University of Wisconsin Press, 1983, pp.15-36.

R.C. BOSANQUET, 'The Pottery', in R.C. Bosanquet and R.M. Dawkins, *The Unpublished Objects from the Palaikastro Excavations, 1902-1906. BSA Supplement No. 1, Part 1,* Macmillan, London, 1923.

H.Th. BOSSERT, *The Art of Ancient Crete,* Zwemmer, London, 1937.

J. BOURRIAU, *Umm el-Ga'ab: pottery from the Nile Valley before the Arab conquest,* Cambridge University Press, 1981.

Jan BOUZEK, 'Die Griechisch-Geometrischen Bronzevögel', in *Eirene,* 6, 1967, pp.115-39.

K. BRANIGAN, *The Foundations of Palatial Crete,* Routledge and Kegan Paul, London, 1970. (Republished, with updated material, as *Pre-palatial,* Hakkert, Amsterdam, 1988.)

K. BRANIGAN, *The Tombs of Mesara: A Study of Funerary Architecture and Ritual in Southern Crete, 2800-1700 B.C.,* Gerald Duckworth, London, 1970 (1970b).

K. BRANIGAN, 'The Tombs of Mesara: new tombs and new evidence', in *BICS,* 22, 1974, pp.200-203.

K. BRANIGAN, 'Myrtos', in *CR,* 25, 1975, pp.116-18.

K. BRANIGAN, 'Craft Specialisation in Minoan Crete', in O. Krzyszkowska and L. Nixon (ed.), *Minoan Society: Proceedings of the Cambridge Colloquium 1981,* Bristol Classical Press, 1983, pp.23-32.

K. BRANIGAN, 'Early Minoan Society: The Evidence of the Mesara Tholoi Reviewed', in *Aux Origines de l'Hellénisme: la Crète et la Grèce. Hommage.à Henri Van Effenterre,* Centre G. Glotz, Publications de la Sorbonne, Paris, 1984.

Keith BRANIGAN (introduced), 'Pre-palatial problems: A Round Table', University of London, Mycenaean Seminar, 19.10.88.

Eva T.H. BRANN, *The Athenian Agora Vol. VIII: Late Geometric and Protoattic pottery,* The American School of Classical Studies at Athens, Princeton, New Jersey, 1962.

Jan BREMMER, *The Early Greek Concept of Soul,* Princeton University Press, 1983.

L. BRISSON, *Le mythe de Tirésias: essai d'analyse structurale,* E.J. Brill, Leiden, 1976.

J.K. BROCK, *Fortetsa: Early Greek Tombs near Knossos,* Cambridge University Press, 1957.

E.A. Wallis BUDGE, *The Gods of the Egyptians Vol. II,* Methuen, London, 1904.

Walter BURKERT, *Structure and History in Greek Mythology and Ritual,* University of California Press, 1979.

Cottie BURLAND, Irene NICHOLSON, Harold OSBORNE, *Mythology of the Americas,* Hamlyn, London/New York/Sydney/Toronto, 1970.

Andrew Robert BURN, *The World of Hesiod,* Kegan Paul, Trench, Trubner and Co., London, 1936.

Ernst BUSCHOR, *Greek Vase-Painting,* transl. G.C. Richards, Chatto & Windus, London, 1921.

G. CADOGAN, *Palaces of Minoan Crete,* Barrie and Jenkins, London, 1976.

Gerald CADOGAN, 'The Relations between Cyprus and Crete circa 2,000-5,000 B.C.', in *Acts of the International Archaeological Symposium,* Departments of Antiquities and Chr. Nikolaou and Sons, Cyprus, 1979.

Rhys CARPENTER, *Folk Tale, Fiction and Saga in the Homeric Epics,* University of California Press, Berkeley and Los Angeles, 1946.

John CARTER, 'The Beginnings of Narrative Art in the Greek Geometric Period', in *BSA,* 67, 1972, pp.25-58.

John L. CASKEY, 'Excavations at Lerna, 1954', in *Hesperia,* XXIV, 1955, pp.25-49.

John L. CASKEY 'Chalandriani in Syros', in Lucy F. Sandler (ed.), *Marsyas: Essays in memory of Karl Lehmann,* Institute of Fine Arts, New York, 1964.

John L. CASKEY, 'Greece, Crete and the Aegean Islands in the Early Bronze Age', in *Cambridge Ancient History Vol. 1 Pt. 2*, Cambridge University Press, 1971, pp.771-807.

Ernst CASSIRER, see Donald Phillip VERENE (ed.), 1979.

John CHADWICK, *The Mycenaean World*, Cambridge University Press, Cambridge, 1976.

John CHADWICK, 'The Mycenaean Dorians', *BICS*, 23, 1976, pp.115-6 (1976b).

S. CHARITONIDES, 'Chamber Tombs of Karpathos', in *A Delt*, 17, 1961-2, pp.32-76.

John F. CHERRY, 'Evolution, Revolution and the Rise of Complex Society in Minoan Crete', summary of paper presented at Cambridge Colloquium on Minoan Society, 1981.

John F. CHERRY, 'Evolution, Revolution and the Origins of Complex Society in Minoan Crete', in O. Krzyszowska and L. Nixon (ed.), *Minoan Society: Proceedings of the Cambridge Colloquium 1981*, Bristol Classical Press, 1983, pp.33-45.

John CHERRY, 'The emergence of Minoan palatial societies: some aspects of the problem', paper presented at University of London, Mycenaean Seminar, 19.2.86.

David B. CLAUS, *Toward the Soul: An Inquiry into the Meaning of 'Psyche' before Plato*, Yale University Press, New Haven and London, 1981.

J.N. COLDSTREAM, 'A Theran Sunrise', in *BICS*, 12, 1965, pp.34-7.

J.N. COLDSTREAM, *Greek Geometric Pottery*, Methuen, London, 1968.

J.N. COLDSTREAM, 'A figured Geometric oinochoe from Italy', in *BICS*, 15, 1968, pp.86-96 (1968b).

J.N. COLDSTREAM, *Knossos, the Sanctuary of Demeter*, British School of Archaeology at Athens, Thames and Hudson, London, 1973.

J.N. COLDSTREAM, 'Deities in Aegean Art: Before and after the Dark Age', Inaugural Lecture presented at Bedford College, London, 27.10.1976, Bedford College, 1977.

J.N. COLDSTREAM, *Geometric Greece*, Methuen, London, 1979.

J.N. COLDSTREAM, 'A Protogeometric Nature Goddess from Knossos', in *BICS*, 31, 1984, pp.93-104.

John E. COLEMAN, '"Frying pans" of the Early Bronze Age Aegean', in *AJA*, 89, 1985, pp.191-219.

Dominique COLLON, *The Seal Impressions from Tell Atchana/Alalakh*, Alter Orient und Alter Testament, Vol. 27, Verlag Butzon & Bercker, Kevelaer, Neukirchener Verlag, Neukirchen-Vluyn, 1975.

Dominique COLLON, *Catalogue of the Western Asiatic Seals in the British Museum: Cylinder Seals, Vol. II*, British Museum Publications, London, 1982.

Dominique COLLON, *Catalogue of the Western Asisatic Seals in the British Museum: Cylinder Seals, Vol. III Isin-Larsa and Old Babylonian periods*, British Museum Publications, 1986.

J.M. COOK, 'Athenian Workshops around 700', in *BSA*, 42, 1947, pp.139-55.

F.M. CORNFORD, *The Unwritten Philosophy and other Essays*, University Press, Cambridge, 1950.

Paul COURBIN, *La Céramique Géometrique de l'Argolide*, Editions E. de Boccard, Paris, 1966.

R.A. CROSSLAND and Ann BIRCHALL (ed.), *Bronze Age Migrations in the Aegean, Proceedings of the First International Colloquium on Aegean Prehistory, Sheffield*, Gerald Duckworth, London, 1973.

F. CUMONT, *Astrology and Religion among the Greeks and Romans*, G.P. Putnam's Sons, New York and London, 1912.

K. DAVARAS, 'Chronika', in *A Delt*, 27, 1972, pp.648-51.

K. DAVARAS, 'Minoan Pottery Kiln in Stylos, Chania', in *AE*, 1973, pp.75-80.

C. DAVARAS, *Guide to Cretan Antiquities*, Noyes Press, New Jersey, 1976.

J.L. DAVIS, 'A Cycladic figure in Chicago from the "Keros hoard" and the non-funereal use of Cycladic marble figurines', paper presented to British Museum Cycladic Colloquium, 1983. See FITTON, 1984, pp.15-21.

Jack. L. DAVIS and John F. CHERRY (ed.), *Papers in Cycladic Prehistory*, Monograph XIV, Institute of Archaeology, University of California, Los Angeles, 1979.

Simon DAVIS, *The Decipherment of the Minoan Linear A and Pictographic Scripts*, Witwatersrand University Press, Johannesberg, 1967.

Pierre DEMARGNE, *La Crète Dédalique*, E. de Boccard, Paris, 1947.

Philippe DERCHAIN, *Hathor Quadrifrons: Recherches sur la syntaxe d'un mythe égyptien*, Nederlands Historisch-Archaeologisch Instituut in het Nabije Oosten, 1972.

V.R. d'A. DESBOROUGH, *The last Mycenaeans and their successors: An archaeological survey c.1200-c.1000 B.C.*, Clarendon Press, Oxford, 1964.

V.R. d'A. DESBOROUGH, *The Greek Dark Ages*, Ernest Benn, London, 1972.

André DESSENNE, 'Le Griffon Créto-Mycénien: inventaire et remarques', in *BCH*, 81, 1957, pp.203-215.

O.T.P.K. DICKINSON, *The Origins of Mycenaean Civilization*, S.I.M.A. 49, Paul Åströms Förlag, Göteberg, 1977.

Oliver DICKINSON, 'Cist Graves and Chamber Tombs', in *BICS*, 29, 1982, pp.123-5.

B.C. DIETRICH, 'Some Evidence of Religious Continuity in the Greek Dark Ages', in *BICS*, 17, 1970, pp.16-31.

B.C. DIETRICH, *The Origins of Greek Religion*, De Gruyter, Berlin, 1974.

E.R. DODDS, *The Greeks and the Irrational*, University of California Press, Berkeley and Los Angeles, 1951.

Mary DOUGLAS, *Natural Symbols*, Penguin Books, Harmondsworth, England, 1973 (first publ. Barrie and Rockliff, 1970).

Christos DOUMAS, 'Korfi t'Aroniou', in *A Delt*, 20, 1965, pp.41-64.

Christos DOUMAS, *The N.P. Goulandris Collection of Early Cycladic Art*, photographs by Ino Ioannidou and Lenio Bartziotis, J. Makris S.A., Athens, 1968.

Christos DOUMAS, *Early Bronze Age Burial Habits in the Cyclades*, S.I.M.A. 48, Paul Åströms Förlag, Göteborg, Sweden, 1977.

Christos DOUMAS, *Cycladic Art: Ancient sculpture and pottery from the N.P. Goulandris Collection*, British Museum Publications, London, 1983.

Page DUBOIS, *Sowing the Body: Psychoanalysis and Ancient Representations of Women*, The University of Chicago Press, 1988.

Émile DURKHEIM, *The Elementary Forms of the Religious Life*, transl. by J.W. Swain, Allen and Unwin, London, 1926.

Émile DURKHEIM and Marcel MAUSS, *Primitive Classification*, transl. and ed. Rodney Needham, University of Chicago Press, 1963.

René DUSSAUD, *Les Civilisations préhelleniques dans le bassin de la Mer Égée*, Librairie Paul Geuthner, Paris, 1914.

Carel J. DU RY, *The Art of the Ancient Near and Middle East*, Harry N. Abrams Inc., New York, London, 1969.

Dr. I.E.S. EDWARDS, 'Some Magical Aspects of the Pyramids', paper presented to Egypt Exploration Society, London, 20.6.1984.

A. ERMAN, *A Handbook of Egyptian Religion*, transl. by A.S. Griffith, Archibald Constable and Co. Ltd., London, 1907.

Arthur J. EVANS, *The Mycenaean Tree and Pillar Cult and Its Mediterranean Relations*, Macmillan, London, 1901.

Arthur J. EVANS, *The Prehistoric Tombs of Knossos*, Quaritch, London, 1906.

Arthur J. EVANS, *Scripta Minoa Vol. I*, Clarendon Press, Oxford, 1909.

Arthur J. EVANS, 'The Ring of Nestor', in *JHS*, 45, 1925, pp.1-75.

Arthur J. EVANS, *The Shaft Graves and Bee-hive Tombs of Mycenae*, Macmillan, London, 1929.

Arthur J. EVANS, *The Earlier Religion of Greece in the Light of Cretan Discoveries*, Macmillan, London, 1931.

Arthur J. EVANS, *Scripta Minoa Vol. II*, Clarendon Press, Oxford, 1952.

Doniert EVELY, 'Minoan Craftsmen: problems of recognition and definition', paper presented at Oxford Aegean Archaeological Seminar, 19.6.1986.

Hugh G. EVELYN-WHITE (transl.), *Hesiod: The Homeric Hymns and Homerica*, The Loeb Classical Library, William Heinemann, London, Harvard University Press, Cambridge, Massachusetts, 1914.

Arthur FAIRBANKS, *Museum of Fine Arts, Boston: Catalogue of Greek and Etruscan vases 1. Early vases preceding Athenian black-figured ware*, Harvard University Press, 1928.

Louis C. FARON, 'Death and Fertility Rites of the Mapuche (Araucanian) Indians of Central Chile' in John Middleton (ed.), *Gods and Rituals: Readings in Religious Beliefs and Practices*, University of Texas Press, Austin and London, 1967, pp.227-254.

J. FAUCOUNAU. 'La civilisation de Syros et l'origine du disque de Phaistos', in *Kretologia*, 7, 1978, pp.101-13.

Paul FAURE, *Fonctions des cavernes crétoises*, Editions E. de Boccard, Paris, 1964.

M.I. FINLEY, *The Ancient Economy*, Chatto and Windus, London, 1973.

M.I. FINLEY, *Early Greece: The Bronze and Archaic Ages*, Chatto and Windus, London, 1981.

Raymond FIRTH, *Symbols, Public and Private*, Cornell University Press, Ithaca, New York, and George Allen and Unwin, 1973.

Lesley FITTON, 'Small monsters made of bits of marble', paper presented to London Classical Society, 18.5.83.

J. Lesley FITTON (ed.), *Cycladica: Studies in Memory of N.P. Goulandris*, Proceedings of the Seventh British Museum Classical Colloquium June 1983, British Museum Publications, 1984.

K. FITTSCHEN, *Untersuchung zum Beginn der Sagendarstellungen bei den Griechen*, Verlag Bruno Hessling, Berlin, 1969.

K.V. FLANNERY, 'Contextual analysis of ritual paraphernalia from Formative Oaxaca', in K.V. Flannery (ed.), *The Early Mesoamerican Village*, Academic Press, New York, San Francisco, London, 1976.

Andrew FLEMING, 'The Myth of the Mother Goddess', in *World Archaeology*, I, 1969, pp.247-61.

J. FONTENROSE, *Python: A Study of Delphic Myth and its Origins*, University of California Press, Los Angeles, 1959.

J. FONTENROSE, *Orion: the myth of the hunter and the huntress*, University of California Publications, Berkeley, 1981.

Hamish FORBES, 'Storage and storage strategies in a modern Greek village: anthropological and archaeological implications', paper presented at Mycenaean Seminar, Institute of Classical Studies, London, 14.11.84.

E.J. FORSDYKE, *Catalogue of Greek and Etruscan Vases in the British Museum Vol. I, Pt. I, Prehistorical Aegean Pottery*, British Museum, London, 1925.

Vassilita FOTOU, 'Some aspects of non-palatial architecture in Crete during the New Palace period', paper presented at University of London, Mycenaean Seminar, 2.12.1987. See *BICS*, 35, 1988, pp.178-9.

Douglas FRAME, *The Myth of Return in Early Greek Epic*, Yale University Press, New Haven and London, 1978.

H. FRANKFORT, *Cylinder Seals*, Macmillan, London, 1939.

H. FRANKFORT, *The Art and Architecture of the Ancient Orient*, Pelican History of Art, Penguin Books, Harmondsworth, 1954.

Sir James George FRAZER, *The Golden Bough* (abridged edition), Macmillan, London, 1941.

Elizabeth FRENCH, 'A chariot larnax from Mycenae', in *BSA*, 56, 1961, pp.88-9.

Elizabeth FRENCH, 'The Development of Mycenaean Terracotta Figurines', in *BSA*, LXVI, 1971, pp.101-87.

E.B. FRENCH and K.A. WARDLE (ed.), *Problems in Greek Prehistory: Papers Presented at the Centenary Conference of the British School of Archaeology at Athens, Manchester, April 1986*, Bristol Classical Press, 1988.

Sigmund FREUD, *Introductory Lectures on Psychoanalysis*, trans. Joan Riviere, George Allen and Unwin, London, 1922.

August FRICKENHAUS, Walter MÜLLER and Franz OELMANN, *Tiryns Vol. 1*, Eleutheroudakis and Barth, Athens, 1912.

Paul FRIEDLÄNDER, *Herakles: Sagengeschichtliche Untersuchungen*, Weidmannsche Buchhandlung, Berlin, 1907.

Paul FRIEDRICH, *The Meaning of Aphrodite*, University of Chicago Press, Chicago and London, 1978.

William D. FURLEY, *Studies in the Use of Fire in Ancient Greek Religion*, Arno Press, New York, 1981.

Arne FURUMARK, *The Mycenaean Pottery: Analysis and Classification*, Kungl. Vitterhets Historie och Antikvitets Akademien, Stockholm, 1941.

N.H. GALE and Z.A. STOS-GALE, 'Cycladic Lead and Silver Metallurgy', in *BSA*, 76, 1981, pp.169-224.

Theodor H. GASTER, *Thespis: Ritual, Myth and Drama in the Ancient Near East*, Henry Schuman, New York, 1950.

Hara S. GEORGIOU, 'Analysis of carbon samples from Katsamba and Knossos, Crete', in *Kretologia*, IV, 1977, pp.133-8.

Patricia GETZ-PREZIOSI, 'Addenda to the Cycladic Exhibition in Karlsruhe', *Archäologischer Anzeiger*, 1978, 1, pp.1-11.

Patricia GETZ-PREZIOSI, *Sculptors of the Cyclades: Individual and Tradition in the Third Millennium B.C.*, University of Michigan Press, Ann Arbor, 1987.

Christopher GILL, 'Snell, Adkins and the Greek Concept of the Person', paper presented to the Hellenic society, London, 17.3.1988.

Margaret A.V. GILL, 'The Minoan Genius', in *Mitteilungen des Deutschen Archäologischen Instituts: Athenische Abteilung*, 79, 1964, pp.1-21.

M.A.V. GILL, 'The Knossos Sealings: Provenance and Identification' in *BSA*, 60, 1965, pp.58-98.

Erving GOFFMAN, 'Gender Advertisements', in *Studies in the Anthropology of Visual Communication*, Vol. 3 No. 2, Society for the Anthropology of Visual Communication, USA, 1976.

Lucy GOODISON, 'A Female sun-deity in the Bronze Age Aegean?', paper presented at the University of London, Mycenaean Seminar, 18.2.1987. See *BICS*, 35, 1988, pp.168-73.

John GOULD, 'Law, Custom and Myth: Aspects of the Social Position of Women in Classical Athens', in *JHS*, 100, 1980, pp.38-59.

Dorothea GRAY, *Seewesen*, Archaeologia Homerica Band 1, Chapter G, Vandenhoeck and Ruprecht, Göttingen, 1974.

L.V. GRINSELL, 'The Boat of the Dead in the Bronze Age', *Antiquity*, 15, 1941, pp.360-70.

Ernst GRUMACH, 'Zur Herkunft des Diskus von Phaistos', in *Proceedings of the Second Cretological Congress (1966), Vol. 1*, Athens, 1968, pp.281-96.

Ernst GRUMACH, 'The Minoan Libation Formula - Again', in *Kadmos*, 7, 1968, pp.7-26 (1968b).

Robin HÄGG, 'Official and Popular Cults in Mycenaean Greece', in Hägg and Marinatos (ed.), *Sanctuaries and Cults in the Aegean Bronze Age*, Paul Åströms Förlag, Stockholm, 1981, pp.35-9.

Robin HÄGG (ed.), *The Greek Renaissance of the Eighth Century B.C.: Tradition and Innovation: Proceedings of the Second International Symposium at the Swedish Institute in Athens, 1-5 June, 1981*, Paul Åströms Förlag, Stockholm, 1983.

Robin HÄGG, 'Epiphany in Minoan Ritual', in *BICS*, 30, 1983, pp.184-5 (1983b).

Robin HÄGG and Nanno MARINATOS (ed.), *Sanctuaries and Cults in the Aegean Bronze Age: Proceedings of the First International Symposium at the Swedish Institute in Athens, 1980*, Paul Åströms Förlag, Stockholm, 1981.

Robin HÄGG and Nanno MARINATOS (ed.), *The Minoan Thalassocracy: Myth and Reality: Proceedings of the Third International Symposium at the Swedish Institute in Athens, 1982*, Paul Åströms Förlag, Stockholm, 1984.

Robin HÄGG and Nanno MARINATOS (ed.), *The Function of the Minoan Palaces: Proceedings of the Fourth International Symposium at the Swedish Institute in Athens, 1984*, Paul Åströms Förlag, Stockholm, 1987.

Edith H. HALL, *Excavations in Eastern Crete: Sphoungaras*, University Museum, Philadelphia, U.S.A., 1912.

H.R. HALL, *The Civilization of Greece in the Bronze Age*, Methuen, London, 1928.

Erik HALLAGER, *The Master Impression: A Clay Sealing from the Greek-Swedish Excavations at Kastelli, Khania*, S.I.M.A. 69, Paul Åströms Förlag, Göteborg, 1985.

Paul HALSTEAD, 'From determinism to uncertainty: Social storage and the rise of the Minoan palace', in Alison Sheridan and Geoff Bailey (ed.), *Economic Archaeology: Towards an Integration of Ecological and Social Approaches*, BAR International series 96, Oxford, 1981, pp.187-213.

Paul HALSTEAD, 'Deconstructing traditional agriculture', paper presented to the Institute of Classical Studies, London, 23.1.86. (Published as 'Traditional and ancient rural economy in Mediterranean Europe: Plus ça change?' in *JHS*, 107, 1987, pp.77-87.)

Friedrich Wilhelm HAMDORF, *Griechische Kultpersonifikationen der vorhellenistischen Zeit*, Verlag Philipp von Zabern, Mainz, 1964.

Jane HARRISON, *Themis: A Study of the Social Origins of Greek Religion*, Cambridge University Press, 1927.

Halford W. HASKELL, 'The Origin of the Aegean Stirrup Jar and its Earliest Evolution and Distribution (MB III-LB I)', in *AJA*, 89, 1985, pp.221-9.

J. HATZIDAKIS, *Les Villas Minoennes de Tylissos*, Librairie Orientaliste Paul Geuthner, Paris, 1934.

Jacquetta HAWKES, *Dawn of the Gods*, Random House, New York, 1968.

W.C. HAYES, *Royal Sarcophagoi of the XVIII Dynasty*, Princeton University Press, Princeton, New Jersey, 1935.

Robert HERTZ, *Death and the Right Hand*, transl. by Rodney and Claudia Needham, with an introduction by E.E. Evans-Pritchard, Cohen and West, London, 1960 (first publ. in Paris, 1907 and 1909).

Reynold HIGGINS, *Minoan and Mycenaean Art*, Thames and Hudson, London, 1967.

R.A. HIGGINS, *Greek Terracottas*, Methuen, London, 1967 (1967b).

Stefan HILLER, 'Possible Historical Reasons for the Rediscovery of Homer', in Hägg (ed.), *The Greek Renaissance of the Eighth Century B.C.*, 1983, pp.9-15.

Stefan HILLER, 'Pax Minoica Versus Minoan Thalassocracy', in R. Hägg and N. Marinatos (eds.), *The Minoan Thalassocracy: Myth and Reality*, 1984, pp.27-30.

Henry HODGES, *Technology in the Ancient World*, Allen Lane, The Penguin Press, London, 1970.

D.G. HOGARTH, 'The Zakro Sealings', in *JHS*, 22, 1902, pp.76-93.

R.G. HOOD 'A Geometric Oenochoe with Ship Scene in Hobart', in *AJA*, 71, 1967, pp.82-7.

Sinclair HOOD, *The Minoans: Crete in the Bronze Age*, Thames and Hudson, London, 1971.

Sinclair HOOD, in Sinclair Hood and Victor Kenna, 'An Early Minoan III sealing from Knossos', in *Antichità Cretesi: Studi in onore di Doro Levi Vol. 1*, Università di Catania - Istituto di Archeologia, 1973, pp.103ff.

Sinclair HOOD, *The Arts in Prehistoric Greece*, Penguin Books, Harmondsworth, England, 1978.

Sinclair HOOD and David SMYTH, *Archaeological Survey of the Knossos Area*, Supplementary Volume No. 14, British School at Athens and Thames and Hudson, 1981.

J.T. HOOKER, *Mycenaean Greece*, Routledge and Kegan Paul, London, Boston and Henley, 1976.

J.T. HOOKER, *The Origin of the Linear B Script*, Ediciones Universidad de Salamanca, 1979.

James HOOKER, *Linear B: An Introduction*, Bristol Classical Press, 1980.

James HOOKER, 'Cult-Personnel in the Pylos tablets', paper presented at Mycenaean Seminar, Institute of Classical Studies, London, 3.11.83.

R.J. HOPPER, *The Early Greeks*, Weidenfeld and Nicholson, London, 1976.

Erik HORNUNG, *Conceptions of God in Ancient Egypt: the one and the many*, transl. John Baines, Routledge and Kegan Paul, London, Melbourne and Henley, 1983 (first publ. 1971 by Wissenschaftliche Buchgesellschaft).

Erik HORNUNG, *Tal der Könige: Die Ruhestätte der Pharaonen*, Artemis Verlag, Zürich und München, 1983 (1983b).

T.P. HOWE 'Linear B and Hesiod's Breadwinners', in *Transactions of the American Philological Association*, 89, 1958, pp.44-65.

S.C. HUMPHREYS, 'Economy and Society in Classical Athens', in *Annali della Scuola Normale Superiore di Pisa*, Serie II, Vol. XXXIX, 1970, pp.1-26.

Sara Anderson IMMERWAHR, *Early Burials from the Agora Cemeteries*, ASCSA, Princeton, New Jersey, 1973.

Silvia Damiani INDELICATO, *Piazza pubblica e palazzo nella Creta Minoica*, Società editoriale Jouvence, Rome, 1982.

Frederic JAMESON, *The Prison House of Language: A Critical Account of Structuralism and Russian Formalism*, Princeton University Press, Princeton, New Jersey, 1972.

Richard JANKO, *Homer, Hesiod and the Hymns: Diachronic development in epic diction*, Cambridge University Press, 1982.

Turham KAMIL, *Yortan Cemetery in the Early Bronze Age*, BAR International Series 145, British Archaeological Reports, Oxford, 1982.

A KANTA, *The Late Minoan III Period in Crete*, S.I.M.A. 58, Paul Åströms Förlag, Göteberg, 1980.

V. KARAGEORGHIS, *Mycenaean Art from Cyprus*, Department of Antiquities, Cyprus, 1968.

Jacqueline KARAGEORGHIS, *La grande déesse de Chypre et son culte*, Maison de l'Orient, Lyons, 1977.

Alexandra KARETSOU, 'The Peak Sanctuary of Mt. Juktas', in R. Hägg and N. Marinatos (ed.), *Sanctuaries and Cults in the Aegean Bronze Age*, Paul Åströms Förlag, Stockholm, 1981, pp.137-53.

Alexandra KARETSOU, 'The Minoan Peak Sanctuary on Mount Juktas', paper presented at University of London, Mycenaean Seminar, 20.5.1987.

G. KARO, *Religion des ägäischen Kreises*, Erlangen A. Deichertsche Verlagsbuchhandlung Dr. Werner Scholl, Leipzig, 1925.

Georg KARO, *Die Schachtgräber von Mykenai*, F. Bruckmann Ag. München, 1930.

V.E.G. KENNA, *Cretan Seals*, Clarendon Press, Oxford, 1960.

V.E.G. KENNA, 'Ancient Crete and the Use of the Cylinder Seal', in *AJA*, 72, 1968, pp.321-36.

V.E.G. KENNA, *The Cretan Talismanic Stone in the Late Minoan Age*, S.I.M.A. 24, Sölvegatan 2, Lund, 1969.

V.E.G. KENNA, 'Three Cylinder Seals found in Crete', in *Kretika Chronika*, Vol. 1, 1969, pp.351-64 (1969b).

Bahija KHALIL ISMAIL, 'Eine Siegesstele des Königs Daduša von Ešnunna', in W. Meid and H. Trenkwalder (ed.), *Im Bannkreis des alten Orients*, = *Innsbrucker Beiträge zur Kulturwissenschaft Vol. 24*, Innsbruck, 1986.

G.S. KIRK, *Homer and the Epic*, Cambridge University Press, 1965.

R.B. KOEHL, 'The Chieftain Cup and a Minoan rite of passage', in *JHS*, 106, 1896, pp.99-110.

H.Z. KOŞAY, 'Disques Solaires mis au jour aux Fouilles d'Alaca-Höyük', in *BSA*, 37, 1936-7, pp.160-5.

O. KRZYSZKOWSKA and L. NIXON (ed.), *Minoan Society: Proceedings of the Cambridge Colloquim 1981*, Bristol Classical Press, 1983.

Donna C. KURTZ and John BOARDMAN, *Greek Burial Customs*, Thames and Hudson, London, 1971.

Jacques LACAN, *The Language of the Self*, transl. with notes and commentary by Anthony Wilden, The John Hopkins University Press, Baltimore and London, 1968.

Michael LANE (ed.), *Structuralism: A Reader*, Jonathan Cape, London, 1970.

Richard LATTIMORE (transl.), *The Iliad of Homer*, University of Chicago Press, Chicago and London, 1951.

Lillian B. LAWLER, *The Dance in Ancient Greece*, Wesleyan University Press, Middletown, Connecticut, U.S.A., 1964.

Edmund LEACH, *Genesis as Myth and Other Essays*, Jonathan Cape, London, 1969.

E.R. LEACH, *Lévi-Strauss*, Modern Masters series, Fontana, 1970.

E.R. LEACH, *Culture and Communication*, Cambridge University Press, 1976.

D.J.N. LEE, *The similes of the Iliad and the Odyssey compared*, Australian Humanities Research Council monograph, 10, Melbourne University Press, Melbourne, 1964.

Doro LEVI, *Festòs e la Civilta' Minoica Tavole 1*, Edizioni dell'Ateneo, Rome, 1976.

Claude LÉVI-STRAUSS, *Structural Anthropology*, transl. Claire Jacobson and Brooke Grundfest Schoepf, Penguin Books, Harmondsworth, England, 1968.

Claude LÉVI-STRAUSS, 'The Sex of the Heavenly Bodies', in M. Lane (ed.), *Structuralism : A Reader*, Jonathan Cape, London, 1970, pp.330-9.

Godfrey LIENHARDT, *Divinity and Experience: The Religion of the Dinka*, Clarendon Press, Oxford, 1961.

G.E.R. LLOYD, *Polarity and Analogy*, University Press, Cambridge, 1966.

P.H.J. LLOYD-JONES, 'Artemis and Iphigenia', in *JHS*, 103, 1983, 87ff.

Charlotte R. LONG, *The Ayia Triadha Sarcophagus: A study of Late Minoan and Mycenaean funerary practices and beliefs*, S.I.M.A. 41, Paul Åströms Förlag, Göteborg, 1974.

Robert H. LOWIE, *Primitive Religion*, George Routledge and Sons, London, 1925.

Kevin McDONNELL and Kevin ROBINS, 'Marxist Cultural Theory: the Althusserian Smokescreen', in K. McDonnell and K. Robins (ed.), *One-Dimensional Marxism*, Allison and Busby, London, 1980, pp.157-231.

J.A. MACGILLIVRAY, 'The end of the Old Palaces in Crete', paper presented at University of London, Mycenaean Seminar, 23.4.86.

J.A. MACGILLIVRAY, 'Excavations at Palaikastro in East Crete', paper presented to British School at Athens at University College, London, 2.2.1988.

J.A. MACGILLIVRAY and R.L.N. BARBER (ed.), *The Prehistoric Cyclades: Contributions to a workshop on Cycladic chronology*, Department of Classical Archaeology, Edinburgh, 1984.

J.A. MACGILLIVRAY with P.M. DAY and R.E. JONES, 'Middle Minoan IA dark faced wares from Knossos', paper presented at BSA Centenary Conference on Problems in Greek Prehistory, Manchester University, April 1986 (1986b). See E.B. French and K.A. Wardle (ed.), *Problems in Greek Prehistory*, Bristol Classical Press, 1988, pp.91-4.

Pierre MARANDA (ed.), *Mythology: Selected Readings*, Penguin Education, Harmondsworth, England, 1972.

Jean-Claude MARGUERON, *Mesopotamia*, Nagel Publishers, Geneva, 1967.

Nanno MARINATOS, *Minoan Sacrificial Ritual: Cult Practice and Symbolism*, Skrifter Utgivna av Svenska Institutet i Athen 8°, IX, Stockholm 1986.

S. MARINATOS, 'La Marine Créto-Mycénienne' in *BCH*, 57, 1933, pp.170-235.

S. MARINATOS, *Excavations at Thera IV* (1970 season), Archaiologiki Etairia, Athens, 1971.

S. MARINATOS and M. HIRMER, *Crete and Mycenae*, transl. J. Boardman, Thames and Hudson, London, 1960.

Karl MARX, *Pre-Capitalist Economic Formations*, Lawrence and Wishart, London, 1964.

Friedrich MATZ, *Die Frühkretischen Siegel*, Walter de Gruyter, Berlin and Leipzig, 1928.

Friedrich MATZ, *Forschungen auf Kreta, 1942*, Walter de Gruyter, Berlin, 1951.

Friedrich MATZ, *Crete and Early Greece*, Methuen, London, 1962.

Marcell MAUSS, *A General Theory of Magic*, transl. by Robert Brain, Routledge and Kegan Paul, London and Boston, 1972 (first publ. by Presses Universitaires de France, 1950).

Caterina MAVRIYANNAKI, *Recherches sur les larnakes minoennes de la Crète occidentale*, Edizioni dell'Ateneo, Rome, 1972.

Margaret MEAD, *Male and Female: A Study of the Sexes in a Changing World*, Penguin Books, London, 1962 (first publ. in the USA, 1950).

E.M. MELAS, *The Islands of Karpathos, Saros and Kasos in the Neolithic and Bronze Age*, S.I.M.A. 68, Paul Åströms Förlag, Göteborg, 1985.

James MELLAART, 'A Neolithic City in Turkey', in *Scientific American*, 210, 1964, pp.94-104.

James MELLAART, 'Excavations at Çatal Hüyük, 1963; Third Preliminary Report' in *Anatolian Studies*, XIV, 1964, pp.39-119 (1964b).

James MELLAART, *Earliest Civilizations of the Near East*, Thames and Hudson, London, 1965.

M. MELLINK, 'The Royal Tombs at Alaca Hüyük', in Saul S. Weinberg (ed.), *The Aegean and the Near East: Studies Presented to Hetty Goldman*, J.J. Augustin, Locust Valley, New York, 1956.

R. MERKELBACH and M.L.WEST (ed.), *Fragmenta Hesiodea*, Clarendon Press, Oxford, 1967.

John MIDDLETON (ed.), *Gods and Rituals: Readings in Religious Beliefs and Practices*, University of Texas Press, Austin and London, 1967.

Jeremy MONTAGU, 'The conch in prehistory: pottery, stone and natural' in *World Archaeology*, 12, 1981, pp.273-9.

Lyvia MORGAN, 'Morphology, Syntax and the issue of Chronology' in J.A. MacGillivray and R.L.N. Barber (ed.), *The Prehistoric Cyclades*, 1984, pp.165-78.

Lyvvia MORGAN, 'A Minoan Larnax from Knossos', in *BSA*, 82, 1987, pp.171-200.

J.S. MORRISON and R.T. WILLIAMS, *Greek Oared Ships 900-322 BC*, Cambridge University Press, 1968.

Louis MOULINIER, *Le Pur et l'Impur dans la Pensée des Grecs*, Librairie C. Klincksieck, Paris, 1952.

Oswyn MURRAY, *Early Greece*, The Harvester Press, Sussex, and The Humanities Press, New Jersey, 1980.

George E. MYLONAS, 'Excavations at Haghios Kosmas', in *AJA*, 38, 1934, pp.258-79.

George E. MYLONAS, 'Homeric and Mycenaean Burial Customs' in *AJA*, 52, 1948, pp.56-81.

George E. MYLONAS, *Aghios Kosmas: An Early Bronze Age Settlement and Cemetery in Attica*, Princeton University Press, Princeton, New Jersey, 1959.

George E. MYLONAS, *Eleusis and the Eleusinian Mysteries*, Princeton University Press, Princeton, New Jersey and Routledge and Kegan Paul, London, 1961 (actually 1962).

George E. MYLONAS, *Mycenae and the Mycenaean Age*, Princeton University Press, Princeton, 1966.

Gregory NAGY, 'Phaethon, Sappho's Phaon, and the White Rock of Leukas', in *Harvard Studies in Classical Philology*, 77, 1973, pp.137-77.

Rodney NEEDHAM, *Symbolic Classification*, Goodyear Publishing Company, Santa Monica, California, 1979.

Grace W. NELSON, 'A Greek votive Iynx-wheel in Boston' in *AJA*, 14, 1940, pp.443-56.

W.-D. NIEMEIER, 'From the Minoan thalassocracy to the Mycenaean expansion', paper presented at University of London, Mycenaean Seminar, 13.11.85.

W.-D. NIEMEIER, 'The "Priest King Fresco" from Knossos: A new reconstruction and interpretation', paper presented at BSA Centenary Conference on Problems in Greek Prehistory, Manchester University, April 1986. See E.B. French and K.A. Wardle (ed.), *Problems in Greek Prehistory*, Bristol Classical Press, 1988, pp.235-44.

Martin P. NILSSON, *The Mycenaean Origin of Greek Mythology*, Cambridge University Press, 1932.

Martin P. NILSSON, *Greek Popular Religion*, Columbia University Press, New York, 1940.

Martin P. NILSSON, *The Minoan-Mycenaean Religion and its Survival in Greek Religion*, C.W.K. Gleerup, Lund, 1950, (first publ. 1927).

Erik OSTENFELD, *Ancient Greek Psychology and the modern mind-body debate*, Aarhus University Press, 1987.

David W. PACKARD, *Minoan Linear A*, University of California Press, Berkeley/Los Angeles/London, 1974.

Ruth PADEL, '"Imagery of the Elsewhere": Two Choral Odes of Euripides' in *CQ*, 24, 1974, pp.227-41.

Ruth PADEL, Review of Artemidorus, *The Interpretation of Dreams*, transl. Dr. Robert J. White, in *Times Literary Supplement*, 1975, p 494.

Ruth PADEL, 'Women: Model for Possession by Greek Daemons' in Averil Cameron and Amélie Kuhrt (ed.), *Images of Women in Antiquity*, Croom Helm, London and Canberra, 1983.

L.R. PALMER, *The Interpretation of Mycenaean Greek Texts*, Clarendon Press, Oxford, 1963.

I.A. PAPAPOSTOLOU, *Ta sfragismata ton Chanion. Symboli sti meleti tis minoikis sfragidoglufias*, Vivliothiki tis en Athenais Archaiologikis Etairias, No. 87, Athens, 1977.

G. PAPATHANASSOPOULOS, *Neolithic and Cycladic Civilization*, 'Milissa' Publishing House for National Archaeological Museum, Athens, 1981.

H.W. PARKE, *Greek Oracles*, Hutchinson University Library, London, 1967.

Robert PARKER, *Miasma: Pollution and Purification in early Greek Religion*, Clarendon Press, Oxford, 1983.

A.A.D. PEATFIELD, 'The Topography of Minoan Peak Sanctuaries' in *BSA*, 78, 1983, pp.273-9.

Alan PEATFIELD, 'Minoan peak sanctuaries', paper presented at University of London, Mycenaean Seminar, 17.2.88.

J.D.S. PENDLEBURY, *The Archaeology of Crete*, Methuen, London, 1939.

J.D.S. PENDLEBURY, *A Handbook to the Palace of Minos, Knossos, with its dependencies*, Max Parrish, London, 1954.

A.W. PERSSON, *The Religion of Greece in Prehistoric Times*, University of California Press, Berkeley and Los Angeles, 1942.

Ernst PFUHL, 'Der archaische Friedhof am Stadtberge von Thera' in *Mitteilungen des Deutschen Archäologischen Instituts: Athenische Abteilung*, 28, 1903, pp.1-288.

A. PIANKOFF, *The Tomb of Ramasses VI*, Pantheon Books, New York, 1954.

A. PIANKOFF, *The Wandering of the Soul*, Bollingen Series XL.6, Princeton University Press, Princeton, 1974.

Charles PICARD, *Les Religions Préhelléniques (Crète et Mycènes)*, Presses Universitaires de France, 108 Boulevard St. Germain, Paris, 1948.

Ingo PINI, 'Kypro-Ägäische Rollsiegel', in *Jahrbuch*, 95, 1980, pp.77-108.

J. PINSENT, 'Bull-Leaping', in O. Krzyszowska and L. Nixon (ed.), *Minoan Society: Proceedings of the Cambridge Colloquium 1981*, Bristol Classical Press, 1983, pp.259-71.

Nicholas PLATON, *Zakros: The Discovery of a Lost Palace of Ancient Crete*, Charles Scribner's Sons, New York, 1971.

N. PLATON, 'Problèmes de Chronologie et de Classification des Sceaux Crétomycéniens', in *Die Kretisch-Mykenische Glyptik und ihre Gegenwärtigen Probleme*, Harald Boldt Verlag KG Boppard, Deutsche Forschungsgemeinschaft, Bonn, 1974.

Elizabeth Ellen PLATT, 'Triangular Jewelry Plaques' in *Bulletin of the American Schools of Oriental Research*, 221, 1976, pp.103-11.

D.F. POCOCK, *Mind, Body and Wealth: A Study of Belief and Practice in an Indian Village*, Basil Blackwell, Oxford, 1973.

Jean-Claude POURSAT, *Catalogue des Ivoires Mycéniens du Musée National d'Athènes*, École Française d'Athènes, Diffusion de Boccard, Paris, 1977.

M.R. POPHAM, 'Some Light on the Dark Ages', paper presented at University of London, Mycenaean Seminar, 15.2.1984.

M. POPHAM and H.W. CATLING, 'Sellopoulo Tombs 3 and 4. Two Late Minoan Graves near Knossos in *BSA*, 69, 1974, pp.195-258.

E. POTTIER, 'Documents céramiques du Musée du Louvre' in *BCH*, 31, 1907, pp.228-69.

Julian READE and David HAWKINS, 'The winged disc emblem in the Ancient Near East', paper presented at Warburg Institute, London, 27.2.84.

Colin RENFREW, *The Emergence of Civilization: The Cyclades and the Aegean in the Third Millenium B.C.*, Methuen, London, 1972.

Colin RENFREW, *Before Civilization: The Radiocarbon Revolution and Prehistoric Europe*, Jonathan Cape, London, 1973.

Colin RENFREW, 'Questions of Minoan and Mycenaean Cult', in Hägg and Marinatos (ed.), *Sanctuaries and Cults in the Aegean Bronze Age*, Paul Åströms Förlag, Stockholm, 1981, pp.27-33.

Colin RENFREW, 'Speculations on the Use of Early Cycladic Sculpture', paper presented at British Museum Cycladic Colloquium, 1983. See FITTON, 1984, pp.24-30.

Colin RENFREW, 'Phases in Development of Aegean religions', paper presented at Oxford Aegean Archaeological Seminar, 1983 (1983b).

Colin RENFREW, *The Archaeology of Cult: The Sanctuary at Phylakopi*, a British School at Athens publication, Thames and Hudson, London, 1985.

G. RETHEMIOTAKIS, 'Larnakes kai aggeia apo to Kavrochori Herakleiou', in *A Delt*, 34, 1979, Vol. I, pp.228-59.

N.J. RICHARDSON (ed.), *The Homeric Hymn to Demeter*, Clarendon Press, Oxford, 1974.

G.M.A. RICHTER, *The Furniture of the Greeks, Etruscans and Romans*, The Phaidon press, London, 1966.

E.V. RIEU (transl.), *Homer: The Odyssey*, Penguin Books, Harmondsworth, 1946.

Roland ROBERTSON (ed.), *Sociology of Religion: Selected Readings*, Penguin Books, Harmondsworth, 1969.

Anna ROES, *Greek Geometric Art: Its Symbolism and its Origin*, H.D. Tjeenk Willink & Zoon, Harlem, and Oxford University Press, Humphrey Milford, London, 1933.

R.T. RUNDLE-CLARK, *Myth and Symbol in Ancient Egypt*, Thames and Hudson, 1959 (first paperback edition 1978).

Bogdan RUTKOWSKI, *Cult Places in the Aegean World*, Polish Academy of Sciences, Warsaw, 1972. (Revised as *The Cult Places of the Aegean*, New Haven, 1986.)

I.M. RUUD, *Minoan Religion: a bibliography*, Universitetsbiblioteket, Oslo, 1980.

Gösta SÄFLUND, 'Cretan and Theran questions', in Hägg and Marinatos (ed.), *Sanctuaries and Cults in the Aegean Bronze Age*, Paul Åströms Förlag, Stockholm, 1981, pp.193-208.

John A. SAKELLARAKIS, 'Minoan Cemeteries at Arkhanes', in *Archaeology*, 20, 1967, pp.276-81.

J. SAKELLARAKIS, public lecture on Archanes (Anemospilia) and human sacrifice, presented to Institute of Classical Studies, Institute of Archaeology and British School at Athens, London, 23.2.1982.

J. SAKELLARAKIS and E. SAPOUNA-SAKELLARAKI, 'Drama of Death in a Minoan Temple', *National Geographic*, Vol. 159, No.2, February 1981, pp.205-22.

John A. and Effie SAKELLARAKIS, 'The Adorant of Myrsine' in *Antichità Cretesi: Studi in onore di Doro Levi Vol 1*, Università di Catania - Istituto di Archeologia, 1973, pp.122-6.

A. SAKELLARIOU and G. PAPATHANASOPOULOS, *National Archaeological Museum A' Prehistoric Collections: A Brief Guide*, Transl. Helen Wace, Elizabeth Wace-French and Ariadne Sanford, Dept. of Antiquities and Restoration, Athens, 1970.

Monique SALIOU, 'The Processes of Women's Subordination in Primitive and Archaic Greece' in Stephanie Coontz and Peta Henderson (ed.), *Women's Work, Men's Property: The Origins of Gender and Class*, Verso, New Left Books, 1986.

Fritz SCHACHERMEYR, *Die minoische Kultur des alten Kreta*, W. Kohlhammer Verlag, Stuttgart, 1964.

Fritz SCHACHERMEYR, *Die ägäische Frühzeit Band 1, Die Vormykenischen Perioden des Griechischen Festlandes und der Kykladen*, Verlag der Österreichischen Akademie der Wissenschaften, Vienna, 1976.

Fritz SCHACHERMEYR, *Die ägäische Frühzeit Band 2, Die Mykenische Zeit und die Gesittung von Thera*, Verlag der Österreichischen Akademie der Wissenschaften, Vienna, 1976 (1976b).

Fritz SCHACHERMEYR, *Die ägäische Frühzeit Band 3, Kreta zur Zeit der Wanderungen*, Verlag der Österreichischen Akademie der Wissenschaften, Vienna, 1979.

K. SCHEFOLD, 'Heroen und Nymphen in Kykladengräber', in *Antike Kunst*, 8, 1965, pp.87-90.

Bernhard SCHWEITZER, '1. Anna Roes: De Oorsprong der geometrische Kunst. 2. Anna Roes: Greek Geometric Art, its Symbolism and its Origin' (Review) in *Gnomon*, 10, 1934, pp.337-353.

Bernhard SCHWEITZER, *Greek Geometric Art*, Transl. P. and C. Usborne, Phaidon Press, London, 1971 (first publ. 1969).

Vincent SCULLY, *The Earth, The Temple and the Gods: Greek Sacred Architecture*, Yale University Press, New Haven and London, 1979 (first publ. 1962).

Richard B. SEAGER, *Excavations on the Island of Pseira, Crete*, University Museum, Philadelphia, 1910.

R.B. SEAGER, *Excavations in the Island of Mochlos*, American School of Classical Studies at Athens, Boston and New York, 1912.

R.B. SEAGER, *The Cemetery of Pachyammos, Crete*, University Museum, Philadelphia, 1916.

J.W. SHAW, 'The Orientation of the Minoan Palaces', in *Antichità Cretesi: Studi in onore di Doro Levi Vol. 1*, Università di Catania - Istituto di Archeologia, 1973, pp.47-59.

J.W. SHAW, 'Evidence for the Minoan Tri-partite Shrine', in *AJA*, 82, 1978, pp.429-48.

Otto SKUTSCH, 'Helen, her Name and Nature' in *JHS*, 107, 1987, pp.188-193.

Morton SMITH, '"Magic", modern definitions and ancient actuality', paper presented at Warburg Institute, London, 6.5.1987.

Bruno SNELL, *The Discovery of the Mind*, Transl. T.G. Rosenmeyr, Basil Blackwell, Oxford, 1953.

A.M. SNODGRASS, *The Dark Age of Greece*, University Press, Edinburgh, 1971.

Jeffrey S. SOLES, 'Social Ranking in Prepalatial Cemeteries', paper presented at BSA Centenary Conference on Problems in Greek Prehistory, Manchester University, April 1986. See E.B. French and K.A. Wardle (edd.), *Problems in Greek Prehistory*, Britstol Classical Press, 1988, pp.49-61.

Christiane SOURVINOU-INWOOD, 'On the lost 'Boat' ring from Mochlos' in *Kadmos*, XII, 2, 1973, pp.149-58.

Christiane SOURVINOU-INWOOD, 'Persephone and Aphrodite at Locri', in *JHS*, 98, 1978, pp.101-21.

Christiane SOURVINOU-INWOOD, 'The Myth of the First Temples at Delphi' in *CQ*, 29, 2, 1979, pp.231-51.

Christiane SOURVINOU-INWOOD, 'Apollo and Delphi: Cultic Realities versus Myths', paper presented at University of London, Mycenaean Seminar, 23.6.1983.

Christiane SOURVINOU-INWOOD, 'A Trauma in Flux: Death in the 8th Century and After', in Hägg (ed.), *The Greek Renaissance of the Eighth Century B.C.*, 1983, pp.33-48 (1983b).

Dan SPERBER, *Rethinking Symbolism*, transl. by Alice L Morton, Cambridge University Press and Hermann, Paris, 1975.

Chester G. STARR, *The Origins of Greek Civilization 1100—650 B.C.*, Jonathan Cape, London, 1962.

Chester G. STARR, 'Minoan Flower Lovers' in R. Hägg and N. Marinatos (ed.), *The Minoan Thalassocracy: Myth and Reality*, Svenska Institutet in Athen, Sweden, 1984, pp.9-12.

Theodore STERN, *The Rubber-ball Games of the Americas*, J.J. Augustin, New York, 1948.

Z.A. STOS-GALE and N.H. GALE, 'The Sources of Mycenaean Silver and Lead', in *Journal of Field Archaeology*, 9, 1982, pp.467-85.

Frank H. STUBBINGS, *Prehistoric Greece*, Rupert Hart-Davies, London, 1972.

Frank H. STUBBINGS, 'The Circus Pot Reconsidered' in *Wandlungen: Studien zur Antiken und Neueren Kunst*, Waldsassen, 1975.

Linda B. SUSSMAN, 'Workers and Drones in Hesiod's Beehive' in John Peradotto and J.P. Sullivan (ed.), *Women in the Ancient World: The Arethusa Papers*, State University of New York Press, Albany, 1984, pp.79-89.

Vivien G. SWAN, *The Pottery Kilns of Roman Britian*, Her Majesty's Satationery Office, London, 1984.

Angela TAMVAKI, 'The Cycladic figurines: some thoughts on their origin, development and parallels', paper presented to British Museum Cycladic Colloquium, 1983.

Veronica TATTON-BROWN (ed.), *Cyprus B.C.: 7000 years of History*, British Museum Publications, London, 1979.]

Lord William TAYLOUR, *The Mycenaeans*, Thames and Hudson, London, 1964.

Lord W. TAYLOUR, 'New Light on Mycenaean Religion' in *Antiquity*, 44, 1970, pp.270-80.

Emmanuel TERRAY, *Marxism and 'Primitive' Societies: Two Studies*, Transl. Mary Klopper, Monthly Review Press, New York and London, 1972.

Jürgen THIMME, 'Die Religiöse Bedeutung der Kykladenidole' in *Antike Kunst*, 8, 1965, pp.72ff.

J. THIMME and P. GETZ-PREZIOSI (ed.), *Art and Culture of the Cyclades*, C.F. Müller, Karlsruhe, 1977.

Carol G. THOMAS, 'The voice of the inarticulate: the products of a non-literate society', paper presented at University of London, Mycenaean Seminar, 15.1.86. See *BICS*, 33, 1986, p 140.

D'Arcy Wentworth THOMPSON, *A Glossary of Greek Birds*, Oxford University Press, Humphrey Milford, London, 1936.

D'Arcy Wentworth THOMPSON, *A Glossary of Greek Fishes*, Oxford University Press, Geoffrey Cumberledge, London, 1947.

George THOMSON, *Studies in Ancient Greek Society: The Prehistoric Aegean*, Lawrence and Wishart, London, 1949.

George THOMSON, *Aeschylus and Athens*, Lawrence and Wishart, London, 1966 (first publ. 1941).

L. THORNDIKE, *A History of Magic and Experimental Science*, i, Macmillan, London, 1923.

Ian A. TODD, *Çatal Hüyük in Perspective*, Cummings Publishing Company, Menlo Park, California, U.S.A., 1976.

Renate TÖLLE, *Frühgriechische Reigentänze*, Hamburg, 1964.

Metaxia TSIPOPOULOU, 'Aghia Photia, Siteia: a protopalatial "Palace"?', paper presented at BSA Centenary Conference on Problems in Greek Prehistory, Manchester University, April 1986. See E.B. French and K.A. Wardle (ed.), *Problems in Greek Prehistory*, Bristol Classical Press, 1988, pp.31-47.

Christos TSOUNTAS, 'Kykladika' in *AE*, 1899, pp.74-134.

Olga TUFNELL, 'Some Gold Bird Ornaments: Falcon or Wryneck?' in *Anatolian Studies*, 33, 1983, pp.57-66.

V.W. TURNER, *The Forest of Symbols*, Cornell University Press, Ithaca, 1970.

P.J. UCKO, 'Interpretation of Prehistoric Anthropomorphic Figurines' in *Journal of Royal Anthropological Institute*, 92, 1962, pp.38-54.

Peter J. UCKO, *Anthropomorphic Figurines of Predynastic Egypt and Neolithic Crete with comparative material from the Prehistoric Near East and Mainland Greece*, Andrew Szmidla, Royal Anthropological Occasional Paper No. 24, 1968.

P.J. UCKO, 'Ethnography and archaeological interpretation of funerary remains', in *World Archaeology*, 1969, I, pp.262-77.

E. Douglas VAN BUREN, *Symbols of the Gods in Mesopotamian Art*, Pontificum Institutum Biblicum, Rome, 1945.

H. und M. VAN EFFENTERRE, 'Vers une grammaire de la Glyptique Créto-Mycénienne', in *Die Kretisch - Mykenische Glyptik und ihre Gegnwärtigen Probleme*, Harald Boldt Verlag KG Boppard, Deutsche Forschungsgemeinschaft, Bonn, 1974.

H. VAN EFFENTERRE, *Le Palais de Mallia et la Cité Minoenne*, Vols I & II, Edizioni dell' Ateneo, Rome, 1980.

Henri VAN EFFENTERRE, 'Le Langage de la Thalassocratie' in R. Hägg and N. Marinatos (ed.), *The Minoan Thalassocracy: Myth and Reality*, 1984, pp.55-7.

Henri VAN EFFENTERRE, *Les Égéens: Aux Origines de la Grèce, Chypre, Cyclades, Crète et Mycènes*, Armand Colin, Paris, 1986.

J.C. VAN LEUVEN, 'Evidence for Mycenaean Religion', paper presented at University of London, Mycenaean Seminar, 15.1.1975, see *BICS*, 22, 1975, pp.203-5.

J.C. VAN LEUVEN, 'The mainland tradition of sanctuaries in prehistoric Greece' in *World Archaeology*, Vol 10 No. 2, 1978, pp.139-48.

R.A. VAN ROYEN and B.H. ISAAC, *The Arrival of the Greeks: the evidence of the settlements*, B.R. Grüner, Amsterdam, 1979.

Donald Phillip VERENE (ed.), *Symbol, Myth and Culture: Essays and Lectures of Ernst Cassirer 1935-1945*, Yale University Press, New Haven and London, 1979.

Emily VERMEULE, *Greece in the Bronze Age*, University of Chicago Press, Chicago and London, 1964.

E.T. VERMEULE, 'Painted Mycenaean Larnakes' in *JHS*, 85, 1965, pp.123-48.

Emily VERMEULE, *Aspects of Death in Early Greek Art and Poetry*, University of California Press, Berkeley, Los Angeles, London, 1979.

Emily VERMEULE and Vassos KARAGEORGHIS, *Mycenaean Pictorial Vase Painting*, Harvard University Press, Cambridge, Massachusetts and London, 1982.

Jean-Pierre VERNANT, *Mythe et Pensée chez les Grecs*, François Maspero, Paris, 1965.

Jean-Pierre VERNANT, 'Le Mythe Prométhéen chez Hésiode', paper presented at Institute of Classical Studies Seminar, London, 20.5.1974.

Jean-Pierre VERNANT, 'À la table des hommes', in *La cuisine du sacrifice en pays grec*, Éditions Gallimard, Paris, 1979, pp.37-132.

Jean-Pierre VERNANT, *Mythe and Society in Ancient Greece*, transl. Janet Lloyd, Methuen, London, 1980 (first publ. in France, 1974).

C.G. VON BRANDENSTEIN, 'The Meaning of Section and Section Names', in *Oceania*, 41, 1970, pp.39-49.

A.J.B. WACE, *Chamber Tombs at Mycenae*, The Society of Antiquaries, Oxford, 1932.

Gisela WALBERG, *Kamares*, Acta Universitatis Upsaliensis Boreas, Uppsala, 1976.

P. WARREN, 'A stone receptacle from the Cave of Hermes Kranaios at Patsos' in *BSA*, 61, 1966, pp.195-6.

Peter WARREN, 'An Early Bronze Age Potter's Workshop in Crete', in *Antiquity*, 43, 1969, pp.224-7.

Peter WARREN, *Myrtos: An Early Bronze Age settlement in Crete*, British School of Archaeology at Athens, Thames and Hudson, 1972.

P.M. WARREN, 'Crete, 3,000-1,400 B.C.: immigration and the archaeological evidence', in R.A. Crossland and Ann Birchall (ed.), *Bronze Age Migrations in the Aegean*, Proceedings of the First International Colloquium on Aegean Prehistory, Sheffield, Duckworth, London, 1973.

Peter WARREN, 'The Beginnings of Minoan Religion', in *Antichità Cretesi: Studi in onore di Doro Levi Vol 1*, Università di Catania - Istituto di Archeologia, 1973, pp.137-47 (1973b).

Peter WARREN, *The Aegean Civilizations*, Elsevier/Phaidon, Oxford, 1975.

Peter WARREN, 'Minoan Crete and ecstatic religion', in Hägg and Marinatos (ed.), *Sanctuaries and Cults in the Aegean Bronze Age*, Paul Åströms Förlag, Stockholm, 1981, pp.155-67.

P.M. WARREN, 'Knossos: the Stratigraphical Museum Excavations 1978-81', paper presented at British School at Athens AGM, London, 2.2.1982. (See also *BSA*, 81, 1986, pp.333-88.)

Peter WARREN, 'Of Squills' in *Aux Origines de l'Hellénisme: la Crète et la Grèce. Hommage à Henri Van Effenterre*, Publications de la Sorbonne, Paris, 1984.

Peter WARREN, 'Early Minoan - Early Cycladic chronological correlations' in J.A. MacGillivray and R.L.N. Barber (eds.), 'The Prehistoric Cyclades', pp.55-62 (1984b).

Peter WARREN, 'New Excavations in the city of Knossos', BSA Centenary Lecture at BM, 15.10.1986.

Peter WARREN, *Minoan Religion as Ritual Action*, Gothenburg University, 1988.

Peter WARREN, 'A new Minoan deposit from Knossos of ca.1600 B.C., and a glance therefrom at contemporary Crete and the Cyclades', paper presented at University of London, Mycenaean seminar, 17.5.1989.

P. WARREN and J. TZEDHAKIS, 'Debla, an Early Minoan Settlement in Western Crete' in *BSA*, 69, 1974, 229-342.

Helen WATERHOUSE, 'Priest-Kings?' in *BICS*, 21, 1974, pp.153-5.

T.B.L. WEBSTER, 'Personification as a Mode of Greek Thought' in *Journal of the Warburg and Courtauld Institutes*, 17, Nos. 1-2, 1954, pp.10-21.

T.B.L. WEBSTER, *From Mycenae to Homer*, Methuen London, 1958.

Saul S. WEINBERG, 'Neolithic Figurines and Aegean Interrelations', in *AJA*, 55, 1951, pp.121-133.

Judith WEINGARTEN, *The Zakro Master and his Place in Prehistory*, Paul Åströms Förlag, Göteborg, 1983.

M.L. WEST (ed.), *Hesiod: Theogony*, Clarendon Press, Oxford, 1966.

M.L. WEST, 'Greek Poetry 2,000-700 B.C.', in *CQ*, 23, 1973, pp.179-92.

M.L. WEST, 'Immortal Helen', Inaugural Lecture delivered on 30.4.75 at Bedford College, University of London.

M.L. WEST, 'Cynaethus' Hymn to Apollo, in *CQ*, 25, 1975, pp.161-70 (1975b).

M.L. WEST (ed.), *Hesiod: Works and Days*, Clarendon Press, Oxford, 1978.

M.L. WEST, *The Hesiodic Catalogue of Women: its Nature, Structure and Origins*, Clarendon Press, Oxford, 1985.

M.L. WEST, 'Greek poetesses', paper presented to Hellenic Society, London, 8.1.1987.

Todd M. WHITELAW, 'The settlement at Fournou Korifi, Myrtos and aspects of Early Minoan social organization', in O. Krzyszkowska and L. Nixon (ed.), *Minoan Society: Proceedings of the Cambridge Colloquium 1981*, Bristol Classical Press, 1983, pp.323-45.

R.F. WILLETTS, *Cretan Cults and Festivals*, Routledge and Kegan Paul, London, 1962.

Raymond WILLIAMS, *Problems in Materialism and Culture: Selected Essays*, Verso Editions and NLB, London, 1980.

Stephanos A. XANTHOUDIDES, 'Ek Kritis' in *AE*, 1907, pp.140-86.

Stephanos A. XANTHOUDIDES, *The Vaulted Tombs of Mesara*, transl. J.P. Droop, University Press of Liverpool, Hodder and Stoughton, 1924.

Agnès XÉNAKI-SAKELLARIOU, *Les cachets Minoens de la collection Giamalakis*, Librairie Orientaliste Paul Geuthner, Paris, 1958.

J.C. YOUNGER, *The Iconography of Late Minoan and Mycenaean Sealstones and Finger Rings*, Bristol Classical Press, 1988.

F. ZAFEIROPOULOU, 'Koufonisi' in Chronika in *A Delt*, 25, 1970, pp.428-30.

F. ZAFEIROPOULOU, 'Protokykladika Euremata ek Ano Koufonesiou' in *AAA*, 3, 1970, pp.48-51 (1970b).

Sir Themistocles ZAMMIT, *Prehistoric Malta: The Tarxien Temples*, Oxford University Press, London, 1930.

Christian ZERVOS, *L'art des Cyclades du début à la fin de l'Âge du Bronze, 2500-1100 avant notre ère*, Éditions 'Cahiers d'art', Paris, 1957.

W. ZSCHIETZSCHMANN, 'Kykladenpfannen' in *AA*, 50, 1935, 652-68.

ABBREVIATIONS

AA - Archäologischer Anzeiger

AAA - Athens Annual of Archaeology

A Delt - Archaiologikon Deltion

AE - Ephemeris Archaiologiki

AJA - American Journal of Archaeology

Antike Gemmen - Antike Gemmen in Deutschen Sammlungen, Vols. I-IV, Munich and Wiesbaden, 1968-75.

AR - Archaeological Reports (publ. by the Society for the Promotion of Hellenic Studies and the British School at Athens)

ASCSA - American School of Classical Studies at Athens

BAR - British Archaeological Reports

BCH - Bullétin de Correspondance Hellénique

BICS - Bulletin of the Institute of Classical Studies

BM - British Museum

BSA - Annual of the British School at Athens

CMS - Corpus der Minoischen und Mykenischen Siegel, Vols I (and Supplement); II,1; II,2; II,3; II,4; II,5; IV; V,1; V,2:, VII; VIII; IX; X; XI; XII; XIII, Verlag Gebr. Mann, Berlin, 1964-88. Also *Beiheft* 1 and 2, 1981 and 1985.

CQ - Classical Quarterly

CR - The Classical Review

Ergon - To Ergon tis Archaiologikis Etaireias

HM - Archaeological Museum of Heraklion

ILN - Illustrated London News

Jahrbuch - Jahrbuch des Deutschen Archäologischen Instituts

JHS - Journal of Hellenic Studies

NAM - National Archaeological Museum in Athens

PAE - Praktika tis en Athenais Archaiologikis Etairias

PM - Sir Arthur Evans, *The Palace of Minos*, Hafner Publishing, London, 1964. 4 volumes and index (first publ. 1921-36).

RSL -Rivista di Studi Liguri

S.I.M.A. - Studies in Mediterranean Archaeology

LIST OF ILLUSTRATIONS

Fig 1   a   Interior of Cycladic 'frying-pan', partly restored.
Reproduced from *AA* 50 (1935), Col. 653-4, Fig 1.

       b   Interior of Bronze Mirror Alaca A 60.
Drawing by Lucy Goodison after Mellink, 1956, Pl. IV Fig 6 (left).

       c   Interior of Bronze Mirror Alaca A' 27.
Drawing by Lucy Goodison after Mellink, 1956, Pl. IV Fig 6 (right).

Fig 2   Front and rear views of three Period 1 figurines from the EBA settlement at Fournou Korifi (Myrtos).
Rough drawing by Lucy Goodison after Warren, 1972, Pl. 71, C and D.

Fig 3   a   EM III - MM IA green steatite paired figurines of Cycladic type, 'from Tekke', Crete. In HM.
Rough drawing by Lucy Goodison

       b   Protopalatial bell-shaped figurines from Tylissos, Crete. In HM.
Rough drawing by Lucy Goodison after a photograph by Carlos Guarita, Reflex.

       c   Protopalatial bell-shaped figurines from Tylissos, Crete. In HM.
Rough drawing by Lucy Goodison after a photograph by Carlos Guarita, Reflex.

       d   Cycladic 'double-idol' in marble. In Badisches Landesmuseum, Karlsruhe, No. B.839, Neg. No. 1666.
Reproduced from Bossert, 1937, 242, No. 411.

Fig 4   Diagram showing the evolutionary development of the Early Cycladic figurines.
Reproduced from Renfrew, 1972, 184, Fig 11.8.

Fig 5   'Sleeping Lady' from the Ggantija temples of Malta (Maltese Middle Neolithic, c. 2,800-2,400 BC).
Drawing by Lucy Goodison after Schachermeyr, 1964, Tafel 43,c.

Fig 6   a   Figurine with marble palette, Karlsruhe No. 87. Skulpturensammlung, Dresden.
Rough drawing by Lucy Goodison after Getz-Preziosi, 1978, 10, Fig 15.

       b   Suggested manner in which figurine Karlsruhe No. 87 may have been secured to palette cat.f. by suspension cords.
Rough drawing by Lucy Goodison after Getz-Preziosi, 1978, 10, Fig 16a.

       c   Cat. e. Marble palette with schematic figurine. Arthur von Arx Collection, Solothurn.
Rough drawing by Lucy Goodison after Getz-Preziosi, 1978, 9, Fig 12.

       d   Stone plaque bearing idol of Louros type in relief. From Ano Koufonesi cemetery.
Rough drawing by Lucy Goodison after *AAA* 3 (1970), 50, Fig 7.

Fig 7   Steatite cruciform figurine wearing a necklace with cruciform pendant shown in relief, from Yialia, Cyprus. Chalcolithic (3,500-2,500 BC). In Cyprus Museum, Nicosia, 1934/111-2/2.
Reproduced from Tatton-Brown, 1979, 19, No. 13. Detail, drawing by Lucy Goodison after same.

Fig 8   Diminutive stone figurine from Crete. In HM No. 3275.
Drawing by Louise London.

Fig 9   a   Figurine from Koumasa H.23.5.
Reproduced from Branigan, 1970b, Fig 16.

       b   Figurine from Platanos H.57.
Reproduced from Branigan, 1970b, Fig 16.

       c   Figurine from Porti H.8.5.
Reproduced from Branigan, 1970b, Fig 16.

Fig 10   Stone 'weights' from Fournou Korifi (Myrtos) Periods 1 and 2.
Drawings by Louise London and Lucy Goodison after Warren, 1972, Pl. 79, C and D.

Fig 11   a   The 'Goddess of Myrtos' P 704. In Aghios Nikolaos Museum.
Reproduced from Warren, 1972, Fig 92.

       b   Neolithic 'Tangas' from Lerna.
Reproduced from Banks, 1977, Pl. 74 Nos. 7-14.

       c   Neolithic 'Tangas' from Lerna.
Reproduced from Banks, 1977, Pl. 76 Nos. 20 and 28.

       d   Triangular clay 'counters' from Fournou Korifi (Myrtos).
Reproduced from Warren, 1972, Pl. 79 E.

       e   Triangular clay counters from Fournou Korifi (Myrtos).
Reproduced from Warren, 1972, Fig 107.

Fig 12   a-c   Star-discs in crescents from the near-Eastern seal repertoire.
Reproduced from Collon, 1982, 132.

       d-e   Variations of the disc in crescent.
Reproduced from Roes, 1933, Fig 1.

       f   Crossed circle of 'wheel' in crescent.
Reproduced from Collon, 1975, 166, No. 122.

g-h	Variations of the disc in crescent.
	Reproduced from Collon, 1986, 48.

i	Winged disc.
	Reproduced from Collon, 1975, 118, No. 215.

j	Astral symbol.
	Reproduced from Roes, 1933, Fig 1.

k	Near-Eastern seal impression, Early Dynastic period (c. 3,000-2,340 BC).
	Reproduced from Frankfort, 1954, Pl. 39 (B).

l-m	Swastika and cross symbols.
	Reproduced from Roes, 1933, Fig 1.

n	Other astral symbols from the near-Eastern repertoire.
	Reproduced from Collon, 1975, Pl. LIII.

Fig 13	a	Babylonian cylinder seal of haematite. Chance find from Western outskirts of Heraklion. In HM No. 132.
	Reproduced from *CMS* II,2 No. 206.

b	Cylinder seal from Platanos. In HM No. 1098.
	Reproduced from Xanthoudides, 1924, 117.

c	Silver cylinder seal from Tomb 1 at Mochlos, Seager's (1912) object No. I*n*. In HM, numbered (in case) as 380, although not so numbered in *CMS*.
	Drawing by Louise London after a photograph by Paul Morrison.

d	Lapislazuli cylinder seal. In HM No. 238.
	Reproduced from *CMS* II, 2 No. 29. Drawing from *PM* IV, 424, Fig 350.

Fig 14	a	Seal from Tholos A at Aghia Triadha. In HM No. 448.
	Reproduced from *CMS* II,1 No. 21.

b	Seal from Tholos II at Lebena. In HM No. 1983.
	Reproduced from *CMS* II,1 No. 198.

c	Sealing from Phaistos. In HM No. 877.
	Reproduced from *CMS* II,5 No. 130.

d	Seal from settlement site at Gournia. In HM No. 391.
	Reproduced from *CMS* II,1 No. 465.

e	Sealing from Phaistos. In HM No. 885.
	Reproduced from *CMS* II,5 No. 125.

f	Seal from Mallia. In HM No. 329.
	Reproduced from *CMS* II,1 No. 417.

g	Steatite seal, chance find from Phaistos. In HM No. 2083.
	Reproduced from *CMS* II,2 No. 202.

h	Black steatite button-seal from near Episkopi. In HM No. 1644. Found in late palatial chamber tomb, belongs stylistically to early palatial period.
	Reproduced from *CMS* II,2 No. 74.

i	Steatite or marble three-sided prism bead. In BM (GR/R) 1876.5-13,5.
	Reproduced from *CMS* VII No. 16.

j	Seal from Messara. In HM No. 1084.
	Reproduced from Xanthoudides, 1924, Pl XV.

k	Seal from Messara. In HM No. 681.
	Reproduced from Xanthoudides, 1924, Pl. VIII.

l	Seal From Trapeza Cave. In HM No. 1565.
	Reproduced from *CMS* II,1 No. 431.

m	Seal from settlement site at Gournia. In HM No. 392.
	Reproduced from *CMS* II,1 No. 466.

n	Seal from Tholos A at Aghia Triadha. In HM No. 494.
	Reproduced from *CMS* II,1 No. 66.

o	Seal from Tholos B at Koumasa. In HM No. 645
	Reproduced from *CMS* II,1 No. 158.

p	Seal from the Messara. In HM No. 1127.
	Drawing by Lucy Goodison after Xanthoudides, 1924, Pl. XV.

q	Sealing from Phaistos. In HM No. 784.
	Reproduced from *CMS* II,5 No. 129.

r	Steatite three-sided prism. In HM No. 90.
	Reproduced from *CMS* II,2 No. 242.

s	Sealing from Phaistos. In HM No. 817.
	Reproduced from *CMS* II,5 No. 124.

t	Steatite seal from Kamilari. In HM No. 1297.
	Reproduced from *CMS* II,1 No. 452.

u	Sealing from Phaistos. In HM No. 879.
	Reproduced from *CMS* II,5 No. 128.

v	Three-sided steatite prism seal of unknown provenance. In HM No. 1474.
	Reproduced from *CMS* II,2 No. 294.

w	Sealing from Phaistos. In HM No. 928.
	Reproduced from *CMS* II,5 No. 126.

Fig 15	a	Dark green steatite prism bead seal. In Fitzwilliam Museum GR. 79. 1901.
	Reproduced from *CMS* VII No. 215.

             c   White steatite three-sided prism. In Metaxas Collection, Heraklion, No. 169.
                    Reproduced from *CMS* IV No. 70.

Fig 23   a   Seal from Crete. In HM No. 1561.
                    Reproduced from *CMS* II,1 No. 427.

             b   Seal from tholos of Aghios Onoufrios. In HM No. 9.
                    Reproduced from *CMS* II,1 No. 111.

Fig 24   a   Minoan jug from Protopalatial period. In HM, Rm 2, Case 27. (The inner circle of dots are executed in red).
                    From a photograph by Lucy Goodison.

             b   Pyxis lid from Vat Room Deposit at Knossos Palace.
                    Reproduced from *PM* I Fig 118 b 2.

             c   Pyxis lid from EM I/II cemetery of Aghia Fotia. In Aghios Nikolaos Museum.
                    Drawing by Lucy Goodison after a photograph by Carlos Guarita.

             d   MM I incised lid from Knossos, Vat Room Deposit. Such lids, reminiscent of the Cycladic 'frying-pans', have recently been discussed by MacGillivray et al. (1986b) who suggest a source for the clay in Central Crete. Evans links them to a Cretan Neolithic tradition (*PM* IV, 87ff).
                    Reproduced from *PM* IV, 89, Fig 56.

Fig 25   a   Grey-green steatite prism from Kastelli Pedeada, south-east of Knossos. In Ashmolean Museum, Oxford, No. CS 39 (1938.746).
                    Drawing reproduced from *PM* I, 124, Fig 93A, b 1.
                    Photograph reproduced from Boardman, 1970, Black and White Pl. 6.

             b   Worship of sun, from table of major religious symbols in ancient Egyptian religion.
                    Reproduced from Rundle Clark, 1959, 259.

Fig 26   a   MM II green jasper prism seal from Heraklion area of Crete. In Ashmolean Museum, Oxford, CS 167 (1938.792).
                    Reproduced from Boardman, 1970, Black and White Pl. 27. Drawing from *PM* I, 277, Fig 207k.

             b   Sealing from Phaistos. In HM No. 824.
                    Reproduced from *CMS* II,5 No. 49.

             c   See Fig 16b.

Fig 27   a   EC II silver diadem from Kastri settlement at Chalandriani on Syros. NAM No. 5234. The silver is believed to be Siphnian (see Gale and Stos-Gale, 1981). May have been a local product of EC II, taken by intruders into their possession (Robert Arnott, *BICS* 36, 1989, 8 n.58).
                    Reproduced from *AE* 1899, Pl. 10 No. 1.

             b   The same object as reconstructed in Caskey, 1964, 65, Fig 5.
                    Drawing by Lucy Goodison after same. (N.B. See also reconstruction in Papathanassopoulos, 1981, 132-3, Fig 61.)

Fig 28   a   Green steatite cone from Stonecutters' workshop at Mallia. In HM No. 1799.
                    From a photograph by Lucy Goodison.

             b   Design on a MM I jug from Mallia. In HM No. 8660.
                    Reproduced from Van Effenterre, 1980, Figs 573 and 574. Rough drawing after same by Lucy Goodison.

Fig 29   Seal from Knossos. In HM No. 676.
                    Reproduced from *CMS* II,2 No. 210.

Fig 30   Onyx three-sided prism, chance find from Mallia. In HM No. 383.
                    Reproduced from *CMS* II,2 No. 230.

Fig 31   a   Seal from Tholos A at Aghia Triadha. In HM No. 1019.
                    Reproduced from *CMS* II,1 No. 94.

             b   Ivory seal from Tholos A at Aghia Triadha. In HM No. 483.
                    Reproduced from *CMS* II,1 No. 55.

Fig 32   a   Figurine from Platanos. In HM.
                    Reproduced from Branigan, 1970b, Fig 16.

             b   Figurine from Aghios Onoufrios. In HM.
                    Reproduced from Branigan, 1970b, Fig 16.

Fig 33   a   Neolithic clay 'idol' from Knossos. In HM.
                    Reproduced from *PM* I, Fig 12, 1a and b.

             b   Neolithic clay 'idol' from Knossos. In HM.
                    Reproduced from *PM* I, Fig 12, 3a and b.

Fig 34   a   Vessel with diminutive figure attached. In HM No. 18358.
                    Drawing by Carlos Guarita.

             b   Diminutive figure from Phaistos. In HM No. 18538.
                    Drawing by Louise London.

             c   'Pebble-shaped', 'tripartite' and 'violin-shaped' figurines from the Cyclades. In NAM.
                    Drawing by Louise London after E. Sapouna-Sakellarakis, *Cycladic Civilization*, (Apollo Editions, Athens), Pl. 29.

             d   Figurine from Aghios Onoufrios. In HM.
                    Drawing by Louise London after a photograph by Carlos Guarita.

Fig 35   (Reading from left to right) see Figs 32a, 32b, Fig 38a and Fig 34c.

Fig 36   a   Clay discoid figures from 'A' layer in second temple of Tarxien, Malta.
                    Reproduced from Zammit, 1930, Figs 3, 5, 8, 9, 10.

             b   Photograph of same, reproduced from Heresies, P.O. Box 1306, New York, Spring 1978, p 133.

             c   Gold pendant from El Ajjul, Gaza, representing Hathor. 17th-16th century B.C.
                    Drawing by Lucy Goodison after ILN, 16.6. 1934.

c   Isis and Nephthys adoring the rising sun. The bird is the sun-god in his hawk form. From the funerary papyrus of Hunefer, high official of 19th Dynasty, c. 1300 BC. In BM No. 9901/1.
Reproduced by courtesy of the Trustees of the British Museum.

d   Isis and Nephthys (identified by accompanying text) stand with arms raised on either side of a sun disc. Detail of decoration on tomb of Ramses VI (see Fig 42b).
Reproduced from Hornung, 1983b, Pl. 89.
(Right) Another version of motif of two female figures and sun from tomb of Ramses VI.
Rough drawing by Lucy Goodison after Piankoff, 1954, Pl. 149.

e   Scene of prayer to the sun by the King and Isis and Nephthys (at the extreme right and left). From over the entrance to the grave of Ramses X.
Reproduced from Hornung, 1983b, 198.

f   Naked sky goddess adorned with sun, moon and stars. From interior of a late sarcophagus lid.
Reproduced from Hornung, 1983b, 136.

g   The 'sun-child' in the belly of the pregnant sky goddess. New Kingdom.
Reproduced from Hornung, 1983b, 136.

h   The sun god as child within the Ouroboros. From 'mythological' mortuary papyrus of Hirweben A, Cairo Museum 'No. 133'. (21st Dynasty).
Reproduced from Hornung, 1983, 164, Fig 18.

i   Here 'a Sun- or Fire-goddess seems to be pictured', according to Frankfort, 1939, 129. Design on a seal of the Sargonid age (2,500-2,400 BC).
Reproduced from Frankfort, 1939, Pl. XVIIIj.

j   Nut giving birth to the sun, the rays of which fall on Hathor in the horizon.
Reproduced from Budge, Vol.II, 1904, 101.

Fig 43 a   Plans of tholoi at Porti and Platanos in Crete.
Reproduced from Xanthoudides, 1924, Pl. LXII.

b   Lebena II tholos tomb showing trilithon door.
Drawing by Lucy Goodison after Branigan, 1970b, Pl. 2, based on original photograph of Dr. S. Alexiou.

Fig 44 a   Aegean rock-cut tombs of the third millenium BC. 1. Manika in Euboea; 2. Manika in Euboea; 3-6 Phylakopi in Melos; 7. Corinth; 8. Athens (final Neolithic).
Reproduced from Renfrew, 1972, Fig 7.6.

b   The 'R Graves' at Steno in the plain of Nidri, Levkas.
Reproduced from Renfrew, 1972, Fig 19.11.

Fig 45   The hypogeum at Knossos.
Reproduced from Renfrew, 1972, Fig 6.9 (after Evans).

Fig 46 a-b 'Foetal' position of skeletons in Cycladic graves (Syros).
Reproduced from AE 1899, Supplementary Plate for Col. 88, Nos. 1 and 3.

c   Rough drawing by Lucy Goodison of Fig 46b.

Fig 47   Skull found in a pottery vase at Archanes, Crete.
Drawing by Louise London after Sakellarakis, 1967, 277.

Fig 48 a   The MM I tholos at Apesokari.
Reproduced from Branigan, 1970b, 135, Fig 28.

b   A reconstruction of the plan of the cemetery area at Platanos, based on the description and incomplete plan published by Xanthoudides; shows trace of paved area.
Reproduced from Branigan, 1970b, Fig 2.

c   Plan of cemetery at Koumasa showing paved area.
Reproduced from Branigan, 1970b, Fig 27.

d   The large tholos at Kamilari (Kamilari I).
Reproduced from Branigan, 1970b, 96, Fig 21.

Fig 49 a   A MM plate, and a fragment of a second, both from Phaistos. In HM No. 10583.
Reproduced from Branigan, 1970b, Fig 29.

b   Scenes of dancing on a reconstructed offerings-table from Phaistos. In HM No. 10576.
Rough drawing by Lucy Goodison after a photograph by Louise London and after Levi, 1976, Tav. LXVI.

c   Steatite cylinder seal from Tholos B at Platanos. In HM No. 1102.
Reproduced from CMS II,1 No. 310.

d   Steatite three-sided prism seal of unknown provenance. In HM No. 116.
Reproduced from CMS II,2 No. 303. Drawing after same by Lucy Goodison.

e   Steatite three-sided prism. In collection of the late R.W. Hutchinson, U.K. (now dispersed).
Drawing by Lucy Goodison after CMS VIII No. 111.

f   Steatite triangular prism seal. In Cabinet des Médailles, Paris, N 4424.
Reproduced from CMS IX No. 25. Drawing after same by Lucy Goodison.

g   Plaque 9 from Korfi t'Aroniou, Naxos.
Reproduced from Doumas, 1965, 57, Fig 11.

Fig 50   Projecting slabs on the outside face of Tholos B, Platanos.
Drawing by Lucy Goodison after Branigan, 1970b, Pl. 4, based on original photograph in Xanthoudides, 1924.

Fig 51 a   The Irish passage grave at Newgrange.
Reproduced from Renfrew, 1973, 121, Fig 23 (after Fergusson 1872).

b   Possible sun symbols from the Irish passage graves.
Reproduced from Fleming, 1969, Fig 33i (after Breuil, Albuquerque e Castro, Eogan, MacWhite, Piggott, and Powell and Daniel).

	b	Steatite three-sided prism from Crete. In HM No. 89.

        b   Steatite three-sided prism from Crete. In HM No. 89.
            Reproduced from *CMS* II,2 No. 241.
        c   Steatite seal from Crete. In HM No. 1399.
            Reproduced from *CMS* II,2 No. 76.
        d   Steatite three-sided prism. In collection of the late R.M. Dawkins, U.K. (now dispersed).
            Reproduced from *CMS* VIII No. 15.

Fig 66 a   Steatite three-sided prism from Stonecutters' workshop, Mallia. In HM No. 1851.
            Reproduced from *CMS* II,2 No. 179.
        b   Three-sided steatite prism from Stonecutters' workshop, Mallia. In HM No. 2292.
            Reproduced from *CMS* II,2 No. 190.
        c   Steatite three-sided prism bead seal. In Metropolitan Museum, New York, No. 25.78.105.
            Reproduced from *CMS* XII No. 28.
        d   Prism seal from Mallia. In HM No. 1815.
            Reproduced from Van Effenterre, 1980, 558, Fig 820.
        e   Three-sided steatite prism seal from Stonecutters' workshop at Mallia. In HM No. 1850.
            Reproduced from *CMS* II,2 No. 178.

Fig 67 a   Seal from Crete, green steatite prism. In Ashmolean Museum, Oxford, CS 51.
            Reproduced from Boardman, 1970, Black and White Pl. 9. Drawing after same by Lucy
            Goodison.
        b   Seal from Crete. In HM No. 2391.
            From a photograph by Lucy Goodison.
        c   Steatite prism seal from Crete. In Giamalakis collection, No. 3183.
            Reproduced from Xénaki-Sakellariou, 1958, Pl. XVIII No. 78c. Drawing after same by Lucy
            Goodison.

Fig 68 a   Triangular prism seal. In Cabinet des Médailles, Paris, No. N4421.
            Reproduced from *CMS* IX No. 22.
        b   As Fig 55c. In Ashmolean Museum, Oxford, CS 71 (1938.760).
            Reproduced from Boardman, 1970, Black and White Pl. 12. Drawing by Lucy Goodison after
            same
        c   No. 2a from Evans' list of hieroglyphic signs.
            Reproduced from Evans, 1909, 181.
        d   Four-sided bead seal from Siteia.
            Reproduced from Evans, 1909, 155, P.29.a.

Fig 69   See Figs 25a and 64a. (Three faces of the same seal.)
            Reproduced from *PM* I, 124, Fig 93A, b 1, 2 and 3.

Fig 70 a   Steatite three-sided prism from plain of Mallia. In HM No. 81.
            Reproduced from *CMS* II,2 No. 237.
        b   Three-sided grey steatite seal from Kastelli Pedeada, south-east of Knossos.
            Reproduced from *PM* I, 124, Fig 93A, a 1.
        c   Steatite three-sided prism from Mallia. In HM No. 1506.
            Reproduced from *CMS* II,2 No. 235.
        d   Steatite three-sided prism from Stonecutters' workshop at Mallia. In HM No. 1788.
            Reproduced from *CMS* II,2 No. 118.
        e   Steatite three-sided prism from Stonecutters' workshop at Mallia. In HM No. 1831.
            Reproduced from *CMS* II,2 No. 159.
        f   Clay sealing from Crete. In HM No. 733.
            Reproduced from *CMS* II,5 No. 239.
        g   Steatite prism seal of unknown provenance. In collection of H. Wiengandt, Marburg.
            Reproduced from *CMS* XI No. 122.
        h   Steatite prism seal of unknown provenance. In Staatliche Ankikensummlungen, Munich.
            Reproduced from *CMS* XI No. 206.

Fig 71 a   Brown steatite three-sided prism seal. In Metaxas Collection, Heraklion, No. 1255.
            Reproduced from *CMS* IV No. 10.
        b   Steatite three-sided prism seal. In collection of M. Velay, New York.
            Reproduced from *CMS* XIII, No. 79. Also drawing after *PM* I, 124, Fig 93A, C 1.
        c   Rock crystal seal bearing hieroglyphic signs, from Mallia. In Giamalakis Collection, No. 3344.
            Reproduced from Xénaki-Sakellariou, 1958, Pl. V and Pl. XX No. 164.

Fig 72 a   Brown steatite three-sided seal from Crete.
            Reproduced from Kenna, 1960, EM seal No. 48.
            (Line drawing of one face only reproduced from Branigan, 1970, 75, Fig 16 F).
        b   Steatite three-sided seal from Crete.
            Reproduced from Evans, 1909, 132, Fig 71.

Fig 73 a   Steatite three-sided prism seal. In Cabinet des Médailles, Paris, No. M 7563.
            Reproduced from *CMS* IX No. 24.
        b   Steatite three-sided prism seal from Stonecutters' workshop, Mallia. In HM No. 1803.
            Reproduced from *CMS* II,2 No. 131.
        c   Steatite three-sided prism seal from Crete, provenance unknown. In NAM No. 4580.
            Reproduced from *CMS* I No. 414.

Fig 74 a   Steatite three-sided prism bead seal. In BM (GR/R) 1934. 11-20,2.
            Reproduced from *CMS* VII No. 8.
        b   Steatite three-sided prism bead seal. In Cabinet des Médailles, Paris, N. 4415.
            Reproduced from *CMS* IX No. 15.

         c   Sealing from Phaistos. In HM No. 683.
                Reproduced from *CMS* II,5 No. 323.

Fig 86   a   Steatite three-sided prism bead seal. In Metropolitan Museum, New York, No. 26.31.123.
                Reproduced from *CMS* XII No. 18.
         b   Steatite three-sided prism bead. In BM (GR/R) 1947. 9-26.3.
                Reproduced from *CMS* VII No. 3.
         c   Steatite three-sided prism from Stonecutters' workshop, Mallia. In HM No. 1772.
                Reproduced from *CMS* II,2 No. 102.
         d   Steatite three-sided prism from Stonecutters' workshop, Mallia. In HM No. 1831.
                Reproduced from *CMS* II,2 No. 159.
         e   Steatite three-sided prism of unknown provenance. In HM No. 119.
                Reproduced from *CMS* II,2 No. 304.
         f   Three-sided seal from Crete, grey steatite.
                Reproduced from *PM* I, 124, Fig 93A, a 2.

Fig 87   a   Seal from Kamilari in Crete. In HM No. 1297.
                Reproduced from *CMS* II,1 No. 452.
         b   Steatite three-sided prism of unknown provenance. In HM No. 625.
                Reproduced from *CMS* II,2 No. 290.
         c   White steatite prism from Praesos.
                Reproduced from Evans, 1909, 150, P.8.a.
         d   Ivory/bone ring bearing concentric circles with 'antithetically disposed leaves' extending from them (Betts, *CMS* X, 70). In collection of H. and M.-L. Erlenmeyr, Basel.
                Reproduced from *CMS* X No. 29.
         e   Sealing from Phaistos. In HM No. 760.
                Reproduced from *CMS* II,5 No. 110.
         f   Chalcedony flattened cylinder from Mallia. In Giamalakis Collection, No. 3075.
                Reproduced from Xénaki-Sakellariou, 1958, Pl. XX No. 122.

Fig 88   a   Steatite three-sided prism. In collection of the late R.M. Dawkins, U.K. (now dispersed).
                Reproduced from *CMS* VIII No. 4.
         b   MM I seal. In Metaxas Collection, Heraklion.
                Reproduced from *CMS* IV No. 70.
         c   Steatite three-sided prism bead seal. In Metropolitan Museum, New York, No. 26.31.103.
                Reproduced from *CMS* XII No. 51.

Fig 89   a   Steatite three-sided prism bead. In Metropolitan Museum, New York, No. 26.31.104.
                Reproduced from *CMS* XII No. 35.
         b   Steatite three-sided prism bead. In Metropolitan Museum, New York, No. 26.31.77.
                Reproduced from *CMS* XII No. 58.

Fig 90   Twelfth dynasty scarab of amethyst engraved with Minoan hieroglyphics. In Ashmolean Museum, Oxford, No. K126 (1938.789).
                Reproduced from *PM* I, 199, Fig 147.

Fig 91   a   Clay sealing from palace of Knossos.
                Reproduced from *PM* I, 281, Fig 213.
          b   Sealing from Phaistos. In HM No. 1489.
                Reproduced from *CMS* II,5 No. 305.
         c   Sealing from Phaistos. In HM No. 937.
                Reproduced from *CMS* II,5 No. 306.
         d   Steatite three-sided prism bead. In Metropolitan Museum, New York, No. 26.31.140.
                Reproduced from *CMS* XII No. 48.

Fig 92   Terracotta shrine model from Cyprus, about 1900 BC. In Cyprus Museum, Nicosia, 1970/IV-28/1.
                Reproduced from Tatton-Brown, 1979, Pl. 54.

Fig 93   Egyptian representation of the inundation making the vegetation grow.
                Reproduced from Rundle Clark, 1959, 101, Fig 14.

Fig 94   a   Mesopotamian cylinder seal, Dynasty of Akkad. In BM 89110.
                Reproduced from Frankfort, 1939, Pl. XVIIIa
         b   Mesopotamian cylinder seal, Dynasty of Akkad. In BM 89115.
                Reproduced from Frankfort, 1939, Pl. XIXa.

Fig 95   a   View of graves at Chalandriani in Syros.
                Reproduced from *AE* 1899, Pl. 7 Nos. 3 and 4.
         b   A view of the tholos tomb at Aghios Kyrillos.
                Drawing by Lucy Goodison after Branigan, 1970b, Pl. 9, based on original photograph of Dr. J. Sakellarakis.

Fig 96   Steatite prism seal from an uncertain locality in Crete. In Staatliche Münzsammlung, Munich, No. 1147.
                Reproduced from Evans, 1909, 149, P.4.a.

Fig 97   Cretan seal, chance find from Olous. In HM No. 1508.
                Reproduced from *CMS* II,2 No. 267.

Fig 98   a   Steatite three-sided prism bead. In Fitzwilliam Museum, Cambridge, GR. 75.1901.
                Reproduced from *CMS* VII No. 207.
          b   Steatite three-sided prism bead. In Metropolitan Museum, New York, No. 26.31.82.
                Reproduced from *CMS* XII No. 32.

b   Head with (?)snake head-dress. In HM No. 9248.
From a photograph by Lucy Goodison.

Fig 111   a   Small gold toad from Platanos.
Drawing by Lucy Goodison after Branigan, 1970, Pl. 13b.

b   Marble pig. In Goulandris Collection No. 285.
Drawing by Lucy Goodison after Doumas, 1983, 72, No. 34.

c   Ivory seal from ossuary at Platanos.
Reproduced from *PM* I, Fig 87,3 a, b and c.

d   Steatite three-sided prism from tholos at Aghios Onoufrios. In HM No. 9.
Reproduced from *CMS* II,1 No. 111.

e   Steatite three-sided prism, chance find from Avdou. In HM No. 1558.
Reproduced from *CMS* II,2 No. 221.

Fig 112   a   Prepalatial seal from Crete. In Giamalakis Collection. Reproduced from Xénaki-Sakellariou, 1958, Pl. XVI, No. 34.

b   Steatite three-sided prism bead. In City Museum, Liverpool, 8.20.
Reproduced from *CMS* VII No. 253.

c   Steatite three-sided prism bead from Sitanos. In Fitzwilliam Museum, Cambridge, GR. 78.1901.
Reproduced from *CMS* VII No. 206.

d   Steatite three-sided prism bead. In Fitzwilliam Museum, Cambridge, GR. 75.1901.
Reproduced from *CMS* VII No. 207.

e   Steatite three-sided prism. In Cabinet des Médailles, Paris, Dépôt du Louvre, AM 1623,14 (=D27).
Reproduced from *CMS* IX No. 5.

f   Three-sided prism bead. In BM (GR/R) 1934.11-20,3.
Reproduced from *CMS* VII No. 17.

g   Steatite three-sided prism. In HM No. 1557.
Reproduced from *CMS* II,2 No. 222. Rough drawing after same by Lucy Goodison.

h   Green steatite lid from Tomb 1 in the cemetery of Mochlos. In HM.
Reproduced from *PM* I, 94, Fig 62. (Compare Platon, 1971, 69.)

Fig 113   a   Ivory seal from tholos site of Siva. In HM No. 995.
Reproduced from *CMS* II,1 No. 369, where it is described as 'Vielleicht Zicke mit Jungem oder Paar in Begattung' (p 428).

b   Steatite three-sided prism of unknown provenance. In HM No. 1298.
Reproduced from *CMS* II,2 No. 306, where it is described by Platon as 'Copulation scene with two horned quadrupeds (goats?)' (p 465). Drawing after same by Lucy Goodison.

c   Diminutive model of the protopalatial period. In HM.
Drawing by Louise London after a photograph by Lucy Goodison.

Fig 114   a   See Fig 54a.

b   Three-sided Cretan seal. In Ashmolean Museum, Oxford, No. 1910.242.
Reproduced from Kenna, 1960, No. K 6. Drawing by Lucy Goodison after same.

Fig 115   a   Three-sided EM Cretan seal in yellowish mottled steatite. In Ashmolean Museum, Oxford, No. 1938.744.
Reproduced from Kenna, 1960, No. K 14. Drawing by Lucy Goodison after same.

b   Three-sided EM Cretan seal in green steatite. In Ashmolean Museum, Oxford, No. 1938.743.
Reproduced from Kenna, 1960, No. K 2.

c   Three-sided seal in blackish-green serpentine from Central Crete. In Ashmolean Museum, Oxford, No. AE. 1221.
Reproduced from Kenna, 1960, No. K 44.

Fig 116   a   Agate MM II seal.
Reproduced from *PM* II, 275, Fig 204s.

b   Steatite three-sided prism. In HM No. 1770.
Reproduced from *CMS* II,2 No. 100.

c   Ivory seal from Tholos B at Platanos. In HM No. 1059.
Reproduced from *CMS* II,1 No. 268.

Fig 117   a   Sealing from Phaistos. In HM No. 703.
Reproduced from *CMS* II,5 No. 253.

b   Sealing from Phaistos. In HM No. 706.
Rough drawing by Lucy Goodison after a photograph by Paul Morrison.

c   Sealing from Phaistos. In HM No. 705.
Drawing by Lucy Goodison after a photograph by Paul Morrison.

d   Steatite three-sided prism. In collection of the late R.M. Dawkins, U.K. (now dispersed).
Reproduced from *CMS* VIII No. 2.

e   Steatite three-sided prism, chance find from Gonies. In HM No. 80.
Reproduced from *CMS* II,2 No. 224.

f   Steatite three-sided prism from Cave of Trapeza. In HM No. 1561.
Reproduced from *CMS* II,1 No. 427.

Fig 118   a   Scene on plaque from Korfi t'Aroniou, Naxos.
Reproduced from Doumas, 1965, 54, Fig 8.

b   White faience scarab. In Metaxas Collection, Heraklion, No. 506.
Reproduced from *CMS* IV No. 98.

c   Steatite three-sided prism from Stonecutters' workshop, Mallia. In HM No. 1835.
Reproduced from *CMS* II,2 No. 163.

f   Seal from 'Gypsum House' at Knossos. No. SEX/81/1393.
Preliminary drawing reproduced by permission of Professor Warren.

g   Lentoid seal, chance find by E. Sapouna-Sakellarakis' staff member at Unexplored Mansion, Knossos.
Rough drawing by Lucy Goodison after *AR* 1986-7, 53, Fig 92.

h   Pottery fragments from Phylakopi.
Drawing by Lucy Goodison after Zervos, 1957, 142, Pl. 172. Warren has remarked the Minoan affinities, cf. my Figs 49a and b (personal communication, 1988).

i   Dark green steatite lentoid, chance find from central Crete. In HM No. 1199.
Reproduced from *CMS* II,4 No. 55.

j   Vase fragment from Phylakopi.
Drawing by Lucy Goodison after Zervos, 1957, 202, Pl. 272. Zervos describes it as showing 'un homme dans l'attitude d'adoration' (p 39).

Fig 132 a   Mould from Palaikastro in East Crete.
Reproduced from Karo, 1925, No. 50.

b   Drawing of details from Palaikastro mould.
Reproduced from *PM* I, 514, Fig 371.

c   Drawing of Palaikastro mould.
Reproduced from Dussaud, 1914, 391, Fig 289.

Fig 133 a   Bronze tablet from Psychro (Dictaean Cave) in Crete. In Ashmolean Museum, Oxford, No. AE.617. Boardman thinks it cannot be later than LM I.
Reproduced from Boardman, 1961, Pl. XV No. 217.

b   Drawing of the same tablet.
Reproduced from Nilsson, 1950, 171, Fig 72.

Fig 134 a   LM IIIA alabastron from Phaistos. In HM No. 1587.
From a photograph by Lucy Goodison.

b   Decoration on Cretan larnax of unknown provenance. In Rethymnon Museum.
Rough drawing by Lucy Goodison after Mavriyannaki, 1972, Pl. XXI, Larnax No. 7.

Fig 135 a   Amethystine quartz bead with convoluted back. In Ashmolean Museum, Oxford (1938.926), K.133.
Reproduced from Kenna, 1960, No. 1331. Drawing after same by Lucy Goodison.

b   Terracotta plaque from tombs of Tanagra, Boeotia.
Drawing by Lucy Goodison after *AR* 1969-70, 17, Fig 26. See *Ergon* 1969, 7, Fig 3.

c   Plaques in position on Tanagra Larnax.
Drawing by Lucy Goodison after Schachermeyr, 1976b, Pl. 44a.

d   Fragments of LH IIIB-C neck-handled jug, painted in the Pictorial Style. From Phylakopi.
Reproduced from Renfrew, 1985, 205, Fig 5.28, No. 508.

e-g Crossed circle designs on larnax from village of Messi, near Rethymnon. In Rethymnon Museum.
Rough drawings by Lucy Goodison after Mavriyannaki, 1972, Pls. X and XI, No. 3. (On Fig 135g Mavriyannaki (p 49) describes 'rays' inside the 'wheel', but I was unable to see them on her photograph Pl. XI).

Fig 136 a-d 'Circus Pot', vase No. 5 from Tomb 521 on Kalkani North Bank, Mycenae. LH III. In Nauplion Museum No. 2530. Side view and details.
Drawings by Lucy Goodison after photographs by Heleni Palaiologou.

e   Drawing of 'Circus Pot' decoration.
Reproduced from Wace, 1932, Pl. XVIII.

f   Bowl from Beth Shemesh, Jerusalem.
Drawing by Lucy Goodison after Stubbings, 1975, Tafel 2a. (Note the contrast between bare and foliate trees.)

Fig 137   Design on false-necked jar from Calymnos. In BM, A 1015.
Reproduced from Forsdyke, 1925, Fig 276.

Fig 138 a   Roundels from Chania bearing the 'armed warrior' ideogram.
Reproduced from *AR* 1973-4, 40, Fig 82. Drawing by Lucy Goodison after same.

b-c Open crater from Karpathos, near Pigadia. From chamber tomb.
Drawing by Lucy Goodison after Vermeule and Karageorghis, 1982, XII.28. Detail (left) drawn by Lucy Goodison and (right) reproduced from Charitonides, 1961-2, 62, Fig 12.

d   Base of the 'Myrsine idol'. In Aghios Nikolaos Museum.
Rough drawing by Lucy Goodison after J. A. and E. Sakellarakis, 1973, 122, Fig 1.

e   Sealing from Zakro. In HM.
From a photograph by Lucy Goodison.

Fig 139 a   Burnt sard lentoid from Crete. In BM (GR/R) 1874.4-5,4.
Reproduced from *CMS* VII No. 130.

b   Sealing from palace of Pylos. In NAM No. 8493.
Reproduced from *CMS* I No. 369.

c   Mycenaean bowl from cemetery site of Ialysos in Rhodes, c.1200-1100 B.C. In BM, A 950.
Reproduced from Forsdyke, 1925, 173, Fig 235. Compare Desborough, 1964, Pl. 7b.

d   Terracotta model from Palaikastro (settlement context). In HM No. 3903.
Reproduced from *PM* III, 72, Fig 41.
(The fragment of circular base may belong to this or another group).

e   Sealing from palace of Pylos. In NAM No. 8491.
Drawing by Lucy Goodison after *CMS* I No. 321.

Fig 158 a   LM IIIB seal. In Metaxas Collection, Heraklion.
             Reproduced from *CMS* IV No. 290.
        b   LM IIIB seal, steatite lentoid. In BM (GR/R) 1947.9-26,39.
             Reproduced from *CMS* VII No. 141.
        c   LM IIIB seal, steatite lentoid. In BM (GR/R) 1952.5-5,1.
             Reproduced from *CMS* VII No. 143.
        d   LM IIIB seal, steatite lentoid. In BM (GR/R) 1947.9-26,43.
             Reproduced from *CMS* VII No. 144.
        e   Steatite lentoid. In HM No. 614. Said to be from Axos.
             Reproduced from *CMS* II,3 No. 4.

Fig 159   Green steatite lentoid. In BM (GR/R) 1947.9-26,41. LM IIIB.
             Reproduced from *CMS* VII No. 142.

Fig 160 a   'Idols' from Karfi, probably of sub-Minoan period.
             (Left) Drawing by Lucy Goodison after Hood, 1978, 109, Fig 93; (right) Drawing by Lucy Goodison after Hawkes, 1968, 275 (detail).
        b   Two gold foil figures with birds from Grave Circle A at Mycenae. Note emphasis on genitals.
             Reproduced from Karo, 1930, Pl. XXVII Nos. 27 and 28.
        c   Limestone lentoid, said to be from Knossos. In HM No. 143.
             Reproduced from *CMS* II,3 No. 170.
        d   Top of a 'goddess' in clay, from Mitropolis in the Messara. Probably LM I, c.1500 B.C. In HM.
             Drawing by Lucy Goodison after Hood, 1978, 108, Fig 91.

Fig 161 a   One of two gems from a tomb in the Kalkani necropolis at Mycenae which show practically identical representations.
             Reproduced from Wace, 1932, Pl. XXVIII No. 31.
        b   'Mother of the Mountains' sealing from Knossos.
             Reproduced from Nilsson, 1950, 353, Fig 162.
        c   Agate gem from Mycenae.
             Reproduced from Nilsson, 1950, 358, Fig. 169.
        d   Lentoid seal from Grave 24 at Armenoi. In Museum of Chania. *CMS* V No. 253.
             Drawing by Lucy Goodison after a photograph by Lucy Goodison.
        e   Sealing from palace of Pylos. In NAM No. 8547.
             Reproduced from *CMS* I No. 374.
        f   Lentoid from Mycenae. In NAM No. 8718.
             Reproduced from *CMS* I No. 167.
        g   Amethyst cylinder seal from Kasarma. In Nauplion Museum.
             Reproduced from *CMS* V No. 584.

Fig 162 a   LH IIB seal. In Metropolitan Museum, New York.
             Reproduced from *CMS* XII No. 286.
        b   Libation vessel shaped like head of a lioness, from Knossos, 'Stone Vase Room'.
             Reproduced from *Archaeologia* LXV, 1914, 85, Fig 91.

Fig 163 a   Jasper three-sided prism bead. In BM (GR/R) 1876.5-13.3.
             Reproduced from *CMS* VII No. 45.
        b   LM II seal. In Metropolitan Museum, New York.
             Reproduced from *CMS* XII No. 244.

Fig 164 a   Lion supporters of the Egyptian solar disc.
             Reproduced from Evans, 1901, 64, Figs 42a and b.
        b   Sealing from a lentoid, from the LM IIIA1 destruction level at Knossos. In HM.
             Reproduced from Boardman, 1970, Fig 122.
         c   Grey steatite lentoid from Amariano. In HM No. 1041.
             Rough drawing by Lucy Goodison after *CMS* IV No. 319

Fig 165   Seal from Rutsi (Pylos). In NAM No. 8327.
             Reproduced from *CMS* I No. 271.

Fig 166 a   Gem from the cave of Psychro in Crete. In Ashmolean Museum, Oxford.
             Reproduced from Nilsson, 1950, 361, Fig 173.
        b   LM II agate lentoid seal from Knossos, Hospital warrior Grave III. In HM.
             Reproduced from Boardman, 1970, Text Fig 113.
        c   LM IIIA1 gold ring from Fourni, Archanes. In HM No. 1017.
             Reproduced from Boardman, 1970, Text Fig 126.
        d   LH IIIC seal. In collection of the late R.M. Dawkins, U.K. (now dispersed).
             Reproduced from *CMS* VIII No. 95.
        e   LH IIIA seal. In collection of V. E. G. Kenna, U.K.
             Reproduced from *CMS* VIII No. 146.

Fig 167 a   LH IIIA/B seal. In Metropolitan Museum, New York.
             Reproduced from *CMS* XII No. 301.
        b   LM/LH seal. In collection of H. and M.-L. Erlenmeyer, Basel.
             Reproduced from *CMS* X No. 134.
        c   Seal with lion and griffin. In Cabinet des Médailles, Paris.
             Reproduced from *CMS* IX No. 148.
        d   LM IIIA lentoid from Aghia Triadha. In HM No. 339.
             Reproduced from *CMS* II,3 No. 118.

Fig 168 a   Faience 'snake-goddess' from Knossos.
             Reproduced from Hall, 1928, 127, Fig 151.

b Green steatite flattened cylinder. In collection of H. and M.-L. Erlenmeyer, Basel.
   Reproduced from *CMS* X No. 68.

c LM II seal. In collection of E. G. Spencer-Churchill, U.K.
   Reproduced from *CMS* VIII No. 147.

d LH III chalcedony lentoid from Akona Tomb I, near Koukounara. In Pylos Museum, No. 145.
   Reproduced from Boardman, 1970, 61, Text Fig 136.

e Red jasper four-sided rectangular bead. In Metropolitan Museum, New York, No. 26.31.151.
   Reproduced from *CMS* XII No. 108.

f Amygdaloid said to be from Psychro. In HM No. 1501.
   Reproduced from *CMS* II,3 No. 289.

g Steatite lentoid from Mallia. In HM No. 1548.
   Reproduced from *CMS* II,3 No. 149.

h Hathor head motif on Egyptian predynastic plaque and on First Dynasty vase; also head of Hathor cow.
   Drawings by Lucy Goodison after Allam, 1963, Pl. I.; also Bleeker, 1973, Pl. I.

i Clay sealing from Room II of Juktas Peak Sanctuary, Crete, showing bull's head with 'star' symbol.
   Drawing by Lucy Goodison after Hägg and Marinatos, 1981, 150, Fig 24.

j The sky as cow. From Tomb of Seti I, Egypt.
   Reproduced from Erman, 1907, 8, Fig 6.

Fig 179 a Typical shape of a Mycenaean chamber tomb.
   Reproduced from Stubbings, 1972, 36, Fig 35.

b Cross-section of tholos tomb of Acharnai-Menidi.
   Reproduced from Wolters, *Jahrbuch* 14, 1899, 116, Fig 24.

c Early Mycenaean tholos tomb at Peristeria. It had been free-standing, without a covering mound. Internal diameter 5.08m.
   Reproduced from *AR* 1977-8, 34, Fig 58.

d Grave Circle A at Mycenae, in plan and (right) as reconstructed by Belger.
   Reproduced from Evans, 1929, 65, Fig 47, and 60, Fig 44.

Fig 180 a Black marble seal from the Messara. In Metaxas Collection, Heraklion.
   Reproduced from *CMS* IV No. 170.

b Seal from Siteia. In Metaxas Collection, Heraklion.
   Reproduced from *CMS* IV No. 164.

Fig 181 a Cornelian prism from Crete. MM III-LM I. In HM No. 130.
   Reproduced from *PM* I, 674, Fig 493 c.

b Chalcedony amygdaloid late palatial seal from Crete. In Heraklion, Giamalakis Collection No. 356.
   Reproduced from Boardman, 1970, 45, Text Fig 96.

c Amygdaloid from Platanos. In HM No. 1139.
   Rough drawing by Lucy Goodison after *CMS* II,3 No. 121.

d Agate amygdaloid from East Crete. In Ashmolean Museum, Oxford, CS 254.
   Reproduced from Boardman, 1970, Black and White Pl. 76.

e Cornelian plump prism. In HM No. 130.
   Rough drawing by Lucy Goodison after Boardman, 1970, Black and White Pl. 73.

f MM III-LM I sealstone.
   Reproduced from *PM* I, 674, Fig 493b.

g MM III-LM I sealstone.
   Reproduced from *PM* I, 674, Fig 493a.

h Cornelian of unknown provenance. In Staatliche Museen, Berlin, No. FG 46.
   Reproduced from *CMS* XI No. 24.

i The 'ba' and shade of the deceased near the tomb (Book of the Dead of Neferubenef, Spell 92).
   Reproduced from Hornung, 1983b, 136.

Fig 182 a MM III seal bearing hieroglyphic signs. In Metropolitan Museum, New York.
   Reproduced from *CMS* XII No. 113.

b MM seal from Mochlos.
   Reproduced from *PM* I, 277, Fig 207b.

c Bead seal with 'template' signs.
   Reproduced from *PM* II, 203, Fig 112c.

Fig 183 a Details of lid of Palaikastro larnax (shown on Figs 149 and 195a). In HM.
   From photographs by Carlos Guarita.

b MM II burial jar from near Knossos.
   Reproduced from Bossert, 1937, 199, Pl. 350.

Fig 184 Group of dancers from tomb I at Kamilari, used MM I-III and reused in LM. In HM No. 15073.
   Photograph by Carlos Guarita.

Fig 185 a Mourning figure on short side of LBA sarcophagus from Tanagra. In Thebes Museum.
   Rough drawing by Lucy Goodison after Kanta, 1980, Pl. 103 No. 1.

b LBA sarcophagus from Tanagra, Tomb 6, with mourning women. The Tanagra tombs date end LH IIIB/ early LH IIIC.
   Drawing by Lucy Goodison after *Ergon*, 1969, 8, Fig 4.

c LBA sarcophagus from Tanagra in Boeotia, with mourning women.
   Drawing by Lucy Goodison after *AR* 1973-4, 19, Fig 30.

          d   Neoplatial seal. In Cabinet des Médailles, Paris.
                Reproduced from *CMS* IX No. 57, where it is described as 'Poisson volant' (p 78).
          e   MM III-LM I seal. In Metropolitan Museum, New York.
                Reproduced from *CMS* XII No. 161, where Kenna describes it as 'Flying fish'.
          f   Cretan seal with fish and birds. In Giamalakis Collection.
                Reproduced from Xénaki-Sakellariou, 1958, Pl. X No. 328.

Fig 197   Bird and fish decoration on bowl. In BM, A 846 (detail).
                Reproduced from Forsdyke, 1925, 150 Fig 201.

Fig 198   a   Fish and bird decoration on sarcophagus lid. In HM.
                From photographs by Lucy Goodison, with rough drawing by Lucy Goodison.
          b   LM III painted sarcophagus.
                Reproduced from Hall, 1928, 190, Fig 247.
          c   LM IIIA painted clay sarcophagus from Anoia, Crete.
                Reproduced from *PM* IV, 338, Fig 281.
          d   MM III-LM I seal. In collection of H. and M.-L. Erlenmeyer, Basel.
                Reproduced from *CMS* X No. 177, where Betts describes it as 'Bird and fish (dolphin?); semi-circles in the field; perhaps in the "talismanic" manner' (p 137).

Fig 199   a   LM IB seal from Knossos.
                Reproduced from Coldstream, 1973, 125, Fig 27.3.
          b   LM IB seal. In collection of V. E. G. Kenna, U.K.
                Reproduced from *CMS* VIII No. 138.
          c   LM IA glandular shaped seal. In BM.
                Reproduced from *CMS* VII No. 73.
          d   Agate amygdaloid seal. In Cabinet des Médailles, Paris, No. M 5814.
                Reproduced from *CMS* IX No. 67.
          e   Sardonyx lentoid seal from Crete. In NAM No. 4661.
                Reproduced from *CMS* I No. 462.
          f   LM I three-sided prism bead. In Metropolitan Museum, New York.
                Reproduced from *CMS* XII No. 181, where Kenna describes it as 'The foreparts of two fish inverted to each other to surround a star' (p 269).
          g   LM I cornelian amygdaloid. In Metropolitan Museum, New York.
                Reproduced from *CMS* XII No. 191, where Kenna describes it as 'A fish between two stars and two vegetable sprays' (p 285).
          h   Neopalatial seal. In Cabinet des Médailles, Paris.
                Reproduced from *CMS* IX No. 71, where the Van Effenterres describe it as 'Poisson (squale) plongeant entre deux étoiles à huit et neuf branches ... Talismanique' (p 92).
          i   Neoplatial seal. In Cabinet des Médailles, Paris.
                Reproduced from *CMS* IX No. 70, where the Van Effenterres describe it as 'Avant-corps d'un poisson entre une étoile à huit branches et une plante aquatique ... Talismanique' (p 91).
          j   Sard lentoid. In HM No. 103.
                Reproduced from *CMS* II,3 No. 375, where it is described as a flying fish with 'Seestern' (p 435).
          k   Lentoid from Mallia. In Giamalakis Collection No. 3067.
                Rough drawing by Lucy Goodison after Xénaki-Sakellariou, 1958, Pl. 10 No. 319, where it is described as three dolphins around an 'étoile' (p 49).

Fig 200   a   Lapislazuli lentoid from Tholos I at Gouvalari, near Koukounara. In Pylos Museum No. 18.
                Reproduced from *CMS* V No. 639, where Pini describes it as 'Vier fische, ... (Delphine?), locker in Form eines Wirbels angeordnet' (p 509).
          b   Lentoid from 'Geometric Graves', Knossos. In HM No. 230.
                Reproduced from *CMS* II,3 No. 75, where it is described as four dolphins or flying fish in 'wirbelförmiger Anordnung' (p 86).

Fig 201   a   LM IA seal. In collection of the late R.M. Dawkins, U.K. (now dispersed).
                Reproduced from *CMS* VIII No. 58.
          b   Neopalatial seal from Crete. In NAM.
                Reproduced from *CMS* I No. 456.
           c   Pink jasper truncated amygdaloid. In Fitzwilliam Museum, Cambridge, GR. 65.1901.
                Reproduced from *CMS* VII No. 229.

Fig 202   a   LM IB seal. In collection of Dilys Russel, U.K.
                Reproduced from *CMS* VIII No. 153.
          b   Amygdaloid from tholos grave at Kasarma. In Nauplion Museum.
                Reproduced from *CMS* V No. 577.

Fig 203   a   LM/LH lentoid seal. In Museum of Fine Arts, Boston No. 65.1317.
                Reproduced from *CMS* XIII No. 18.
          b   Red jasper lentoid, from grave at Mikro Kastelli. In Thebes Museum.
                Reproduced from *CMS* V No. 667.

Fig 204   a   Seal impression from the palace of Pylos, LH IIIB. In NAM.
                Reproduced from *CMS* I No. 344.
           b   LM IIIB seal. In collection of the late R.W. Hutchinson, U.K. (now dispersed).
                Reproduced from *CMS* VIII No. 128.
          c   Jasper lentoid of unknown provenance. In HM No. 944.
                Reproduced from *CMS* II,3 No. 327.
          d   Terracotta dolphin from the temple of Aghia Irini, Kea.
                Rough drawing by Lucy Goodison after Hägg and Marinatos, 1981, 132, Fig 9.

c   Horses and fish on collared jar from Dodekanese. In Toronto.
Drawing by Lucy Goodison after Vermeule and Karageorghis, 1982, XII.42. (Note the circular symbols on the horses' bodies; on the reverse side of the vessel one of those symbols is rayed).

d   Three-sided Cretan seal. In Chania Museum.
Photograph by Lucy Goodison.

Fig 217   a   The Episkopi larnax, from LM III tomb. In Ierapetra Archaeological Collection.
Drawing by Lucy Goodison after Vermeule, 1979, 67, Fig 25 and Warren, 1975, 108.

b   Larnax from Tanagra, Grave 22. (One of its short ends shows a scene of placing the corpse in a larnax, see *AAA*, 3, 1970, 195, Fig. 15.)
Drawing by Lucy Goodison after *Ergon*, 1969, 11, Fig 7.

Fig 218   a   Section of chariot-fresco from palace of Tiryns.
Reproduced from Hall, 1928, 231, Fig 305.

b   LH I-II seal from tholos tomb at Kasarma. In Nauplion Museum.
Reproduced from *CMS* V No. 585.

c   Clay figurine of female figure on horse, from Attica. In Stathatos collection.
Rough drawing by Lucy Goodison after Mylonas, 1966, Fig 118.

d   Design on LM three-handled Cretan jar from grave context.
Rough drawing by Lucy Goodison after Benson, 1970, Pl. VII Fig 1. (See Matz, 1951, 740, Pl. 3, 1.)

e   Design on vase from Mycenae.
Reproduced from Benson, 1970, Pl. VII Fig 2.

f   Chariot krater from Ialysos in Rhodes.
Reproduced from Vermeule and Karageorghis, 1982, XII.6.

g   Terracotta chariot group from the West Shrine at Phylakopi. Find No. 1558.
Reproduced from Renfrew, 1985, 253, Fig 6.25.

h   Figurine of horse and rider from Archanes in Crete. In HM No. 18505.
Drawing by Lucy Goodison after a photograph by Carlos Guarita.

Fig 219   a   Skeleton of horse cut into pieces, found near door of inner chamber of tomb at Archanes.
Rough drawing by Lucy Goodison after J. Sakellarakis, 1967, 279, Pl. 9.

b   Skeletons of horses found in dromos of tholos tomb at Marathon.
Drawing by Louise London after Mylonas, 1966, Pl. III.

Fig 220   a   Design of seal from Rutsi near Pylos. In NAM.
Reproduced from *CMS* I No. 279.

b   Ivory signet ring from Phylakopi, LB I, bears red pigment in incisions.
Reproduced from Nilsson, 1950, 171, Fig 73.

c   Sealing from Chania destruction level dated to end of LM I. Probably from a ring, see Papapostolou, 1977, 27ff and 69ff.
Rough drawing by Lucy Goodison after Hallager, 1985, Fig 24.

Fig 221   Clay figure with poppies from Gazi, probably LM IIIA. In HM.
Rough drawing by Lucy Goodison after Hood, 1978, 109, Fig 92 (detail).

Fig 222   a   Steatite lentoid from Mycenae. In NAM No. 5409.
Reproduced from *CMS* I No. 42.

b   Haematite lentoid seal from Midea. In NAM No. 8771.
Reproduced from *CMS* I No. 195.

c   LM III serpentine lentoid from Grave 15 at Armenoi. In Chania Museum.
Reproduced from *CMS* V No. 244.

Fig 223   Dark green steatite lentoid, LM IIIA. In Metropolitan Museum, New York.
Reproduced from *CMS* XII No. 264.

Fig 224   a   LH III chalcedony lentoid from Mycenae. In NAM.
Reproduced from *PM* IV, 502, Fig. 444.

b   Flattened cylinder seal from Knossos area. Dated by Boardman to the late palace period (1970, 100). In Ashmolean Museum, Oxford, CS 204.
Reproduced from *PM* IV, 502, Fig 443.

Fig 225   a   Gold ring, the 'Isopata ring'. In HM No. 424.
Reproduced from Nilsson, 1950, Fig 139.

b   Black serpentine lentoid. In Cabinet des Médailles, Paris.
Reproduced from *CMS* IX No. 164.

c   Seal impression from Aghia Triadha. In HM No. 505.
Reproduced from Nilsson, 1950, Fig 134.

d   Seal design from Crete. In HM.
Reproduced from *Annuario della Scuola Archeologica di Atene*, 8-9, 1925-6, 139, Fig 153.

e   Haematite cylinder seal from Palaikastro. In HM No. 565.
Reproduced from *CMS* II,3 No. 279.

f   Bronze seal said to be from Kavoussi. In HM Bronze No. 970.
Reproduced from *CMS* II,3 No. 305.

Fig 226   a   Agate lentoid from Vafio tomb. In NAM, No. 1776.
Reproduced from *PM* IV, 453, Fig 378.

b   Glass plaque from Mycenae.
Reproduced from Nilsson, 1950, Fig 54.

c   Haematite amygdaloid. In Metropolitan Museum, New York. LM I.
Reproduced from *CMS* XII No. 212.

d   Late Mycenaean stirrup jar, from grave context. In BM No. A 914.
Reproduced from Forsdyke, 1925, 165, Fig 222.

e   Small stirrup jar from a tomb at Makresia, near Olympia.
Drawing by Lucy Goodison after Hawkes, 1968, Pl. 38 (detail).

f   Stirrup jar from Gurob. In BM No. A 989.
Reproduced from Forsdyke, 1925, 183, Fig 258.

g   LM III stirrup jar from cemetery at Kritsa. In Aghios Nikolaos Museum No. 135.
From a photograph by Carlos Guarita.

h   Late Minoan stirrup jar. In Aghios Nikolaos Museum.
Drawing by Lucy Goodison.

i   Stirrup jar from Galia. In HM.
Reproduced from Kanta, 1980, Pl. 116 No. 4.

Fig 239   a   Vessel from Sub-Minoan Karfi, Crete. In HM.
Drawing by Lucy Goodison after a photograph by Carlos Guarita.

b   Red polished ware pyxis from Tomb 2 at Vounous. In Cyprus Museum, Nicosia.
Reproduced from Tatton-Brown, 1979, 31, No. 64.

Fig 240   Jasper three-sided prism bead, MM III. In Metropolitan Museum, New York No. 26.31.115.
Reproduced from *CMS* XII No. 94.

Fig 241   a   Gold ring in Ashmolean Museum, Oxford 1919.56.
Reproduced from Nilsson, 1950, Fig 155.

b   LH III ring from the Vafio tomb in Laconia. In NAM.
Reproduced from Nilsson, 1950, 275, Fig 138.

c   LM IIIA1 gold signet ring from larnax at Archanes, Crete. In HM No. 989.
Rough drawing by Lucy Goodison after Sakellarakis, 1967, 280, Fig 13.

d   Gold ring from the necropolis of Kalyvia, Tombe dei Nobili Grave 11. See *CMS* II, 3 No. 114. In HM.
Reproduced from Nilsson, 1950, Fig 133.

e   Sealing from Aghia Triadha. In HM.
Photograph by Lucy Goodison.

f   Seal impression in HM.
Photograph by Lucy Goodison.

g   Ring sealing from Chania, dated before end of LM I. In Chania Museum No. 1024.
Photograph by Lucy Goodison.

h   LH II-III engraved steatite plaque from Eleusis. In Eleusis Museum.
Reproduced from *CMS* V No. 422.

i   Bronze ring from Knossos area. In HM Bronze No. 2490.
Reproduced from *CMS* II,3 No. 15.

j   Gold ring, bought in Cnania. In Staatliche Museen, Berlin, No. Misc. 11886.
Reproduced from *CMS* XI No. 29.

k   Gold ring from Sellopoulou, Crete, Tomb 4. LM III A. In HM No. 1034.
Reproduced from Popham and Catling, 1974, Fig 14d.

l   Fragments of LM IIIA1 larnax from Knossos, T.107.214. Note the bird above.
Drawing of reconstructed design reproduced from Morgan, 1987, 181, Fig 7. The short end of the larnax, towards which this figure is facing, bears a stylized tree.

Fig 242   a   Interior of inner coffin, Nesi-Pa-Ur-Shefit. In the Fitzwilliam Museum, Cambridge, No. E.1-1822. Egyptian, 21st Dynasty (approx. 1100-950 B.C.).
Photograph reproduced by permission of Fitzwilliam Museum, Cambridge. Drawing of detail reproduced from Hornung, 1983b, 181.

b   Egyptian jar personified as the goddess Hathor. Early 18th Dynasty, c.1551-1490 B.C. There is also an unpublished 12th Dynasty example (c.1991-1785 B.C.) from Karnak North.
Reproduced from Bourriau, 1981, 38, No. 52.

Fig 243   a   LM/LH green steatite lentoid. In collection of H. and M.-L. Erlenmeyer, Basel.
Reproduced from *CMS* X No. 160.

b   Scene on lid of Episkopi larnax (see Fig 217a above).

c   Plaque from Korfi t'Aroniou, Naxos.
After Doumas, 1965, 54, Fig 8.

d   Black steatite seal of uncertain provenance. In Ashmolean Museum, Oxford, 1938.1097.
Reproduced from Kenna, 1960, No. 21 P. Drawing after same by Lucy Goodison.

Fig 244   a   Gold ring from the necropolis of Phaistos.
Reproduced from Nilsson, 1950, 257, Fig 125.

b   Sealing from the palace of Pylos. In NAM.
Reproduced from *CMS* I No. 377, where A. Sakellariou describes it as 'Kultszene: Mensch vor einem Affengott (?) mit Hundekofp' (p 386).

c   Limestone lentoid said to be from Knossos. In HM No. 1461.
Reproduced from *CMS* II,3 No. 168.

d   Sard amygdaloid from Mochlos. In HM No. 750.
Reproduced from *CMS* II,3 No. 258.

e   Black steatite lentoid from Makryteikos, Knossos. In HM No. 1411.
Reproduced from *CMS* II,4 No. 136.

f   Black steatite lentoid from 'Gonies'. In HM No. 724.
Reproduced from *CMS* II,4 No. 196.

| | e | Painted plaster tablet from Mycenae. |

e   Painted plaster tablet from Mycenae.
Reproduced from Bossert, 1937, 32, Pl. 43.

f   Limestone lentoid from the necropolis of Mavro Spilio, Knossos. In HM No. 1315.
Reproduced from *CMS* II,3 No. 32.

Fig 254   Flat cylinder from Knossos, belonging to start of LM I period.
Reproduced from Nilsson, 1950, 349, Fig 160.

Fig 255 a Seal impression from Knossos, of which eleven examples were found.
Reproduced from Nilsson, 1950, Fig 165.

b   LH IIIC seal from Grave B at Aplomata. In Naxos Museum.
Reproduced from *CMS* V No. 608.

c   LM IB-LM II clay sealing from Kastelli, Khania.
Reproduced from Hallager, 1985, Fig 11.

Fig 256   Fresco from Knossos palace (reconstruction). In HM.
Rough drawing by Lucy Goodison after a photograph by Asimokopouli Brothers, Athens.

Fig 257 a Gold signet ring from Mycenae.
Reproduced from Evans, 1901, 85, Fig 57.

b   Green steatite lentoid. In collection of H. Seyring, Neuchatel.
Reproduced from *CMS* X No. 270.

Fig 258 a Haematite lentoid. In Fogg Art Museum, Cambridge, Mass., U.S.A.
Reproduced from *CMS* XIII No. 39.

b   Near-Eastern seal of Sargonid Age.
Reproduced from Frankfort, 1939, 116, Text Fig 32, where he describes it as showing the goddess of vegetation: 'seated before her own statue, she carries a bowl from which water streams'.

c   Steatite lentoid. In Musée d'Art et d'Histoire, Geneva.
Reproduced from *CMS* X No. 261.

d   Sealing No. 1 from Zakro.
Reproduced from Nilsson, 1950, 283, Fig 142.

Fig 259 a Gold ring from Thebes. (See Fig 129).

b   Gold ring said to come from near Sestos in Northern Greece. In Staatliche Museen, Berlin, No. 30219, 512.
Reproduced from Nilsson, 1950, 266, Fig 130. See also *CMS* XI No. 28.

c   Gold ring from Knossos. In Ashmolean Museum, Oxford, No. K 250.1938.1127. My identification of rays rather than locks is tentative.
Reproduced from Nilsson, 1950, 256, Fig 123.

d   Painted end of larnax from LM IIIB-IIIC chamber-tomb at Milatus. In HM No. 1617.
Reproduced from Evans, 1906, 99, Fig 107. (Alexiou identifies the figure as female).

Fig 260 a Figurine from Crete. in HM No. 8345.
Rough drawing by Lucy Goodison after J. A. Sakellarakis, *Herakleion Museum*, Ekdotike Athenon, Athens, 1980, 53.

b   Terracotta figurine from chamber tomb at Mycenae. In NAM.
Drawing by Lucy Goodison after a photograph by E. Tzaferis, Athens.

c   Two 'phi-shaped' figurines with an infant on their shoulders, from chamber tomb at Mycenae.
Drawing by Lucy Goodison after Mylonas, 1966, No. 108.

d   Ivory group from Mycenae.
Reproduced from Immerwahr, 1973, Fig 17.

Fig 261 a Gem from Vafio. In NAM.
Reproduced from Nilsson, 1950, 146, Fig 53.

b   Lentoid from West Crete. In Benaki Museum, No. 105/11.
Reproduced from Nilsson, 1950, Fig 56.

c   Lentoid of unknown provenance. In Museo di Villa Giulia, Rome, No. 53852.
Reproduced from *PM* IV, 465, Fig 389a.

d   Seal showing male figure between two genii. LB II/III lentoid 'from Figalia'. In Staatliche Museen, Berlin, No. FG 10.
Reproduced from *PM* IV, 466, Fig 390.

Fig 262 a Glass plaque from Mycenae.
Reproduced from Nilsson, 1950, 146, Fig 54.

b   Plaque showing genii with columns, from Mycenae.
Reproduced from Evans, 1901, 19, Fig 13.

c   Impressed glass plaque from a tomb at Mycenae.
Reproduced from Evans, 1901, 19, Fig 14.

Fig 263 a Green stone lentoid seal showing two genii(?) with column. In Ashmolean Museum, Oxford, 1967.138.
Reproduced from Boardman, 1970, Black and White Pl. 192. Drawing by Lucy Goodison after same.

b   Cretan lentoid. In NAM.
Reproduced from *CMS* I No. 513.

c   Seal cylinder from Mycenae.
Reproduced from Nilsson, 1950, 257, Fig 126.

d   Vase fragment from Old Salamis, Cyprus.
Reproduced from Evans, 1901, Fig 6, where he describes it as showing 'Pillar Shrines and Votaries' (p 14).

Fig 276   a   Fragment of a vessel from the Argive Heraion. In NAM.
              Reproduced from Schweitzer, 1971, Fig 21.
          b   Kantharos in NAM No. 14477.
              From a photograph by Lucy Goodison, with drawing after same by Lucy Goodison.
          c   Bowl from the Kerameikos. In NAM No. 784.
              Reproduced from Schweitzer, 1971, Pl. 65, with rough drawing after same by Lucy Goodison.
          d   Eighth century B.C. gold cylinder from Kamiros. In Munich.
              Drawing by Lucy Goodison after *Antike Gemmen* I-1 No. 98.
Fig 277   a   Bronze pendant from Tomb P at Fortetsa near Knossos. No. 1570.
              Reproduced from Brock, 1957, Pl. 114 i and ii.
          b   Dedalic plaque showing a female figure, from Crete, seventh century B.C.
              Drawing by Lucy Goodison after Higgins, 1967b, Pl. 10 A.
          c   Detail of Fig 277e.
          d   Bronze Age Cretan seal (see Fig 25a).
          e   Frieze from the shoulder of a belly amphora from Fortetsa, near Knossos.
              Reproduced from Schweitzer, 1971, 72, Fig 35.
          f   Figurines from Lindos, Rhodes.
              Reproduced from Blinkenberg, 1931, Nos. 2038 and 2043 (from left to right).
          g   Chalcedony scarab from Cyprus, of sixth-century orientalizing style. In Oxford 1966.595.
              Reproduced from Boardman, 1968, Pl. III No. 40. Boardman notes that 'Rays may be shown
              above the disc' (p 31).
          h   Scaraboid from Emporio in Chios, late eighth century.
              Reproduced from Boardman, 1967, Pl. 95 No. 536, and p 237, where he comments that it was
              probably made in Cilicia.
          i   Scaraboid from Lindos in Rhodes.
              Reproduced from Blinkenberg, 1931, No. 521. Drawing after same by Lucy Goodison.
Fig 278   a   Assemblage from Tiryns attributed to eighth century B.C. In Nauplion Museum.
              Photograph by Lucy Goodison.
          b   Clay ring and disc from Tiryns.
              Reproduced from Schliemann, *Tiryns*, 1886, 148, Nos. 73 and 74 (left to right).
Fig 279   a   Detail of decoration on a krater from the Kerameikos. In Louvre, Paris, No. A 517.
              Reproduced from Schweitzer, 1971, Pl. 36. Rough drawing by Lucy Goodison after same.
          b   Neck-handled amphora. In Benaki Museum, Athens, No. 7675.
              Reproduced from Schweitzer, 1971, Pl. 46. (Detail) Drawing by Lucy Goodison after Ahlberg,
              1971b, Fig 46b.
          c   Detail of belly-handled amphora.
              Reproduced from Schweitzer, 1971, Pl. 31. (Detail) Rough drawing by Lucy Goodison after same.
          d   Krater from the Kerameikos. In NAM, No. 990.
              Reproduced from Schweitzer, 1971, Pl. 40.
          e   Terracotta figurine of a mourner, eighth century B.C. grave offering from Athens.
              Drawing by Lucy Goodison after Kurtz and Boardman, 1971, Fig 6.
          f   Detail of krater in Louvre No. A 522.
              Reproduced from Ahlberg, 1971b, Fig 5b.
Fig 280   a   Hand-made incised doll-shaped clay figures and a pyxis (right) from Athens, the Kerameikos.
              Reproduced from *Jahrbuch*, 1962, No. 77, 97 Abb. 15 Nos. 6 and 7, and 98 Abb. 16 No. 12.
          b   Fragments of coffins from Assarlik. In BM, Nos. A 1113,25; A 1114,1; A 1114,2; A 1114,3; A
              1115 (from top left).
              Reproduced from Forsdyke, 1925, 215, Fig 302 (left) and 216, Fig 303 (the rest).
          c   Green steatite gem, probably from Melos, Archaic. In collection of the British School at Athens.
              Reproduced from Betts, 1971b, Pl. 4b.
          d   Lead 'wheel' from Crete, allegedly from a 'cave-tomb' at Kissamo. In Ashmolean Museum,
              Oxford, No. AE.146; 1891.666.
              Reproduced from Boardman, 1961, 90, No. 394.
          e   Gold pendant with crystal and amber inlays on crescents and discs respectively, from eighth or
              early seventh century B.C., found in Tekke Tomb 2.
              Reproduced from Boardman, 1967b, Pl. 10.
Fig 281   a   Plan of Chamber Tomb XI at Fortetsa near Knossos.
              Reproduced from Snodgrass, 1971, 167, Fig 64.
          b   Cross-section and plan of tumulus at Vodhine in Epirus.
              Reproduced from Snodgrass, 1971, 258, Fig 90.
Fig 282   a   Bronze bowl from Idalion in Cyprus. In Metropolitan Museum, New York.
              Reproduced from Schweitzer, 1971, 53, Fig 18. Schweitzer points out that the subject matter
              draws on oriental models, although the style is Geometric.
          b   Fragment from Tiryns. In NAM No. 1504.
              Drawing by Lucy Goodison after Ahlberg, 1971b, Fig 56e.
          c   Detail of a krater from Athens. In NAM, Athens No. 810.
              Reproduced from Schweitzer, 1971, Pl. 63.
          d   Hydria from Analatos in Attica. In NAM.
              Reproduced from Schweitzer, 1971, Pls. 52-55 (details).
          e   Fragment of a cup from Amyclae in Laconia. In NAM.
              Reproduced from Schweitzer, 1971, 67, Fig 28 (detail).

    f 'Lid' with bird decoration from Fortetsa.
       Reproduced from Brock, 1957, Pl. 46 and Pl. 153 No. 678.
    g Eighth century figurine from Boeotia.
       Drawing by Lucy Goodison after Higgins, 1967b, Pl. 9 E.
Fig 293 a Detail of decoration on a krater from the Kerameikos. In Louvre, Paris, No. A 517.
       Reproduced from Schweitzer, 1971, Pl. 36.
    b Detail of decoration on the same krater shown on Fig 293a.
       Reproduced from Schweitzer, 1971, Pl. 37. Drawing by Lucy Goodison after same.
    c Minoan larnax in HM (see Fig 206a).
       Rough drawing by Lucy Goodison.
    d Bow fibula in BM.
       Reproduced from Schweitzer, 1971, 213, Fig 125.
    e Detail of krater from the Kerameikos. In Louvre, Paris, No. A 522.
       Reproduced from Schweitzer, 1971, Pl. 39.
    f Design on locally made pyxis from mid-ninth century tomb at Lefkandi, Toumba.
       Drawing by Lucy Goodison after *AR* 1986-7, 14, Fig 18.
    g Attic cup from market area, Athens, last half of ninth century.
       Reproduced from *BSA* 44, 1949, 96, Fig 1.
Fig 294 a Attic krater fragments. In Warsaw 142172 (ex Königsberg A.18).
       Reproduced from Morrison and Williams, 1968, Pl. 4c(i) after Antike Kleinkunst in Königsberg,
       II, Pl. 2, 1935.
    b Western Greek Geometric krater from Pithecusae.
       Reproduced from Mitteilungen des Deutschen Archäologischen Instituts: Römische Abteilung,
       1953-4, Vol. 42, 42, Fig 1.
Fig 295 a Fragments of a krater from the Kerameikos. In Louvre, Paris, No. A 527.
       Reproduced from Schweitzer, 1971, Pl. 38.
    b Fragments of a krater in the Louvre, Paris, CA 3362.
       Reproduced from Ahlberg, 1971, 26, Fig 26.
    c Fragments of a krater in the Louvre, Paris, A 528.
       Reproduced from Ahlberg, 1971, 31, Fig 34.
    d Fragments of a krater in the Louvre, Paris, A 537.
       Reproduced from Ahlberg, 1971, 31, Fig 35.
Fig 296   Design on fragmentary krater in the Louvre, Paris.
       Reproduced from Ahlberg, 1971, 36, Fig 44.
Fig 297 a Detail of the figured zone on the belly of a krater in New York, 34.11.2.
       Reproduced from Ahlberg, 1971, 28, Fig 30.
    b General view of krater detailed in Fig 297a. (A different boat scene appears in the figured zone on
       the other side of the krater).
       Reproduced from Ahlberg, 1971, 27, Fig 28.
Fig 298 a Late Geometric vase from Thebes. (See Fig 275a).
    b Gold signet-ring from Crete (see Fig 212e).
       Reproduced from *PM* II, 250, Fig 147b.
Fig 299 a Fragments of an openwork bronze stand from the Idaean Cave, Crete.
       Reproduced from Boardman, 1961, 133, Fig 49A.
    b Model of boat from Tomb X at Fortetsa near Knossos.
       Reproduced from Brock, 1957, Pl. 36 No. 542i.
    c Decoration on Geometric oinochoe in University Museum, Hobart.
       Reproduced from Fittschen, 1969, Abb. 14.
    d Ivory relief from the sanctuary of Artemis Orthia.
       Reproduced from *BSA* Vol. 13, 1906-7, Pl. 4.
Fig 300 a-f Diminutive figurines from Cave of Inatos (Tsoutsouros) in S. Crete. In HM.
       Rough drawings by Carlos Guarita. Most of these items are unpublished, and for permission to
       use these drawings I am grateful to Dr Davaras.
Fig 301   'Artemis' amphora from Thebes. In NAM 5893.
       Reproduced from *AE* 1892, Pl. 10, No. 1.
Fig 302 a Birds carry fish on Geometric pottery design from necropolis of Eleusis.
       Reproduced from *AE* 1898, Pl. 5 No. 2a.
    b Bird and fish juxtaposed on Argive sherd.
       Reproduced from Roes, 1933, 60, Fig 47.
    c Bow fibula. In Staatlichen Museen, Berlin.
       Reproduced from Schweitzer, 1971, 212, Fig 123.
Fig 303 a Upper half of a krater from the Kerameikos. In NAM, No. 990.
       Rough drawing by Lucy Goodison after Schweitzer (see Fig 279d).
    b Detail of Fig 303a.
       Reproduced from Schweitzer, 1971, Pl. 40.
    c Krater in Metropolitan Museum, New York, No. 14.130.14.
       Reproduced from Schweitzer, 1971, Pl. 41.
       (Details) Rough drawings by Lucy Goodison after Ahlberg, 1971b, Fig 25.
    d Late Geometric amphora from the Agora, Athens, P 4990.
       Drawings by Lucy Goodison after reconstruction in Hesperia, Suppl. II, 1939.
    e Neck-handled amphora from Attica. In NAM, Stathatos collection.
       Reproduced from Schweitzer, 1971, Pl. 47.

	e	Argive Late Geometric. In Nauplion Museum No. 1915. Rough drawing by Lucy Goodison after Coldstream, 1968, Pl. 29f.
	f	Argive Late Geometric. In NAM No. 231. Reproduced from Coldstream, 1968, Pl. 28e.
	g	Design showing horse with fish on Argive sherd. Reproduced from Roes, 1933, 66, Fig 54.
Fig 317	a	Krater from Kourion in Cyprus. In Metropolitan Museum, New York. Reproduced from Schweitzer, 1971, Pl. 82 (detail).
	b	Krater in Allard Pierson Museum, Amsterdam. Drawing by Lucy Goodison after Schweitzer, 1971, Pl. 80 (detail).
	c	Amphora from Attica (?) in Museum of Fine Arts, Boston. Drawing by Lucy Goodison after Fairbanks, 1928, Pl. XX No. 261 (detail).
	d	Decoration on vase in Scheurleer collection, The Hague. Reproduced from Roes, 1933, 71, Fig 59.
Fig 318	a	Steatite lentoid showing a winged horse, probably from Melos. In collection of British School at Athens. Reproduced from Boardman, 1970, Black and White Pl. 231.
	b	Steatite lentoid showing forepart of winged horse. In collection of Dilys Russell, U.K. Reproduced from Boardman, 1970, Black and White Pl. 252.
	c	Steatite lentoid showing winged horse. In Dresden No. 1614. Reproduced from Boardman, 1970, Black and White Pl. 255.
Fig 319	a	Funerary oinochoe from Kamirus, Rhodes. In Staatliche Museen, Berlin. Reproduced from Schweitzer, 1971, 82, Fig 43.
	b	Detail of design on straight-sided pithos from Fortetsa, No. 1440, H.41. Rough drawing by Lucy Goodison after Coldstream, 1979, 69, Fig 21b.
Fig 320		Design on neck of oinochoe from Rheneia, Delos. In Mykonos Museum. Reproduced from Schweitzer, 1971, 69, Fig 30.
Fig 321	a	Steatite amygdaloid showing the foreparts of two winged goats joined in a whirl, from Melos. In BM. Reproduced from Boardman, 1970, Black and White Pl. 251.
	b	Grey stone lentoid showing a contorted winged goat. In BM. Reproduced from Boardman, 1970, Black and White Pl. 242.
	c	Steatite lentoid showing a winged goat-fish and on the reverse a contorted winged horse and dolphin. In Metropolitan Museum, New York. Reproduced from Boardman, 1970, Black and White Pl. 235.
Fig 322	a	Serpentine disc in collection of Dilys Russell, U.K. Reproduced from Boardman, 1970, Black and White Pl. 211. His interpretation of the squiggly lines as 'reins' in both cases seems dubious. Drawings by Lucy Goodison after Boardman.
	b	Pottery design showing the horse with (?)snake in mouth. Reproduced from Roes, 1933, 57, Fig 43.
Fig 323	a	Steatite lentoid from Galaxidi showing bird, 'snake' and dolphin. In BM. Reproduced from Boardman, 1970, Black and White Pl. 237.
	b	7th or early 6th century B.C. steatite amygdaloid from Melos. In Staatliche Museen, Berlin, No. FG 93. Reproduced from Boardman, 1970, Black and White Pl. 241.
Fig 324		Steatite amygdaloid showing a palm tree with goats. In BM 1934.1-20.7. Reproduced from Boardman, 1970, Black and White Pl. 234.
Fig 325	a	Green steatite amygdaloid showing goat with disc and branch. Once in collection of the late R.M. Dawkins, U.K. Reproduced from Boardman, 1970, 119, Text Fig 175.
	b	Seal from Melos. In Ashmolean Museum, Oxford, 1894. 5A (xxvii). Reproduced from Boardman, 1970, Black and White Pl. 212.
	c	Ivory disc, perhaps from Mykonos. In Metropolitan Museum, New York. Reproduced from Boardman, 1970, Black and White Pl. 213, where he describes it as showing 'A lion and star' (p 135).
	d	Ivory disc from Siphnos. Reproduced from Boardman, 1970, Black and White Pl. 217, where he describes it as showing a centaur holding branches with a bird (p 135).
	e	Green steatite lentoid in Bard Collection, London. Reproduced from Boardman, 1970, Black and White Pl. 228.
	f	Grey steatite amygdaloid. In BM. Reproduced from Boardman, 1970, Black and White Pl. 236.
	g	Amygdaloid in Hermitage Museum, Leningrad, No. 517. Reproduced from Boardman, 1970, Black and White Pl. 253, where he describes it as '1. A goat without horns. 2. A winged horse' (p 136).
Fig 326	a	Design on krater from Tomb F at Tekke, near Knossos. Reproduced from *AR* 1976-7, 16, Fig 35.
	b	Design on bell krater from Fortetsa Tomb VI near Knossos. Reproduced from Brock, 1957, Pl. 135 No. 45.
Fig 327		'Lid' from Tomb P at Fortetsa near Knossos. Drawings by Lucy Goodison after Brock, 1957, Pl.107i and ii, No. 1414.

Fig. 1

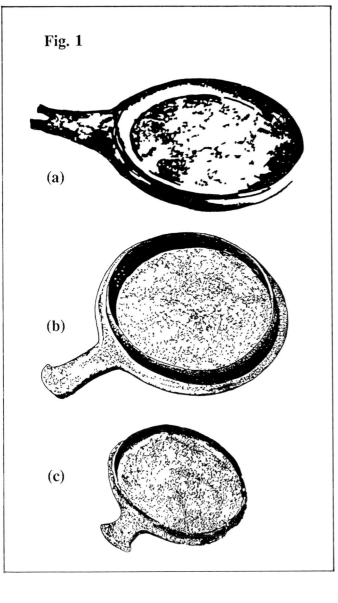

(a)

(b)

(c)

Fig. 2

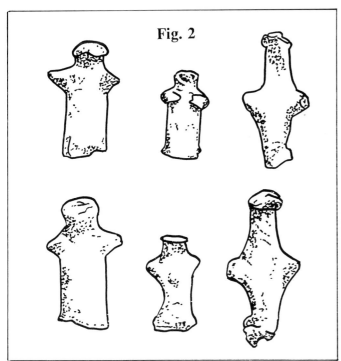

Fig. 3

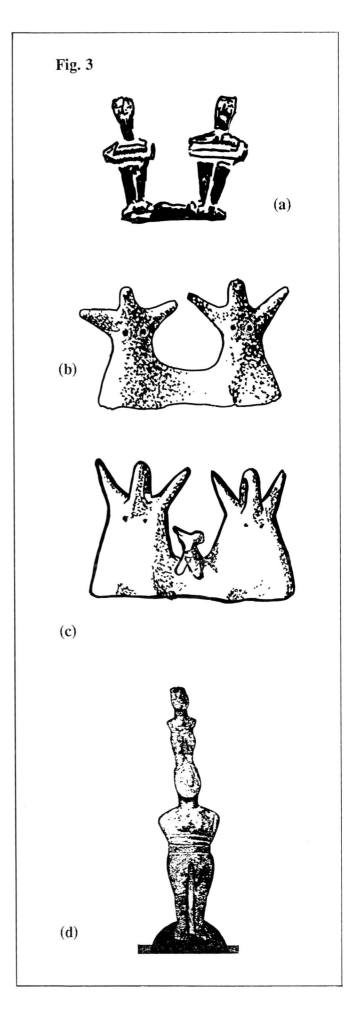

(a)

(b)

(c)

(d)

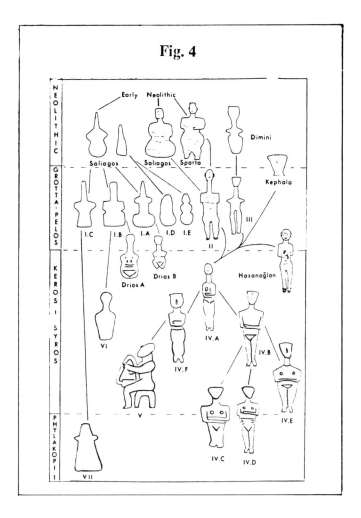

Fig. 4

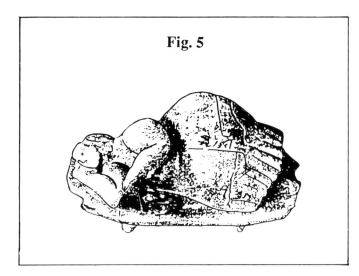

Fig. 5

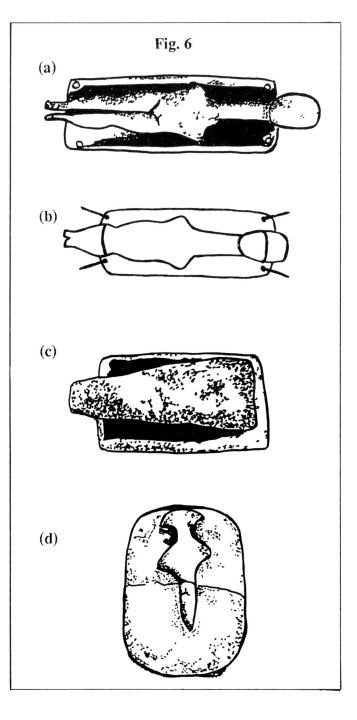

Fig. 6

(a)

(b)

(c)

(d)

Fig. 7

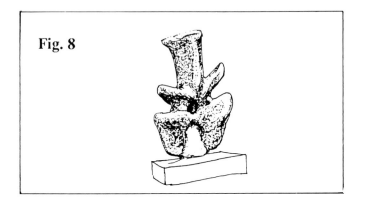

Fig. 8

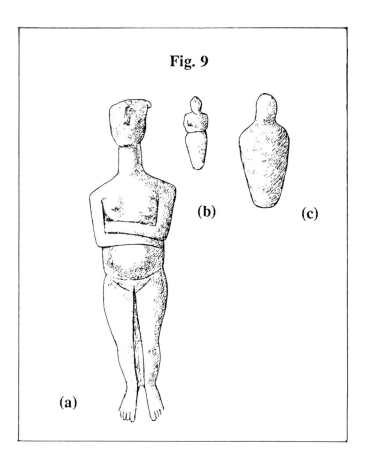

Fig. 9

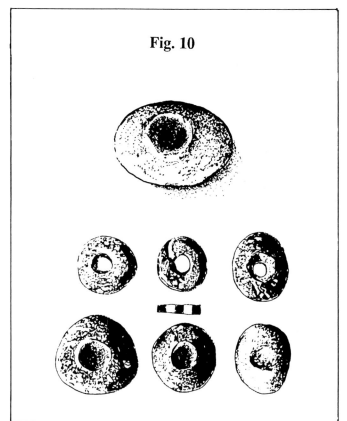

Fig. 10

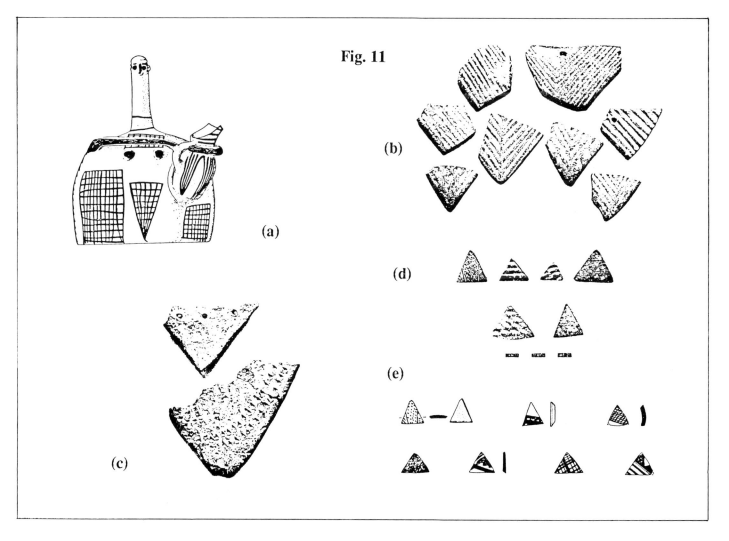

Fig. 11

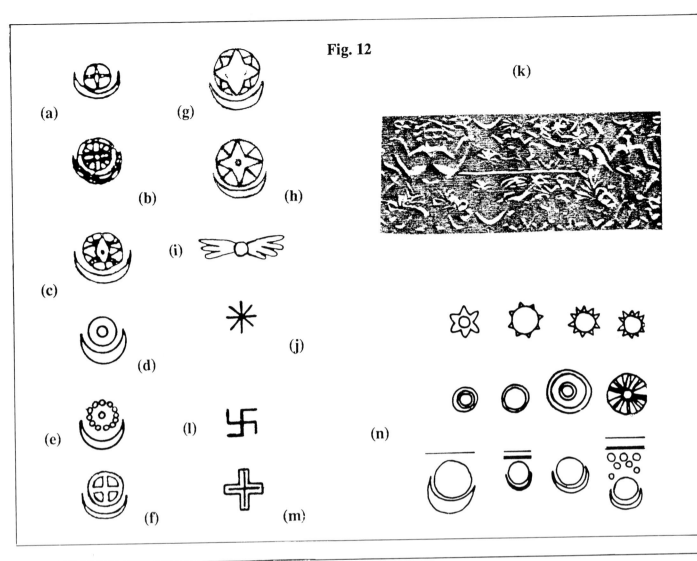

Fig. 12

(a) (b) (c) (d) (e) (f) (g) (h) (i) (j) (k) (l) (m) (n)

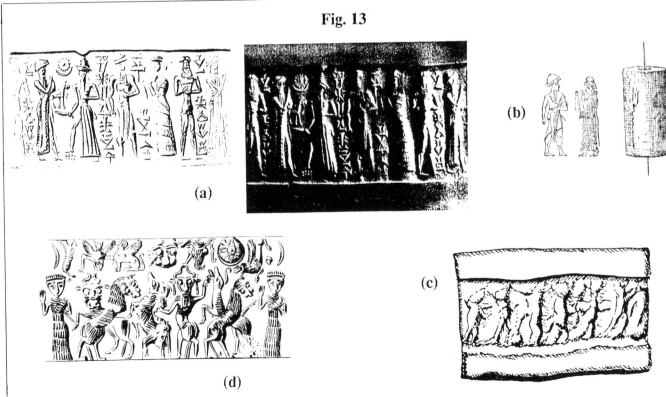

Fig. 13

(a) (b) (c) (d)

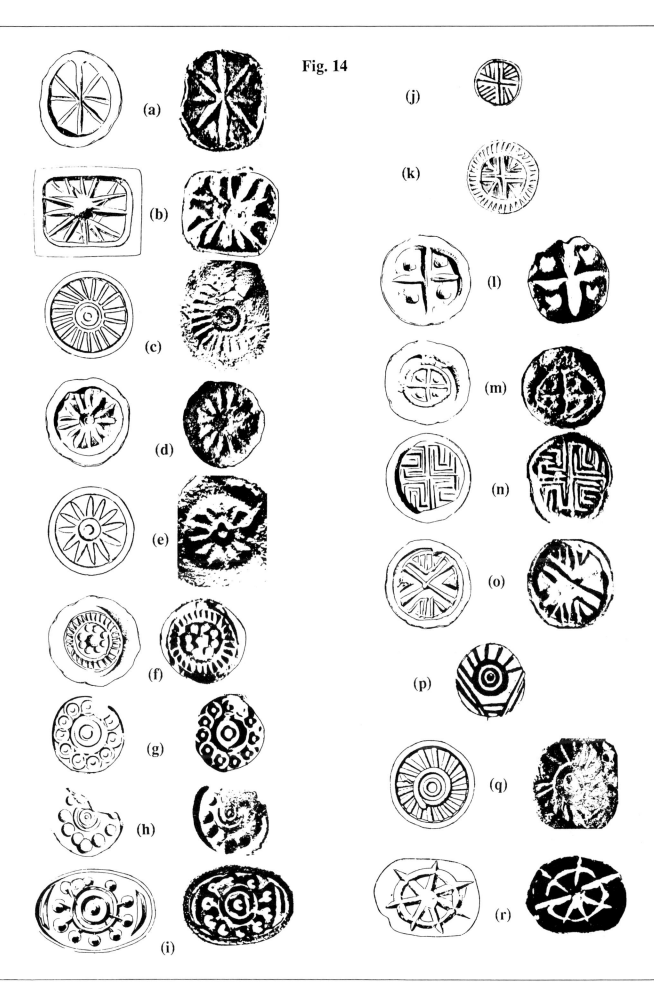

Fig. 14

Fig. 14

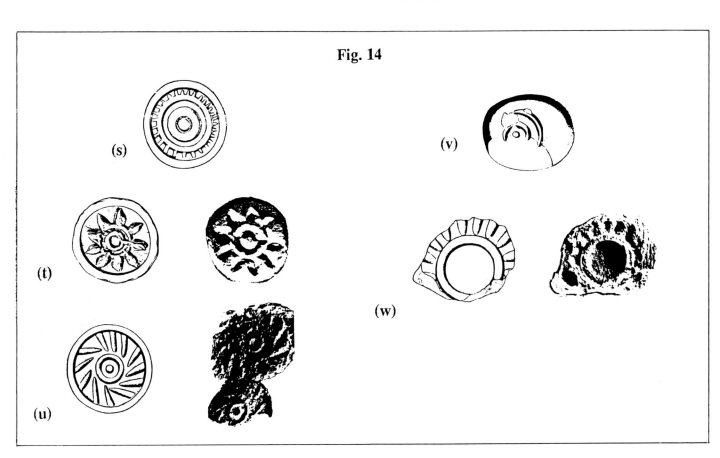

Fig. 15

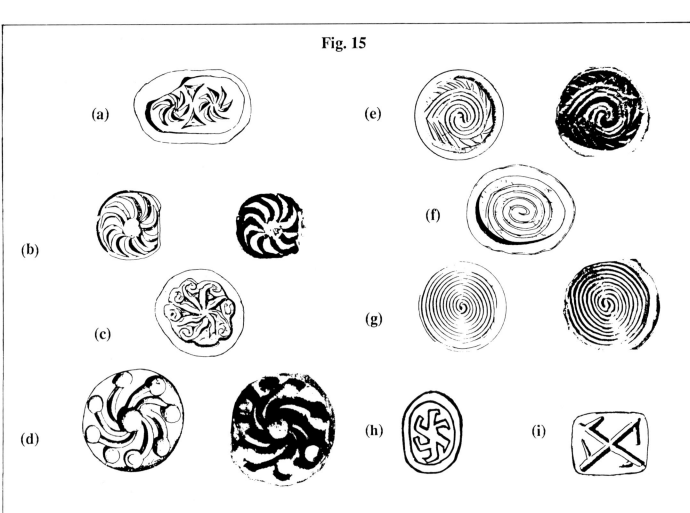

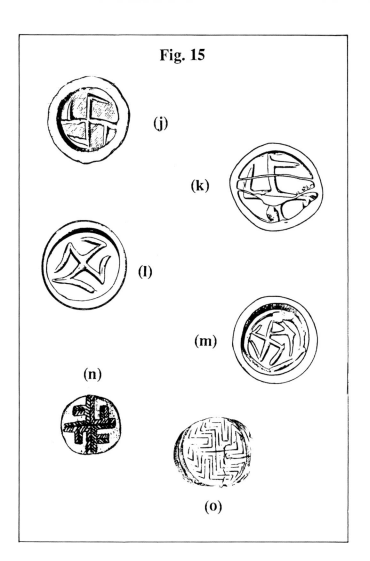

Fig. 15

(j) (k) (l) (m) (n) (o)

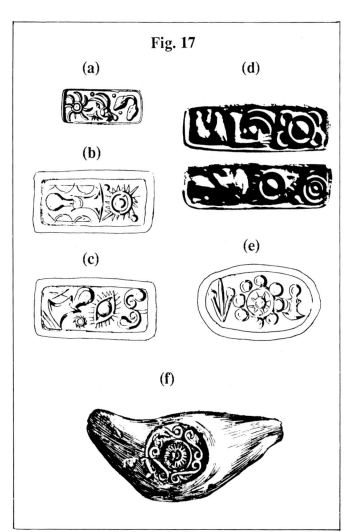

Fig. 17

(a) (b) (c) (d) (e) (f)

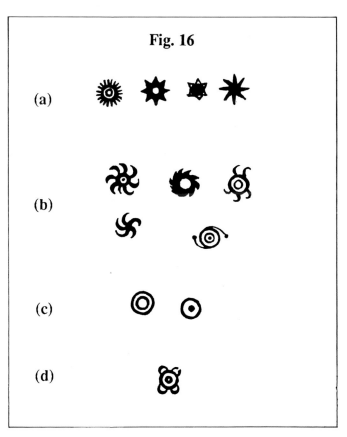

Fig. 16

(a)

(b)

(c)

(d)

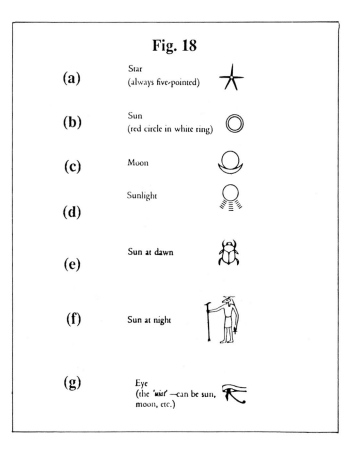

Fig. 18

(a) Star
(always five-pointed)

(b) Sun
(red circle in white ring)

(c) Moon

(d) Sunlight

(e) Sun at dawn

(f) Sun at night

(g) Eye
(the 'wiat'—can be sun,
moon, etc.)

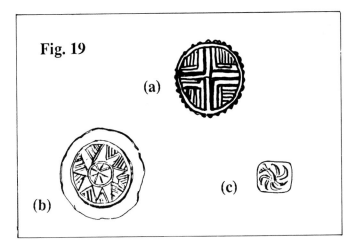

Fig. 19

(a)

(b)

(c)

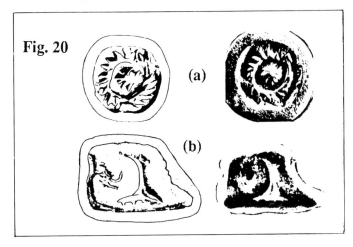

Fig. 20

(a)

(b)

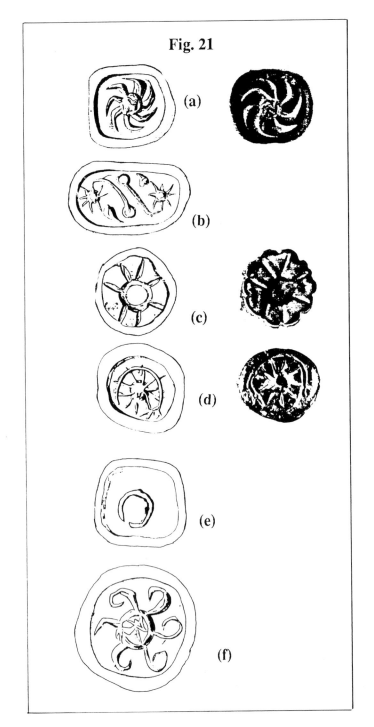

Fig. 21

(a)

(b)

(c)

(d)

(e)

(f)

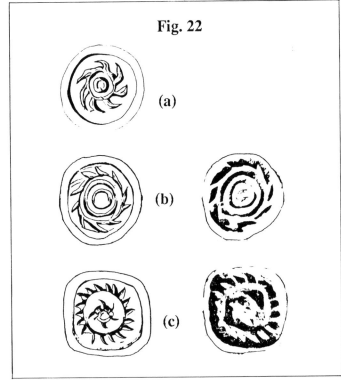

Fig. 22

(a)

(b)

(c)

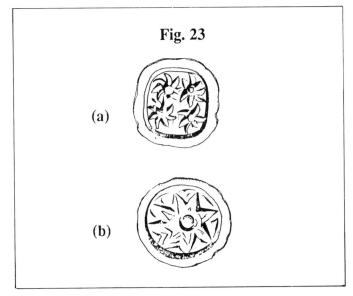

Fig. 23

(a)

(b)

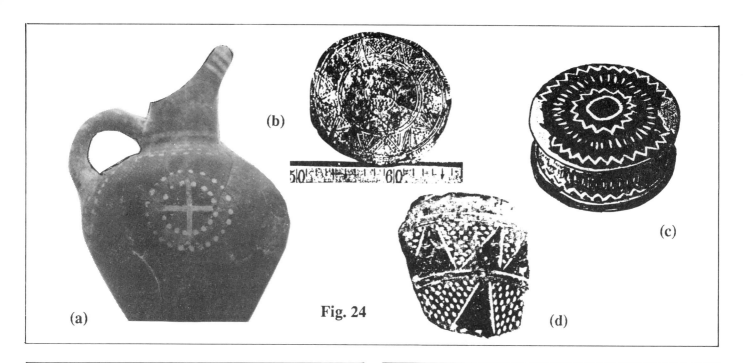

Fig. 24

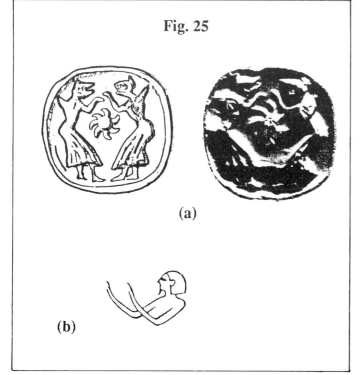

Fig. 25

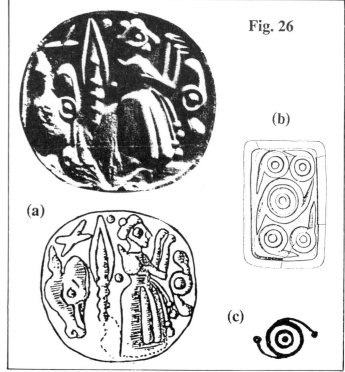

Fig. 26

Fig. 27

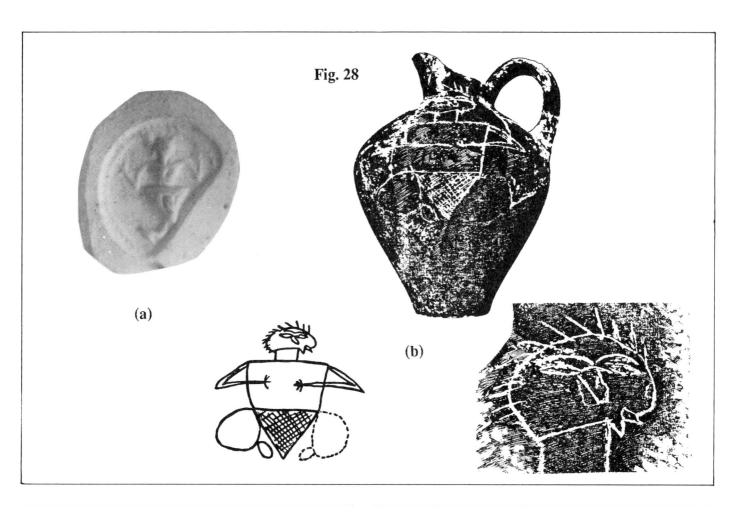

Fig. 28

(a)

(b)

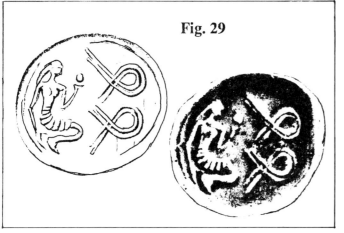

Fig. 29

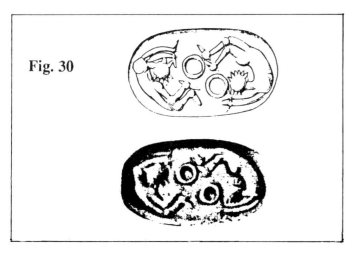

Fig. 30

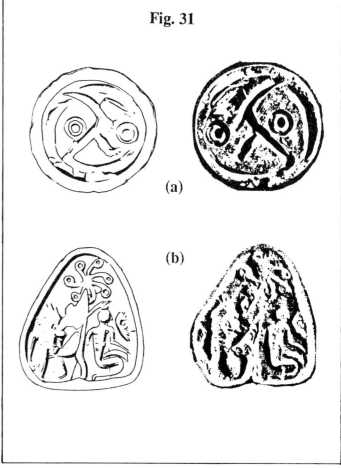

Fig. 31

(a)

(b)

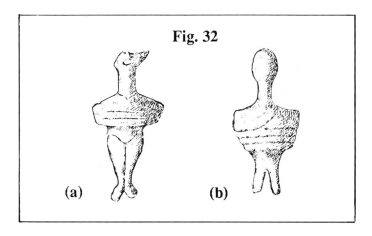

Fig. 32

(a)   (b)

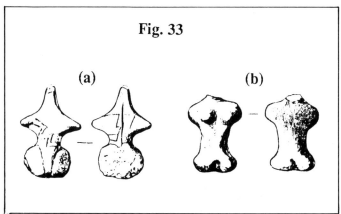

Fig. 33

(a)   (b)

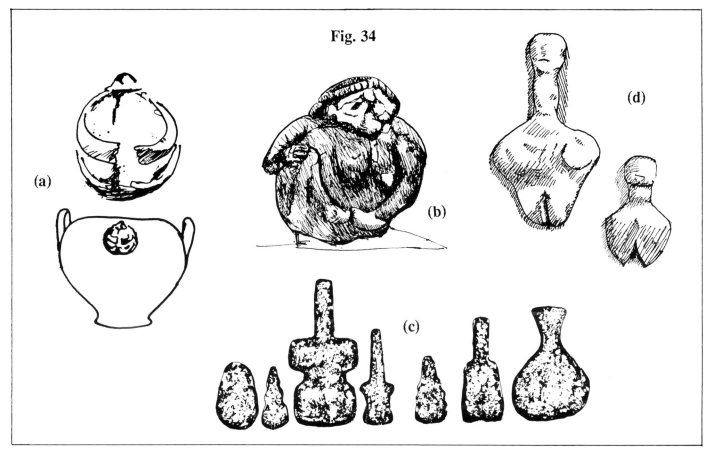

Fig. 34

(a)   (b)   (c)   (d)

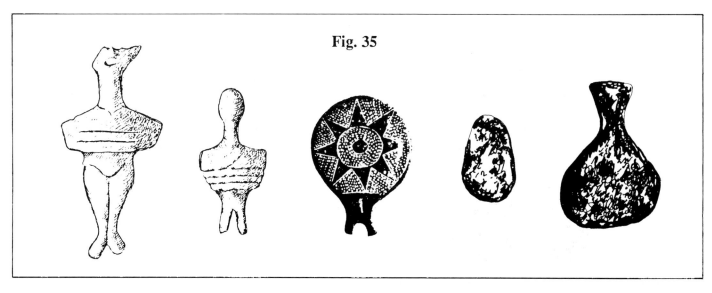

Fig. 35

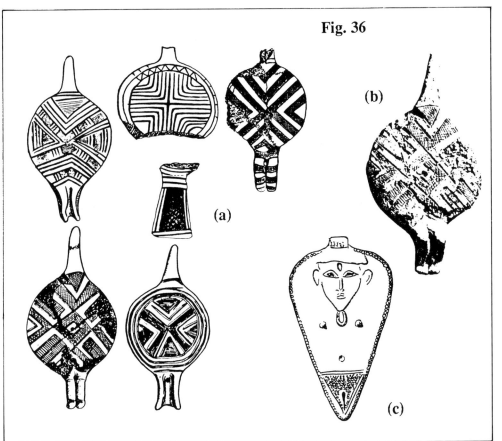

Fig. 36

(a) (b) (c)

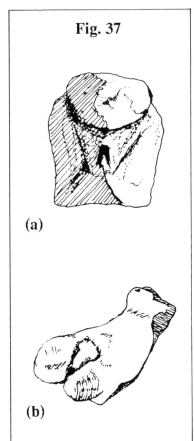

Fig. 37

(a) (b)

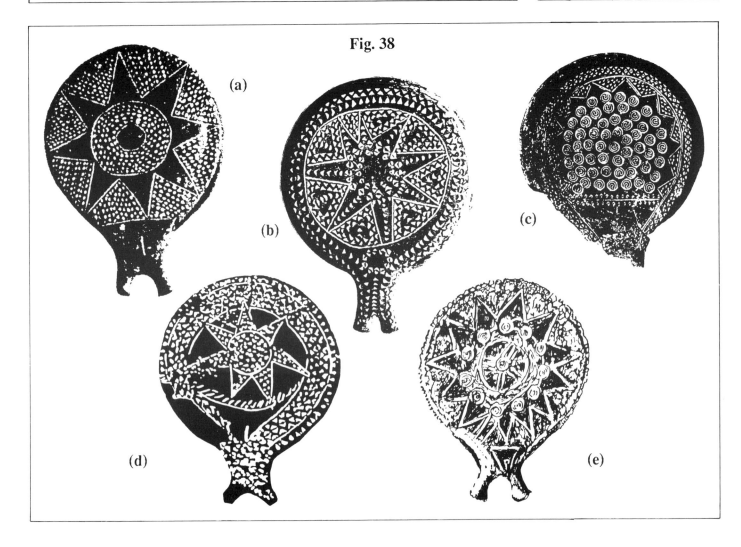

Fig. 38

(a) (b) (c) (d) (e)

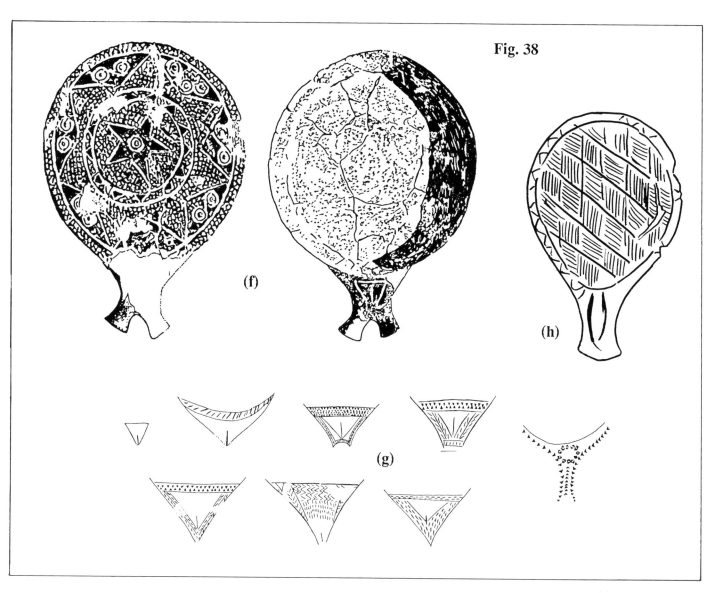

Fig. 38

(f)

(g)

(h)

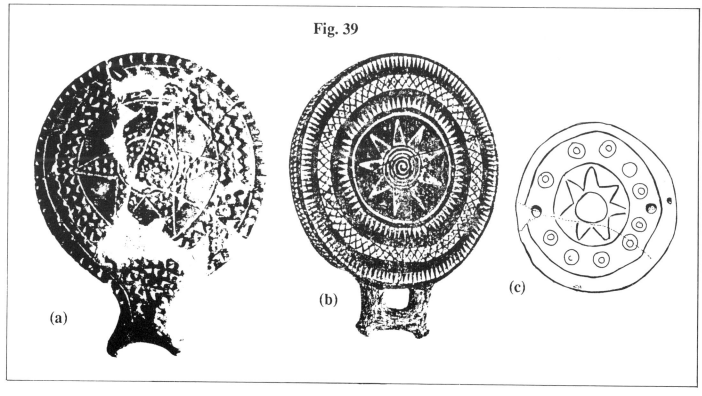

Fig. 39

(a)

(b)

(c)

Fig. 39

(d)

(e)

(f)

(g)

(h)

(i)

(j)

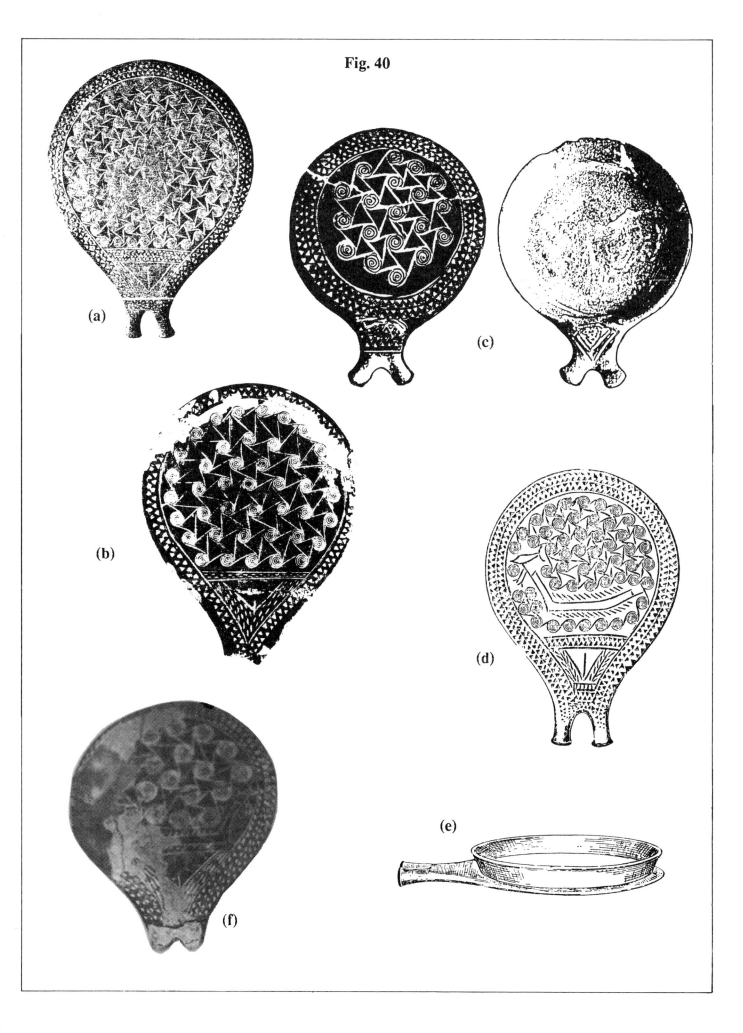

Fig. 40

Fig. 41

(a)

(b)

(c)

Fig. 42

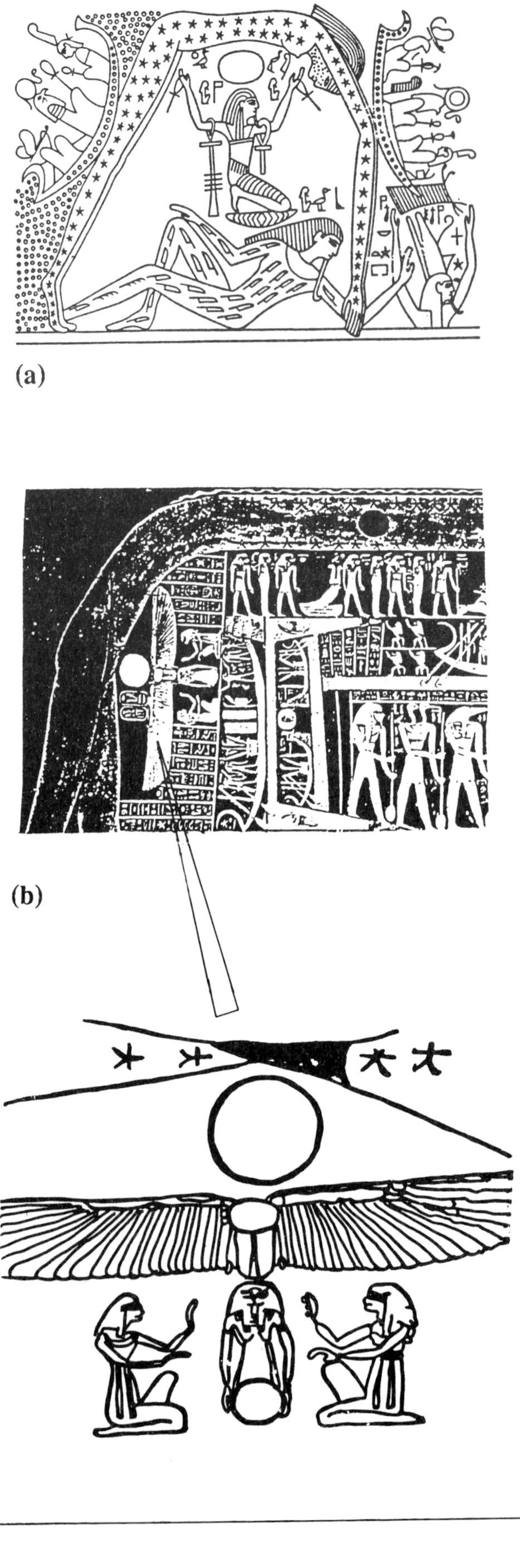

(a)

(b)

Fig. 42

(c)

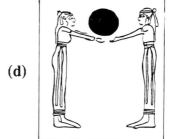

(d)

(e)

(f)

(g)
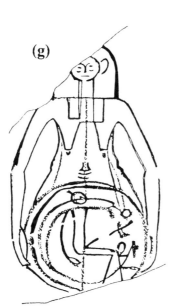

(h)
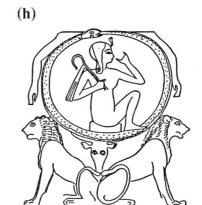

(i)

(j)
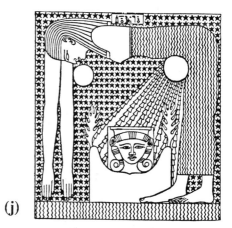

Fig. 43

(a)

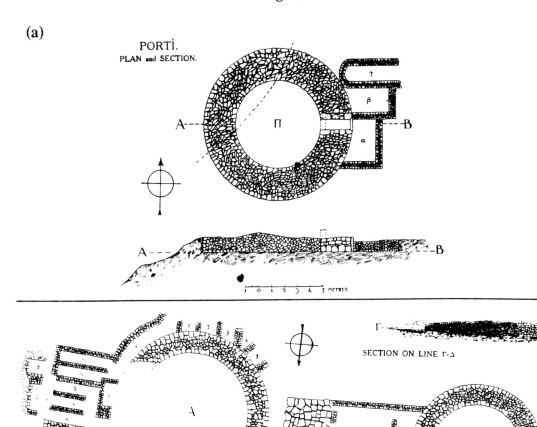

PORTÍ.
PLAN and SECTION.

A - - - B

A - - - B

1 0 1 2 3 4 5 METRES

Γ - - - Δ

SECTION ON LINE Γ-Δ

A

Γ - - - Δ

B

PLÁTANOS.

THOLOI A and B, PLAN.
THOLOS B, SECTION.

1 0 1 2 3 4 5 METRES.

(b)

Fig. 44

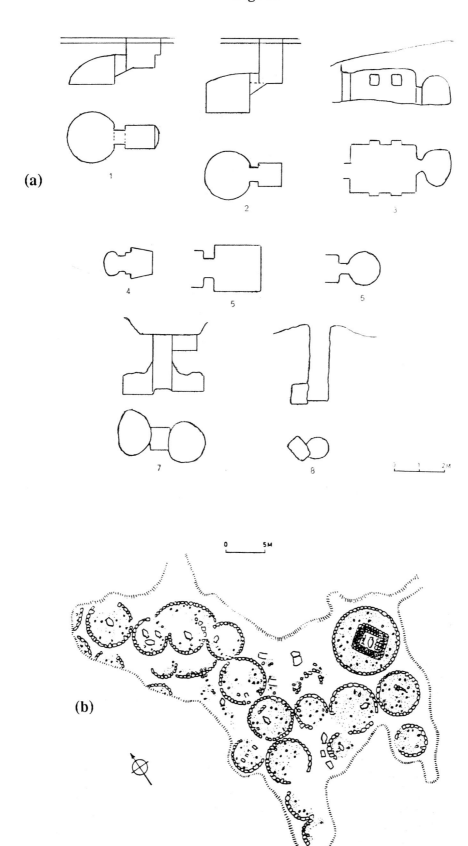

(a)

(b)

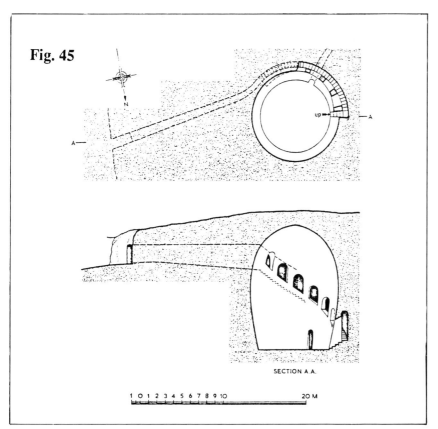

Fig. 45

SECTION A A.

1 0 1 2 3 4 5 6 7 8 9 10   20 M

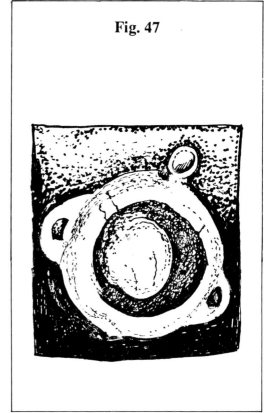

Fig. 47

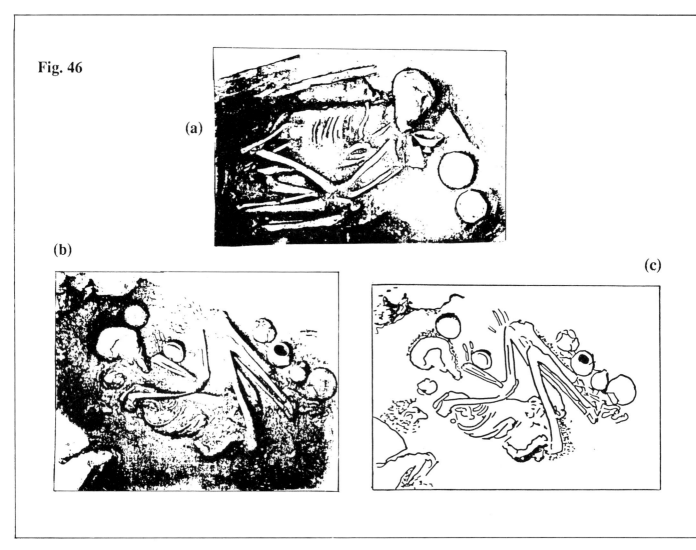

Fig. 46

(a)

(b)

(c)

Fig. 48

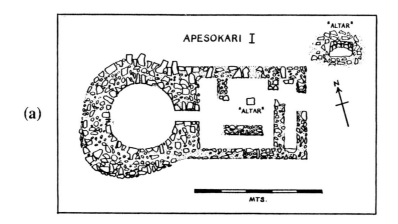

APESOKARI I

"ALTAR"

"ALTAR"

N

MTS.

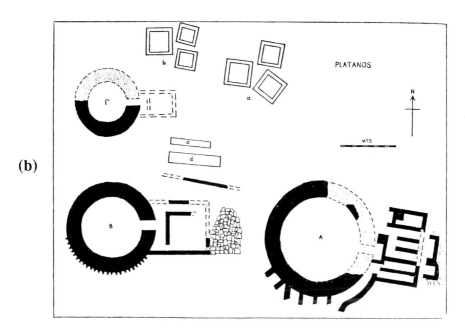

(b)

PLATANOS

b.

a.

e

d

B

A

N

MTS.

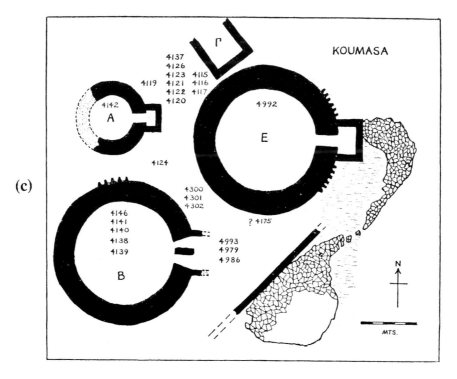

(c)

KOUMASA

Γ

4137
4126
4123   4115
4119   4121   4116
        4122   4117
        4120

4142

A

4992

E

4124

4300
4301
4302

? 4175

4146
4141
4140
4138
4139

4993
4979
4986

B

N

MTS.

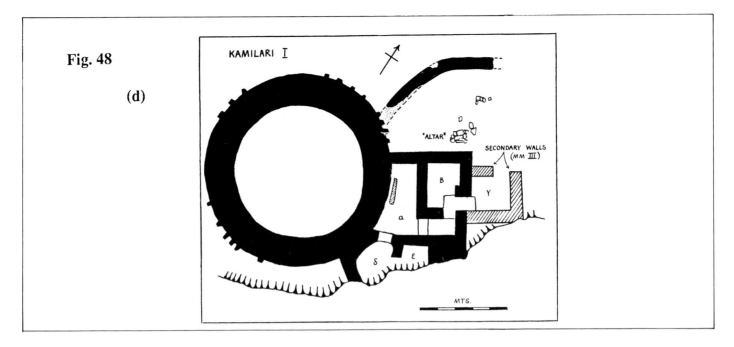

Fig. 48

(d)

KAMILARI I

"ALTAR"

SECONDARY WALLS (MM III)

MTS.

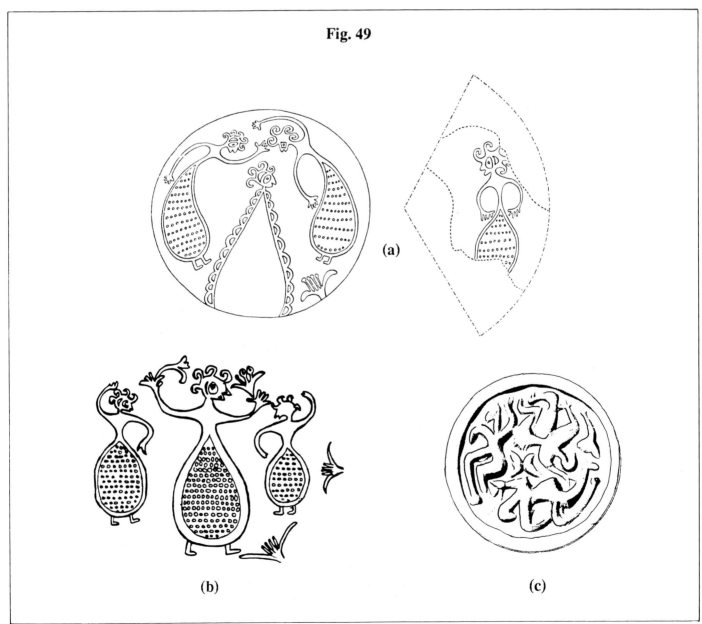

Fig. 49

(a)

(b)

(c)

Fig. 49

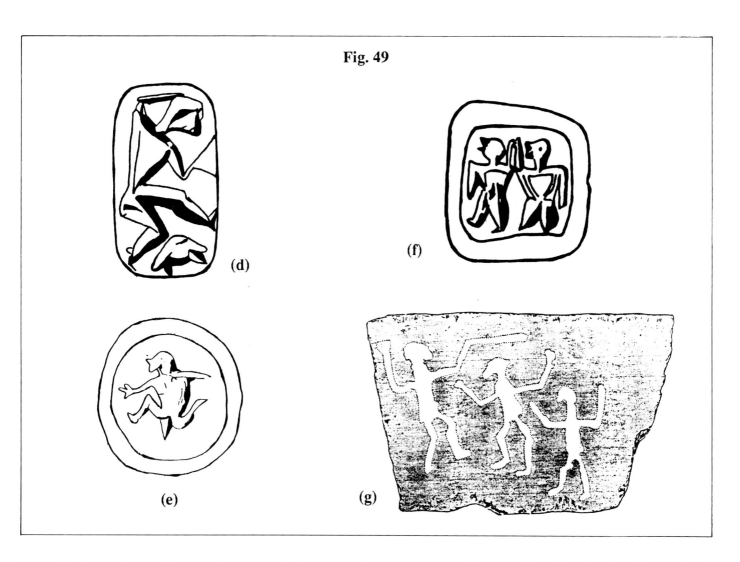

(d)

(f)

(e)

(g)

Fig. 50

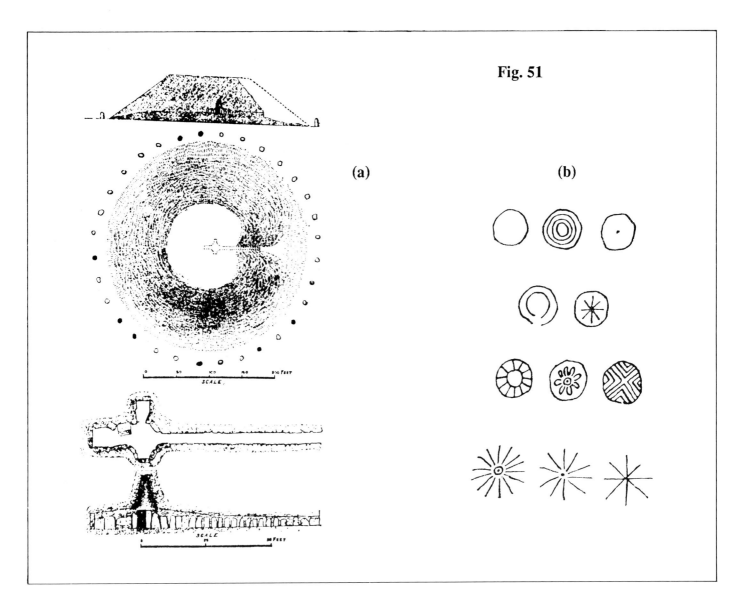

Fig. 51

(a)

(b)

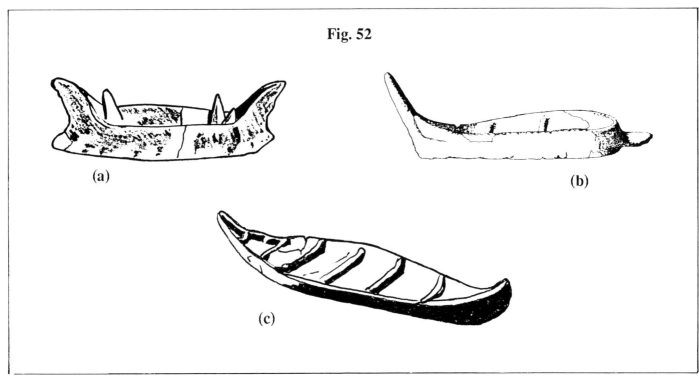

Fig. 52

(a)

(b)

(c)

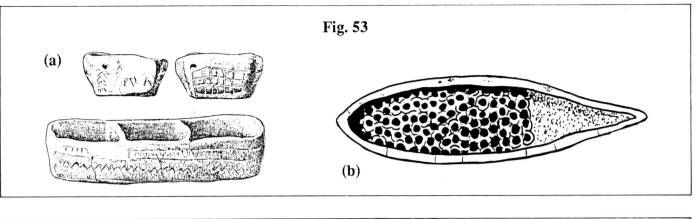

Fig. 53

(a)

(b)

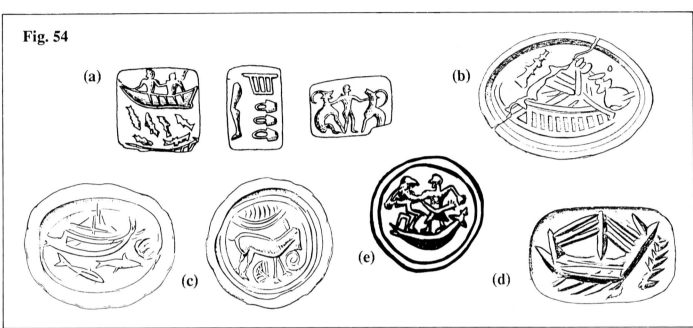

Fig. 54

(a)

(b)

(c)

(e)

(d)

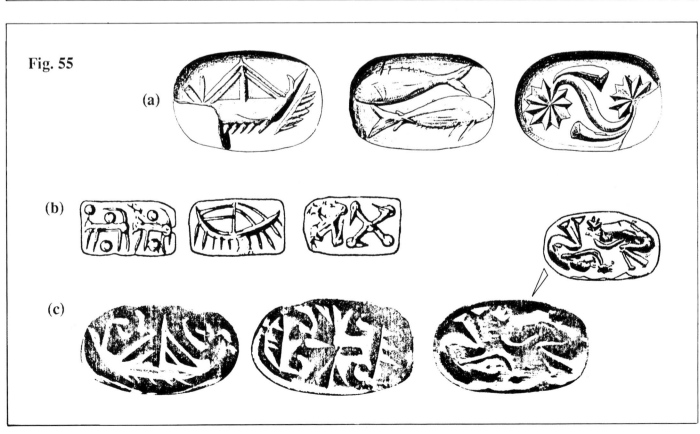

Fig. 55

(a)

(b)

(c)

Fig. 56

(a)

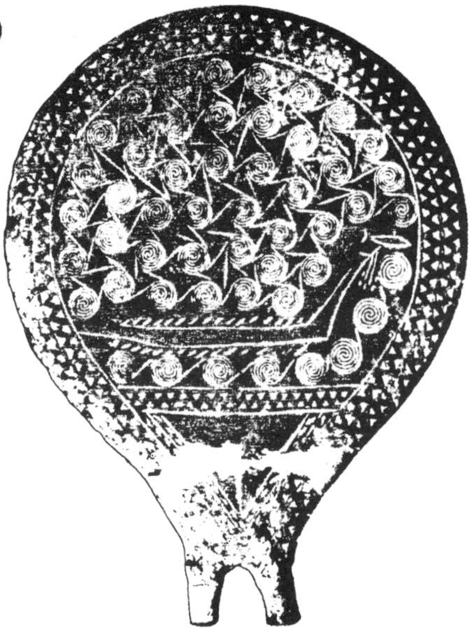

(b)

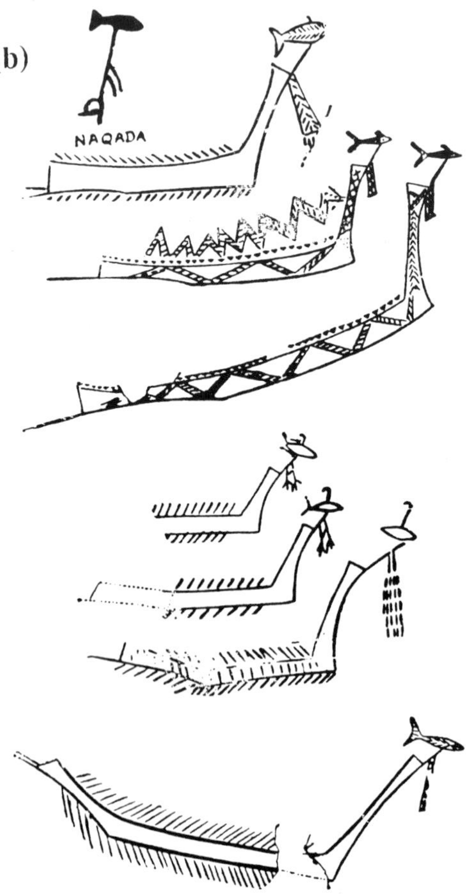

NAQADA

Fig. 57

(a)

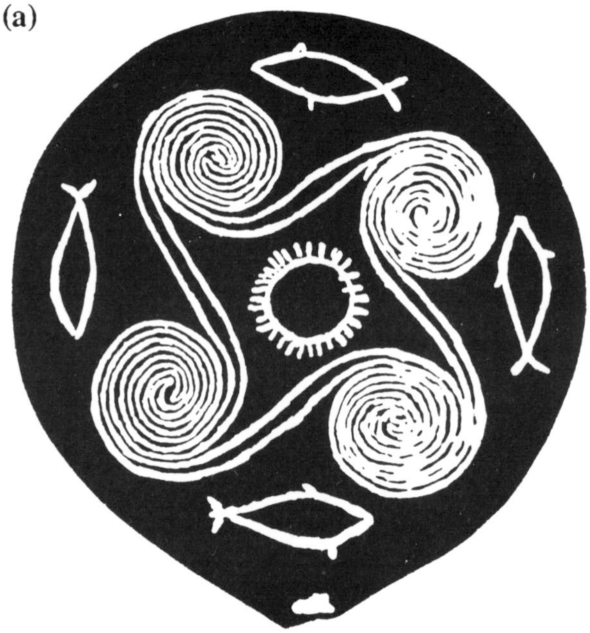

(b)

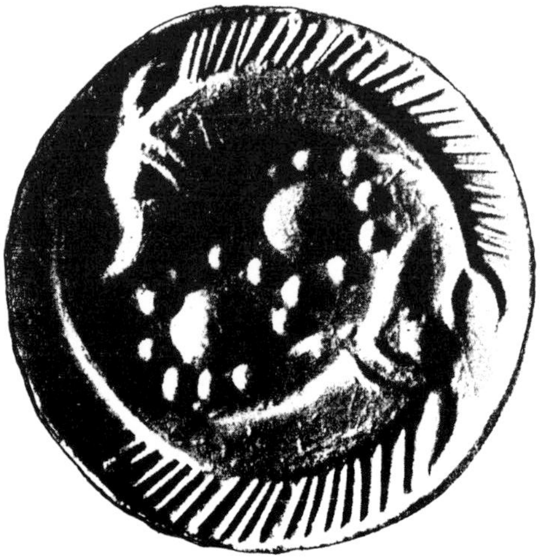

(c)

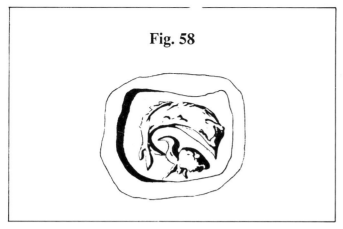

Fig. 58

Fig. 59

Fig. 60

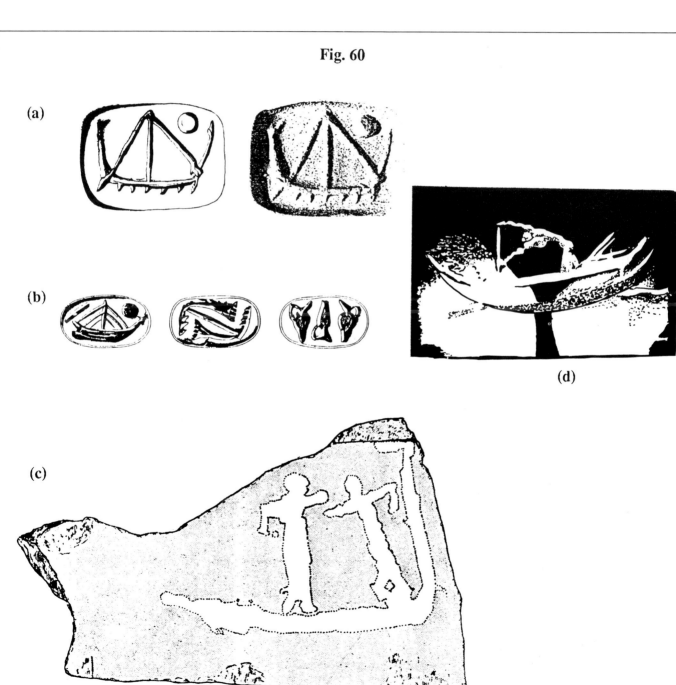

(a)

(b)

(c)

(d)

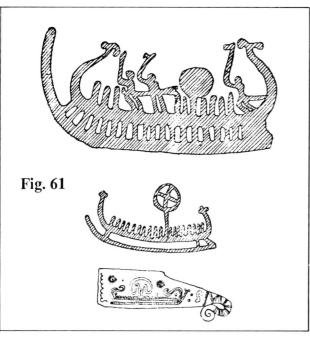

Fig. 61

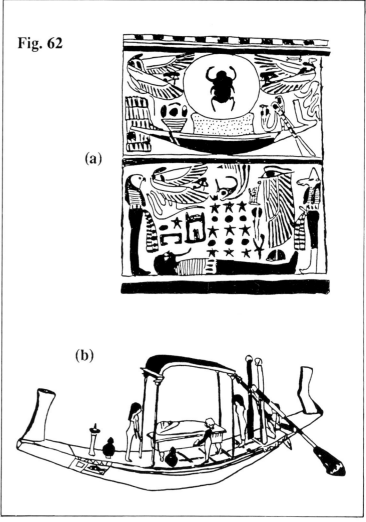

Fig. 62

(a)

(b)

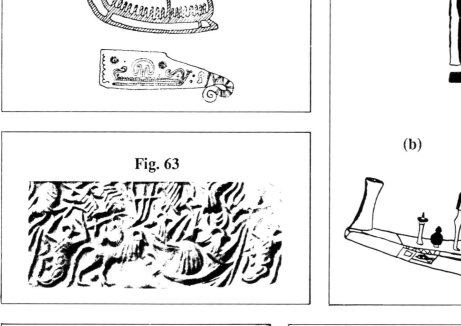

Fig. 63

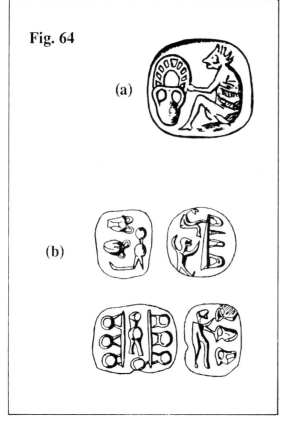

Fig. 64

(a)

(b)

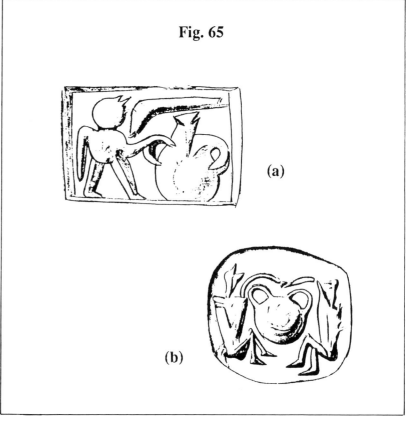

Fig. 65

(a)

(b)

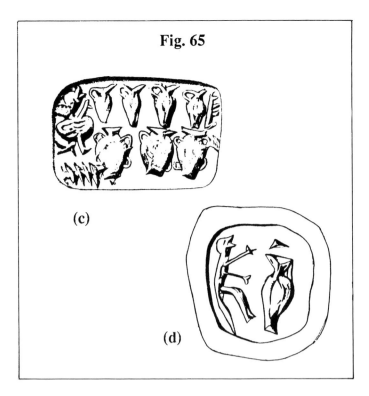

Fig. 65

(c)

(d)

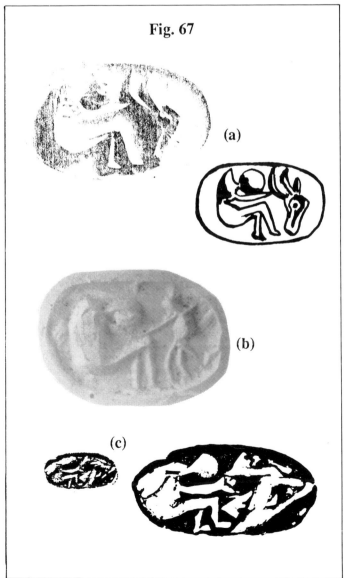

Fig. 67

(a)

(b)

(c)

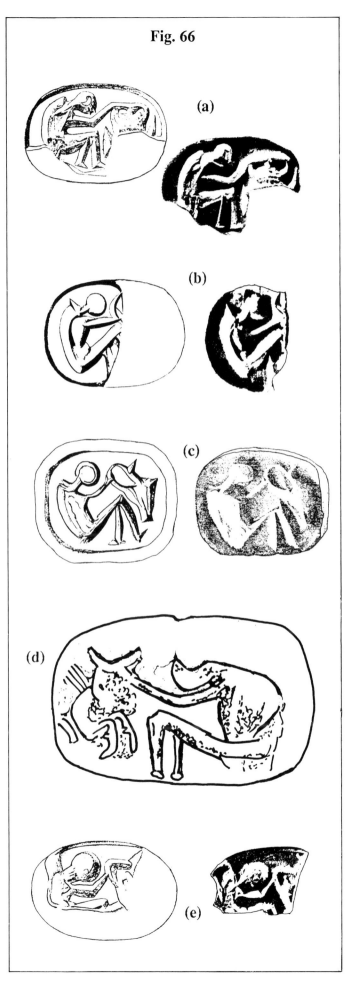

Fig. 66

(a)

(b)

(c)

(d)

(e)

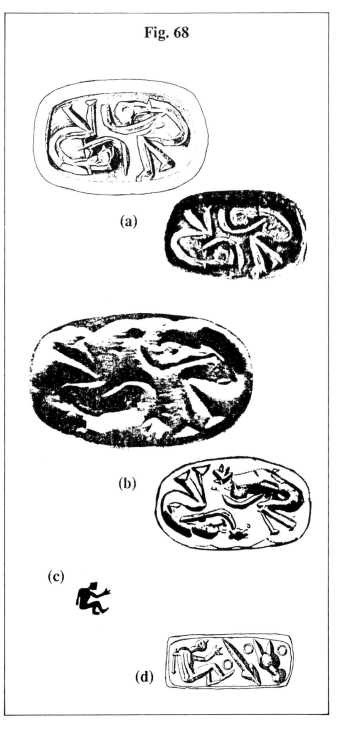

Fig. 68

(a)

(b)

(c)

(d)

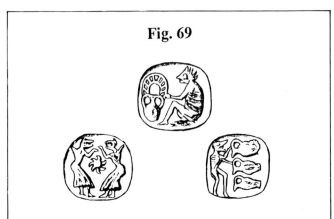

Fig. 69

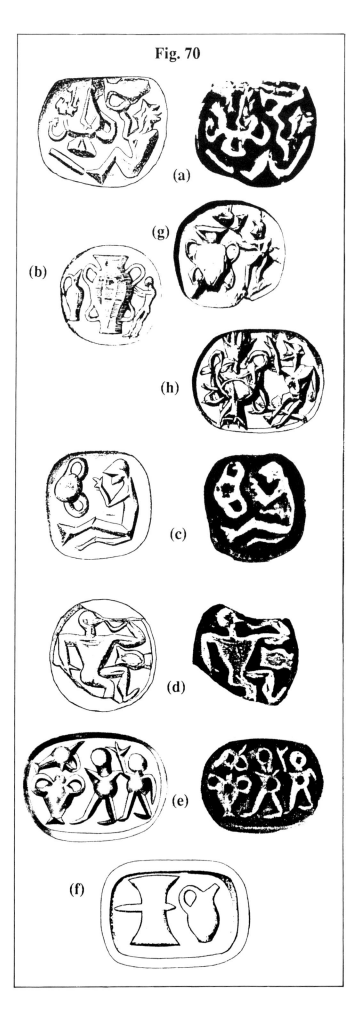

Fig. 70

(a)

(g)

(b)

(h)

(c)

(d)

(e)

(f)

Fig. 71

(a)

(b)

(c)

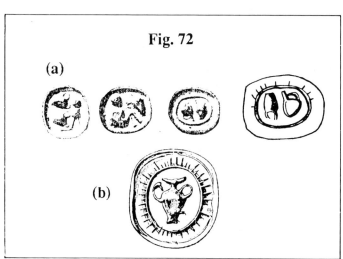

Fig. 72

(a)

(b)

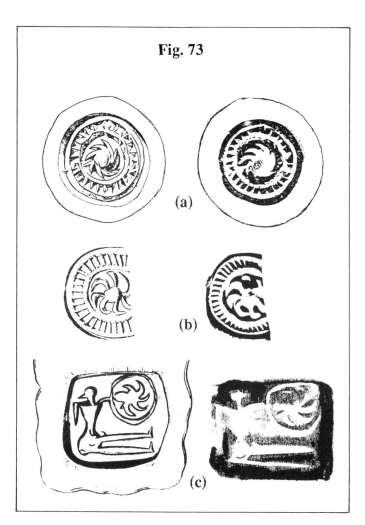

Fig. 73

(a)

(b)

(c)

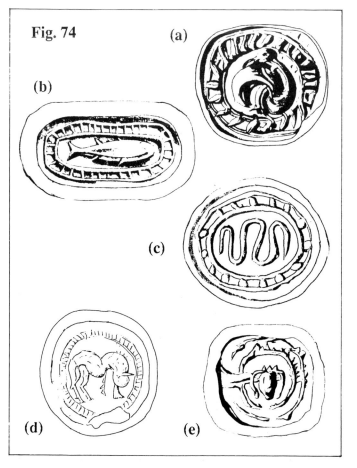

Fig. 74

(a)

(b)

(c)

(d)

(e)

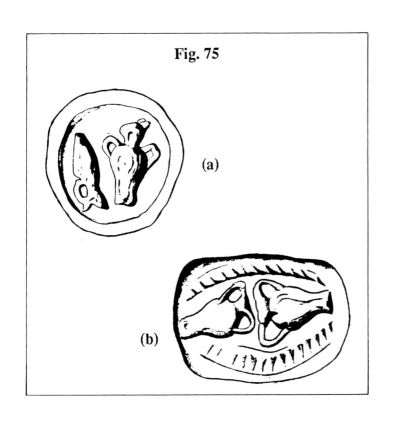

Fig. 75

(a)

(b)

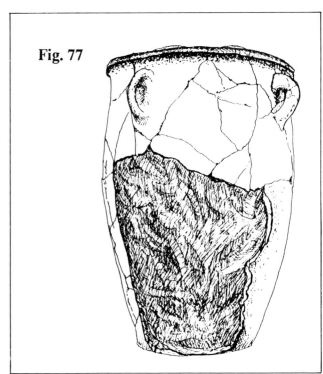

Fig. 77

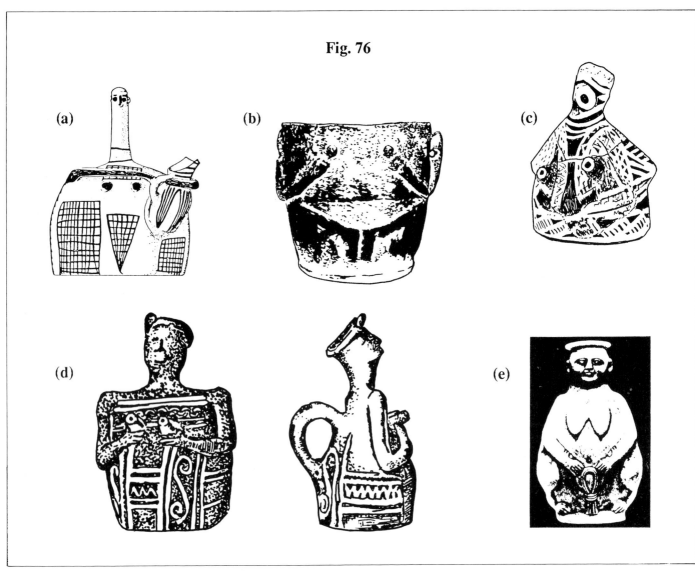

Fig. 76

(a)

(b)

(c)

(d)

(e)

Fig. 78

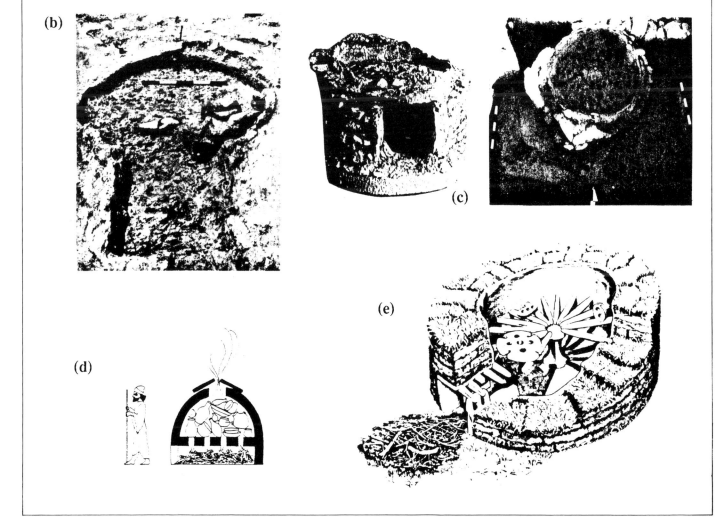

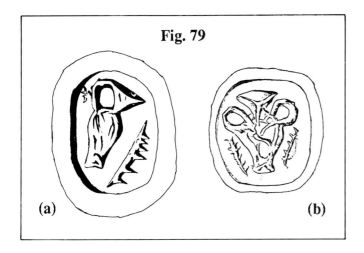

Fig. 79

(a)   (b)

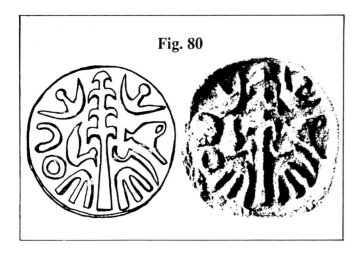

Fig. 80

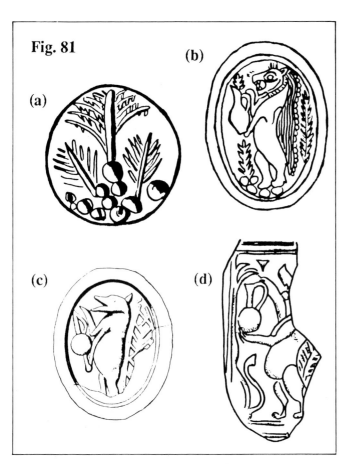

Fig. 81

(a)   (b)

(c)   (d)

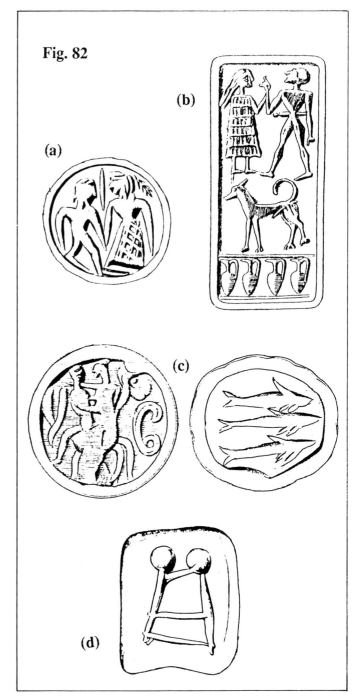

Fig. 82

(a)

(b)

(c)

(d)

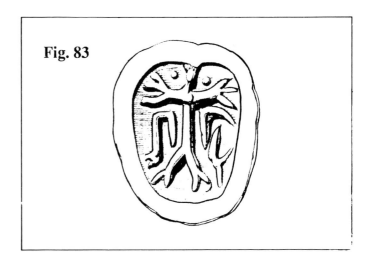

Fig. 83

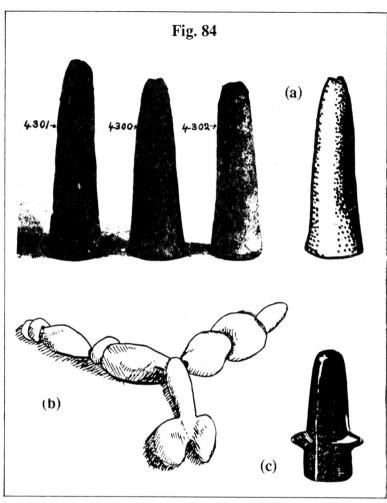

Fig. 84

(a)

(b)

(c)

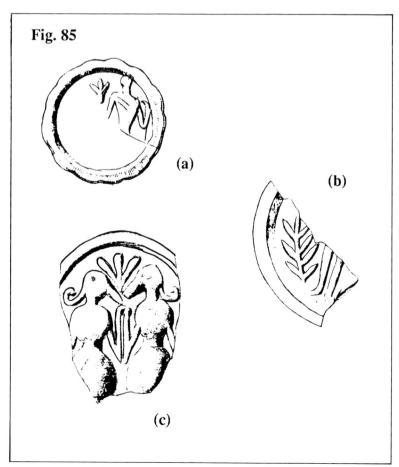

Fig. 85

(a)

(b)

(c)

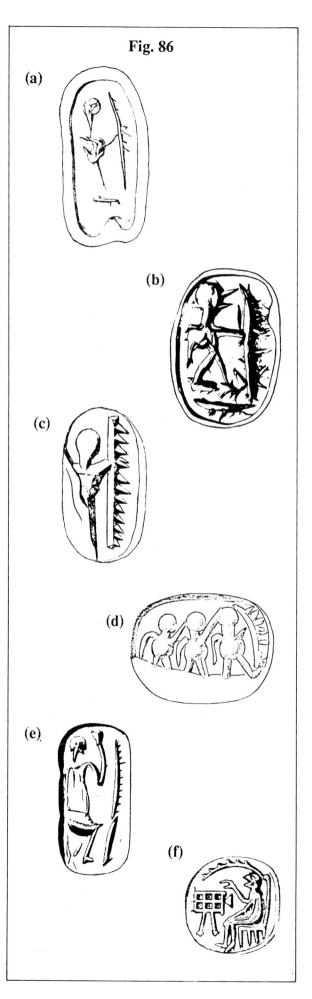

Fig. 86

(a)

(b)

(c)

(d)

(e)

(f)

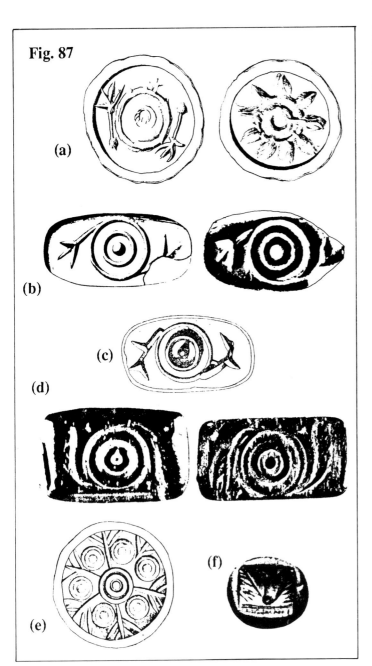

Fig. 87

(a)

(b)

(c)

(d)

(e)

(f)

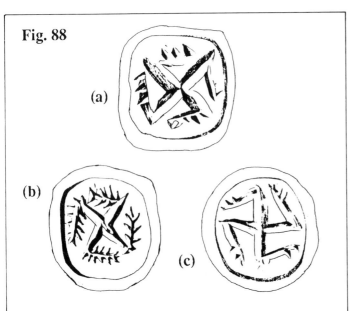

Fig. 88

(a)

(b)

(c)

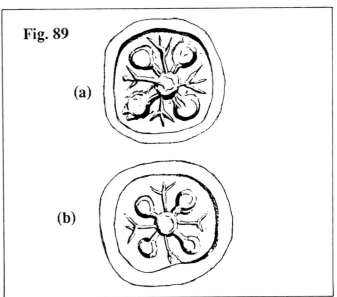

Fig. 89

(a)

(b)

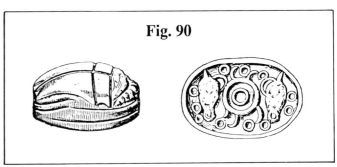

Fig. 90

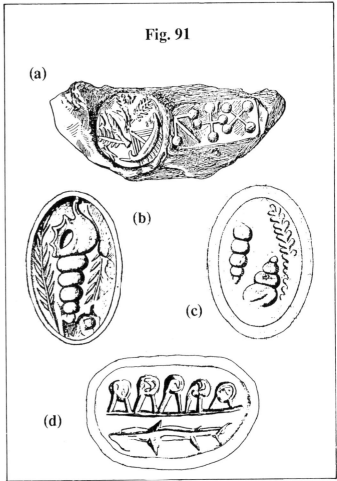

Fig. 91

(a)

(b)

(c)

(d)

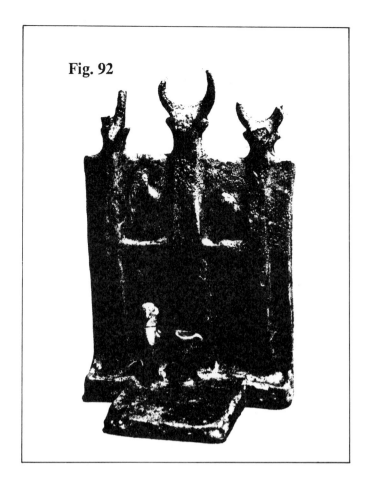

Fig. 92

Fig. 93

Fig. 94

(a)

(b)

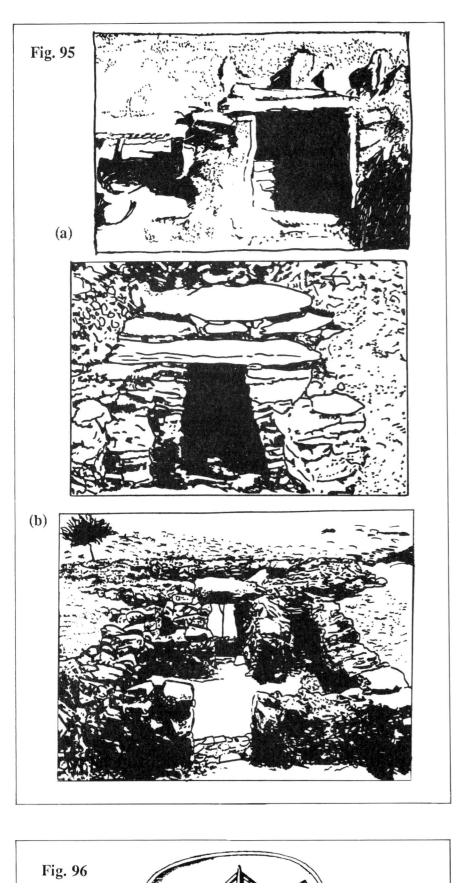

Fig. 95

(a)

(b)

Fig. 96

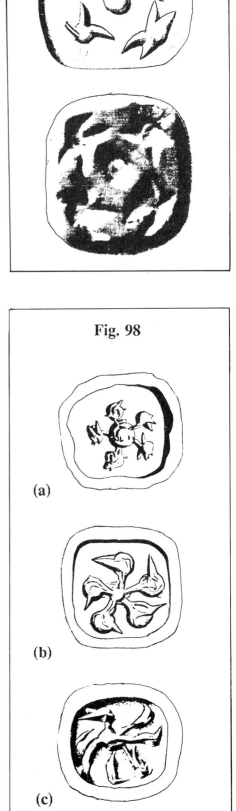

Fig. 97

Fig. 98

(a)

(b)

(c)

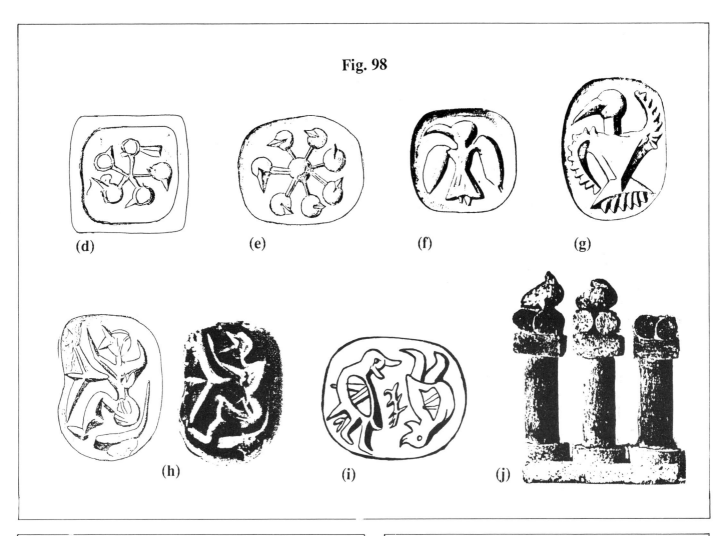

Fig. 98

(d)

(e)

(f)

(g)

(h)

(i)

(j)

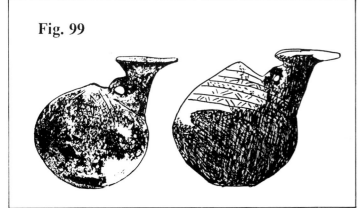

Fig. 99

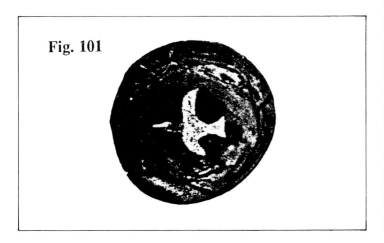

Fig. 101

Fig. 100

(a)

(b)

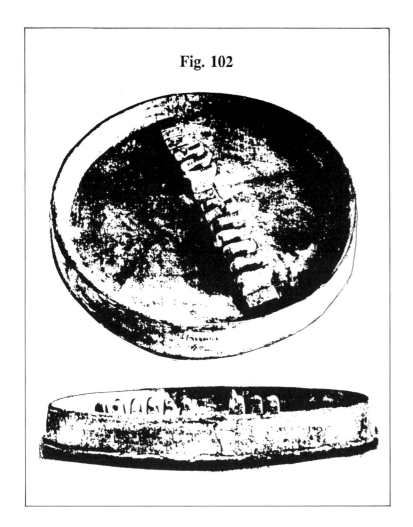

Fig. 102

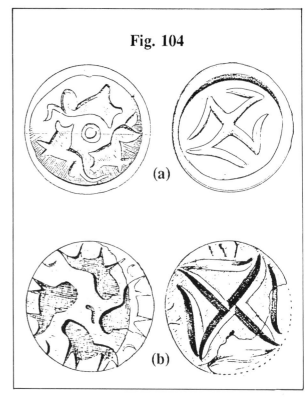

Fig. 104

(a)

(b)

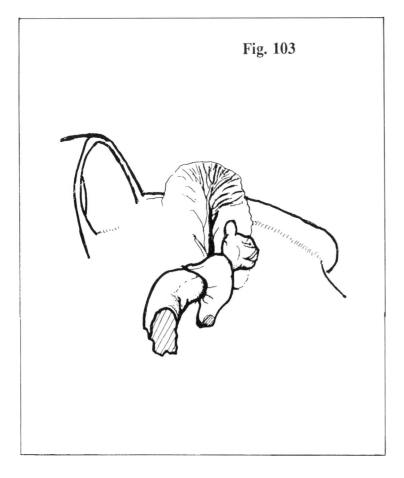

Fig. 103

Fig. 105

(a)   (b)

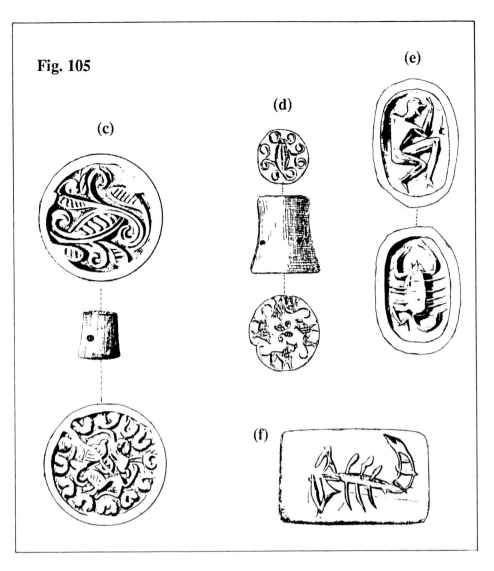

Fig. 105

(c)

(d)

(e)

(f)

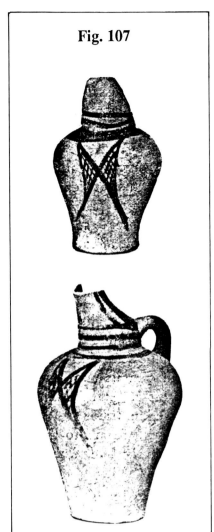

Fig. 107

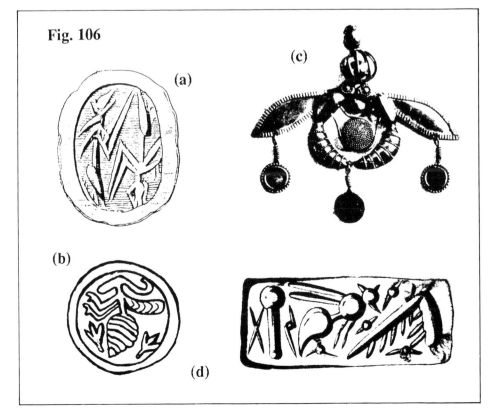

Fig. 106

(a)

(c)

(b)

(d)

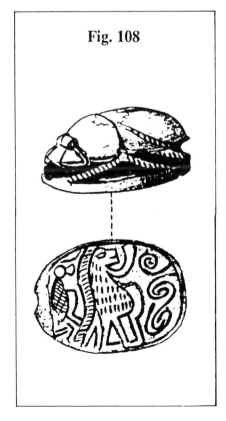

Fig. 108

Fig. 109

(a)

(b)

(c)

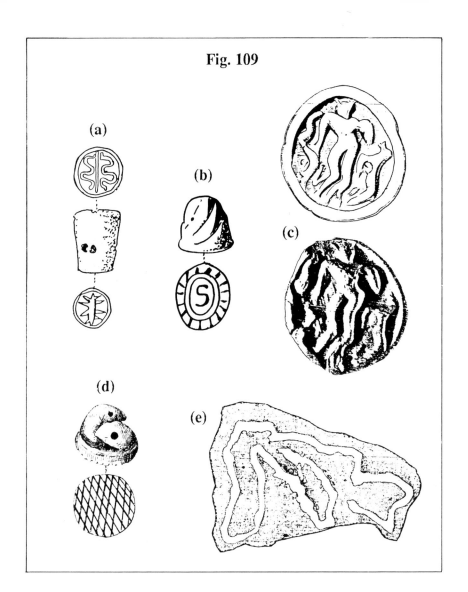

(d)

(e)

Fig. 110

(a)

(b)

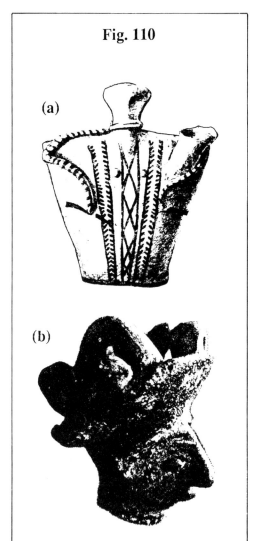

Fig. 111

(a)

(b)

(c)

(d)

(e)

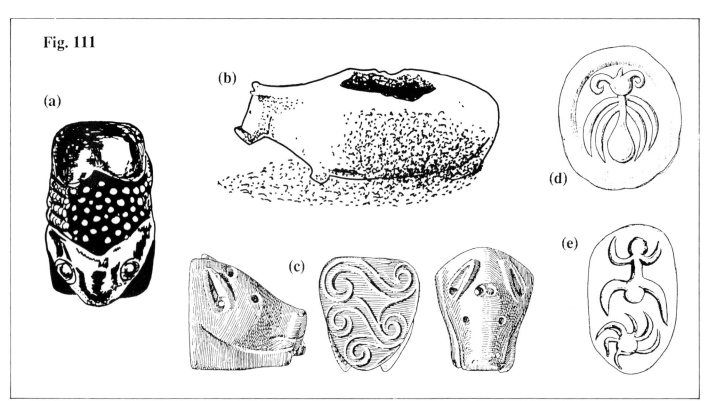

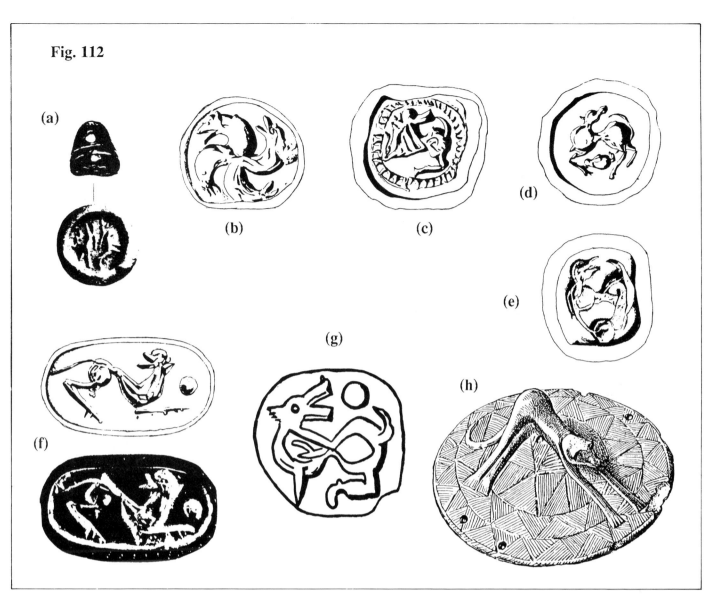

Fig. 112

(a) (b) (c) (d) (e) (f) (g) (h)

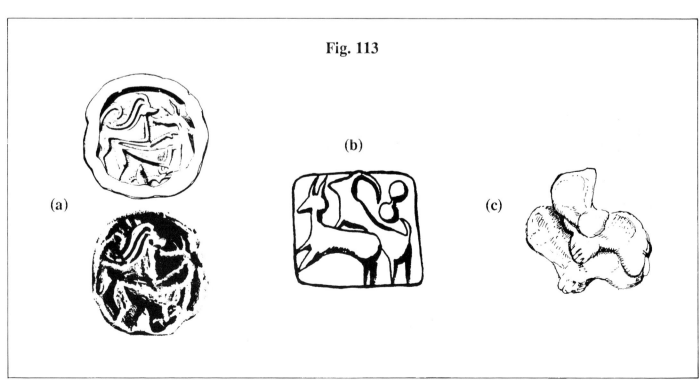

Fig. 113

(a) (b) (c)

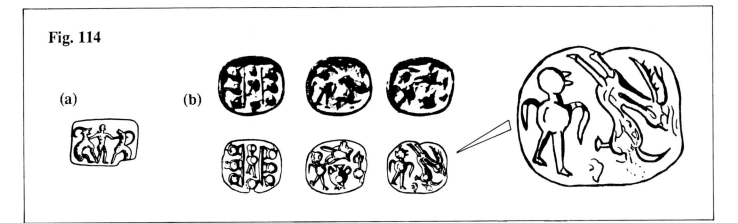

Fig. 114

(a) (b)

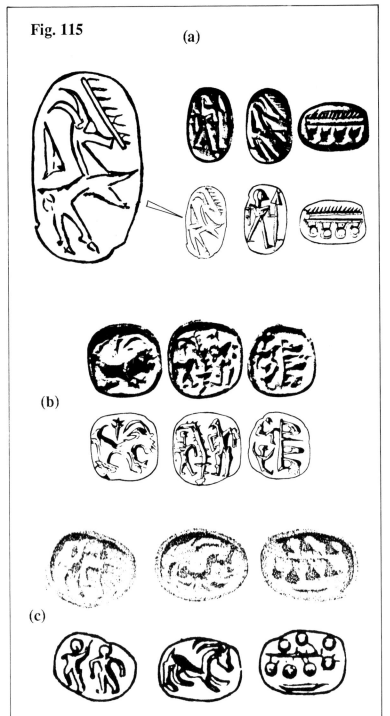

Fig. 115

(a)

(b)

(c)

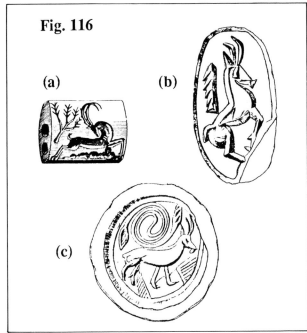

Fig. 116

(a) (b)

(c)

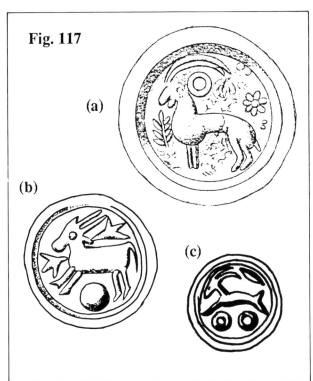

Fig. 117

(a)

(b)

(c)

Fig. 117

(d)

(e)

(f)

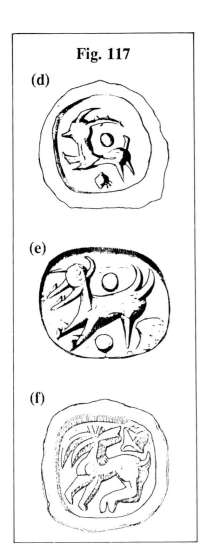

Fig. 118

(a)

(b)

(c)

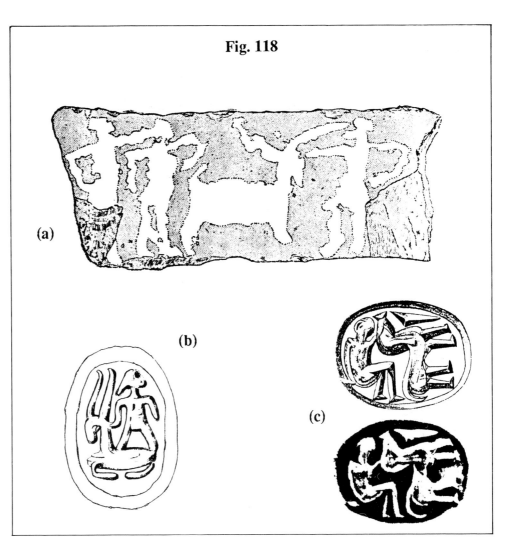

Fig. 119

(b)

(a)

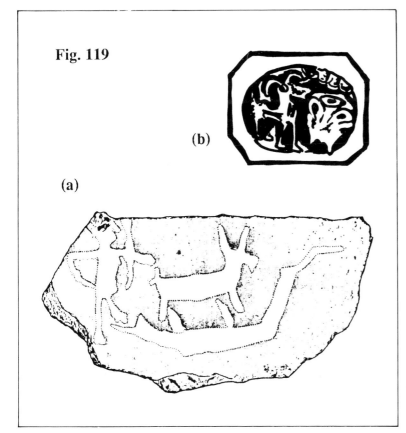

Fig. 120

(a)

(b)

(c)

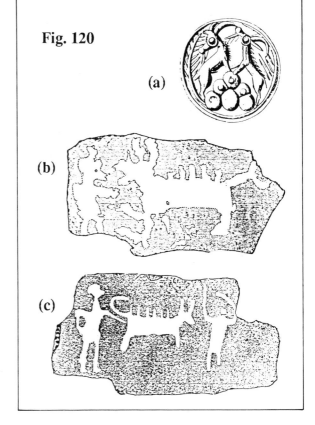

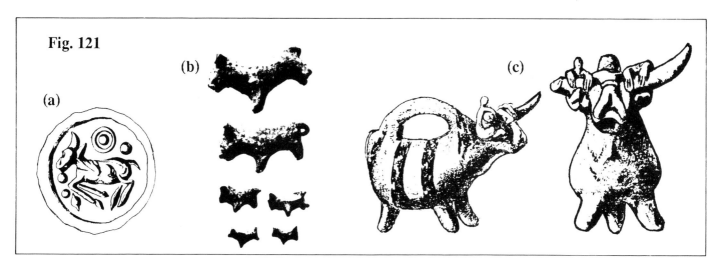

Fig. 121 (a) (b) (c)

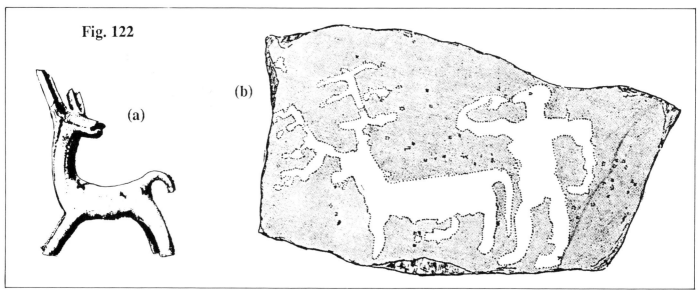

Fig. 122 (a) (b)

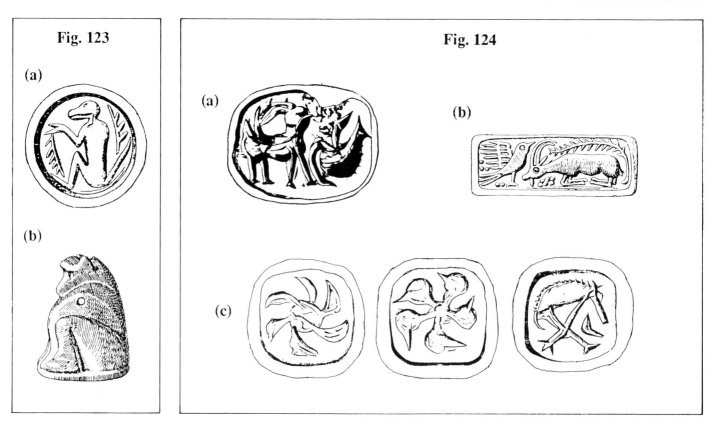

Fig. 123 (a) (b)

Fig. 124 (a) (b) (c)

Fig. 124

(d)

(e)

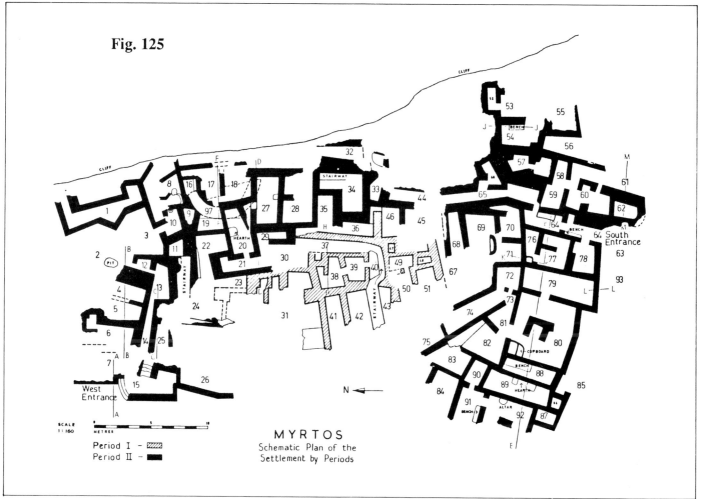

Fig. 125

MYRTOS
Schematic Plan of the
Settlement by Periods

Period I –
Period II –

SCALE
1:160

West
Entrance

South
Entrance

N

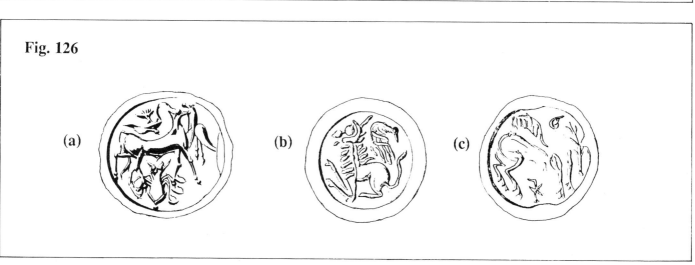

Fig. 126

(a)

(b)

(c)

Fig. 127

(a)

(b)

(c)

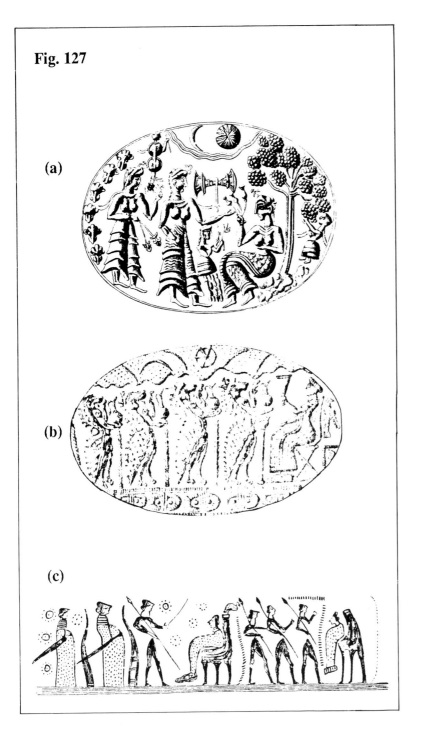

Fig. 129

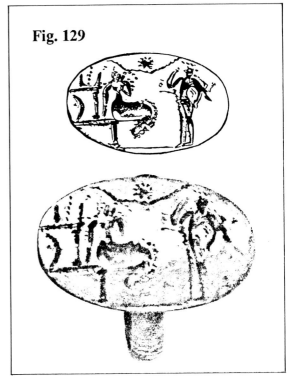

Fig. 130

(a)

(b)

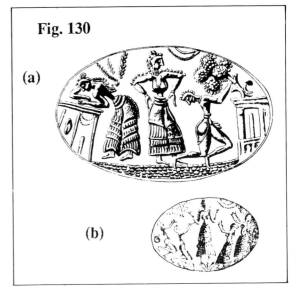

Fig. 128

(a)

(b)

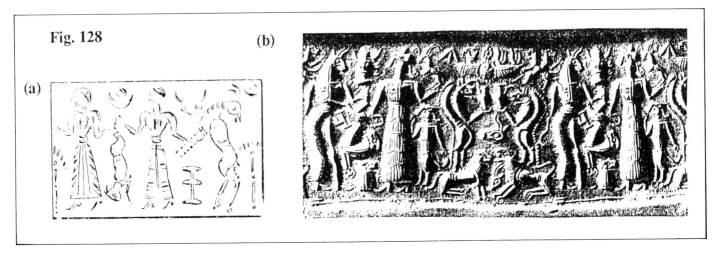

Fig. 131

Fig. 132

(a)

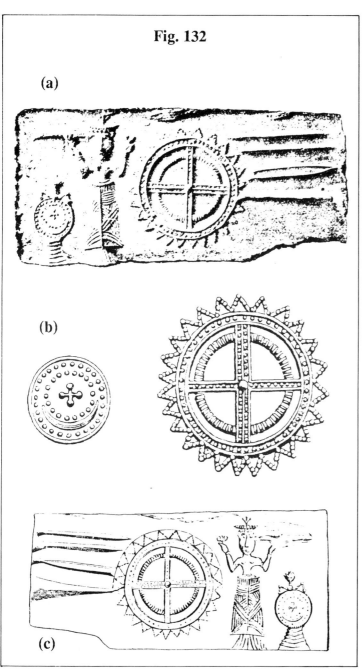

(b)

(c)

Fig. 134

(a)

(b)

Fig. 133

(b)

(a)

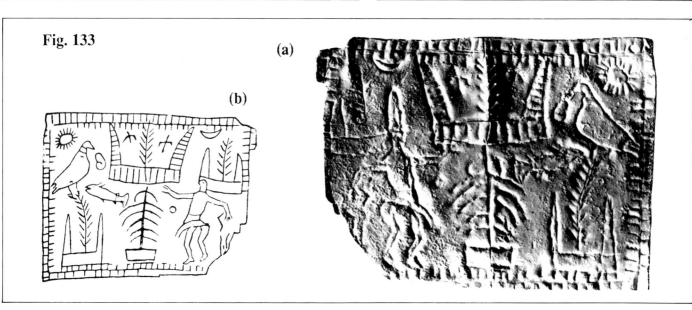

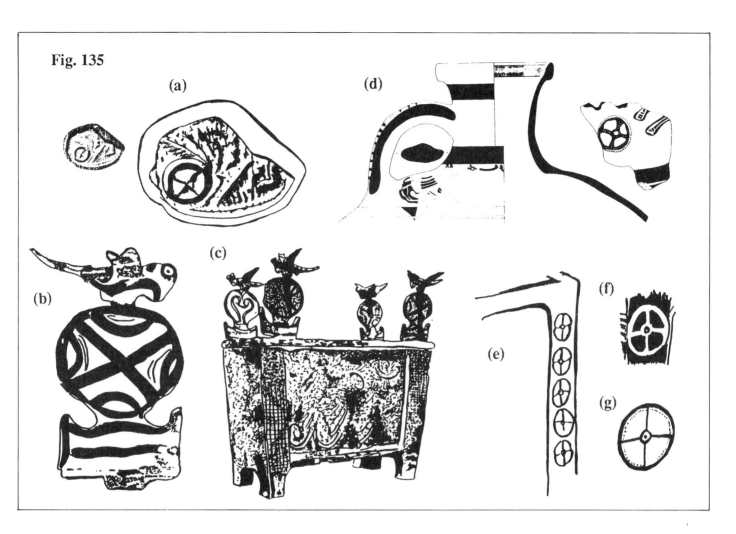

Fig. 135

(a) (d) (b) (c) (e) (f) (g)

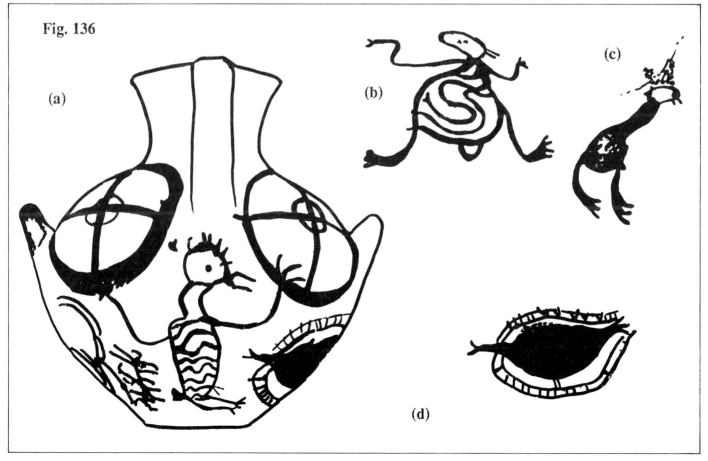

Fig. 136

(a) (b) (c) (d)

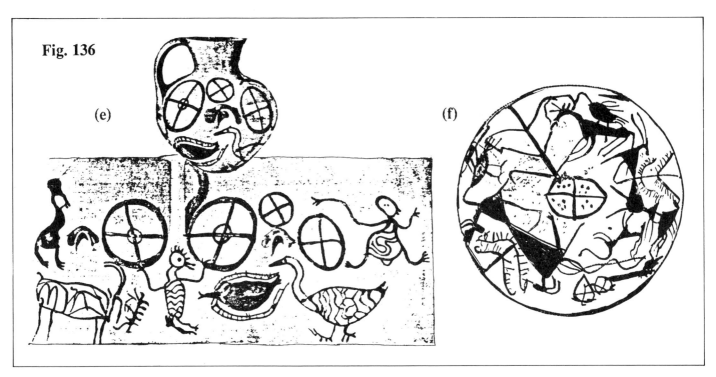

Fig. 136

(e)

(f)

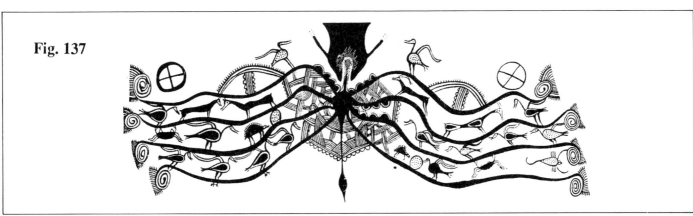

Fig. 137

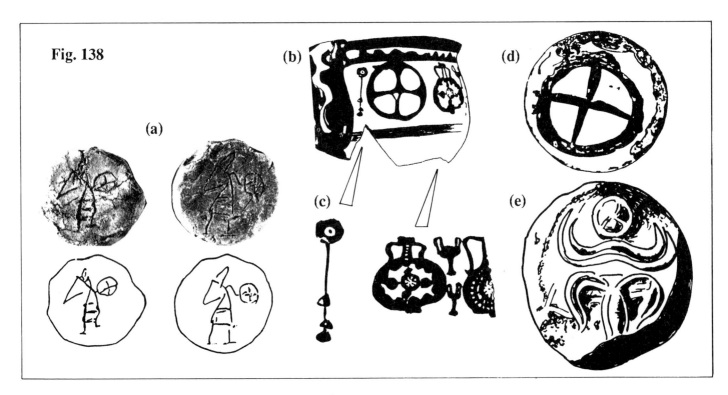

Fig. 138

(a)

(b)

(c)

(d)

(e)

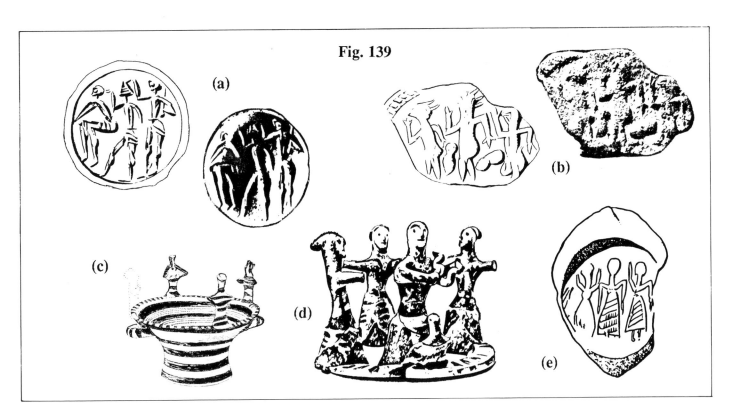

Fig. 139

(a)

(b)

(c)

(d)

(e)

Fig. 140

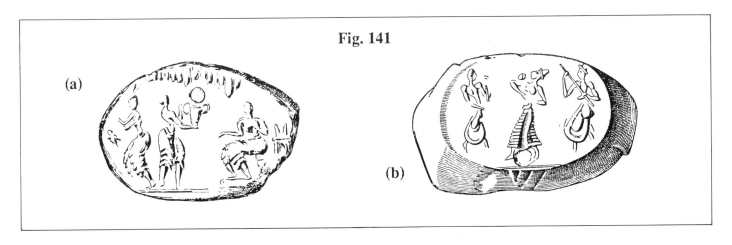

Fig. 141

(a)

(b)

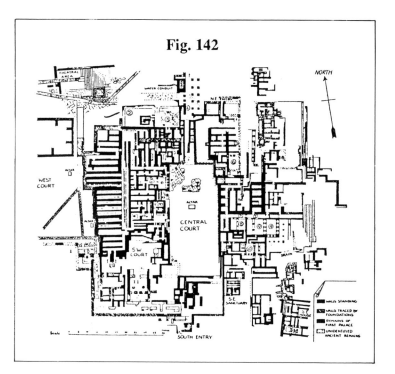

Fig. 142

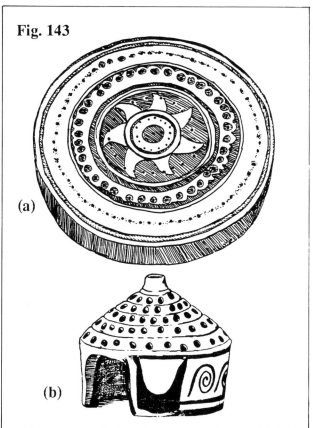

Fig. 143

(a)

(b)

Fig. 144

Fig. 146

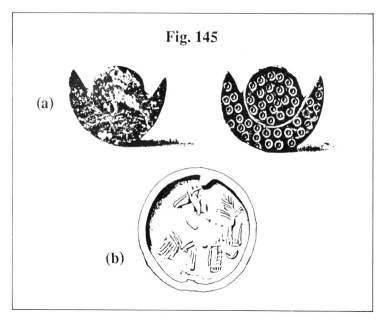

Fig. 145

(a)

(b)

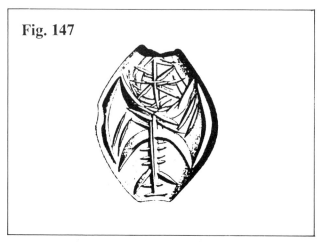

Fig. 147

Fig. 148

(a)

(b)

(c)

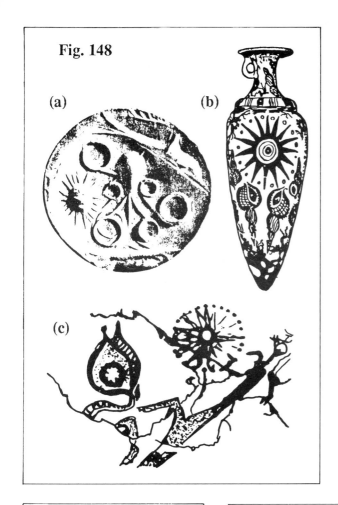

Fig. 149

Fig. 150

Fig. 151

Fig. 152

(a)

(b)

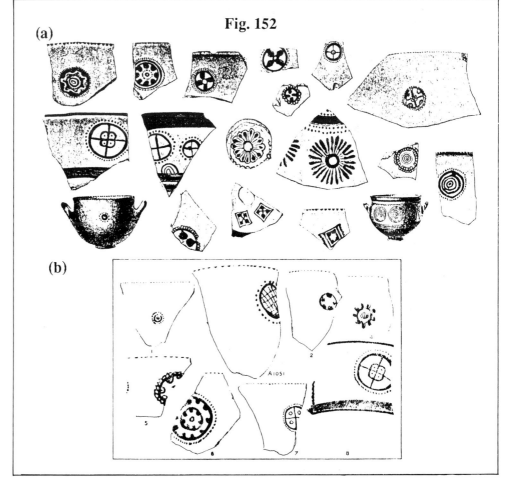

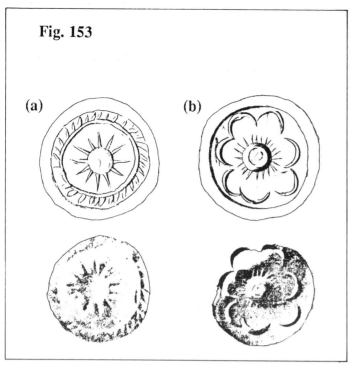

Fig. 153

(a) (b)

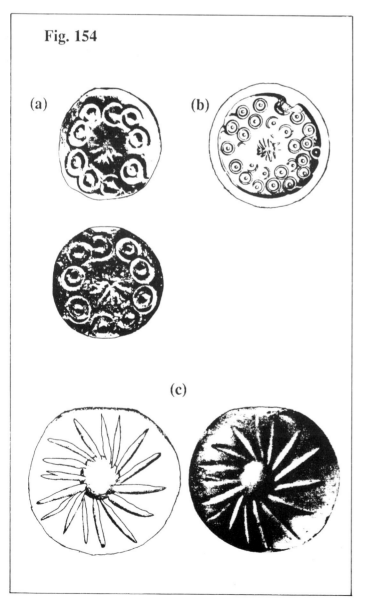

Fig. 154

(a) (b)

(c)

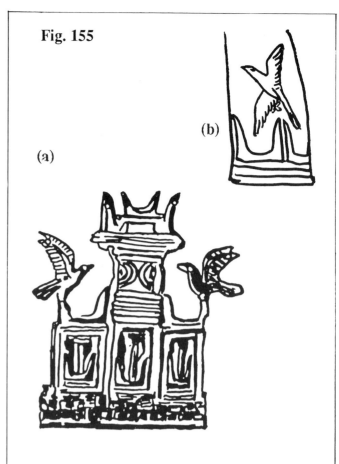

Fig. 155

(a) (b)

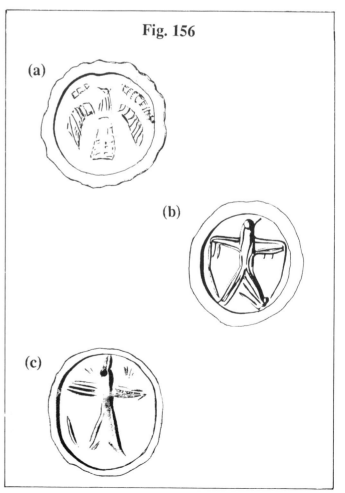

Fig. 156

(a)

(b)

(c)

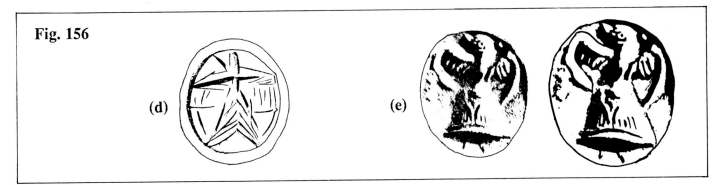

Fig. 156

(d)

(e)

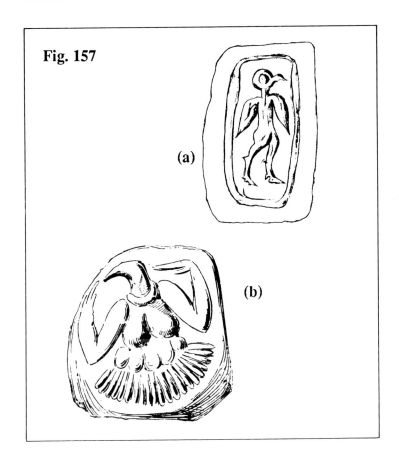

Fig. 157

(a)

(b)

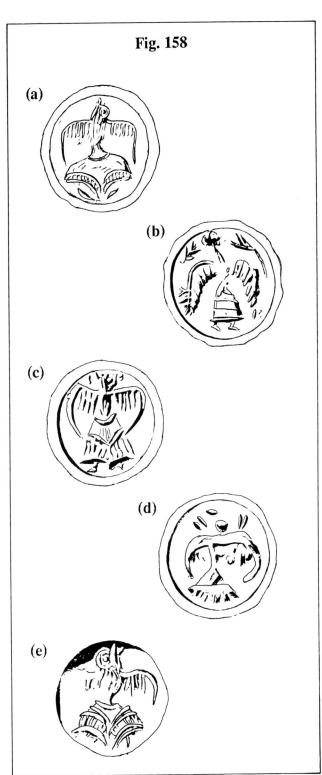

Fig. 158

(a)

(b)

(c)

(d)

(e)

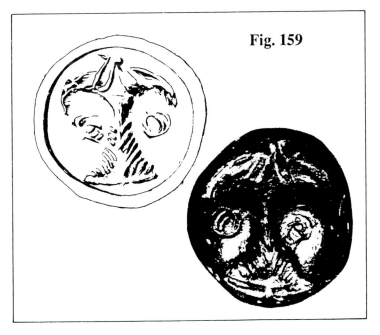

Fig. 159

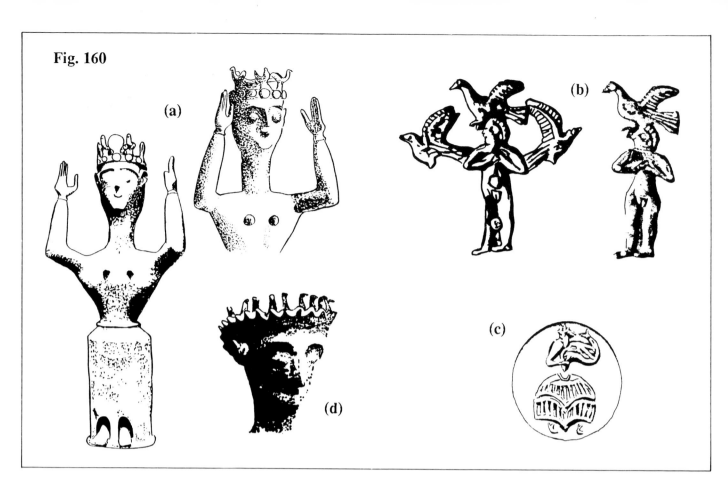

Fig. 160

(a)

(b)

(c)

(d)

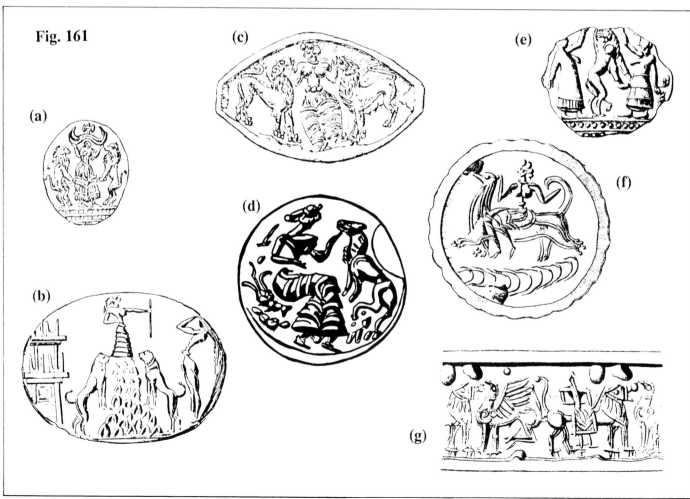

Fig. 161

(a)

(b)

(c)

(d)

(e)

(f)

(g)

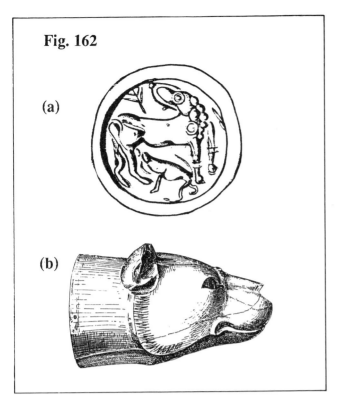

Fig. 162

(a)

(b)

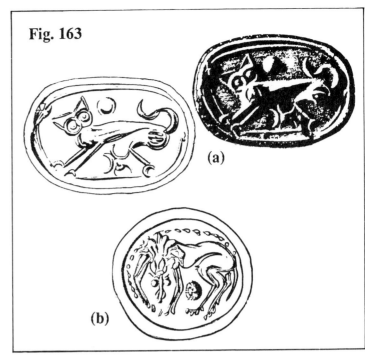

Fig. 163

(a)

(b)

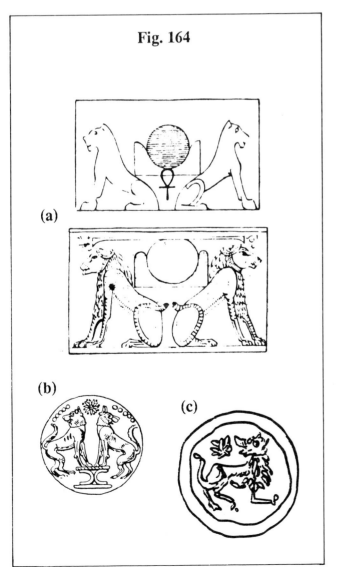

Fig. 164

(a)

(b)

(c)

Fig. 165

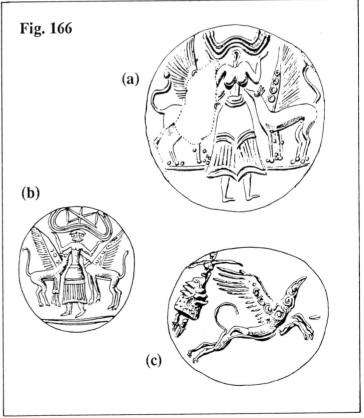

Fig. 166

(a)

(b)

(c)

Fig. 166

(d) (e)

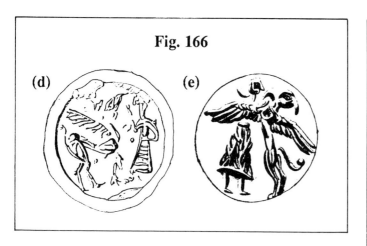

Fig. 167

(a)

(b)

(c)

(d)

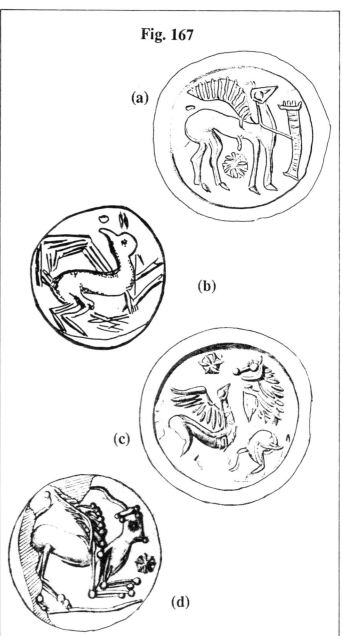

Fig. 168

(a) (b)

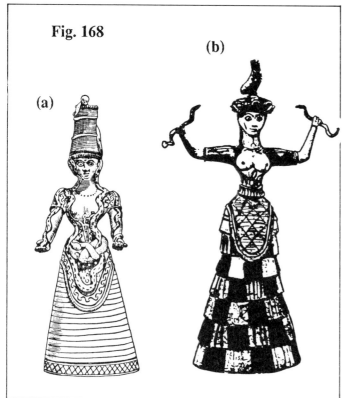

Fig. 169

(a)

(b)

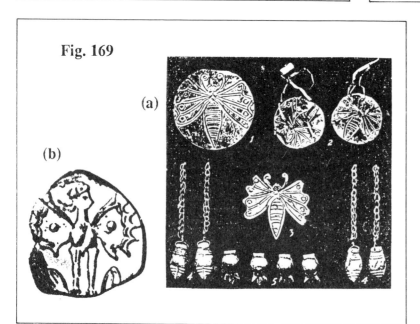

Fig. 170 (a)

(c)

(b)

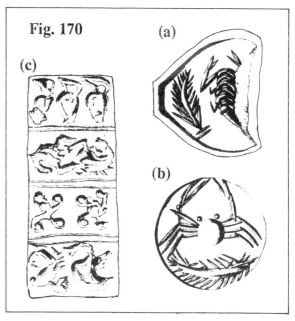

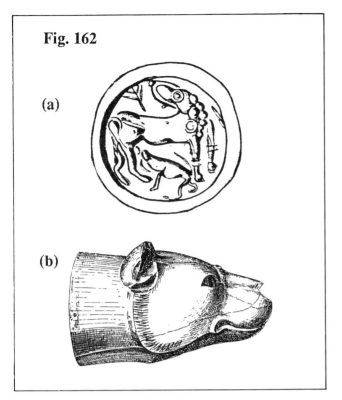

Fig. 162

(a)

(b)

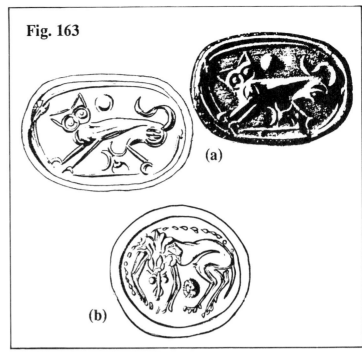

Fig. 163

(a)

(b)

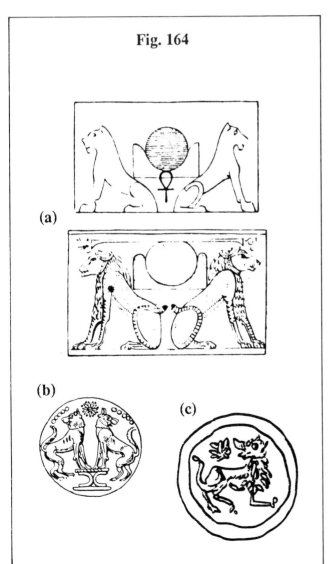

Fig. 164

(a)

(b)

(c)

Fig. 165

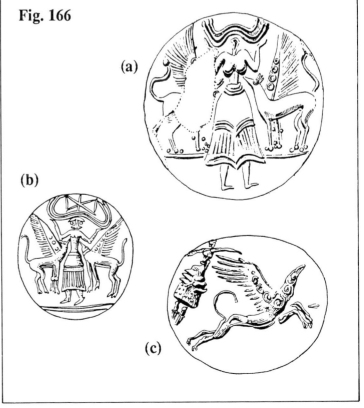

Fig. 166

(a)

(b)

(c)

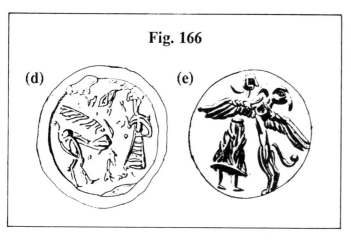

Fig. 166

(d)   (e)

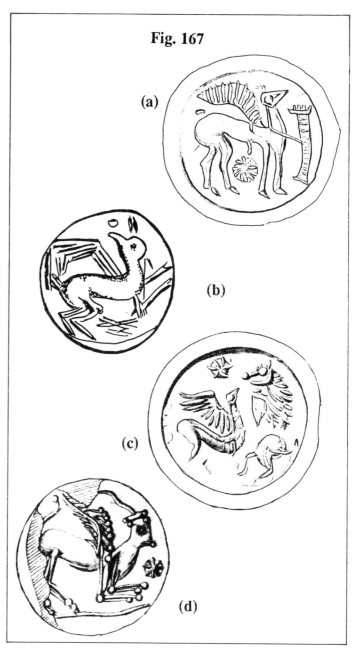

Fig. 167

(a)

(b)

(c)

(d)

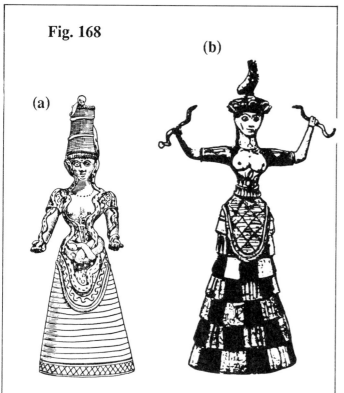

Fig. 168

(a)   (b)

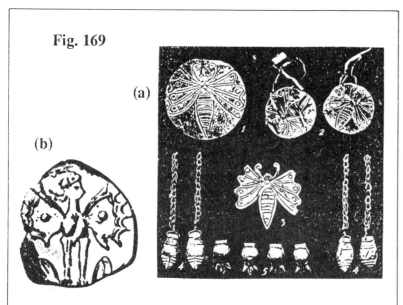

Fig. 169

(a)

(b)

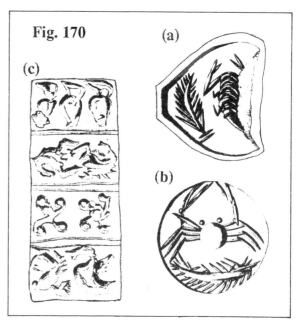

Fig. 170   (a)

(c)

(b)

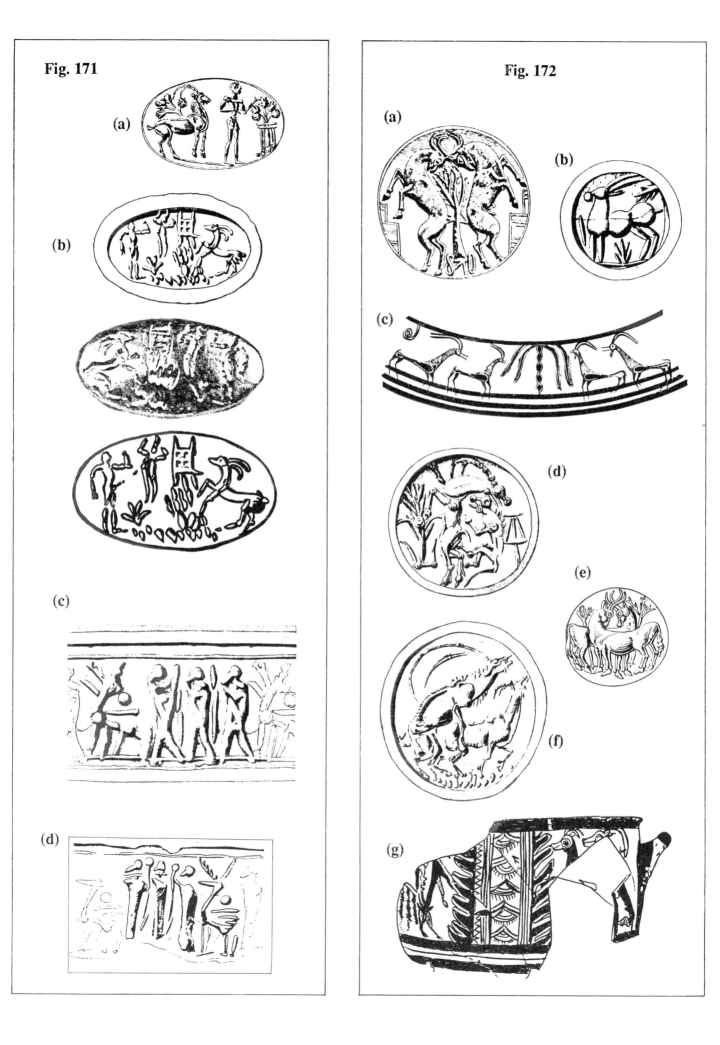

Fig. 171

(a)

(b)

(c)

(d)

Fig. 172

(a)

(b)

(c)

(d)

(e)

(f)

(g)

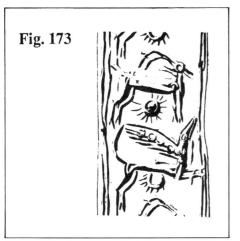

Fig. 173

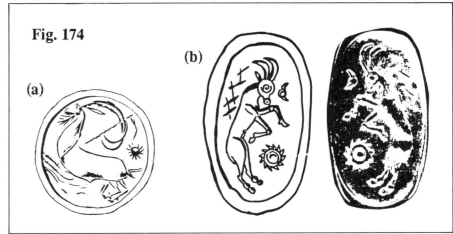

Fig. 174

(a) (b)

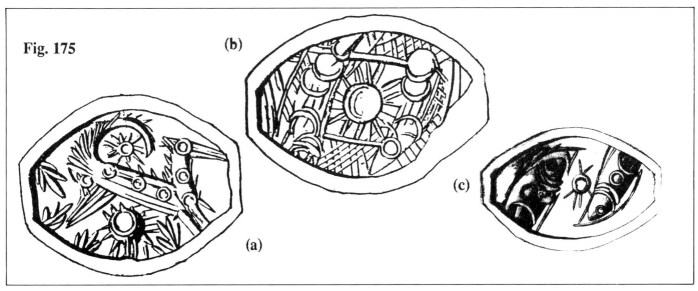

Fig. 175

(b)

(a)

(c)

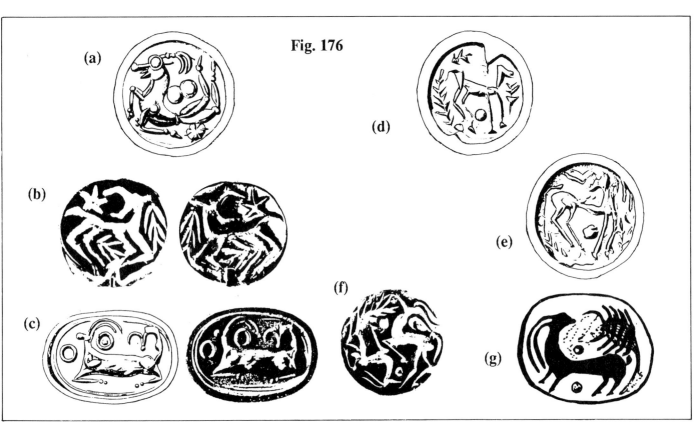

Fig. 176

(a)

(b)

(c)

(d)

(e)

(f)

(g)

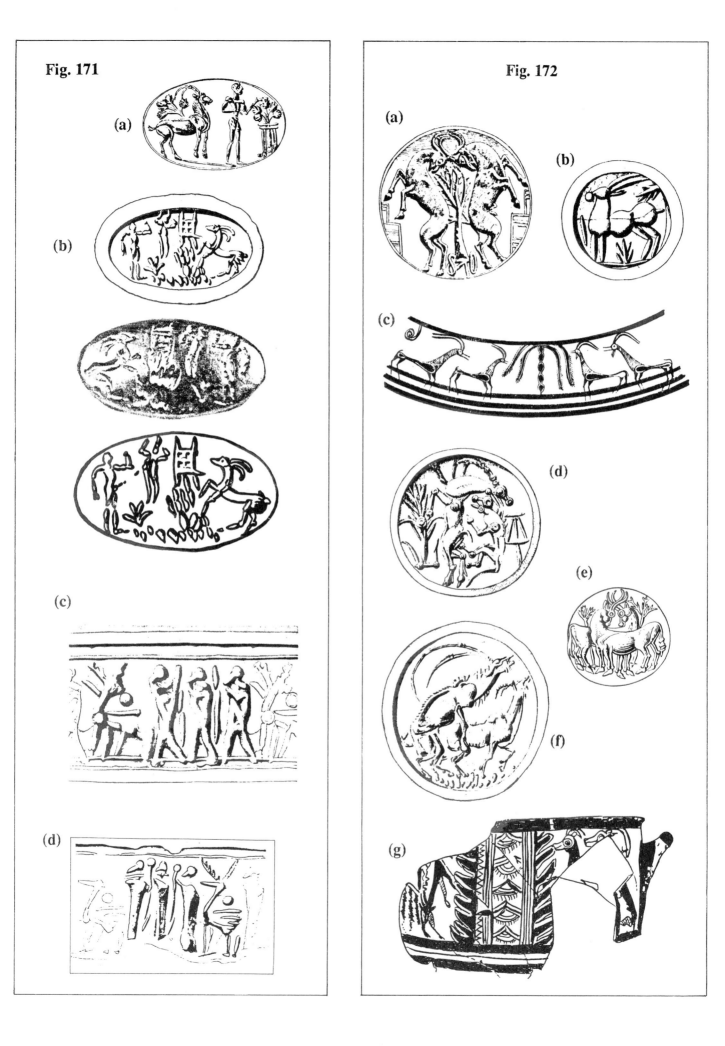

Fig. 171

(a)

(b)

(c)

(d)

Fig. 172

(a)

(b)

(c)

(d)

(e)

(f)

(g)

Fig. 173

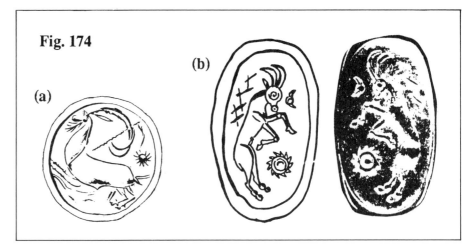

Fig. 174

(a)

(b)

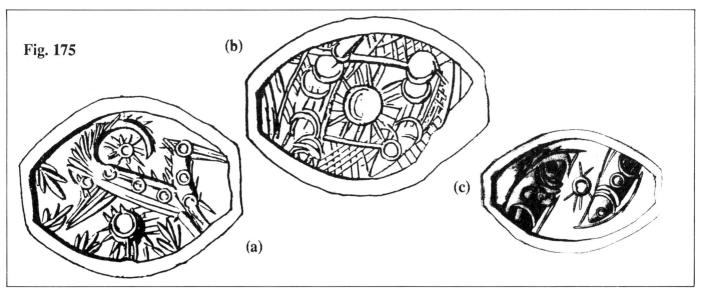

Fig. 175

(b)

(a)

(c)

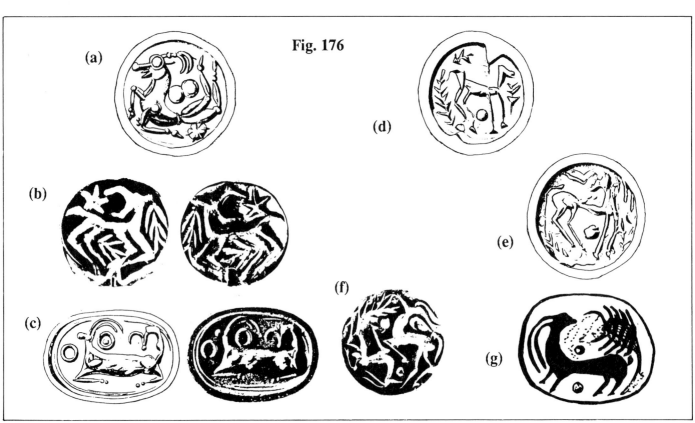

Fig. 176

(a)

(d)

(b)

(e)

(c)

(f)

(g)

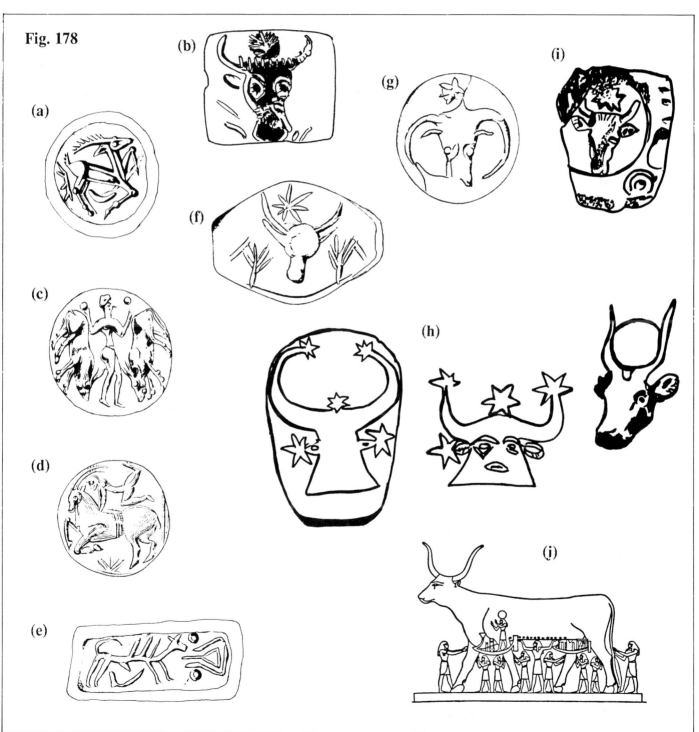

Fig. 177

(a)   (b)   (c)   (d)

Fig. 178

(a)   (b)   (g)   (i)

(f)

(c)   (h)

(d)

(e)   (j)

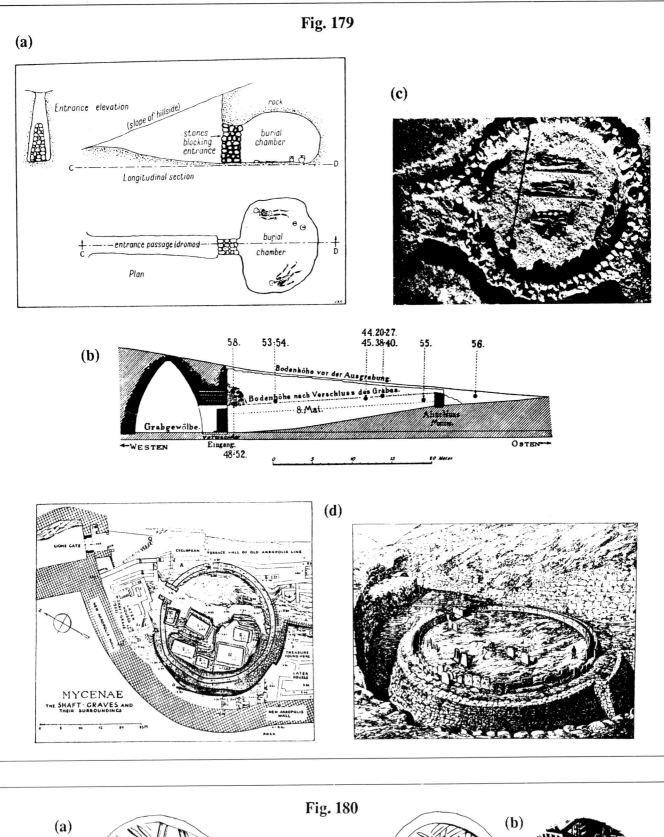

Fig. 179

(a)

Entrance elevation
(slope of hillside)
rock
stones blocking entrance
burial chamber
C ——————— D
Longitudinal section

entrance passage (dromos)
burial chamber
C ———————— D
Plan

(c)

(b)

58. 53·54. 44.20-27. 45.38·40. 55. 56.

Bodenhöhe vor der Ausgrabung.
Bodenhöhe nach Verschluss des Grabes.
8. Mai.

Grabgewölbe.
Eingang.
48·52.

← WESTEN
Abschluss Mauer
OSTEN →

0   5   10   15   20 Meter

MYCENAE
THE SHAFT · GRAVES AND
THEIR SURROUNDINGS

0   5   10   15   20 25 M

LIONS GATE
CYCLOPEAN TERRACE WALL OF OLD ACROPOLIS LINE
TREASURE FOUND HERE
LATER HOUSES
NEW ACROPOLIS WALL
ROCK

(d)

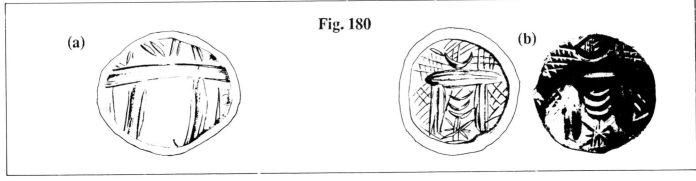

Fig. 180

(a)

(b)

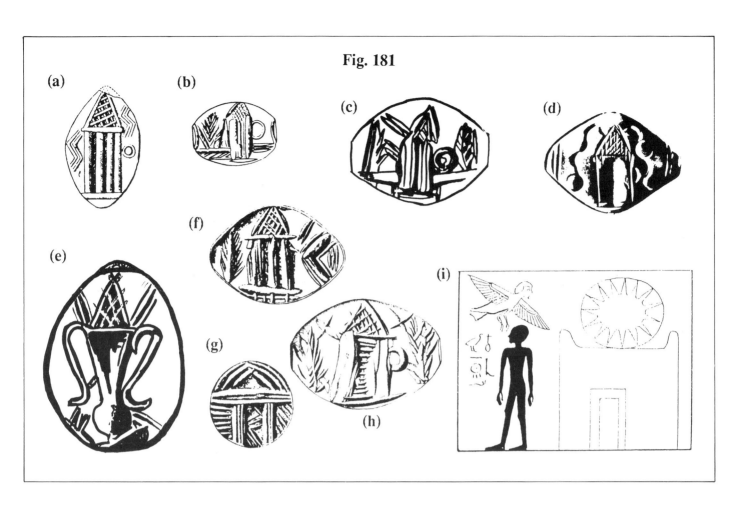

Fig. 181

(a) (b) (c) (d)

(e) (f)

(g) (h)

(i)

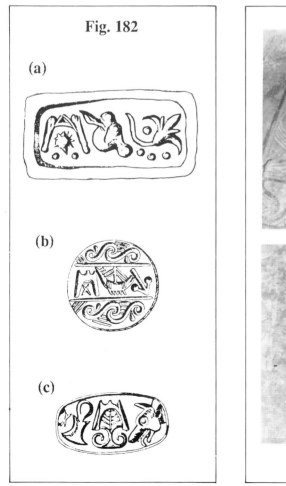

Fig. 182

(a)

(b)

(c)

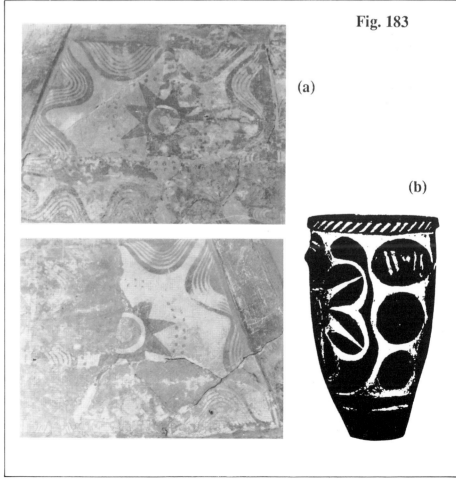

Fig. 183

(a)

(b)

Fig. 184

Fig. 186

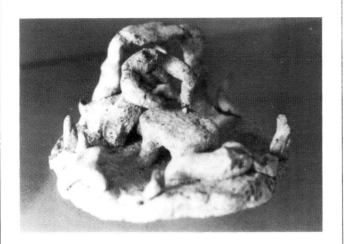

Fig. 185

(a)

(e)

(b)

(c)

(d)

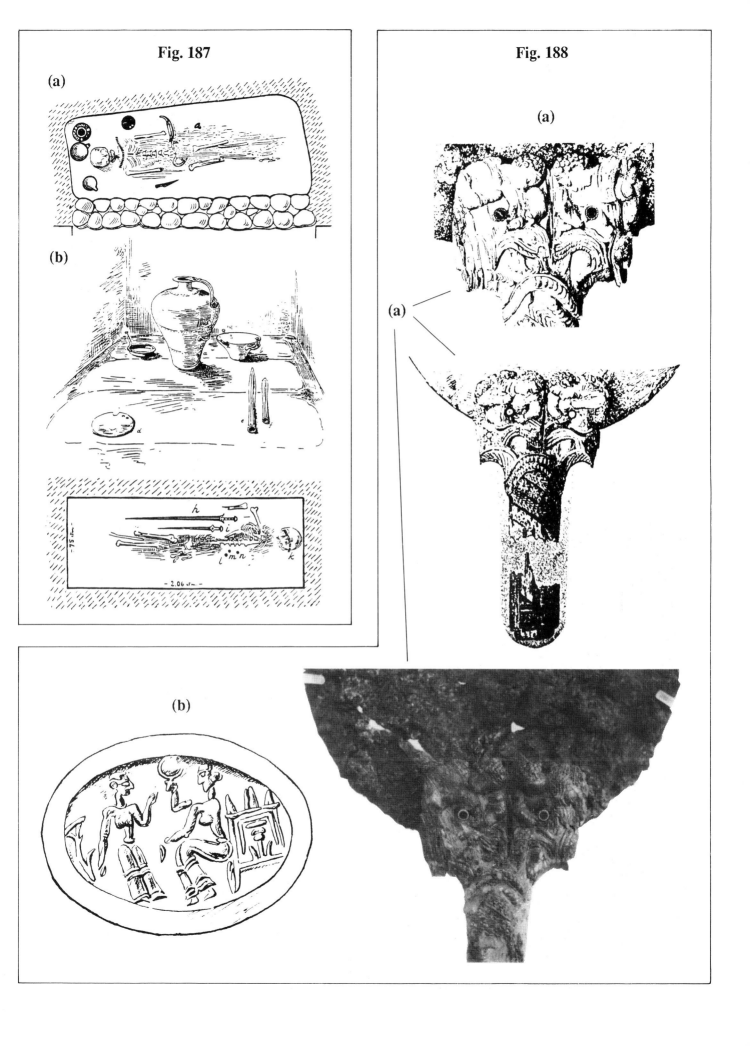

Fig. 187

(a)

(b)

Fig. 188

(a)

(a)

(b)

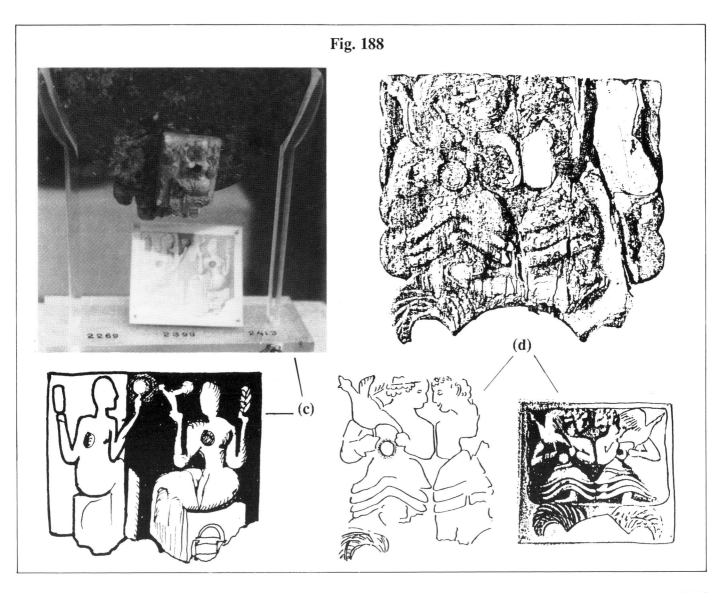

Fig. 188

(c)

(d)

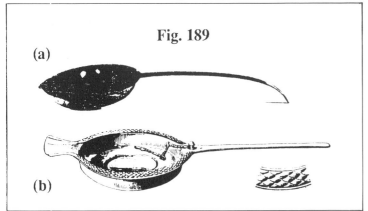

Fig. 189

(a)

(b)

Fig. 190

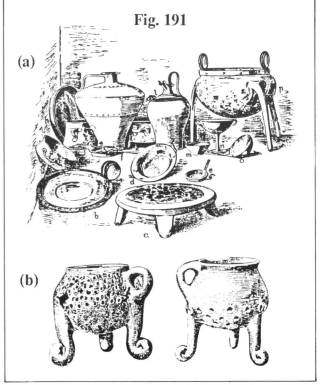

Fig. 191

(a)

(b)

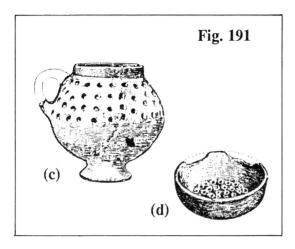

Fig. 191

(c)

(d)

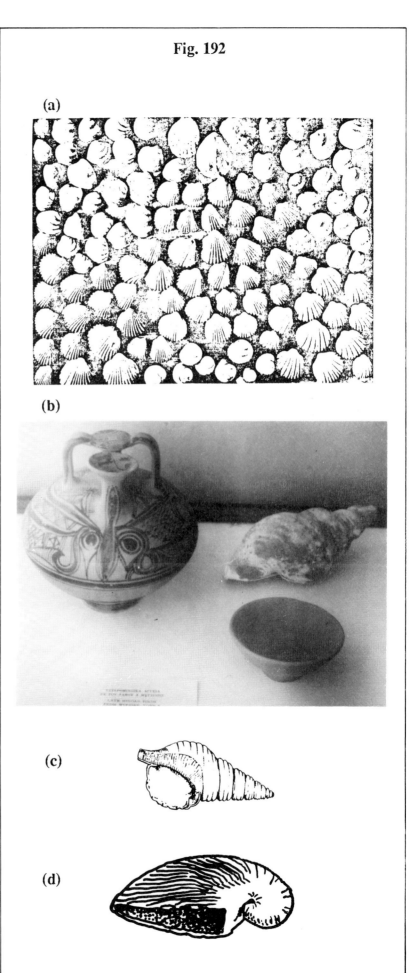

Fig. 192

(a)

(b)

(c)

(d)

Fig. 193

Fig. 194

Fig. 195

(a)

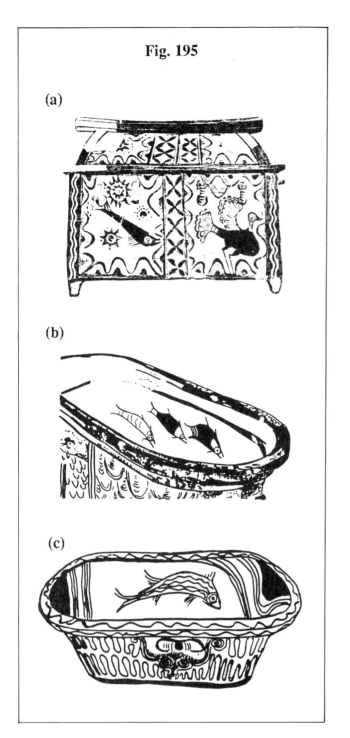

(b)

(c)

Fig. 196

(a)   (b)

(c)   (d)

(e)   (f)

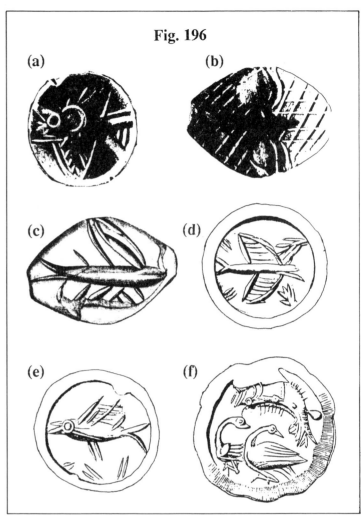

Fig. 197

Fig. 198

(a)

(a) contd ...

Fig. 198

… contd (a)

(b)

(c)

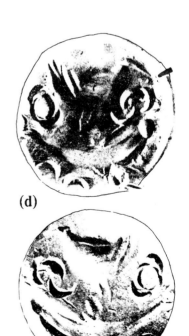

(d)

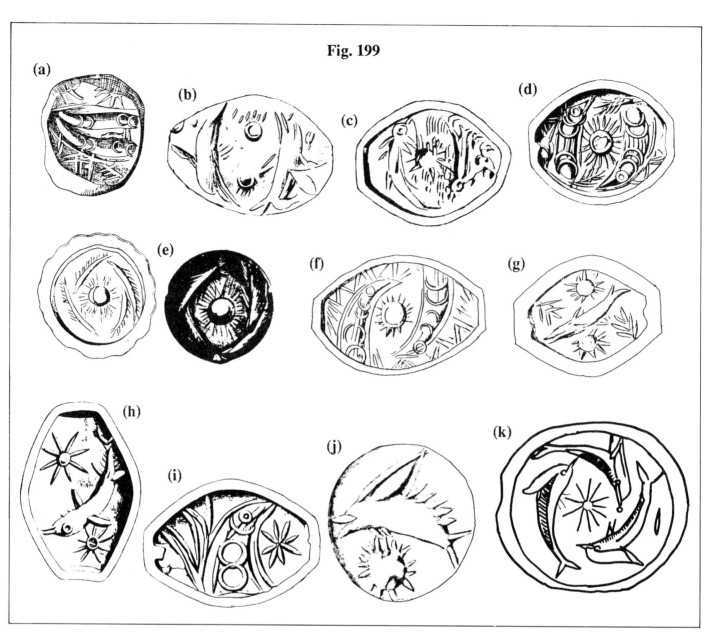

Fig. 199

(a) (b) (c) (d) (e) (f) (g) (h) (i) (j) (k)

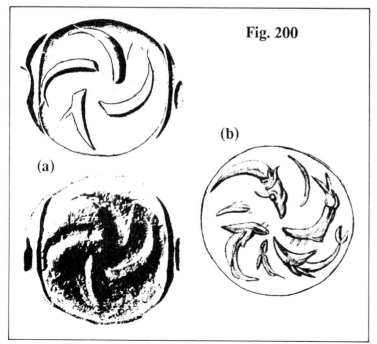

Fig. 200

(a) (b)

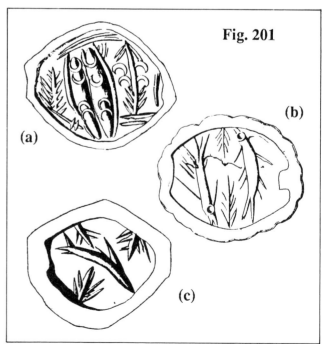

Fig. 201

(a) (b) (c)

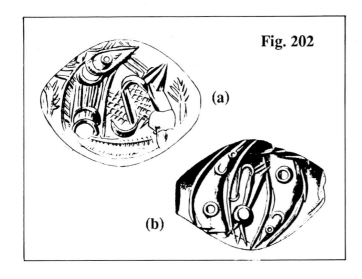

Fig. 202

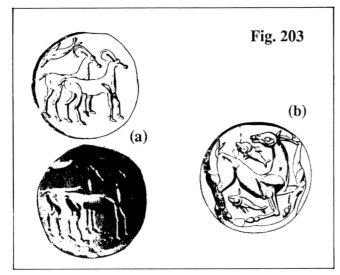

Fig. 203

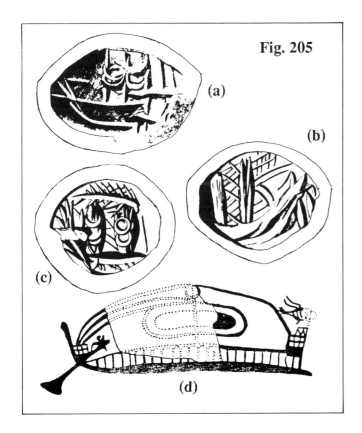

Fig. 205

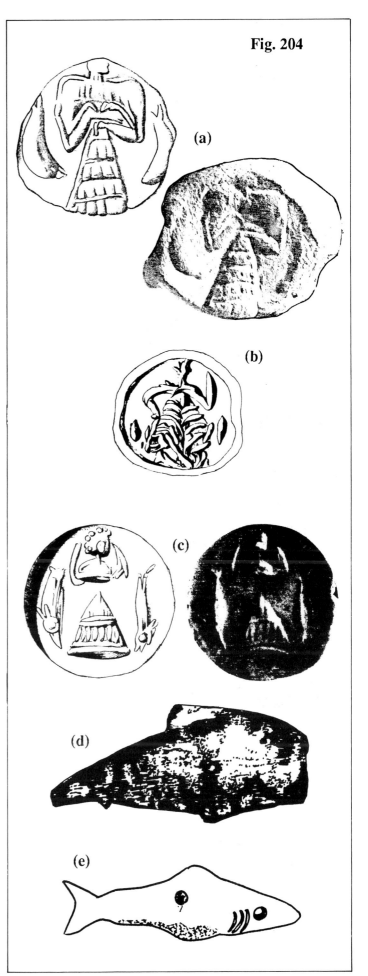

Fig. 204

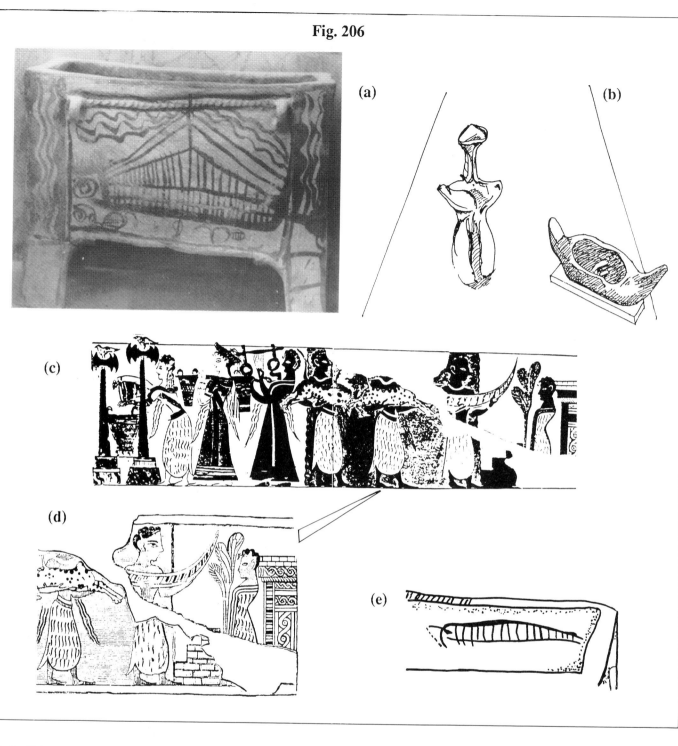

Fig. 206

(a)

(b)

(c)

(d)

(e)

Fig. 207

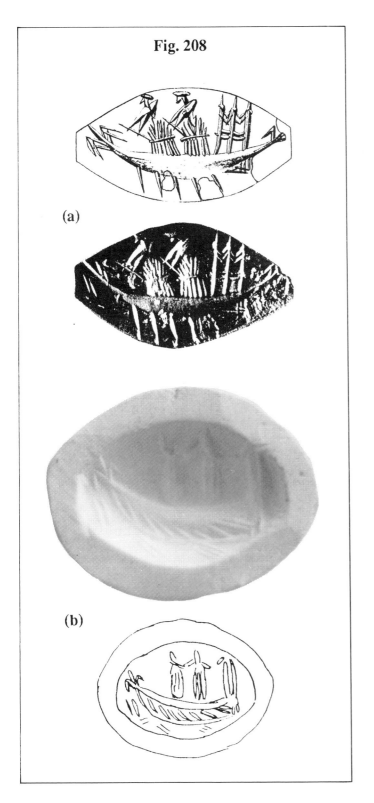

Fig. 208

(a)

(b)

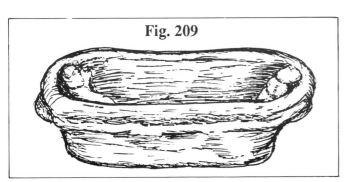

Fig. 209

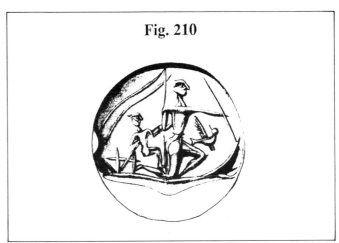

Fig. 210

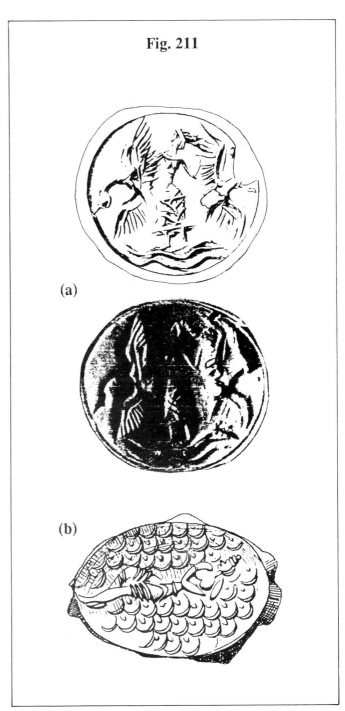

Fig. 211

(a)

(b)

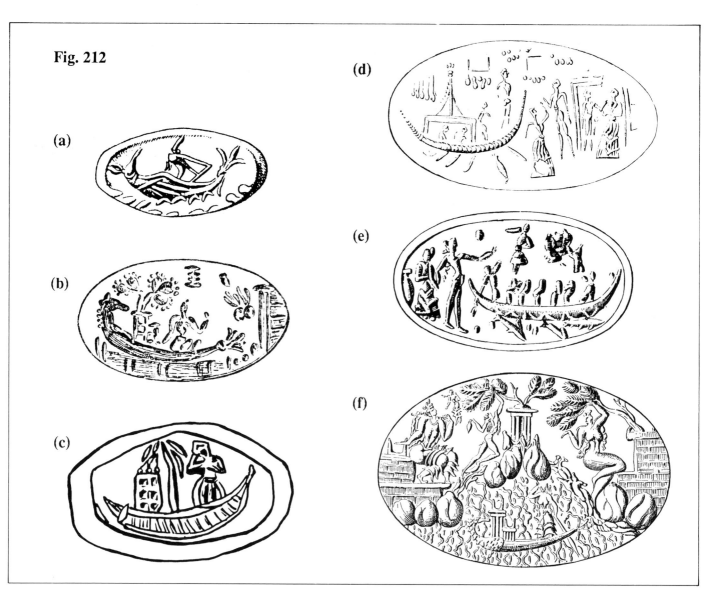

Fig. 212

(a)

(b)

(c)

(d)

(e)

(f)

Fig. 213

(a)

(b)

Fig. 214

(a)

(b)

(c)

Fig. 215

(a)

(b)

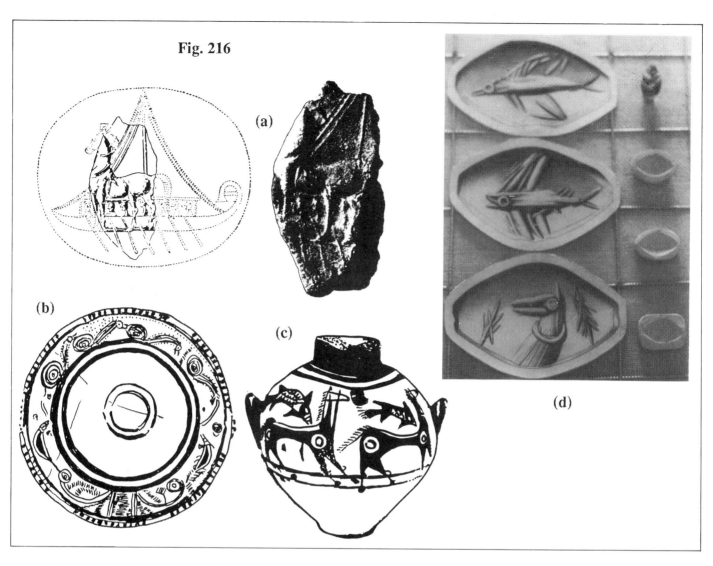

Fig. 216

(a)

(b)

(c)

(d)

Fig. 217

(a)

Fig. 217

(b)

Fig. 218

(a)

(b)

(c)

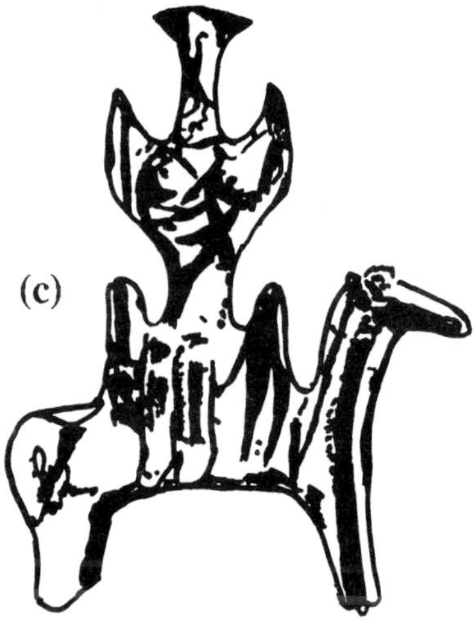

(h)

(d)

(e)

(g)

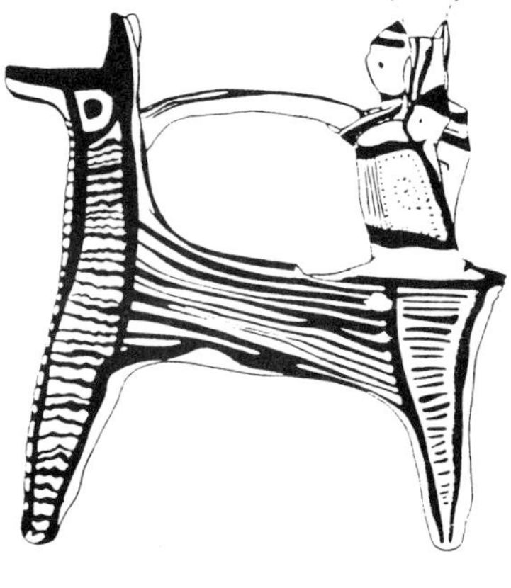

(f)

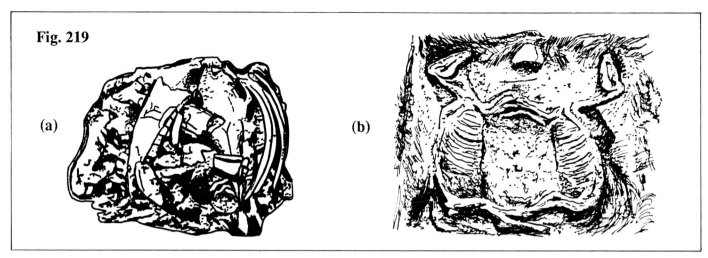

Fig. 219

(a)

(b)

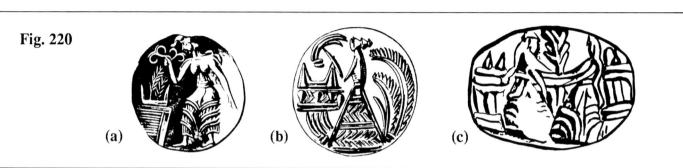

Fig. 220

(a)

(b)

(c)

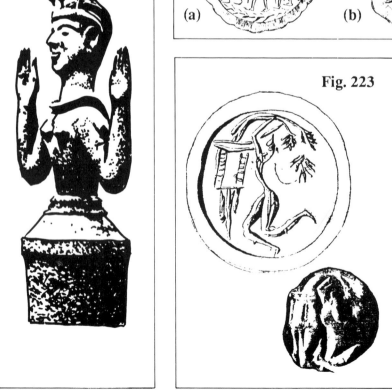

Fig. 221

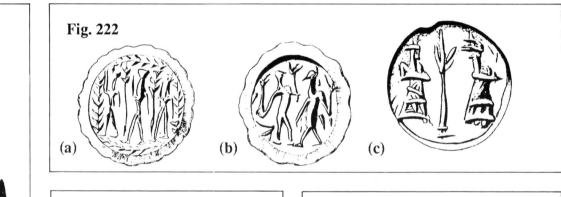

Fig. 222

(a)

(b)

(c)

Fig. 223

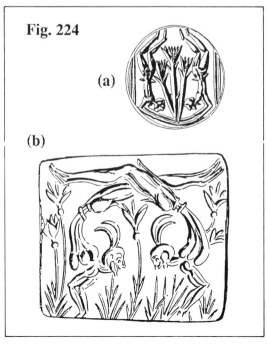

Fig. 224

(a)

(b)

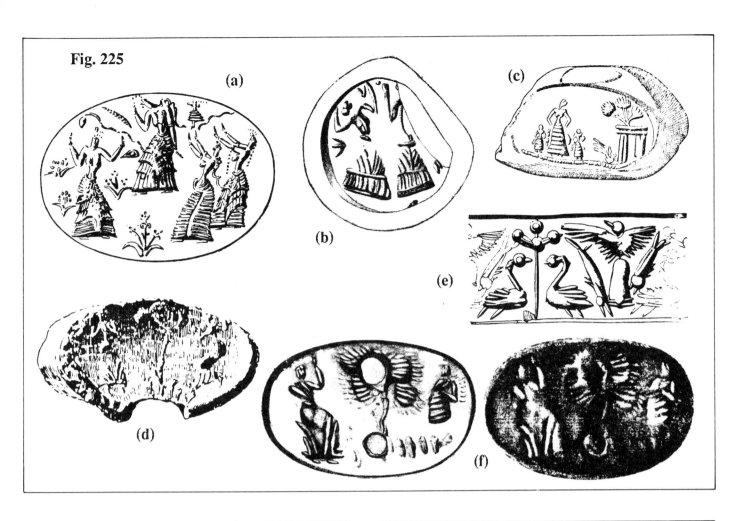

Fig. 225

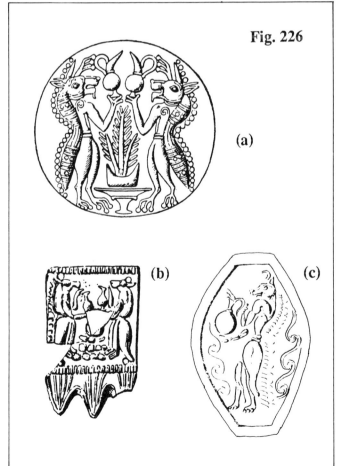

Fig. 226

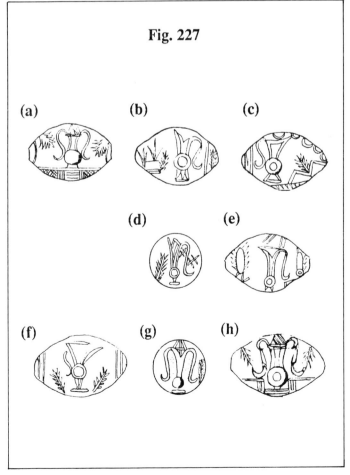

Fig. 227

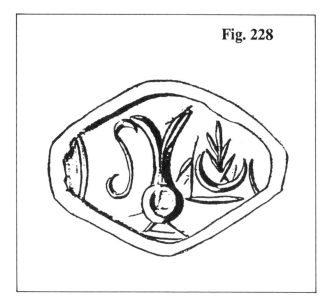

Fig. 228

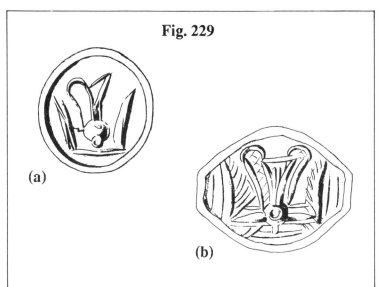

Fig. 229

(a)

(b)

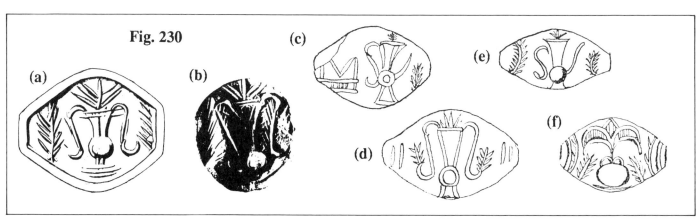

Fig. 230

(a)

(b)

(c)

(d)

(e)

(f)

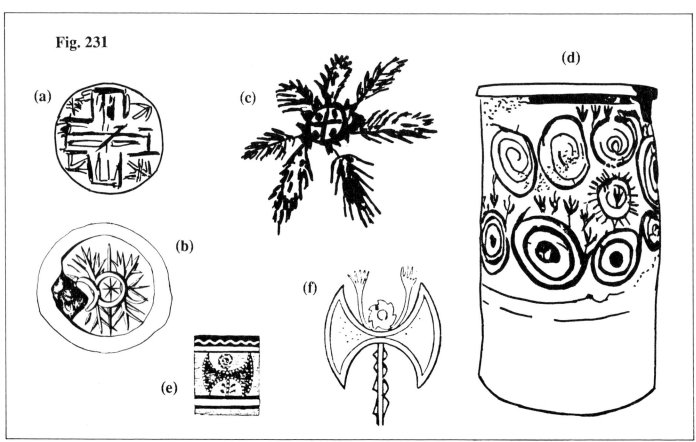

Fig. 231

(a)

(b)

(c)

(d)

(e)

(f)

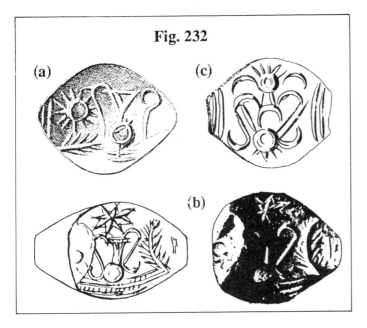

Fig. 232

(a)   (c)

(b)

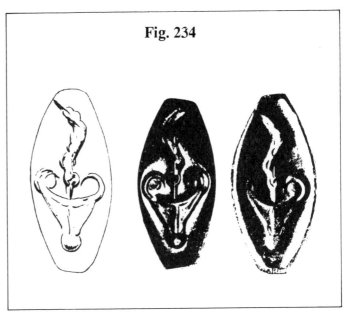

Fig. 234

Fig. 233

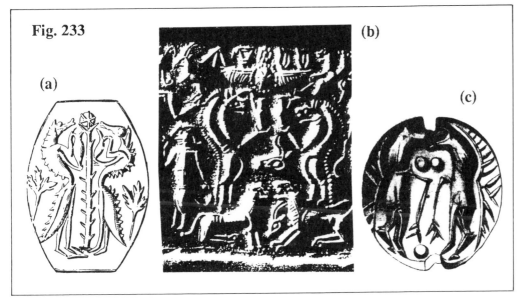

(a)   (b)   (c)

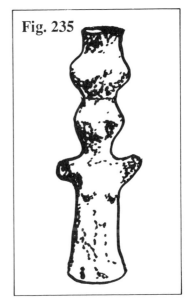

Fig. 235

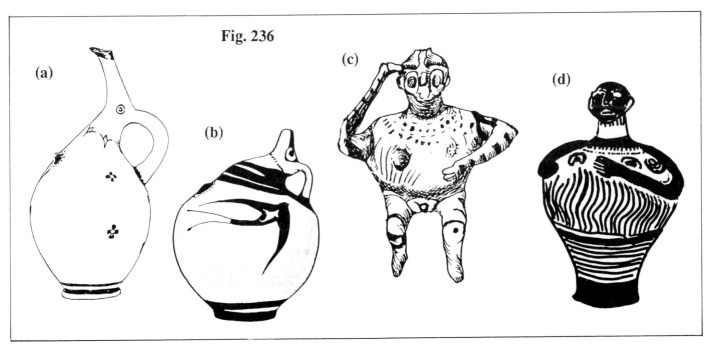

Fig. 236

(a)   (b)   (c)   (d)

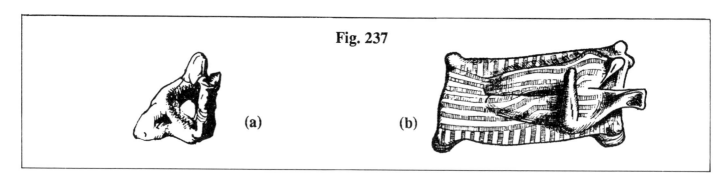

Fig. 237

(a)

(b)

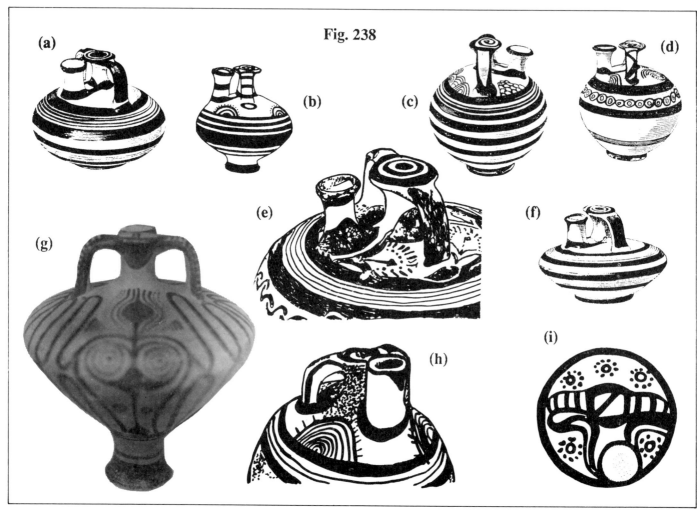

Fig. 238

(a)

(b)

(c)

(d)

(e)

(g)

(f)

(h)

(i)

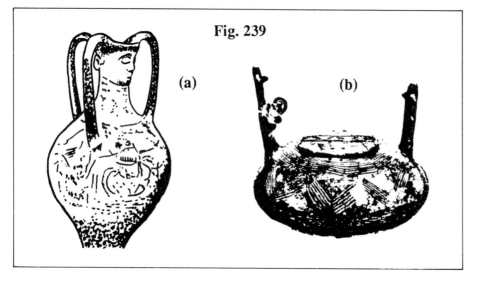

Fig. 239

(a)

(b)

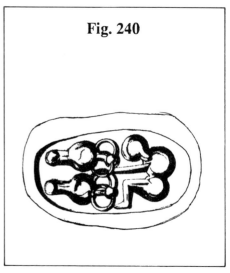

Fig. 240

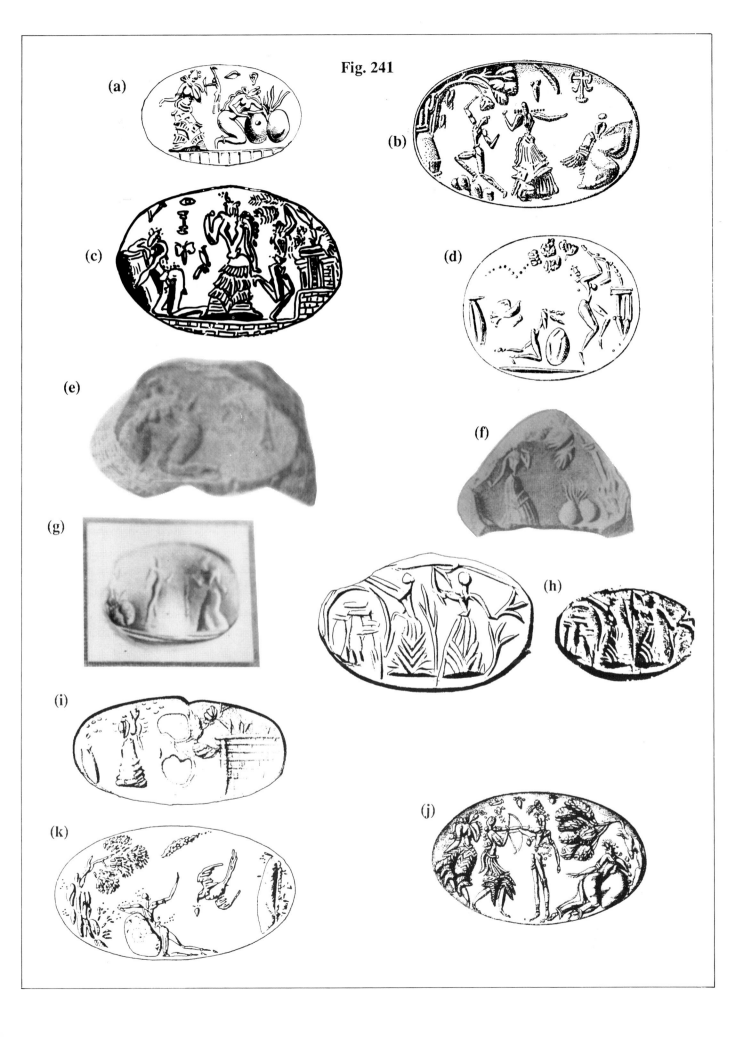

Fig. 241

Fig. 241

(l)

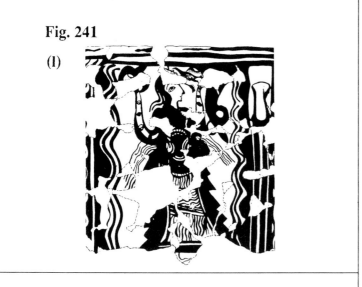

(a)   **Fig. 242**

(b)

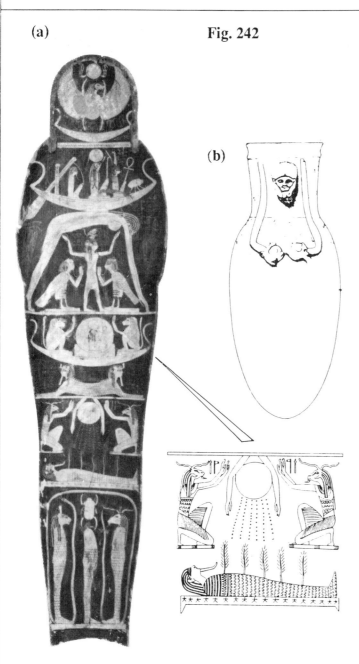

Fig. 243

(a)

(b)

(c)

(d)

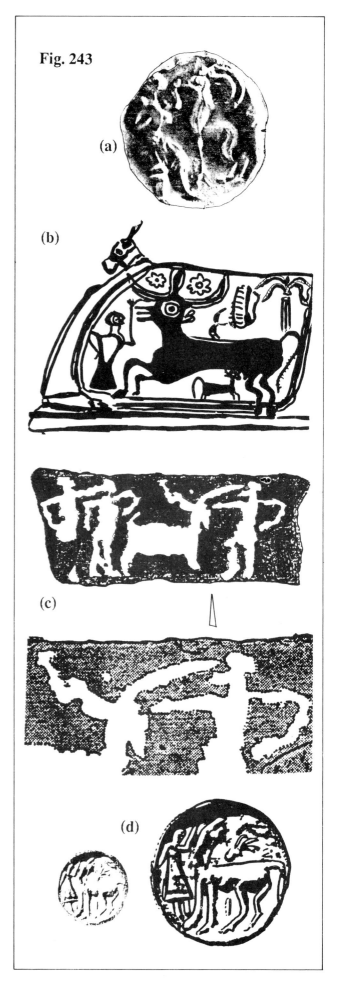

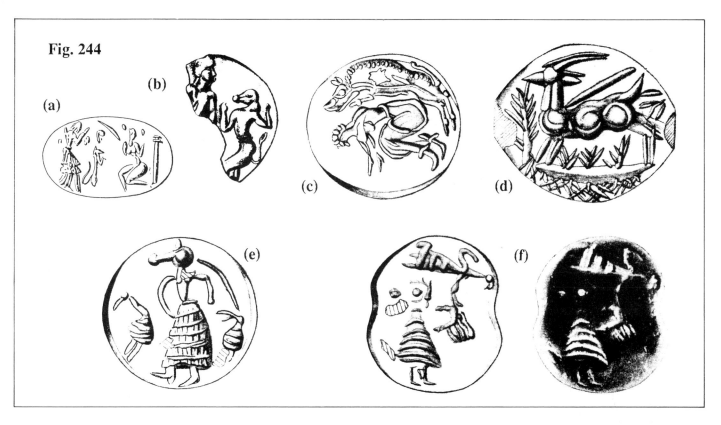

Fig. 244

(a)

(b)

(c)

(d)

(e)

(f)

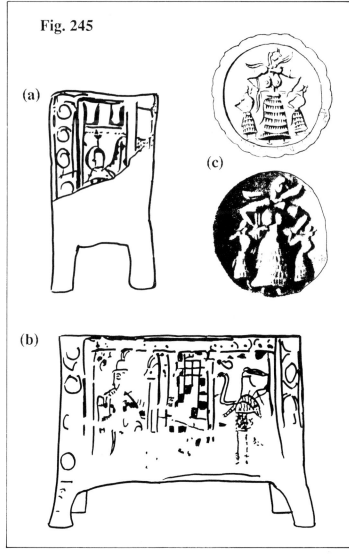

Fig. 245

(a)

(b)

(c)

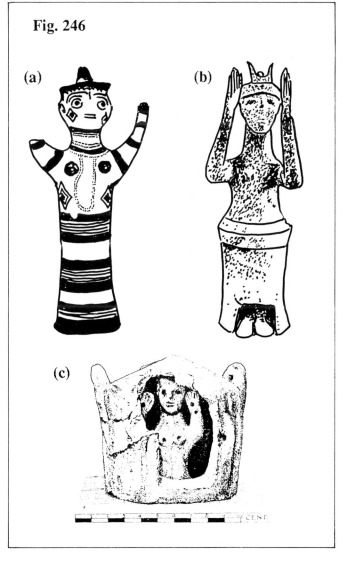

Fig. 246

(a)

(b)

(c)

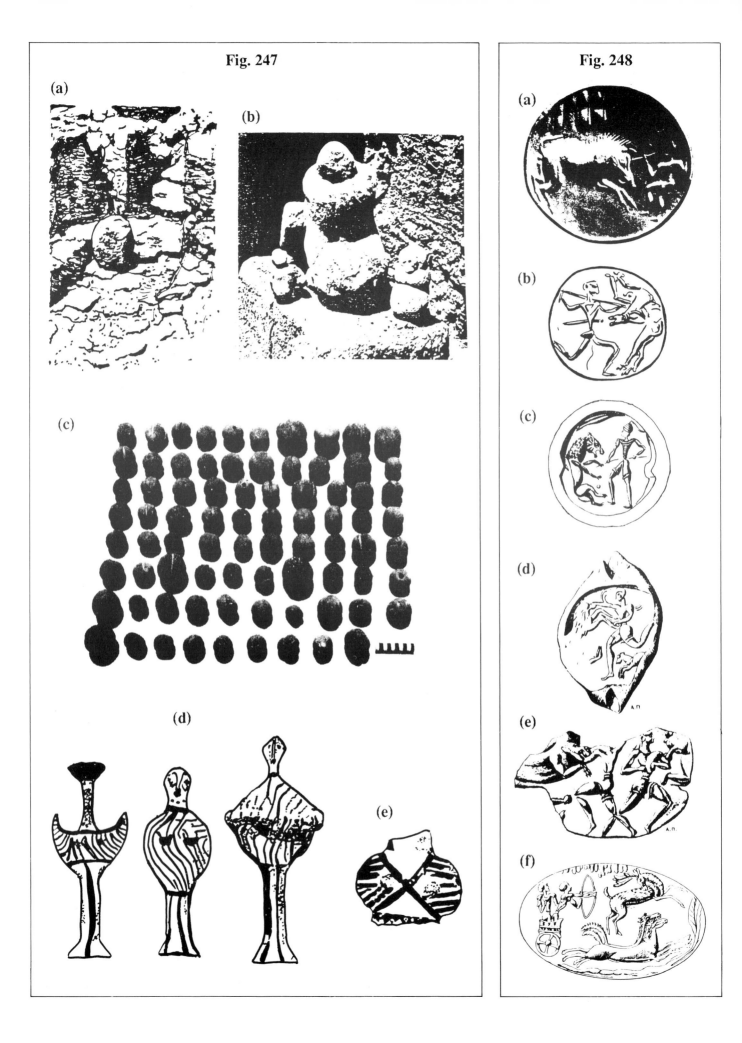

Fig. 247

(a)

(b)

(c)

(d)

(e)

Fig. 248

(a)

(b)

(c)

(d)

(e)

(f)

Fig. 248

(g)

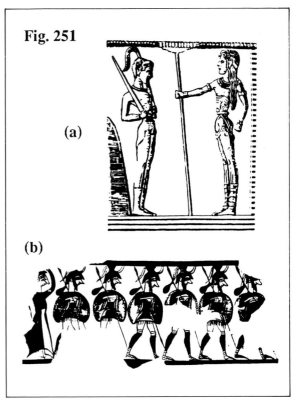

Fig. 251

(a)

(b)

Fig. 249

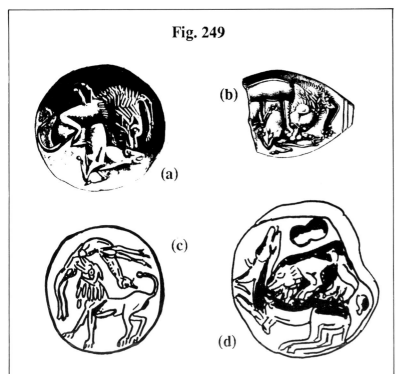

(a)

(b)

(c)

(d)

Fig. 252

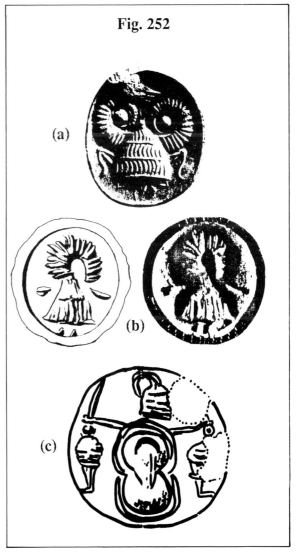

(a)

(b)

(c)

Fig. 250

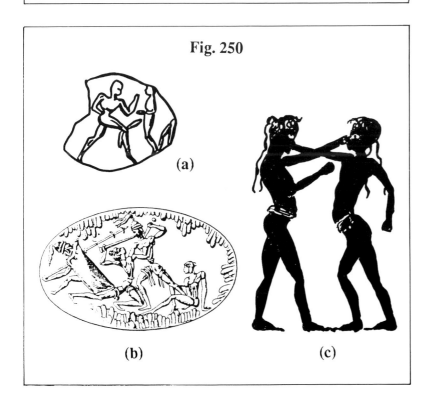

(a)

(b)

(c)

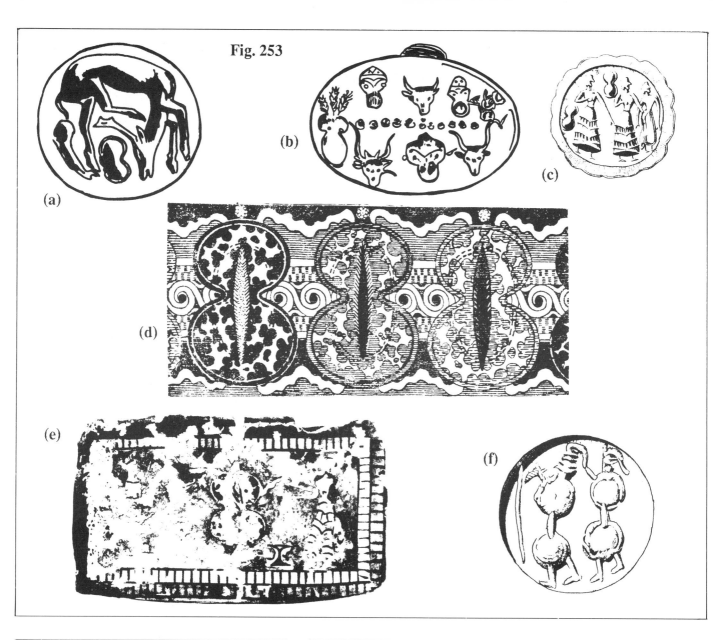

Fig. 253

(a)

(b)

(c)

(d)

(e)

(f)

Fig. 254

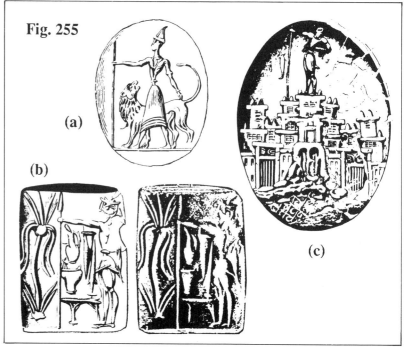

Fig. 255

(a)

(b)

(c)

Fig. 256

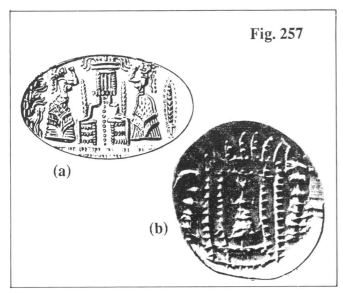

Fig. 257

(a)

(b)

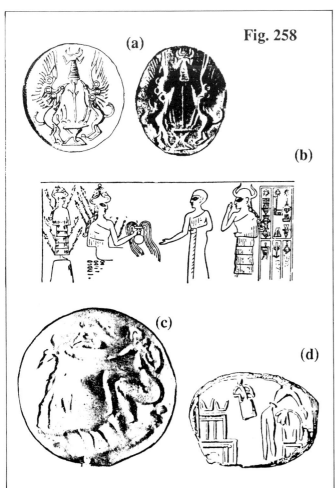

Fig. 258

(a)

(b)

(c)

(d)

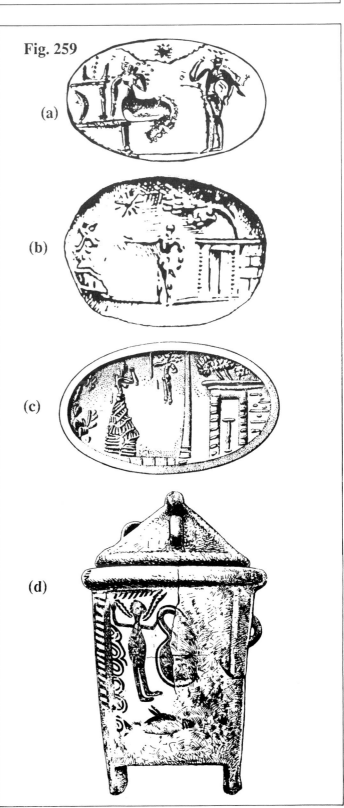

Fig. 259

(a)

(b)

(c)

(d)

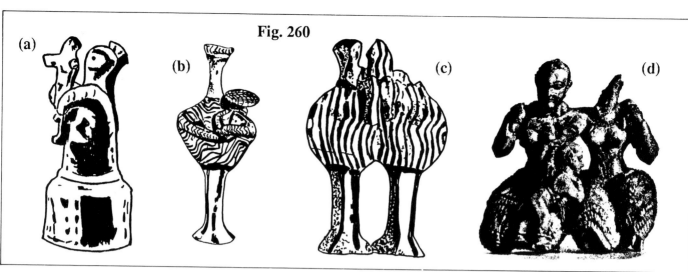

Fig. 260

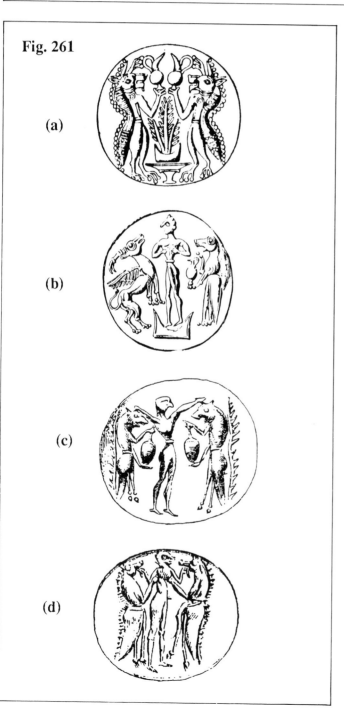

Fig. 261

(a)

(b)

(c)

(d)

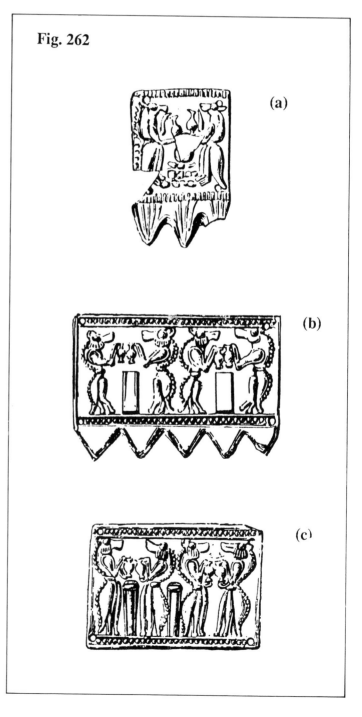

Fig. 262

(a)

(b)

(c)

Fig. 263

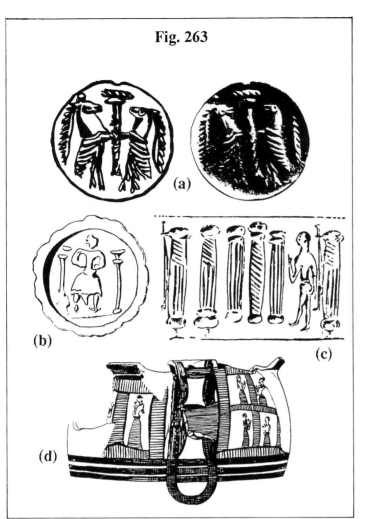

(a)

(b)

(c)

(d)

Fig. 264

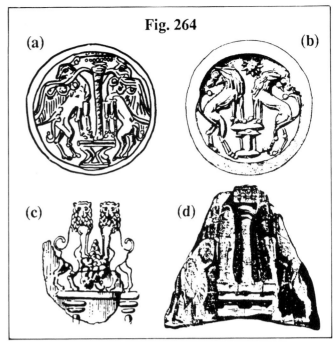

(a)

(b)

(c)

(d)

Fig. 265

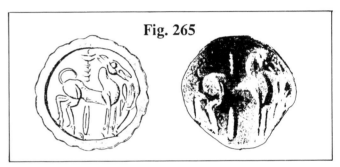

Fig. 266

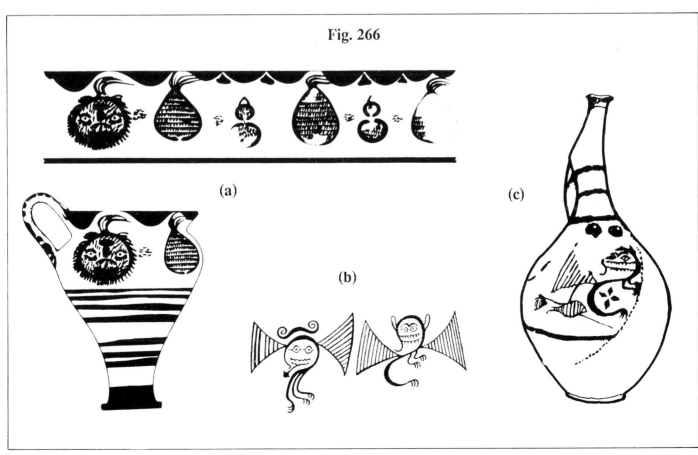

(a)

(b)

(c)

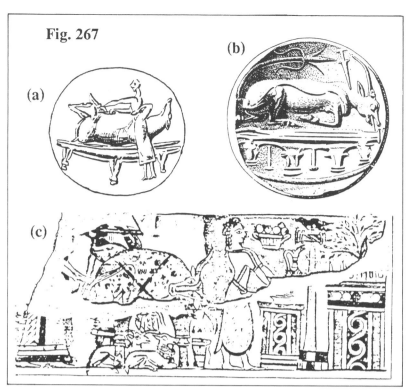

Fig. 267

(a)

(b)

(c)

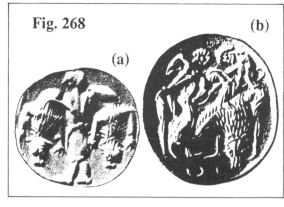

Fig. 268

(a)

(b)

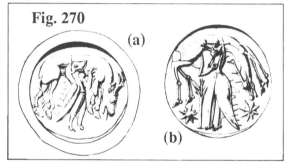

Fig. 270

(a)

(b)

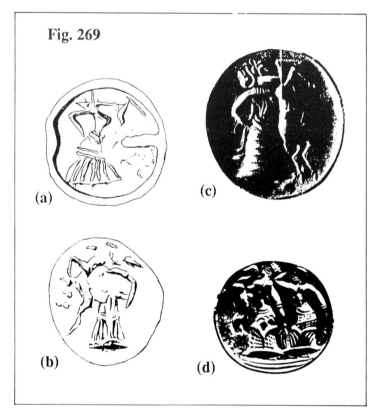

Fig. 269

(a)

(b)

(c)

(d)

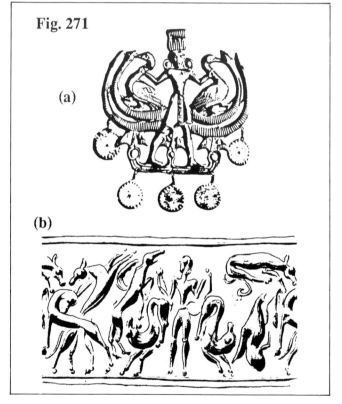

Fig. 271

(a)

(b)

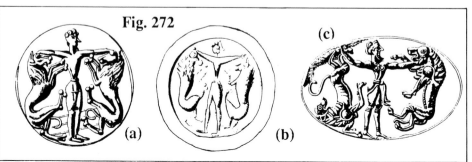

Fig. 272

(a)

(b)

(c)

Fig. 273

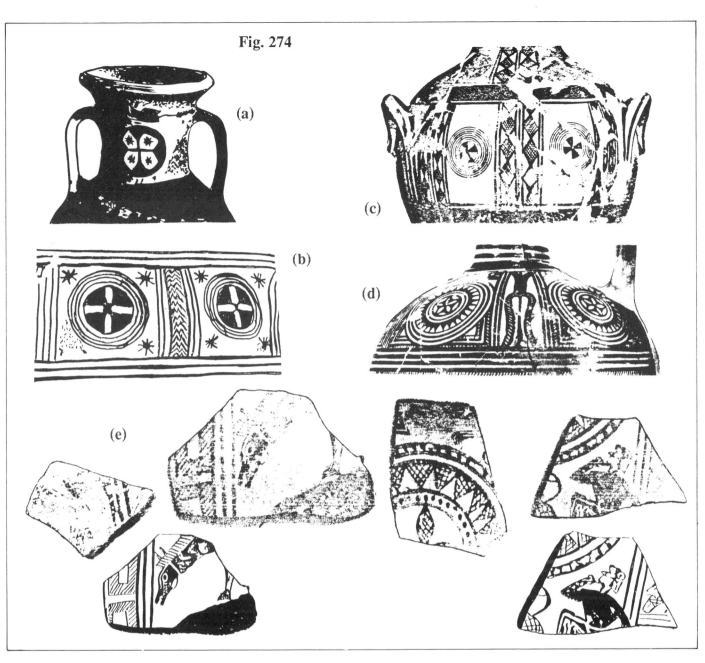

Fig. 274

(a)

(b)

(c)

(d)

(e)

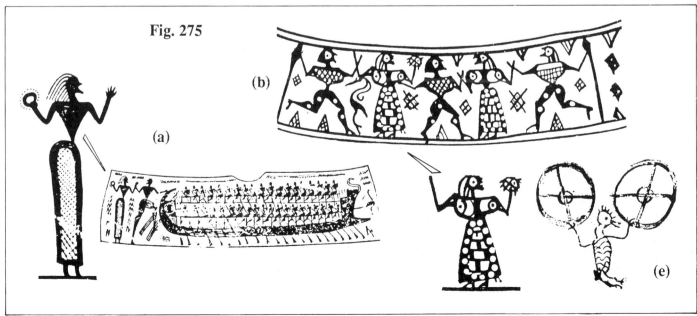

Fig. 275

(a)

(b)

(e)

Fig. 275

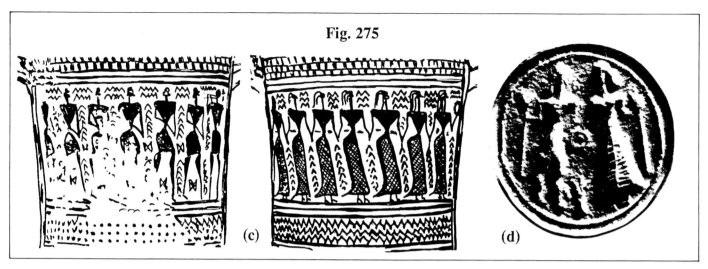

(c)

(d)

Fig. 276

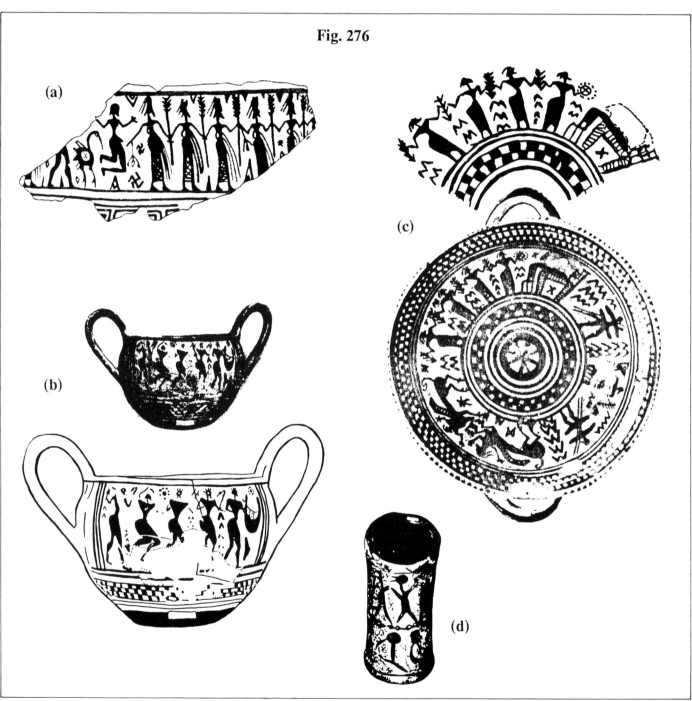

(a)

(b)

(c)

(d)

Fig. 277

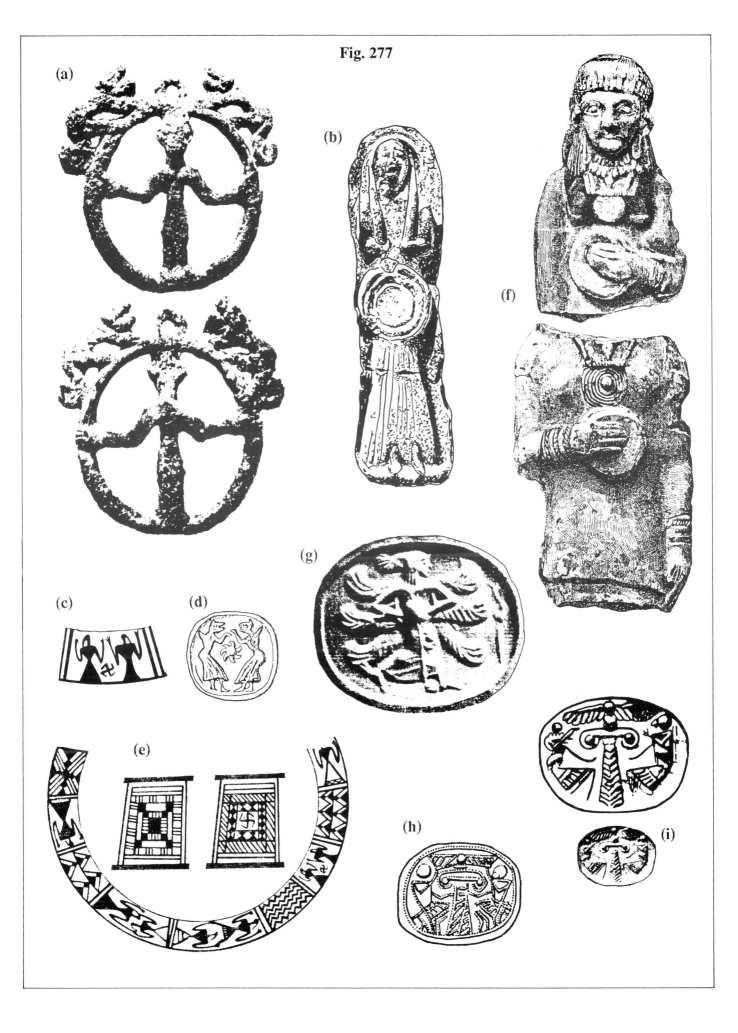

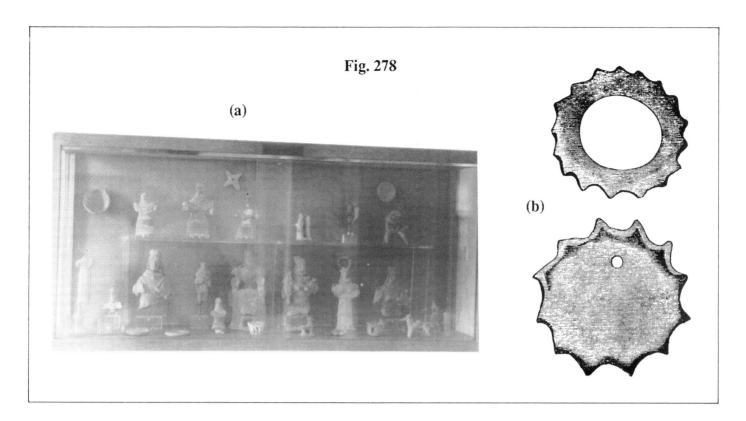

Fig. 278

(a)

(b)

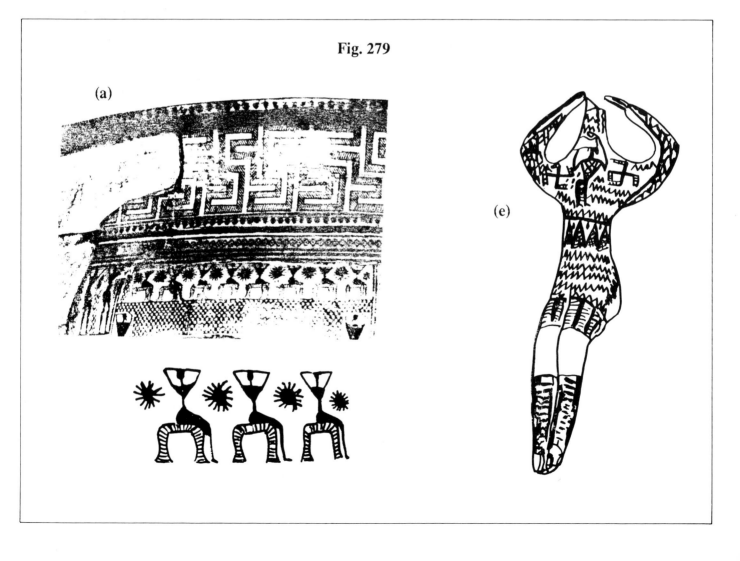

Fig. 279

(a)

(e)

Fig. 279

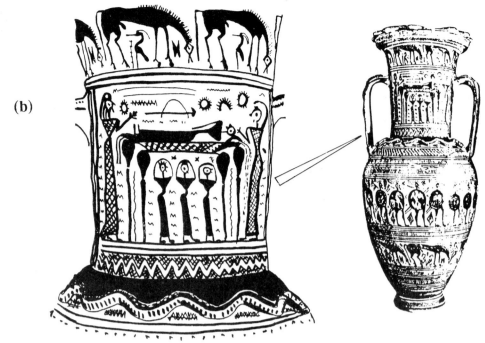

(b)

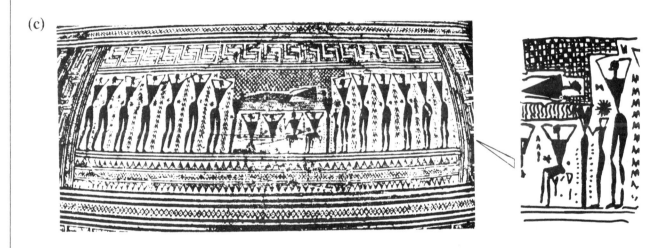

(c)

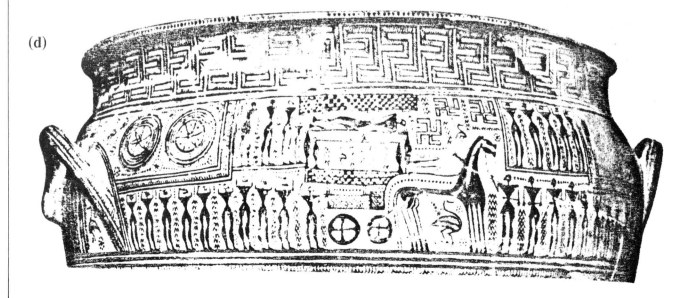

(d)

Fig. 279

(f)

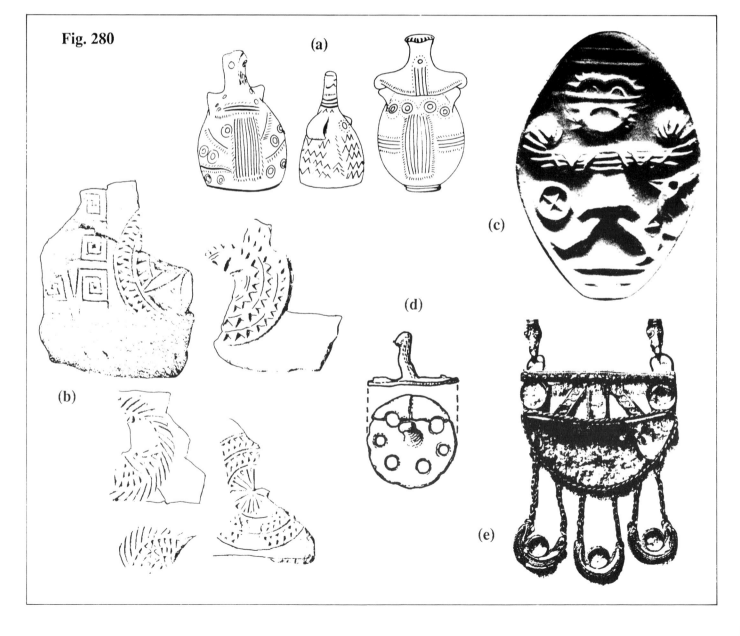

Fig. 280

(a)

(b)

(c)

(d)

(e)

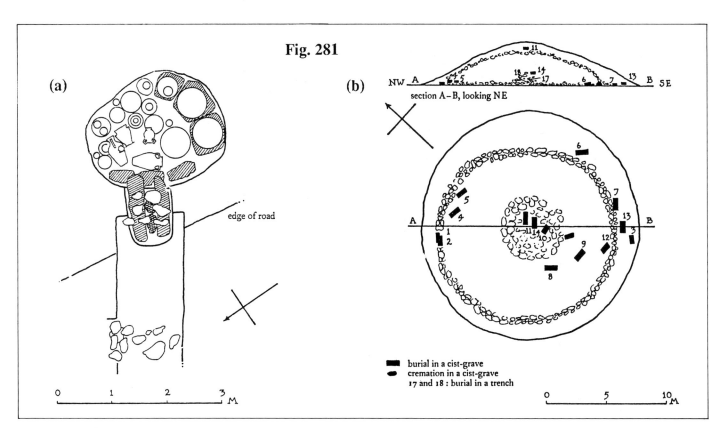

Fig. 281

(a)

(b)

edge of road

NW A ... B SE

section A–B, looking NE

■ burial in a cist-grave
● cremation in a cist-grave
17 and 18 : burial in a trench

0   1   2   3
M

0   5   10
M

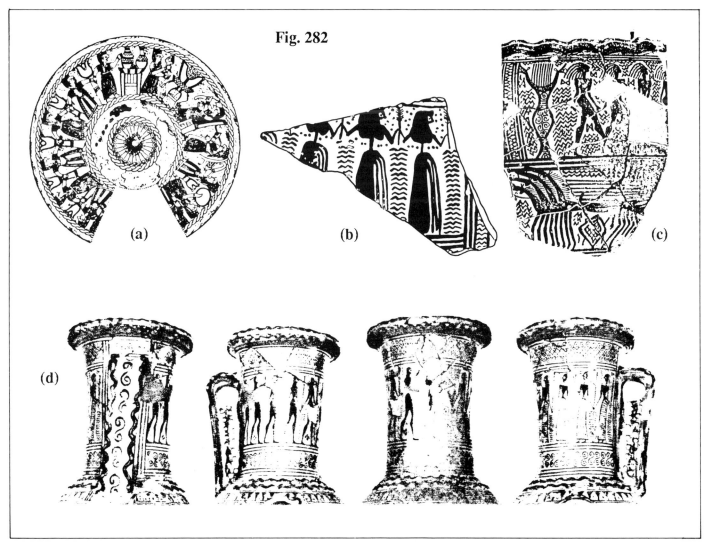

Fig. 282

(a)   (b)   (c)

(d)

Fig. 282

(e)

Fig. 283

(a)

(b)

(c)

(e)

(d)

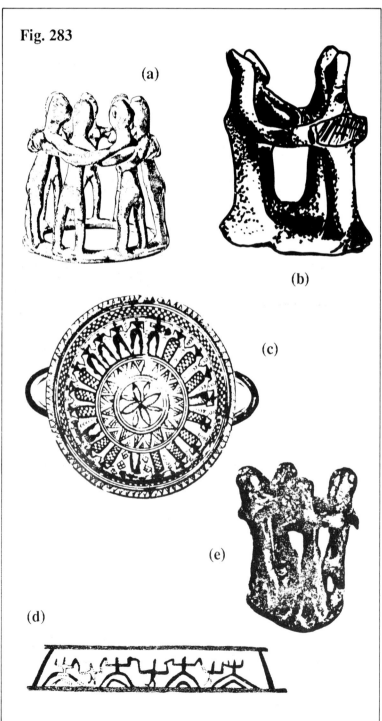

Fig. 284

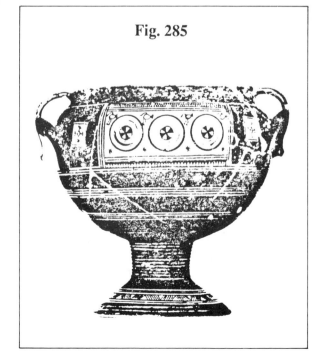

Fig. 285

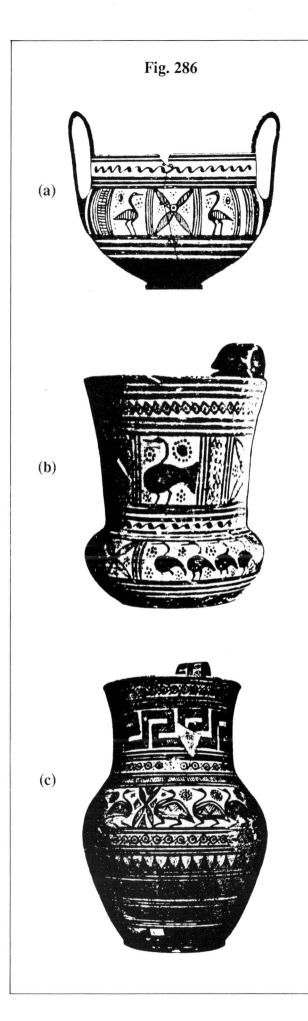

Fig. 286

(a)

(b)

(c)

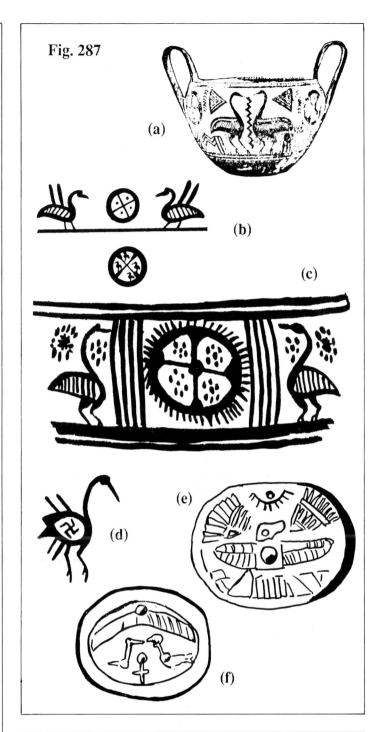

Fig. 287

(a)

(b)

(c)

(d)

(e)

(f)

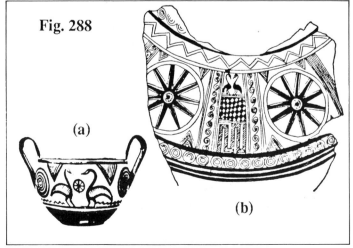

Fig. 288

(a)

(b)

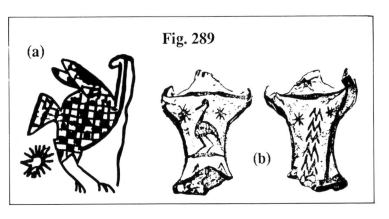

Fig. 289

(a)   (b)

Fig. 290

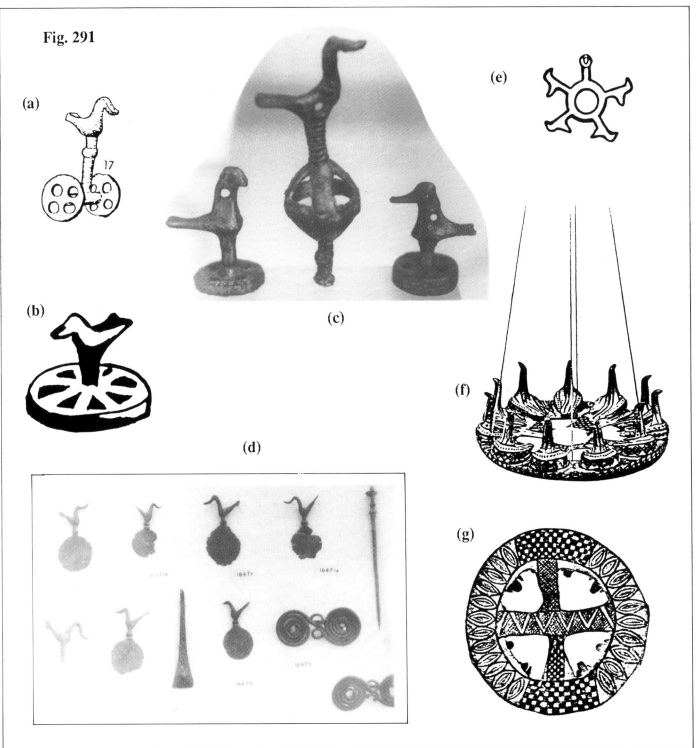

Fig. 291

(a)   (b)   (c)   (d)   (e)   (f)   (g)

Fig. 292

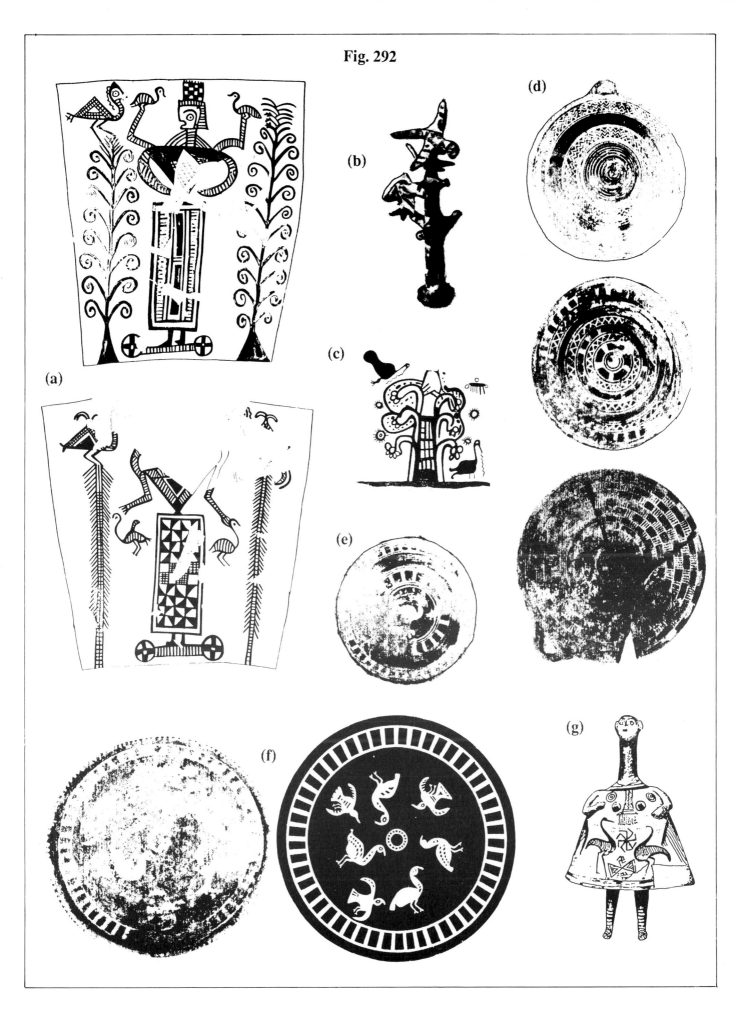

Fig. 293

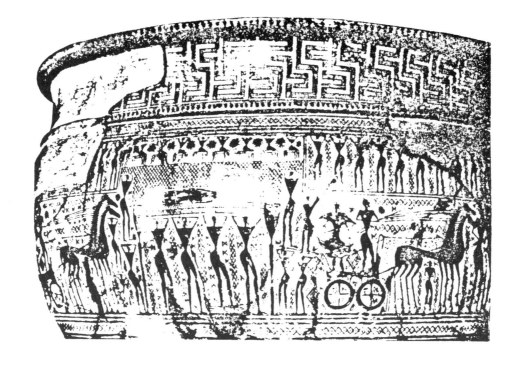

(a)

(b)

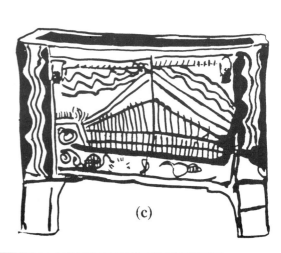

(c)

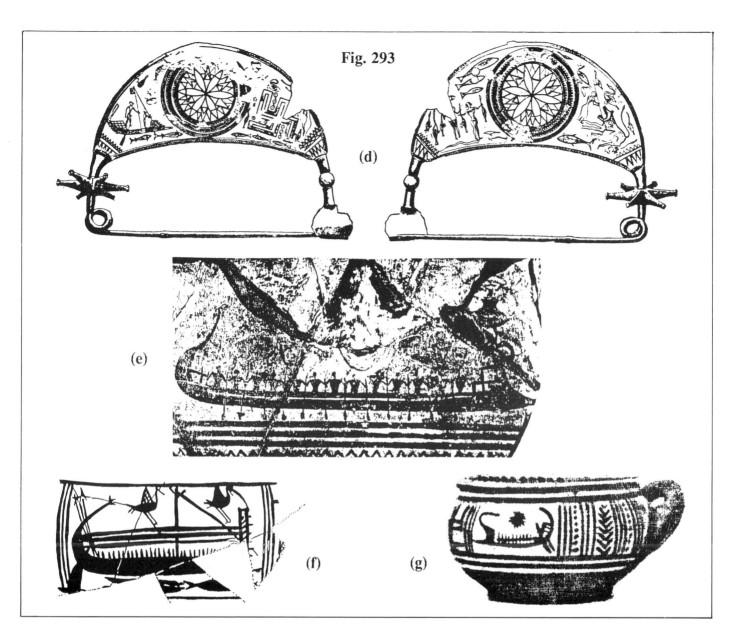

Fig. 293

(d)

(e)

(f)

(g)

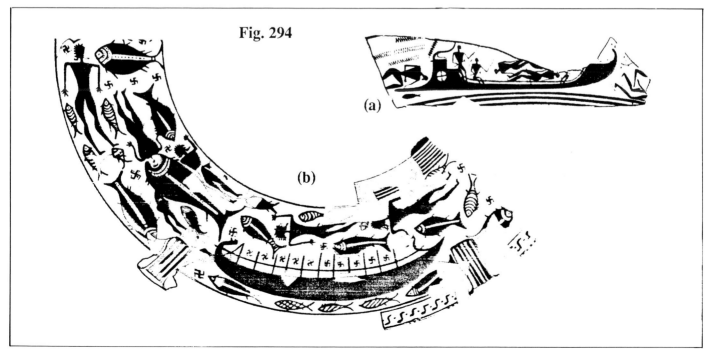

Fig. 294

(a)

(b)

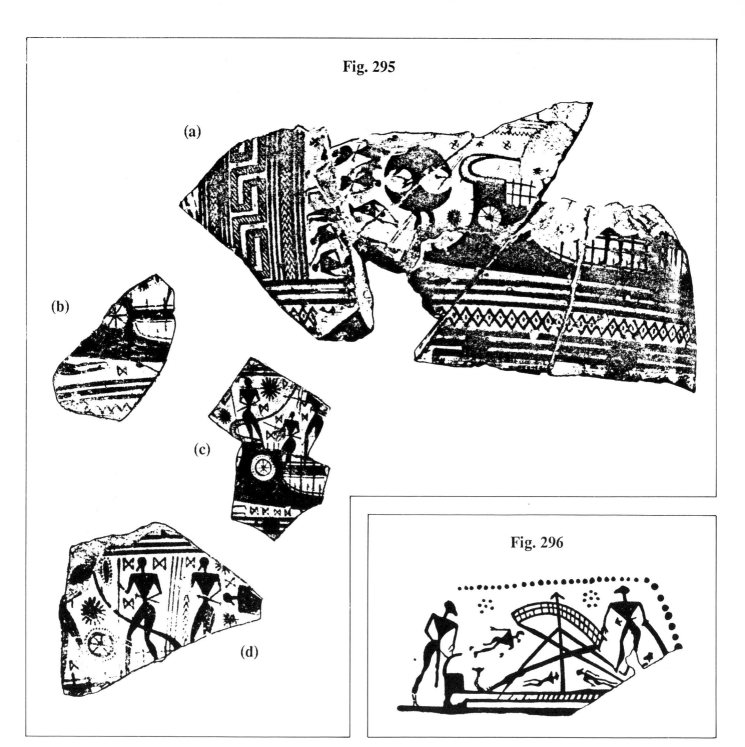

Fig. 295

(a)

(b)

(c)

(d)

Fig. 296

Fig. 297

(a)

(b)

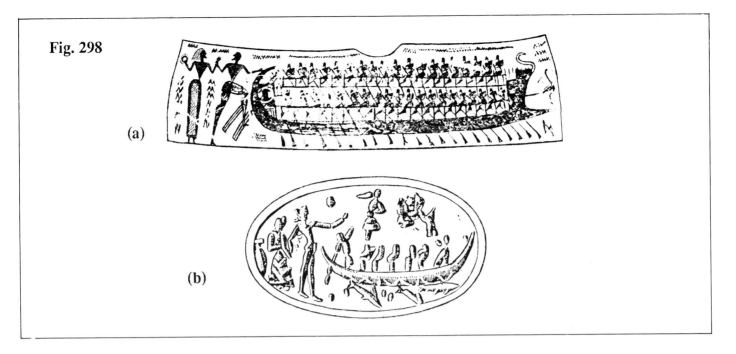

Fig. 298

(a)

(b)

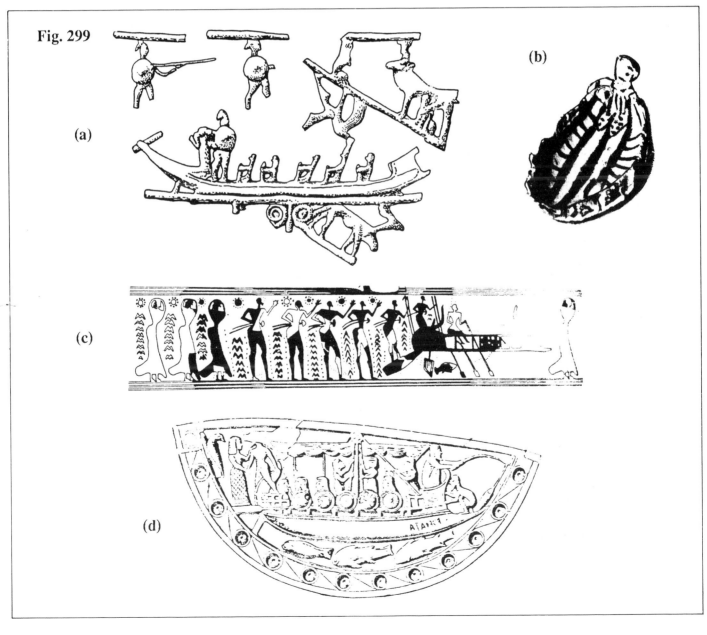

Fig. 299

(a)

(b)

(c)

(d)

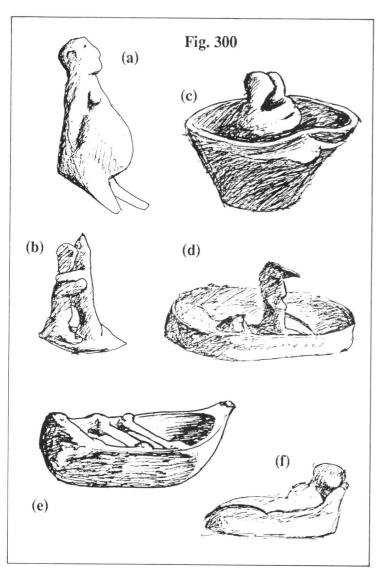

Fig. 300

(a)
(b)
(c)
(d)
(e)
(f)

Fig. 301

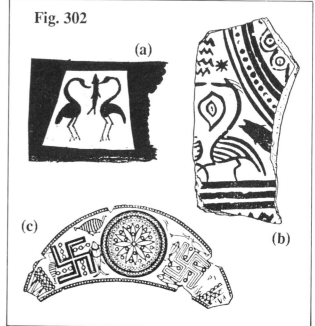

Fig. 302

(a)
(b)
(c)

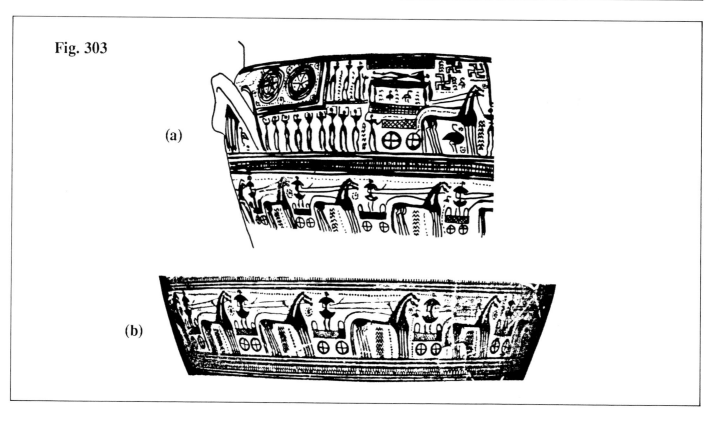

Fig. 303

(a)
(b)

Fig. 303

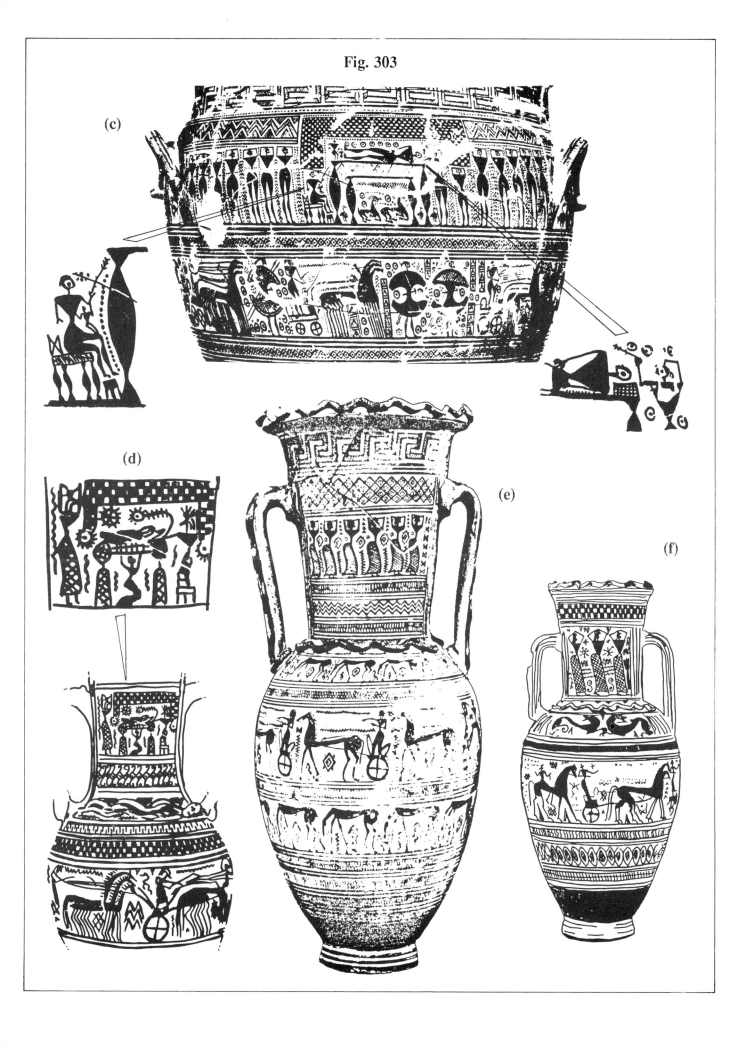

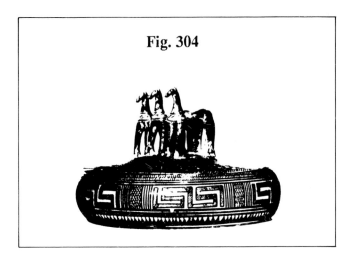

Fig. 304

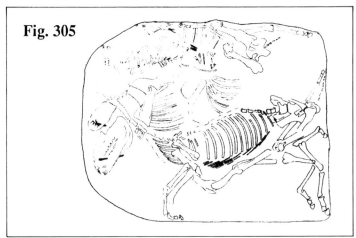

Fig. 305

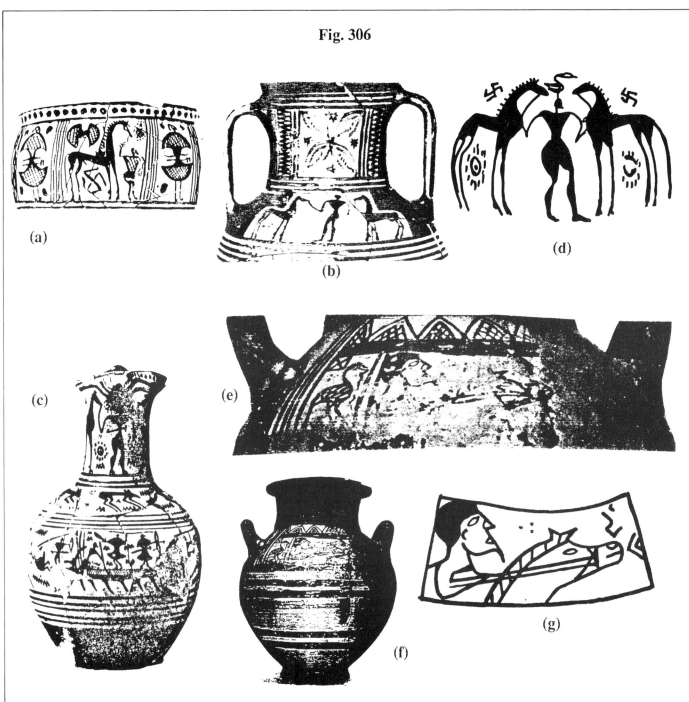

Fig. 306

(a)

(b)

(c)

(d)

(e)

(f)

(g)

Fig. 307

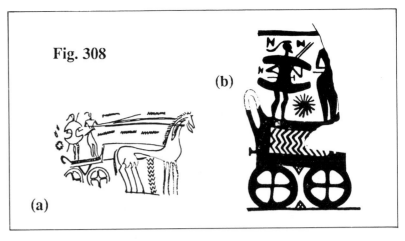

Fig. 308

(a)

(b)

Fig. 309

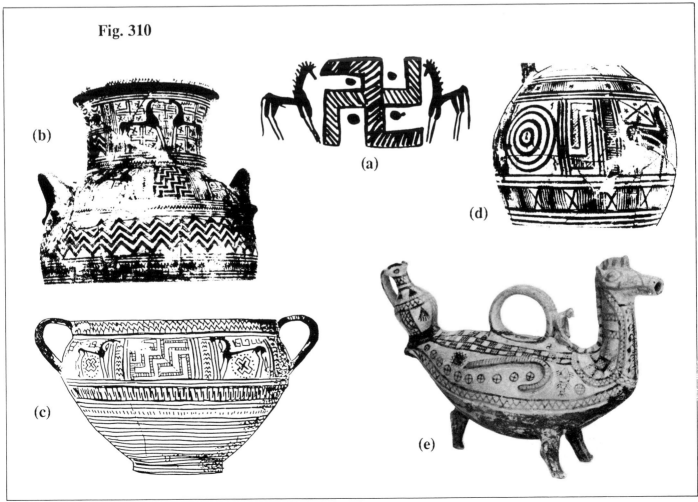

Fig. 310

(a)

(b)

(c)

(d)

(e)

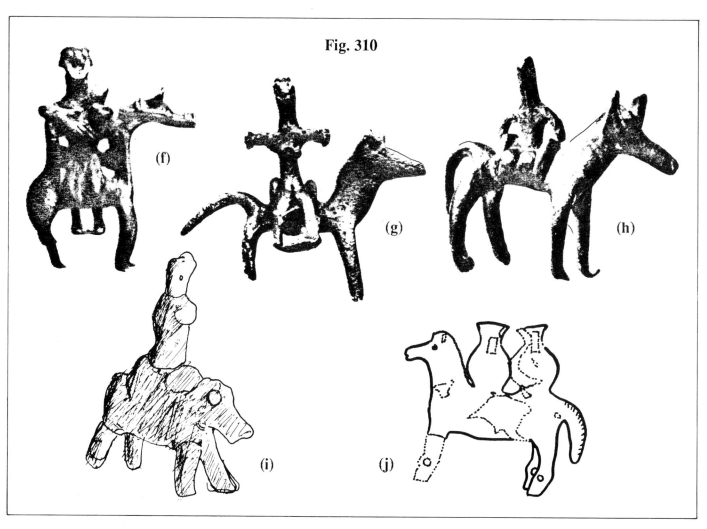

Fig. 310

(f)

(g)

(h)

(i)

(j)

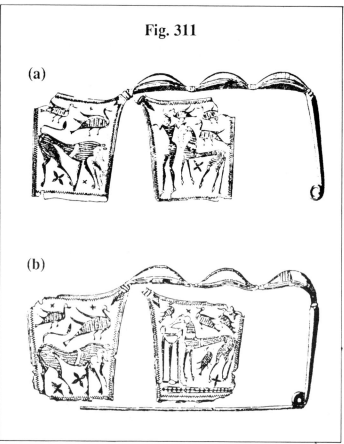

Fig. 311

(a)

(b)

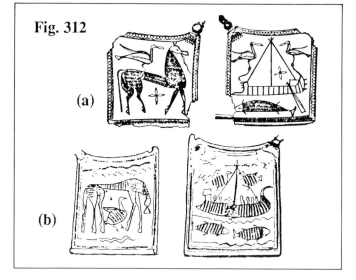

Fig. 312

(a)

(b)

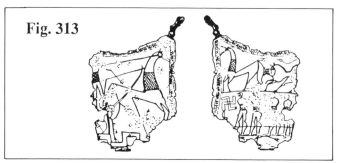

Fig. 313

Fig. 314

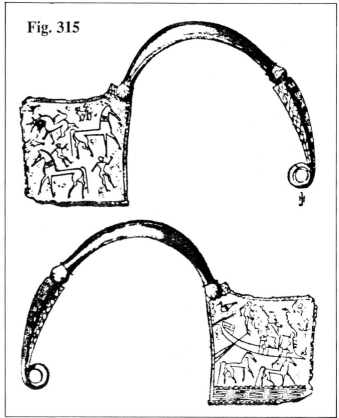

Fig. 315

Fig. 316

(a)

(b)

(c)

(d)

(e)

(f)

(g)

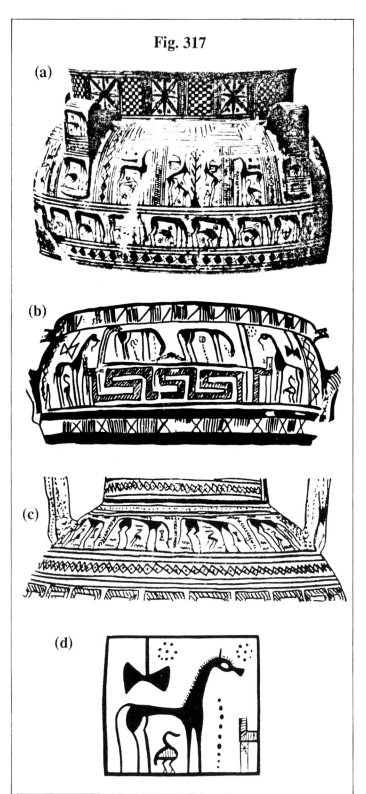

Fig. 317

(a)

(b)

(c)

(d)

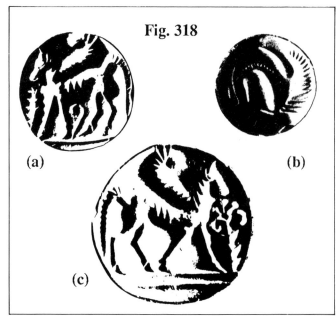

Fig. 318

(a)

(b)

(c)

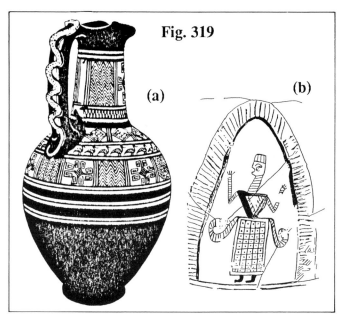

Fig. 319

(a)

(b)

Fig. 320

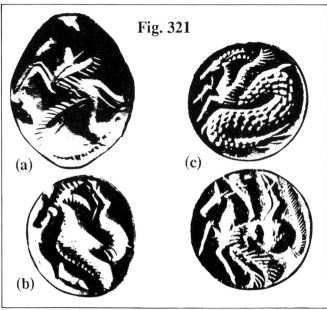

Fig. 321

(a)

(b)

(c)

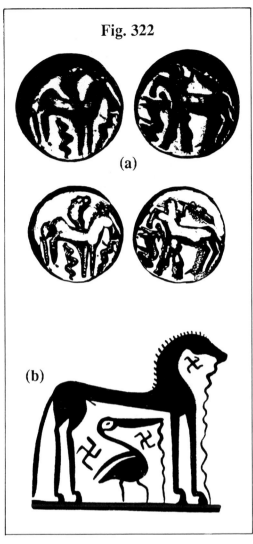

Fig. 322

(a)

(b)

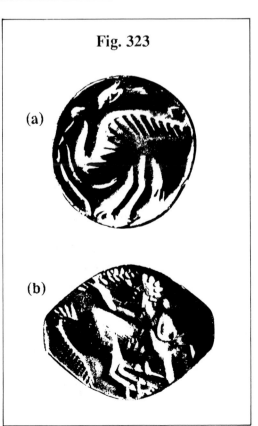

Fig. 323

(a)

(b)

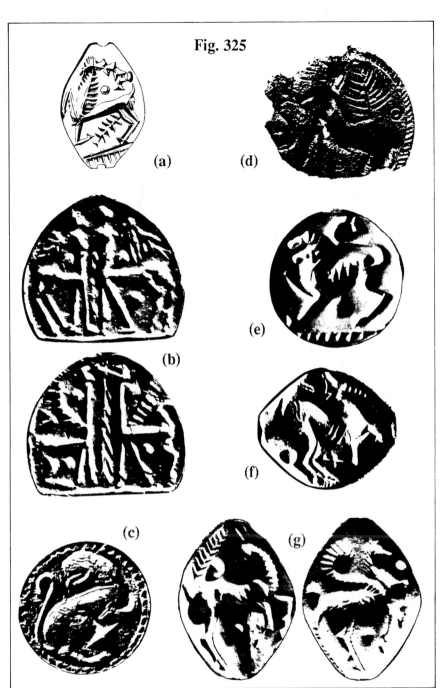

Fig. 325

(a)

(b)

(c)

(d)

(e)

(f)

(g)

Fig. 324

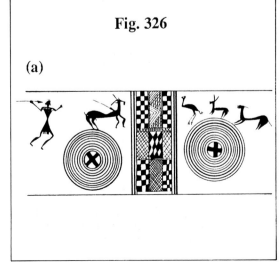

Fig. 326

(a)

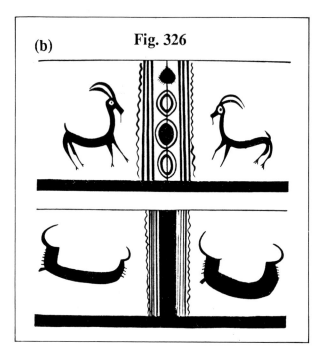

(b)

Fig. 326

Fig. 327

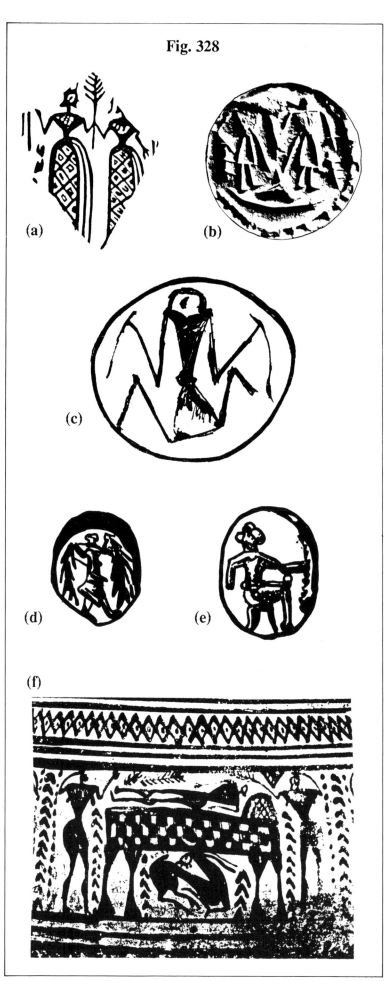

Fig. 328

(a)　(b)

(c)

(d)　(e)

(f)

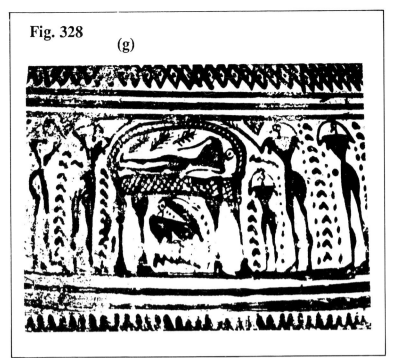

Fig. 328 (g)

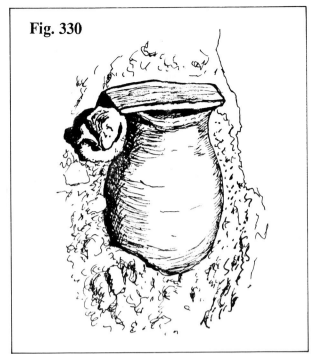

Fig. 330

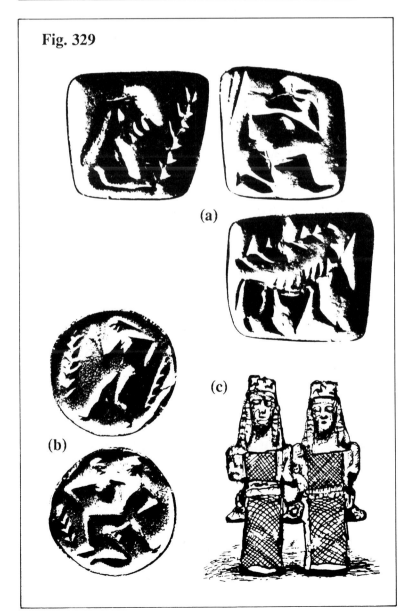

Fig. 329

(a)

(c)

(b)

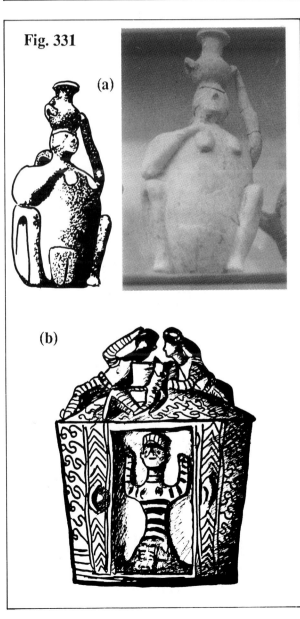

Fig. 331

(a)

(b)

Fig. 331

(c)

(d)

Fig. 332

(a)

(b)

(c)

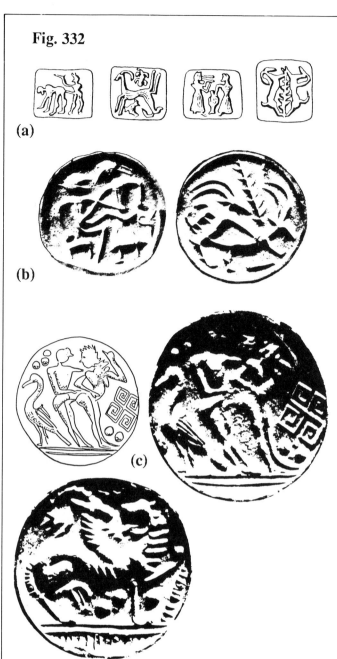

Fig. 333

(a)

(b)

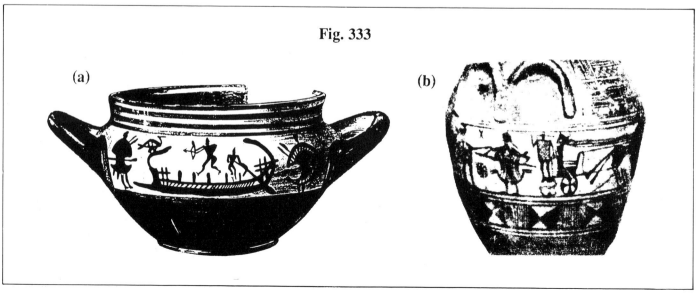

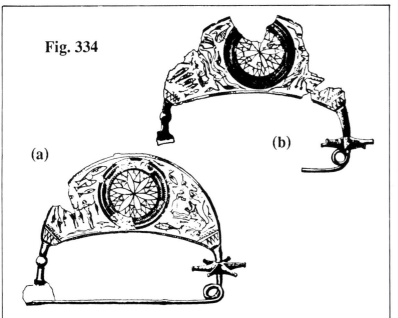

Fig. 334

(a)

(b)

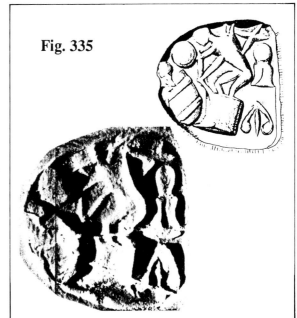

Fig. 335

Fig. 336

(a)

(b)

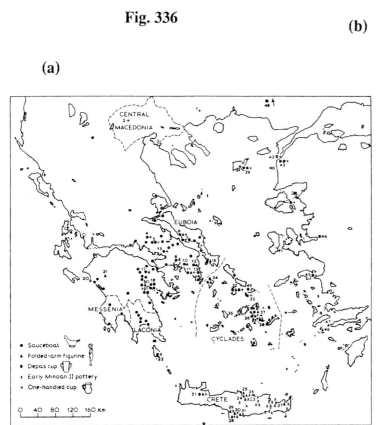

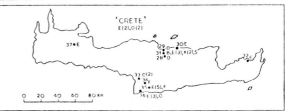

The international spirit of the Aegean Early Bronze 2 period. Findspots of certain types of wide distribution. (There are many additional finds, not indicated on the map, of Early Minoan II pottery in Crete, of folded-arm figurines in the Cyclades, and of *depas* cups elsewhere in Anatolia. The distribution of 'sauceboats' in mainland Greece, based on French 1968, is a simplified one.)

Findspots: 1, Sitagroi; 2, Vardarophtsa; 3, Kritsana; 4, Aghia Marina; 5, Orchomenos; 6, Manika; 7, Lefkandi; 8, Eleusis; 9, Piraeus; 10, Athens; 11, Aghios Kosmas; 12, Brauron; 13, Raphina; 14, Sounion; 15, Eutresis, 16, Styra; 17, Zygouries; 18, Tiryns; 19, Lerna; 20, Aghios Andreas; 21, Neraidha; 22, Kastri; 23, Knossos; 24, Teke; 25, Herakleion; 26, Pyrgos; 27, Siteia; 28, Lebena; 29, Aghios Onouphrios; 30, Platanos; 31, Koumasa; 32, Chalandriani; 33, Kynthos; 34, Aghia Irini; 35, Akrotiraki; 36, Spedos; 37, south-east Naxos, uncertain location; 38, Dhaskalio; 39. Poliochni; 40, Thermi; 41, Emborio; 42, Protesilaos; 43, Troy; 44, Bayrakli; 45, Heraion; 46, Karpathos; 47, Kap Krio; 48, Michailitch; 49, Dhiakophtis; 50, Argos; 51, Platyvola.

Finds of folded-arm figurines in the Cyclades and Crete. In each case the site number is followed by a letter or letters indicating the variety of the figurines and, when several were found, the number of examples.

The varieties are indicated as follows:

A, Kapsala; B, Dokathismata; C, Chalandriani; D, Kea; E, Koumasa; F, Spedos; S, Special variant (seated or double); O, unspecified; X, prehistoric copy.

(For findspots, see notes to figures.)

Fig. 336

(c)

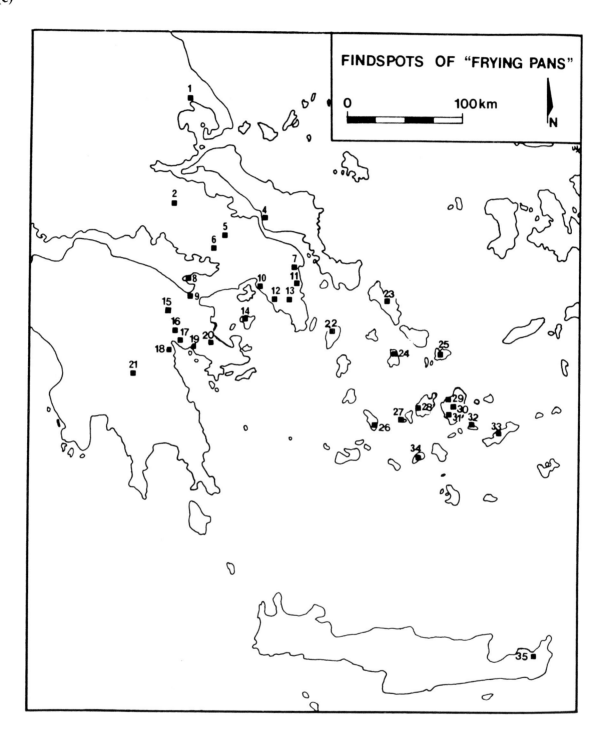

FINDSPOTS OF "FRYING PANS"

0   100km   N

Findspots of Early Bronze Age "frying pans" in the Aegean. Key: 1. Pefkakia; 2. Manesi; 4. Manika; 5. Lithares; 6. Eutresis; 7. Marathon; 8. Perachora; 9. Corinth; 10. Palaia Kokkinia; 11. Raphina; 12. Ayios Kosmas; 13. Markopoulo; 14. Aegina; 15. Nemea; 16. Berbati; 17. Tiryns; 18. Lerna; 19. Asine; 20. Epidauros; 21. Asea; 22. Keos, Ayia Irini; 23. Andros; 24. Syros, Chalandriani; 25. Mykonos; 26. Siphnos, Akrotiraki; 27. Despotikon; 28. Paros, Kampos; 29. Naxos, Grotta and Aplomata; 30. Naxos, Ayioi Anargyroi; 31. Naxos, Louros; 32. Ano Kouphonisi; 33. Amorgos, Kato Akroterion; 34. Sikinos; 35. Crete, Ayia Photia. Not shown: Alaca Hüyük.

Fig. 336

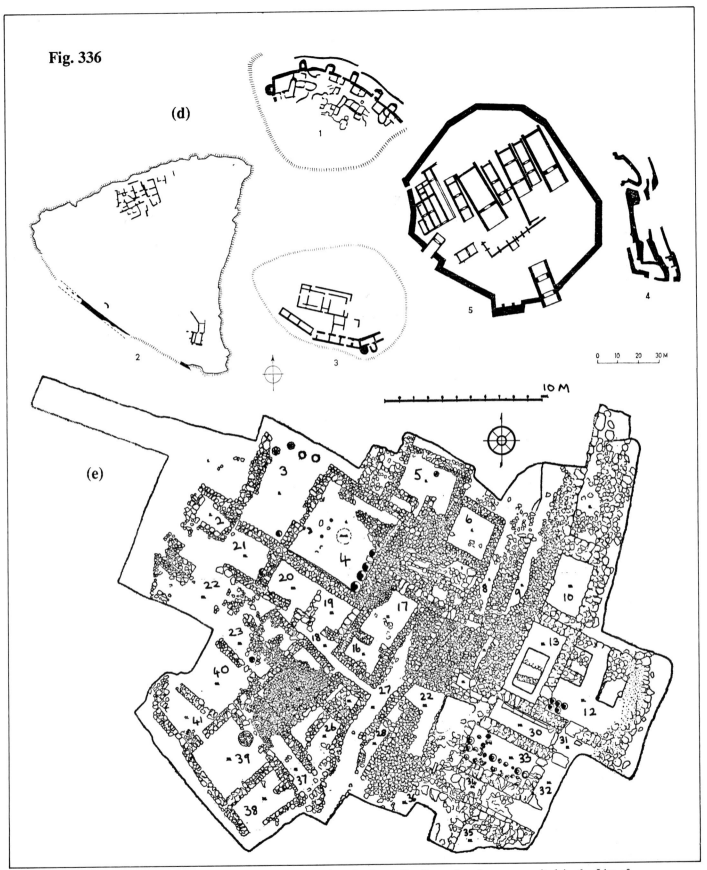

Please note: the following figures are now drawings by Lucy Goodison after the sources cited in the List of Illustrations (pp.229ff.): 1a, 15h, 46a, 57a, 66d, 78a, 95a, 100b, 109 a and b, 138e, 144, 155a, 160b (left), 167b, 168b, 178b, 231a, 249d, 253a, 274a, 291b, 292b, 297a, 299b.

PUBLICATIONS

BULLETIN NUMBER 34 (1987): ESSAYS ON GREEK DRAMA Ed. B. Gredley.
ISSN 0076-0730. £22.50.

BULLETIN NUMBER 35 (1988). ISSN 0076-0730. £25.

CULTS OF BOIOTIA, Fascicle 2 — Herakles to Poseidon By Albert Schachter (1986). Bulletin
Supplement Number 38. Fascicle 3 in preparation. Fascicles 1 and 4 available. SBN 900587 41 5.
1 £20, 2 £25, 4 £10.

RESOLUTIONS AND CHRONOLOGY IN EURIPIDES: the Fragmentary Tragedies
By Martin Cropp and Gordon Fick (1985). Bulletin Supplement Number 43. SBN 900587 46 6. £15.

THE PENDENT SEMI-CIRCLE SKYPHOS By Rosalinde Kearsley. Bulletin Supplement 44.
SBN 900587 58 X. £30.

PROLEGOMENA TO CLAUDIAN By J. B. Hall (1986). Bulletin Supplement Number 45.
SBN 900587 49 0. £30.

GREEK MANUSCRIPTS OF THE ANCIENT WORLD By E. G. Turner. Second edition
revised and enlarged, edited by P. J. Parsons (1987). Bulletin Supplement Number 46.
SBN 900587 48 2. £30.

GREEK BOOKHANDS OF THE EARLY BYZANTINE PERIOD: AD 300-800
By G. Cavallo and H. Maehler (1987). Bulletin Supplement Number 47. SBN 900587 51 2. £30.

SOPATROS THE RHETOR By Michael Winterbottom and Doreen Innes (1988).
Bulletin Supplement Number 48. SBN 900587 54 7. £30.

THE CREATIVE POET: Studies on the Treatment of Myths in Greek Poetry
By Jennifer R. March (1987). Bulletin Supplement Number 49. SBN 900587 52 0. £25.

**VIR BONUS DISCENDI PERITUS: Studies in Celebration of Otto Skutsch's Eightieth
Birthday** (1988). Bulletin Supplement Number 51. SBN 900587 55 5. £30.

ROMAN MYTH AND MYTHOGRAPHY By J. N. Bremmer and N. M. Horsfall (1987).
Bulletin Supplement Number 52. SBN 900587 53 9. £20.

DEATH, WOMEN AND THE SUN By Lucy Goodison (1989). Bulletin Supplement Number 53.
SBN 900587 56 3. £40.

GREEK AND LATIN PAPYROLOGY By Italo Gallo, translated by Maria Rosaria Falivene
and Jennifer R. March (1986). Bulletin Supplement Number 54, Classical Handbook 1.
SBN 900587 50 4. £9. (A5 format.)

**THE GREEK RENAISSANCE IN THE ROMAN EMPIRE: PAPERS FROM THE
TENTH BRITISH MUSEUM CLASSICAL COLLOQUIUM** Edited by Susan Walker
and Averil Cameron (1989). Bulletin Supplement 55. SBN 900587 59 8. £40.

PLUTARCH: *LIFE OF KIMON* Edited, with translation and commentary, by A. Blamire (1989).
Bulletin Supplement Number 56, Classical Handbook 2. SBN 900587 57 1. £10. (A5 format.)

THE HEROES OF ATTICA By Emily Kearns (1989). Bulletin Supplement Number 57.
SBN 900587 60 1. £30.

Forthcoming:

BULLETIN NUMBER 36 (1989). ISSN 0076-0730. £25.

MONUMENTS ILLUSTRATING NEW COMEDY Third edition. By A. Seeberg and J. R. Green.
Bulletin Supplement 50.

Full details of these and other Publications are available from:-
Institute of Classical Studies
31-34 Gordon Square
London WC1H 0PY

Редактор: Гэри Грот
Помощник редактора: Майкл Кетрон
Дизайнер обложки: Джейкоб Коуви
Макет: Тони Онг
Художник по цвету: Рич Томмасо
Производство: Пол Бэреш
Помощник издателя: Эрик Рейнолдс
Издатели: Гэри Грот и Ким Томпсон

Disney

Дональд Дак

Рождество в Беднотауне

Карл Баркс

УДК 821.111(73)-053.2
ББК 84(7Сое)-44
  Б25

Walt Disney's Donald Duck
"A Christmas For Shacktown"
Originally published in the English language by Fantagraphics Books
under the title Walt Disney's Donald Duck: "A Christmas For Shacktown"

Баркс, Карл.
Б25   Дональд Дак. Рождество в Беднотауне / Карл Баркс; пер. с англ. Ксении
Жолудевой. — Москва : Издательство АСТ, 2019. — 240 с. —
(Disney Comics. Утиные истории).

ISBN 978-5-17-112211-9

Утята Билли, Вилли и Дилли решают устроить настоящее Рождество для бедных детишек из городского района Беднотаун. Конечно, без помощи дядюшки Скруджа им не обойтись! Но самый богатый селезень в мире только что пережил трагедию: он потерял все свои деньги, каждый цент... Помимо классической рождественской истории Карла Баркса вас ждут новые невероятные приключения Дональда и племянников: путешествия по тропическим лесам, поиски легендарного артефакта – Золотого шлема, и битву умов со знаменитым Позолочённым Человеком. В одной из историй впервые появляется легендарное деньгохранилище Скруджа Макдака!

Перед вами новый сборник «Утиных историй» знаменитого художника Карла Баркса с дополнительными материалами и коллекцией оригинальных обложек!

ISBN 978-5-17-112211-9

УДК 821.111(73)-053.2
ББК 84(7Сое)-44

Содержание

Disney

Дональд Дак

"РОЖДЕСТВО В БЕДНОТАУНЕ"

ВЕЗДЕ ДЕТИ С НЕТЕРПЕНИЕМ ЖДУТ РОЖДЕСТВА, НО, ПОХОЖЕ, В БЕДНОТАУНЕ ЭТО БУДЕТ ВСЕГО ЛИШЬ ЕЩЁ ОДИН ОБЫЧНЫЙ ХОЛОДНЫЙ И ГОЛОДНЫЙ ДЕНЬ!

СДАЁТСЯ КОМНАТА

ЗРЯ МЫ ПОШЛИ ИЗ ШКОЛЫ ЭТИМ ПУТЁМ!

ДА УЖ! ТУТ ЧУВСТВУЕШЬ СЕБЯ ПЕРЕКОРМЛЕННЫМ ПОРОСЁНКОМ!

А МЕСТНЫЕ ДЕТИШКИ НА ТОЛСТЯЧКОВ ТОЧНО НЕ ТЯНУТ!

СПОРИМ, ОНИ НИКОГДА НЕ ЕЛИ КОНФЕТ, КЕКСОВ ИЛИ ДРУГИХ СЛАДОСТЕЙ!

СПОРИМ, ОНИ В ЖИЗНИ НЕ ПОЛУЧАЛИ НА РОЖДЕСТВО *ИГРУШКИ*, КАК ДРУГИЕ ДЕТИ!

ТОЧНО! И ЁЛОК ЗДЕСЬ НЕТ!

ЧТО Ж, НЕ ПОВЕЗЛО ИМ! НО У НАС ЕЩЁ СТОЛЬКО ХЛОПОТ С НАШИМ РОЖДЕСТВОМ!

ДА, ТОЛЬКО...

БЕДНЯЖКИ ИЗ БЕДНОТАУНА НИКОГДА НЕ ВОЛНОВАЛИСЬ, КАК ПРОЙДЁТ РОЖДЕСТВО! ЭТО-ТО МЕНЯ И БЕСПОКОИТ!

ТАК-ТАК! БИЛЛИ, ВИЛЛИ И ДИЛЛИ! ОГО! ЧТО ЗА **КИСЛЫЕ ЛИЦА**?

ВЫ ДОЛЖНЫ ЛУЧИТЬСЯ СЧАСТЬЕМ! СКОРО **РОЖДЕСТВО**, И ВАС ЖДЁТ МОРЕ КЕКСОВ, КОНФЕТ И ПРЕКРАСНЫХ **ИГРУШЕК**!

В ТОМ-ТО И БЕДА, ДЕЙЗИ!

МЫ ПОЛУЧИМ ГОРУ ПОДАРКОВ И ОТ ЭТОГО ЧУВСТВУЕМ СЕБЯ **ПЕРЕКОРМЛЕННЫМИ ПОРОСЯТАМИ**!

НО ПОЧЕМУ?

ТЕБЕ НАС НЕ ПОНЯТЬ!

МЫ ТОЛЬКО ЧТО ИЗ **БЕДНОТАУНА**!

!

О, ЭТО ЖУТКОЕ МЕСТО В ОВРАГЕ... ТАМ ЖИВУТ ТЕ, КОГО ЖИЗНЬ ЗАБРОСИЛА НА САМОЕ ДНО!

ДА, ДЕЙЗИ! ТАМ ДЕТИ, КОТОРЫМ НИКОГДА НЕ ВЕЗЛО!

К-КАЖЕТСЯ, ТЕПЕРЬ ПОНЯЛА!

ДАМЫ ИЗ МОЕГО КЛУБА ХОТЕЛИ **ЧЕМ-НИБУДЬ** ЗАНЯТЬСЯ! ХМ!

БЕГИТЕ ДОМОЙ, МАЛЬЧИКИ, И НЕ ВОЛНУЙТЕСЬ О МАЛЕНЬКИХ НЕСЧАСТНЫХ БЕДНОТАУНЦАХ! МЫ О НИХ **ПОЗАБОТИМСЯ**!

КАЖДЫЙ ГОД В КАНУН РОЖДЕСТВА У ДОНАЛЬДА ОДНА И ТА ЖЕ ГОЛОВНАЯ БОЛЬ!

КАК МНЕ КУПИТЬ МАЛЬЧИКАМ ПОДАРКИ, ЕСЛИ НА СЧЕТУ ВСЕГО **ПЯТЬ** ДОЛЛАРОВ?

ЖАЛОВАНЬЯ ДО **СЛЕДУЮЩЕГО ГОДА** НЕ ЖДИ! И НИКТО НЕ ОДОЛЖИТ МНЕ НИ ЦЕНТА!

А ВЕДЬ СТОЛЬКО ВСЕГО НАДО КУПИТЬ: КОНФЕТЫ, ОРЕШКИ, ПЕЧЕНЬЕ!

И ХУЖЕ ВСЕГО, ЧТО МАЛЬЧИКИ СОБИРАЮТСЯ ПОТРАТИТЬ ПЯТЬ ДОЛЛАРОВ НА ПОДАРОК **МНЕ**! ЧУВСТВУЮ СЕБЯ **НИКЧЁМНЫМ**!

ХОТЕЛ БЫ Я ВСТРЕТИТЬ ТОГО, У КОГО **БОЛЬШЕ** ПРОБЛЕМ НА РОЖДЕСТВО!

ТУК! ТУК!

ДОНАЛЬД, Я ПРИШЛА ЗА ПОМОЩЬЮ! ТЕБЕ ВЕДЬ НА РОЖДЕСТВО НЕ О ЧЕМ ВОЛНОВАТЬСЯ?

ЭТО УЖ **ТОЧНО**!

А МОЙ КЛУБ ДОЛЖЕН СОБРАТЬ **ПЯТЬДЕСЯТ ДОЛЛАРОВ**!

ТЕБЕ ВЫДАТЬ ЦЕНТАМИ, ПЯТИЦЕНТОВИКАМИ ИЛИ ОЖЕРЕЛЬЯМИ ИЗ РАКУШЕК?

О, Я НЕ ПРОШУ **ТЕБЯ** ДАТЬ МНЕ **ВСЮ** СУММУ!

ОБИДИШЬ, ЕСЛИ НЕ ВОЗЬМЁШЬ!

Я УГОВОРИЛА ДЕВОЧЕК УСТРОИТЬ РОЖДЕСТВЕНСКИЙ УЖИН ДЛЯ ДЕТЕЙ БЕДНОТАУНА!

ВСЕ БЫЛИ ОЧЕНЬ ЩЕДРЫ, НЕ ХВАТАЕТ КАКИХ-ТО ПЯТИДЕСЯТИ ДОЛЛАРОВ!

И ТУТ ТЫ ВСПОМНИЛА БОГАТОГО И ПРОЦВЕТАЮЩЕГО **МЕНЯ**!

НЕТ, НЕТ! НО НАДЕЯЛАСЬ, ЧТО ТЫ ЗНАЕШЬ **КОГО-ТО ПОДХОДЯЩЕГО**!

ДЯДЯ ДОНАЛЬД!

ПОЧЕМУ БЫ НЕ ПОПРОСИТЬ ДЕНЕГ У ДЯДИ СКРУДЖА?

ОН ЖЕ САМЫЙ БОГАТЫЙ СЕЛЕЗЕНЬ В МИРЕ!

И МОЖЕТ ДАТЬ ПОЛСОТНИ НА **БЛАГОЕ ДЕЛО**!

ПОЛСОТНИ ТУМАКОВ ДАСТ, ЭТО ТОЧНО! Я ЕГО ЗНАЮ!

ДОНАЛЬД, СХОДИ К НЕМУ! СКАЖИ, ЧТО МЫ ПОТРАТИМ ДВАДЦАТЬ ПЯТЬ ДОЛЛАРОВ НА ИНДЮШЕК И ДВАДЦАТЬ ПЯТЬ — НА ИГРУШЕЧНЫЙ ПОЕЗД!

ИГРУШЕЧНЫЙ ПОЕЗД!

УВЕРЕН, НА ПОЕЗД ОН НЕ СОГЛАСИТСЯ!

ДОЛЖЕН СОГЛАСИТЬСЯ! МЫ УЖЕ **ПООБЕЩАЛИ** ДЕТЯМ, ЧТО КУПИМ!

У НЕСЧАСТНЫХ ДЕТОК БЕДНОТАУНА **НИКОГДА** НЕ БЫЛО ИГРУШЕК! ПОНИМАЕШЬ?

Я-ТО ПОНИМАЮ, А ДЯДЯ СКРУДЖ ВРЯД ЛИ!

ДЯДЯ ДОНАЛЬД, **ОДИН** ИГРУШЕЧНЫЙ ПОЕЗД — ПУСТЯК ДАЖЕ ДЛЯ СТАРОГО СКРЯГИ ВРОДЕ ДЯДЮШКИ СКРУДЖА!

ЛАДНО! СХОЖУ!

РАНЬШЕ Я ДУМАЛ, ЧТО ДЕЛА ПЛОХИ! НО ТЕПЕРЬ ПО-НАСТОЯЩЕМУ ВЛИП!

ПРОДАЁТСЯ 10,000 ПОДЕРЖАННЫХ НЕФТЯНЫХ ВЫШЕК СПРОСИТЬ СКРУДЖА МАКДАКА

ХОП СИНГ «ТРАВЫ И КОР...»

У ДЯДИ СКРУДЖА СВОИ ЗАБОТЫ!

СИЛ МОИХ НЕТ! В СЫРУЮ ПОГОДУ БАНКНОТЫ ТАК РАЗБУХАЮТ! ПРИДЁТСЯ ПОДНЯТЬ КРЫШУ ЕЩЁ НА ДВА МЕТРА!

ДЕНЬГО-ХРАНИЛИЩЕ НЕ ВХОДИТЬ

С ТРЕМЯ КУБИЧЕСКИМИ АКРАМИ ДЕНЕГ СТОЛЬКО ПРОБЛЕМ! ИХ СОДЕРЖАНИЕ ВЛЕТАЕТ МНЕ В КОПЕЕЧКУ!

ТУК! ТУК!

КОГО ТАМ ПРИНЕСЛО? ОЧЕРЕДНОГО ПОПРОШАЙКУ ЗА РОЖДЕСТВЕНСКИМИ ДАРАМИ?

ВОЙДИТЕ!

А, ЭТО **ТЫ**! Я ЧУТЬ БЫЛО НЕ ПОТРАТИЛ ЯДРО ЗРЯ!

ГЛЫК! ОН НЕ В ДУХЕ! ГОТОВ МЕТАТЬ ГРОМЫ И МОЛНИИ!

ИГРУШЕЧНЫЙ ПОЕЗД! ДУРАЦКИЙ, **БЕСПОЛЕЗНЫЙ** ИГРУШЕЧНЫЙ ПОЕЗД!

ДЕТЯМ ТАК НЕ КАЖЕТСЯ!

ПОСЛУШАЙ, ПЛЕМЯННИЧЕК! Я ДАМ ДВАДЦАТЬ ПЯТЬ ДОЛЛАРОВ НА ИНДЮШЕК, И ТОЧКА!

МАЛО ТОГО! Я ДАМ ИХ, ТОЛЬКО ЕСЛИ ТЫ САМ ДОСТАНЕШЬ ЕЩЁ ДВАДЦАТЬ ПЯТЬ!

КОГДА НАЙДЁШЬ ДЕНЬГИ НА ПОЕЗД, **ПОКАЖИ** ИХ МНЕ, И ПОЛУЧИШЬ ЧЕТВЕРТЬ СОТНИ НА ИНДЮШЕК!

ПОЖАРНЫЙ ВЫХОД ←

ХЛЮП!

СКРУДЖ МАКДАК, САМЫЙ БОГАТЫЙ **СЕЛЕЗЕНЬ** В МИРЕ

И СОБИРАЕТСЯ ТАКОВЫМ ОСТАТЬСЯ!

ВОТ ДЕЛА!

КАК ТЕПЕРЬ БЫТЬ?

МЫ НЕ МОЖЕМ ПОДВЕСТИ БЕДНЫХ ДЕТЕЙ!

ПРИДЁТСЯ ВСЁ ЖЕ СОБРАТЬ ДЕНЬГИ!

ТОЧНО!

НАЧНЁМ ПРЯМО СЕЙЧАС!

С СЕБЯ!

ДЯДЯ ДОНАЛЬД, СКОЛЬКО ТЫ СОБИРАЛСЯ ПОТРАТИТЬ НА ПОДАРКИ ДЛЯ НАС?

ПЯТЬ ДОЛЛАРОВ... (ГЛЫК!)

ОТДАЙ ИХ ДЕЙЗИ!

И НАМ ОСТАЁТСЯ СОБРАТЬ...

...ЕЩЁ ДВАДЦАТЬ!

А ВОТ ПЯТЬ ДОЛЛАРОВ, ЧТО ШЛИ НА ПОДАРОК ДЛЯ ДЯДИ ДОНАЛЬДА! ОСТАЁТСЯ ПЯТНАДЦАТЬ!

ТЕПЕРЬ МЫ СОБЕРЁМ ЮНЫХ СУРКОВ И ПОЙДЁМ ЧИСТИТЬ ДОРОЖКИ ОТ СНЕГА! ТАК МЫ ЗАРАБОТАЕМ ЕЩЁ ПЯТЁРКУ!

ЕСЛИ МАЛЬЧИКИ ТАК СТАРАЮТСЯ, Я ПРОДАМ СВОЁ ВЯЗАНИЕ И ВЫРУЧУ ЕЩЁ ПЯТЬ ДОЛЛАРОВ!

ОЙ, ДА Я ТУТ ОДИН ОСТАЛСЯ!

ЧТО Ж, ПРОЩАЙ РОЖДЕСТВО И ДЛЯ МЕНЯ, И ДЛЯ МАЛЬЧИКОВ, И ДЛЯ ДЕЙЗИ!

НАДЕЮСЬ, ЭТИ ЧУМАЗЯТА ИЗ БЕДНОТАУНА ПОРАДУЮТСЯ ИГРУШЕЧНОМУ ПОЕЗДУ, КОТОРЫЙ ТАК ДОРОГО НАМ ДОСТАЛСЯ!

ПОХОЖЕ, ОСТАВШАЯСЯ ПЯТЁРКА НА МНЕ!

МИСТЕР, ВЫ НЕ ПОЖЕРТВУЕТЕ НА РОЖДЕСТВЕНСКИЙ УЖИН ДЛЯ БЕДНЫХ ДЕТЕЙ?

КОНЕЧНО! СКОЛЬКО ДЕТЕЙ ВАМ НУЖНО?

ПОДТЯЖКИ

5 НА 10

БЛЕСТЯЩИЙ ОТВЕТ, КАК НИ КРУТИ!

МИСТЕР, ВЫ НЕ ПОЖЕРТВУЕТЕ...

МИСТЕР, ВЫ НЕ ПОЖЕРТВУЕТЕ НА РОЖДЕСТВЕНСКИЙ УЖИН ДЛЯ КОВБОЕВ, КОТОРЫЕ НЕ УМЕЮТ ПЕТЬ ЙОДЛЕМ?

СОШЛИСЬ НА НИЧЬЕЙ!

ПРОДАЕТ... 300 ПОДЕРЖАННЫХ ЗОЛОТЫХ ШАХТ ОТЛИЧНЫЕ ТУННЕЛИ СПРОСИТЬ СКРУДЖА МАКДАКА

МИСТЕР, ВЫ ПОЖЕРТВУЕТЕ НА РОЖДЕСТВЕНСКИЙ УЖИН ДЛЯ БЕДНЫХ ДЕТЕЙ!

ПРИЯТЕЛЬ, Я БЫ С РАДОСТЬЮ! НО ИДУ ВОЗВРАЩАТЬ ДОЛГ СКРУДЖУ МАКДАКУ!

СНОГСШИБАТЕЛЬНЫЙ АРГУМЕНТ!

Я зря трачу время, ведь все деньги в руках дяди Скруджа!

Должен же быть способ получить от него лишнюю пятёрку! Может, его **РАЗЖАЛОБИТЬ** или **ЗАПУГАТЬ**? Попробую!

Придумал! Заставлю его прослезиться! Где наш семейный альбом?

Вот то, что надо! Фотография старого Джейка Макдака, родного дядюшки самого Скруджа!

С этой бородой я точь-в-точь, как он!

Поведаю дядюшке Скруджу жалостную историю, и его сердце растает!

ТУК! ТУК!

ВОЙДИТЕ!

А ТЫ ЕЩЁ КТО ТАКОЙ?

ТВОЙ СТА-АР-РЫЙ **БЕ-ЕДНЫЙ** ДЯДЮШКА ДЖЕЙК, ПЛЕМЯННИЧЕК СКРУДЖИ! НЕ ПОМНИШШЬ МЕНЯ?

КОНЕЧНО, **ПОМНЮ! ДОРОГОЙ** СТАРЫЙ ДЯДЮШКА ДЖЕЙК ИЗ ШОТЛАНДИИ! ТЫ КАЧАЛ МЕНЯ НА КОЛЕНКЕ, КОГДА Я БЫЛ МАЛЕНЬКИМ!

И ОДОЛЖИЛ ШИЛЛИНГ **ШЕСТЬДЕСЯТ ЛЕТ** НАЗАД, ЗЛОСТНЫЙ НЕПЛАТЕЛЬЩИК!

ТАК, С УЧЁТОМ ПРОЦЕНТОВ И ТЕКУЩЕГО КУРСА ТЫ ДОЛЖЕН МНЕ...

...ВОСЕМЬ ТЫСЯЧ ТРИСТА ДВАДЦАТЬ ШЕСТЬ ДОЛЛАРОВ! ПЛАТИ НЕМЕДЛЯ!

НЕ ВЫШЛО РАСТРОГАТЬ, ТАК НАПУГАЮ ДО ИКОТЫ!

СТОИЛО ПОЛУЧШЕ ИЗУЧИТЬ ПРОШЛОЕ ДЯДЮШКИ ДЖЕЙКА!

СОХРАНИ СВОЙ ГОРОД В ЧИСТОТЕ

ДУМАЙ! ДУМАЙ! ЧТО ЕМУ СТРАШНЕЕ ВСЕГО? ПРИВИДЕНИЯ? ВЗЛОМЩИКИ? ТЕРМИТЫ?

ПРИДУМАЛ! ПРОЩЕ ЧЕМ ЗАБРАТЬ ШПИНАТ У МЛАДЕНЦА!

ДЗЫНЬ!

РОЖДЕСТВЕНСКИЙ ПРАЗДНИК ДЛЯ РЕБЯТ ИЗ БЕДНОТАУНА НАЧНЁТСЯ ПО РАСПИСАНИЮ!

DОНАЛЬD

МНЕ ПОНАДОБИТСЯ РУЧНАЯ **КРЫСА** МАЛЬЧИКОВ!

НАКОНЕЦ-ТО Я ЗАТОЛКАЛ ВСЕ ДЕНЬГИ ОБРАТНО... ИК! ТЕПЕРЬ КОГО ПРИНЕСЛО?

ТУК! ТУК!

ВОЙДИТЕ!

ОПЯТЬ ТЫ!

ДА! НА УЛИЦЕ ТАК ХОЛОДНО, ЧТО Я ПРИШЁЛ СПРОСИТЬ, НЕ МОГУ ЛИ Я ПОРАБОТАТЬ НА ТЕБЯ... **ВНУТРИ?**

ВНУТРИ? МНЕ НЕ НУЖНЫ **ПРОБЛЕМЫ В ДОМЕ!**

ЭХ ТЫ, ДЯДЯ СКРУДЖ!

КРЫСА! ВИЖУ **КРЫСУ!**

КРЫСА! ООО, ОНА СЪЕСТ БАНКНОТ НА МИЛЛИОН ДОЛЛАРОВ!

А НУ ИДИ СЮДА, ЗУБАСТАЯ ОБЖОРА!

ПОМОГИ ПОЙМАТЬ ЕЁ ДО ТОГО, КАК ОНА СЛОПАЕТ ВСЕ МОИ ДЕНЬГИ! ДАЮ ДЕСЯТЬ ЦЕНТОВ!

НЕ ПРИТРОНУСЬ К ЭТОМУ ОПАСНОМУ ЗВЕРЮ МЕНЬШЕ ЧЕМ ЗА ПЯТЬ ДОЛЛАРОВ!

НУ, ХОРОШО, ХОРОШО! ДАМ ТЕБЕ ПЯТЁРКУ... ТОЛЬКО ИЗЛОВИ КРЫСУ!

КРЫСИК, КРЫСИК, ИДИ СЮДА! СМОТРИ, КАКОЕ СОВПАДЕНИЕ — У МЕНЯ В КАРМАНЕ КУСОЧЕК СЫРА!

ТАК... ПОШЛА НА ЗАПАХ СЫРА... ОП, Я СХВАТИЛ ЕЁ!

ДЕРЖИ СВОЮ ПЯТЁРКУ, ПЛЕМЯННИЧЕК... НО, СДАЁТСЯ МНЕ, КРЫСА ОКАЗАЛАСЬ В ДОМЕ НЕСПРОСТА!

ЭЙ, МАЛЬЧИКИ! КАК ВАШИ ДЕЛА?

ОТЛИЧНО, ДЯДЯ ДОНАЛЬД! ЮНЫЕ СУРКИ ЗАРАБОТАЛИ ПЯТЬ ДОЛЛАРОВ, РАСЧИЩАЯ СНЕГ!

МАК ДАК АВЕНЮ

А МНЕ ВАША КРЫСА ПОМОГЛА НАПУГАТЬ ДЯДЮ СКРУДЖА И ПОЛУЧИТЬ ЕЩЁ ПЯТЬ! ИДЁМ, НУЖНО НАЙТИ ДЕЙЗИ!

О, ДОНАЛЬД! Я ПРОДАЛА МОЁ ВЯЗАНИЕ ЗА ПЯТЬ ДОЛЛАРОВ!

ПО ГАЗОНУ НЕ ХОДИТЬ

УРА! ВМЕСТЕ МЫ СОБРАЛИ ЦЕЛОЕ СОСТОЯНИЕ!

ВОТ ПЯТЬ ДОЛЛАРОВ ОТ ЮНЫХ СУРКОВ!

И ПЯТЬ — ЗА МОЁ ВЯЗАНИЕ!

А ВОТ ПЯТЬ ДОЛЛАРОВ ОТ ДЯДИ СКРУДЖА!

О, НЕТ!

Я ПОЛОЖИЛ БАНКНОТУ В ОДИН КАРМАН С КРЫСОЙ!

СЭКОНОМЛЮ-КА Я ПЯТИЦЕНТОВИК И ПОЙДУ ДОМОЙ ЧЕРЕЗ ПАРК ПЕШКОМ!

ЗАЙМ

ЗДАНИЕ МАКДАКА

ЧТО Я ВИЖУ? МОЙ ПЛЕМЯННИК ДОНАЛЬД ПОПРОШАЙНИЧАЕТ, СЛОВНО ОБЫЧНЫЙ БРОДЯГА!

ДОНАЛЬД! У ТЕБЯ СОВСЕМ НЕТ АМБИЦИЙ?

ЕСЛИ Я МОГУ ЗАРАБОТАТЬ ДОЛЛАР ЗА ПЯТЬ МИНУТ — НЕТ!

ТЫ БЫЛ ЗДЕСЬ ВСЕГО ПЯТЬ МИНУТ, И... И...

ПОДВИНЬСЯ! ПОЖАЛУЙ, Я ВЫТЕСНЮ ТЕБЯ С РЫНКА ЛЁГКИХ ДЕНЕГ!

ЕДИНСТВЕННАЯ ГОДНАЯ СКАМЕЙКА В ПАРКЕ, И ОН ЕЁ ЗАНЯЛ!

НАДЕЮСЬ, НИКТО МЕНЯ НЕ УЗНАЕТ! ПОДНИМУ ВОРОТНИК И ПРИКИНУСЬ БЕДНЯКОМ!

ТЕМ ВРЕМЕНЕМ ДЕТИ В БЕДНОТАУНЕ СТРОЯТ РАДУЖНЫЕ ПЛАНЫ!

ИГРУШЕЧНЫЙ ПОЕЗД! МЫ ПРАВДА ПОЛУЧИМ НА РОЖДЕСТВО ИГРУШЕЧНЫЙ ПОЕЗД?

ТАК ПООБЕЩАЛИ ЭТИ МИЛЫЕ ЛЕДИ!

ДАВАЙТЕ ПОСТРОИМ ЖЕЛЕЗНУЮ ДОРОГУ ВОЗЛЕ ЛАЧУГИ ИНВАЛИДА ДЖО, ЧТОБЫ ОН СМОГ УВИДЕТЬ НАШ ПОЕЗД!

ПРОТЯНЕМ ШНУР К ЕГО ПОСТЕЛИ, И ОН БУДЕТ ГУДЕТЬ В ГУДОК!

МЫ ВСЕ ПОВЕСЕЛИМСЯ!

ТАКОГО ВЕСЕЛЬЯ У НАС В ЖИЗНИ НЕ БЫВАЛО!

МНЕ ВСЁ ЕЩЁ НУЖНО НАЙТИ **ЧЕТЫРЕ** ДОЛЛАРА! МЕЛОЧЬ, КОГДА У ТЕБЯ **ЕСТЬ** ДЕНЬГИ, И **УЖАСНО МНОГО**, КОГДА ИХ НЕТ!

НУ И НУ! **КОГО** Я ВИЖУ!

ГЛЭДСТОУН ГАНДЕР! МОЙ **ВЕЗУЧИЙ** КУЗЕН!

СЛАДОС

ТЫ КАК РАЗ ТОТ, КТО МОЖЕТ МНЕ ПОМОЧЬ, ГЛЭДСТОУН!

КАКИЕ ПУСТЯКИ ТЕБЯ ВОЛНУЮТ, КУЗЕН?

МНЕ НУЖНО ЧЕТЫРЕ ДОЛЛАРА! У ТЕБЯ ЕСТЬ ДЕНЬГИ?

У МЕНЯ ИХ **ОТРОДЯСЬ НЕ БЫЛО!** ЗАЧЕМ МНЕ?

НУ ТОГДА **НАЙДИ** НЕМНОГО ДЛЯ МЕНЯ! ТЫ **ВСЕГДА** НАХОДИШЬ КОШЕЛЬКИ И ЦЕННОСТИ!

СЕЙЧАС **НЕ СЕЗОН,** КУЗЕН! ВСЕ КОШЕЛЬКИ ПОГРЕБЕНЫ ПОД СЛОЕМ СНЕГА!

НО ТЫ ТАКОЙ ВЕЗУЧИЙ, ЧТО НЕПРЕМЕННО НАЙДЁШЬ!

ДОНАЛЬД РАССКАЗЫВАЕТ ГЛЭДСТОУНУ ОБ УЖИНЕ ДЛЯ БЕДНОТАУНА!

РАДИ ТАКОГО БЛАГОРОДНОГО ДЕЛА ПОПЫТАЮСЬ!

ОЙ-ОЙ! МНЕ ПРИДЁТСЯ **ЖЕЛАТЬ** ОЧЕНЬ СИЛЬНО — А ЭТО ПОХОЖЕ НА РАБОТУ...

ДА ЛАДНО, ПОЙДЁМ!

НАЙДУТСЯ ЛИ БУМАЖНИКИ В ТОМ БОЛЬШОМ ОТЕЛЕ?

ВОЗМОЖНО, КУЗЕН! ВСЁ ВОЗМОЖНО!

ПРОВЕРИМ! Я ПРОЙДУСЬ И ВЫТЯНУ ШЛЯПУ! ВДРУГ ДЕНЬГИ ВЫПАДУТ ИЗ ОКНА!

ДАВАЙ ВСТАНЕМ В СНЕГУ ПОД ЭТИМИ ОКНАМИ! СЮДА ВЫХОДЯТ НОМЕРА БОГАТЕЕВ!

ЧУВСТВУЮ СЕБЯ ГЛУПО, СТОЯ ТУТ У ВСЕХ НА ВИДУ!

ПЛЮХ

КАКОЙ-ТО ШУТНИК КИНУЛ **РАСКАЛЁННУЮ** МОНЕТКУ В ТВОЮ ШЛЯПУ!

МОНЕТА ПРОЖГЛА ЕЁ НАСКВОЗЬ!

ПОЙДУ И РАСКВАШУ ЭТОМУ УМНИКУ НОС!

НЕТ! СТОЙ!

МОНЕТКА РАСПЛАВИЛА ДЫРУ В СНЕГУ! Я ЗНАЛ, ЧТО МОЯ УДАЧА НЕ ПОДВЕДЁТ!

СМОТРИ! ПОД СНЕГОМ **БУМАЖНИК**! ДЕНЕЖКА УКАЗАЛА МНЕ, ГДЕ ИСКАТЬ!

УХ ТЫ, НУ И НУ! ЗА ТАКУЮ **НАХОДКУ** ПРИЧИТАЕТСЯ ХОРОШАЯ **НАГРАДА**!

ПРИВЕТ, ДЯДЮШКА! КАК ИДЁТ БИЗНЕС?

НЕ ТВОЁ ДЕЛО!

БА, ВЫШЕ КЛЮВ! ВОТ ТЕБЕ БОЛЬШАЯ БЛЕСТЯЩАЯ МОНЕТКА!

ГРРР!

ЕСЛИ БЫ ДОНАЛЬД ЗНАЛ, КАКИЕ БЕДЫ ПРИНЕСУТ ЭТИ ДЕСЯТЬ ЦЕНТОВ!

ПОЙДУ, НАЙДУ ДЕЙЗИ!

ЧУДЕСНО! ТЫ РАЗДОБЫЛ ДЕНЬГИ НА ПОЕЗД!

У ДЕТЕЙ ИЗ БЕДНОТАУНА ВСЁ-ТАКИ БУДЕТ РОЖДЕСТВО!

ДАВАЙ ПОКАЖЕМ НАШИ ДВАДЦАТЬ ПЯТЬ ДОЛЛАРОВ И ЗАБЕРЁМ ТЕ ДВАДЦАТЬ ПЯТЬ, ЧТО ОБЕЩАЛ ДЯДЯ СКРУДЖ!

ЗВЕНИТЕ, КОЛОКОЛЬЧИКИ! ЗВЕНИТЕ, КОЛОКОЛЬЧИКИ! ЗВЕНИТЕ ВСЮ ДОРОГУ!

ТЕМ ВРЕМЕНЕМ ДЯДЯ СКРУДЖ НАЧИНАЕТ ЗЛИТЬСЯ!

ТЬФУ! ПРОСИДЕЛ ЗДЕСЬ УЖЕ ПОЛЧАСА, А ЗАРАБОТАЛ ЛИШЬ ДЕСЯТЬ ЦЕНТОВ ОТ ДОНАЛЬДА!

И ВСЁ ЖЕ ДЕСЯТЬ ЦЕНТОВ — ЭТО ДЕСЯТЬ ЦЕНТОВ! ПОЙДУ, ПОЛОЖУ ИХ В СЕЙФ!

Я НЕ РИСКНУ ОТКРЫВАТЬ ЭТУ ДВЕРЬ!

ПРИДУМАЛ! ЗАКИНУ МОНЕТКУ ЧЕРЕЗ ЧЕРДАЧНЫЙ ЛЮК!

ТРУХЛЯВОЕ МУЧЕНЬЕ, А НЕ КРЫША! ТОГО И ГЛЯДИ ПРОЛОМИТСЯ!

ВРЯД ЛИ Я ПОЛОЖУ СЮДА ЕЩЁ ХОТЬ ОДНУ МОНЕТКУ!

АХ, КАК ТЫ ПРАВ, ДЯДЯ СКРУДЖ!

СИЛЫ НЕБЕСНЫЕ! ЧТО СТРЯСЛОСЬ? О, НЕТ!

ДЯДЯ СКРУДЖ ДОЛЖЕН БЫТЬ ГДЕ-ТО ТУТ! ДВЕРЬ НЕ ЗАПЕРТА!

ЕСЛИ ПРИШЁЛ ЗА СВОИМИ ДЕНЬГАМИ, ПЛЕМЯННИЧЕК, ТЫ ОПОЗДАЛ НА ДЕСЯТЬ... ЦЕНТОВ!

ЧТО ЗНАЧИТ «ОПОЗДАЛ»? ТЫ НЕ МОЖЕШЬ УВИЛЬНУТЬ, РАЗ ОБЕЩАЛ!

Я И НЕ УВИЛИВАЮ, Я СТРАДАЮ!

МОЖЕШЬ НЕ ВЕРИТЬ... НО Я РАЗОРЁН!

ТЫ И РАНЬШЕ ПЫТАЛСЯ МЕНЯ ОБМАНУТЬ, НО БОЛЬШЕЙ ЛЖИ Я НЕ СЛЫШАЛ!

МОИ ДЕНЬГИ ПРОПАЛИ! ДО ПОСЛЕДНЕГО ЦЕНТА!

ОТКРЫВАЙ СВОЙ СЕЙФ И ДОСТАНЬ МОИ ДВАДЦАТЬ ПЯТЬ ДОЛЛАРОВ! А ТО И ПАЛЬТО СВОЕГО ЛИШИШЬСЯ!

ВОТ! СЕЙФ ОТКРЫТ! ИДИ И САМ ДОСТАВАЙ!

ВОТ ЖУТЬ! НА МЕСТЕ СЕЙФА БЕЗДОННАЯ ЯМА!

МОИ ДЕНЬГИ ПРОПАЛИ! Я ВСЕГО ЛИШЬ БЕДНЫЙ СТАРИЧОК! (ХНЫК! ХНЫК!) УА-А-А!

ЭТО ВСЁ **ТВОЯ** ВИНА! ТЫ ДАЛ МНЕ ПОСЛЕДНЮЮ **МОНЕТКУ**, КОТОРАЯ ВЫЗВАЛА ОБВАЛ!

САМОЕ **ПЕЧАЛЬНОЕ**, ЧТО ТЕПЕРЬ ДЕТИ ИЗ БЕДНОТАУНА ЛИШАТСЯ СВОЕГО РОЖДЕСТВЕНСКОГО ПРАЗДНИКА!

НУ УЖ НЕТ, НЕ ЛИШАТСЯ! ДЕНЬГИ ГДЕ-ТО ТАМ! НАДО ТОЛЬКО **ДОСТАТЬ** ИХ!

НО ЭТО БУДЕТ **НЕЛЕГКО**! ДЯДЯ СКРУДЖ ОБРАЩАЕТСЯ К ВЕДУЩИМ ИНЖЕНЕРАМ МИРА!

ПОЛАГАЮ, ДЕНЬГИ ПРОВАЛИЛИСЬ В ГИГАНТСКУЮ НОРУ СУСЛИКА!

НАСКОЛЬКО ЖЕ **ГЛУБОКА** НОРА И НАСКОЛЬКО **ВЕЛИК** СУСЛИК?

МОИ ОЧКИ УПАЛИ ВНИЗ, И Я НЕ УСЛЫШАЛ УДАРА ОБ **ДНО**!

ПОЗВОЛЬТЕ НЕМНОГО ПОШУМЕТЬ, И МОЙ ШУМОМЕР ОПРЕДЕЛИТ ГЛУБИНУ ПО ЭХО!

ХОТЕЛ БЫ Я **ПОТОРОПИТЬ** ЭТИХ РЕБЯТ!

ДО РОЖДЕСТВА ОСТАЛОСЬ...

...ВСЕГО **ДВА ДНЯ**!

ЧТО Ж, ТОГДА МЫ ПРОСТО СПУСТИМ В ПЕЩЕРУ ВЁДРА И ВЫЧЕРПАЕМ ВСЕ ДЕНЬГИ! ПОЧЕМУ БЫ ТАК НЕ СДЕЛАТЬ?

ПОТОМУ ЧТО **ПОД** ДЕНЬГАМИ **ЕЩЁ ОДИН** ТОНКИЙ СЛОЙ!

ЗЫБУЧИЕ ПЕСКИ

МАЛЕЙШАЯ **ВИБРАЦИЯ** — И ДЕНЬГИ ПРОВАЛЯТСЯ В БЕЗДОННЫЕ **ЗЫБУЧИЕ ПЕСКИ**!

НУ, ПРОБУРИТЕ **ТУННЕЛЬ**! ПРИМЕРНО ТАКОЙ!

ТУННЕЛИ СТРОЯТ МАШИНЫ! А МАШИНЫ **ВИБРИРУЮТ**!

ВСЕГО ХОРОШЕГО, МИСТЕР МАКДАК! СОВЕТУЮ **ЗАБЫТЬ** ПРО ЭТИ ДЕНЬГИ! ВЫ **НИКОГДА** ИХ НЕ ДОСТАНЕТЕ!

ОПТИМИСТЫ, НИЧЕГО НЕ СКАЖЕШЬ!

У НИХ ОТ САНТА-КЛАУСА ТОЛЬКО БОРОДА!

ХНЫ-ЫК ХНЫ-ЫК ХНЫ-Ы-ЫК! (ВСХЛИП! ХНЫК!) Я БЕДНЫЙ СТАРИЧОК БЕЗ ГРОША! (ВСХЛИП! ХНЫК! ХНЫК!)

УТКИ В УНЫНИИ! ОНИ СОБРАЛИСЬ И РЕШАЮТ, КАК БЫТЬ ДАЛЬШЕ!

УСТРОИМ ВЕЧЕРИНКУ В ЛЮБОМ СЛУЧАЕ! НА ЭТИ ДЕНЬГИ КУПИМ ИНДЕЕК!

НО ИГРУШЕЧНОГО ПОЕЗДА НЕ БУДЕТ!

НЕТ!

ЭТО НЕЧЕСТНО! НЕЧЕСТНО!

СПОРИМ, ДЕТИ ХОТЕЛИ ПОЕЗД БОЛЬШЕ ВСЕГО НА СВЕТЕ!

ОХО-ХО! ЕСЛИ Б ТОЛЬКО БЫЛ СПОСОБ СПАСТИ ДЕНЬГИ ДЯДИ СКРУДЖА...

НА СЛЕДУЮЩЕЕ УТРО!

ПОРА ВСТАВАТЬ, ЛОДЫРИ! ВРЕМЯ ЗАВТРАКАТЬ!

МЫ ДУМАЕМ, ДЯДЯ ДОНАЛЬД!

ТАК ПРИДУМАЙТЕ, КАК МНЕ СВЕСТИ КОНЦЫ С КОНЦАМИ!

С ТЕХ ПОР КАК ДЯДЯ СКРУДЖ ЛИШИЛСЯ СОСТОЯНИЯ, ОН ПЕРЕЕХАЛ К НАМ!

ЭТО УЖЕ ТРЕТЬЯ ИЛИ ЧЕТВЁРТАЯ МОЯ ПОРЦИЯ ОВСЯНКИ, ПЛЕМЯННИЧЕК? СЛЁЗЫ МЕШАЮТ МНЕ РАССМОТРЕТЬ СТОЛ!

ЕЩЁ ПОЗЖЕ!

ОЙ-ЁЙ, КОНЕЧНАЯ!

ВОТ НЕВЕЗЕНИЕ! МЫ ДОЛЖНЫ БЫТЬ **ПРЯМО ПОД** ТВОИМИ ДЕНЬГАМИ, НО ДО НИХ НЕ ДОБРАТЬСЯ!

ОГО! ТУТ ГДЕ-ТО ЕСТЬ **ПРОХОД!** Я ЧУЮ ДЕНЬГИ!

НЮХ! НЮХ!

НЮХ НЮХ

ТОЧНО! ТУТ **БАРСУЧЬЯ НОРА!** И ДЕНЬГИ С ДРУГОЙ СТОРОНЫ!

УЖЕ ЧТО-ТО! НО КАКОЙ ОТ НЕЁ ПРОК?

МЫ НЕ РИСКНЁМ РАСШИРЯТЬ ДЫРУ!

АГА! ИНАЧЕ ВСЁ РУХНЕТ! СЛЫШИТЕ? КАМНИ УЖЕ ТРЕЩАТ!

ПРЕДОСТАВЬТЕ ЭТУ ПРОБЛЕМУ ЮНЫМ СУРКАМ!

ЮНЫМ СУРКАМ

ВСЁ ПО ПЛЕЧУ!

НЕЧЕГО И ГОВОРИТЬ, У ДЕТЕЙ ИЗ БЕДНОТАУНА БЫЛО **ПОТРЯСАЮЩЕЕ** РОЖДЕСТВО! С НАРЯЖЕННЫМИ РОЖДЕСТВЕНСКИМИ ЁЛКАМИ, ТОРТАМИ, КОНФЕТАМИ И ИНДЕЙКОЙ!

И С ДЕСЯТКАМИ ИГРУШЕЧНЫХ ПОЕЗДОВ!

ГДЕ ЖЕ **ДОБРЕЙШИЙ** СТАРЫЙ СКРУДЖ МАКДАК, ЧЕЙ ЩЕДРЫЙ ВЗНОС СДЕЛАЛ ЭТОТ ПРАЗДНИК ЯВЬЮ?

Я ЗНАЮ, ГДЕ! ОТНЕСУ ЕМУ ЖАРЕНУЮ НОЖКУ!

ТАК И ЗНАЛ, ЧТО НАЙДУ ТЕБЯ ЗДЕСЬ, ДЯДЮШКА!

ОХХХ! Я ТУТ **НАДОЛГО** ЗАСТРЯЛ!

ЭТОТ ДУРАЦКИЙ ПОЕЗД ВЫВОЗИТ МОИ ДЕНЕЖКИ С ТАКОЙ СКОРОСТЬЮ...

...ЧТО ПРИДЁТСЯ СИДЕТЬ ЗДЕСЬ ЕЩЁ ДВЕСТИ СЕМЬДЕСЯТ ДВА ГОДА ОДИННАДЦАТЬ МЕСЯЦЕВ ТРИ НЕДЕЛИ И ЧЕТЫРЕ ДНЯ!

ЧУХ ЧУХ

Disney
Дональд Дак

ДЯДЯ ДОНАЛЬД, А ЧТО ЭТО ЗА БОЛЬШОЕ ЗДАНИЕ НА ХОЛМЕ КИЛМОТОР?

ЭТО **НОВОЕ ДЕНЬГОХРАНИЛИЩЕ** ДЯДЮШКИ СКРУДЖА, МАЛЬЧИКИ!

УХ ТЫ! ОНО УЖ ТОЧНО БРОСАЕТСЯ ВСЕМ В ГЛАЗА!

ДА! А ЧЕРЕЗ ПОТАЙНЫЕ ОТВЕРСТИЯ И ДЯДЯ СКРУДЖ ВИДИТ **ВСЁ**, ЧТО ТВОРИТСЯ ВОКРУГ!

ОН ОТСЕЛИЛ ДВАДЦАТЬ КВАРТАЛОВ, ЧТОБЫ **ГРАБИТЕЛИ** НЕ МОГЛИ ПОДОБРАТЬСЯ К НЕМУ!

КРОМЕ ТОГО, СТЕНЫ И КРЫША **ТОЛЩИНОЙ В ТРИ МЕТРА**!

ОГО! НИЧЕГО СЕБЕ! **ПОХОЖЕ**, ПОЛУЧИЛАСЬ НЕПРИСТУПНАЯ КРЕПОСТЬ!

ДОНАЛЬД ДАК

ДА! НАКОНЕЦ-ТО ДЕНЕЖКИ ДЯДИ СКРУДЖА В **БЕЗОПАСНОСТИ**!

ЭЙ! ТЕЛЕФОН ЗВОНИТ!

ДА, ДА, ДЯДЯ СКРУДЖ... КОНЕЧНО! МЫ С ПЛЕМЯННИКАМИ БУДЕМ В МГНОВЕНИЕ ОКА!

ДЯДЯ СКРУДЖ ПРИГЛАШАЕТ НАС ОСМОТРЕТЬ ЕГО НОВОЕ ДЕНЬГОХРАНИЛИЩЕ!

ЗДОРОВО! КЛАСС!

ДА, ДЯДЯ СКРУДЖ... ЧТО? ХОРОШО... ЗАПИШУ! МЫ ТАК И СДЕЛАЕМ... СПАСИБО! ПОКА!

ДЯДЯ СКРУДЖ ОСТАВИЛ КОЕ-КАКИЕ ИНСТРУКЦИИ, КАК К НЕМУ ПОПАСТЬ!

ТЕПЕРЬ, КОГДА МЫ ДОБРАЛИСЬ ДО ПУСТЫРЯ, ЖДИТЕ МОИХ УКАЗАНИЙ!

МЫ ЗДЕСЬ! ТАК, ВЫСТРАИВАЙТЕСЬ В ШЕРЕНГУ И БЕРИТЕ ПО КАРТОНКЕ!

УХОДИТЕ!

ЗАЧЕМ ОНИ НАМ, ДЯДЯ ДОНАЛЬД?

ЧТОБЫ НА РАДАРЕ ДЯДИ СКРУДЖА МЫ ОТОБРАЗИЛИСЬ В ВИДЕ КВАДРАТОВ!

СТОП!

ВОН

ПРОЧЬ!

ОТЛИЧНО! БРОСАЙТЕ КАРТОНКИ И ИДИТЕ ЗА МНОЙ СЛЕД В СЛЕД!

УХОДИТЕ!

НУ, МАЛЬЧИКИ, ЧТО СКАЖЕТЕ?

КАК-ТО ТУТ НЕУЮТНО! БРРР!

ЗДЕСЬ ВЕЗДЕ ПРОТИВОВЗЛОМНАЯ СИГНАЛИЗАЦИЯ! В КАЖДОМ УГЛУ КАМЕРЫ! НИ ОДНОМУ ГРАБИТЕЛЮ СЮДА НЕ ПОПАСТЬ!

БОМ БОМ

СКРИП

ГАВ! ГАВ!

А ТЕПЕРЬ ПОДНИМЕМСЯ СЮДА И ВЗГЛЯНЕМ НА МОИ ДЕНЕЖКИ! ВСЕ НА БОРТ!

ВОТ МОЁ СОСТОЯНИЕ, МАЛЬЧИКИ! ДЕСЯТЬ ЭТАЖЕЙ В ВЫСОТУ И ПЛОЩАДЬЮ С ЦЕЛЫЙ КВАРТАЛ!

О, НА НИХ МОЖНО КУПИТЬ МОРЕ ЖВАЧКИ!

ЧТО ТЫ СОБИРАЕШЬСЯ ДЕЛАТЬ С ЭТИМИ ДЕНЬГАМИ, ДЯДЯ СКРУДЖ?

БУДУ ХРАНИТЬ ПРЯМО ЗДЕСЬ, РАЗУМЕЕТСЯ!

НО ЭТО ЖЕ СОВСЕМ НЕ ВЕСЕЛО! НЕУЖЕЛИ ТЫ НЕ ХОЧЕШЬ ИХ НА ЧТО-НИБУДЬ ПОТРАТИТЬ?

КТО ГОВОРИЛ ПРО ТРАТЫ?

ОБОЖАЮ ЛЮБОВАТЬСЯ ДЕНЕЖКАМИ!

А ЕЩЁ БЕГАТЬ ПО НИМ БОСИКОМ И СЛЫШАТЬ ХРУСТ ТЫСЯЧЕДОЛЛАРОВЫХ КУПЮР ПОД НОГАМИ!

СОРЯТ ДЕНЬГАМИ ТОЛЬКО БОЛВАНЫ! ОНИ НЕ ПОНИМАЮТ, ЧТО ЗНАЧИТ ИСТИННОЕ **НАСЛАЖДЕНИЕ**!

ПЛЮХ
ФЫРК

ДОНАЛЬД, МОЖЕШЬ ВЫГЛЯНУТЬ В ГЛАЗОК? ПРОВЕРЬ, НЕ ШНЫРЯЕТ ЛИ КТО ВОКРУГ!

ТАК И ЗНАЛ, ЧТО ОН ПОПРОСИТ ОБ УСЛУГЕ... **ЗАБЕСПЛАТНО**!

ПЕРИСКОП
СМОТРОВАЯ ТРУБКА

О, ОТСЮДА И ПРАВДА ВИДНО ВСЮ ОКРУГУ!

ОЙ-ЁЙ!

ДЯДЯ СКРУДЖ, БЕГИ СЮДА! Я ЗАМЕТИЛ НЕЧТО ПОДОЗРИТЕЛЬНОЕ!

БРАТЬЯ ГАВС ВЫШЛИ ИЗ ТЮРЬМЫ! ОНИ НА НИЧЕЙНОМ КЛОЧКЕ ЗЕМЛИ ПОД ХОЛМОМ!

ДЕЛАЮТ **ПОДКОП**! О, МИЛОСТИВЫЕ УТКИ!

БРАТЬЯ ГАВС!
УЖАСНЫЕ БРАТЬЯ ГАВС!

ОНИ ЧТО-ТО ЗАДУМАЛИ!
НО ИМ НЕ ДОБРАТЬСЯ
ДО ТВОИХ ДЕНЕГ!

У НИХ НЕТ
ШАНСОВ! ЭТИ
СТЕНЫ ТРИ МЕТРА
ТОЛЩИНОЙ!

ДА, Я ЗАКАЗАЛ СТЕНЫ И КРЫШУ
ТОЛЩИНОЙ В ТРИ МЕТРА...

...НО РАДИ ЭКОНОМИИ НЕ ДЕЛАЛ
ФУНДАМЕНТ!

О-ХО-ХО!

ТЕПЕРЬ БРАТЬЯ ГАВС ПРОКОПАЮТ ТУННЕЛЬ
ПОД ЗЕМЛЁЙ И ВЫКАЧАЮТ ВСЕ МОИ ДЕНЕЖКИ,
СЛОВНО ФАСОЛИНЫ
ИЗ ДЫРЯВОГО МЕШКА!

ХНЫК!
ХНЫК!

НУ, ПРИЧИТАНИЯМИ ИХ НЕ ОСТАНОВИШЬ!
ПОШЛИ! СПУСТИМСЯ ВНИЗ И НАЧИСТИМ
ИМ НОСЫ!

ТЫ ПРАВ! РАЗБЕРЁМСЯ
ПО-МУЖСКИ И ЗАСТАВИМ
ИХ УЙТИ!

ПЯТЬСОТ ТРИПЛИКАТИЛЛИОНОВ
МУЛЬТИПЛУДИЛЛИОНОВ КВАДРУПЛИКАТИЛЛИОНОВ
ЦЕНТРИФУГАЛИЛЛИОНОВ ДОЛЛАРОВ И ШЕСТНАДЦАТЬ
ЦЕНТОВ СТОЯТ ТОГО, ЧТОБ ЗА НИХ БОРОТЬСЯ,
НЕ БУДЬ Я СКРУДЖ МАКДАК!

О, НЕТ! Я ЗАБЫЛ ПРО МИННОЕ ПОЛЕ!

БАБАХ!

ОЙ-ЁЙ, ОПЯТЬ!

ЖИВЕЕ, ВНУТРЬ!

В ЧЁМ ДЕЛО?

ЗАБЫЛ О МИНАХ-СЮРПРИЗАХ!

ВСЁ УСТРОЕНО ТАК, ЧТО ЕСЛИ ЧУЖАК ЗАБЕРЁТСЯ, ЕМУ НИКОГДА ОТСЮДА НЕ ВЫБРАТЬСЯ!

НАМ ТОЖЕ ПРИДЁТСЯ ЗДЕСЬ СИДЕТЬ?

ДА! ЧТОБЫ ОБЕЗВРЕДИТЬ ВСЕ ЛОВУШКИ, НУЖНА НЕДЕЛЯ! А ПОКА...

...ЛУЧШЕ СДЕЛАЙ ЧТО-НИБУДЬ ПРЯМО СЕЙЧАС! БРАТЬЯ ГАВС ТАЩАТ БУРЫ И СВЁРЛА!

О, ЭТИ БРАТЬЯ ГАВС! УЖАСНЫЕ БРАТЬЯ ГАВС!

ХОРОШЕНЬКИЕ ДЕЛА!

ПОКА МЫ ЗАСТРЯЛИ ТУТ, БРАТЬЯ ГАВС ЗА НЕДЕЛЮ ОПУСТОШАТ ВСЁ ТВОЁ ДЕНЬГОХРАНИЛИЩЕ!

МОГУЧИЙ ДОЛЛАР

О, КРЯК ТЕБЕ! ТВОЯ ГОЛОВА ПОЛНА ГЕНИАЛЬНЫХ ИДЕЙ! ВОТ И ПРИДУМАЙ, КАК ОДУРАЧИТЬ ЭТИХ БАНДИТОВ!

БЫСТРЫЙ БАКС

НУЖНО КАК-ТО ЗАДЕРЖАТЬ ГАВСОВ, ПОКА МЫ НЕ ВЫБЕРЕМСЯ! МОЖЕТ, НАУЧИМ ДЯТЛОВ ДОЛБИТЬ ДЫРЫ В ИХ ИНСТРУМЕНТАХ?

ДУМАЙ КАК СЛЕДУЕТ!

ЭВРИКА! ЗАПОЛНИМ ДЕНЬГОХРАНИЛИЩЕ ВОДОЙ!

ДЕНЬГИ ВОДА НЕ ИСПОРТИТ, А ВОТ БРАТЬЕВ ГАВС ВЫМОЕТ ИЗ ИХ ТОННЕЛЕЙ, СЛОВНО КРЫС!

ДОНАЛЬД! ЧТО БЫ Я ДЕЛАЛ БЕЗ ТВОИХ ВЫДУМОК!

ЗАПОЛНЮ ДЕНЬГОХРАНИЛИЩЕ ВОДОЙ ДО САМОГО ПОТОЛКА! БРАТЬЯМ ГАВС ДАВНО ПОРА ПРИНЯТЬ ВАННУ!

ВЕЧЕРОМ ТОГО ЖЕ ДНЯ!

ЭЙ, ДЯДЯ ДОНАЛЬД, ПОСЛУШАЙ, ЧТО ГОВОРЯТ ПО РАДИО!

ЗАГЛУШИТЕ СВОИ АВТО! ПОЛОЖИТЕ ДОПОЛНИТЕЛЬНЫЕ ОДЕЯЛА НА КРОВАТЬ! СЕГОДНЯШНЯЯ НОЧЬ БУДЕТ САМОЙ ХОЛОДНОЙ ЗА ВСЮ ИСТОРИЮ ДАКСБУРГА!

У ТЕБЯ ЗДЕСЬ НЕТ ПЕЧКИ, ДЯДЯ СКРУДЖ?

ТОЛЬКО МОЯ ГАЗОВАЯ ПЛИТКА, НО ОНА НЕ РАБОТАЕТ — Я ОТКАЗАЛСЯ ПЛАТИТЬ ЗА ГАЗ!

К ПОЛУНОЧИ ГОРОД ЗАМИРАЕТ! ДЕРЕВЬЯ ТРЕСКАЮТСЯ ОТ ЖУТКОГО ХОЛОДА! ПОЖАРНЫЕ ГИДРАНТЫ ВЗРЫВАЮТСЯ ЛЕДЯНЫМИ ФОНТАНАМИ!

ХРУСТ!

ЖУТКИЙ МОРОЗ ПРОБИРАЕТСЯ ДАЖЕ СКВОЗЬ ТРЁХМЕТРОВЫЕ СТЕНЫ ДЕНЬГОХРАНИЛИЩА ДЯДЮШКИ СКРУДЖА!

Я БЫ ОТДАЛ ЦЕЛЫЙ ГРОШ ЗА СУХИЕ КУПЮРЫ ДЛЯ РАСТОПКИ!

ТРЕСК

А ЭТО ЕЩЁ ЧТО?

ВОДА ВНУТРИ ХРАНИЛИЩА ПРЕВРАЩАЕТСЯ В ЛЁД И РАЗЛАМЫВАЕТ СТЕНЫ!

ГОРЕ МНЕ, ГОРЕ!

К УТРУ ДЕНЬГОХРАНИЛИЩЕ ДЯДИ СКРУДЖА ПРЕВРАЩАЕТСЯ В РАЗВАЛИНЫ! НА ЕГО МЕСТЕ СТОИТ ГИГАНТСКИЙ ЛЕДЯНОЙ КУБ!

БЕРЕГИСЬ! ОН НАЧИНАЕТ СЪЕЗЖАТЬ!

ОДИН ЗА ДРУГИМ УТКИ ВЫЛЕЗАЮТ ИЗ-ПОД ОБЛОМКОВ ХРАНИЛИЩА!

ИЩЕШЬ МОИ **ДЕНЕЖКИ**, ДОНАЛЬД?

ДА! ЧТО С НИМИ СТАЛО?

ОНИ СОСКОЛЬЗНУЛИ С ХОЛМА ПРЯМО В ЛАПЫ БРАТЬЯМ ГАВС!

ВОТ ОНИ, ТВОИ **ГЕНИАЛЬНЫЕ ИДЕИ**!

О-ХО-ХО! У МЕНЯ БЫЛ ТЯЖЁЛЫЙ ГОД! БОЮСЬ, НЕ ВИДАТЬ НАМ С МАЛЬЧИКАМИ ИНДЕЙКИ НА РОЖДЕСТВО!

А У МЕНЯ ВСЁ ОТЛИЧНО... КАК ВСЕГДА!

И В РОЖДЕСТВО СЪЕМ СТОЛЬКО ИНДЕЕК, СКОЛЬКО ВЛЕЗЕТ! ВЕДЬ Я ТАКОЙ ВЕЗУЧИЙ!

ЗА ТВОЁ РОЖДЕСТВО Я СПОКОЕН, ГЛЭДСТОУН! ТАК ЧТО НЕ БОЛТАЙ ПОПУСТУ!

ВИДИШЬ, Я ГОЛ КАК СОКОЛ, НО К РОЖДЕСТВУ...

СЭР!

ЧТО?

КАЖДОЕ РОЖДЕСТВО Я ДАЮ ПО ДОЛЛАРУ СЕЛЕЗНЮ С КУРЧАВЫМИ ВОЛОСАМИ В ГЕТРАХ И БАБОЧКЕ!

ПРАВДА?

ЭТО КУДА ЛУЧШЕ, ЧЕМ ДАВАТЬ ДЕНЬГИ ГНОМУ В ДЕРЕВЯННЫХ БАШМАКАХ, ШЁЛКОВОМ КОЛПАКЕ И МЕХОВЫХ ШТАНАХ!

ВИДИШЬ? ТОЛЬКО ЧТО БЫЛ НА МЕЛИ, И ВОТ Я УЖЕ ПРИ ДЕНЬГАХ! УДАЧА ГЛЭДСТОУНА ПОБЕДИТ ВСЁ И ВСЯ!

ГРРР! БРРР!

ТОЧНО! ЭТОТ ДОЛЛАР — ОТЛИЧНОЕ НАЧАЛО НА ПУТИ К РОЖДЕСТВЕНСКОЙ ИНДЕЙКЕ! ВОТ Я ВЕЗУНЧИК!

А КУДА ДЕЛСЯ ДОНАЛЬД? А, УШЁЛ МРАЧНЕЕ ТУЧИ! МОЯ УДАЧА ЯВНО ЕМУ ПРЕТИТ!

ГЛЭДСТОУН ПОЛУЧИТ СВОЮ ИНДЕЙКУ, НЕ СОМНЕВАЮСЬ! НО ЧТО БУДЕТ НА УЖИН В МОЁМ ДОМЕ?

НУЖНО ЕЩЁ РАЗ ПРОВЕРИТЬ НАЛОГОВУЮ ДЕКЛАРАЦИЮ! МОЖЕТ, НАМ ВООБЩЕ ЕСТЬ НЕ ПРИДЁТСЯ!

ВЫЧТЕМ 10 СТРОКИ 14 ИЗ ПОЛОВИНЫ ОБЩЕЙ СУММЫ СТРОК 11 И 13, ВЫЧТЕМ КВАДРАТНЫЙ КОРЕНЬ ИЗ 16 СТРОКИ 12 ПОМНОЖЕННОЙ НА ЧЕТЫРЕ...

ОГО! Я ПЕРЕПУТАЛ ВСЕ ЦИФРЫ И ПЕРЕПЛАТИЛ ПЯТЬДЕСЯТ ДОЛЛАРОВ!

ДЕНЕГ, КОТОРЫЕ МНЕ ВЕРНУЛИ, ХВАТИТ НЕ ТОЛЬКО НА РОЖДЕСТВЕНСКУЮ ИНДЮШКУ!

ТЕПЕРЬ КУПИТЬ ЕЁ ТАК ПРОСТО, ЧТО ДАЖЕ НЕ ИНТЕРЕСНО!

ДЯДЯ ДОНАЛЬД! УФФ! ПФФ!

ТЫ НАМ ПОМОЖЕШЬ?

УФФ! ПФФ!

МЫ ДОЛЖНЫ ПРОДАТЬ ВСЕ ЭТИ БИЛЕТЫ НА РОЗЫГРЫШ ИНДЕЙКИ ОТ ЮНЫХ СУРКОВ!

НО ЗА ВЕСЬ ДЕНЬ ВСУЧИЛИ ВСЕГО ОДИН БИЛЕТ!

ПОЖАЛУЙСТА, ДЯДЯ ДОНАЛЬД! У ВСЕХ СЕМЕЙ, КРОМЕ НАС, ЕСТЬ ИНДЕЙКА!

ГОВОРИШЬ, ВЫ ПРОДАЛИ ВСЕГО ОДИН БИЛЕТ?

ХММ... ВЫИГРАТЬ ИНДЕЙКУ УВЛЕКАТЕЛЬНЕЕ, ЧЕМ ПРОСТО КУПИТЬ!

Я ВЕДЬ ПРИ ДЕНЬГАХ И НИКОГДА РАНЬШЕ НЕ ПОБЕЖДАЛ В ЛОТЕРЕЕ!

СКОЛЬКО У ВАС БИЛЕТОВ? Я КУПЛЮ ВСЕ!

У МЕНЯ СОРОК ДЕВЯТЬ БИЛЕТОВ, А У КОГО-ТО ВСЕГО ОДИН! ПТИЧКА ТОЧНО БУДЕТ МОЕЙ!

НАПИШИ СВОЁ ИМЯ НА БИЛЕТАХ И ОПУСТИ ИХ В ЯЩИК В ШТАБЕ ЮНЫХ СУРКОВ! САМ РОЗЫГРЫШ БУДЕТ ЗАВТРА!

ТЕМ ЖЕ ВЕЧЕРОМ!

ВОТ! Я ВСЁ ПОДПИСАЛ! ШАНСЫ ВЫИГРАТЬ ИНДЕЙКУ — СОРОК ДЕВЯТЬ К ОДНОМУ!

КСТАТИ, МАЛЬЧИКИ, ВЫ НЕ ПОМНИТЕ, КТО КУПИЛ ОСТАВШИЙСЯ БИЛЕТИК?

ПОМНИМ!

ТВОЙ КУЗЕН ГЛЭДСТОУН!

ГЛЭДСТОУН!

ВИЛЛИ, НЕСИ НАШАТЫРЬ! ДЯДЮ ДОНАЛЬДА ПОДКОСИЛА НОВОСТЬ!

ПОЗЖЕ!

НУЖНО ЧТО-ТО ПРИДУМАТЬ, ЧТОБЫ ВЫИГРАТЬ ИНДЮШКУ! СОРОК ДЕВЯТЬ ШАНСОВ ПРОТИВ УДАЧИ ГЛЭДСТОУНА — ПШИК!

ПОБЕДНЫЙ БИЛЕТИК ИЗ ЯЩИКА ВЫТАЩИТ КАКОЙ-НИБУДЬ МАЛЫШ! КАК БЫТЬ УВЕРЕННЫМ, ЧТО ВЫТЯНУТ ОДИН ИЗ МОИХ?

ИДЕЯ! ПРОТКНУ БИЛЕТЫ БУЛАВКОЙ, ЧТОБЫ ОНИ ЦЕПЛЯЛИСЬ К РУКАМ!

УТРОМ!

ПОТРАТИЛ ВСЮ НОЧЬ, ЗАТО ТЕПЕРЬ МОИ БИЛЕТЫ ГОТОВЫ К ПОБЕДЕ! ОНИ ПРАКТИЧЕСКИ ПРИЛИПАЮТ К ПАЛЬЦАМ!

НАСТУПАЕТ РЕШАЮЩИЙ МОМЕНТ!

МНЕ КЛАСТЬ СВОИ БИЛЕТИКИ СЮДА?

ВЕРРРНО!

ЛЕЙТЕНАНТ-ГЕНЕРАЛ СВЕРХГЕРОЙСКИ ХРЮК ВЫТАЩИТ ВЫИГРЫШНЫЙ!

ПОДОЖДИТЕ МИНУТКУ! Я ПОЛОЖУ **МОЙ** БИЛЕТ!

МЕДАЛИ ЮНЫХ СУРКОВ

ХЕ-ХЕ! УНИКАЛЬНАЯ ЛОТЕРЕЯ, КОГДА У ВЕЗУНЧИКА ГЛЭДСТОУНА НЕТ ШАНСОВ!

ТАК-ТАК! У НАС ТУТ КАКТУСОВЫЙ КОТ?

НЕТ, СЭР! ЭТО БУЛАВОЧНЫЙ ПИТ, ДИКОБРАЗ И НАШ СИМВОЛ!

ОН КУСАЕТСЯ?

ЧИК!

НЕТ! НО ДЕРЁТСЯ ХВОСТОМ!

ЧИК! БИЛЕТ ВЕСЬ В ДЫРКАХ, КАК ДУРШЛАГ! НО ВДРУГ ЭТО ПРИНЕСЁТ УДАЧУ!

ХА! ХА! ХОТЯ Я И ТАК СЧАСТЛИВЧИК!

БИЛЕТЫ ПЕРЕМЕШАНЫ, ВЫИГРЫШНЫЙ БИЛЕТ ВЫНУТ! КТО ЖЕ ОБЛАДАТЕЛЬ ИНДЕЙКИ?

ГЛЭДСТОУН ГАНДЕР!

Я ВСЁ ЕЩЁ МОГУ **КУПИТЬ** ИНДЕЙКУ, НО НЕ ХОЧУ... Я ДОЛЖЕН ХОТЬ РАЗ ВЫИГРАТЬ В ЛОТЕРЕЮ, ПРОСТО ЧТОБ ДОКАЗАТЬ СЕБЕ, ЧТО МОГУ!

ТЫ МЕНЯ ВЗБЕСИЛ, ПОЭТОМУ Я НЕПРЕМЕННО ОБСТАВЛЮ В ЛОТЕРЕЮ ИМЕННО **ТЕБЯ!**

НАПРАШИВАЕШЬСЯ НА НЕПРИЯТНОСТИ, ПАРЕНЬ!

РОЗЫГРЫШ ИНDЕЕК! РАDИ БЕЗГОЛОСЫХ УХАЮЩИХ СОВ

ЗАГЛЯНЕМ СЮДА И ПОПЫТАЕМ УДАЧУ!

МНОГО У ВАС ОСТАЛОСЬ БИЛЕТОВ, МЭМ?

ВСЕ ДО ОДНОГО! СОТНЯ! (ОХ!) НИКТО НЕ ХОЧЕТ ИХ ПОКУПАТЬ! ПОХОЖЕ, У ВСЕХ ЕСТЬ ИНДЕЙКА!

ВЫИГРАЙ В ЛОТЕРЕЮ

ПРОДАЙТЕ **ОДИН** БИЛЕТ ГЛЭДСТОУНУ, А Я КУПЛЮ ОСТАЛЬНЫЕ!

РОЗЫГРЫШ ТУТ

О, БЛАГОДАРЮ ВАС, ДЖЕНТЛЬМЕНЫ! МАЛЕНЬКАЯ ДЕВОЧКА ВЫТАЩИТ ВЫИГРЫШНЫЙ БИЛЕТ В ЧЕТЫРЕ!

МЫ ПРИДЁМ!

ДУМАЕШЬ, СМОЖЕШЬ ПОБЕДИТЬ МЕНЯ С ШАНСАМИ ДЕВЯНОСТО ДЕВЯТЬ К ОДНОМУ? ХА! ХА!

УЖ **ПОПЫТАТЬСЯ-ТО** Я МОГУ?

НА ЭТОТ РАЗ ОБОЙДЁМСЯ БЕЗ СЮРПРИЗОВ! Я ПРИДУМАЛ, **КАК** ЗАСТАВИТЬ УДАЧУ МНЕ УЛЫБНУТЬСЯ!

DOНАЛЬD DAK

ПОБЕДИТЕЛЯ НАЗОВЁТ **МАЛЕНЬКАЯ ДЕВОЧКА?** ЭТОЙ ДЕВОЧКОЙ БУДУ **Я!**

ВО ВСЕХ МОИХ БИЛЕТАХ БУДЕТ **СТАЛЬНАЯ БУЛАВКА!**

А В ЛАДОНИ СПРЯЧУ **МАГНИТ**... ВУАЛЯ! ВОТ ВАМ БИЛЕТИК!

НЕЗАДОЛГО ДО ЧЕТЫРЁХ ЧАСОВ!

ВОТ МОИ БИЛЕТЫ, МЭМ! ПОДПИСАНЫ И **ВСЁ ТАКОЕ!**

ОЧЕНЬ ХОРОШО, МИСТЕР ДАК!

А ТЕПЕРЬ ПОРА ПЕРЕОДЕТЬСЯ!

БЕДНЫЙ ДЯДЯ ДОНАЛЬД!

ВОТ БЫ ХОТЬ **КАК-ТО** ПОМОЧЬ ЕМУ ВЫИГРАТЬ!

ЭЙ! У МЕНЯ ИДЕЯ!

ШУ! ШУ! ШУ!

НО ТАК ВЕДЬ **НЕЧЕСТНО!**

НЕЧЕСТНАЯ ИГРА ПРОТИВ ГЛЭДСТОУНА — ПРОСТО **САМОЗАЩИТА!**

ГЛЭДСТОУН, МОЖЕМ МЫ ОПУСТИТЬ ТВОЙ БИЛЕТ В ЯЩИК?

ХОТИМ УБЕДИТЬСЯ, ЧТО ТЫ НЕ ЖУЛЬНИЧА-ЕШЬ!

ХОРОШО! КИДАЙТЕ САМИ, РАЗ ТАК ВОЛНУЕТЕСЬ!

ВЫШЛО ПРОЩЕ,

ЧЕМ МЫ

ДУМАЛИ!

ВОТ БИЛЕТ ГЛЭДСТОУНА ГАНДЕРА, МЭМ!

СПАСИБО, МАЛЬЧИКИ!

ВСЁ.

ГОТОВО?

АГА! ВОТКНУЛ С КАЖДОЙ СТОРОНЫ ПО БУЛАВКЕ!

ВОТ ТАК! НИКОМУ НЕ ВЫТЯНУТЬ ЭТОТ КОЛЮЧИЙ БИЛЕТИК!

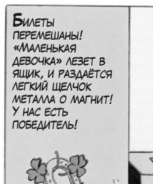

БИЛЕТЫ ПЕРЕМЕШАНЫ! «МАЛЕНЬКАЯ ДЕВОЧКА» ЛЕЗЕТ В ЯЩИК, И РАЗДАЁТСЯ ЛЕГКИЙ ЩЕЛЧОК МЕТАЛЛА О МАГНИТ! У НАС ЕСТЬ ПОБЕДИТЕЛЬ!

ГЛЭДСТОУН ГАНДЕР? КАК ТАКОЕ ВОЗМОЖНО?

НО ДОНАЛЬД НЕ СДАЁТСЯ!

У МЕНЯ ХВАТИТ ДЕНЕГ НА ЕЩЁ ОДНУ ЛОТЕРЕЮ! И УЖ НА ЭТОТ РАЗ ГЛЭДСТОУНУ НЕ ВЫИГРАТЬ!

ПОЗЖЕ!

ХА! ХА! ТЕБЕ ВСЁ-ТАКИ ПРИШЛОСЬ **КУПИТЬ** ИНДЕЙКУ?

ДА, ДЛЯ МОЕЙ ЛОТЕРЕИ!

Я РАЗЫГРЫВАЮ ЭТУ ИНДЮШКУ! ПОПЫТАЕШЬ УДАЧУ?

УДАЧА — МОЁ ВТОРОЕ ИМЯ!

ОТЛИЧНО! ПРИХОДИ КО МНЕ ДОМОЙ ПРЯМО **СЕЙЧАС!** ВОТ ТВОЙ БИЛЕТ!

ТЕПЕРЬ, КЛАДИ СВОЙ БИЛЕТ **СЮДА!**

А ЭТО ЕЩЁ ЧТО ТАКОЕ?

МОИ БИЛЕТЫ!

БИЛЛИ, ЗАЛЕЗАЙ НА СТУЛ И ВЫТАСКИВАЙ ОТТУДА ВЫИГРЫШНЫЙ БИЛЕТ!

НО ЕМУ НИКОГДА НЕ ДОТЯНУТЬСЯ ДО МОЕГО БИЛЕТА! СНАЧАЛА НУЖНО **ВСТРЯХНУТЬ** АКВАРИУМ!

НЕТ ВРЕМЕНИ! РОЗЫГРЫШ СОСТОИТСЯ СИЮ МИНУТУ!

ПРОТЕСТУЮ!

ПРОТЕСТ ОТКЛОНЁН! ЭТО **МОЯ** ЛОТЕРЕЯ, И Я УСТАНАВЛИВАЮ ПРАВИЛА... БИЛЛИ, ВЫТЯГИВАЙ БИЛЕТ!

НО ПРЕЖДЕ ЧЕМ БИЛЛИ УСПЕЛ ВЫТЯНУТЬ БИЛЕТ, ВСЁ ПОЛЕТЕЛО ВВЕРХ ДНОМ!

ЗЕМЛЕТРЯСЕНИЕ! ЗЕМЛЕТРЯСЕНИЕ!

ОНО УЖЕ ЗАКОНЧИЛОСЬ! БИЛЛИ, ТЫ СЛЫШАЛ СВОЕГО ДЯДЮ! ВЫТАСКИВАЙ БИЛЕТ!

ДЕРЖИ, ДЯДЯ ДОНАЛЬД! КАКОЙ ТУТ НОМЕР?

НОМЕР? АХ, ДА... НОМЕР!

17674!

ЭТО МОЙ НОМЕР!

ИК?

НО БЫВАЮТ ДНИ, КОГДА УДАЧА ПЕРЕБОРЩИЛА С ПОДАРКАМИ!

Я ВЫИГРАЛ В ЛОТЕРЕЮ ТРЁХ ИНДЕЕК! ПРОДАШЬ ИХ ЗА МЕНЯ?

ПРИЯТЕЛЬ, Я СВОИХ-ТО НЕ МОГУ ПРОДАТЬ! У ВСЕХ В ГОРОДЕ ЕСТЬ ИНДЕЙКА!

ДАЖЕ ДОНАЛЬД С ПЛЕМЯННИКАМИ ОТВЕДАЮТ ИНДЮШКИ... В ГОСТЯХ У ДЕЙЗИ!

СЧАСТЛИВОГО РОЖДЕСТВА, ДОНАЛЬД! ОХ! ТЫ ВЫГЛЯДИШЬ НЕСЧАСТНЫМ!

ХА! ЕСЛИ ДУМАЕШЬ, ЧТО ОН НЕСЧАСТЕН, ВЫГЛЯНИ В ОКНО!

ЭТО ГЛЭДСТОУН!

ПОЖАЛУЙСТА! НУ, ПОЖАЛУЙСТА! БУДЬТЕ МИЛОСЕРДНЫ И ЗАБЕРИТЕ ЭТИХ ПРОКЛЯТЫХ ИНДЕЕК!

КАК-ТО ЗДЕСЬ БЕЗЛЮДНО!

А ГДЕ ВСЕ?

ПЕРЕЕХАЛИ В ДОМИКИ НА ДНЕ ДОЛИНЫ! ЭТИМ УТРОМ ЗДЕСЬ СОШЛО ТРИ ЛАВИНЫ!

ЭТО ПЛОХО, ДЯДЯ ДОНАЛЬД!

ЛУЧШЕ ПОЕДЕМ В ДРУГОЕ МЕСТО!

МИНУТОЧКУ!

Я ВИЖУ МУЗЫКАЛЬНЫЙ АВТОМАТ! ИНТЕРЕСНО...

ДА! ВОТ ОН, МОЙ «ВОПЯЩИЙ КОВБОЙ»! УЖЕ В ЗАПИСЯХ!

НЕТ, НЕТ, ДЯДЯ ДОНАЛЬД! ДАВАЙ УЕДЕМ СЕЙЧАС ЖЕ!

ЗДЕСЬ ОПАСНО!

«О, ПОХОРОНИ МЕНЯ ТАМ, С МОЕЙ ПОТРЁПАННОЙ ГИТА-А-А-АРОЙ...»

КАНТРИ-ОРКЕСТР В УДАРЕ!

РААР

СНОВА ЛАВИНА! СПАСАЙСЯ, КТО МОЖЕТ!

ЭТА САМАЯ БОЛЬШАЯ! НО ОНА ПРОШЛА МИМО ГОСТИНИЦЫ!

РААР

ФУХ! НАС ЧУТЬ НЕ НАКРЫЛО!

ЧЕТВЁРТЫЙ РАЗ ЗА ДЕНЬ — ЭТО СЛИШКОМ! ЕСЛИ Б Я НЕ БЫЛ ХОЗЯИНОМ ОТЕЛЯ, УЕХАЛ БЫ СО ВСЕМИ!

А ПОЧЕМУ СХОДЯТ ЛАВИНЫ, МИСТЕР?

ОБЫЧНО ИЗ-ЗА ВНЕЗАПНЫХ ОТТЕПЕЛЕЙ... НО СЕЙЧАС ДЕЛО НЕЧИСТО!

ЕСТЕСТВЕННЫХ ПРИЧИН НЕТ! МОЖЕТ, ЛАВИНЫ ВЫЗЫВАЕТ СНЕЖНЫЙ ОТШЕЛЬНИК!

СНЕЖНЫЙ ОТШЕЛЬНИК?

КТО ЭТО?

СТРАННЫЙ СТАРЫЙ ЧУДАК, КОТОРЫЙ ЖИВЁТ В ПЕЩЕРЕ В ГОРАХ! ЛЮДИ ВЕЧНО ШУТЯТ, ЧТО ОН НАСЫЛАЕТ ЛАВИНЫ!

НУ, ПУСТЬ ПОКА СОБИРАЕТСЯ С СИЛАМИ, А Я ПОЙДУ ВНУТРЬ И ВКЛЮЧУ «ВОПЯЩЕГО КОВБОЯ»!

ДА! КАКОЕ-ТО ВРЕМЯ ТУТ БУДЕТ БЕЗОПАСНО!

ТЕПЕРЬ Я НЕ ХОЧУ ОТСЮДА УЕЗЖАТЬ!

И Я ТОЖЕ!

ЗДЕСЬ КАКАЯ-ТО ЗАГАДКА, БРАТЦЫ! САМАЯ НАСТОЯЩАЯ ТАЙНА!

«ВОПЯЩИЙ КОВБОЙ»! ЕГО НАПИСАЛ Я, МИСТЕР!

ТЫ ПОДУМАЙ! А С ВИДУ ВЫ НЕ ПОХОЖИ НА БОЛЬНОГО!

И МНОГИЕ СТАВИЛИ ЭТУ ЗАПИСЬ?

ДО ВАШЕГО ПРИХОДА — ТРОЕ!

«О, ПОХОРОНИ МЕНЯ ТАМ, С МОЕЙ ПОТРЁПАННОЙ ГИТАААААРОЙ...»

ЗАТЫКАЙТЕ УШИ! СНОВА ШЕДЕВР ДЯДИ ДОНАЛЬДА!

РААР

И СНОВА ЛАВИНА!

ДВА ОПОЛЗНЯ ЗА ДЕСЯТЬ МИНУТ!

СНЕЖНЫЙ ОТШЕЛЬНИК, ПОХОЖЕ, КУ-КУ!

ЛАВИНА ПРОШЛА СЛИШКОМ БЛИЗКО К ОТЕЛЮ!

А МОЖНО АРЕНДОВАТЬ ОДИН ИЗ ДОМИКОВ В ДОЛИНЕ?

КОНЕЧНО! Я САМ ТУДА НАПРАВЛЯЮСЬ!

РАЗ УЖ МЫ ОСТАЁМСЯ ЗДЕСЬ, МОЖЕТ, СХОДИМ В ГОРЫ И ПОИЩЕМ ЭТОГО СНЕЖНОГО ОТШЕЛЬНИКА?

Я С ВАМИ, СТО ПРОЦЕНТОВ!

Я с радостью начищу нос этому полоумному старикашке! Он дважды не дал мне послушать «Вопящего ковбоя»!

Утки арендуют лыжи и отправляются в гору!

Выходи, покажись! Не прячься в сугробах, снежный змей!

Оползни двинулись отсюда! Любопытно, вокруг никаких следов!

Ага! Вон его пещера!

Тут записка! Здесь сказано: «Я переехал! Не могу больше слышать «Вопящего ковбоя»! С. Отшельник».

Я переехал! Не могу больше слышать «Вопящего ковбоя»! С. Отшельник.

Ах, так! Песня моя не угодила! Теперь точно до него доберусь!

Зато мы узнали, зачем снежному отшельнику пускать лавины!

А ещё — нашли способ, как его выманить!

Билли, дай мне зеркало!

НАДЕЮСЬ, СРЕДИ ПОСТОЯЛЬЦЕВ ЕСТЬ **ЮНЫЙ СУРОК**!

И ПРАВДА ЕСТЬ!

НЕУЖЕЛИ ЭТО?.. ТОЧНО! КТО-ТО СОЛНЕЧНЫМИ ЗАЙЧИКАМИ ПЕРЕДАЁТ ПОСЛАНИЕ КОДОМ ЮНЫХ СУРКОВ! ДАМ ИМ ЗНАК ПРОДОЛЖАТЬ!

П-О-Л-О-Ж-И Ц-Е-Н-Т В А-В-Т-О-М-А-Т И В-К-Л-Ю-Ч-И В-О-П-Я-Щ-Е-Г-О К-О-В-Б-О-Я!

СТРАННАЯ ПРОСЬБА! НО ЭТИ РЕБЯТА НАВЕРХУ — **ДЕСЯТИЗВЁЗДНЫЕ ГЕНЕРАЛЫ**! НАВЕРНЯКА, У НИХ СВОИ ПРИЧИНЫ!

ТЕПЕРЬ ПРИСТУПИМ К ДЕЛУ! КОГДА СНЕЖНЫЙ ОТШЕЛЬНИК ПОЯВИТСЯ, ЧТОБ СПУСТИТЬ ОЧЕРЕДНУЮ ЛАВИНУ, ПОЙМАЕМ ЕГО С ПОЛИЧНЫМ!

ДА, НО КАК ОН УСЛЫШИТ ПЕСНЮ НА ТАКОЙ ВЫСОТЕ?

ОЙ-ЁЙ! ОБ ЭТОМ Я НЕ ПОДУМАЛ!

«ВОПЯЩИЙ КОВБОЙ»! ОПУЩУ МОНЕТКУ И ПОБЕГУ ПРОЧЬ СО ВСЕХ НОГ! А КТО БЫ ОСТАЛСЯ?

СЛУШАЙ! МУЗЫКА ДОНОСИТСЯ СЮДА СЛОВНО ВОЙ ТЫСЯЧИ КОЙОТОВ!

АЖ УШИ ЗАКЛАДЫВАЕТ!

О, ПОХОРОНИ МЕНЯ ТАМ, С ♫♪ МОЕЙ ПОТРЁПАННОЙ ГИТА-А-АРОЙ ♪ #

НЕУДИВИТЕЛЬНО, ЧТО СНЕЖНЫЙ ОТШЕЛЬНИК ОБЕЗУМЕЛ!

КАНЬОН УСИЛИВАЕТ ЗВУК, СЛОВНО МЕГАФОН! НО ТОЛЬКО У ОДНОЙ МЕЛОДИИ!

ОСТАЛЬНЫЕ ЗВУКИ СЮДА НЕ ДОЛЕТАЮТ!

СМОТРИТЕ! ОПЯТЬ *ЛАВИНА!*

ДЯДЯ ДОНАЛЬД!

ГДЕ ДЯДЯ ДОНАЛЬД?

АХ! ЛЮБЛЮ ЭТОТ КАНТРИ-БЭНД!

ШМЯК

БЕДНЫЙ ДЯДЯ ДОНАЛЬД! ОН НА ПУТИ ЛАВИНЫ!

ПЛЮХ

УЖЕ *ТРИЖДЫ* СНЕЖНЫЙ ОТШЕЛЬНИК ИСПОРТИЛ МНЕ ПЕСНЮ!

ОН ЦЕЛ!

НИ КАПЕЛЬКИ НЕ ПОСТРАДАЛ!

ВСЁ ЕМУ НИПОЧЁМ, НАШЕМУ ДЯДЕ ДОНАЛЬДУ!

ТЕПЕРЬ МЫ ЗНАЕМ, ЧТО СНЕЖНЫЙ ОТШЕЛЬНИК ПРЯЧЕТСЯ ГДЕ-ТО ТАМ!

НЕТ, РЕБЯТКИ! Я ПРЯМО ЗДЕСЬ!

НО... НО ВИД У ВАС НЕ СВИРЕПЫЙ!

Я В ЖИЗНИ НЕ ОБИДЕЛ НИ ОДНО ЖИВОЕ СУЩЕСТВО!

И ПРИШЁЛ УБЕДИТЬСЯ, ЧТО ВЫ, РЕБЯТКИ, НЕ ПОСТРАДАЛИ!

УЖЕ СЛИШКОМ ПОЗДНО СПУСКАТЬСЯ ВНИЗ! ЛУЧШЕ ПЕРЕНОЧУЙТЕ ЗДЕСЬ ВМЕСТЕ СО МНОЙ!

ОН, КАЖЕТСЯ ВПОЛНЕ МИРНЫМ! РИСКНЁМ?

К ТОМУ ЖЕ МЕТЕЛЬ НАДВИГАЕТСЯ! ЧУВСТВУЕТЕ, КАК ЩИПЛЕТ МОРОЗ?

ШУ! ШУ!

ТЫ ПРАВ! БУДЕМ ДЕРЖАТЬ УШКИ НА МАКУШКЕ!

И, МОЖЕТ, ТОГДА ПОЙМЁМ, КАК ОН ВЫЗЫВАЕТ ЛАВИНЫ!

МАЛЬЧИКИ СООБЩАЮТ ВНИЗ, ЧТО У НИХ ВСЁ В ПОРЯДКЕ И ОНИ ПРОВЕДУТ НОЧЬ В ТЁПЛОЙ ПЕЩЕРЕ! ДОНАЛЬД ЛОЖИТСЯ СПАТЬ, И ЕМУ СНИТСЯ СОН, БУДТО УТЯТА В ГОСТЯХ У СТРАШНОГО СНЕЖНОГО ОТШЕЛЬНИКА!

МИЛОЕ У ВАС ТУТ МЕСТЕЧКО, МИСТЕР ОТШЕЛЬНИК!

ДА! НЕ САМАЯ ЛУЧШАЯ МОЯ ПЕЩЕРА, ЗАТО ДАЛЕКО ОТ ЖУТКОГО МУЗЫКАЛЬНОГО АВТОМАТА!

НЕ МОГУ УСНУТЬ! ПОЙДУ ПОСЛУШАЮ МОЮ ПЕСНЮ, УЖ ОЧЕНЬ ЗДОРОВО ИГРАЕТ КАНТРИ-ОРКЕСТР! УВЕРЕН, ЧТО ОТЕЛЬ НЕ ЗАПЕРТ!

ВСЕ БЛАГИЕ ЗВЁЗДЫ! ОПЯТЬ ЭТОТ «ВОПЯЩИЙ КОВБОЙ»!

О, ПОХОРОНИ МЕНЯ ТАМ ♪♫

РААР

А ВОТ И ЕЩЁ ОДНА ЛАВИНА!

СНОВА ПРОШЛА МИМО ОТЕЛЯ!

НО ЕЩЁ БЫ МИЛЛИМЕТР, И КАПУТ!

ПРОСИМ ПРОЩЕНИЯ, МИСТЕР ОТШЕЛЬНИК! МЫ ДУМАЛИ, ЛАВИНЫ ВЫЗЫВАЕТЕ ВЫ!

ЛАВИНЫ ВЫЗЫВАЕТ ТОТ, КТО НАПИСАЛ ЭТУ ПЕСНЮ! ОПОЛЗНИ СХОДЯТ ИЗ-ЗА ВИБРАЦИЙ В СКАЛАХ!

ВСЮ НОЧЬ ЗАВЫВАЕТ ВЬЮГА, ЗАТЕМ НАСТУПАЕТ УТРО...

СНЕЖНЫЕ ШАПКИ ПО ВСЕЙ ДОЛИНЕ!!! ВОТ БЕДА! ЕСЛИ ДЯДЯ ДОНАЛЬД ЕЩЁ РАЗ ПОСТАВИТ СВОЮ ПЕСНЮ...

ПРОЩАЙТЕ, МИСТЕР ОТШЕЛЬНИК! И СПАСИБО ВАМ ОГРОМНОЕ!

НУЖНО СКОРЕЕ СПУСТИТЬСЯ ВНИЗ И **ПРЕДУПРЕДИТЬ** ДЯДЮ ДОНАЛЬДА!

А В ЭТО ВРЕМЯ...

ДОЛЖНО БЫТЬ, ОТШЕЛЬНИКА СОВСЕМ ЗАМЕЛО! Я СМОГУ СЛУШАТЬ «ВОПЯЩЕГО КОВБОЯ» СКОЛЬКО ДУШЕ УГОДНО!

СЛИШКОМ ПОЗДНО!

«О, ПОХОРОНИ МЕНЯ ТАМ...»

ПЛЮЮЮЮХ

ДЯДЯ ДОНАЛЬД!

ДЯДЯ ДОНАЛЬД! ТЫ В ПОРЯДКЕ?

ЛУЧШЕ НЕ БЫВАЕТ! СКИНЬТЕ МНЕ НЕМНОГО МОНЕТ! ДОСТАТОЧНО, ЧТОБЫ Я ПРОТЯНУЛ ТУТ ДО ВЕСНЫ!

И ВОТ...

«О, ПОХОРОНИ МЕНЯ ТАМ С МОЕЙ ПОТРЁПАННОЙ ГИТА-А-АРОЙ... МОЁ СЕРДЦЕ ВЗЫВАЕТ К ТЕБЕ-Е-Е!»

ЗНАЕТЕ, ЧТО МЕНЯ ТЕПЕРЬ БЕСПОКОИТ?

ЕЩЁ ОДНА ЛАВИНА?

НЕТ! РАННЯЯ ВЕСНА!

СМОТРИ! ЭТО ЖЕ МЭР И УПРАВЛЯЮЩИЙ ПАРКАМИ!

ИХ ВЫШВЫРНУЛИ ИЗ ОФИСА ДЯДЮШКИ СКРУДЖА!

DISNEY
ДОНАЛЬД ДАК

А ЕЩЁ НАЗЫВАЕТ СЕБЯ САМЫМ БОГАТЫМ СЕЛЕЗНЕМ В МИРЕ! СТАРЫЙ **СКРЯГА**! ДЕСЯТЬ ЦЕНТОВ ПОЖАЛЕЛ!

ТЫ МЕЛОЧНЫЙ, ЖАДНЫЙ, СТАРЫЙ СКУПЕРДЯЙ!

ОФИС

СКРУДЖ МАКДАК

САМЫЙ БОГАТЫЙ СЕЛЕЗЕНЬ В МИРЕ

СКАЖИТЕ, А ЧТО ОН СДЕЛАЛ?

ЛУЧШЕ СПРОСИТЕ, ЧТО ОН **НЕ СДЕЛАЛ**!

МЫ ПРОСИЛИ У НЕГО НЕСКОЛЬКО ЖАЛКИХ ТЫСЯЧ ЕГО ЗАПЛЕСНЕВЕЛЫХ ДОЛЛАРОВ!

ХОТИМ ВОЗВЕСТИ СТАТУЮ КОРНЕЛИУСА КУТА, **ОСНОВАТЕЛЯ** НАШЕГО СЛАВНОГО ГОРОДА!

ТАК БЫ МЫ ОТДАЛИ **ДОЛГ ЧЕСТИ** ЭТОМУ ХРАБРОМУ ПОЧТЕННОМУ ПЕРВОПРОХОДЦУ, КОТОРЫЙ ПРЕВРАТИЛ ДИКУЮ ПУСТОШЬ В ПРОЦВЕТАЮЩИЙ ГОРОДОК!

В ЭТОМ ГОРОДЕ **ПРОЦВЕТАЮТ** ТОЛЬКО ПОПРОШАЙКИ ВРОДЕ ВАС! ИЩИТЕ ДРУГОГО ДУРАЧКА, КОТОРЫЙ ОПЛАТИТ ВАШ **ДОЛГ**!

И ПРЕКРАТИТЕ ГОВОРИТЬ, ЧТО Я **НЕ** САМЫЙ БОГАТЫЙ СЕЛЕЗЕНЬ В МИРЕ! А ТО РАЗОЗЛЮСЬ И **РАЗОБЛАЧУ** ВАШИ **ПЛУТНИ**!

ХОЧЕШЬ ВЫВЕСТИ ИЗ СЕБЯ ДЯДЮ СКРУДЖА, ПОПРОСИ У НЕГО ДЕНЕГ!

ЭЙ! ТАМ НА УЛИЦЕ ПЕРЕПОЛОХ!

ВСТРЕЧАЮТ КАКУЮ-ТО ВАЖНУЮ ШИШКУ С ВОСТОКА!

ОН ПРИЕХАЛ В ДАКСБУРГ НА КАНИКУЛЫ!

ЭТО ЖЕ МАХАРАДЖА КАКОНТАМСТАНА!

ГОВОРЯТ, ОН САМЫЙ БОГАТЫЙ БОГАЧ В МИРЕ!

ЭТИ ПРОСТОЛЮДИНЫ ОЧАРОВАНЫ МОИМ ВЕЛИКОЛЕПИЕМ! ПРИТОРМОЗИ, Я ШВЫРНУ ЭТИМ БЕДНЯКАМ НЕСКОЛЬКО ТЫСЯЧ ДРУПИЙ!

ВЫ ВИДИТЕ ТО ЖЕ, ЧТО И Я?

ДА! И ДУМАЮ О ТОМ ЖЕ, О ЧЁМ И ВЫ!

СОЗОВИТЕ ГОРОДСКОЙ ОРКЕСТР! ВЫЗОВИТЕ КОМАНДУЮЩЕГО ПАРАДОМ! МЫ ДОЛЖНЫ ПОПРИВЕТСТВОВАТЬ ЭТОГО КОРОЛЕВСКОГО ГОСТЯ С РАЗМАХОМ, ДОСТОЙНЫМ ЕГО ЧЕКОВОЙ КНИЖКИ... ТО ЕСТЬ, ЕГО... ЕГО ВЕЛИЧИЯ!

ДЯДЯ ДОНАЛЬД, ТЫ ДУМАЕШЬ, МАХАРАДЖА БОГАЧЕ ДЯДИ СКРУДЖА?

ПОЖИВЁМ – УВИДИМ!

НА СЛЕДУЮЩИЙ ДЕНЬ!

СВЯТЫЕ УТКИ! ВЫ ТОЛЬКО ПОСМОТРИТЕ!

«МАХАРАДЖА КАКОНТАМСТАНА, *САМЫЙ БОГАТЫЙ БОГАЧ В МИРЕ*, ПОЖЕРТВУЕТ ДАКСБУРГУ ДВАДЦАТЬ ТЫСЯЧ ДОЛЛАРОВ НА ВОЗВЕДЕНИЕ СТАТУИ КОРНЕЛИУСА КУТА»!

«ДВАДЦАТЬ ТЫСЯЧ! ПУСТЯКИ! СУЩИЕ ГРОШИ», — ЗАЯВИЛ НЕОБЫЧАЙНО БОГАТЫЙ ГОСТЬ С ПРОЦВЕТАЮЩЕГО ВОСТОКА!

УХ, МАЛЬЧИКИ! ТЕПЕРЬ *ПОВЕСЕЛИМСЯ!* Я ДОЛЖЕН ПОКАЗАТЬ ЭТУ СТАТЬЮ ДЯДЕ СКРУДЖУ!

ТЫ НЕ ПОТРАТИШЬСЯ НА ГАЗЕТЫ, ТАК ЧТО Я ПРИНЁС ТЕБЕ ОДНУ ПОЧИТАТЬ!

БА-А! Я ЧИТАЮ ТОЛЬКО СУММЫ НА СЧЕТАХ!

ОЙ-ЁЙ! ОЙ-ЁЙ!

«МАХАРАДЖА... *БОГАТЕЙШИЙ БОГАЧ В МИРЕ*... ДВАДЦАТЬ ТЫСЯЧ ДОЛЛАРОВ... СУЩИЕ ГРОШИ»!

ВЫСКОЧКА! КРИКЛИВЫЙ ХВАСТУН! ОН НЕ МОЖЕТ БЫТЬ ПЕРВЫМ БОГАЧОМ МИРА! *САМЫЙ БОГАТЫЙ — Я!*

НУ, ОН СВОИ ДЕНЬГИ НЕ ПРЯЧЕТ!

КАКОЙ-ТО ВТОРОСОРТНЫЙ МИЛЛИАРДЕРИШКА ХОЧЕТ ОБСКАКАТЬ МЕНЯ!

ТОЧНО, ЭТИМ ОН И ЗАНЯТ!

ЧТО Ж! РАЗ ТЕПЕРЬ БОГАТСТВО ДОКАЗЫВАЮТ ТРАТАМИ, ПЕРЕЩЕГОЛЯЮ ЕГО В РАСХОДАХ!

НУ-НУ! ГОВОРЯТ, ОН ТРАТИТ МИЛЛИОНЫ ДОЛЛАРОВ В ГОД!

МИЛЛИОНЫ! ДА ЦЫПЛЁНОК ТРАТИТ БОЛЬШЕ! ПОЙДИ И ВЫВЕДАЙ ВСЁ О СТАТУЕ!

УЗНАЙ, НАСКОЛЬКО ОНА БОЛЬШАЯ И НА ЧТО ПОХОЖА!

ВХОД ВОСПРЕЩЁН

О, БЕЗУМНЫЙ МИР! ИЗМЕРЯЮТ СОСТОЯНИЕ НЕ В ЗАРАБОТКАХ, А В ТРАТАХ!

НЕДЕЛЮ СПУСТЯ! ЖИТЕЛИ ДАКСБУРГА СОБРАЛИСЬ В ПАРКЕ НА ТОРЖЕСТВЕННОЕ ОТКРЫТИЕ ПАМЯТНИКА!

УРА МАХАРАДЖЕ!

ТРИЖДЫ УРА ЕГО ЧЕКОВОЙ КНИЖКЕ!

НО КОГДА ЗАВЕСА СПАДАЕТ, ТОЛПА ИЗУМЛЁННО АХАЕТ, ИБО ЧУТОЧКУ ЛЕВЕЕ СПАДАЕТ ЕЩЁ ОДНО ПОКРЫВАЛО!

ЕЩЁ ОДНА СТАТУЯ КОРНЕЛИУСА КУТА!

ТОЛЬКО БОЛЬШЕ!

В ДВА РАЗА БОЛЬШЕ!

КТО ПОСМЕЛ ПРЕВЗОЙТИ МЕНЯ? КТО **ПРЕВРАТИЛ** МОИ ДВАДЦАТЬ ТЫСЯЧ ДОЛЛАРОВ В ЖАЛКУЮ МЕЛОЧЬ?

«ВОЗВЕДЕНО В ЧЕСТЬ ХРАБРОГО ПОЧТЕННОГО КОРНЕЛИУСА КУТА СКРУДЖЕМ МАКДАКОМ, **ВЕЛИЧАЙШИМ БОГАЧОМ В МИРЕ**»!

И СЛОВА **«ВЕЛИЧАЙШИМ БОГАЧОМ»** ВЫЛОЖЕНЫ ЗОЛОТЫМИ СЛИТКАМИ В 22 КАРАТА!

ВЫСКОЧКА! ДЕРЗКИЙ ХВАСТУН! **НИКТО** НЕ СМЕЕТ ПРЕВЗОЙТИ МАХАРАДЖУ КАКОНТАМСТАНА!

ВЫЗВАТЬ МАСТЕРОВ! ВЫРУБИТЬ БОЛЬШЕ ДЕРЕВЬЕВ! Я ВОЗВЕДУ **ЕЩЁ ОДНУ** СТАТУЮ КОРНЕЛИУСА КУТА!

ВЫВЕДАЙ ВСЁ ПРО НОВУЮ СТАТУЮ! КАКОЙ ПЛАНИРУЮТ РАЗМЕР И УКРАШЕНИЯ!

К ВЕЧЕРУ БУДЕТ СДЕЛАНО!

ОН СНОВА ЭТО СДЕЛАЛ! ЗА НОЧЬ УСТАНОВИЛ СТАТУЮ **БОЛЬШЕ** МОЕЙ!

ЕЩЁ ОДНА НЕДЕЛЯ! ЗАНАВЕС ВНОВЬ ПАДАЕТ!

КОРНЕЛИУС КУТ

СВЯЖИТЕСЬ С МОЕЙ СОКРОВИЩНИЦЕЙ В КАКОНТАМСТАНЕ! ПУСТЬ ПРИШЛЮТ ДЕСЯТОК СЛОНОВ, ГРУЖЁНЫХ ДРУПИЯМИ! Я ВОЗВЕДУ **ЕЩЁ ОДНУ** СТАТУЮ! **НЕБЫВАЛУЮ!**

ДОНАЛЬД, ЗА РАБОТУ!

СЛУШАЮСЬ, ДЯДЯ СКРУДЖ!

СДЕЛАЙТЕ ФИГУРУ ИЗ ЗАМОРСКОГО **МРАМОРА** **ДЕВЯНОСТО** ЭТАЖЕЙ В ВЫСОТУ!

ДА, МАХАРАДЖА!

ДА, ВАШЕ КНЯЖЕСТВО!

НЕСКОЛЬКО НЕДЕЛЬ МАШИНЫ ГРОМЫХАЮТ И ГРОХОЧУТ ВНУТРИ ГРОМАДНЫХ ЭКРАНОВ, КОНКУРИРУЮЩИЕ КОМАНДЫ РАБОЧИХ СОПЕРНИЧАЮТ В ПОГОНЕ ЗА ВЕЛИЧАЙШЕЙ СТАТУЕЙ, КОТОРАЯ ПРИНЕСЁТ ВЕЛИЧАЙШУЮ ЧЕСТЬ ПОБЕДИТЕЛЮ!

БОЛЬШЕ ВСЕГО, НУ, КРОМЕ МОИХ ДЕНЕГ, Я ЛЮБЛЮ ДОБРУЮ **СХВАТКУ!**

И ВОТ, КАМЕРА СИЛЬНО ОТЪЕЗЖАЕТ НАЗАД, ЧТОБЫ ПОКАЗАТЬ ПОТРЯСАЮЩИЙ ФИНИШ ТРЕТЬЕГО РАУНДА БИТВЫ ТИТАНОВ!

ДЕСЯТЬ ТЫСЯЧ ДЕМОНОВ НА ГОЛОВУ ЭТОГО ВЫСКОЧКИ! ОН СНОВА МЕНЯ ПРЕВЗОШЁЛ!

БОЛЬШЕ КАРАВАНОВ, ГРУЖЁННЫХ ДРУПИЯМИ! БОЛЬШЕ ПОСТАВОК МРАМОРА! Я В БЕШЕНСТВЕ!

НЕТ, НЕТ, ВАШЕ КНЯЖЕСТВО! УМОЛЯЮ! СТАТУИ КОРНЕЛИУСА КУТА УЖЕ НЕКУДА СТАВИТЬ!

КАК НАСЧЁТ ВАШЕЙ СТАТУИ? ДЛЯ РАЗНООБРАЗИЯ?

ХО!

СТАТУЯ МЕНЯ! ВОТ ГДЕ Я СМОГУ ПРЕВЗОЙТИ ЭТОГО МАЛЕНЬКОГО ВЫСУШЕННОГО ЛАПЧАТОГО КОРОТЫШКУ!

СЛЕДИ!

УВИДИМСЯ!

СДЕЛАЙТЕ МОЮ СТАТУЮ ВСЮ ИЗ ЗОЛОТА! ДВЕНАДЦАТЬ МЕТРОВ В ВЫСОТУ!

ДА, МАХАРАДЖА!

МОЙ ТЮРБАН... СДЕЛАЙТЕ ЕГО ИЗ БРИЛЛИАНТОВ В ПЕРЛАМУТРОВОЙ ОПРАВЕ!

ДА, ВАШЕ ВЫСОКОКНЯЖИЕ!

А ДЛЯ ГЛАЗ Я ХОЧУ ИЗУМРУДЫ ВЕЛИЧИНОЙ С ЯБЛОКО!

ДА, ВАШЕ ИМПЕРАТОРСКОЕ ПРЕВЕЛИЧИЕ!

КАК Я ЖАЛЕЮ, ЧТО ВТЯНУЛ ДЯДЮ СКРУДЖА В ЭТО ГЛУПОЕ СОСТЯЗАНИЕ!

(ХМММ! МММ!) ИЗУМРУДЫ ДЛЯ ГЛАЗ... ИЗУМРУДЫ ЗЕЛЁНЫЕ, НЕ ТАК ЛИ?

ЗЕЛЁНЫЕ ГЛАЗА! ХА! ДА ОН ВЕСЬ ПОЗЕЛЕНЕЕТ ОТ ЗАВИСТИ, КОГДА УВИДИТ МОЮ СТАТУЮ!

ДАКСБУРГ СГОРАЕТ ОТ НЕТЕРПЕНИЯ! ПРИБЛИЖАЕТСЯ РЕШАЮЩИЙ ДЕНЬ!

ОДИН ИЗ ЭТОЙ ПАРОЧКИ НЕПРЕМЕННО РАЗОРИТСЯ!

СПОРИМ, МАХАРАДЖА ОБСТАВИТ СТАРИКА СКРУДЖА!

КОРНЕЛИУС КУТ

ВОЗДВИГНУТО СКРУДЖЕМ МАКДАКОМ ВЕЛИЧАЙШИМ БО...М

НУ, НЕТ! СТАВЛЮ НА СТАРИНУ МАКДАКА!

ТЫ ПОДУМАЙ! ДВА ВЕЛИЧАЙШИХ БОГАЧА МИРА ПЫТАЮТСЯ ПЕРЕТРАНЖИРИТЬ ДРУГ ДРУГА! ЭТО ЖЕ КОЛОССАЛЬНО!

НАСТУПАЕТ ДЕНЬ БОЛЬШОГО ПРЕДСТАВЛЕНИЯ!

О, УЖАС! ДЯДЯ СКРУДЖ СДАЁТ ПОЗИЦИИ! ЕГО СТАТУЯ НЕ БОЛЬШЕ МАХАРАДЖИ!

ОН ПРОИГРАЛ!

СТАТУЯ МАХАРАДЖИ ОТКРЫТА!

СПЛОШНОЕ ЗОЛОТО!

ДВЕНАДЦАТЬ МЕТРОВ В ВЫСОТУ!

ВЗГЛЯНИТЕ НА ТЮРБАН!

А ЭТИ ИЗУМРУДНЫЕ ГЛАЗА!

И ПУСТЬ ВЫСКОЧКА МАКДАК ТЕПЕРЬ ПОПРОБУЕТ МЕНЯ ПРЕВЗОЙТИ! ПОСМОТРИМ!

ПОКРЫВАЛО СПАДАЕТ СО СТАТУИ ДЯДИ СКРУДЖА!

ЭТО ВСЕГО ЛИШЬ ЦИЛИНДР!

ХА! ХА! ОН НЕ СМОГ ПОЗВОЛИТЬ СЕБЕ ОСТАЛЬНОЕ!

ХА! ХА! ВОТ ВАМ ВСЕМ!

ПРЫГ

СТАТУЯ ВЫСКОЧИЛА ИЗ-ПОД ЗЕМЛИ НА ГИДРАВЛИЧЕСКОЙ ПРУЖИНЕ!

ДВАДЦАТЬ ПЯТЬ МЕТРОВ В ВЫСОТУ!

ЦЕЛЬНЫЕ БРИЛЛИАНТЫ ЗАКРЕПЛЕНЫ НА ПЛАТИНЕ!

А ПОСМОТРИТЕ НА ЭТИ ГЛАЗА! ЗВЁЗДЧАТЫЕ САПФИРЫ ВЕЛИЧИНОЙ С ФУТБОЛЬНЫЙ МЯЧ!

ДЯДЯ ДОНАЛЬД В ОБМОРОКЕ! ВСЁ ВЕСЕЛЬЕ ПРОПУСТИТ!

ЧТО С МОИМ СОСТОЯНИЕМ, ВЕРНЫЙ ПЁС? ХВАТИТ НА ЕЩЁ ОДНУ ПОПЫТКУ?

НЕ ХВАТИТ ДАЖЕ НА БОБОВУЮ ПОХЛЁБКУ, ГЛУПЫЙ ТРАНЖИРА! ТЫ РАЗОРЁН!

А У МЕНЯ ЗАКЛАДНАЯ НА ВАШ РОСКОШНЫЙ ГАРДЕРОБ! ВОЗВРАЩАЙТЕСЬ В ОТЕЛЬ И ИЗВОЛЬТЕ ОТДАТЬ ВСЮ ОДЕЖДУ!

ПОЗЖЕ! ДЯДЯ СКРУДЖ ПРИНИМАЕТ ПОСЕТИТЕЛЯ!

МАХАРАДЖА! МИЛОСТИ ПРОСИМ!

ПРИСАЖИВАЙСЯ! Я ТАК РАД, ЧТО ТЫ ЗАШЁЛ!

АГА!

ТВОЙ СЕЙФ ПУСТ! ТАК ТЫ ТОЖЕ РАЗОРЁН!

РАЗОРЁН? Я?

ТУТ У МЕНЯ ВСЕГО ЛИШЬ СЕЙФ ДЛЯ МЕЛОЧИ!

А ОСНОВНОЕ ХРАНИЛИЩЕ — ТРИ КУБИЧЕСКИХ АКРА ДЕНЕГ В ПОДВАЛЕ!

ЕЩЁ ПОЗЖЕ!

ДЯДЯ СКРУДЖ, ПОЧЕМУ БЫ ТЕБЕ НЕ ПОЖАЛЕТЬ МАХАРАДЖУ И НЕ ПОДАТЬ ЕМУ ДЕСЯТЬ ЦЕНТОВ НА ЧАШКУ КОФЕ?

ЦЕЛЫХ ДЕСЯТЬ ЦЕНТОВ? Я, ПО-ТВОЕМУ, КТО? ПРОКЛЯТЫЙ ТРАНЖИРА?

Disney

Дональд Дак

ВЕСНОЙ ВООБРАЖЕНИЕ ЮНОШИ С ЛЁГКОСТЬЮ ПОВОРАЧИВАЕТСЯ К МЫСЛЯМ О...

У-У-У-У-У-У! ВУ-У-ВУ-У-ВУ! У-У-У-У-У-У!

ОХ, ДОНАЛЬД, Я БУДУ **ТАК** СКУЧАТЬ, КОГДА ТЫ ЗАВТРА УПЛЫВЁШЬ К ОСТРОВУ САН-МАКРЕЛЬ!

НО ЭТО ЖЕ ВСЕГО НА **ОДИН** ДЕНЬ, ДЕЙЗИ!

ОХ! ЦЕЛЫЙ УЖАСНО **ДЛИННЫЙ** ДЕНЬ! ЧАС ЗА ЧАСОМ НИ ЕДИНОЙ ВЕСТОЧКИ ОТ ТЕБЯ!

С ЭТИМ НИЧЕГО НЕ ПОДЕЛАЕШЬ! НА САН-МАКРЕЛЕ НЕТ ТЕЛЕФОНОВ!

ВЕСНОЙ ВООБРАЖЕНИЕ МАЛЬЧИШЕК ОХВАЧЕНО МЫСЛЯМИ О ЗВЕРИНЫХ И ПТИЧЬИХ СОСТЯЗАНИЯХ!

РАКЕТОКРЫЛ, НАШ ПОЧТОВЫЙ ГОЛУБЬ, ПОЧТИ ГОТОВ К ПЕРВОМУ ТРЕНИРОВОЧНОМУ ПОЛЁТУ!

КАКОЙ ОТКОРМЛЕННЫЙ! АЖ БЛЕСТИТ, КАК НОВЕНЬКАЯ ПУЛЯ!

ПОДУМАТЬ ТОЛЬКО, ОН ДОСТАЛСЯ НАМ ВСЕГО ЗА **ДЕСЯТЬ ЦЕНТОВ**, ВЕДЬ ПРЕЖНИЙ ХОЗЯИН В НЁМ РАЗОЧАРОВАЛСЯ!

УГУ! НО У РАКЕТОКРЫЛА ЕСТЬ **КЛАСС**! ОН ФИНИШИРОВАЛ **27-М** В БОЛЬШОЙ ГОНКЕ ИЗ ГЛЕНДЕЙЛА В БЕРБАНК ВОСЕМЬ ЛЕТ НАЗАД!

ЗНАЮ! НО БЫВШИЙ ВЛАДЕЛЕЦ СЧИТАЛ ЕГО ЛЕНТЯЕМ ИЗ-ЗА ПОСТОЯННЫХ ОСТАНОВОК НА СОРЕВНОВАНИЯХ!

ВЫЯСНИМ, **ПОЧЕМУ** ОН ОСТАНАВЛИВАЛСЯ, И ВСЁ ИСПРАВИМ... ВОЗМОЖНО!

ОХ, ДОНАЛЬД, ВОТ БЫ НАЙТИ *СПОСОБ* ПРИСЛАТЬ МНЕ ХОТЬ КОРОТЕНЬКУЮ ЗАПИСКУ, ЧТОБЫ СКРАСИТЬ БЕСКОНЕЧНЫЕ ЧАСЫ ЗАВТРАШНЕГО ОЖИДАНИЯ!

ПРИДУМАЛ! УКРАДУ...ТО ЕСТЬ *ОДОЛЖУ* У РЕБЯТ ИХ ПОЧТОВОГО ГОЛУБЯ!

ПИСЬМО ГОЛУБИНОЙ ПОЧТОЙ! КАК *РОМАНТИЧНО!*

НА СЛЕДУЮЩЕЕ УТРО ДОНАЛЬД ПРИСТУПИЛ К ОСУЩЕСТВЛЕНИЮ СВОЕГО КОВАРНОГО ПЛАНА!

ТАК! ВЫ, ЛОДЫРИ, СЕГОДНЯ ОТПРАВЛЯЕТЕСЬ В ПОГРЕБ ПЕРЕБИРАТЬ КАРТОШКУ НА СЕМЕНА, ПОКА Я ПЛАВАЮ ДО САН-МАКРЕЛЯ! ШАГОМ МАРШ!

НО, ДЯДЯ ДОНАЛЬД...

НИКАКИХ «НО»! РАБОТА УДЕРЖИТ ВАС ОТ ПРОКАЗ!

НО, ДЯДЯ ДОНАЛЬД, МЫ НЕ МОЖЕМ ПОЙТИ *СЕЙЧАС!* РАКЕТОКРЫЛ ЖДЁТ СВОЙ ЗАВТРАК!

Я ПОКОРМЛЮ ВАШЕГО ГОЛУБЯ! ЗА РАБОТУ!

НО ЕМУ ЕЩЁ НУЖНО *ПОУПРАЖНЯТЬСЯ!*

Я УСТРОЮ ЕМУ УПРАЖНЕНИЯ! (МНОГО УПРАЖНЕНИЙ! ХЕ-ХЕ!)

И ВОТ!

МАЛЬЧИКИ МЕНЯ В ПОРОШОК СОТРУТ, ЕСЛИ УЗНАЮТ, ЧТО Я ВЗЯЛ ИХ ДРАГОЦЕННУЮ СТАРУЮ ПТИЧКУ!

ПОЧТИ ПОЛДЕНЬ! ВРЕМЯ ОТПРАВИТЬ МОЁ ПОСЛАНИЕ ДЕЙЗИ!

ЭТА МАЛЕНЬКАЯ ПОЭМА ЗАСТАВИТ ЕЁ СЕРДЦЕ ТРЕПЕТАТЬ, КАК ЛИСТ НА ВЕТРУ... «У ЗВЁЗД ГЛАЗА ТВОИМ ПОД СТАТЬ...»

«ИНАЧЕ КАК ИМ ТАК СИЯТЬ?»... Я НАПИСАЛ БЫ БОЛЬШЕ, НО ЭТОМУ ГОЛУБЮ МНОГО НЕ УНЕСТИ!

НУ, ДАВАЙ, ЖИВАЯ РАКЕТА! НЕСИ ПОЧТУ!

ДЕЙЗИ БУДЕТ ЖДАТЬ ВЕСТОЧКУ У КЛЕТКИ РАКЕТОКРЫЛА! АХ! РАЗВЕ ВЕСНА НЕ ПРЕКРАСНА?

ЧТО ЗА ЖИЗНЬ! ЧТО ЗА ЖИЗНЬ!

ЭЙ, СМОТРИТЕ, ЧТО Я ВЫРЕЗАЛ ИЗ КАРТОШКИ!

ПАРОВОЗ ЧТО НАДО!

ПОИГРАЕМ В ЖЕЛЕЗНУЮ ДОРОГУ!

ТУ-У-ТУ-У-У!

ТУ-У-У-ТУ-У-У! ТУ-У-У-У-ТУ-У-У-У!

ОЙ! К НАМ ВЛЕТЕЛ ГОЛУБЬ!

РАКЕТОКРЫЛ!

ТОЧНО РАКЕТОКРЫЛ!

КАК ТЫ СЮДА ПОПАЛ?

КТО ТЕБЯ ВЫПУСТИЛ?

К ЕГО ЛАПЕ ПРИВЯЗАНА **ЗАПИСКА**!

«ДЕЙЗИ! У ЗВЁЗД ГЛАЗА ТВОИМ ПОД СТАТЬ, ИНАЧЕ КАК ИМ ТАК СИЯТЬ? ДОНАЛЬД.»

АХ ТАК!

ДЯДЯ ДОНАЛЬД, ЗНАЧИТ?

ИСПОЛЬЗУЕТ НАШЕГО ГОЛУБЯ, ЧТОБЫ ДОСТАВЛЯТЬ СВОИ СЛАЩАВЫЕ ЛЮБОВНЫЕ ЗАПИСКИ!

У, ПОХИТИТЕЛЬ ГОЛУБЕЙ! УХ, ЗМЕЙ!

ЕСТЬ КАРАНДАШ? МЫ С НИМ ПОКВИТАЕМСЯ!

ОТЛИЧНО, РАКЕТОКРЫЛ! ДОСТАВЬ ЭТО ПИСЬМО ДЕЙЗИ!

О ДА! ЭТО НАУЧИТ ДЯДЮ НЕ ТРОГАТЬ НАШЕГО ГОЛУБЯ!

«ДЕЙЗИ! КАРТОФЕЛЯ ГЛАЗКИ ТВОИМ ПОД СТАТЬ, ИНАЧЕ И ОНИ МОГЛИ Б СИЯТЬ! ДОНАЛЬД»!

ИНТЕРЕСНО, ПОЧЕМУ РАКЕТОКРЫЛА СЮДА **ПРИНЕСЛО**?

САМ УДИВЛЯЮСЬ!

ОН НЕ МОГ **УВИДЕТЬ** НАС В ТЁМНОМ ПОГРЕБЕ!

ВЕЧЕРОМ!

ДОМОЙ ВОЗВРАТИЛСЯ МОРЯК ИЗ МОРЕЙ!

ТЕПЕРЬ В ГОСТИ К МОЕЙ СЛАДКОЙ ВИШЕНКЕ! ОНА МЕНЯ ЖДЁТ НЕ ДОЖДЁТСЯ!

ТАК И ЕСТЬ!

ТРЕСЬ!

ДЕЙЗИ ДАК

В ЧЁМ ДЕЛО, ДЕЙЗИ? ТЫ НЕ ПОЛУЧИЛА МОЮ ЗАПИСКУ?

О, Я ЕЁ КАК РАЗ ПОЛУЧИЛА!

И ВЕРНУЛА ОТПРАВИТЕЛЮ В ЭТОЙ ВАЗЕ!

ПРИДУМАЛ ЖЕ НАПИСАТЬ, ЧТО У МЕНЯ ГЛАЗА, КАК КАРТОФЕЛИНЫ!

ХЛОП!

ОЙ-ЁЙ!

«КАРТОФЕЛЯ ГЛАЗКИ ТВОИМ ПОД СТАТЬ...»

ЭТО ДЕЛО РУК МАЛЬЧИКОВ!

ОНИ КАК-ТО ПЕРЕХВАТИЛИ МОЁ ПИСЬМО К ДЕЙЗИ! НУ, Я ИМ УСТРОЮ! СЕЙЧАС ПОЛУЧАТ!

ХОТЯ... СТОП! ЛУЧШЕ НЕ СЕЙЧАС! ЗАДАТЬ ОБЫЧНУЮ ТРЁПКУ — СЛИШКОМ ПРОСТО!

ДОНАЛЬД DAK

НАДО СТАТЬ ИЗВОРОТЛИВЫМ, КАК ЗМЕЙ, И НАЙТИ ДРУГОЙ СПОСОБ ПОКВИТАТЬСЯ!

ШЛИ ДНИ! РЕБЯТА ТРЕНИРОВАЛИ РАКЕТОКРЫЛА, ПОКА ОН НЕ НАУЧИЛСЯ ЛЕТАТЬ СО СКОРОСТЬЮ РЕАКТИВНОЙ ПУЛИ!

ЕСЛИ Б ТОЛЬКО УЗНАТЬ, ЗАЧЕМ ОН ДЕЛАЕТ ОСТАНОВКУ ВО ВРЕМЯ ГОНКИ!

И ПОЧЕМУ ВЛЕТЕЛ В ПОГРЕБ, КОГДА МЫ ЧИСТИЛИ КАРТОШКУ?

Я ПОНЯЛ! ОН НАС УСЛЫШАЛ!

МЫ СВИСТЕЛИ, КАК ПАРОВОЗНЫЕ ГУДКИ! ПОМНИТЕ?

ПАРОВОЗНЫЕ ГУДКИ... СВИСТ! ТОЧНО!

ОНИ ИСПЫТАЛИ СВИСТ НА РАКЕТОКРЫЛЕ!

ФЬЮЮТЬ!

ВСЁ СХОДИТСЯ! ВОТ ПОЧЕМУ ОН ОСТАНАВЛИВАЕТСЯ! НЕ МОЖЕТ ПРОЛЕТЕТЬ МИМО, КОГДА СВИСТЯТ!

ЧТО Ж, ХОРОШО, ЧТО ВСЁ ВЫЯСНИЛОСЬ!

ДАЖЕ НЕ ПРЕДСТАВЛЯЕТЕ, КАК ЭТО ХОРОШО! ХЕ-ХЕ-ХЕ-ХЕ!

МАЛЬЧИКИ СЛЕДИЛИ ЗА РАСПИСАНИЕМ ГОНОК, И ВОТ ПОДВЕРНУЛАСЬ ПОДХОДЯЩАЯ!

МАРШРУТ ГОНКИ ОТ ОДИНОКОЙ ГОРЫ ЧЕРЕЗ ПУСТЫНЮ!

СПОРТ

ПРИЗ $

СМОТРИТЕ! ПОЛЁТ ПРОЙДЁТ ВДОЛЬ ЭТОЙ ЛИНИИ! НЕТ НИ ЖЕЛЕЗНЫХ ДОРОГ, НИ ЗАВОДОВ! СОВЕРШЕННО НЕЧЕМУ СВИСТЕТЬ!

ЗНАЧИТ, РАКЕТОКРЫЛ ПОЛЕТИТ НАПРЯМИК И БЕЗ ОСТАНОВОК!

ОН ТОЧНО ПОБЕДИТ!

ХЕ! ХЕ! ХЕ! ХЕ! ХЕ!

ГОНКА ПОЧТОВЫХ ГОЛУБЕЙ ОФИЦИАЛЬНО СТАРТОВАЛА С ОДИНОКОЙ ГОРЫ!

РЕАКТИВНЫЙ КЛИНОК, СТАРТОВАЛ В 8:02!

РАКЕТОКРЫЛ СТАРТОВАЛ В 8:02:05!

РАКЕТОКРЫЛ БЫСТРО ВЫХОДИТ В ЛИДЕРЫ! У ЭТОЙ ПТИЦЫ ТОЧНО ЕСТЬ КЛАСС!

ВНИЗУ ПРОНОСЯТСЯ МИЛИ ЗА МИЛЯМИ! ГОРЫ, ПУСТЫНИ, РЕКИ И ФЕРМЫ!

НА ПОДЛЁТЕ К ДАКСБУРГУ РАКЕТОКРЫЛ ДАЛЕКО ВПЕРЕДИ ВСЕХ!

А ВОТ И ОН!

ФЬЮТЬ!

АХ! НУ И МЕСТЬ Я ПРИДУМАЛ! СЛАДКИЙ, СЛАДКИЙ МИГ!

ФЬЮТЬ-ФЬЮТЬ!

ПОЗЖЕ, КОГДА ВСЕ ПТИЦЫ ПРОЛЕТЕЛИ МИМО!

НУ, СВИСТОЛЮБ, ТЕПЕРЬ МОЖЕШЬ ОТПРАВЛЯТЬСЯ!

ВОТ И ОН!

УЖЕ НЕ ВАЖНО!

ОН ФИНИШИРОВАЛ 99-М ИЗ 100 ГОЛУБЕЙ!

РАКЕТОКРЫЛ! КАК ТЫ МОГ?

МЫ ЖЕ В ТЕБЯ СТОЛЬКО СИЛ И ВИТАМИНОВ ВЛОЖИЛИ!

НАСКОЛЬКО НЕБЛАГОДАРНОЙ МОЖЕТ БЫТЬ ПТИЦА?

ДОНАЛЬД В ОЧЕРЕДНОЙ РАЗ ПЫТАЕТСЯ ПОМИРИТЬСЯ С ДЕЙЗИ!

НУ, ХОРОШО! ПОЛОЖИМ, Я ПОВЕРЮ В ТВОЮ ИСТОРИЮ И ПРОЩУ, НО ПРИ ОДНОМ УСЛОВИИ — ПРОДАЙ ЭТУ УЖАСНУЮ ПТИЦУ, ИЗ-ЗА КОТОРОЙ ВСЁ НАЧАЛОСЬ!

ПОПРО-БУЮ!

ПОЗЖЕ!

УНЫНИЕ!

КОНЕЧНО, ПРОДАВАЙ! И ДУМАТЬ НЕЧЕГО!

ОТЛИЧНО! У МЕНЯ ЕСТЬ ПОКУПАТЕЛЬ НА ОСТРОВЕ САН-МАКРЕЛЬ!

ТЕПЕРЬ ДОНАЛЬД И ДЕЙЗИ ПУСТИЛИСЬ В ПЛАВАНИЕ К ОСТРОВУ САН-МАКРЕЛЬ ВМЕСТЕ — ПРОДАТЬ РАКЕТОКРЫЛА!

ПРОЩАЙ, СТАРЫЙ ДРУГ!

ДА, ПРОЩАЙ, ЛОДЫРЬ!

ЛОБОТРЯС!

В НЕСКОЛЬКИХ МИЛЯХ ОТ БЕРЕГА!

БАТЮШКИ, ДОНАЛЬД! ЧТО ЭТО?

О-ХО-ХО! НЕ ВЕЗЁТ, ТАК НЕ ВЕЗЁТ! ВОДЯНОЙ СМЕРЧ НА НАС ИДЁТ!

ЛОДКА ТРЕЩИТ! СИГНАЛЬ ПО РАДИО О ПОМОЩИ!

БУЛЬК!

НЕ МОГУ! ЗДЕСЬ НЕТ РАДИО!

ПАРУС УНЕСЛО! МЫ ТОНЕМ!

НУЖНО КАК-ТО ПОЗВАТЬ НА ПОМОЩЬ! СДЕЛАЙ ЧТО-НИБУДЬ!

МЫ ПРОПАЛИ! ПОМОГИТЕ! СПАСИТЕ!

СТОП! А ЧТО ЕСЛИ НАС СПАСЁТ ЗЛОСЧАСТНЫЙ ГОЛУБЬ?

ВТОРОПЯХ ОНИ НАЦАРАПАЛИ «SOS», И РАКЕТОКРЫЛ ВЗМЫЛ В НЕБО!

И НЕ ОТВЛЕКАЙСЯ НА СВИСТ! ПОЖАЛУЙСТА!

ВЖУХ

НА БЕРЕГУ СТОИТ КОНСЕРВНЫЙ ЗАВОД! И ВОТ ДОСАДА — КАК РАЗ ВРЕМЯ ОБЕДА!

ТУУУ

ТУТУТУТУ

ЭТО ПОСЛАНИЕ!

ПОЗЖЕ!

ЭЙ, СМОТРИТЕ! РАКЕТОКРЫЛ!

ОН ВЕРНУЛСЯ! НО КАК?

ЗДЕСЬ БЫЛО КАКОЕ-ТО ПОСЛАНИЕ, НО ОНО ВЫПАЛО ПО ПУТИ!

ДЯДЯ ДОНАЛЬД ОТПРАВИЛ БЫ ЗАПИСКУ, ТОЛЬКО ЕСЛИ ОН В БЕДЕ!

МЫ ДОЛЖНЫ ОТЫСКАТЬ ПИСЬМО!

РАСХОДИМСЯ И ИЩЕМ ВОКРУГ ВСЕГО, ЧТО СВИСТИТ И ГУДИТ!

ПОИСКИ ВИЛЛИ ПРИВЕЛИ К КОНСЕРВНОМУ ЗАВОДУ!

КЛОЧОК БУМАГИ НА КРЫШЕ! УВЕРЕН, ЭТО ТА САМАЯ ЗАПИСКА!

МГНОВЕНИЕ СПУСТЯ!

«СПАСИТЕ! МЫ ТОНЕМ В ТРЁХ МИЛЯХ К ВОСТОКУ ОТ МЫСА ВЕДЬМИН ЗУБ! ДОНАЛЬД + ДЕЙЗИ»

БЕРЕГОВАЯ ОХРАНА!

СПАСЛИ ЛИ ИХ? НУ КОНЕЧНО! И ВОТ, НЕСКОЛЬКО ДНЕЙ СПУСТЯ...

НОВАЯ ГОЛУБИНАЯ ГОНКА!

МОЛНИЯ СТАРТОВАЛ В 08:06!

РАКЕТОКРЫЛ СТАРТОВАЛ В 08:06:04!

ПТИЦЫ ПОДЛЕТАЮТ К ДАКСБУРГУ! ЧЕРЕЗ СЕКУНДУ МЫ НАЗОВЁМ ПОБЕДИТЕЛЯ!

И ВОТ ЗВУЧИТ СИГНАЛ С КЛЕТКИ! ПЕРВЫЙ ВНОВЬ РАКЕТОКРЫЛ! ПТИЦА-СЕНСАЦИЯ, ЧТО ВЫИГРЫВАЕТ КАЖДУЮ ГОНКУ!

А ВАМ СЛАБО? И, УЧТИТЕ, ДРУЗЬЯ, ОН ДЕЛАЕТ ЭТО В НАУШНИКАХ!

УГУ! ТЕПЕРЬ ПОБЕДА ТОЧНО НЕ УСВИСТИТ! ХЕ! ХЕ!

Disney

Дональд Дак

Уже очень давно Дональд с племянниками ломают головы над тем, насколько удачлив Глэдстоун Гандер и ПОЧЕМУ!

Проследим за ним! Вот верный способ всё выяснить!

Пусть выйдет из дома! Будем за ним хвостом ходить и узнаем, ВСЕГДА ли он так удачлив, как когда мы с ним вместе!

Да! Он бахвалится, что НИКОГДА НЕ РАБОТАЛ и всегда всё идёт ему в руки ДАРОМ!

Посмотрим!

Шшш! Вот и он, с корзиной! Пошёл за покупками!

«Когда найду я четырёхлистный клевер в долине счастливых подков»

Клочок бумаги из его корзины! СПИСОК ПОКУПОК!

Ага! Вот и узнаем, что он обычно получает за так! ЕСЛИ получает!

А У НЕГО БОЛЬШИЕ ЗАПРОСЫ! «ДЕСЯТОК ЯИЦ, БАТОН ХЛЕБА, БАРАНЬЯ НОГА, ЯБЛОЧНЫЙ ПИРОГ, КВАРТА СЛИВОК И ПРЫГАЛКИ «КУЗНЕЧИК»!

ЕСЛИ ЕМУ ВСЁ ДОСТАНЕТСЯ БЕСПЛАТНО, ОН ПРОСТО ЧУДО ПРИРОДЫ, НЕ МЕНЬШЕ!

ХММ! ЭТО КУДАХЧЕТ КУРИЦА-НЕСУШКА МИССИС ДЖОНС!

КО-КО-КО!

КУДАХТАЮЩИЕ НЕСУШКИ ОТКЛАДЫВАЮТ ЯЙЦА! АГА!

СПРЯТАЛА ГНЕЗДО НА ОБЩЕСТВЕННОЙ ТЕРРИТОРИИ, А В НЁМ — ДЕСЯТОК ЯИЦ! ДА ТЫ ВЕЗУНЧИК, ГЛЭДСТОУН!

ЧТО ТАМ ШЛО ПЕРВЫМ ПУНКТОМ В СПИСКЕ, ДЯДЯ ДОНАЛЬД? ДЕСЯТОК ЯИЦ?

ДА! ДЕСЯТОК ЯИЦ!

НО ЭТО НЕ ТАК УЖ НЕВЕРОЯТНО! КТО УГОДНО МОГ НАЙТИ ТАМ ГНЕЗДО!

МУЧИТЕЛЬ! НЕБЛАГОДАРНЫЙ ПРОХВОСТ!

НУ ВСЁ, ДОРОГУША!

МОЛОДОЖЁНЫ МЁРФИ СНОВА ССОРЯТСЯ!

Я УВЕРЕН — УДАЧА ГЛЭДСТОУНА **НЕ ИМЕЕТ ГРАНИЦ!**

ВСЁ ЕЩЁ ЕСТЬ ШАНС, ЧТО ОН СЯДЕТ В ЛУЖУ!

ВИДИТЕ? ПОКА НЕ **ВЕСЬ СПИСОК СОБРАЛ!** ОСТАЛАСЬ КВАРТА СЛИВОК И ПРЫГАЛКИ!

А ОН ПОЧТИ ДОМА!

КАЖЕТСЯ, Я ЧТО-ТО ЗАБЫЛ! ЖАЛЬ, СПИСОК ПОТЕРЯЛСЯ!

ОЙ-ОЙ! ТАМ КТО-ТО ПРЫГАЕТ НА «КУЗНЕЧИКЕ»! ВЫГЛЯДИТ НЕВАЖНО!

ЭТО ЖЕ САМ ВИНТ РАЗБОЛТАЙЛО, ИЗОБРЕТАТЕЛЬ! КАК ДЕЛА, ВИНТ?

ПЛОХО! (ОХХ! УФФ!) ОЧЕНЬ ПЛОХО!

Я ДУМАЛ, ЧТО НАШЁЛ НОВЫЙ СПОСОБ ВЗБИВАТЬ МАСЛО! (УФФ! УФФ!)

НО ПОСЛЕ ЧАСА ПРЫЖКОВ НА «КУЗНЕЧИКЕ» ЭТА КВАРТА СЛИВОК ТАК И ОСТАЛАСЬ *СЛИВКАМИ!*

ЗАБИРАЙ ПРЫГАЛКИ И СЛИВКИ ТОЖЕ! ПОЙДУ ДОМОЙ ИЗОБРЕТАТЬ ПОПКОРН СО ВКУСОМ МАСЛА БЕЗ МАСЛА!

СТОН!

А ПОКА ДОНАЛЬД ЯРОСТНО ТОЛКАЛ ГЛЭДСТОУНА В СТОРОНУ ОФИСА ДЯДЮШКИ СКРУДЖА, СТАРЫЙ СКРЯГА ТОНУЛ В ГЛУБИНАХ СВОЕЙ ТОСКИ!

ЧТО СО МНОЙ НЕ ТАК В ПОСЛЕДНИЕ ДНИ? МОИ ДОХОДЫ УПАЛИ ДО МИЛЛИАРДА ДОЛЛАРОВ В ЧАС!

ДОЛЖНА БЫТЬ **ПРИЧИНА**! УДАЧА **НИКОГДА** РАНЬШЕ МЕНЯ НЕ ПОКИДАЛА!

ЗАЧЕМ ТОРОПИТЬСЯ! МОЖЕТ, СЕЙЧАС **НЕПОДХОДЯЩИЙ** МОМЕНТ ПРОСИТЬ ДЕНЕГ У ТВОЕГО СКУПЕРДЯЯ-ДЯДЮШКИ!

НА ЭТО ВСЯ НАДЕЖДА!

В СТАРИННОЙ КНИГЕ НАРОДНЫХ ПРИМЕТ СКАЗАНО: «ЧТОБЫ ПРЕРВАТЬ ПОЛОСУ НЕУДАЧ, СДЕЛАЙ ТО, ЧЕГО НИКОГДА НЕ ДЕЛАЛ»!

ЧТО ЖЕ Я НИКОГДА НЕ ДЕЛАЛ... ХМММ!

ТОЧНО! Я НИКОГДА НЕ ДЕЛИЛСЯ ДЕНЬГАМИ! ЭТО ВЕРНЁТ МНЕ УДАЧУ!

ХЕЙ, ВОТ КТО МНЕ НУЖЕН! ГЛЭДСТОУН ГАНДЕР!

ГЛЭДДИ, СТАРИНА! Я ТУТ РЕШИЛ ВРУЧИТЬ МЕШОК МОНЕТ ПЕРВОМУ, КТО ВОЙДЁТ В ЭТУ ДВЕРЬ! НА, ДЕРЖИ! ОНИ **ТВОИ**!

ГУСИ И ГУСЫНИ! ОНИ РУХНУЛИ В ОБМОРОК ВСЕЙ ТОЛПОЙ!

ДОНАЛЬД И РЕБЯТА УБЕДИЛИСЬ, ЧТО УДАЧА ГЛЭДСТОУНА БЕЗГРАНИЧНА!

НО ПОЧЕМУ? ПОЧЕМУ ЕМУ ТАК ВЕЗЁТ?

ДУМАЮ, У НЕГО ЕСТЬ СЧАСТЛИВЫЙ ТАЛИСМАН! ВО МНОГО РАЗ СИЛЬНЕЕ ПОДКОВЫ!

ПОХОЖЕ НА ПРАВДУ! ЕСЛИ ВЫЯСНИМ, КАКОЙ АМУЛЕТ, МОЖЕТ, САМИ ТАКИМ ОБЗАВЕДЁМСЯ!

ГЛЭДСТОУН НИКОГДА НЕ ПРИЗНАЕТСЯ!

ЗНАЮ, НО МЫ НАВЕСТИМ ЕГО И РАЗВЕДАЕМ, ЧТО К ЧЕМУ!

И ВОТ!

НИКОГДА РАНЬШЕ НЕ ВСТРЕЧАЛ ГОСТЕЙ, КОТОРЫЕ ВЕЗДЕ СУЮТ СВОЙ КЛЮВ!

МЫ НЕ ИЗ ТАКИХ!

А В СЕЙФЕ ЧТО?

НЕ ТВОЁ ДЕЛО!

ЕСЛИ ОН ДЛЯ ЦЕННОСТЕЙ, ПОЧЕМУ ДЕНЬГИ СНАРУЖИ?

НЕ ТВОЁ... ЛАДНО, СЕЙФ НУЖЕН ДЛЯ ЧЕГО-ТО ДРУГОГО! ТЕПЕРЬ УХОДИТЕ!

ЗВУК, КАК БУДТО ТАМ ПУСТО! ОТКРЫВАЙ, И ПОСМОТРИМ!

ТУК ТУК

НЕТ! НЕТ! НИКТО НЕ ЗАГЛЯДЫВАЕТ В ЭТОТ СЕЙФ! ДАЖЕ Я!

НО ПОЧЕМУ?

ПОТОМУ ЧТО ВНУТРИ НЕЧТО, ЧТО МЕНЯ ПОГУБИТ, ЕСЛИ... НЕВАЖНО! ПРОВАЛИВАЙ!

ЧТО БЫ НИ ХРАНИЛОСЬ В СЕЙФЕ, ОНО НУ ОЧЕНЬ ОСОБЕННОЕ!

НЕ СОМНЕВАЮСЬ, ТАМ ЕГО ТАЛИСМАН УДАЧИ!

ПРИВЕТ, ДЯДЯ СКРУДЖ! ЧТО ЗА УГРЮМЫЙ ВИД?

У МЕНЯ ЧЁРНАЯ ПОЛОСА!

Я ДАЖЕ ВРУЧИЛ ГЛЭДСТОУНУ МЕШОК С ДЕНЬГАМИ, НАДЕЯЛСЯ ПРИВЛЕЧЬ НАЗАД ВЕЗЕНЬЕ, НО И ЭТО НЕ ПОМОГЛО!

ВЫШЕ КЛЮВ, ДЯДЮШКА! МЫ УЗНАЛИ, ГДЕ НАЙТИ ТО, ЧТО СДЕЛАЕТ ВСЕХ НАС ВЕЗУНЧИКАМИ!

О ЧЁМ ТЫ?

О СЧАСТЛИВОМ ТАЛИСМАНЕ ГЛЭДСТОУНА! ОН ПРЯЧЕТ ЕГО В СЕЙФЕ!

ОГО! СКОРЕЕ ВЫЯСНИМ, ЧТО ТАМ!

ДА! ЕСЛИ ПРОСТАЯ **МОНЕТА** — **ТВОЙ** СЧАСТЛИВЫЙ ТАЛИСМАН, ПОЧЕМУ **НАШИ** МОНЕТКИ НЕ ПРИНОСЯТ НАМ УДАЧИ!

ДА ПОТОМУ, ЧТО ТАМ **НЕ** СЧАСТЛИВЫЙ ТАЛИСМАН! ЭТО... ВПРОЧЕМ, НЕ ВАШЕ ДЕЛО!

НЕТ, ТЕПЕРЬ УЖЕ НАШЕ! МЫ УСТАЛИ ОТ ТВОЕЙ ПРОКЛЯТОЙ **ТАЙНЫ!**

ХОРОШО! ХОРОШО! Я **ПРИЗНАЮСЬ!**

ОДНАЖДЫ, ДАВНЫМ-ДАВНО, В **МОМЕНТ КРАЙНЕЙ СЛАБОСТИ,** Я ВЫШЕЛ НА РАБОТУ!

НА РАБОТУ?

ДА! И Я **ЗАРАБОТАЛ** ЭТУ МОНЕТУ!

НО МНЕ БЫЛО ТАК **СТЫДНО,** ЧТО Я **ЗАПЕР** ЕЁ В СЕЙФЕ И НИКОГДА НЕ ОТКРЫВАЛ ЕГО!

ЕСТЬ КОММЕНТАРИИ?

ТОЛЬКО НЕ ДЛЯ ПЕЧАТИ!

БАМ! ПУХ! СКРИИИП!

ЧТО ТАМ ЗА КАНОНАДА? САЛЮТ К ЧЕТВЁРТОМУ ИЮЛЯ?

ИЛИ МАРСИАНСКОЕ ВТОРЖЕНИЕ?

ПУХ! ВРУМ!

ДА ТАМ ВИНТ РАЗБОЛТАЙЛО, НАШ БЕЗУМНЫЙ ИЗОБРЕТАТЕЛЬ!

ТЫР

ПРИВЕТ, ДЯДЯ ДОНАЛЬД!

ЧТО ЭТО ЗА ШТУКА, ВИНТ?

МОЙ НОВЫЙ РЕАКТИВНЫЙ БАГГИ ДЛЯ БАГАЖА, ДОНАЛЬД!

ПРОЛЕТАЕТ ДВА КВАРТАЛА НА ПАРЕ ФЕЙЕРВЕРКОВ!

ПОСТОРОНИСЬ! ОЧИСТИТЬ УЛИЦУ! СТАРТУЕМ!

ТОЛЬКО ПРЕДСТАВЬТЕ УЛИЦЫ, ЗАБИТЫЕ КУРЬЕРАМИ НА ТАКИХ ТАРАТАЙКАХ!

ВИНТ РАЗБОЛТАЙЛО УЖЕ ДЕСЯТЬ ЛЕТ ПЫТАЕТСЯ ИЗОБРЕСТИ ЧТО-НИБУДЬ ПОЛЕЗНОЕ! И ЭТО ЕЩЁ САМЫЙ УДАЧНЫЙ ПРОЕКТ!

ПРОСЛЕЖУ ЗА НИМ И ПОСМОТРЮ, ЧЕМ ВСЁ КОНЧИТСЯ! А ТО УЖЕ НЕСКОЛЬКО НЕДЕЛЬ НЕ СМЕЯЛСЯ ДО КОЛИКОВ!

БАМ! ПУУ

БУМС!

ХА! ХА! ТЫ ВРЕЗАЛСЯ В ДЕРЕВО!

КОНЕЧНО! ЗДЕСЬ МНЕ НУЖНО БЫЛО ОСТАНОВИТЬСЯ!

ВОТ ТАК ИЗОБРЕТЕНИЕ!

НЕ БЫЛО ВРЕМЕНИ ДОВЕСТИ ЕГО ДО УМА! Я СЕЙЧАС СЛИШКОМ ЗАНЯТ — СОЗДАВАЛ МОЗГОЯЩИКИ!

ОТЛИЧНО, РЕБЯТА! ХВАТАЙТЕ ПО ЯЩИКУ И НЕСИТЕ В ЛЕС!

ТЫ НАЗВАЛ ЭТИ КОРОБКИ **МОЗГОЯЩИКАМИ?** ТОЛЬКО НЕ ДУМАЙ, ЧТО Я СУЮ НОС...

ВОВСЕ НЕТ, ДОНАЛЬД! ЭТИ ЯЩИКИ — ПРЕДМЕТ МОЕЙ ГОРДОСТИ, НОВЕЙШЕЕ И ВЕЛИЧАЙШЕЕ ИЗОБРЕТЕНИЕ!

ОНИ НАБИТЫ ПРИБОРАМИ, КОТОРЫЕ ПОСЫЛАЮТ ЭЛЕКТРИЧЕСКИЕ МЫСЛЕЛУЧИ, ДЯДЯ ДОНАЛЬД!

СМОТРИ! УСТАНАВЛИВАЕМ ПО ЯЩИКУ НА КАЖДОЙ СТОРОНЕ ЗВЕРИНОЙ ТРОПЫ, И КАЖДЫЙ ЗВЕРЬ, КОТОРЫЙ ПРОЙДЁТ МИМО, НАУЧИТСЯ **ДУМАТЬ!**

БОЛЬШЕ ТОГО, ДЯДЯ ДОНАЛЬД! ЖИВОТНЫЕ СМОГУТ **ГОВОРИТЬ** И **ВЕСТИ СЕБЯ КАК ЛЮДИ!**

ТЕПЕРЬ Я ВКЛЮЧУ МЫСЛЕЛУЧИ И ЗАВТРА УТРОМ МЫ ВЕРНЁМСЯ, ЧТОБЫ ВЫЯСНИТЬ, КАК ОНИ СРАБОТАЛИ!

(У-У-УХ!) ВАУ! А Я-ТО СЧИТАЛ БАГГИ ДЛЯ БАГАЖА **БЕЗУМНЫМ** ИЗОБРЕТЕНИЕМ!

ЭЙ! А ВЫ КАК ВВЯЗАЛИСЬ В ЭТУ **БЕЛИБЕРДУ?**

МЫ **РАБОТАЕМ** НА МИСТЕРА РАЗБОЛТАЙЛО!

МЫ ЕГО **АССИСТЕНТЫ!**

НИКОГДА РАНЬШЕ **СЕЛЕЗНИ** НЕ ОПУСКАЛИСЬ ДО ТАКОГО!

ТЕМ ЖЕ ВЕЧЕРОМ!

МАЛЬЧИКИ, ВЫ ДОЛЖНЫ ПРЕКРАТИТЬ РАБОТАТЬ НА ЭТОГО СУМАСБРОДА ВИНТА!

ПОЧЕМУ, ДЯДЯ ДОНАЛЬД?

ВЫ... ВЫ... НУ, ВЫ ОПОЗОРИТЕСЬ ПЕРЕД ВСЕМ ГОРОДОМ! СТАНЕТЕ ПОСМЕШИЩЕМ!

ОХ!

ПОДУМАЙТЕ! ВСЕ УЗНАЮТ, ЧТО ВЫ ПОМОГАЕТЕ ВИНТУ С ЕГО МОЗГОЯЩИКАМИ И БУДУТ ДРАЗНИТЬ ВАС ДО КОНЦА ДНЕЙ!

МЫ РИСКНЁМ!

ЛЮДИ НЕДОЛГО СМЕЯЛИСЬ НАД ЭДИСОНОМ ИЛИ МАРКОНИ*!

НО ВИНТ НЕ ЭДИСОН! ОН ВСЕГО ЛИШЬ БЕЗОБИДНЫЙ ЧУДАК!

КАК И ЭДИСОН, ПОКА ЕГО ИЗОБРЕТЕНИЕ НЕ СРАБОТАЛО!

ПОХОЖЕ, УТЯТ ТАК ПРОСТО НЕ ОТГОВОРИТЬ! ОНИ КУПИЛИСЬ НА ЭТИ БРЕДОВЫЕ ИДЕИ!

ЧТО Ж, ИСПОЛЬЗУЮ СТРАТЕГИЮ! ЗАСТАВЛЮ ИХ СГОРАТЬ ОТ СТЫДА, ТОГДА САМИ УЙДУТ!

102

* ТОМАС ЭДИСОН (1847-1931) И ГУЛЬЕЛЬМО МАРКОНИ (1874-1931) - ИЗВЕСТНЫЕ ИЗОБРЕТАТЕЛИ.

ПОЗЖЕ!

ЭЙ, ТАМ! ПРОСЫПАЙТЕСЬ! Я ХОЧУ ВЗЯТЬ НАПРОКАТ КОСТЮМ!

ПАРИ МАСК КОСТЮМЫ

У ВАС ЕСТЬ КОСТЮМ ВОЛКА, ДО ЖУТИ ПОХОЖИЙ НА НАСТОЯЩЕГО?

ТАКОЙ?

ДА! ТО, ЧТО НАДО!

КОГДА ВИНТ И МАЛЬЧИКИ ПРИДУТ УТРОМ В ЛЕС, ОНИ ПОВСТРЕЧАЮТ «ВОЛКА», КОТОРЫЙ НАУЧИЛСЯ ДУМАТЬ, КАК ЧЕЛОВЕК!

СЛЕДУЮЩИМ УТРОМ!

НЕ МОГУ ДОЖДАТЬСЯ КОГДА СМОГУ ВЗГЛЯНУТЬ, КАКИЕ ЧУДЕСА СОТВОРИЛИ МОИ МОЗГОЯЩИКИ!

СУДЯ ПО СЛЕДАМ, ТУТ ПРОШЛА ТОЛПА ЖИВОТНЫХ!

ДАЖЕ ВОЛК ПРОБЕГАЛ!

О ДА, ДЖЕНТЛЬМЕНЫ! ЭТО БЫЛ Я! ДОБРОГО УТРЕЧКА!

ВОЛК! ВОЛК!

И ОН РАЗГОВА- РИВАЕТ!

МОЁ ИЗОБРЕТЕНИЕ РАБОТАЕТ!

И ВДРУГ, СОВЕРШЕННО ВНЕЗАПНО, РАСХОТЕЛОСЬ МНЕ СЫРОЙ КУРЯТИНЫ! ЗАХОТЕЛ **ПРИГОТОВЛЕННОЙ** ЕДЫ!

ЖАРЕНАЯ УТКА! НЯ-Я-Я-Я-ЯМ!

ЧТО Ж ТАМ В ЭТИХ КОРОБКАХ, ПРИЯТЕЛЬ? КАКИЕ-ТО ЛУЧИ ДЛЯ **АППЕТИТА**?

БОЮСЬ, ЧТО ТАК!

ЭЙ, ВОЛК ОТ НАС ОТСТАЛ! ИСПАРИЛСЯ!

ТОГДА ВЕРНЁМСЯ И УЗНАЕМ, КАК ТАМ ВИНТ!

СМОТРИТЕ! ЗДЕСЬ СЛЕДЫ БОРЬБЫ!

И СЛЕДЫ ДЯДИ ДОНАЛЬДА!

ДА! ЕГО ЗАБРАЛ ВОЛК! **НАСТОЯЩИЙ** ВОЛК!

Т-ТЫ **РАЗГОВА-РИВАЕШЬ**!

НО ТЫ КРОЛИК!

АГА! ЗАБАВНАЯ ШТУКА! МЫ С МОЕЙ СТАРУШКОЙ ГУЛЯЛИ ВЧЕРА ПО ТРОПЕ! МИНОВАЛИ ДВЕ СМЕШНЫЕ КОРОБОЧКИ!

НО СЕЙЧАС НЕ ОБ ЭТОМ! ХОТИТЕ СПАСТИ ДЯДЮ, ТОГДА ПОРА БЕЖАТЬ ВПРИПРЫЖКУ! ОНИ УШЛИ ТУДА!

ДЛЯ ДЯДИ ДОНАЛЬДА ДЕЛО ПАХНЕТ ЖАРЕНЫМ!

ДЯДЯ ДОНАЛЬД! ДЯДЯ ДОНАЛЬД!

ЧЕГО ВОЛКУ ОТ НЕГО НАДО?

ОЙ-ЁЙ!

О, ДА! ВДРУГ СТРАСТЬ КАК ЗАХОТЕЛОСЬ ЖАРКОГО ИЗ УТЯТИНЫ!

НАМ НЕ СПРАВИТЬСЯ С ВОЛКОМ ГОЛЫМИ РУКАМИ! ПОЗОВЁМ НА ПОМОЩЬ ВИНТА!

ВИНТ! МИСТЕР РАЗБОЛТАЙЛО! МОЖЕТЕ ВКЛЮЧИТЬ У МОЗГОЯЩИКОВ ОБРАТНЫХ ХОД?

ЗАСТАВИТЬ ИХ ОГЛУПИТЬ ВОЛКА?

В ОБЩЕМ, ДА! НАДО ПЕРЕНАПРАВИТЬ ЛУЧ ИЗ ЯЩИКА «Б» В ЯЩИК «А», ЧТО СМЕНИТ ОТРИЦАТЕЛЬНЫЙ ПОЛЮС НА ПОЛОЖИТЕЛЬНЫЙ...

ДЕТАЛИ НЕ ВАЖНЫ! НАМ НУЖНО ПРЕРВАТЬ ЗВАНЫЙ УЖИН!

МОЗГОЯЩИКИ УСТАНОВИЛИ ПО ПРОТИВОПОЛОЖНЫМ СТОРОНАМ ОТ СЧАСТЛИВОГО ВОЛКА-ПОВАРА!

ТАК, СЛЕГКА ПРИПРАВИМ ТЕБЯ ШАЛФЕЕМ!

ЩЁЛК!

ГРРРР!.. РРРВУФ!

У-У-У! УА-АЙ! УА-А!

ТЫ СПАСЁН, ДЯДЯ ДОНАЛЬД! ВОЛК СНОВА ДУМАЕТ, КАК ВОЛК!

И ВОТ!

ТЕПЕРЬ, ДЯДЯ ДОНАЛЬД, ТЫ ПОНЯЛ, ПОЧЕМУ ЛЮДИ ПЕРЕСТАЛИ СМЕЯТЬСЯ НАД ЭДИСОНОМ, МАРКОНИ И АЛЕКСАНДРОМ ГРЭМОМ БЭЛЛОМ!

НИКОГДА НЕ ЗНАЕШЬ, КАКИЕ УДИВИТЕЛЬНЫЕ ОТКРЫТИЯ МОЖЕТ СДЕЛАТЬ ТОТ, КОГО ТЫ НАЗЫВАЕШЬ «ЧУДАКОМ»!

МИСТЕР, ПОДАЙТЕ МОНЕТКУ НА ПУЧОК МОРКОВКИ!

ОЙ, ДА НУ ТЕБЯ!

Disney

Дональд Дак

"Золотой шлем"

Дональд — помощник сторожа в Даксбургском музее!

Иэх!

ДРЕВНЯЯ ЛАДЬЯ ВИКИНГОВ

Эта древняя махина была найдена в Херринге, Норвегия, где была захоронена викингами около 920 г.н.э.

ДОИСТОРИЧЕСКАЯ КОРОВА

Иэх!

ПАРИК ВСАДНИКА БЕЗ ГОЛОВЫ

БОГ ТРЁПА

Работаю уже третий месяц, и хоть бы что-нибудь произошло!

МЕШОК ДЛЯ СТИРКИ ЛЕДИ ГОДИВЫ

ЗАЛ. 10

Платят хорошо, смены маленькие! Наверное, не стоит жаловаться!

ВЕСЕЛЬЕ

БОРЬБА

Но я любитель СУРОВЫХ БУДНЕЙ! Обожаю ПРИКЛЮЧЕНИЯ и весёлое житьё, которое наверняка было у ВИКИНГОВ!

ТОЛЬКО ПОДУМАТЬ! ЛЮДИ ПЕРЕСЕКАЛИ ОКЕАН В ЭТОЙ СТАРОЙ ЛОХАНКЕ И ОРИЕНТИРОВАЛИСЬ ЛИШЬ ПО СОЛНЦУ И ЗВЁЗДАМ!

ПЛАВАЛИ В ИСЛАНДИЮ И ГРЕНЛАНДИЮ, А МОЖЕТ И В **АМЕРИКУ**, ЗА СОТНИ ЛЕТ ДО «КОРОЛЕВЫ МЭРИ»!

МИСТЕР, КАК НАЙТИ ЭКСПОЗИЦИЮ БАБОЧЕК?

ЭТО В ВОСТОЧНОМ КРЫЛЕ! ИДИТЕ ПО КОРИДОРУ «К», ЗАТЕМ НАЛЕВО, ПО КОРИДОРУ 9! ПЕРВАЯ КОМНАТА ПОСЛЕ ЧУЧЕЛА ЖИРАФА!

ДРЕВНИЕ ВИКИНГИ ОХОТИЛИСЬ НА МОРЖЕЙ И КИТОВ, БИЛИСЬ С ДИКИМИ ПЛЕМЕНАМИ, А Я РАССКАЗЫВАЮ РАЗНЫМ БОТАНИКАМ, КАК ОТЫСКАТЬ БАБОЧЕК!

ЧТО СТАЛО С СОВРЕМЕННЫМИ МУЖЧИНАМИ?

МИСТЕР СТОРОЖ! КАК ПОПАСТЬ В ЗАЛ ВЫШИВКИ И КРУЖЕВ?

ВТОРАЯ ДВЕРЬ ПОСЛЕ ВЯЗАНЫХ САЛФЕТОК! (СВЯТЫЕ КУРОПАТКИ!)

НА ПАРУ МИНУТ ПОДНИМУСЬ НА БОРТ СТАРОЙ ПОСУДИНЫ — ВООБРАЖУ СЕБЯ ВИКИНГОМ!

ЧУЖИЕ ПАРУСА ПО КУРСУ, ХРАБРЫЕ НОРМАННЫ! ГОТОВЬТЕСЬ ПОТОПИТЬ ЦЕЛЫЙ ФЛОТ!

СКРИИП

ВИДНО, В ТРЮМЕ ОГРОМНАЯ КРЫСА!

НЕТ, ЗДЕСЬ ЧЕЛОВЕК! КТО ЭТОТ ТИП?

ЭЙ, ТЫ! МАРШ ОТСЮДА! КОРАБЛЬ ДЛЯ ОСМОТРА, А НЕ ЧТОБЫ РАЗНЮХИВАТЬ!

Я НИЧЕГО НЕ ТРОГАЛ! ПРОСТО ХОТЕЛ ПОСМОТРЕТЬ, КАК СКРЕПЛЕНЫ СНИЗУ ДОСКИ!

В БИБЛИОТЕКЕ ВЫ НАЙДЁТЕ **ЧЕРТЕЖИ** КОРАБЛЯ! ТРЕТЬЯ ДВЕРЬ НАЛЕВО ПОСЛЕ КЛАДКИ С ЯЙЦАМИ ДИНОЗАВРА!

ЧЕРТЕЖИ! ВОТ ЕЩЁ!

Я УЖЕ ВИДЕЛ ЕГО ЗДЕСЬ! ВЕЧНО КРУТИТСЯ У ЭТОЙ ЛАДЬИ ВИКИНГОВ!

ОН ПОЛЗАЛ ПО ТРЮМУ ТАК, БУДТО **ЧТО-ТО ИСКАЛ!**

ЭММ! ЧТО Ж ТУТ МОЖНО НАЙТИ, КРОМЕ ЖУКОВ-ДРЕВОТОЧЦЕВ?

ЗОЛОТО И ДРАГОЦЕННОСТИ ВЫВЕЗЛИ С КОРАБЛЯ ЕЩЁ ДО ТОГО, КАК ВИКИНГИ ЕГО ЗАТОПИЛИ!

ВИДНО, ЭТОТ ПАРЕНЬ ИСКАЛ НЕЧТО, О ЧЁМ УЗНАЛ ИЗ СТАРИННЫХ КНИГ!

ПЕРЕВОДЧИКИ ДРЕВНИХ ТЕКСТОВ ПОРОЙ НАТЫКАЮТСЯ НА УДИВИТЕЛЬНЫЕ ТАЙНЫ!

СТУК! СТУК!

ХММ! ЗАГЛУШКА ШЕВЕЛИТСЯ!

ТЫ ГЛЯДИ! ЕСЛИ КОТЕЛОК ВАРИТ — ВСЁ ИДЁТ КАК ПО МАСЛУ!

СВИТОК ИЗ КОЖИ ОЛЕНЯ! ПОХОЖЕ НА **КАРТУ**!

НА НЕЙ — ДРЕВНИЕ ПИСЬМЕНА! НАДО ПОКАЗАТЬ КУРАТОРУ!

ДЕВЯНОСТО СЕВЕРНЫХ СИЯНИЙ ТЕБЕ НА ХВОСТ! ГЛУПЫЙ СТОРОЖ **НАШЁЛ** ТО, ЧТО Я ИСКАЛ!

ПОЗЖЕ!

ДОНАЛЬД, ТЫ СОВЕРШИЛ ОДНО ИЗ ВЕЛИЧАЙШИХ ОТКРЫТИЙ В ИСТОРИИ! ЭТА КАРТА ИЗ ОЛЕНЬЕЙ КОЖИ — **СУДОВОЙ ЖУРНАЛ** ДРЕВНЕЙ ЛАДЬИ! ОН ПОВЕСТВУЕТ ОБО ВСЕХ ЕЁ ПОХОДАХ!

СМОТРИ! ЕЮ КОМАНДОВАЛ ВИКИНГ ПО ИМЕНИ ОЛАФ СИНИЙ! ОН ПЛАВАЛ К ЗЕМЛЯМ ИСЛАНДИИ В 900 ГОДУ Н.Э. — ЗА ГОДЫ ДО ЭРИКА РЫЖЕГО!

А В 901 ГОДУ ПРИВЁЛ ЛАДЬЮ К БЕРЕГАМ **СЕВЕРНОЙ АМЕРИКИ**!

И КАК ДОКАЗАТЕЛЬСТВО, ЧТО ОН БЫЛ ЗДЕСЬ, ЗАРЫЛ **ЗОЛОТОЙ ШЛЕМ** НА ПЯТЬДЕСЯТ ДЕВЯТОЙ ПАРАЛЛЕЛИ, НА ПОБЕРЕЖЬЕ **ЛАБРАДОРА**!

ШЛЕМ! КОРАБЛЬ! **КАРТА**! ВСЕ ОБРЫВКИ ИСТОРИИ, КОТОРУЮ Я ПЕРЕВОДИЛ В НОРВЕГИИ, СОШЛИСЬ! ПОРА ДЕЙСТВОВАТЬ!

КУРАТОР

ДОНАЛЬД, НАКОНЕЦ-ТО МЫ **ТОЧНО ЗНАЕМ**, КТО ОТКРЫЛ АМЕРИКУ!

ТЫ **ПРОСЛАВИШЬСЯ**! МУЗЕЙ ПРОСЛАВИТСЯ! МИЛЛИОНЫ ЛЮДЕЙ ПРИДУТ ПОСМОТРЕТЬ НА ЛАДЬЮ ОЛАФА И ЗОЛОТОЙ ШЛЕМ!

НО СНАЧАЛА НЕПЛОХО БЫ **ОТЫСКАТЬ** ЭТОТ ШЛЕМ!

ВЕРНО!

Я НЕМЕДЛЕННО ОТПРАВЛЮ ЭКСПЕДИЦИЮ НА ЛАБРАДОР!

ВЫ НИЧЕГО НЕ СТАНЕТЕ ДЕЛАТЬ!

Я АДВОКАТ ШАРКИ! ЭТА КАРТА ПРИНАДЛЕЖИТ МОЕМУ КЛИЕНТУ, АЗУРУ СИНЕМУ, ПРЯМОМУ ПОТОМКУ ОЛАФА СИНЕГО!

ПО КАКОМУ ПРАВУ ВЫ ПРЕДЪЯВЛЯЕТЕ СТОЛЬ АБСУРДНЫЕ ТРЕБОВАНИЯ?

ПО НОРМАМ ПРАВА «КОДЕКСА ОБ ОТКРЫТИЯХ», БОРОДАЧ!

Что ж, похоже, во время правления Карла Великого, в 792 г. н.э., правители всех народов собрались в Риме и подписали закон, который гласил: «Любой, кто открыл за морем новые земли, становится их владельцем, если не завещает своему королю»!

Поскольку Олаф Синий открыл Северную Америку ДЛЯ СЕБЯ, теперь она принадлежит ЕГО БЛИЖАЙШЕМУ РОДСТВЕННИКУ!

Призрак великого Цезаря! Такой закон И ВПРЯМЬ существует и не был аннулирован!

Хе-хе!

А теперь передайте карту моему клиенту! Или нам арестовать вас и каждого жителя Америки за ВТОРЖЕНИЕ в частные владения?

Чушь и пустая болтовня! Как он ДОКАЖЕТ, что РОДСТВЕННИК Олафа Синего?

Фокус, покус, филипокус!

Что на языке закона значит: «А как ВЫ докажете ОБРАТНОЕ»?

Карту, пожалуйста!

Теперь я удаляюсь на поиски шлема! А потом вернусь и взыщу дань с вас, моих РАБОВ!

Хокус, локус, джокус! Что означает: «Владыка земли владеет и подданными!»

ДОНАЛЬД, ЭТО САМОЕ **УЖАСНОЕ**, ЧТО СЛУЧАЛОСЬ С НАШЕЙ СТРАНОЙ! **ВСЕ** МЫ **РАБЫ** ЭТОГО ЧЕЛОВЕКА!

ХОТИТЕ СКАЗАТЬ, ТЕПЕРЬ ЭТОТ СКОЛЬЗКИЙ ТИП — **ПРАВИТЕЛЬ** СЕВЕРНОЙ АМЕРИКИ?

ДА, ЕСЛИ ТОЛЬКО МЫ НЕ ПОМЕШАЕМ ЕМУ **НАЙТИ** ЗОЛОТОЙ ШЛЕМ! ДАВАЙ СЯДЕМ И ПОДУМАЕМ!

ОТПРАВЛЮ ПО ЕГО СЛЕДУ ПОЛИЦИЮ! ВОТ И ВСЕ ДЕЛА!

ЕГО НЕ **ОСТАНОВЯТ** НИ ПОЛИЦИЯ, НИ АРМИЯ, НИКТО! У НЕГО ЕСТЬ ПОЛНОЕ **ПРАВО** ИСКАТЬ ШЛЕМ! ТАКОВ **ЗАКОН**!

ТОГДА ОГРЕЮ ЕГО ДУБИНКОЙ! С СОТРЯСЕНИЕМ МОЗГА ДАЛЕКО НЕ УПЛЫВЁШЬ!

А ВДРУГ ПРОМАХНЁШЬСЯ? ЕСТЬ ВЫХОД **ПОЛУЧШЕ**! НАЙДИ МНЕ БУМАГУ!

ВОТ КАРТА ОЛАФА, КАК Я ЕЁ ЗАПОМНИЛ! ОТМЕЧЕННЫЙ КРЕСТИКОМ МЫС И ЕСТЬ МЕСТО, ГДЕ ОН ЗАРЫЛ ШЛЕМ!

ОТЛИЧНАЯ РАБОТА, СЭР! НО **НАМ-ТО** ЧТО С ЭТОГО?

МНОГОЕ, ДОНАЛЬД! МЫ С ТОБОЙ НАЙДЁМ ШЛЕМ ПРЕЖДЕ АЗУРА СИНЕГО!

СЭР, МЫ ЧТО ЖЕ, ОТПРАВИМСЯ НА ЛАБРАДОР? К АЙСБЕРГАМ И ПОЛЯРНЫМ МЕДВЕДЯМ?

ОЛАФ СИНИЙ СМОГ! РАЗВЕ МЫ МЕНЕЕ МУЖЕСТВЕННЫ?

УГХ!

КАЖДЫЙ ИЗ НАС ВОЗЬМЁТ ПО КАРТЕ! ТЫ ПОПРОБУЕШЬ ДОСТИГНУТЬ МЫСА ПО МОРЮ! Я ОТПРАВЛЮСЬ ПО СУШЕ! ОДИН ИЗ НАС ДОЛЖЕН ДОБРАТЬСЯ ТУДА РАНЬШЕ АЗУРА СИНЕГО!

ПОНИМАЮ, СЭР! ЛИБО ТАК, ЛИБО НЕВОЛЯ!

ЛИБО ТАК, ЛИБО РАБСТВО!

ВОТ ТВОЯ КАРТА И ДЕНЬГИ НА РАСХОДЫ! САДИСЬ НА НОЧНОЙ САМОЛЁТ ДО НЬЮФАУНДЛЕНДА!

ОТТУДА САМ ПРОЛОЖИШЬ ПУТЬ ПО МОРЮ В МАЛЕНЬКОЙ ЛОДКЕ, КАК ЭТО ДЕЛАЛИ ДРЕВНИЕ ВИКИНГИ! ТЫ В ДЕЛЕ?

Д-ДА! КОНЕЧНО, СЭР!

НУ И НУ! А Я ЕЩЁ ВОРЧАЛ, ЧТО СО МНОЙ НИЧЕГО ИНТЕРЕСНОГО НЕ СЛУЧАЕТСЯ! ХОРОШО, ЧТО Я АВАНТЮРИСТ!

ЕЩЁ КОЕ-ЧТО, ДОНАЛЬД! ЕСЛИ ОТЫЩЕШЬ ЗОЛОТОЙ ШЛЕМ, ВЫКИНИ В МОРЕ, ЧТОБЫ НИКТО НИКОГДА БОЛЬШЕ ЕГО НЕ НАШЁЛ! ОН ОПАСЕН!

Утром Дональд проснулся воодушевлённым! Впереди **приключения!** Первоклассное **веселье,** достойное настоящих викингов!

БОЛЬШЕ НИКАКИХ ЗАТХЛЫХ МУЗЕЙНЫХ ЗАЛОВ! ОТНЫНЕ Я ДОНАЛЬД — ГРОЗА СЕВЕРНЫХ МОРЕЙ!

ПУСТЬ **НЕЖЕНКИ** ИЗУЧАЮТ СВОИХ БАБОЧЕК И ВЫШИВАЮТ УЗОРЫ НА САЛФЕТКАХ! МЕНЯ ЖДУТ СКРИП МОРСКОЙ СОЛИ НА ЗУБАХ И ВОЙ ШТОРМА В ПАРУСАХ!

ТЕБЯ ЖДЁТ РЕЙС ОБРАТНО В ДАКСБУРГ, ЕСЛИ НЕ ВСТАНЕШЬ С КРОВАТИ! СКОРО САДИМСЯ НА НЬЮФАУНДЛЕНДЕ!

Вскоре утки выяснили, что Азур Синий времени не теряет!

ГРУЗИТЕ ПРИПАСЫ НА БОРТ! ОТПЛЫВАЕМ **НЕМЕДЛЕННО!**

ЭТОТ МАЛЫЙ ОТПРАВЛЯЕТСЯ НА ПОИСКИ ЗОЛОТОГО ШЛЕМА, КОТОРЫЙ СДЕЛАЕТ ЕГО **ПРАВИТЕЛЕМ** СЕВЕРНОЙ АМЕРИКИ!

НУ, ДЕЛА! Я ЧИТАЛ ОБ ЭТОМ В УТРЕННЕЙ ГАЗЕТЕ!

ЗНАЧИТ, ОН УЖЕ И В ГАЗЕТЫ РАСТРУБИЛ!

ХОЧЕТ, ЧТОБЫ ВСЕ ЗНАЛИ!

ПОСМОТРИТЕ ТУДА! ПРИХВАТИЛ СВИДЕТЕЛЕЙ, ЧТОБЫ **ПОДТВЕРДИТЬ** НАХОДКУ ШЛЕМА!

К СЛОВУ О СВИДЕТЕЛЯХ! С НИМ ЦЕЛАЯ ШАЙКА ГАЗЕТЧИКОВ!

ВО ВРЕМЯ ПОИСКОВ ШЛЕМА ЕГО ДАЖЕ ВОЕННЫЙ КОРАБЛЬ БУДЕТ ОХРАНЯТЬ!

ДОНАЛЬД С ПЛЕМЯННИКАМИ АРЕНДОВАЛИ ЛОДКУ, НО ПРОШЁЛ НЕ ОДИН ЧАС, ПРЕЖДЕ ЧЕМ ОНИ НАПАЛИ НА СЛЕД АЗУРА СИНЕГО!

ПОХОЖЕ, ОН УЖЕ В СОТНЕ МИЛЬ ВПЕРЕДИ!

С ТАКОЙ БЫСТРОЙ ЛОДКОЙ И ХОРОШИМ ЭКИПАЖЕМ ОН УВЕЛИЧИВАЕТ ОТРЫВ КАЖДУЮ МИНУТУ!

ПУСТЬ УДИРАЕТ! В ЭТОЙ ГОНКЕ НУЖНА НЕ СКОРОСТЬ, А ЖИВУЧЕСТЬ!

ОНИ ШЛИ КУРСОМ НА СЕВЕР! НА ГОРИЗОНТЕ ПОЯВИЛИСЬ АЙСБЕРГИ!

ПЕРЕСЕКАЕМ ПЯТЬДЕСЯТ ПЯТУЮ ПАРАЛЛЕЛЬ!

КАК ТЫ УЗНАЛ, ДЯДЯ ДОНАЛЬД?

РАССЧИТАЛ ПО СОЛНЦУ ПРИ ПОМОЩИ СЕКСТАНТА, НЕДОТЁПА!

ОЙ!

А ЕСЛИ ХОЧЕШЬ УБЕДИТЬСЯ, ЧТО МЫ ИДЁМ НА СЕВЕР, СВЕРЬСЯ С КОМПАСОМ!

И ПРАВДА!

НАМ ПОВЕЗЛО, ЧТО ТЫ ПРИХВАТИЛ ЭТИ ШТУКИ! БЕЗ НИХ МЫ БЫ ТОЧНО СБИЛИСЬ С ПУТИ!

НА 56 ПАРАЛЛЕЛИ СЕВЕРНОЙ ШИРОТЫ ПОГОДА НАЧИНАЕТ ПОРТИТЬСЯ!

МОРСКИЕ ПТИЦЫ ИЩУТ УКРЫТИЯ! НАДВИГАЕТСЯ УЖАСНЫЙ ШТОРМ!

МОЖЕТ, ПЕРЕЖДЁМ НЕПОГОДУ В ОДНОМ ИЗ ЭТИХ ФЬОРДОВ, ДЯДЯ ДОНАЛЬД?

НЕТ! ИДЁМ НА СЕВЕР!

ПУСТЬ АЗУР СИНИЙ ПРЯЧЕТСЯ! ТОГДА У НАС БУДЕТ ШАНС ЕГО ОБОГНАТЬ!

И ПОТОМ, ЕСЛИ ХОТИМ БЫТЬ, КАК ВИКИНГИ, МЫ И ПЛАВАТЬ ДОЛЖНЫ, КАК ВИКИНГИ! ПРЕОДОЛЕЕМ ВСЁ, ЧТО ПОДКИНЕТ НАМ МОРЕ!

БРР! ЛУЧШЕ БЫ ДЯДЯ ДОНАЛЬД ХОТЬ НЕНАДОЛГО ЗАБЫЛ О СВОЕЙ ЖИВУЧЕСТИ!

ДАЛЕКО ВПЕРЕДИ КОРАБЛИ АЗУРА СИНЕГО ПРИНИМАЮТ УДАРЫ СТИХИИ!

ПОВОРАЧИВАЕМ! ПОВОРАЧИВАЕМ! ПОПРОБУЕМ ДОБРАТЬСЯ ПО ВЕТРУ ДО САГЛИК-БЭЙ!

НЕ СЛЫШИМ ВАС!

ЦЕПОЧКА АЙСБЕРГОВ РАЗДЕЛЯЕТ КОРАБЛИ!

МЫ УХОДИМ ОТСЮДА!

ВОЕННЫЙ КОРАБЛЬ ИДЁТ НАЗАД, СЭР! НАМ ТОЖЕ РАЗВОРАЧИВАТЬСЯ?

ДЕРЖАТЬ КУРС! ЗДЕСЬ Я ОТДАЮ ПРИКАЗЫ!

И АЗУР СИНИЙ БЕЗРАССУДНО ВЕДЁТ СВОЙ КОРАБЛЬ ПРЯМО МЕЖДУ АЙСБЕРГАМИ!

ДАЛЬШЕ НЕЛЬЗЯ, СЭР! СЛИШКОМ **РИСКОВАННО**!

ПОВЕРНУТЬ НАЗАД **ЕЩЁ РИСКОВАННЕЕ**! СКАЗАНО ВАМ — ДЕРЖАТЬ КУРС!

Я СТАНУ ВЛАСТЕЛИНОМ СЕВЕРНОЙ АМЕРИКИ, ТОЛЬКО ЕСЛИ НАЙДУ ШЛЕМ **ПЕРВЫМ**! И Я ДОБЕРУСЬ ДО НЕГО ПЕРВЫМ!

БОССУС, ШЕФУС, ПРАВДУС! ЧТО ОЗНАЧАЕТ: «СЛОВО БОССА — ЗАКОН!»

ТРЕСЬ

ОТЛИЧНО, МИСТЕР СИНИЙ! ЧТО **ТЕПЕРЬ** ГОВОРИТ ЗАКОН?

ЧАСАМИ ПОЗЖЕ!

ШТОРМ ОТСТУПАЕТ, ДЯДЯ ДОНАЛЬД! ЭЙ! ЧТО ВИДНО ВОКРУГ?

СПАСАТЕЛЬНЫЕ ШЛЮПКИ ИДУТ НА ЮГ! ЭТО КОМАНДА АЗУРА И ЕГО **СВИДЕТЕЛИ**! ОНИ ПОТЕРПЕЛИ КРУШЕНИЕ!

УРА!

ТЕПЕРЬ АЗУРУ СИНЕМУ НЕ ОБОГНАТЬ НАС НА ПУТИ!

К ШЛЕМУ!

ПОХОЖЕ, ТЕПЕРЬ МЫ ВПЕРЕДИ! НО ГДЕ ЖЕ САМ АЗУР? ЕГО НЕТ НИ В ОДНОЙ ЛОДКЕ!

ЭТО ЖЕ ВРЕМЯ! МНОГО МИЛЬ СЕВЕРНЕЕ!

ГОВОРЮ ВАМ, СЭР, ДОВОЛЬНО ГЛУПО ПЫТАТЬСЯ ДОСТИЧЬ ПЯТЬДЕСЯТ ДЕВЯТОЙ ПАРАЛЛЕЛИ НА ЭТОЙ УТЛОЙ ЛОДЧОНКЕ!

И КАК ВЫ, БЕЗ СЕКСТАНТА И КОМПАСА, НАЙДЁТЕ ПУТЬ ЧЕРЕЗ БЕСКРАЙНЕЕ МОРЕ?

НИКАК! НО ПРОДОЛЖАЙ ГРЕСТИ! КАК-НИБУДЬ ВЫКРУТИМСЯ!

ЭТОЙ НОЧЬЮ ОПУСТИЛСЯ ТУМАН! ГУСТОЙ, КАК ГОРОХОВЫЙ СУП!

МОЖЕТ НАМ ЗАГЛУШИТЬ МОТОР И ПЕРЕЖДАТЬ ТУМАН, ДЯДЯ ДОНАЛЬД?

НЕТ! ПРОДОЛЖАЕМ ПЛЫТЬ! Я ОРИЕНТИРУЮСЬ ПО КОМПАСУ!

НО АЙСБЕРГИ, ДЯДЯ ДОНАЛЬД! ТЫ ВРЕЖЕШЬСЯ В НИХ В ТЕМНОТЕ!

ОСТОРОЖНО!

ЭЙ! Я КОЕ-ЧТО ПРИДУМАЛ! ЕСЛИ КРИЧАТЬ, МЫ СМОЖЕМ «УВИДЕТЬ» АЙСБЕРГИ УШАМИ — БУДЕМ СЛУШАТЬ ЭХО!

СУПЕРИДЕЯ! КРИ-ИК НАЧИНА-АЙ!

МИЛИ СПУСТЯ!

ПРИВЕТ!

АЙСБЕРГ ПРЯМО ПО КУРСУ!

ПРИВЕТ

ПРИВЕТ!

АЙСБЕРГ ПО ПРАВОМУ БОРТУ! ДАЛЕКО!

ПРИВЕТ

ПРИВЕТ!

ПРИВЕТ!

ДОБРЫЙ ВЕЧЕР!

ВАШИ КРИКИ НАМ ОЧЕНЬ ПОМОГЛИ! МЫ УСЛЫШАЛИ ВАС ЗА НЕСКОЛЬКО МИЛЬ!

КАРАМБА! АЗУР СИНИЙ!

НА СЛЕДУЮЩЕЕ УТРО!

ИТАК, ДЯДЯ ДОНАЛЬД, ЧТО ТЕПЕРЬ ДЕЛАТЬ?

УЖ ТОЧНО НЕ ШУМЕТЬ И ДЕРЖАТЬ РОТ НА ЗАМКЕ!

АЗУР СИНИЙ УКРАЛ НАШУ ЛОДКУ, И КОМПАС, И СЕКСТАНТ! МЫ ВЫБЫЛИ ИЗ ГОНКИ ЗА ЗОЛОТЫМ ШЛЕМОМ!

ДА, СЕЙЧАС НЕ ДО ШУТОК!

БУДЬ У НАС ПАРУС И ВЕТЕР, ОНИ БЫ ТЯНУЛИ ЛОДКУ!

ЕЩЁ СКАЖИ, БУДЬ У НАС КРЫЛЬЯ, МЫ БЫ ЛЕТЕЛИ И САМИ ТЯНУЛИ!

УТКИ ПЫТАЮТСЯ ГРЕСТИ, НО ВСЁ НАПРАСНО!

Я ГДЕ-ТО ЧИТАЛ, ЧТО ВИКИНГИ БЫЛИ ВЫНОСЛИВЫЕ, КАК ЛОШАДИ! ДОЛЖНЫ БЫЛИ БЫТЬ!

ОСТАЁТСЯ НАДЕЯТЬСЯ, ЧТО КУРАТОР ДОБЕРЁТСЯ ДО МЫСА РАНЬШЕ, ЧЕМ НЕГОДЯЙ АЗУР СОРВЁТ ДЖЕКПОТ!

НО У КУРАТОРА СВОИ ПРОБЛЕМЫ!

МОТОР СГОРЕЛ, СЭР! РЕМОНТ ЗАЙМЁТ ТРИ ДНЯ!

НО Я НЕ МОГУ ЖДАТЬ ТАК ДОЛГО! Я СПЕШУ!

ТОГДА ВАМ ЛУЧШЕ ПОЙТИ ПЕШКОМ! НУЖНОЕ МЕСТО В СТА МИЛЯХ ВО-О-ОН В ТУ СТОРОНУ!

О НЕТ!

СТО МИЛЬ! МНЕ НЕ УСПЕТЬ ВОВРЕМЯ! ДОНАЛЬД — ПОСЛЕДНЯЯ НАДЕЖДА АМЕРИКИ!

МОРЕ ЧАСТО ЖЕСТОКО, НО ИНОГДА ДЕЛАЕТ ПОДАРКИ!

КРУШЕНИЕ! ОБЛОМКИ ПЛАВАЮТ В ВОДЕ!

ЭТО БАК С КОРАБЛЯ АЗУРА!

И ПАРУСИНА! Я ВИЖУ ПАРУСИНУ!

ОБЛОМКИ ОКАЗАЛИСЬ БЕСЦЕННОЙ НАХОДКОЙ — ИЗ НИХ УТКИ СООРУДИЛИ МАЧТУ! А ИЗ НАЙДЕННОЙ ТКАНИ СДЕЛАЛИ ПАРУС!

МЫ СНОВА В ДЕЛЕ!

ДО ТЕМНОТЫ Я ПОВЕДУ СУДНО ПО СОЛНЦУ! А ПОТОМ БУДЕМ ДЕРЖАТЬСЯ ПОЛЯРНОЙ ЗВЕЗДЫ!

ЗАМЕТИЛ, МЫ ПЛЫВЁМ ТОЧЬ-В-ТОЧЬ КАК ВИКИНГИ ТЫСЯЧУ ЛЕТ НАЗАД?

ДА, НАШ ДЯДЯ-АВАНТЮРИСТ ДОЛЖЕН БЫТЬ СЧАСТЛИВ!

ТОЙ ЖЕ НОЧЬЮ!

КАК ДАЛЕКО НА СЕВЕР НАМ ПЛЫТЬ, ДЯДЯ ДОНАЛЬД?

СОГЛАСНО КАРТЕ, ПОКА ПОЛЯРНАЯ ЗВЕЗДА НЕ ОКАЖЕТСЯ ПОД ПРЯМЫМ УГЛОМ К МОЕЙ СОГНУТОЙ РУКЕ!

ЕЩЁ ДВА ДНЯ ПУТИ НА СЕВЕРО-ВОСТОК В ЭТОЙ УТЛОЙ ЛОХАНКЕ, И МЫ НА МЕСТЕ!

ДВА ДНЯ! ОХ!..

НАКОНЕЦ, ОНИ ДОСТИГЛИ ПЯТЬДЕСЯТ ДЕВЯТОЙ ПАРАЛЛЕЛИ И ПОВЕРНУЛИ НА ЗАПАД К БЕРЕГУ!

ВИДИТЕ МЫС В ФОРМЕ КРЕСТА?

НЕТ! НО ПРОСТО ВИДЕТЬ ЗЕМЛЮ — УЖЕ СЧАСТЬЕ!

ОЛАФ СИНИЙ, ПОХОЖЕ, ДУМАЛ ТАКЖЕ! ЭТО САМЫЙ ОТВРАТИТЕЛЬНЫЙ МАРШРУТ ДО АМЕРИКИ, ЧТО Я ЗНАЮ!

ОНИ ЧАСАМИ ОБЫСКИВАЮТ БЕРЕГ ВДОЛЬ И ПОПЕРЁК!

НИ ОДНОГО ПОДХОДЯЩЕГО МЫСА! НАВЕРНОЕ, МЫ ВЗЯЛИ СЛИШКОМ ДАЛЕКО НА СЕВЕР!

ИЛИ НА ЮГ!

МОЖЕТ, КУРАТОР **ОШИБСЯ**, КОГДА ПЕРЕРИСОВЫВАЛ КАРТУ?

ДА! Я ЗАМЕТИЛ, ЧТО АЗУР СИНИЙ ЗДЕСЬ **НЕ** ИЩЕТ!

ЗРЯ ТЫ ТАК ДУМАЕШЬ, ДОНАЛЬД!

ТЫСЯЧА ЧЕРТЕЙ! ЭТОТ СВИТОК ЧУДОВИЩНЫЙ **ОБМАН**!

ЗДЕСЬ **НЕТ** МЫСА В ФОРМЕ КРЕСТА!

ПРЕДЛАГАЮ **ЗАСУДИТЬ** КОГО-НИБУДЬ — НЕ ВАЖНО КОГО — НА МИЛЛИОНЫ ДОЛЛАРОВ ИЗ-ЗА ВАШЕГО РАЗОЧАРОВАНИЯ, СЭР!

И ЗАСУЖУ! НО СНАЧАЛА МЫ ОБОГНЁМ ОСТРОВ И ОСМОТРИМ ЕГО С ЮГА! СТАРИК ОЛАФ МОГ **ОШИБИТЬСЯ**, ОРИЕНТИРУЯСЬ ПО ЗВЁЗДАМ!

КАК УДАЧНО!

АЗУР СИНИЙ!

ТАРАНЬ ИХ ЛОДКУ, ШАРКИ! ЭТОМУ ЖАЛКОМУ МУЗЕЙНОМУ СТОРОЖУ НИ ЗА ЧТО **НЕ ОБОЙТИ** МЕНЯ В ГОНКЕ ЗА ЗОЛОТЫМ ШЛЕМОМ!

НУ, АВАНТЮРИСТЫ, МОЙ КУЛАК ПОЗАБОТИТСЯ О МЕЛЮЗГЕ ВРОДЕ ВАС!

ВЕЛИКОДУШНЫЙ ПРАВИТЕЛЬ, ПРАВДА, МАЛЬЧИКИ?

НУ, ХОТЬ ПИСТОЛЕТ В ХОД НЕ ПУСТИЛ!

О ДА! ЭТО ТАК ПО-ДЖЕНТЕЛЬМЕНСКИ! ТАК ЩЕДРО!

ЛЕДИ, ЧТО ЗОВЕТСЯ УДАЧЕЙ, — ДАМА КРАЙНЕ ПЕРЕМЕНЧИВАЯ! ВНЕЗАПНО ОНА, КАЖЕТСЯ, ОТВЕРНУЛАСЬ ОТ АЗУРА СИНЕГО!

ПРОКЛЯТЬЕ! ДВИГАТЕЛЬ ЗАГЛОХ!

СТОЛЬКО ЧАСОВ ПОТЕРЯЕМ, ПОКА Я ЧИНЮ ЭТУ ПРОКЛЯТУЮ ЖЕЛЕЗЯКУ!

ВЫ МОЖЕТЕ ЗАСУДИТЬ КОМПАНИЮ-ПРОИЗВОДИТЕЛЯ НА МИЛЛИОНЫ ДОЛЛАРОВ!

ЗАТЕМ ЛЕДИ УДАЧА УЛЫБАЕТСЯ НЕСЧАСТНЫМ УТКАМ!

ДЯДЯ ДОНАЛЬД, А ДАВНО ОЛАФ РИСОВАЛ СВОЮ КАРТУ?

ТЫСЯЧУ ЛЕТ НАЗАД! И ЧТО ЭТО МЕНЯЕТ?

НИЧЕГО! ВОТ ТОЛЬКО ЗА ТЫСЯЧУ ЛЕТ ВОЛНЫ МОГЛИ ОТРЕЗАТЬ МЫС ОТ МАТЕРИКА!

ТЫ ПРАВ, ВИЛЛИ! МЫ НАШЛИ МЫС! И ПЕРЕХИТРИЛИ АЗУРА СИНЕГО!

НУ, СОГЛАСНО КАРТЕ, ШЛЕМ ЗАРЫТ ГДЕ-ТО...

ТАМ!

ПИРАМИДА ИЗ КАМНЕЙ! ВПЕРЁД, МАЛЬЧИКИ! ПОИЩЕМ ЗДЕСЬ!

ОГО, ДЯДЯ ДОНАЛЬД!

МЫ НЕ ОЖИДАЛИ, ЧТО ТЫ ТАК БЫСТРО ПРИМЕРИШЬ «ЗОЛОТОЙ ШЛЕМ»!

МОТОР ВНОВЬ ЗАРАБОТАЛ! НАВЕРНОЕ, МЫ ПОВРЕДИЛИ ПРОВОДКУ, КОГДА ТАРАНИЛИ ЭТИХ УТОК!

ПРЕЖДЕ ЧЕМ ПОПЛЫВЁМ ДАЛЬШЕ, ХОЧУ УБЕДИТЬСЯ, ЧТО С НИМИ ПОКОНЧЕНО!

«СЕМЬ КЛЫКОВ МОРСКОЙ ВЕДЬМЫ! — ВСКРИЧАЛ АЗУР СИНИЙ! — ОНИ НАШЛИ ЗОЛОТОЙ ШЛЕМ!»

СТАРАЯ КАРТА И ЗОЛОТОЙ ШЛЕМ — **КЛЮЧИ** К СУДЬБЕ СЕВЕРНОЙ АМЕРИКИ! НАКОНЕЦ-ТО ОНИ В МОИХ РУКАХ!

ОКТУС, СОКТУС, БОМБИФФИКУС! ЧТО ОЗНАЧАЕТ: «ЗАДАЙТЕ-КА ИМ, БОСС!»

С ЭТОГО ДНЯ ВСЕ ЖИТЕЛИ СЕВЕРНОЙ АМЕРИКИ — МОИ **РАБЫ**! ОНИ БУДУТ РАБОТАТЬ НА МЕНЯ БЕЗ ВЫХОДНЫХ ДО КОНЦА СВОЕЙ ЖИЗНИ!

ИХ ДОМА ТЕПЕРЬ **МОИ**! И МАШИНЫ, ТАРЕЛКИ, КАСТРЮЛИ И СКОВОРОДКИ! Я ВЛАДЕЮ **ВСЕМ**, И **ЗАБЕРУ** ВСЁ!

ТЫ НЕ ПОЛУЧИШЬ НАШИ МЕДАЛИ ЮНЫХ СУРКОВ!

И МОЙ НОВЫЙ ТЕЛЕВИЗОР!

ЕЩЁ КАК ПОЛУЧИТ! ФИГУС, БРЕДУС, СКУНСУС! В ПЕРЕВОДЕ: «ТАКОВ ЗАКОН»!

А ТЕПЕРЬ МАРШ В ЛОДКУ, ХОЛОПЫ! БУДЕТЕ МОЕЙ КОМАНДОЙ, ПОКА ПЛЫВЁМ В НЬЮФАУНДЛЕНД, ГДЕ МЕНЯ **КОРОНУЮТ**!

ЗАЧЕМ ВОЗВРАЩАТЬСЯ В НЬЮФАУНДЛЕНД, СИНИЙ! ТЕБЯ КОРОНУЮТ ПРЯМО ЗДЕСЬ!

КУРАТОР!

ХВАЛА НЕБЕСАМ, ДОНАЛЬД, Я УСПЕЛ СЮДА ВОВРЕМЯ! СВЯЖИТЕ ЭТОГО ЗЛОДЕЯ, МАЛЬЧИКИ!

ШЛЕМ НЕ ДОЛЖЕН СНОВА ПОПАСТЬ К НЕМУ В РУКИ!

ЛУЧШЕ СРАЗУ ОТПЛЫТЬ И БРОСИТЬ КАРТУ И ШЛЕМ **ДАЛЕКО** В МОРЕ!

ИТАК, ХОТЬ НА ВРЕМЯ **С**ЕВЕРНАЯ **А**МЕРИКА В БЕЗОПАСНОСТИ!

КУРС НА ВОСТОК, ДОНАЛЬД! НУЖНО ВЫЙТИ НА ГЛУБИНУ!

ПОЗЖЕ!

КУРАТОР ВЫГЛЯДИТ УСТАЛЫМ!

ДА УЖ! ОН ПРОШЁЛ СОТНИ МИЛЬ БЕЗ ОТДЫХА! БЕДНЫЙ СТАРИЧОК!

ПОЗВОЛЬТЕ МНЕ ПРИСМОТРЕТЬ ЗА НИМИ, ПОКА ВЫ СПИТЕ, СЭР!

НЕТ, ДОНАЛЬД! Я **НИКОМУ** НЕ МОГУ ИХ ДОВЕРИТЬ, ДАЖЕ ТЕБЕ!

ОЧЕНЬ ВЕРНОЕ РЕШЕНИЕ, СЭР! ПОКА ОНИ В ВАШИХ РУКАХ — НЕ **ВЫПУСКАЙТЕ**!

ЭТО **ВАШ** КЛЮЧ К **С**ЕВЕРНОЙ **А**МЕРИКЕ! ЕСЛИ **ЗАХВАТИТЕ** КОНТИНЕНТ, БУДУ РАД ПРЕДСТАВЛЯТЬ ВАШИ ИНТЕРЕСЫ!

СКОЛЬКО ЖЕ СТОЯТ ТВОИ УСЛУГИ, ШАРКИ?

ЧАСТЬ КОНТИНЕНТА! СКАЖЕМ, **КАНАДА**!

КОНЕЧНО, ЕСЛИ ДЕЛО ЗАТЯНЕТСЯ В СУДЕ, МОЙ ГОНОРАР **ВОЗРАСТЁТ**! НАПРИМЕР, ТЕХАС! ЗАТЕМ НЬЮ-ЙОРК!

ЯСНО!

ШЛИ МИНУТЫ, И УСТАЛЫЙ КУРАТОР НАЧАЛ МЕНЯТЬСЯ!

У СТАРИКА В ГЛАЗАХ ПОЯВИЛСЯ **СТРАННЫЙ БЛЕСК**!

И ВДРУГ!

ПОВОРАЧИВАЙ НА ЮГ, ДОНАЛЬД! РЕШЕНО! **Я** СТАНУ ПРАВИТЕЛЕМ СЕВЕРНОЙ АМЕРИКИ!

ЧТО? ВОТ НЕЛЕПОСТЬ! ВЫ ЖЕ **НЕ ПОТОМОК** ОЛАФА СИНЕГО!

ФОКУСУС, ПОКУСУС, ФИЛИПОКУСУС! «ЧЕМ ВЫ ДОКАЖЕТЕ, ЧТО ЭТО **НЕ ТАК?**»

ШАРКИ ПРАВ! **Я МОГУ** ВЛАДЕТЬ СЕВЕРНОЙ АМЕРИКОЙ! КАРТА И ШЛЕМ ПОДТВЕРДЯТ МОИ ПРАВА!

НУ ДЕЛА, БРАТЕЦ! ПОХОЖЕ, ИСТОРИЯ **ПОВТОРЯЕТСЯ**!

Я БУДУ ПРАВИТЬ ЭТОЙ СТРАНОЙ РАДИ МУЗЕЕВ! ОБЯЖУ ВСЕХ ПОСЕЩАТЬ МУЗЕИ ДВАЖДЫ В ДЕНЬ!

КРЯК! ПЛАНЫ АЗУРА МНЕ БОЛЬШЕ ПО ВКУСУ!

КАЖДОЕ ВОСКРЕСЕНЬЕ МУЗЕЙНЫЕ ВЕЧЕРА! ЛЮДИ БУДУТ ПРИНОСИТЬ СВОИ ЗАКУСКИ И ИЗУЧАТЬ ДРЕВНИЕ БЕЗДЕЛУШКИ!

А В ОСТАЛЬНЫЕ ДНИ ПУСТЬ СТРОЯТ НОВЫЕ МУЗЕИ! ХОЧУ МУЗЕИ НА КАЖДОМ УГЛУ, НА КАЖДОМ... КАЖДОМ...

СТОМИЛЬНЫЙ ПОХОД НАКОНЕЦ-ТО ВЗЯЛ СВОЁ!

ХР-Р-Р-Р-Р-Р...

ОН ОТКЛЮЧИЛСЯ! ПОЗАБОТЬТЕСЬ О НЕМ, МАЛЬЧИКИ, ПОКА Я ПОЗАБОЧУСЬ ОБ ЭТИХ ПРОКЛЯТЫХ РАРИТЕТАХ!

ЗАШВЫРНУ ИХ ТАК ДАЛЕКО, ЧТОБ НИ ОДНА РЫБА НЕ НАШЛА!

НУ ЖЕ, БРОСАЙ! НЕ ЖДИ ТОГО ЖЕ СТРАННОГО БЛЕСКА У СЕБЯ ГЛАЗАХ!

ЗАМАНЧИВАЯ КАРТИНА, НЕ ТАК ЛИ? БУДУ СЧАСТЛИВ СТАТЬ ВАШИМ АДВОКАТОМ! ЗА ПЛАТУ, РАЗУМЕЕТСЯ!

ДЯДЯ ДОНАЛЬД! ШВЫРЯЙ ПРОКЛЯТЫЙ ШЛЕМ В ОКЕАН!

НЕТ! ПОЧЕМУ Я НЕ МОГУ БЫТЬ ПРАВИТЕЛЕМ СЕВЕРНОЙ АМЕРИКИ? СТАНУ КОРОЛЁМ ДОНАЛЬДОМ, НАСЛЕДНИКОМ ВИКИНГОВ!

ФОКУСУС, БРЯКУС, ШМЯКУС! ЧТО ОЗНАЧАЕТ: «МЫ СНОВА НА КРЮЧКЕ!»

Я ПОЗВОЛЮ ЛЮДЯМ ЖИТЬ, КАК ИМ ХОЧЕТСЯ! И НЕ БУДУ ТРЕБОВАТЬ ИХ ВЕЩИ! ПУСТЬ ЗАБИРАЮТ ВСЕ ЗЕМЛИ, НЕФТЯНЫЕ МЕСТОРОЖДЕНИЯ И ШАХТЫ, КАКИЕ ХОТЯТ!

НО, СЭР! ЧЕМ ЖЕ ВЫ БУДЕТЕ ВЛАДЕТЬ?

ХА!

ВОЗДУХОМ! ЕДИНСТВЕННОЙ ВЕЩЬЮ, БЕЗ КОТОРОЙ НИКОМУ НЕ ПРОЖИТЬ!

Я ЗАСТАВЛЮ ВСЕХ **ИЗМЕРИТЬ** ОБЪЕМ СВОИХ ЛЕГКИХ! И КАЖДЫЙ ВДОХ БУДЕТ **СТОИТЬ ДЕНЕГ!**

ВЕЛИКОЛЕПНАЯ ИДЕЯ, СЭР! ВЗДОХ ЗА ПЯТЬ ЦЕНТОВ, А **ЗЕВОК** ЗА ДЕСЯТЬ!

ШАРКИ, ТЫ ЗНАЕШЬ ТОЛК В КИСЛОРОДЕ!

ОХУС, АХУС, ВЗДОХУС! ЧТО ОЗНАЧАЕТ: «ДЯДЯ ДОНАЛЬД ПРЕВРАТИЛСЯ В ПОДЛУЮ ГАДЮКУ!»

ДОЛЖНО БЫТЬ, ШЛЕМ СТАРОГО ОЛАФА ОБЛАДАЛ ЗЛЫМИ ЧАРАМИ, РАЗ ДОНАЛЬД ВДРУГ ВООБРАЗИЛ СЕБЯ **ЗЛОБНЫМ** ДРЕВНИМ ВИКИНГОМ!

ЭТИ ПРЕЗРЕННЫЕ БЕСТИИ МОГУТ УКРАСТЬ МОЙ ШЛЕМ! ОТ НИХ НУЖНО ИЗБАВИТЬСЯ!

МОЖЕМ ВЫСАДИТЬ ИХ НА **АЙСБЕРГЕ,** СЭР!

И ВОТ...

Я ВЫШЛЮ ЗА ВАМИ КОРАБЛЬ, КАК СТАНУ КОРОЛЕМ!

КАК МИЛО СО СТОРОНЫ ВАШЕГО ВЕЛИЧЕСТВА!

БОБЫ

ВОТ ТЕПЕРЬ ЖИТЕЛИ СЕВЕРНОЙ АМЕРИКИ ТОЧНО ОБРЕЧЕНЫ!

НЕ ОТЧАИВАЙСЯ! ДЯДЕ ДОНАЛЬДУ ЕЩЁ НУЖНО ДОБРАТЬСЯ ДО **СУШИ!**

НЕ УВЕРЕН, ЧТО ОН **НАЙДЕТ** ЕЁ В ЭТОМ ТУМАНЕ! ВЕДЬ Я УКРАЛ ЕГО **КОМПАС!**

ЧТО? ТОГДА КТО СПАСЁТ НАС?

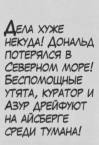

ДЕЛА ХУЖЕ НЕКУДА! ДОНАЛЬД ПОТЕРЯЛСЯ В СЕВЕРНОМ МОРЕ! БЕСПОМОЩНЫЕ УТЯТА, КУРАТОР И АЗУР ДРЕЙФУЮТ НА АЙСБЕРГЕ СРЕДИ ТУМАНА!

ЕСЛИ ПОЯВИТСЯ СОЛНЦЕ, Я СМОГУ СОРИЕНТИРОВАТЬСЯ!

ПРОГНОЗ ПОГОДЫ ОБЕЩАЕТ НЕСКОЛЬКО ДНЕЙ ПАСМУРНОЙ ПОГОДЫ!

ПРОКЛЯТЬЕ! Я НАЧИНАЮ ДУМАТЬ, ЧТО ВИКИНГИ БЫЛИ ВЕЗУНЧИКАМИ, В ОТЛИЧИЕ ОТ НАС!

МАЛЬЧИКИ УСТРОИЛИ СОВЕТ!

В ШКОЛЕ НАС УЧИЛИ, ЧТО АЙСБЕРГИ ДРЕЙФУЮТ К ЮГУ!

И МЫ ЗНАЕМ, ЧТО ВЕТРА ДУЮТ С СЕВЕРА, ЗНАЧИТ, МЫ ИДЁМ ВЕРНЫМ КУРСОМ!

ДЯДЯ ДОНАЛЬД ОСТАВИЛ НЕСКОЛЬКО ТОПОРОВ! МОЖЕТ НАМ УДАСТСЯ ПРИДАТЬ АЙСБЕРГУ ФОРМУ, С КОТОРОЙ ОН БУДЕТ ПЛЫТЬ БЫСТРЕЕ?

ТОЙ ЖЕ НОЧЬЮ!

БОЮСЬ, МЫ ПЛАВАЕМ КРУГАМИ, МИСТЕР ДАК! ЛУЧШЕ ЗАГЛУШИТЬ ДВИГАТЕЛЬ И ПОБЕРЕЧЬ ГОРЮЧЕЕ!

НЕТ, ПОГОДИ МИНУТУ!

ВИЖУ ОГНИ! ДВА ОГОНЬКА МИГАЮТ ПРЯМО ПО КУРСУ!

ТРЕСК

ЧТО ТАКОЕ? Я ВО ЧТО-ТО ВРЕЗАЛСЯ?

ДА! ЭТО ЛЬДИНА, СЭР! А ОГОНЬКИ — ГЛАЗА ПОЛЯРНОГО МЕДВЕДЯ!

ЭЙ, ТАМ! НЕ ПОМОЖЕТЕ? У НАС НЕПРИЯТНОСТИ!

ТИХО, ШАРКИ! ЭТО ОЛАФ СИНИЙ!

О, НЕТ! ЭТО НЕ ОН!

И НЕ ЛАДЬЯ ВИКИНГОВ!

У НАС ГОНОЧНЫЙ АЙСБЕРГ!

БИЛЛИ, ДИЛЛИ И ВИЛЛИ!

НЕ СПЕШИТЕ, СЭР! ЗАХВАТИМ ИХ КОМПАС И ПРИПАСЫ! ВЫ ВСЁ ЕЩЁ МОЖЕТЕ СТАТЬ КОРОЛЕМ ДОНАЛЬДОМ, НАСЛЕДНИКОМ ВИКИНГОВ!

ДА, МОГУ!

НО НЕТУС, НИКОГДАКУС, НИЗАЧТОКУС! ЧТО ЗНАЧИТ: «НЕ ХОЧУ!»

ТОГДА Я БУДУ ВЛАСТИТЕЛЕМ СЕВЕРНОЙ АМЕРИКИ! Я, ШАРКИ, ИМПЕРАТОР ВСЕГО!

ВАМ НЕ КАЖЕТСЯ, ЧТО ЭТА БОРЬБА ЗА СОБСТВЕННОСТЬ ДОСТИГЛА ПИКА?

ЭТУС, ПРАВДУС, ТОЧНЯКУС! ЧТО ЗНАЧИТ: «ДА!»

ШЛЁП

ПЮЛХ

ТЕПЕРЬ **НИКТО** НЕ БУДЕТ ВЛАДЕТЬ СЕВЕРНОЙ АМЕРИКОЙ! ПРОЩАЙ, ЗОЛОТОЙ ШЛЕМ!

ВЕРНО! И ХВАТИТ СЛЕДИТЬ ЗА НИМ ВЗГЛЯДОМ!

ВСТРЯХНИСЬ, У ТЕБЯ В ГЛАЗАХ ОПАСНЫЙ БЛЕСК!

И ВОТ НАШ ДОНАЛЬД СНОВА СТОРОЖ В МУЗЕЕ!

ЖИЗНЬ **АВАНТЮРИСТА**, КОНЕЧНО, ИМЕЕТ СВОИ ПЛЮСЫ! НО ВООБЩЕ-ТО...

МИСТЕР СТОРОЖ, НЕ ПОДСКАЖЕТЕ, ГДЕ НАЙТИ КРУЖЕВНЫЕ АБАЖУРЫ?

ОХ... ТРЕТЬЯ СЕКЦИЯ МЕЖДУ... А, НЕ ВАЖНО!

ПОЙДЁМТЕ ВМЕСТЕ! И Я БУДУ НЕ Я, ЕСЛИ САМ НЕ ПОЛЮБУЮСЬ КРУЖЕВНЫМИ АБАЖУРАМИ!

Племянники Дональда

Disney

ШУ! ШУ! ШУ!

ПОЛОТЕНЦА
10 центов

ЗАВТРА ЗАКАНЧИВАЮТСЯ ЗАНЯТИЯ В ШКОЛЕ, И ТВОИ ПЛЕМЯННИКИ ВЕРНУТСЯ ДОМОЙ НА ЛЕТНИЕ КАНИКУЛЫ!

Я УЖЕ ПОДУМАЛ ОБ ЭТОМ!

Disney

Дональд Дак

ОНИ БУДУТ ДНИ НАПРОЛЁТ СЛОНЯТЬСЯ ВОКРУГ БЕЗ ДЕЛА! И ПОПАДАТЬ В НЕПРИЯТНОСТИ!

Я УЖЕ ПОДУМАЛ ОБ ЭТОМ!

ОНИ ЗАСТАВЯТ ТЕБЯ **ПОВОЛНОВАТЬСЯ**! БУДУТ КУПАТЬСЯ, ГДЕ ОПАСНО, К СОСЕДЯМ ЛАЗИТЬ!

И ОБ ЭТОМ УЖЕ ПОДУМАЛ!

Я СОСТАВИЛ СПИСОК ВСЕХ ПЕРЕДРЯГ, В КОТОРЫЕ МОГУТ УГОДИТЬ МАЛЬЧИКИ, И ПРИДУМАЛ СПОСОБ, КАК **ВСЁ ЭТО** ПРЕДОТВРАТИТЬ!

В КУПАНИИ НЕТ НИКАКИХ ПРОБЛЕМ, ЕСЛИ ДЕТИ ПЛАВАЮТ **НА МЕЛКОВОДЬЕ**!

ТОЧНО!

И ОНИ НЕ СМОГУТ ВЛЕЗТЬ В ДРАКУ, ЗАБРАТЬСЯ К СОСЕДЯМ, ПОПАСТЬ ПОД МАШИНУ, СВАЛИТЬСЯ С ДЕРЕВА И ТОМУ ПОДОБНОЕ, ЕСЛИ ПОБЛИЗОСТИ НЕ БУДЕТ МАШИН, ДЕРЕВЬЕВ, ЛЮДЕЙ ИЛИ ДОМОВ!

ЭТО ТОЧНО! НО ГДЕ...

ХОЧЕШЬ СПРОСИТЬ, ГДЕ Я НАЙДУ ТАКОЕ МЕСТО, ГДЕ МАЛЬЧИКИ НИЧЕГО НЕ НАТВОРЯТ? ОНО УЖЕ НАЙДЕНО!

КАРТА

СОСЕДУШКА, Я ПРОВЕДУ С МАЛЬЧИШКАМИ ЛЕТО В ПЛАВУЧЕМ ДОМИКЕ, НА ОТМЕЛИ, ПОСРЕДИ ОЗЕРА ЭРИ, В ДЕСЯТИ МИЛЯХ ОТ БЕРЕГА!

ТЫ... ТЫ ШУТИШЬ!

НЕТ! ЭТО **ЕДИНСТВЕННОЕ** МЕСТО, ГДЕ СПЛОШНЫЕ ПЛЮСЫ И **НИ ОДНОГО** МИНУСА! И ДЕТИ ВСЁ ВРЕМЯ БУДУТ У МЕНЯ НА ГЛАЗАХ!

НО ТЕБЕ ВСЁ РАВНО НЕ УДАСТСЯ УДЕРЖАТЬ ИХ ОТ НЕПРИЯТНОСТЕЙ! **ЧТО-НИБУДЬ,** ДА СЛУЧИТСЯ! Я КУПЛЮ ТЕБЕ ИНДЕЙКУ НА УЖИН, ЕСЛИ ОШИБАЮСЬ!

ХОРОШО! А Я КУПЛЮ ИНДЕЙКУ ТЕБЕ, ЕСЛИ ЭТО БУДУТ НЕ САМЫЕ ТИХИЕ, БЕЗОПАСНЫЕ И **ЛУЧШИЕ** В ЖИЗНИ ЛЕТНИЕ КАНИКУЛЫ!

И ВОТ — НЕДЕЛЮ СПУСТЯ!

ВОТ ОНО, МАЛЬЧИКИ! ИДЕАЛЬНОЕ МЕСТО ВДАЛИ ОТ НАПАСТЕЙ!

ОГО!

МОЖНО НАМ **ПОРЫБАЧИТЬ,** ДЯДЯ ДОНАЛЬД?

ДА! И НЕТ НИКАКОЙ ОПАСКИ, ЧТО ВЫ ВЛЕЗЕТЕ НА ЧУЖОЙ УЧАСТОК!

И ПОПЛАВАТЬ МОЖНО?

ДА! БЕЗ РИСКА УТОНУТЬ НА ГЛУБИНЕ! ВЕДЬ МЫ НА МЕЛКОВОДЬЕ!

ЕСЛИ СРЕЖЕМ ВЕРХ У ЭТОЙ КАНИСТРЫ С ГОРЮЧИМ, ПОЛУЧИТСЯ НЕПЛОХОЙ СОВОК!

ДА!

ПОЧЕМУ НЕТ?

И ВОТ!

УРА! ГЛЯДИТЕ! ЯМА МНЕ УЖЕ ПО УШИ!

ДАБЛ-ПЛЭЙ! ВЗРЫВУЦКИ НА ТОЛКУЦКИ, ТОТ НА ВЖИЖУЦКИ!

СОЛНЦЕ ЖАРИТ! УЖАСНО ПИТЬ ХОЧЕТСЯ!

ПОЙДУ ГЛОТНУ ХОЛОДНОЙ, ЧИСТОЙ ПРЕСНОЙ ВОДИЧКИ!

ЭЙ! КАК РЫБИНА УГОДИЛА В БОЧКУ С ВОДОЙ?

МЫ ЕЁ ТУДА ПУСТИЛИ!

А ЧТО НЕ ТАК?

ЕЩЁ СПРАШИВАЕШЬ?! ТАМ ЖЕ ПИТЬЕВАЯ ВОДА!

НУ ДА! НО РАЗВЕ ТАКАЯ МАЛЕНЬКАЯ РЫБКА ИСПОРТИТ ЕЁ?

ОНА ЖЕ ЧИСТАЯ!

ЧИСТАЯ, КАК ЖЕ! НА НЕЙ НАВЕРНЯКА МИЛЛИОН БАКТЕРИЙ!

О НЕТ!

ОТПРАВИЛИ ГОРЮЧЕЕ ЗА БОРТ! НУ И НУ!

МАТЬ МОЯ УТКА! Я ТОЛЬКО ЧТО КИНУЛ В ОКНО ГОРЯЩУЮ СПИЧКУ!

ЗАВОДИТЕ МОТОР! ПОДНИМАЙТЕ ЯКОРЬ! ХВАТАЙТЕ ВЁСЛА! НУЖНО УБИРАТЬСЯ ОТСЮДА!

СКОРЕЕ! СКОРЕЕ! ПЛАМЯ ПОДБИРАЕТСЯ К ЛОДКЕ!

ЧТО Ж, МАЛЬЧИКИ! МЫ УПЛЫЛИ ИЗ ПЕКЛА!

И ПОЧТИ НЕ ПОСТРАДАЛИ, ТОЛЬКО ПАРА ДОСОК ГОРИТ!

НАША БОЧКА С ВОДОЙ ПОЗАБОТИТЬСЯ ОБ ЭТОМ!

А ВОТ ТЕПЕРЬ МЫ УГОДИЛИ В ПЕРЕПЛЁТ!

О ЧЁМ ТЫ?

ЧТО ОПЯТЬ НЕ ТАК?

У НАС **НЕТ** ПИТЬЕВОЙ ВОДЫ! И **НЕТ** ГОРЮЧЕГО, ЧТОБЫ КИПЯТИТЬ ВОДУ ИЗ ОЗЕРА!

И НЕТ ГОРЮЧЕГО, ЧТОБЫ ДОБРАТЬСЯ ДО БЕРЕГА И ВЗЯТЬ ЕЩЁ ГОРЮЧЕГО!

ПРОСТЫЕ ЧЕЛОВЕЧЕСКИЕ МЕЧТЫ! КАК БЫСТРО ОНИ ПРЕВРАЩАЮТСЯ В **КОШМАР**!

ЛУЧШЕ НАМ ЗАТАИТЬСЯ В ТРЮМЕ И НЕ ПОПАДАТЬСЯ ЕМУ НА ГЛАЗА КАКОЕ-ТО ВРЕМЯ!

ПОЗЖЕ!

ВСЁ ЕЩЁ ХОЧЕТСЯ ПИТЬ! МОЖЕТ, В БОЧКЕ ОСТАЛАСЬ ХОТЬ **КАПЛЯ ВОДЫ**?

НЕ ВАЖНО, ЧТО ТАМ БЫЛА **РЫБА**! Я ДОЛЖЕН ПОПИТЬ!

ОЙ! СОСКАЛЬЗЫВАЮ!

БУМС

УХМФ!

СИЛЬНЫЙ ЗАПАДНЫЙ ВЕТЕР ПОДХВАТИЛ БОЧКУ, ДОТАЩИЛ ДО ГРАНИЦЫ ОЗЕРА И УРОНИЛ В РЕКУ!

СКОРО Я БУДУ ПРОПЛЫВАТЬ МИМО ГОРОДА! ЗДЕСЬ РЯДОМ БУФФАЛО, ЛАКАВАННА, И НИАГАРСКИЙ ВОДОПАД С КУЧЕЙ ТУРИСТОВ!

КТО-НИБУДЬ НЕПРЕМЕННО ЗАМЕТИТ БОЧКУ И ЗАИНТЕРЕСУЕТСЯ ЕЮ!

ЛЮБОПЫТНЫЕ НАШЛИСЬ! НО СПЕРВА...

СПАСИТЕ!

КАЖЕТСЯ, ВНУТРИ КТО-ТО ЕСТЬ!

ТОЛЬКО НЕ ГОВОРИ, ЧТО ЕЩЁ ОДИН ШУТНИК СПРЫГНУЛ С НИАГАРЫ В БОЧКЕ!

НЕДЕЛЮ СПУСТЯ!

ЭЙ, ДОНАЛЬД! УЖЕ ВЕРНУЛИСЬ?

ДА! И ВОТ ИНДЕЙКА, КОТОРУЮ Я ОБЕЩАЛ!

ОГО! ИДЕАЛЬНОЕ МЕСТО ОКАЗАЛОСЬ ПРОВАЛЬНЫМ? ЧТО-ТО СЛУЧИЛОСЬ С ДЕТЬМИ?

НЕТ, С ДЕТЬМИ ВСЁ ХОРОШО!

А ВОТ СО МНОЙ... ЛУЧШЕ НЕ ВСПОМИНАТЬ!

И ОСВОИЛ БЕЗРОДНЫЙ КУЗЕН ПОВАДКИ ОХОТНИКОВ ЗА КАМУШКАМИ, И УЖЕ МЧИТСЯ ОН ИСКАТЬ БОГАТСТВА!

АМЕТИСТЫ, ОПАЛЫ, ГРАНАТЫ И ИЗУМРУДЫ! ТОЛЬКО И ЖДУТ, КОГДА ИХ НАЙДУТ! ПОДУМАТЬ ТОЛЬКО!

ПУСТЬ ГЛЭДСТОУН И ДАЛЬШЕ СОБИРАЕТ ПО КАМЕШКУ! Я ВЕРНУСЬ В ГОРОД С ГРУЗОВИКОМ ДРАГОЦЕННОСТЕЙ!

СОГЛАСНО СПРАВОЧНИКУ, ПЕРЕД НАМИ ОТЛИЧНОЕ МЕСТО ДЛЯ ПОИСКА ОНИКСОВ И ЯШМЫ, ДЯДЯ ДОНАЛЬД!

А ЕЩЁ БИРЮЗЫ, ТОПАЗОВ, СЕРДОЛИКА И ГРАНАТОВ!

СКОРО ОСТАНОВИМСЯ И ПЕШКОМ ОБСЛЕДУЕМ ОДИН ИЗ ЭТИХ КАНЬОНОВ!

ПОЗЖЕ!

МЕШОК ГРАНАТОВ ЗАСТАВИТ **ВЕЗУНЧИКА** ГЛЭДСТОУНА ПОКРАСНЕТЬ... ОТ СТЫДА!

МОЖЕТ, СНАЧАЛА УБЕДИТЬСЯ, ЧТО ЗДЕСЬ РАЗРЕШЕНЫ ПОИСКИ? ЭТА ЗЕМЛЯ МОЖЕТ КОМУ-ТО **ПРИНАДЛЕЖАТЬ!**

БАА!

КОМУ НУЖЕН БЕСПОЛЕЗНЫЙ КЛОЧОК ЗЕМЛИ С ГОРСТКОЙ БУЛЫЖНИКОВ И КАКТУСОВ? ЛУЧШЕ СМОТРИТЕ ПО СТОРОНАМ!

ВДРУГ!

ДЯДЯ ДОНАЛЬД!

ЦЕЛАЯ ГРУДА ОПАЛОВ, АГАТОВ И ИЗУМРУДОВ!

ТЫ ПРАВ, ВИЛЛИ! ТОЛЬКО ЭТО БИРЮЗА, ГРАНАТЫ И ОНИКСЫ!

А СОГЛАСНО СПРАВОЧНИКУ, ТУТ СЕРДОЛИК, «КОШАЧИЙ ГЛАЗ» И ПЕРИДОТЫ!

НЕ БУДЕМ СПОРИТЬ! ТАК ИЛИ ИНАЧЕ, СМОТРЯТСЯ ОНИ РОСКОШНО!

А ЛУЧШЕ ВСЕГО ТО, ЧТО ПОБЛИЗОСТИ ДОЛЖНЫ БЫТЬ ЕЩЁ РОССЫПИ! ТОННЫ ДРАГОЦЕННОСТЕЙ ЖДУТ-ПОЖДУТ ПУТЕШЕСТВИЯ В ГРУЗОВИКЕ!

ХЕ! ХЕ!

СКЛАДЫВАЙТЕ ВСЁ В МЕШОК! БЫСТРЕЕ, РЕБЯТА! НЕЛЬЗЯ, ЧТОБЫ КТО-НИБУДЬ УЗНАЛ О НАШЕЙ НАХОДКЕ!

ТСС! ДЯДЯ ДОНАЛЬД! ШАГИ!

ТАК-ТАК! ГОРОДСКИЕ, ПОДИ? ЧТОЙ-ТО ВЫ ПОЗАБЫЛИ НА МОЕЙ ЗЕМЛЕ?

ЭТ-ТА ГРУДА КАМНЕЙ — ВАША?

А ТО Ж! ЕНТО МОЙ УЧАСТОК! СОРОК АКРОВ ТАКЕННОЙ ГЛУХОМАНИ!

ОХ! АХ! ЭМ!

ЦВЕТОЧКИ ДИКИЕ ИЩЕТЕ, ПОДИ?

ЧТО... ОХ, НЕТ! ТО ЕСТЬ, ДА!

ЭТОТ ГЛУПЫЙ ДЕРЕВЕНЩИНА И НЕ ПОДОЗРЕВАЕТ О БОГАТСТВЕ У НЕГО ПОД НОГАМИ!

МЫ... ОХ... Я ПОДЫСКИВАЮ ЗЕМЛЮ ДЛЯ ПОКУПКИ! УЧАСТОК ВРОДЕ ЭТОГО!

ЧТО Ж, ПРИШЛЫЙ, ДОГОВОРИЛИСЬ! ГОНИ ПЯТЬДЕСЯТ ДОЛЛАРОВ, И ЗЕМЕЛЬКА ТВОЯ!

Позже!

УМНО ПРИДУМАНО, А, МАЛЬЧИКИ?

ПРЕДСТАВЬ СЕБЕ! ПЯТЬДЕСЯТ ДОЛЛАРОВ ЗА ФЕРМУ ДРАГОЦЕННЫХ КАМНЕЙ!

УЖЕ ТРЕТИЙ УЧАСТОК ЗА НЕДЕЛЮ! ГОД УДИВИТЕЛЬНО БОГАТ НА ПРОСТОФИЛЬ!

НЕСИТЕ КАМНИ! ВЕРНЁМСЯ В ГОРОД, ВОЗЬМЁМ БОЛЬШЕ ПРИПАСОВ!

ПОТОМ ВЕРНЁМСЯ И ЗАДЕРЖИМСЯ ТУТ НА **НЕДЕЛЮ!** БУДЕМ КАЖДЫЙ ДЕНЬ ВЫГРЕБАТЬ БОГАТСТВА ИЗ ЭТОГО КАНЬОНА!

По возвращении в город!

ЭЙ! ЭТО ГЛЭДСТОУН! ПОКАЖЕМ ЕМУ НАШ МЕШОК САМОЦВЕТОВ?

НЕПРЕМЕННО, МАЛЬЧИКИ! НЕПРЕМЕННО!

ВОТ ВЕДЬ ЧУДЕСА!

ГДЕ ТЫ НАШЕЛ ВСЕ ЭТИ **КАМНИ?** МОЖЕТ, Я ПОМОГУ ИСКАТЬ ДАЛЬШЕ?

КАК ЖЕ!

ТЫ ЖЕ ТАКОЙ, ТАКОЙ, **ТАКОЙ** ВЕЗУЧИЙ! ПОЙДИ НАЙДИ **ДРАГОЦЕННУЮ ЖИЛУ** ГДЕ-НИБУДЬ **В ПАРКЕ!**

КАК МОГ ДОНАЛЬД **ОБСКАКАТЬ** МЕНЯ В ПОИСКЕ САМОЦВЕТОВ? ТУТ ДЕЛО **НЕЧИСТО!**

СНАЧАЛА ПОМОЕМ КАМНИ, А ЗАТЕМ ОТПОЛИРУЕМ! ТОГДА УЗНАЕМ, СКОЛЬКО СРЕДИ НИХ ПЕРВОКЛАССНЫХ БРИЛЛИАНТОВ!

НАМ С МАЛЬЧИКАМИ НЕ НУЖНЫ **ВСЕ** ЭТИ КАМЕШКИ! ТАКОЕ БОГАТСТВО МЫ В ЖИЗНИ НЕ ПОТРАТИМ!

Я... Я ГОТОВ ВОЙТИ В ДОЛЮ! ПЛАЧУ ЭТИМ **БРИЛЛИАНТОМ**!

НУ, ТЫ МОЙ **КУЗЕН,** ТАК ЧТО УСТУПЛЮ ТЕБЕ ДВАДЦАТЬ АКРОВ ЭТОЙ ЗЕМЛИ ЗА КАМЕНЬ!

ДОНАЛЬД, СТАРИНА! ТЫ НАСТОЯЩИЙ **ПРИНЦ**! ПРОЩАЮ ТЕБЕ ВСЕ РАЗЫ, КОГДА МЫ ОБИЖАЛИ ДРУГ ДРУГА!

ДЯДЯ ДОНАЛЬД ПРОСТО **ПЛУТ**! ОН ЕЩЁ ПОЖАЛЕЕТ О СВОЁМ КОВАРСТВЕ!

ВОТ ТВОЯ КУПЧАЯ, ГЛЭДСТОУН! МОЖЕШЬ СОБИРАТЬ ЗДЕСЬ САМОЦВЕТЫ!

УХ ТЫ! ДВАДЦАТЬ АКРОВ ГРАНАТОВ, ОПАЛОВ И АГАТОВ! МОИ! ВСЕ МОИ!

ОЙ! СТРАННО... ЦВЕТА СТИРАЮТСЯ!

ТАК ПОЧЕМУ БЫ ТЕБЕ НЕ ПРИКУПИТЬ ТАКУЮ?

И ПРОВЕСТИ ОСТАТОК ЖИЗНИ, ВЫПЛАЧИВАЯ ЗА НЕЁ!

ТОГДА ТОЧНО СМОЖЕШЬ КОЛЛЕКЦИОНИРОВАНИЕ ЗАБРОСИТЬ!

Я НЕ ХОЧУ **КУПИТЬ**! Я НАМЕРЕН ЕЁ **ПРОДАТЬ**!

НО СПЕРВА МАРКУ НАДО **НАЙТИ**! (КХМ! КХМ!)

И ВОТ МОЯ ИДЕЯ! Я СОБИРАЮ И ПРОДАЮ МАРКИ И ПЫТАЮСЬ НАКОПИТЬ НАМ ДЕНЕГ НА БИЛЕТЫ В ГВИАНУ! ТАМ МЫ **МОЖЕМ** НАЙТИ ОДНУ ИЗ ЭТИХ КРОШЕК ЦЕНОЙ В ПЯТИДЕСЯТИ ТЫСЯЧ ДОЛЛАРОВ!

ЭКСПЕДИЦИЯ В ГВИАНУ РАДИ **МАРКИ**?

КОНЕЧНО! ПЯТЬДЕСЯТ ТЫСЯЧ ХРУСТЯЩИХ КУПЮР — НЕ МЕЛОЧЬ!

УХ, ТЫ! ДЖУНГЛИ! ПИРАТСКИЕ ТАЙНИКИ! ЗАБРОШЕННЫЕ ПЛАНТАЦИИ!

ДУМАЮ, БУДЕТ ВЕСЕЛО! ПРАВДА, МАРКУ ПРИДЁТСЯ ПОИСКАТЬ!

КАЖДЫЙ ДЕНЬ ДОНАЛЬД ОТПРАВЛЯЕТСЯ НА ВОКЗАЛ ПОКОПАТЬСЯ В МУСОРНЫХ КОРЗИНАХ!

АХ! ЗЕЛЁНАЯ БЕРМУДСКАЯ ЗА 60 ЦЕНТОВ!

И АВСТРАЛИЙСКАЯ «КУКАБАРА» 1932 ГОДА ЗА 30 ЦЕНТОВ!

?

МОЙ БЕДНЫЙ, НЕУДАЧЛИВЫЙ КУЗЕН! НЕУЖЕЛИ ДЕЛА ТАК ПЛОХИ, ЧТО ТЫ РОЕШЬСЯ В ПОМОЙКАХ И МУСОРКАХ?

НЕТ, ГЛЭДСТОУН ГАНДЕР! НЕ ПЕРЕЖИВАЙ, У МЕНЯ ТУТ БИЗНЕС!

Я КОЛЛЕКЦИОНЕР МАРОК, А ТАКИЕ РЕБЯТА, САМ ЗНАЕШЬ, НЕ БЕДСТВУЮТ!

СМОТРИ! Я НАБРАЛ МАРОК НА ДЕВЯНОСТО ЦЕНТОВ МЕНЬШЕ ЧЕМ ЗА ДЕСЯТЬ МИНУТ!

БЫТЬ НЕ МОЖЕТ!

А КОГДА НАЙДУ ТУ, ЧТО СТОИТ ТЫСЯЧИ ДОЛЛАРОВ, ПРОДАМ ЕЁ И ОТПРАВЛЮСЬ НА...

ДЕВЯНОСТО ЦЕНТОВ ЗА ДЕСЯТЬ МИНУТ!

К ПОЕЗДАМ

С МОИМ ВЕЗЕНИЕМ Я НАЙДУ ЦЕЛОЕ СОСТОЯНИЕ ЗА ДЕСЯТЬ СЕКУНД!

О НЕТ! МОЙ ДЛИННЫЙ ЯЗЫК! Я ЗАИНТЕРЕСОВАЛ ГЛЭДСТОУНА МАРКАМИ!

ДЕСЯТЬ СЕКУНД СПУСТЯ!

ТАК-ТАК, ПОХОЖЕ, ЗДЕСЬ ЕСТЬ ИЗ ЧЕГО ВЫБРАТЬ!

Я НАШЁЛ **ЦЕЛУЮ КОЛЛЕКЦИЮ**! И ДАЖЕ КНИЖКУ ДЛЯ ЕЁ ХРАНЕНИЯ!

К ПОЕЗДА

БОЛВАН! ЭТО ЧЕЙ-ТО АЛЬБОМ! ГДЕ ТЫ ЕГО НАШЁЛ?

НА СКАМЕЙКЕ, ПОЗАДИ МУСОРНОЙ КОРЗИНЫ! ОН ПРОСТО ЛЕЖАЛ ТАМ И ЖДАЛ, КТО ЕГО ЗАБЕРЁТ!

ОГО! ЭТОТ АЛЬБОМ — **НАСТОЯЩЕЕ СОКРОВИЩЕ**! ВЛАДЕЛЕЦ БУДЕТ ЕГО ИСКАТЬ!

ЛУЧШЕ И БЫТЬ НЕ МОГЛО, МММ! И ОН БУДЕТ ГОТОВ ОТВАЛИТЬ **КРУГЛЕНЬКУЮ СУММУ**, ДА?

ПУТЕШЕ

ЗДЕСЬ УКАЗАНО ИМЯ! ЕГО ЗОВУТ ФИЛО Т. ЭЛЛИСТ, ЖИВЁТ В ДОМЕ 120 ПО РОСКОШ' ДРАЙВ!

ЭТО ЖЕ УЛИЦА МИЛЛИОНЕРОВ!

ТЫ ДОЛЖЕН НЕМЕДЛЕННО ВЕРНУТЬ ЕМУ АЛЬБОМ!

НУ, **НЕТ**, КУЗЕН! ПУСТЬ ПОНЕРВНИЧАЕТ! ЭТО **УВЕЛИЧИТ** НАГРАДУ!

ПОЙДЁШЬ К НЕМУ **СЕЙЧАС**! КОЛЛЕКЦИЯ СЛИШКОМ ЦЕННАЯ, НЕЧЕГО ТЯНУТЬ!

И вот...

Я ПОЙДУ С ТОБОЙ, ПРИСМОТРЮ, ЧТОБ ТЫ НЕ ВЫКИНУЛ КАКОЙ-НИБУДЬ ФОКУС!

ФИЛО Т. ЭЛЛИСТ

В ДОМЕ!

ГОВОРИТЕ, ЭТОТ ДЖЕНТЛЬМЕН НАШЁЛ ОДИН ИЗ МОИХ АЛЬБОМОВ?

ДА, СЭР! МИСТЕР ГЛЭДСТОУН ГАНДЕР, СЭР!

ЭТО ЖЕ МОЯ ЗНАМЕНИТАЯ ВОСТОЧНАЯ КОЛЛЕКЦИЯ! ГДЕ ВЫ ЕЁ НАШЛИ?

НА СКАМЕЙКЕ В ЗДАНИИ ВОКЗАЛА!

БАТЮШКИ! **КАК** ТАКОЕ МОГЛО СЛУЧИТЬСЯ? ОХ, КОНЕЧНО! ВСПОМНИЛ! Я ОСТАВИЛ ЕЁ ТАМ!

ПРИЕХАЛ НА ВОКЗАЛ, ЧТОБЫ СЕСТЬ НА ПОЕЗД! ПЛАНИРОВАЛ ОТПРАВИТЬСЯ В КАКОЙ-ТО ГОРОД ИСКАТЬ МАРКИ, НО ЗАБЫЛ И НАЗВАНИЕ ГОРОДА, И НОМЕР ПОЕЗДА!

ЗАТЕМ ВЕРНУЛСЯ ДОМОЙ, НО ЗАБЫЛ АЛЬБОМ! КАКАЯ РАССЕЯННОСТЬ! ХА-ХА!

ПРЕЖДЕ ЧЕМ Я ЗАБУДУ О НАГРАДЕ ЗА ВАШУ ЧЕСТНОСТЬ, МИСТЕР ГАРФИЛД... ВОЗЬМИТЕ ЭТО!

ТЫСЯЧА ДОЛЛАРОВ!

ЭТОГО ХВАТИЛО БЫ НА БИЛЕТЫ ДО ГВИАНЫ! А ИХ ПОЛУЧИЛ ГЛЭДСТОУН!

ТАК, ТАК! НУЖНО ПОТОРОПИТЬСЯ И ПОТРАТИТЬ ДЕНЬГИ ПРЕЖДЕ, ЧЕМ ОНИ НАЧНУТ ОТТЯГИВАТЬ КАРМАН!

ДОГОНЮ ТЕБЯ ПОЗЖЕ! Я СЕЙЧАС СЛИШКОМ СЛАБ, ЧТОБЫ ДВИГАТЬСЯ!

ЧЕРЕЗ НЕКОТОРОЕ ВРЕМЯ!

ОХ-ХО! КТО ВЫ, СЭР?

АХ, ДА! ВСПОМНИЛ! ВЫ МИСТЕР ГАЛСТОУН ГИНКЛ, ЮНОША, КОТОРЫЙ ВЕРНУЛ МНЕ ЗАБЫТЫЙ АЛЬБОМ!

Я ЖЕ ЗАБЫЛ ПОБЛАГОДАРИТЬ ВАС! КАКАЯ РАССЕЯННОСТЬ!

НЕТ-НЕТ, МИСТЕР ЭЛЛИСТ! ВЫ ВСЁ ПЕРЕПУТАЛИ! Я НЕ...

ХОТИТЕ СКАЗАТЬ, ЧТО НЕ ХОТИТЕ НАГРАДЫ?

СПРИГЛИ, ПОКАЖИТЕ МИСТЕРУ ГИЛФУНКЛУ ВЫХОД! И ПРОСЛЕДИТЕ, ЧТОБЫ ОН ПРИНЯЛ ДЕНЬГИ!

ДА, СЭР

ПОДУМАТЬ ТОЛЬКО! МИСТЕР ГАРЛАНД ГУСЕПИМПЛ НЕ ХОТЕЛ НАГРАДЫ! КАКОЕ ПОРАЗИТЕЛЬНОЕ БЛАГОРОДСТВО!

ЩЁЛК

ТЫСЯЧА ДОЛЛАРОВ! ОН ДАЛ МНЕ ТЫСЯЧУ ДОЛЛАРОВ!

Я ДОЛЖЕН ИХ ВЕРНУТЬ! НЕЛЬЗЯ БРАТЬ ДЕНЬГИ, КОТОРЫЕ МНЕ НЕ ПРИНАДЛЕЖАТ!

НО ЭТО ПОСТАВИТ **ЕГО** В **ГЛУПОЕ** ПОЛОЖЕНИЕ...

А Я НЕ ХОЧУ **РАССТРАИВАТЬ** ТАКОГО ХОРОШЕГО ЧЕЛОВЕКА!

И ПОТОМ, ЕМУ ЭТИ ТРАТЫ ПО КАРМАНУ!

А ЕСЛИ Я НАЙДУ МАРКУ, ЕМУ ПЕРВОМУ ПРЕДЛОЖУ ЕЁ КУПИТЬ!

ЧТО Ж, РАЗ МИСТЕР ФИЛО Т. ЭЛЛИСТ СЧАСТЛИВ, ДУМАЮ, И МНЕ СТОИТ УСПОКОИТЬСЯ!

СОБИРАЙТЕСЬ, МАЛЬЧИКИ! МЫ ЕДЕМ В БРИТАНСКУЮ ГВИАНУ!

ЗА ВРЕМЯ ДОЛГОГО ПУТИ БИЛЛИ, ВИЛЛИ И ДИЛЛИ КОЕ-ЧТО ПОЧИТАЛИ!

ДЯДЯ ДОНАЛЬД, ЗДЕСЬ СКАЗАНО, ЧТО В ШЕСТНАДЦАТОМ ВЕКЕ ПУТЕШЕСТВЕННИКИ ЧАСТО ПОСЕЩАЛИ ГВИАНУ В ПОИСКАХ ЭЛЯ ДОРАДО!

ЭТО ГОРОД, ШАХТА ИЛИ МАРКА СИГАР?

ЭЛЬ ДОРАДО — ЛЕГЕНДАРНЫЙ **ПОЗОЛОЧЁННЫЙ ЧЕЛОВЕК**! ЗДЕСЬ НАПИСАНО, ЧТО ОН ЦЕЛИКОМ ПОКРЫЛ СЕБЯ **ЗОЛОТОМ**!

СЭР УОЛТЕР РЭЛИ ПРЕДПРИНЯЛ ТРИ ЭКСПЕДИЦИИ К ВЕРХОВЬЯМ ОРИНОКО, НО ТАК И НЕ НАШЁЛ ЕГО!

ОХ-ХО! ЕСЛИ УЖ ТАМ ПОЗОЛОЧЁННОГО ЧЕЛОВЕКА НЕ СМОГЛИ НАЙТИ, КАКИЕ У МЕНЯ ШАНСЫ НАЙТИ **МАРКУ**?

НУ, ДАЖЕ ЕСЛИ МЫ **НИЧЕГО** НЕ НАЙДЁМ, ХОТЬ ОТ ДУШИ ПОВЕСЕЛИМСЯ, ПОКА ИЩЕМ!

НИКОГДА ЕЩЁ ДОНАЛЬД ТАК НЕ ЗАБЛУЖДАЛСЯ! НЕДЕЛЯ ОБШАРИВАНИЯ СТАРЫХ ЧЕРДАКОВ И СУНДУКОВ ВЫМОТАЛА УТОК И ЛИШИЛА ВСЯКОЙ НАДЕЖДЫ!

ЕЩЁ ОДИН ТАКОЙ ДЕНЬ, И ХОТЬ К ПАУКАМ В ЛАПЫ!

ДОМО-ВЛАДЕЛЬЦЫ ПРИВЕТЛИВЫ! ДАЖЕ СЛИШКОМ!

МАДАМ, У ВАС ЕСТЬ СТАРЫЕ ПИСЬМА?

СИ, СИ, СЕНЬОР! ЦЕЛЫЙ СУНДУК НА ЧЕРДАК! ВЫ ПЛАТИТЬ ДОЛЛАР И СМОТРЕТЬ ЕГО!

ЕЩЁ ПЯТЬ КОЛЛЕКЦИОНЕР! МЫ ИМЕТЬ ДОЛЛАР ЗА НЕДЕЛЮ, ПЭДРО!

МАРИЯ, ЭТОТ СТАРЫЙ СУНДУК ПОМОЧЬ НАМ ЖИТЬ В РОСКОШЬ!

ОБЛЕЙСЯ КАСТОРКОЙ, ДЕДУЛЯ!

КАСТОРОВОЕ МАСЛО

ВЫ СПАСЛИ МНЕ ЖИЗНЬ, МАЛЬЧИКИ!

Я ГОТОВ НА ВСЁ, ЧТОБЫ ВАС ОТБЛАГОДАРИТЬ! НА ВСЁ!

ЧТО ВЫ! НЕ СТОИТ!

ПОСТОЙТЕ! МОЖЕТ, ВЫ ПОДСКАЖЕТЕ НАМ, ГДЕ ИСКАТЬ ОДНОЦЕНТОВУЮ РОЗОВУЮ МАРКУ 1856 ГОДА?

ВСЕ В ГВИАНЕ ДАВНО СМЕЮТСЯ, КОГДА СЛЫШАТ ЭТОТ ВОПРОС! НО ВЫ СПАСЛИ МНЕ ЖИЗНЬ...

НЕ УДИВЛЯЙТЕСЬ МОИМ СЛОВАМ! Я НЕ ЗНАЮ, ГДЕ МАРКА, НО ЗНАЮ, У КОГО ОНА!

И У КОГО?

У ЭЛЯ ДОРАДО, ПОЗОЛОЧЁННОГО ЧЕЛОВЕКА!

ДЯДЯ ДОНАЛЬД!

СТАРЫЙ РЫБАК РАССКАЗАЛ ЗАХВАТЫВАЮЩУЮ ИСТОРИЮ!

В 1856 ГОДУ МОЙ ОТЕЦ БЫЛ ПОЧТОВЫМ КУРЬЕРОМ МЕЖДУ РЕЧНЫМИ ПОСЕЛЕНИЯМИ И ДЖОРДЖТАУНОМ! ОДНАЖДЫ ОН ОТПРАВИЛСЯ СО СВОЕЙ ПОЧТОВОЙ СУМКОЙ ВНИЗ ПО РЕКЕ...

СРЕДИ ПОЧТЫ БЫЛ И КОНВЕРТ С ОДНОЦЕНТОВОЙ РОЗОВОЙ МАРКОЙ!

НО ДО ДЖОРДЖТАУНА ОН ТАК И НЕ ДОБРАЛСЯ! В ПЯТИДЕСЯТИ МИЛЯХ ВЫШЕ ПО ТЕЧЕНИЮ ПЛЕМЯ СТРАННЫХ ИНДЕЙЦЕВ СХВАТИЛО ЕГО И УТАЩИЛО В ДЖУНГЛИ!

А СУМКА С ПОЧТОЙ? ЧТО С НЕЙ?

ИХ ВОЖДЬ ЗАБРАЛ ЕЁ! ЕМУ ОЧЕНЬ БЫЛИ ПО ДУШЕ БОЛЬШИЕ СЕРЕБРЯНЫЕ ЗАСТЁЖКИ!

ИХ ВОЖДЬ?

ЭЛЬ ДОРАДО, ОГРОМНЫЙ ИНДЕЕЦ, С ГОЛОВЫ ДО НОГ ПОКРЫТЫЙ ЗОЛОТОМ!

ОГО! СПОРИМ, ОН ВЕСИТ ТОННУ!

ДВЕ ТОННЫ!

ЧТО СЛУЧИЛОСЬ С ВАШИМ ОТЦОМ?

ОН СБЕЖАЛ! НО, НАСКОЛЬКО ВСЕМ ИЗВЕСТНО, СУМКА ТАК И ОСТАЛАСЬ У ЭЛЯ ДОРАДО!

ДЕЛО БЫЛО В 1856 ГОДУ! УЖЕ ТОГДА ЛЮДИ СЧИТАЛИ СЕБЯ СЛИШКОМ ЗДРАВОМЫСЛЯЩИМИ, ЧТОБЫ ПОВЕРИТЬ В СУЩЕСТВОВАНИЕ ПОЗОЛОЧЁННОГО ЧЕЛОВЕКА! ОН ПОСМЕЯЛИСЬ НАД ИСТОРИЕЙ ОТЦА! СКАЗАЛИ, ЧТО У НЕГО БЫЛА ГОРЯЧКА!

ЗНАЧИТ, НИКТО НЕ ПОШЁЛ ПО ЕГО СЛЕДУ, ЧТОБЫ ВЕРНУТЬ СУМКУ?

ТОЛЬКО Я! ШЕСТЬДЕСЯТ ЛЕТ Я ПЫТАЛСЯ НАПАСТЬ НА СЛЕД, КОТОРЫЙ ДАВНЫМ-ДАВНО ОСТЫЛ!

А ВАМ УДАЛОСЬ ПОДОБРАТЬСЯ К НЕМУ?

ОДНАЖДЫ! КАК-ТО В САВАННЕ Я ИЗДАЛИ РАЗГЛЯДЕЛ ПОЗОЛОЧЁННОГО ЧЕЛОВЕКА!

КХМ... ЭМ... В ВАШИ ГОДЫ УЖЕ ТРУДНО ГОНЯТЬСЯ ЗА СУМКОЙ! КАК НАСЧЁТ СДЕЛКИ?

НА СЛЕДУЮЩИЙ ДЕНЬ!

ВПЕРЁД, НА ПОИСКИ ЗОЛОТОГО ЧЕЛОВЕКА И РОЗОВОЙ МАРКИ!

КРАСОЧНАЯ ПОЕЗДОЧКА, ГОЛУБЧИКИ МОИ!

И ЛУЧШЕ ВСЕГО ТО, ЧТО СТАРЫЙ РЫБАК ОТКАЗАЛСЯ ОТ СВОЕЙ ДОЛИ!

ОН ТОЛЬКО ХОЧЕТ ОБЕЛИТЬ ИМЯ ОТЦА!

ЕСЛИ НАМ ПОВЕЗЁТ, ОН ТОЖЕ БУДЕТ В ВЫИГРЫШЕ!

ПОЗЖЕ!

ЧТО ЭТО ЗА РАВНИНА?

САВАННА!

ИМЕННО ЗДЕСЬ РЫБАК ВИДЕЛ ЭЛЯ ДОРАДО!

ДА! МНОГО ЛЕТ НАЗАД!

ВПОЛНЕ ВОЗМОЖНО! НО В **НАШИ ДНИ** ИНДЕЕЦ В ЗОЛОТЫХ ПАНТАЛОНАХ СМОТРЕЛСЯ БЫ ТУТ ОЧЕНЬ ГЛУПО!

ПИЛОТ, ВЫСАДИТЕ НАС У ГРАНИЦЫ ДЖУНГЛЕЙ! ДАЛЬШЕ ПОЙДЁМ ПЕШКОМ!

СЛУШАЮСЬ! НО НИЧЕГО БЕЗУМНЕЕ ВАШЕЙ ЗАТЕИ Я В ЖИЗНИ НЕ СЛЫХАЛ!

ПУСТЬ ЭТО ЗВУЧИТ **БЕЗУМНО**, НО У НАС ЕСТЬ ЛУЧШАЯ ПОДСКАЗКА ПРО МАРКУ ЗА ПЯТЬДЕСЯТ ТЫСЯЧ ДОЛЛАРОВ!

МИЛИ СПУСТЯ В СУЩЕСТВОВАНИЕ ПОЗОЛОЧЁННОГО ЧЕЛОВЕКА ВЕРИТСЯ УЖЕ ОХОТНЕЕ!

ЗДЕСЬ ДАЖЕ ДИНОЗАВРЫ МОГЛИ БЫ ОСТАТЬСЯ НЕЗАМЕЧЕННЫМИ!

КАК ТОТ ЯГУАР, ЧТО СОБИРАЕТСЯ ПРЫГНУТЬ НА ТЕБЯ?

ГДЕ?

ТЕПЕРЬ УЖЕ **ВОТ ТАМ**! УДАВ **ПРЫГНУЛ** ПЕРВЫМ!

ОТ ЭТИХ ДЖУНГЛЕЙ У МЕНЯ МУРАШКИ ПО КОЖЕ!

НЕУДИВИТЕЛЬНО!

ТЫ СТОИШЬ НА МУРАВЕЙНИКЕ!

НЕСКОЛЬКО ДНЕЙ ОНИ ШЛИ, БРЕЛИ, КАРАБКАЛИСЬ И ПОЛЗЛИ СРЕДИ МУРАВЬЁВ, ЗМЕЙ, ЯЩЕРИЦ, ЛЕТУЧИХ МЫШЕЙ-ВАМПИРОВ, ЯГУАРОВ, ЛЕНИВЦЕВ, БРОНЕНОСЦЕВ, ЛАМАНТИНОВ, ОБЕЗЬЯН И МОСКИТОВ!

ДЯДЯ ДОНАЛЬД, ТЫ УЖЕ НАТОПАЛ НА ПЯТЬДЕСЯТ ТЫСЯЧ ДОЛЛАРОВ! СО СЛЕДУЮЩЕГО ШАГА ДОЛЖНЫ КАПАТЬ ПРОЦЕНТЫ!

А ВЕДЬ МЫ ЕЩЁ НЕ ДОШЛИ ДО НОВЫХ ТЕРРИТОРИЙ! СТАРИК ЗДЕСЬ УЖЕ ВСЁ ОБШАРИЛ!

ДЯДЯ ДОНАЛЬД, РАЗВЕ МОЖНО ОБШАРИТЬ ДЖУНГЛИ?! МЫ МОЖЕМ БЫТЬ В ПЯТИДЕСЯТИ МЕТРАХ ОТ ГОРОДА И НЕ ЗАМЕТИТЬ ЕГО!

ВОТ ЧТО Я СКАЖУ! ДАВАЙТЕ ВЕРНЁМСЯ В ДАКСБУРГ!

ЭЙ, НА ПЛЕЧЕ У ВИЛЛИ — ОБЕЗЬЯНА!

АГА! РУЧНАЯ, КАК КОТЁНОК!

ОБЕЗЬЯНУ ПРИРУЧИЛИ! ЗДЕСЬ КТО-ТО ЖИВЁТ!

ДО БЛИЖАЙШЕЙ ИЗВЕСТНОЙ ДЕРЕВНИ ПАРУ ДНЕЙ ПУТИ! А ЗНАЧИТ ТУТ...

... ПЛЕМЯ НАШЕГО ЗОЛОТОШТАННИКА!

СПУГНИТЕ ОБЕЗЬЯНУ! ПОСМОТРИМ, КУДА ОНА ПОБЕЖИТ!

КЫШ!

ПШЛА!

ИДИ ДОМОЙ!

ОНА БЕЖИТ ВО-О-ОН ТУДА!

ВПЕРЁД!

НЕСКОЛЬКО ЗАРОСЛЕЙ СПУСТЯ!

УХ ТЫ, МОЩЁНАЯ ТРОПА!

СНОВА УХ ТЫ!

ПОХОЖЕ НА ЗАБРОШЕННЫЙ ХРАМ!

ДА, НА ХРАМ МАЙЯ! РУИНЫ, КАК В МЕКСИКЕ!

Я НЕ ВИЖУ НИКОГО, **КРОМЕ** ОБЕЗЬЯН!

ДА, НО ГДЕ-ТО ДОЛЖЕН БЫТЬ ТОТ, КТО ИХ **ПРИРУЧИЛ**!

Я НЕ ВИЖУ ТУТ **ДЫМА**! ЕСЛИ ПОБЛИЗОСТИ И ЖИВУТ ЛЮДИ, ОНИ ЯВНО НЕ ЛЮБЯТ **ГОТОВИТЬ**!

ХОРОШО БЫ ОНИ НЕ ПЕРЕДУМАЛИ, КОГДА УВИДЯТ НАС!

ЧТО Ж, ЕСЛИ **МЫ** НЕ ВИДИМ **ИХ**, ТО И ОНИ **НАС** ТОЖЕ... НАДЕЮСЬ!

УВЕРЕН, ЭТОТ ВИГВАМ ПРИНАДЛЕЖИТ ЭЛЮ ДОРАДО! СПРЯЧЕМ РЮКЗАКИ ЗДЕСЬ И ПРОКРАДЁМСЯ ВНУТРЬ ЧЕРЕЗ ЧЁРНЫЙ ХОД!

БАТЮШКИ! ДА ТУТ ЦЕЛЫЙ МУЗЕЙ!

СТАРЫЕ РЖАВЫЕ ИСПАНСКИЕ ДОСПЕХИ!

КТО БЫ ИХ НИ НОСИЛ, ОН **ВИДЕЛ** ЭЛЯ ДОРАДО, НО НЕ СМОГ ВЕРНУТЬСЯ И РАССКАЗАТЬ ОБ ЭТОМ!

СТАРЫЕ САБЛИ! КРЕМНИЕВЫЕ МУШКЕТЫ! ПИРАТСКИЕ ПОЯСА! ЭТОТ ЭЛЬ ДОРАДО ТОТ ЕЩЁ КОЛЛЕКЦИОНЕР!

А-АЙ!

ЧТО ТАКОЕ? ТЫ ЧТО-ТО УВИДЕЛ?

ДА! ЧУЧЕЛА УТОК!

ИДЁМ! ПОРА ПОКОНЧИТЬ С ПОИСКАМИ!

ГДЕ-ТО ДОЛЖНА БЫТЬ КОМНАТА, ГДЕ ОН ХРАНИТ ЭКСПОНАТЫ ИЗ СЕРЕБРА!

ВОТ! ВОТ ОНА!

А ВОТ, КАК ПОДАРОЧЕК ПОД ЁЛКОЙ, НАША СТАРАЯ ЗНАКОМАЯ — ПОЧТОВАЯ СУМКА!

ОЙ, ПРОСТИТЕ! МЫ РЕШИЛИ, ЧТО ВАС НЕТ ДОМА!

ДЖАКАРУНИ! САКАРУНИ! МАКАРУНИ!

ГЛЫК!

И ВОТ...

(ПЕРЕВОД): ЗАВТРА КОРОТЫШКИ, КОТОРЫЕ ПОСМЕЛИ КОСНУТЬСЯ МОЕГО СЕРЕБРА, УЗНАЮТ ВСЮ ТЯЖЕСТЬ КОРОЛЕВСКОЙ КАРЫ!

ЛЮБОПЫТНО! ЭТИ РЕБЯТА ПОЯВИЛИСЬ ТАК ВНЕЗАПНО!

НАВЕРНО, ЗА НАМИ С САМОГО НАЧАЛА СЛЕДИЛИ!

ВСЁ ШЛО ПРЕКРАСНО, ПОКА Я НЕ ОТКРЫЛ СУМКУ!

ДА... ПОКА ТЫ НЕ ТРОНУЛ СЕРЕБРЯНЫЕ ЗАСТЕЖКИ!

ВСПОМНИТЕ, СТАРЫЙ РЫБАК ГОВОРИЛ, ЧТО ЭЛЬ ДОРАДО ПОМЕШАН НА СЕРЕБРЕ!

ОХ! НЕУДИВИТЕЛЬНО! ЭТИ ЗАСТЁЖКИ ЕДИНСТВЕННОЕ СЕРЕБРО В ЕГО КОЛЛЕКЦИИ!

СПОРИМ, БУДЬ У НАС ХОТЬ КУСОЧЕК СЕРЕБРА, МЫ БЫ СМОГЛИ ОТКУПИТЬСЯ!

МЫ ПОДУМАЛИ ОБ ЭТОМ ЕЩЁ В ДЖОРДЖТАУНЕ!

НО ДЕНЕГ НА ЧТО-НИБУДЬ СЕРЕБРЯНОЕ НЕ ХВАТИЛО!

ПОЭТОМУ МЫ КУПИЛИ НА БАРАХОЛКЕ БАЛЛОНЧИК С СЕРЕБРЯНОЙ КРАСКОЙ!

МАЛЬЧИКИ, ЕСЛИ ДЕЙСТВОВАТЬ С УМОМ, ДАЖЕ КРАСКА МОЖЕТ СПАСТИ НАШИ ШЕИ!

ВСЮ НОЧЬ!

ЕСТЬ ИДЕИ, ВИЛЛИ?

НЕТ, НО Я ДУМАЮ!

УТРОМ!

ОЙ-ЁЙ! ПОХОЖЕ, МОЙ ВЫХОД!

КУКУРАРИ! БУБУРАРИ! ТОМДИКУНАРИ! (ПЕРЕВОД): БОЛЬШОГО КАЗНИТЕ ПЕРВЫМ!

ОНИ ПРОВОДЯТ СВОЙ РИТУАЛ ПРЯМО НАД НАМИ!

ТОЧНО! ЭЛЬ ДОРАДО ДОЛЖЕН СТОЯТЬ ГДЕ-ТО ТУТ!

НУ, СЕЙЧАС НАЧНЁТСЯ! ОН ВЫБИРАЕТСЯ ИЗ ДЫРЫ!

ЭЛЬ ДОРАДО! УТКИ СОТВОРИЛИ **ВЕЛИКОЕ ЧУДО**!

ТЫ ТЕПЕРЬ НЕ **ЗОЛОТОЙ**, А **СЕРЕБРЯНЫЙ**!

СИПАРУНИ! МАМПАРУНИ! УХТТТЫЗЗ! (ПЕРЕВОД): ОХ, МММ-МАМОЧКИ!

СУМКА У НАС! УНОСИМ НОГИ, ПОКА ЭТИ РЕБЯТА НЕ ПОЧУЯЛИ ПОДВОХ!

КАК ВЫ ДОГАДАЛИСЬ **ЕГО** ПОКРАСИТЬ?

МЫ ПРОСТО ПОДУМАЛИ, ЧТО ЕСЛИ ОН ЩЕГОЛЯЕТ В **ЗОЛОТОМ** СО ВРЕМЕН УОЛТЕРА РЭЛИ, ТО ОБРАДУЕТСЯ НОВЫМ ЦВЕТАМ В ЛЕТНЕЙ КОЛЛЕКЦИИ!

БЫСТРЕЕ!

СЕКУНДОЧКУ! КАЖЕТСЯ, ТУТ **ГАРДЕРОБНАЯ**! И Я ВИЖУ ТАМ КОЕ-ЧТО ПОЛЕЗНОЕ!

И ВОТ УТКИ И СТАРЫЙ РЫБАК ВСТРЕЧАЮТСЯ СНОВА!

ВЫ НАШЛИ ЕЁ! **ПОЧТОВАЯ СУМКА**!

АГА! А ЕСЛИ КТО-НИБУДЬ **ОПЯТЬ ЗАСОМНЕВАЕТСЯ** В СЛОВАХ ВАШЕГО ОТЦА, ЗАПАСНАЯ ПАРА КАЛЬСОН ЭЛЯ ДОРАДО ПОМОЖЕТ УБЕДИТЬ НЕДОВЕРЧИВЫХ!

ПОСЛЕ БЕСЧИСЛЕННЫХ ПИРУШЕК И ПОХВАЛ!

ТЕПЕРЬ НАМ ОСТАЛОСЬ ЛИШЬ ДОСТАВИТЬ СВОЙ ПРИЗ ДОМОЙ И ПРОДАТЬ ФИЛО Т. ЭЛЛИСТУ!

ДОКИ

ТАК ЛИ?

МИНУТОЧКУ! ДУМАЕТЕ, ВЫ МОЖЕТЕ ПОКИНУТЬ СТРАНУ С СУМКОЙ ПОЧТОВОЙ СЛУЖБЫ ЕГО ВЕЛИЧЕСТВА?

НО ЭТА СУМКА — АНТИКВАРИАТ! ЕЙ ДЕВЯНОСТО ШЕСТЬ ЛЕТ!

ПОЧТА ЕГО ВЕЛИЧЕСТВА ВСЕГДА ПРИХОДИТ, ДАЖЕ С ОПОЗДАНИЕМ НА ДЕВЯНОСТО ШЕСТЬ ЛЕТ!

ЧТО НАМ ТЕПЕРЬ ДЕЛАТЬ, ДЯДЯ ДОНАЛЬД?

СЛЕДУЕМ ЗА ПИСЬМОМ!

ПОРТОВАЯ ПОЧТОВАЯ СЛУЖБА

МЫ В КУРСЕ ВАШИХ ПРИКЛЮЧЕНИЙ С ПОЗОЛОЧЁННЫМ ЧЕЛОВЕКОМ! МЫ ГАДАЛИ, КОГДА ЖЕ ВЫ ВЕРНЁТЕ СУМКУ!

А НЕЛЬЗЯ МНЕ ОСТАВИТЬ ТОЛЬКО ЭТО ПИСЬМО? Я РАДИ НЕГО ЖИЗНЬЮ РИСКОВАЛ!

ПРОСТИ, СТАРИНА, НО ВСЕ ЭТИ ПИСЬМА ДОЛЖНЫ БЫТЬ ДОСТАВЛЕНЫ!

ПРАВИЛА

РОЗОВАЯ МАРКА!

СМОТРИТЕ! НЕУДИВИТЕЛЬНО, ЧТО СЕЛЕЗЕНЬ ПРОСИТ ПИСЬМО!

ЛЮБОЙ БЫ ПОПРОСИЛ!

ЛАДНО, СДЕЛАЕМ ПОБЛАЖКУ! ЗАПИШИ ДЛЯ НЕГО АДРЕС!

«МИСС СЮЗИБЕЛЬ СУОН, ДОМ 60 ПО ХОНКЕР СТРИТ, МАДХЕН, ОГАЙО, США.»

ВОТ! ЕСЛИ МИСС СУОН ЕЩЁ ЖИВА, МОЖЕТ, ОНА СОГЛАСИТЬСЯ ОТДАТЬ ВАМ КОНВЕРТ!

УДАЧИ!

ДЯДЯ ДОНАЛЬД,

ТЕПЕРЬ

В МАДХЕН, ОГАЙО?

УГАДАЛИ!

В МАДХЕНЕ!

НЕТ... НИКАКАЯ МИСС СЮЗИБЕЛЬ СУОН ЗДЕСЬ НЕ ЖИВЁТ!

АВИАПОЧТА

ПИСЬМА

ОНА СЪЕХАЛА В 1880 ГОДУ! НОВЫЙ АДРЕС: 10, КРЯК-РОУД, ВЕБФУТ, ШТАТ ОРЕГОН!

ВЕБФУТ, ОРЕГОН!

НЕТ... НИКАКАЯ МИСС СЮЗИБЕЛЬ СУОН ЗДЕСЬ НЕ ЖИВЁТ

ПОЧТА

МАГАЗИН

ОНА УПЛЫЛА ОТСЮДА В 1901 ГОДУ! ПРОСИЛА ПЕРЕСЫЛАТЬ ПОЧТУ ПО АДРЕСУ: ДОМ 45 НА КРЯКВЕННОЙ УЛИЦЕ, ДАКСБУРГ, КАЛИСОТА!

ДАКСБУРГ!

ЭТО ЖЕ НАШ

РОДНОЙ ГОРОД!

КАК УДАЧНО, ЧТО ЭТО НАШ ДАКСБУРГ! Я БЫ НЕ СМОГ СЛЕДОВАТЬ ЗА ПИСЬМОМ С ПУСТЫМИ КАРМАНАМИ!

ДОМА!

ЕДЕМ НА КРЯКВЕННУЮ УЛИЦУ И ПОСМОТРИМ, ГДЕ ОСЕЛА НАША МИСС СУОН!

ИНСТРУМЕНТЫ ГИЗМО

ОЙ-ЁЙ! ЗДЕСЬ ТЕПЕРЬ ОГРОМНАЯ ФАБРИКА!

45

ЛАДНО, ПОЕХАЛИ ОБРАТНО НА ПОЧТУ!

ПРИВЕТИК! СМОТРИТЕ, КТО ВЕРНУЛСЯ В ГОРОД!

ПАРКОВКИ НЕТ

ПОЧТ

СТАРЫЙ ДОБРЫЙ КУЗЕН ДОНАЛЬД! НЕ УХОДИ ДАЛЕКО! УВИДИМСЯ, КОГДА Я ЗАБЕРУ СВОЮ ПОЧТУ!

ПОДУМАТЬ ТОЛЬКО, МОЯ УСОПШАЯ ТЁТУШКА ПОЛУЧИЛА ПИСЬМО ИЗ ЮЖНОЙ АМЕРИКИ! И ОНО ПРОШТАМПОВАНО 1856 ГОДОМ!

КАКАЯ СТРАННАЯ СТАРАЯ МАРКА!

СПОРИМ, ФИЛО Т. ЭЛЛИСТ КУПИТ ЕЁ У МЕНЯ! Я ЖЕ ВЕЗУНЧИК!

И ВОТ...

ОН ЗАШЁЛ В ТОТ ДОМ, ДЯДЯ ДОНАЛЬД!

ЭТОГО Я И БОЯЛСЯ!

ФИЛО Т. ЭЛЛИСТ

МОЖЕМ РАССЛАБИТЬСЯ, МАЛЬЧИКИ! ВСЁ, КОНЕЦ!

ДВЕ МИНУТЫ СПУСТЯ!

УХ ТЫ! НУ ДЕЛА!

ЭЙ, ДА ТУТ СЕМЕЙКА ДАК! Я ТОЛЬКО ЧТО ПРОДАЛ МАРКУ ЗА ПЯТЬДЕСЯТ ТЫСЯЧ ДОЛЛАРОВ! ПРЕДСТАВЛЯЕТЕ! МАРКУ!

КСТАТИ, ВЫ ЖЕ СОБИРАЛИСЬ В ЮЖНУЮ АМЕРИКУ ИСКАТЬ КАКУЮ-ТО МАРКУ! УДАЧНО СЪЕЗДИЛИ?

АХ! ХОЛОДНЫЕ, ТЁМНЫЕ ВОДЫ! МОЖНО ЛИ НАЙТИ ЛУЧШЕЕ МЕСТО ДЛЯ МОИХ ГОРЬКИХ СЛЁЗ!

ХНЫК!

Я СОБИРАЛСЯ СЕСТЬ НА **ПОЕЗД** ДО СЕНТ-ЛУИСА ИЛИ НА САМОЛЕТ?

КОНЕЧНО, НА **ПОЕЗД**! НО ПОЧЕМУ МНЕ ПРИШЛОСЬ **БЕЖАТЬ** ДО СТАНЦИИ?

ДОЛЖНО БЫТЬ, Я ЗАБЫЛ СВОЮ МАШИНУ! КАКАЯ РАССЕЯННОСТЬ!

НУЖНО ПОЙМАТЬ ТАКСИ!

ТАКСИ! ТАКСИ!

НА ВОКЗАЛ! Я ДОЛЖЕН УСПЕТЬ НА ПОЕЗД!

КАЖЕТСЯ, СТАЛО ПОЛЕГЧЕ! Я... ОЙ!

Я ЗАБЫЛ СВОИ МАРКИ! ОСТАВИЛ АЛЬБОМ НА ПЕРИЛАХ МОСТА, ПОКА ВЫЗЫВАЛ ТАКСИ!

КОШМАР! ЕЩЁ И У ПОЕЗДА НЕТ ОСТАНОВОК ДО САМОГО САН-ФРАНЦИСКО!

ТАМ ОН ТОЖЕ НЕ ОСТАНОВИТСЯ, МИСТЕР ЭЛЛИСТ! ЭТО ПОЕЗД ДО ЧИКАГО!

!

АЛЬБОМ ДЛЯ МАРОК

МОЙ СТАРЫЙ ДРУГ, ГРИНДСТОУН ГИММИК!

ПОЗЖЕ!

ЭТО ДЯДЯ ДОНАЛЬД! ОН ГДЕ-ТО ЗА ГОРОДОМ!

КОМИКСЫ

ОТТУДА ПУТЬ НЕБЛИЗКИЙ, ДЯДЯ ДОНАЛЬД! У ТЕБЯ ДОСТАТОЧНО ДЕНЕГ НА ТАКСИ ДО ДОМА?

О, У МЕНЯ ЕСТЬ ПЯТЬДЕСЯТ ТЫСЯЧ ДОЛЛАРОВ! ДУМАЮ, ЭТОГО ХВАТИТ!

И ТАК ДАЛЕЕ, И ТАК ДАЛЕЕ!

ЗДЕСЬ КАК МИНИМУМ ТРИДЦАТЬ ТОНН ДЕНЕГ! И ХРАНИТЬ ИХ НЕГДЕ!

ЧТО ДЕЛАТЬ? ЧТО ЖЕ ДЕЛАТЬ?

И КТО ЕЩЁ МОГ ПОЯВИТЬСЯ В ЭТУ СЕКУНДУ, ЕСЛИ НЕ...

МОЙ НЕПУТЁВЫЙ ПЛЕМЯННИЧЕК! ДОНАЛЬД!

ПРИВЕТ, ДЯДЯ СКРУДЖ!

ЧТО ТЫ ТАК СКРИВИЛСЯ, ДЯДЬ? КТО-ТО ПОДСУНУЛ ДЕРЕВЯННУЮ МОНЕТКУ?

ЕЩЁ СКАЖИ, ДЕРЕВЯННЫЙ ПУДИНГ! НЕЧЕГО ОСТРИТЬ!

У МЕНЯ УЖАСНАЯ ПРОБЛЕМА, ДОНАЛЬД! НЕ ЗНАЮ, ЧТО ДЕЛАТЬ С ЭТИМИ ДЕНЬГАМИ!

В СЕЙФЕ НЕ ПОМЕЩАЮТСЯ?

ДЕНЬГО ХРАНИЛИ ВХОД ВОС

ДА! А Я НЕ МОГУ ОСТАВИТЬ ИХ ЗДЕСЬ — ВДРУГ УКРАДУТ! И СТОРОЖИТЬ ТУТ ТОЖЕ НЕ МОГУ!

ХММ!

ПРИДУМАЛ! ПОСТРОЙ ДЕНЬГОХРАНИЛИЩЕ ПОБОЛЬШЕ!

ОНО ОБОЙДЁТСЯ В МИЛЛИАРДЫ ДОЛЛАРОВ!

НЕТ СМЫСЛА ТРАТИТЬ МИЛЛИАРДЫ, ЧТОБЫ СОХРАНИТЬ МИЛЛИОНЫ!

ПЕРВЫМ ДЕЛОМ НАДО КУПИТЬ МАШИНУ!

ЭТА МАЛЫШКА МОЖЕТ МНОГО МИЛЬ ПРОТЯНУТЬ НА КАПЛЕ БЕНЗИНА!

ДЕНЬГИ ТРАЧУ Я!

$302

И ВОТ МОЙ ВЫБОР!

ЛИХАЧ V24!

ПОЧЁМ ТАКОЙ ЗВЕРЬ?

КАК ЕСТЬ — ПЯТЬДЕСЯТ ТЫСЯЧ! А ЕСЛИ С ЧЕХЛАМИ ДЛЯ КРЕСЕЛ ИЗ МЕХА ГОРНОСТАЯ, ТО СТО!

НАДЕНЬТЕ ЧЕХЛЫ И ОТСЧИТАЙТЕ СТО ТЫСЯЧ ИЗ ЭТОЙ ГОРЫ!

ТЕПЕРЬ ПРИКУПИМ МОДНЫЙ ПРИЦЕП!

ПРИЦЕП! ЗАЧЕМ?

ЧТОБЫ ЗАГРУЗИТЬ ТУДА ДЕНЬГИ! МЫ ЕДЕМ В ПУТЕШЕСТВИЕ!

И ВОТ...

КАК ЖЕ ТЫ ПОТРАТИШЬ ДЕНЬГИ **В ПУТИ**, ПЛЕМЯННИК?

УВИДИШЬ!

КТО ГОТОВ ПЕРЕКУСИТЬ?

МЫ!

ТАМ ЧИСТАЯ МАЛЕНЬКАЯ ЗАКУСОЧНАЯ! И БУРГЕРЫ ВСЕГО ПО ДВАДЦАТЬ ЦЕНТОВ!

ТОГДА, ДЯДЯ СКРУДЖ, ВЕЧНОСТЬ УЙДЁТ, ЧТОБ ОСВОБОДИТЬ ПРИЦЕП! ПОЕДИМ ТУТ!

НУ И ЦЕНЫ! ВЛАДЕЛЬЦА ЭТОЙ ОБДИРАЛОВКИ ДАВНО ПОРА СУДИТЬ ЗА РАЗБОЙ!

ЗАБУДЬ О ЦЕНАХ! ДУМАЙ О ДЕНЬГАХ, КОТОРЫЕ НУЖНО ПОТРАТИТЬ!

ПЯТЬ ДВОЙНЫХ ПОРЦИЙ ЖАРЕНЫХ ГРУДОК КАЛЕДОНСКИХ ПЕРЕПЕЛОВ СО ВСЕМИ ДОБАВКАМИ ОТ СУПА ДО ОРЕШКОВ!

ВЗБИТЫЕ СЛИВКИ К ОРЕШКАМ, СЭР?

ДА! И ВИШЕНКОЙ УКРАСЬТЕ!

ВИШНЯ ПЯТЬ ДОЛЛАРОВ СВЕРХУ!

ОТЛИЧНО! БРОСЬТЕ СРАЗУ ГОРСТЬ!

СМОТРИТЕ! МИМО МАРШИРУЕТ ОТРЯД ЮНЫХ СУРКОВ!

ТАК ДЕЙСТВУЙТЕ! ПРИГЛАСИТЕ ИХ ПООБЕДАТЬ С НАМИ!

ЭТО ПРИЯТЕЛИ МОИХ ПЛЕМЯННИКОВ! ОБСЛУЖИТЕ ИХ ПО **ВЫСШЕМУ** РАЗРЯДУ!

ПЛАТУ ВОЗЬМИТЕ ОТСЮДА! ЕСЛИ ТАМ ОСТАНЕТСЯ ПАРА ТЫСЯЧ ОСТАВЬТЕ СЕБЕ! ВЫ ЗАСЛУЖИЛИ ЧАЕВЫЕ!

С ЭТОГО МОМЕНТА ПИТАЕМСЯ ТОЛЬКО ТАК!

ПРИЗНАЮ, **ТРАТИТЬ** ДЕНЬГИ ТЫ УМЕЕШЬ, ДОНАЛЬД! НО ЗАЧЕМ С ТАКИМ **РАЗМАХОМ?**

ТЫ ГОТОВ **ГОДАМИ** ПЛАТИТЬ МНЕ ТРИДЦАТЬ ЦЕНТОВ В ЧАС, ИЛИ ХОЧЕШЬ, ЧТОБЫ Я ЗАКОНЧИЛ ПОБЫСТРЕЕ?

ХОРОШО! СДАЮСЬ! НО КАК ВЫНЕСТИ ЭТИ СТРАДАНИЯ!

ЭЙ! ТАМ ИНДЕЙСКИЕ СЕРЕБРЯНЫЕ БЕЗДЕЛУШКИ!

ЧУЮ БОГАТЕНЬКИХ ТУРИСТОВ, ЗМЕЙ-В-ТРАВЕ!

ВИЖУ-ВИЖУ!

Я ПРОСТО ОБЯЗАН НАКУПИТЬ БРАСЛЕТОВ И ЗАКОЛОК ДЛЯ ДЕЙЗИ И ВСЕХ ДАМ ЕЁ КЛУБА!

И НЕСКОЛЬКО ПОДКОВ НА УДАЧУ ДЛЯ ГЛЭДСТОУНА!

$50

НАСТОЯЩЕЕ СЕРЕБРО

О-ХО-ХО! ПОРА ПОКУПАТЬ НОВУЮ МАШИНУ!

ОПЯТЬ?

У ЭТОЙ ЦВЕТ НЕ ТОТ! НУЖЕН БОЛЕЕ ПОДХОДЯЩИЙ К ПЕЙЗАЖУ!

ЛАЗУРНЫЕ ГОРЫ

ШЕСТЬ ДНЕЙ И СЕМЬ АВТОМОБИЛЕЙ СПУСТЯ!

Я СОВСЕМ ИЗМОТАН! ТРАТИЛ ДЕНЬГИ НАПРАВО И НАЛЕВО!

ЗАТО МЫ ВЕСЕЛИЛИСЬ НА ПОЛНУЮ!

ПОЧЕМУ БЫ НЕ ПУТЕШЕСТВОВАТЬ ТАК ПОЧАЩЕ?

СЪЕДИТЕ ЕЩЁ НЕСКОЛЬКО ЖАРЕНЫХ КАЛЕДОНСКИХ ПЕРЕПЕЛОВ?

НЕТ!

ПОНИМАЮ И НЕ ВИНЮ! Я ТОЖЕ ЛЮБЛЮ ПЕРЕМЕНЫ!

БУРГЕРЫ ПО ТРИДЦАТЬ ЦЕНТОВ ЗА ШТУКУ!

ЗНАЮ! ЗАВЕРНЁТЕ ИХ В ЗОЛОТУЮ ФОЛЬГУ, ЧТОБЫ ВЫГЛЯДЕЛИ ДОРОЖЕ?

НАКОНЕЦ!

У МЕНЯ ПОЛУЧИЛОСЬ! ВСЕ ДЕНЬГИ ПОТРАЧЕНЫ!

И ОСТАЛОСЬ ДОСТАТОЧНО БЕНЗИНА, ЧТОБЫ ДОБРАТЬСЯ ДОМОЙ!

ОТ ТАКИХ НОВОСТЕЙ МОЁ СЕРДЦЕ СНОВА ОЖИВАЕТ!

ДЕЛЬЦЕ СДЕЛАНО!

ПОЙДЁМ В ОФИС, ДОНАЛЬД, ВЫПЛАЧУ ТВОЁ ЖАЛОВАНЬЕ!

УЖАСНЕЕ ПЫТКИ В МОЕЙ ЖИЗНИ НЕ БЫЛО! ХОРОШО, ЧТО ВСЁ ЗАКОНЧИЛОСЬ!

WALT DISNEY'S
Donald Duck
in "A CHRISTMAS FOR SHACKTOWN

10¢

Комментарии

ТЕМ ВРЕМЕНЕМ ДЕТИ В БЕДНОТАУНЕ СТРОЯТ РАДУЖНЫЕ ПЛАНЫ!

ИГРУШЕЧНЫЙ ПОЕЗД! МЫ ПРАВДА ПОЛУЧИМ НА РОЖДЕСТВО ИГРУШЕЧНЫЙ ПОЕЗД?

ТАК ПООБЕЩАЛИ ЭТИ МИЛЫЕ ЛЕДИ!

РОЖДЕСТВО В БЕДНОТАУНЕ, *стр. 7*

Хотя Карла Баркса и нельзя назвать бунтарём, его взгляды на Рождество сильно расходились с общепринятыми. Праздник, который большинство обывателей ждёт с таким же нетерпением, как день зарплаты, для Баркса был лишь ещё одним днём, обнажавшим самые безнравственные черты человеческой натуры.

Сюжет «Рождества в Беднотауне» стал, пожалуй, самой значительной уступкой автора праздничным дням, которые он сам воспринимал не иначе, как парад человеческой жадности, стяжательства и фальшивых эмоций. Билли, Вилли и Дилли уже мечтают о рождественском ужине и сладостях, которые ждут их дома, торопятся и решают срезать путь, пройдя через Беднотаун. Жители этого района настолько обнищали, что один взгляд на них заставил бы известного фотографа и ярого борца с социальной несправедливостью Якоба Рииса рвануть за фотоаппаратом.

Ясно, что никакому празднику не под силу вытеснить из сердца столь печальные картины. И вот наша троица чувствительных утят твёрдо решает пожертвовать собственным весельем и убедить более удачливых жителей Даксбурга принести Рождество детям Беднотауна. Дональд, естественно, готов поддержать эту затею, правда, за счёт любимого дядюшки.

Но пока Дональд считает, что у Скруджа достаточно денег, чтобы осуществить любую мечту, сам дядюшка искренне полагает, что понятие «достаточно» к деньгам неприменимо даже тогда, когда вес его богатства уже не выдерживает земная кора.

Как в сцене из фильма «Парни и куколки», где Нейтан Детройт пытается втянуть Ская Мастерсона в аферу, а вместо этого заключает пари на собственное имущество, так и Скрудж с истинно шотландской расчётливостью готов дать денег, только если Дональд прежде принесёт ему свою часть суммы на подарки. (Я никогда не одобрял мультипликационный образ Скруджа за его шотландский акцент, поскольку для меня он такое же американское детище, как прохладительные напитки, но в этом комиксе Баркс вспоминает о маленьком Скрудже, которого качал на коленке шотландский дядюшка, так что пусть всё будет по-шотландски). И всё же, несмотря на обещание Дональду и шотландские корни, Скрудж избегает Рождества с таким упорством, словно за ним гонятся все духи дома с привидениями.

Кстати, барксовское «Рождество в Беднотауне» вдохновило молодого и подающего надежды художника-комиксиста по имени Роберт Крамб на создание первого в своей жизни комикса.

Р. ФЬОРЕ

БОЛЬШОЕ ХРАНИЛИЩЕ НА ХОЛМЕ КИЛМОТОР, *стр. 39*

Наконец-то король обретает свой замок. Именно в истории «Большое хранилище на холме Килмотор» впервые появляется центральный элемент мифологии Скруджа Макдака — деньгохранилище. Высокое, прямо-таки исполинское здание венчает вершину холма Килмотор и возвышается над Даксбургом. Хранилище одновременно и замок, и тюрьма. Здесь, за мощными крепостными стенами, Скрудж хранит всё своё

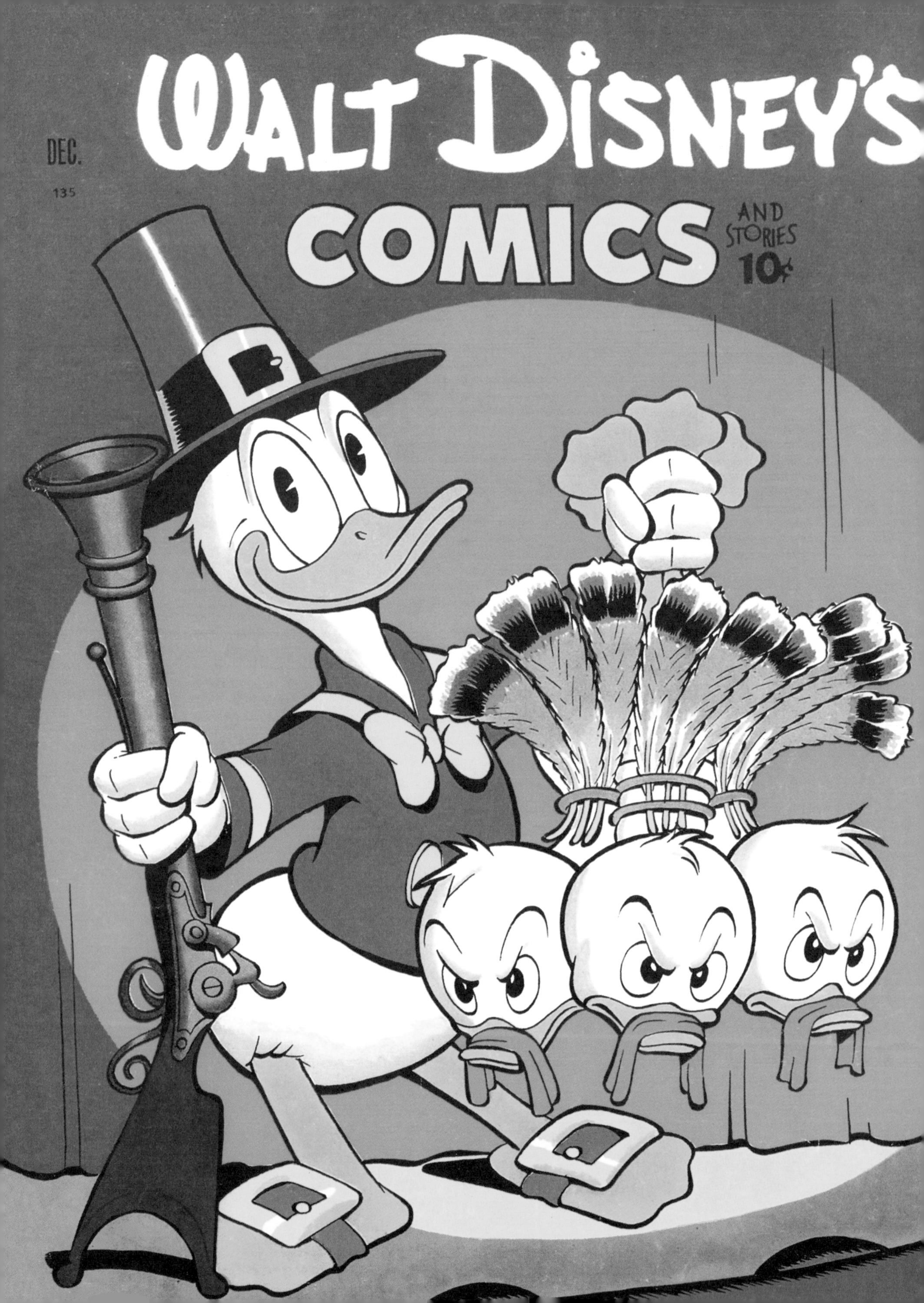
DEC.
135
WALT DISNEY'S
COMICS
AND STORIES
10¢

состояние, ну или ту часть, которая особенно дорога его сердцу. Здесь он предаётся маленьким радостям: прикасается к деньгам, любуется ими, купается в них (возможно Скрудж относится к деньгам, как к живым созданиям, самым любимым созданиям этого мира). Но затем появляется тема хранилища как тюрьмы. Под надёжной защитой разнообразных ловушек и следящих систем хранилище выглядит совершенно неприступным для любого взломщика. Но эта история о том, что в здание не только сложно войти, но из него практически невозможно выйти.

Комиксист Дон Роса в заметках к своей серии «Жизнь и времена Скруджа Макдака», писал, что хотя Карл Баркс «впервые пришёл к своей хрестоматийной идее деньгохранилища именно в "Большом хранилище на холме Килмотор", позднее он использовал хранилище так, словно оно существовало всегда».

В наши дни просто невозможно подумать о Скрудже, чтобы перед мысленным взором не возникли неприступные стены его деньгохранилища. Именно поэтому в своей собственной версии прошлого Утиной вселенной Роса показывает, что молодой Скрудж начинает строить хранилище сразу, как появляется в Даксбурге.

История реального прототипа деньгохранилища начинается на берегу огромного

водохранилища, принадлежащего мультимиллионеру Уильяму Ф. Уиттеру. Основатель города Хемет в штате Калифорния — города, где Баркс жил в течение многих лет — Уиттер перекачивал воду из водохранилища на огромную очистную установку, построенную на холме Хеметс Парк Хилл. Это знаменитое сооружение и стало источником вдохновения для создания хранилища богатств Скруджа.

А вместе с хранилищем пришли и братья Гавс. Эта банда грабителей впервые появилась на страницах журнала «Комиксы и истории Уолта Диснея» месяцем ранее и с тех пор стала неразрывно связанной с хранилищем. Кажется, что взлом хранилища является единственной целью жизни братьев Гавс. Иногда сам Скрудж от излишнего беспокойства за свои денежки невольно облегчает Гавсам их задачу, что мы и видим в этой истории.

С созданием деньгохранилища и появлением братьев Гавс Баркс практически завершил формирование того хрестоматийного образа Скруджа, каким мы знаем его сегодня. Да, Баркс ещё не сделал своего героя более отзывчивым любителем приключений, но и этого события оставалось ждать совсем недолго. Комикс «Всего лишь бедный старичок» увидит свет через каких-то три месяца после «Большого хранилища на холме Килмотор» (см. комикс «Дядюшка Скрудж: Всего лишь бедный старичок», вышедший в этой серии ранее).

СТЕФАНО ПРИАРОНЕ

ОБЫЧНОЕ ВЕЗЕНИЕ ГЛЭДСТОУНА, стр. 49

Если бы кто-то взялся описать историю комиксов на манер «Исторического справочника по бейсболу», то сухая выжимка из «Обычного везения Глэдстоуна» и разыгравшейся на его страницах дуэли двух ведущих питчеров, Дональда и Глэдстоуна, выглядела бы примерно так:

Цель: Дональд хочет выиграть индейку в лотерею, для чего скупает все билеты кроме одного, доставшегося Глэдстоуну.

Число попыток, предпринятых Дональдом: Три.

Средства, использованные Дональдом для жульничества: В первом розыгрыше Дональд проделывает во всех своих билетах множество отверстий, чтобы их проще было подцепить. Во втором розыгрыше он вставляет булавки внутрь каждого билета, чтобы их можно было достать из корзины магнитом. В третий раз он организовывает собственную лотерею, и единственный билет Глэдстоуна засыпает горой своих билетов.

Средства, благодаря которым Глэдстоуну неизменно удаётся победить Дональда: В первом розыгрыше билет Глэдстоуна случайно падает на дикобраза и становится более шероховатым, поэтому его вытаскивают первым; во второй раз всё срывается из-за попытки племянников Дональда сжульничать ему на пользу; в третью лотерею вмешивается землетрясение, опрокинувшее гору билетов.

Характеристика состояния Дональда: Бессильная ярость.

Р. ФЬОРЕ

ТАЙНА «ВОПЯЩЕГО КОВБОЯ», стр. 59

В возрасте восьми лет Карл Баркс был совершенно очарован ковбоями, которых встречал в период сенокоса на ранчо в Орегоне. Он уважал прямоту и стойкость этих людей — день за днём они выполняли самые сложные работы, довольствуясь лишь самыми необходимыми инструментами. Повзрослевший Баркс восхищался популярными «поющими ковбоями» 1930-х—1940-х годов, звёздами вроде Джина Отри и Роя Роджерса, которые пели о погонщиках скота, водивших стада по американскому Западу. В «Вопящем ковбое» Баркс беззлобно пародирует Отри и его последователей, создав двойственный образ

самовлюблённой утки, которая, как следует из названия, любит заунывно вопить.

Этот комикс легко принять за очередную комедийную историю, в которой самомнение Дональда в сотый раз становится причиной череды неприятностей — в данном случае его пение вызывает целый каскад лавин. Как говорил сам Баркс, одной из его любимых всегда была поговорка «гордость предшествует падению» (или лавине), а в этой истории гордость Дональда проявляется в его желании снова и снова прослушивать мелодию собственного сочинения. Но подобное прочтение комикса слишком поверхностно. Дональд жаждет слушать сельскую музыку, исполненную на самодельных инструментах и записанную на пластинку. Подобную музыку горячо любил сам Баркс. Автор видел в ней своеобразное противоядие от излишеств современной музыки: «Ах! Эту группу!» (любовь Дональда столь глубока, что её невозможно выразить словами). Высоко оценивая простоту ковбойского уклада жизни, Баркс точно также обожал старомодные репертуары американских фолк-групп.

Сам Барк однажды описал свой вкус в музыке как «подчеркнуто деревенский». При всей своей элегантности и изобретательности, его художественный стиль также можно охарактеризовать как «подчеркнуто деревенский». Подобно любимой Барксом чёткой схеме дуэта гитары и мандолины в песне «Индюшка в соломе», его сюжеты, особенно десятистраничные, наподобие «Вопящего ковбоя», выстраивались по строгой формуле. Сначала идёт вступление, задающее основную тему или проблему (например, песня «Вопящий ковбой»), далее следует серия комических ситуаций, основанных на этой проблеме (в каждой ситуации повторяется новая вариация), в финале герои находят решение, уже понятное из сюжета. В этом рассказе первая строчка песни, звучащая как «О, похороните меня там с моей потрёпанной гитарой», сбывается в финале, когда Дональд счастливо

погребён под снегом в обнимку со старым музыкальным автоматом, проигрывающим столь любимые его сердцу песни в стиле фолк.

И пока мы наслаждаемся лёгкостью и прозрачной ясностью таких историй, как «Вопящий ковбой», Баркс, скорее всего, старается напомнить нам и о том, сколько кропотливой, а, подчас, и мучительной работы нужно вложить, чтобы получить такую лёгкость. Подобно ковбоям из своего детства, он отдаётся делу без остатка. Используя лишь самые необходимые инструменты — карандаш, чернила и бумагу — Баркс день за днём решал крайне сложные художественные задачи.

КЕН ПЭРИЛЛ

МОНУМЕНТАЛЬНЫЕ МОТЫ, стр. 69

Спустя почти двадцать лет после публикации некоторых из своих рассказов Карл Баркс недоумевал, как ему позволили разрабатывать такие сюжеты. «Я думал, как, чёрт побери, мне вообще удалось всё это проверить», — вспоминал он в интервью Дональду Олту. А говоря об истории «Монументальные моты», он отмечал: «О, господи, да там же сплошной цинизм».

Чёрный юмор «Мотов» рождается из хлёсткой сатиры, в то время как шутовские выходки персонажей мгновенно вызывают гомерический смех. Мотивации персонажей и их внутреннее состояние переданы исключительно выражениями лиц. Позы и лица героев читаются легко, как в немых кинокомедиях. Но это вовсе не значит, что выражения лиц лишены глубины: посмотрите на тот диапазон эмоций, что отражается в глазах Дональда, когда тот навещает дядюшку Скруджа в деньгохранилище в надежде спровоцировать старого скрягу ввязаться в спор с махараджей.

Сюжет развивается по строго выверенной схеме с головокружительной скоростью. С такой же скоростью городской пейзаж Даксбурга заполоняют возмутительно гигантские статуи, превосходящие все мыслимые габариты человека и природы и пугающие зверюшек на полях. Никто не вмешивается в это безумное состязание: молчат сбитые с толку даксбургцы, молчат плывущие по течению городские чиновники и, конечно, молчит Дональд, который сначала заварил всю эту кашу, а затем превратился в соучастника действа. Никем не сдерживаемое, соревнование превращается в фарс, финал которого явно будет печальным.

Зная читательский вкус Баркса, можно предположить, что он был знаком с «потлачем», церемониальным обрядом коренных народов Америки, некогда населявших северо-западное побережье Тихого океана. «Потлач» — это обряд дарения подарков, например, на свадьбу или другое официальное торжество. В смутные времена таким способом решали конфликты. Желая продемонстрировать материальное превосходство, соперничающие вожди раздавали всё более и более впечатляющие подарки, тем самым показывая противнику размер своего богатства и щедрости. Соперничество продолжалось до тех пор, пока одна из сторон не оказывалась в шаге от разорения, а иногда и впадала в нищету, прямо как в случае с махараджей.

Баркс скрупулёзно избегал в своих комиксах спорных тем. Но в этой истории сложно не заметить параллели с набирающей в те времена обороты ядерной гонкой, в частности, с непрекращающимися испытаниями всё более мощных бомб со стороны Соединённых штатов и Советского Союза. В этом свете ошеломлённые, горестные физиономии уток в нижней части страницы 75 и паника на лицах политиков, осознавших, что они выпустили на волю силы, которые не способны сдерживать, принимают куда более глубокий смысл.

В эру ядерного оружия Баркс рисует даксбургских гигантских колоссов. Они — никому не нужные памятники бездумного соперничества, которые ещё долго будут напоминать о наших ошибках.

РИЧ КРЕЙНЕР

РАКЕТОКРЫЛ СПАСАЕТ ПОЛОЖЕНИЕ, стр. 79

Карл Баркс начинает историю «Ракетокрыл спасает положение» со знаменитой строчки Альфреда Теннисона, поэта девятнадцатого столетия, почитаемого за музыкальность и метрическую точность: «Весной воображение молодого человека с легкостью поворачивается к мыслям о…»

Баркс обрывает цитату Теннисона, не дав появиться на свет последнему слову («любви»), и отдаёт поводья в руки Дональду, который буквально оглушает Дейзи чередой своих «ууу». Чтобы лишний раз подчеркнуть отсутствие у Дональда музыкальных талантов, Баркс рисует рядом подслушивающую чайку, во взгляде которой и насмешка, и страдание.

Для Баркса «звучание» его текстов имеет ничуть не меньшую важность, чем правдоподобие его персонажей и точный выбор времени для шутки. Подобно поэту, он уделяет огромное внимание размеру, порой даже высчитывая количество слогов в реплике, не позволяя ей выбиться из общего ритма. Такая практика, по словам самого Баркса, помогает «создать ровный, непрерывный поток, чтобы голоса уток звучали словно поэзия в прозе».

Баркс считал, что хороший комикс по определению должен читаться очень легко. Язык для такой истории необходим минималистичный и музыкальный. Даже во время бедствия на море Дональд умудряется найти рифму, подходящую ситуации: «Не везёт, так не везёт! Водяной смерч на нас идёт!»

Баркс также хотел, чтобы имена его героев звучали интересно на слух, прямо как состоящее из повторяющихся согласных имя Дейзи Дак или ритмически выверенные имена Билли, Вилли и Дилли. Клички голубей Баркс связал с достижениями военных технологий того времени, которые славились своими скоростными качествами — с названиями боевых ракет и реактивных двигателей времён Второй мировой войны. Заглавный персонаж, голубь Ракетокрыл, назван в честь первого американского ракетоплана Northrop MX-324 Rocket Wing. Дональд позже награждает питомца уничижительным звукоподражательным прозвищем «Жужжалка» — так во время войны англичане окрестили немецкую ракету «Фау-1», печально известную характерным жужжащим звуком двигателя. Одним из соперников Ракетокрыла в гонке выступает Реактивный Клинок, кличка которого перекликается с названием американского реактивного истребителя F-86 «Сейбр» («Сабля»), широко применяемого в армии США на момент первой публикации комикса.

Основная интрига сюжета строится вокруг полётов и звука — свиста, который отвлекает Ракетокрыла от его задания. Точно также, как «завывания» Дональда привлекают внимание чайки, так и племянники призывают своего голубя звуками «ту-ту», а окружающий мир наполнен разнообразными «фьють», «свирк», «фу-у-ух» и «пффу-ух». Всегда заинтересованный в тематической (и акустической) завершённости своих историй, Баркс аккуратно подводит черту в этом повествовании о полётах и свисте в двух последних панелях. Сначала звонит колокольчик, а затем рассказ завершается картиной искусственно созданной тишины: Ракетокрыл выиграл гонку, потому что находчивые утята надели ему звукоизолирующие наушники.

КЕН ПЭРИЛЛ

УЖАСНЫЙ СЕКРЕТ ГЛЭДСТОУНА, стр. 89

Если и был в Утиной вселенной персонаж, к которому сам Карл Баркс питал искреннее отвращение, то это определённо Глэдстоун Гандер. Дядюшка Скрудж может быть скупцом и брюзгой, но его состояние нажито ценой труда и тяжких лишений. Даже бандиты, братья Гавс, нередко проявляют поразительную

изобретательность в своих бесконечных попытках избавить Скруджа от его золота. То, какими средствами они пользуются, нередко заставляет улыбнуться даже самого Скруджа, который считает Гавсов своими самыми достойными противниками.

А вот Глэдстоун вызывает у Баркса и его героев лишь отрицательные эмоции — возмущение, зависть, недоумение и отчаяние. Всю эту гамму чувств автор рисует в «Ужасном секрете Глэдстоуна», когда Дональд и племянники проходят путь от глубокого уныния (Глэдстоун заставляет всех остальных «чувствовать себя неудачниками!», до решительной ярости прямо в следующей же панели («Но и его везенью должен быть предел! Наверняка есть нечто, что ему не под силу!»).

Конечно, никакого предела нет. Но наверняка есть секрет, а его можно было бы украсть, скопировать или запатентовать. В отличие от богатств Скруджа, которые каждую секунду могут пасть жертвой грабителей, рыночной экономики или стихийного бедствия, удача Глэдстоуна пока необъяснима, но кто знает...

В своих попытках раскрыть ужасную тайну Глэдстоуна, Дональд, Скрудж и племянники обнаруживают, что секрет вовсе не в счастливом талисмане, а в памятном сувенире из самого позорного дня в жизни Глэдстоуна, когда он, поддавшись слабости, единственный раз зарабатывал деньги. «Да потому что там не счастливый талисман!» — кричит Глэдстоун взломщикам, — «Это... впрочем, не ваше дело!».

И, действительно, эта десятицентовая монетка никогда не была в деле, и именно так Глэдстоун надеется обезопасить себя — запирает её в сейфе, навсегда изъяв из обращения, чтобы уничтожить (или хотя бы выбросить из головы) все воспоминания о сделке, которая едва не связала Глэдстоуна с рыночной экономикой и чьим-либо делом.

Этот десятицентовик, похороненный в недрах его сейфа, нетронутый с того самого дня, как был заработан, способен «погубить» Глэдстоуна, и не только потому, что навсегда подорвёт его репутацию в глазах Скруджа и Дональда. Ужаснее всего, что Глэдстоун сам верит — лишь фанатичный отказ от труда и рыночных отношений позволяет ему вести беззаботный образ жизни, к которому он так привык.

И даже попытка устроить своей удаче «действительно серьёзную» проверку слишком напоминает Гандеру «работу». Секрет его удачи, по крайней мере, так думает сам Глэдстоун, в его абсолютной уверенности в собственном умении получать что-то — всё, что угодно — даром. А монетка напоминает о единственном миге сомнений, являет собой единственную связь с возможным «крахом».

Но все эти глубокие переживания при виде

монетки доступны лишь самому Глэдстоуну. Дональд, Скрудж и племянники пережили совершенно иной опыт, и все их комментарии по этому поводу «не для печати». На самом деле, Дональд и остальные настолько потрясены услышанным, что практически утратили дар речи. Они изображены лишь силуэтами, словно после всех отрицательных эмоций, которые пришлось пережить за время этой истории, просто нет такого выражения, которое могло бы в полной мере передать всю глубину их отвращения к Глэдстоуну. Ну, или глубину отвращения самого Баркса.

ДЖАРЕД ГАРДНЕР

НЕПРИЯТНОСТИ С МОЗГОЯЩИКАМИ, стр. 99

Вряд ли кто-то сомневался, что героями комиксов Баркса всегда были люди, которые лишь в силу обстоятельств выглядели как утки. В этом комиксе Баркс решил вволю позабавиться над человеческим тщеславием и создал иногда пугающий, но в то же время бесконечно комичный рассказ о смешных животных, которые «говорят и ведут себя как люди».

Баркс использует обычный для мультфильма приём, чтобы стереть различия, задающие привычный порядок вещей. Утки, воспринимающие себя как «человеческие существа», создают «мозгоящики», которые перепутают личности и запустят вереницу событий, где поступки людей и животных будут отзеркалены.

Когда Дональд наряжается волком, чтобы проучить Винта и ребят, он выглядит совсем как настоящий волчище, если не брать в расчёт пуговицы на груди (заметные только читателю). Утят его дразнящий крик «Жареная утятина» приводит в самый настоящий ужас. Они забывают о своём самопровозглашённом человекоподобии и ведут себя как самая настоящая пернатая добыча.

В типичном для Баркса ироничном подходе к причинно-следственным связям, следующий поворот

MAY
140

WALT DISNEY'S
COMICS
AND STORIES 10¢

SCORE

сюжета кажется совершенно логичным после высокомерного вмешательства Дональда. Настоящий волк скрывается за маской обывателя. Баркс регулярно рисовал подобных персонажей, когда хотел ввести в повествование человека, но в рисовке образа сохранял черты прототипа — собаки.

В этом комиксе Баркс крайне умело смешивает комедию и ужасы. Образы волка и селезня, сбрасывающих свои маски, вносят в повествование оттенок сюрреализма. А вспомним сцену, где Дональд осознаёт леденящую кровь истину, что из охотника он сам превратился в «жареную утятину» для своего обидчика! Она описана в красках, знакомых любому ребёнку, который хоть раз попадал в ситуации, когда обычная игра внезапно становилась чем-то опасным.

Историю можно рассматривать и как самоанализ, размышления автора над основной задачей художника-комиксиста. В его рассказах животные должны говорить и вести себя как люди. Но параллели, которые панель за панелью проводятся между Дональдом и волком, добавляют повествованию более глубокий смысл. Дональд собирался просто позабавиться, но в его «превращении» присутствует нечто звериное. А волк становится настоящей угрозой только тогда, когда мыслелучи дают ему способность мыслить по-человечески. Эта история о «человеческой мысли», стоящей будто бы выше наших естественных инстинктов, и о том, как мы подсознательно маскируем эти инстинкты, находясь в обществе.

Винт Разболтайло, которого Баркс ранее представлял в качестве проходного персонажа, здесь впервые играет важную роль в первой из нескольких историй о возможностях и опасностях науки. Его изобретение работает, но приводит к ужасающим последствиям, а его подход к ситуации неизменно остаётся отстранённым — для него это просто «игры разума».

Но когда утята сравнивают Винта с Эдисоном, это совсем не кажется незаслуженным. И хотя им пришлось прыгнуть в кроличью нору и приложить немалые усилия, чтобы ликвидировать последствия эксперимента, мальчики всё равно сохраняют наивную веру в возможности науки. Дональд осознаёт своё бессилие и только отмахивается от надоедливого кролика, который напоминает ему, что науку не остановить.

МАТТИАС УАЙВЕЛ

ЗОЛОТОЙ ШЛЕМ, *стр. 111*

«Золотой шлем» — это самая настоящая симфония, созданная из мотивов и элементов, будораживших воображение Карла Баркса на протяжении всей его карьеры.

«Золотой шлем» похож на рискованное приключение, квест по поиску предмета невероятной ценности и странной силы, гонку сквозь коварные препятствия к экзотическим и суровым краям.

Испытания героев становятся всё тяжелее из-за постоянных поворотов сюжета и кривых усмешек фортуны. Смена позиций и новые и новые альянсы с включением довольно большого числа действующих лиц двигают повествование вперёд и закручивают

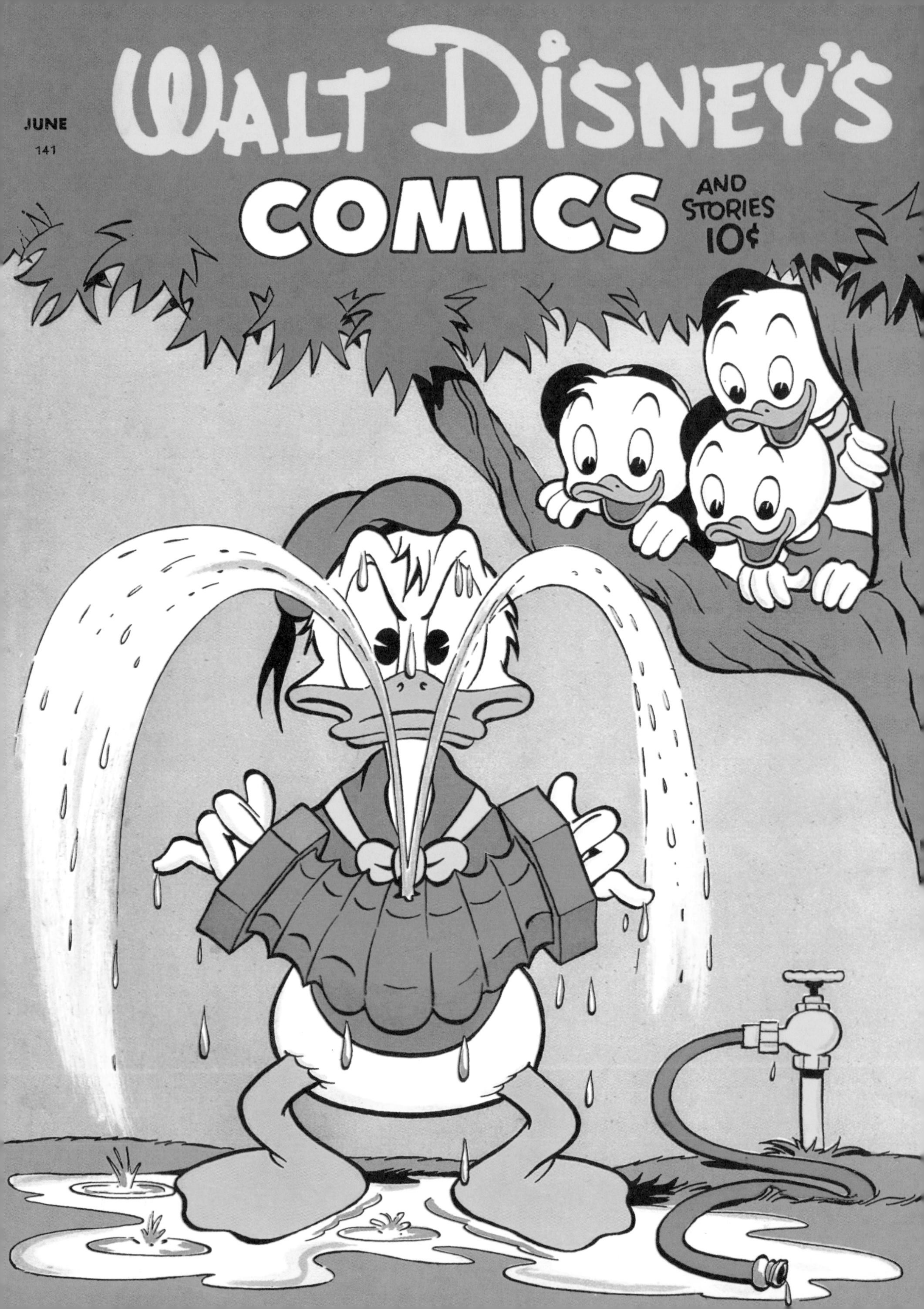
WALT DISNEY'S
JUNE
141
COMICS
AND
STORIES
10¢

интригу. В отличие от великих героев мифов и легенд, любой из персонажей этой истории вряд ли достоин стать обладателем искомого трофея.

Юмор и опасность следуют клюв к клюву. Комедийные карикатуры соседствуют с хмурыми взглядами и подлыми злодействами. Глаза у героев живые и выразительные, гротеск сведён к минимуму. В образе Шарки Баркс создаёт классический образчик нечистого на руку юриста, беспринципного адвокатишки по найму, несущего полную тарабарщину на латыни от имени любого, кто его нанял и моментально переходящего на сторону победителя. Плюс есть сюжеты, которые ставят нас в тупик!

Помимо удивительной насыщенности повествования выделяются две дополнительные особенности этого комикса. Во-первых, динамика повествования, сохраняющаяся на протяжении всей истории. Каждая сцена полностью детализирована, каждый перерыв чётко запланирован. Напряжение не ослабевает ни на секунду, все отдельные элементы этой энергичной истории идеально проработаны. В комиксной индустрии высочайшей похвалой считается замечание, что в комиксе нет проходных панелей, и этот рассказ полностью заслуживает такого комплимента. Каждая иллюстрация рассказывает историю.

А взгляните на сами изображения! На первой же панели сражённый унынием Дональд зримо передаёт нам состояние хронического недовольства, которое излечат последующие испытания! На первой панели второй страницы мы, прямо как солнце и звёзды, о которых вспоминает Дональд, смотрим вниз на извлечённый археологами корабль. Его уключины для вёсел теперь выглядят более чётко и показывают, с каким вниманием Баркс относился к деталям и мелочам на своих рисунках. Каждая уключина расположена в точности на своём месте, рядышком со скамьями, на которых некогда сидели гребцы.

В другом месте иллюстрации Баркса вызывают совершенно иной спектр эмоций. Как, например, в сцене, где Азур Синий таранит лодку уток, буквально разбивая судёнышко пополам и оставляя героев барахтаться в морской воде. Подобная картина по-настоящему пугает.

Второй заслуживающей внимания особенностью остаётся безусловное признание Барксом некой общности стремлений, движущей поступками всего человечества, что наглядно иллюстрируют персонажи автора. Мечта о величии, охватившая одного за другим всех героев, по сути своей определяет, что значит быть человеком. Каждый может сбиться с пути или, по крайней мере, встать на скользкую дорожку. Например, фантазии куратора о власти музейных работников и обязательном посещении музеев душераздирающе смешны в своей ограниченности, прямо как наивные и глупые мечты, которые заботят всех остальных. Конечно, кроме нас самих.

РИЧ КРЕЙНЕР

КАНИКУЛЫ НА ЯХТЕ, стр. 145

Среди профессиональных комиков присутствует такое понятие как «правило трёх» или «комедийная троица», смысл которого сводится к следующему: трёхкратное повторение одного и того же действия в течение одной истории или шутки сочнее, смешнее и полнее, чем любое другое количество повторений. Вот почему в домике у трёх медведей Златовласка портит именно три предмета (тарелки, стулья и кровати), в анекдоте в бар постоянно заходят именно три духовных лица (священник, раввин и мулла), а знаменитый художник и признанный комиксист Карл Баркс строит сюжет «Каникул на яхте» вокруг нескольких комических троиц.

Сюжет комикса состоит из трёх частей: Дональд заключает пари с соседом, страдает от неурядиц на яхте, а потом возвращается домой и вручает соседу

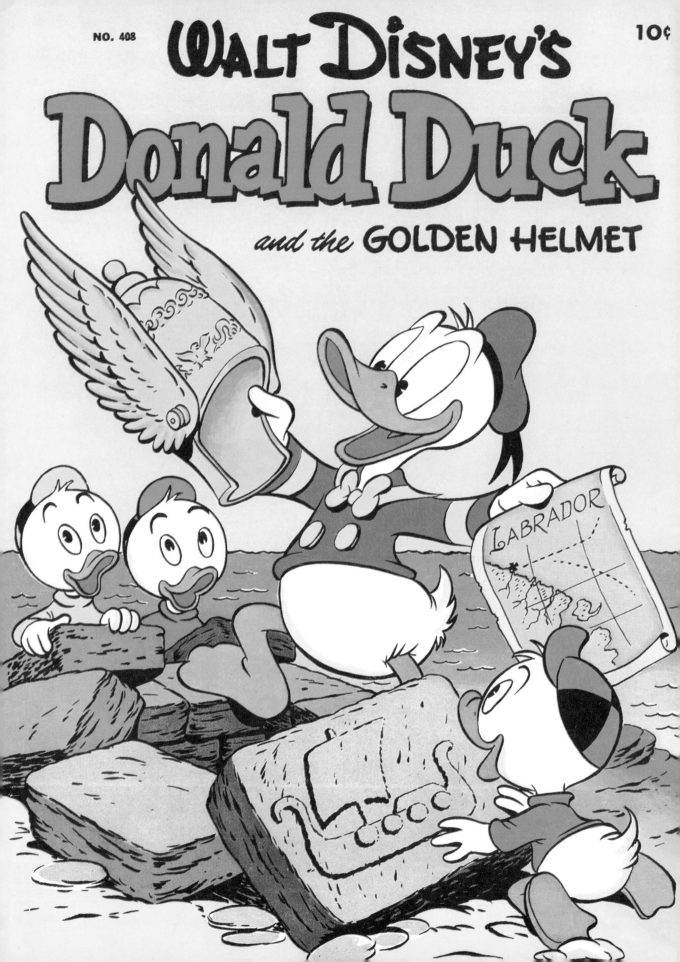

проигранную индейку. На первых трёх панелях комикса сосед описывает возможные (вскоре ставшие реальными) сценарии того, что может пойти не так. И всякий раз Дональд самоуверенно отвечает, что он «обо всём подумал».

Разумеется, план разработан не слишком глубоко, а потому почти сразу всё идёт наперекосяк.

На третьей странице комикса Дональд нежится в гамаке — на протяжении истории мы увидим его в этом гамаке ровно три раза, и каждый раз градус его волнения будет расти всё выше и выше — и хвастается собственным планом по ограждению племянников от неприятностей. «Вот это я понимаю! Идеально!» — радуется он.

А для Баркса это идеальное начало для истории, которую он хочет рассказать.

Тем временем во второй, развёрнутой части комикса Билли, Вилли и Дилли запускают пойманную рыбу в бочку с питьевой водой, выливают в озеро горючее и выбрасывают за борт бочку, внутри которой — просьба о помощи. Все три действия ведут к трём комическим последствиям: питьевая вода испорчена, лодку окружает стена пламени, а их дядюшка падает в бочке с Ниагарского водопада (обратите внимание на состоящую из трёх частей фразу Дональда «Здесь рядом Буффало, и Лакаванна, и Ниагарский водопад», которую он произносит, пока его бочка неумолимо приближается к водопаду).

«Каникулы на яхте» — не самая лучшая или новаторская работа Баркса, но это отличная шутовская машинка, которая после трёх поворотов ключика заставляет нас смеяться от души.

КРЕЙГ ФИШЕР

ОХОТНИКИ ЗА БРИЛЛИАНТАМИ, *стр. 155*

В кульминации «Охотников за бриллиантами», «небеса внезапно озарились бриллиантовой вспышкой» и полный драгоценных камней метеорит падает

на землю, принадлежащую «великому королю удачи» Глэдстоуну Гандеру. Событие кажется удивительным, даже сказочным, и лишь слова из самого начала комикса «будь эта история сказкой…», наводят на мысль об обратном.

Дональд отчаянно стремится превзойти Глэдстоуна в поиске бриллиантов и самоцветов, поэтому приобретает 40 гектаров усыпанной драгоценными камнями земли, но на поверку драгоценности оказываются фальшивками. Поняв, что его обманули, Дональд проделать то же самое и надуть Глэдстоуна. План срабатывает — наконец-то Гандер побеждён и унижен. Но всё это ровно до той минуты, как на его землю не падает метеорит, битком набитый драгоценными камнями.

Центральная сюжетная линия заканчивается авторским текстом, одновременно подтверждая и опровергая сказочную природу происходящего: «В сказке великий король…»

Графически Карл Баркс подчёркивает ироничную сказочную атмосферу, изображая ореол из линий различной длины над каждым драгоценным камнем, а также над головами персонажей в моменты удивления, гнева или разочарования. Вторые по величине экспрессивные линии появляются вокруг Глэдстоуна, когда он злорадствует, что по-прежнему является «королём удачи», а самые короткие линии возникают в глазах у Дональда, когда он узнаёт, что «бриллиант», с помощью которого Глэдстоун купил землю Дональда, на самом деле никчёмный циркон. В противовес миниатюрным линиям в глазах Дональда на следующей панели мы видим самые длинные линии ореола в этой истории, излучаемые солнцем. В этой сцене силуэты уезжающих в закат уток изображены на фоне лучей заходящего светила, тепло которого дарит жизнь всему земному. Отличное напоминание об настоящих ценностях и незначительности земных богатств.

ДОНАЛЬД ОЛТ

ПОЗОЛОЧЁННЫЙ ЧЕЛОВЕК, *стр. 165*

«Позолочённый человек» изящно объединяет в себе сразу несколько ключевых тем, которые волновали Баркса как художника. Это динамичная, насыщенная история, закрученная вокруг капризов фортуны, морального долга и колониальной политики.

Сюжетным центром притяжения становится экзотический город доколумбовой эпохи, схожий с легендами конкистадоров об Эльдорадо, населённый суеверными отшельниками, которыми правит тот самый гигантский позолочённый человек из названия истории. Но в этот раз Баркс в нетипичной для себя

манере разделяет повествование на две равные части. В первой части действие разворачивается в родном городе уток, вторая же посвящена путешествию. При этом Баркс не только подчёркивает резкий контраст между аккуратно подстриженными лужайками Улицы Миллионеров и песчаными берегами реки Эссекибо, но и показывает перенос городского пейзажа на первобытный. И вот уже шикарные бунгало усеивают саванну, а старые колониальные дома гниют в запустении на фоне вздымающихся в небо дымовых труб Джорджтауна.

(Британская) Гвиана — объект неиссякаемого интереса филателистов. Действительно существующая розовая марка номиналом в один цент и вдохновила Баркса описать эту абсурдную погоню за эфемерным реликтом прошлого, ставшим бесценным по логике капитализма. Этой же логикой руководствуются и символические антагонисты. В «домашней» половине истории Фило Т. Эллист, добродушный, но крайне рассеянный миллиардер с говорящим именем, а в Южной Америке это Эль Дорадо, разгневанный золотой гигант. Оба — заядлые коллекционеры редкостей, носящих сугубо символический смысл, будь то редкие марки или посеребрённые доспехи, оба действуют в схожем (можно сказать, едином) материалистическом порыве.

По своему обыкновению Глэдстоун Гандер олицетворяет здесь несправедливость существующей системы. Раз за разом он пожинает плоды честных усилий Дональда, раз за разом вырывает из рук кузена плоды успеха. Таким образом, эта история вписывает первостепенные для Баркса вопросы моральности тех или иных поступков в абсурдном мире в явственно материалистичную оправу. Подобный симбиоз предвосхищает многие тематические элементы, которые сыграют свою роль в ряде будущих знаменитых историй о Скрудже.

История завершается в характерной для Баркса манере.

Дональда ждёт хэппи-энд, возможный лишь благодаря счастливой случайности, хотя прежде обстоятельства всякий раз оборачивались против него. Редчайшая марка, за которой с таким упорством гонялся Дональд, которая на каждом шагу от него ускользала, внезапно оказывается в его руках. Наш селезень совершает совершенно бескорыстный поступок, который, к счастью, приносит ему денежную награду, за которой он и гонялся с самого начала. Это один из самых ироничных и в то же время обнадёживающих комиксов Баркса.

МАТТИАС УАЙВЕЛ

НЕУДАЧЛИВЫЕ ТРАНЖИРЫ, стр. 199

В «Ужасном секрете Глэдстоуна» мы уже выяснили, что самым большим страхом Глэдстоуна Гандера является необходимость зарабатывать себе на жизнь, так как она поставит крест на его блаженном

существовании вне рыночной экономики. Скрудж в «Неудачливом транжире» поставлен перед схожей дилеммой, ведь и Скрудж, и Глэдстоун обладают стойкой аллергией к процессу денежного оборота, но причины этой аллергии у них совершенно различны, как и мировоззрение и суть героев.

С точки зрения Скруджа, существует лишь два способа обращения с деньгами. Вы или скупаете новые предприятия, гарантируя себе в будущем увеличение доходов, или же, как это показано в томе «Всего лишь бедный старичок», в прямом смысле «купаетесь» в них. То есть, наполняете деньгами бассейн и с наслаждением плаваете, причем каждая монетка в этом океане богатств несёт с собой какое-то ценное воспоминание о пережитом опыте, триумфе или окупившемся риске.

Но что произойдёт, когда все предприятия уже будут принадлежать вам, а в вашем деньгохранилище кончится место? Именно с такой проблемой сталкивается Скрудж в «Неудачливом транжире». Наступает время делать нечто невозможное — тратить деньги не на бизнес, а на себя. Другими словами, Скрудж вынужден стать частью культуры потребителей, которая, по

его мнению, всегда была уделом простофиль.

К счастью, рядом есть готовый помочь Дональд. За скромную плату в тридцать центов за час Дональд приглашает дядюшку в головокружительное путешествие по стране, чтобы избавиться от тридцати тонн лишних денег. В первый раз за свою бытность миллиардером Скрудж знакомится с миром роскоши и расточительности: жареными каледонскими перепелами и шикарными лимузинами, где на сиденьях чехлы из меха горностаев. На индейских территориях он попадает в ловушки для туристов, которых инстинктивно избегал всю жизнь. Пожалуй, единственный эпизод, который во время путешествия заставил его порадоваться — момент, когда он снабжает деньгами на обувь бедняка и всех членов его многочисленной босоногой семьи.

Но для нашего бедного богача в этой истории нет счастливой развязки. В современной экономике Скрудж занимает такое положение, что уже никогда больше не сможет играть роль обычного потребителя, ибо все истраченные деньги рано или поздно вернутся к нему. Любая трата денег, где угодно и на что угодно, лишь увеличивает состояние Макдака, который теперь и представляет собой экономику — всю целиком. Перспектива утонуть в океане денег становится для него всё более ужасающе реальной.

ДЖАРЕД ГАРДНЕР

ОДНОСТРАНИЧНЫЕ ИСТОРИИ О ДОНАЛЬДЕ ДАКЕ

Одностраничные истории, вошедшие в настоящий том, удивительно разнородны.

Да, Карл Баркс зарекомендовал себя мастером-комиксистом во всех аспектах своего ремесла и

NO. 422

10¢

Walt Disney's
Donald Duck
and THE GILDED MAN

издатель часто отдавал на откуп художнику создание всей книги комиксов. Но архивные записи свидетельствуют о том, что шесть из девяти коротких историй, собранных в этом сборнике, были придуманы другими сценаристами, затем отданы Барксу для переработки и только после этого были выпущены на бумаге.

Одностраничный комикс имеет простую и строгую структуру, состоящую из «супружеской пары» — завязки и развязки. Залог успеха такого произведения в том, чтобы как можно раньше закрутить интригу и получить как можно большую отдачу.

В этой подборке представлено несколько тактик построения сюжета. Примером одного из них может служить обманчивое замешательство Дональда, снимающего стекло с собственной витрины, чтобы опробовать кое-что в «Блестящей идее Дональда» (стр. 109). В «Ёлочных игрушках» (стр. 209) правдоподобный рассказ о том, что мальчишки всегда остаются мальчишками, до последнего не раскрывает, чем закончатся попытки утят стать ёлочными декораторами. Последняя панель здесь нарочно увеличена, чтобы читатель мог увидеть ёлку целиком и в полной мере оценить юмор финала. Другой автор ставит перед героями изначально невыполнимую задачу, вроде той, что даёт племянникам Дональд в «Списке желаний» (стр. 211).

Совершенно очевидно, что нужно быть подлинным мастером своего дела, чтобы создать финальную панель, которая буквально побеждает читателя юмором. И здесь Баркс великолепен. Мы не замечаем ничего, кроме шутки. К примеру, наслаждаясь изобретательностью и превосходным художественным оформлением истории «Самодельная газонокосилка» (стр. 110), мы совершенно упускаем из виду те физические страдания, которым подвергают себя утята, пытаясь выйти из положения. Благодаря превосходной графике в «Прибыльной поломке» (стр. 143) — комиксе, повествующем о финансовом предприятии племянников — мы не задаёмся вопросом, почему же никто из искупавшихся неудачников не стремится предупредить идущих следом. В концовке «Рождественского поцелуя» (стр. 210), мы настолько увлечены комичным выражением лица Дональда, получившего поцелуй от вантуза, что забываем про распухший клюв селезня.

Менее успешные одностраничные комиксы страдают недостаточным вниманием к структуре произведения. Они экономят на вступлении, затягивают развязку, позволяют истории скатиться в дешёвый анекдот, но ударные фразы дают им шанс на реабилитацию. Баркс, в отличие от остальных сценаристов, разворачивает перед читателем настоящую микродраму. Те три комикса, что он сочинил сам — «Выгодная арифметика», «Опасная вылазка» и «Умная глупость Дональда» — смотрятся наиболее выигрышно из-за плавного развития сюжета и мощного финала. История протекает равномерно, без лишних рывков. Интрига и комическое напряжение устанавливаются в самом начале и не отпускают до последней панели.

Для «Выгодной арифметики» (стр. 144) неторопливый темп повествования имеет решающее значение (особенно для нас, тех, кому предстоит высчитывать математическую закономерность). В «Опасной вылазке» (стр.197) логичность и строгая последовательность действий делают странное поведение Дональда почти обычным. Сначала Дональд предстаёт перед нами в трико, а в финале он уже в полной боевой экипировке. А зачем же наш селезень сознательно загнал себя в угол в «Умной глупости Дональда» (стр.198)? Ответ на этот вопрос будет совершенно неожиданным, но вполне оправданным в рамках комикса. Каждая короткая история в этом томе демонстрирует нам разницу между просто хорошей шуткой и шуткой, которая безоговорочно покорила наши сердца.

РИЧ КРЕЙНЕР

О комментаторах

Дональд Олт — профессор английского языка в Университете Флориды; основатель и редактор академического журнала «ImageTexT: междисциплинарные исследования комиксов»; редактор книги «Карл Баркс: разговоры»; исполнительный продюсер документального фильма «Человек Дака: интервью с Карлом Барксом».

Р. Фьоре, по собственным словам, зарабатывает на жизнь честным трудом, когда на то есть возможность, неподалёку от исторического Даксбурга. Такое маргинальное существование время от времени приводит его в компанию Walt Disney — довольно интересное местечко. А вообще он пишет о комиксах и мультфильмах дольше, чем ты живёшь на этом свете, дитя моё.

Крейг Фишер — адъюнкт-профессор английского языка в Аппалачском государственном университете. Его колонку о различных жанрах комикса «Монстры питаются критиками» можно прочитать на сайте The Comics Journal (tcj.com).

Джаред Гарднер изучает и преподаёт искусство комикса в Университете штата Огайо; из-под его пера вышли три книги; также является одним из авторов журнала The Comics Journal.

Рич Крейнер в течение долгого времени пишет для журнала The Comics Journal и ещё дольше читает Карла Баркса. Живёт с супругой и кошкой в штате Мэн.

Кен Пэрилл — автор книги «Читая Дэниела Клоуза» (Fantagraphics, 2012), эссе о Луизе Мэй Олкотт и отрочестве, отношениях матерей и сыновей в Америке во времена до войны между Севером и Югом, о музыканте и телеведущем Лоренсе Велке и, конечно, о комиксах. Его тексты появляются в таких изданиях как The Nathaniel Hawthorne Review, The Journal of Popular Culture, The Boston Review, The Believer and The Comics Journal. Кен преподаёт литературу в Университете Восточной Каролины.

Стефано Приароне родился в северо-западной Италии в то время, когда вышедший на пенсию Карл Баркс дописывал свои последние истории о Юных сурках. Стефано пишет о популярной культуре для многих итальянских газет и журналов, внёс существенный вклад в полное итальянское собрание работ Баркса и написал диссертацию по экономике на тему предпринимательской жилки дядюшки Скруджа (за что винит свою тётушку, которая читала ему Баркса, когда Стефано было всего три годика).

Маттиас Уайвел — куратор отдела итальянской живописи XVI столетия в Национальной галерее Лондона. Вот уже 15 лет активно пишет о комиксах.

Где были впервые напечатаны эти утиные истории?

ОТ РЕДАКТОРА: «Полное собрание Карла Баркса» от Disney включает в себя комиксы о Дональде Даке и дядюшке Скрудже, которые были впервые напечатаны в традиционном американском формате четырёхцветного журнала. Первая утиная история Баркса увидела свет в октябре 1942 года. Истории из этого сборника в списке даны в хронологической последовательности, но в самом томе публикуются в другом порядке. Это одиннадцатый том.

Исходные журналы комиксов печатались под логотипом Dell, часть из них появилась в так называемой серии «Четыре цвета» — название этой серии в самих комиксах никогда не появлялось, но в большинстве случаев среди специалистов принято ссылаться на серию «разовых изданий» комиксов «Делл», имеющих последовательную нумерацию. Также номера серии «Четыре цвета» иногда называют просто «разовыми изданиями».

Большая часть историй в данном томе изначально публиковалась без названия. Иногда они именовались при последующих переизданиях. Заголовки некоторых историй взяты из переписки или интервью Баркса. (Впрочем, иногда Баркс называл один и тот же комикс по-разному.) Некоторые истории так и не получили официального названия, но имели неформальные заголовки, данные поклонниками или индексаторами. В настоящем томе для таких комиксов были выбраны наиболее подходящие названия. Неофициальные заголовки обозначены звёздочкой в круглых скобках — (*).

В списке ниже истории из этого тома размещены в порядке их первой публикации.

Комиксы и истории Уолта Диснея №135 (декабрь 1951)
Обложка
Большое хранилище на холме Килмотор
(Деньгохранилище с подвохом) (*)

Четыре цвета №367 (январь 1952)
Обложка
Ёлочные игрушки (*)
Рождество в Беднотауне
Рождественский поцелуй (*)
Список желаний (*) (также известный как «Список желаний размером с почтовую марку)

Комиксы и истории Уолта Диснея №136 (январь 1952)
Обложка
Обычное везение Глэдстоуна (*)

Комиксы и истории Уолта Диснея №137 (февраль 1952)
Обложка
Тайна «Вопящего ковбоя» (*)

Комиксы и истории Уолта Диснея №138 (март 1952)
Обложка
Монументальные моты (*)

Комиксы и истории Уолта Диснея №139 (апрель 1952)
Обложка
Ракетокрыл спасает положение (*)

Комиксы и истории Уолта Диснея №140 (май 1952)
Обложка
Ужасный секрет Глэдстоуна

Комиксы и истории Уолта Диснея №141 (июнь 1952)
Обложка
Неприятности с мозгоящиками (*)

Четыре цвета №408 (июль-август 1952)
Обложка
Блестящая идея Дональда (*)
Золотой шлем
Самодельная газонокосилка (*)
Прибыльная поломка (*)

Комиксы и истории Уолта Диснея №142 (июль 1952)
Обложка
Каникулы на яхте (*)

Комиксы и истории Уолта Диснея №143 (август 1952)
Обложка
Охотники за бриллиантами (*)

Четыре цвета №422 (сентябрь-октябрь 1952)
Обложка
Выгодная арифметика (*)
Позолочённый человек
Опасная вылазка (*) (также известная как «Опасная вылазка за котом»)
Умная глупость Дональда (*)

Комиксы и истории Уолта Диснея №144 (сентябрь 1952)
Обложка
Неудачливые транжиры (*)

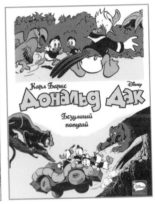

Литературно-художественное издание
әдеби-көркем басылым

Для среднего и старшего школьного возраста
Орта және жоғарғы жасқа арналған

Серия «Disney Comics. Утиные истории»

Карл Баркс

Дональд Дак
Рождество в Беднотауне

Заведующий редакцией *Сергей Тишков*
Ответственный редактор *Елизавета Нефедова*
Переводчик *Ксения Жолудева*
Редактор *Юлия Богатырева*
Корректор *Арина Христофорова*
Ретушь и отрисовка звуков: *Константин Миронов*
Компьютерная вёрстка: *Радик Садыков*
Оформление обложки: *Екатерина Климова*

Подписано в печать 08.08.2019. Формат 84x108/16. Усл. печ. л. 25,2.
Печать офсетная. Гарнитура LaffayetteComicPro. Бумага офсетная
Тираж 3 000 экз. Заказ № 8761.

Произведено в Российской Федерации
Изготовлено в 2019 г.
Изготовитель: ООО «Издательство АСТ»
129085, г. Москва, Звёздный бульвар, д. 21, стр. 1, ком. 705, пом. I, этаж 7
Наш электронный адрес: www.ast.ru

Общероссийский классификатор продукции ОК-034-2014 (КПЕС 2008);
58.11.1 - книги, брошюры печатные
Соответствует ТР ТС 007/2011

Өндіруші: ЖШҚ «АСТ баспасы»
129085, Мәскеу қ., Звёздный бульвары, 21-үй, 1-құрылыс, 705-бөлме, I жай, 7-қабат
Біздің злектрондық мекенжаймыз : www.ast.ru
E-mail: mainstream@ast.ru
Интернет-магазин: www.book24.kz Интернет-дүкен: www.book24.kz
Импортер в Республику Казахстан ТОО «РДЦ-Алматы».
Қазақстан Республикасындағы импорттаушы «РДЦ-Алматы» ЖШС.
Дистрибьютор и представитель по приему претензий на продукцию в республике Казахстан:
ТОО «РДЦ-Алматы»
Қазақстан Республикасында дистрибьютор
және өнім бойынша арыз-талаптарды қабылдаушының
өкілі «РДЦ-Алматы» ЖШС, Алматы қ., Домбровский көш., 3«а», литер Б, офис 1.
Тел.: 8 (727) 2 51 59 89,90,91,92
Факс: 8 (727) 251 58 12, вн. 107; E-mail: RDC-Almaty@eksmo.kz
Өнімнің жарамдылық мерзімі шектелмеген.
Өндірген мемлекет: Ресей
Сертификация қарастырылған

Отпечатано с электронных носителей издательства.
ОАО "Тверской полиграфический комбинат". 170024, Россия, г. Тверь, пр-т Ленина, 5.
Телефон: (4822) 44-52-03, 44-50-34, Телефон/факс: (4822)44-42-15
Home page - www.tverpk.ru Электронная почта (E-mail) - sales@tverpk.ru

EAC

12+